PHYSICAL ANTHROPOLOGY

PHYSICAL

Philip L. Stein
Bruce M. Rowe
Los Angeles Pierce College

ANTHROPOLOGY

SECOND EDITION

McGraw-Hill Book Company

New York St. Louis San Francisco Auckland Bogotá
Düsseldorf Johannesburg London Madrid
Mexico Montreal New Delhi Panama Paris
São Paulo Singapore Sydney Tokyo Toronto

This book was set in Souvenir Light by Ruttle, Shaw & Wetherill, Inc.
The editors were Lyle Linder and Laura D. Warner;
the designer was Anne Canevari Green;
the cover photograph was taken by Gebhard Fröhlich;
the production supervisor was Dennis J. Conroy.
New drawings were done by J & R Services, Inc.
Von Hoffmann Press, Inc., was printer and binder.

PHYSICAL ANTHROPOLOGY

1 2 3 4 5 6 7 8 9 0 V H V H 7 8 3 2 1 0 9 8

Library of Congress Cataloging in Publication Data

Stein, Philip L.
    Physical anthropology.

    Includes index.
    1. Physical anthropology.   I.   Rowe, Bruce M., joint
author.   II.   Title.
GN60.S72 1978   573   77-9442
ISBN 0-07-061116-5

To Our Families

Contents

Preface

The people of Western cultures have traditionally seen humans as the center of a universe created for humans to occupy, utilize, and control. Recently, however, the mass media's reports of overpopulation, worldwide food and energy shortages, pollution, and social unrest have made it evident to many that humans are not above and beyond the influence of nature.

We are an integral part of the natural scheme. Our survival, like that of other organisms, depends upon maintaining a balance with the environments that support us. We are dependent upon the natural world, and when we ignore this dependence—by polluting the environment, for example—our survival itself is threatened.

Through its unique viewpoint—the holistic approach—anthropology provides insights into the dynamic interrelationships of the biological, environmental, cultural, and social aspects of human existence. Humans as biological beings cannot be studied apart from humans as cultural and social beings. By examining our biological limitations and potentials, we can gain a fuller understanding of how cultural innovations affect biology and environment. By discovering our relationships to the rest of the animal world and our evolutionary history, we can appreciate more clearly our place in nature and the requirements for persistence.

The subject of anthropology is humankind, an unbelievably complex product of the evolutionary process—organisms that celebrate birth, form complex social bonds, and sometimes consider death to be a transition to a new life. With a large brain and precise hands, humans have created, destroyed, and rebuilt monuments to individuals, governments, and gods. Humans also have invented slavery, racial stereotypes, pollution, and wars.

This text is concerned with physical anthropology, the study of the biological nature of humankind. The first part deals with the nature of anthropology, particularly physical anthropology, and certain basic philosophical concerns. This is followed by the development of basic concepts necessary to the proper understanding of evolutionary theory. Next, the problems of human variation are explored. Attention then focuses on humankind's relationship with the animal world, especially with our closest living relatives, the primates. Through comparative studies of these forms—prosimians, monkeys, and apes—anthropology attempts to reconstruct many aspects of human evolution. The fifth and final part discusses the fossil record, the physical remains of human evolutionary history. The text concludes with a look at our evolutionary present and future.

The twentieth century is characterized by rapid accumulation of new information in areas of scientific investigation. It seems as if a week does not go by without a journal report of some major new hypothesis of relevance to physical anthropology. In the past few years new discoveries in areas such as genetics, growth and development, primatology, and paleoanthropology have had major impact on our concepts of human evolution and behavior. As a result of these new ideas and data many changes and additions have been made in the second edition of this text. For example, we have introduced many concepts which, although not new in themselves, have recently taken on new significance. These include hypotheses that deal with regulatory genes and neoteny. We have added a section on growth and development, an area of active research in physical anthropology. The material on the fossil hominids has been greatly expanded and revised in light of new finds and concepts.

A book does not develop in a vacuum. We wish to acknowledge those who have counseled us, encouraged us, and aided us in the tasks of reviewing, typing, and photography. First, we

would like to thank the following persons who read all or portions of the manuscript or aided in its development: Everett and Janet Frost, Mildred Dickeman, Leslie Aiello, Rita Castellano, Glenn A. Gorelick, Van K. Hainline, Ronald Farrar, Robert L. Pence, Eleanor F. Michael, Arnold L. Freed, Gail Kennedy, Mary L. Walek, Robert L. Blakely, Karen Kovac, Roland A. Gangloff, Vinson Sutlive, Allen C. Beck, Robert L. Van Burkleo, Philip G. Grant, Douglas R. Givens, Paul E. Simonds, L. Lewis Johnson, and Mark E. Harlan. Second, we would like to pay tribute to the memory of the late Ronald D. Kissack, the editor of the first edition, in deep appreciation of his faith and encouragement. We also wish to thank our editors of the second edition, Lyle Linder and Laura Warner; our designer Anne Green; and production supervisor Dennis Conroy. Finally, special thanks go to Rick Freed and Dodie Stoneburner for much of the original photography and to Carol Stein for her long hours spent in reading and typing the manuscript and in developing the Glossarial Index.

Philip L. Stein
Bruce M. Rowe

PHYSICAL ANTHROPOLOGY

PART ONE
WHAT IS HUMANKIND?

I am Atum, who appeared alone on the primeval hill, rising from the waters of chaos. When I appeared, heaven had not come into being; neither had the earth, nor the creatures of the earth. I lifted myself up from the water and made a foundation upon which to stand. Then I made every form to come from my mouth. First I made Shu and Tefnut by spewing them from my mouth. They became gods with me.

My eye followed after them as I observed them through the long periods of time. Finally they returned and restored my eye. I shed tears and men were made from the tears. After my eye returned, it was angry with me because I had made another one in its place.

I arose from the plants and created reptiles and all creeping things. Shu and Tefnut gave birth to Geb and Nut. Geb and Nut brought forth Osiris, Horus, Seth, Isis, and Nephthys. From them came forth many children to multiply the earth.

These gods were sent forth to destroy Apophis, my archenemy who is no more. I put a curse upon him and all his chlidren. The enemy of Re is consumed. Re shall drive across the heavens in peace. Life! Prosperity! Health![1]

Thus the ancient Egyptians explained creation and the origin of human beings. All societies have ideas as to the origin and nature of people. This also is the subject matter of physical anthropology. In this first part we will examine some of the facts that have been obtained through scientific investigations of people. The scientific method itself will be explored, as will the development and nature of anthropology and evolutionary theory.

[1] From Fred G. Bratton, *Myths and Legends of the Ancient Near East.* Copyright © 1970 by Fred G. Bratton. With permission of the publishers, Thomas Y. Crowell Company, Inc.

Chapter One

Investigating the Nature of Humankind

THE NATURE OF HUMANKIND

What is it to be human? This question has been satisfactorily answered for some, has puzzled others, and has tormented many. Plato defined people as "bipeds without feathers," an amusing image but also an early attempt at classifying people as animals. Mark Twain observed, "Man is the only animal that blushes—or needs to." He recognized the human social consciousness, the ability to be embarrassed. An anonymous author wrote, "Man is the only animal that eats when he is not hungry, drinks when he is not thirsty, and makes love at all seasons."

Fundamental questions of physical anthropology are: What is it to be human and what is the nature of humankind? The attempt to solve these puzzles throws light on the even more intriguing question: What am I?

Of Termites and People

The investigation of these queries will begin with a comparison and contrast of the behavior of termites and people. Like humans, termites survive through complex patterns of social behavior. But the bases of these patterns differ.

Termites   A motherless world awaits. Emerging from their pupae, termites need no pampering, no tutelage. Nature is complete in preparing the various castes of termites with all the equipment and behavior they will need to fulfill their respective functions.

No decision has to be made as to who will do what. Their division of labor is programmed from the start. Once their reproductive organs begin to function, the reproductive castes will do nothing but produce new offspring. They will not feed themselves or do any other type of work.

The egg-laying queen can attain a volume many times larger than that of her subjects (Figure 1-1). The bulkiness of this egg-laying machine will often prevent her even from moving under her own power. In times of danger the workers will roll their valuable procreator into a royal cell and seal it in order to protect her.

The soldier caste is specialized for the protection of the termite city. The blind, wingless, sterile soldiers cannot even attempt a coup d'etat, nor can they desert the citizens for whom they provide protection. Even if their lack of sight and wings did not prevent their escape, the size of their jaws would. These viselike mandibles are more than 500 times as large as those of other castes and render the soldiers incapable of feeding themselves.

The reproductive castes and the soldiers are dependent on the workers for food. The worker, like the soldier, is totally blind and incapable of reproduction. It tunnels to subterranean sources

Figure 1-1 Termite colony. *Subterranean termite queen surrounded by workers of various ages.*

of cellulose and ingests this food. It is then digested by microscopic organisms which reside in special organs in the termite body. Upon conversion of the cellulose, the usable nutrients are regurgitated into the mouths of reproductive individuals and soldiers.

When the total population of any caste becomes too large for peak functioning of the community as a whole, the workers are programmed through inborn mechanisms to stop feeding the unwanted. Without the adult workers' help, the individuals of the other castes, along with "infant" workers, are doomed. In this manner the population size is maintained in balance.

Through their mindless efficiency the termites have done well. They have been around longer than humans, are more numerous, and are widely distributed. The problems of population control and starvation, which continue to baffle us, have been solved for the termites through inborn mechanisms. The termites' behavior pattern has proved to be one among many successful modes of survival.

People as hunter-gatherers Children born into a Bushman society of South Africa are completely dependent on their family for food. While they are very young, their mother's milk will be the primary means of nourishment. Later their fathers, uncles, and brothers will supply them with meat, and their mothers, aunts, and sisters with wild plant foods. Not until the children are five or six, perhaps much older, will they contribute to the group's subsistence.

Children live in the camps of their parents until they marry. In the interim they learn the rules by which they must live. To survive, they must listen well to the elders who have experienced nature, its rewards and punishments (Figure 1-2).

The children grow and develop. They learn that it is the job of the males to provide the camp with meat. Skill in hunting is developed by children's games and by watching and listening to fathers and uncles. The boys also learn that it will be their responsibility as adults to protect their groups from the wrongdoings of other groups.

The children learn that the females are the gatherers. Roots, nuts, berries, stems, and leaves are collected and brought back for the day's meal. It is the women who supply the camp with the majority of the food. Their gathering activities account for up to 80 percent of the food by weight.[1] Elizabeth Marshall Thomas describes the gathering of Bushman women in the following excerpt:

[1] R. B. Lee, "What Hunters Do for a Living, or How to Make Out on Scarce Resources," in R. B. Lee and I. DeVore (eds.), *Man the Hunter* (Chicago: Aldine, 1968), pp. 30–48. It is generally true that modern hunter-gatherers depend more on vegetable material, and in some cases shellfish, eggs, lizards, fish, etc., than they do on meat—although meat is a highly valued food. The exception to this occurs in areas where vegetation is scarce, such as in the far north. It is likely that the dependence on plant material and other gathered food sources was common in the past; and, therefore, in many areas of the world women have been the major breadwinners of the family for most of human development.

Dasino, Twikwe, Tsetchwe walked in front, each with a digging-stick thrust in her belt like an enormous knife, each wearing a heavy cape, and Tsetchwe carrying her baby, who rode, carefree and swinging his feet, on her shoulder. . . . We walked until we came to a patch of tsama melons, perhaps twenty of them lying together, shiny, smooth, and green in the grass. . . . The women stopped and began to gather up the green melons. . . . [Later, after finding evidence of a deeply buried root, Thomas observed the results of Twikwe's labor.] She had made a hole three feet deep, a foot across, and at the bottom, dim in shadow, lay an immense gray root wedged securely between two stones. . . . Again she bent over the hole, leaning over so far that her head came between her knees, and grasped the huge root with both hands. She tugged so hard that I heard her joints crack, but the root was wedged and she couldn't move it. . . . We would leave it.[2]

[2] Elizabeth Marshall Thomas, *The Harmless People* (New York: Knopf, 1958), pp. 103–104, 108–109. Copyright 1958 by Alfred A. Knopf. Used with permission of the publisher.

Figure 1-2 Bushman family. *Human survival depends on the prolonged protection and tutelage of offspring. Family ties can last a lifetime.*

The human dimension   Human life depends on technology. A person stripped of clothes, shelter, tools, and weapons has no chance in this world, where biological equipment alone is not sufficient for survival. Human beings substitute spears for long canine teeth, fire for fur, and other technological achievements to compensate for the lack of inborn adaptations.

Nevertheless, survival is only a part-time task. Humans may take time to ponder the nature of the universe or their own nature. They may paint a picture and dedicate it to their sacred spirit, or they may play magic upon it. Thoughts of awe, of understanding, of fear, and contentment can occupy their minds. And their ideas are transmittable; thoughts, through language, can enter the minds of others, and there they can incubate to new heights of development.

Termites are mindless machines. They have no choice of the route through life they will travel. Nevertheless, they have been extremely successful in their adaptations to a variety of habitats. Humans, on the other hand, are almost totally dependent on learned behavior. In fact, the emergence of the human species and its continuance are dependent upon what is called *culture*.

The Culture Concept

Culture is one of those words which everyone uses and almost everyone uses differently. A person may say, "Those people belong to the Art Society; they certainly are cultured." To the anthropologist there is one thing culture is not, and that is a level of sophistication or an amount of formal education. Culture is not something that one society or person has and another does not.

Culture has been defined by anthropologists in hundreds of ways. Fortunately, most definitions have points in common, and these points will be included in our definition. They are the facts that culture is learned, nonrandom, systematic behavior that can be transmitted from person to person and from generation to generation.

Culture is learned   First, culture is learned behavior as opposed to *innate*. By innate is meant biologically determined, coded by the hereditary material. When termites emerge from their pupae, workers, soldiers, and queens crawl away to their respective predetermined tasks. They are innately equipped to brave the hazards of their environment. Humans do not function in this manner. A baby abandoned at birth has *no* chance of surviving by itself. In fact, most six- or seven-year-olds would probably perish if left to their own resources.

What would we be without culture? There are people without culture who can be observed in back wards of mental institutions.[3] They have virtually no mental functions. We refer not to persons with such afflictions as schizophrenia or paranoia but to those individuals who have virtually no potential to learn. They cannot speak or feed themselves. Nor can they be toilet-trained or taught to dress. From one day to the next they do not recognize people they have lived with for years. A person without culture is not like a nonhuman animal. Without the potential for culture, such a person is an incomplete being with the body of a person, even the somewhat damaged brain of one; what is lacking is a functioning mind.

Culture is nonrandom, systematic behavior   Culture is patterned in two ways. First, it is nonrandom behavior. That is, specific actions or thoughts are usually the same for particular situations. For example, in Western societies when two people meet, they usually shake hands. A specific behavioral pattern, such as shaking hands, in a particular situation, such as two people meeting, is called a *norm*. A norm is the most frequent behavior that the members of a group will show in a specific situation.

[3] Craig MacAndrew and Robert Edgerton, "The Everyday Life of Institutionalized 'Idiots,' " *Human Organization*, 23 (1964), 312–318.

Culture also is patterned in the sense that it is systematic. That is, one aspect of behavior is related to all the others, and taken together, they form a *system*. A system can be defined as a collection of parts which are interrelated so that a change in any one part may bring about changes in the others. In addition, a group's cultural traditions and the way they relate to each other reflect certain underlying principles about the basic characteristics of people and nature.

Culture is transmittable   Culture is transmittable; it spreads. You can teach Fido to respond to his name and other verbal commands, but this newly acquired "vocabulary" is not going to be used to discuss world problems with the other dogs on the block. The dog has certainly learned something but has learned it as a response to a stimulus which was rewarded in some way. Probably no great mental processes, no interpretations, were involved. With humans, information can be learned, stored in the cortex of the brain, interpreted, and then transmitted to other people. The person doing the transmitting may accomplish this directly, or, for that matter, may even be dead. These ideas and accomplishments are passed on through those who knew the dead person or through written and other records. This process continues, so that knowledge builds on the basis of past generations. In societies with writing, each generation can continue to influence following generations indefinitely. A particular culture is the result, therefore, of its history as well as its present state. Although there is now evidence that certain animals also possess some ability to pass on acquired behavior (Chapter 11),[4] none have developed this to the same degree as humans.

[4] Topics to be developed later are indicated by parenthetical references to subsequent chapters.

Two aspects of culture   There are two aspects of the cultural phenomenon. First, culture is an *extrasomatic* adaptation to an environment. On the other hand a culture is an environment.

Nonhuman animals usually adapt to their environments through changes in their *somatic* form. Somatic means "bodily," and a somatic change would be an alteration in the body. So an extrasomatic change would be a change in behavior.

Of course, somatic changes also have been important in human evolution and partially account for why we no longer look like our distant ancestors. More than the human body evolved, however; the mind also developed to the point where it was sometimes able to substitute cultural innovation for biological alteration. If you were to transplant a group of temperate-zone animals to an arctic environment, they might all die, or conceivably only those who were somewhat different from the average, perhaps by having more fur, might survive. Put people in the same environment, and they could build an igloo, start a fire, or kill a polar bear to make a coat.

The human biological potential for culture allows people to adapt to environments through culture as well as biology. This is one reason why the human species is one of the most widely dispersed on earth. Humans have climbed to the top of the highest mountains with the aid of bottled oxygen and other supplies; they have descended to the deepest parts of the ocean by using bathyspheres; they have occupied every climatic zone by using the appropriate clothing, shelter, and temperature-controlling devices. The flexibility that culture allows has recently been displayed to the extreme. In space travel, humans, who like other animals need air to breathe, food to eat, and water to drink, can rocket to an airless, foodless, waterless environment. Somatic features do not need to change to accomplish this. Instead, biological potential responds to the desires of a conquering mind.

Culture is a means of adaptation, but a *particular* culture is also an environment. Examine the area in which you are reading this book. If it is your room, you may be surrounded by curtains, glass windows, plaster walls, light fixtures, and so on, all of which are cultural innovations. Even if you are reading outdoors, the bench you are sitting on, the buildings around you, the smog in the air are all parts of the cultural environment. Even the grass and trees, if transplanted or sown by humans, are where they are because learned behavior allowed them to be put there. In either case, the room or the courtyard, your surroundings are basically made by human hands. In the room, you may not even be able to hear or see or smell the natural environment.

The Relationship of Brain to Mind

The human *mind* consists of internalized cultural elements organized into an original personality. The mind has the potential to combine these elements into unique configurations which allow for the creativity and innovational ability of human thought.

The formation and development of mind depend on the brain, specifically the *cerebral cortex*. It is here that complex thought takes place and here that the highly efficient communication system, language, resides. Through the use of the symbolic logic of language and other appropriate mechanisms, such as memory and mental images, things can be thought about which are not directly present or obvious (Chapter 11).

The brain is responsible for *all* levels of behavior beyond reflexes. One of these levels is that of awareness. There is some evidence that a chimpanzee can recognize itself in a mirror. What it is most likely aware of, as Jane Goodall has said, is that the body reflected in the glass is its own.[5]

Human awareness goes far beyond this. An individual looks in the mirror and sees "a person with great potential in the business world." In other words, human awareness is not restricted to recognition of a physical entity. It also includes the concept of the uniqueness of self and the relationship of self to others and to the environment.

The concept of self is one attribute of the mind, an attribute that creates a power that can exert control over the body. If people imagine themselves to be sick, even when there is no organic cause, the very conception can produce physical symptoms of illness. Certain types of backaches, headaches, and asthma are among the many known *psychosomatic illnesses,* and some people maintain that nearly all illnesses have a mental aspect.[6]

The mind can cause more than discomfort: it can kill. A sorcerer points a bone at a man. The victim's face distorts with fear. His eyes glaze. He attempts to cry out, but the sounds do not come. He trembles and twitches uncontrollably. He falls to the ground. His arms sway as if to ward off the poison that he believes is entering his body. He crawls back to his hut. A couple of weeks later he is dead.

Cases like this one, based on the observations of Herbert Basedow,[7] occur in a wide range of societies. What happens is this: the victim believes so strongly in the powers of the sorcerer that his mind, in a state of fear, triggers the biological processes that kill him. There is no need for the sorcerer to harm the victim physically. The actual cause of death is a lowering of blood pressure caused by prolonged activity of the *sympathicoadrenal* system. In situations of fear, this system is activated for the purpose of preparing the body

[5] Jane van Lawick-Goodall, *In the Shadow of Man* (Boston: Houghton Mifflin, 1971), pp. 250–251.

[6] Walter B. Cannon, "Voodoo Death," *American Anthropologist,* 44 (1942), 169.

[7] Herbert Basedow, *The Australian Aboriginal* (Adelaide: Preece, 1925).

for extreme physical activity, such as warding off an attack. When the crisis is over, the system usually shuts down and the body is returned to a more stable state. If the fear persists, the sympathicoadrenal system continues to work, eventually causing death.

Understanding the relationship of mind to body will become increasingly important to us in the future. Fear is but one thing which can lead to biological breakdown; frustration and confusion also play a part. As our cities become more crowded, and as life becomes generally more difficult, mental illness appears to be increasing (Chapter 16).

The Characteristics of Humankind

Biologically people are not as different from other animals, especially other *primates*, as many of us would like to believe. We share some characteristics with all animals, more with all *vertebrates*, and even more with all *mammals*. It is not surprising that people should be quite similar to our primate relatives (Chapter 10).

The anatomical differences between people and the chimpanzee are, to a degree, matters of size and proportion. Not only does the chimpanzee have the same bones and muscles as humans, but most of these structures are found in nearly the same places and in most cases serve the same or similar functions. The internal organs of both types of animal are similar. Even the body fluids, such as blood, are alike. Genetic similarities, which are reflected in the outward manifestation of the characteristics mentioned, are also striking. For instance, the genetic material in chimps is remarkably close to that of people (Chapter 12).

Nevertheless, all populations of organisms display some differences from all others. The following discussion presents a few human biological idiosyncrasies. Note, however, that even these are mostly matters of *degree* rather than type. Here we will simply say a few words about each of these characteristics, for all of them will be considered in later chapters.

The human brain and its ability to symbolize
One important characteristic of humans is the development of the brain in a way that provides the potential for cultural behavior. One of the things that makes the human brain a revolutionary instrument is the potential for speech. Other animals can create and respond to a limited number of *signals*, and, in some cases, *symbols*. Chimpanzees can be taught to communicate to a limited degree in systems similar to language (Chapter 11). Yet, the human cortex has the greatest ability to organize symbols into an effective system that can relate and create experiences and ideas. Note, however, that this is a matter of degree. It also must be emphasized that the great potential to use symbols is but one way to accomplish the task of survival and has nothing to do with "superiority."

A symbol is anything, whether it be *visual, oral, tactile,* or *olfactory,* that represents something else that is distant in time and space from it. A word, for instance, is a symbol of what it refers to. In order to understand the meaning of the symbol, the thing that it refers to need not be present. Such things as stop signs, trademarks, Morse code, and Braille are all symbolic. At a higher level of abstraction, a symbol can be substituted physically for its object. For example, a general's insignia not only represent the general and his or her authority, they *are* authority. Similarly, some people consider an attack on the flag to be an attack on the country or on its people.

The symbol itself is arbitrary. That is, there is no intrinsic relationship between the symbol and what it represents. For instance, the word *pen* denotes the object it refers to only because in English it has been designated to do so. To an Italian, a Bushman, or another non-English speaker, the sound "pen" might have no meaning or a different meaning. Since each culture codes its unique complex of knowledge and experiences into different sets of symbols, its conception of itself and the world which surrounds it differs. This is one main reason for the different configurations that culture takes.

Bipedalism Habitual *bipedalism* is another human trait, yet other animals are bipedal. Bipedalism serves several functions. For one, it frees the hands for use in activities other than movement. In time of danger the young monkey clings quickly to the furry belly of its mother as she flees, but the human baby is snatched into the arms of an adult and carried to safety. Second, food can easily be carried back to the camp; it need not be carried in the mouth or eaten where it is acquired. This allows people to protect their food from scavengers that could otherwise steal it from their larger-brained but weaker neighbors. By transporting food to a home base, a person can share it with those who were not along during the search for food. Third, a dog cannot throw a spear. A human's dangling arms and grasping hands make it possible to throw weapons. This arm-hand combination also aids in unparalleled manipulation of the environment.

Birds walk on two legs, yet their upper limbs have been modified into wings and are useless for manipulating objects. A kangaroo moves on three "legs"; its tail acts as an efficient locomotor device. Bears, dogs, monkeys, and apes, among others, often rear up on their hind legs and even walk a short distance on them. But people are habitually bipedal, and their upper limbs are highly efficient structures for grasping, holding, and manipulating objects (Figure 1-3).

A fourth advantage of bipedalism is the increase in the range of the visual field that results from the elevation of the eyes. A crocodile may weigh as much as a human, but its eyes are only a short distance from the ground. Even though some quadrupeds, such as the giraffe, have eyes off the ground, most animals must be content to stare into a field of grass or a clump of bushes. The human two-legged posture allows people to see over those bushes and grasses. This has great significance because it permits sighting predators from a distance.

Ostrich　　　　Kangaroo　　　　Human

Figure 1-3　Bipedal animals. *Although many animals are bipedal, human posture is structured for more efficient use of the arms and hands than is true in other animals.*

Advantages in one area often mean disadvantages in others. With the development of human bipedalism certain structural weaknesses developed. For instance, humans cannot run as fast as many other animals. In addition, the bipedal configuration of the human body has meant a weakening of the back and abdomen, problems in circulation, and a loss of manipulatory abilities of the toes, as well as other structural alterations.[8]

Human reproduction In nonhuman mammals, the female is usually receptive to males during certain times of the year. Because of this, for most mammals births peak within specific seasons, such as the onset of spring or of the rainy season. People have the biological potential to mate and produce offspring the year around. This difference between humans and other animals is recognized by most people. It is no wonder that early explorers were amazed to find that births among the Yurok Indians of California occurred predominantly in one season. They thought they had found a biologically primitive people whose mating behavior was closer to apes than to humans. What was actually occurring was a cultural phenomenon. The explorers did not realize that the Yuroks' ideas of marriage and cohabitation were completely different from the European model. For reasons seeded in tradition, the Yurok men spent most of the year living together, apart from their wives, in a men's sweathouse and clubhouse. It was there that they kept all their possessions. During the summer couples slept together outside. Nine months later babies abounded.[9]

[8] For further information see Wilton M. Krogman, "The Scars of Human Evolution," *Scientific American,* 185 (December 1951), 54–57.

[9] A. L. Kroeber, *Handbook of the Indians of California* (Berkeley: California Book, 1953), p. 44.

Not only are humans biologically able to breed in all seasons, but their *reproductive risk* is low. In fish, the number of eggs produced must be phenomenal to promote the continuance of the population. Because of the harshness of the marine environment, the hazards of external fertilization and development, and the always present predators, a single codfish must generate 30 million eggs, of which 50,000 might hatch and only two reach maturity. More than two might overpopulate and lead to the degeneration of the environment; fewer would eventually shrink the population to a level at which extinction would be probable. An average of two offspring per two adults is the magic number for animal populations that are in equilibrium with their environments. The greater the hazards of birth and life, the greater the number of eggs needed to assure that two offspring will survive to reproduce.

As we progress from fish to amphibians, to reptiles, and finally to mammals, the number of eggs needed to assure two offspring diminishes. Human reproduction is among the least risky systems, with an average of five births resulting in two individuals who will reproduce. This represents the number for nonindustrial societies. Today in countries with advanced medical procedures and relatively stable food supplies the ratio is even more favorable.

This low risk is due to the fact that in humans, as in most mammals, fertilization and development occur within a controlled environment, the mother's body. The fish mother is long gone when the baby fish hatch, whereas the mammalian progeny will be nourished and protected by its mother even after it is born. While the human mother is pregnant and after the child is born, cultural factors such as providing adequate shelter, food, and general care can help lower the reproductive risk. However, since the efficiency of these depend on what the physical environment can provide and on the acquired knowledge of the specific group, reproductive risk will vary from culture to culture.

In humans the mother-child relationship is extended in two ways. First, other relatives and friends can aid directly in the child's survival, and second, the period of dependence is long. In fact, a child may remain at least partially dependent on kin for life. Or the adults, whose protection allowed the child to survive, might eventually become dependent on their offspring. This type of relationship is unknown in the rest of the animal world.

People and Nature

People are biological entities. But with the development of the biological potential for culture, people began to interact consciously with the natural environment. Culture became the main method of adaptation to environments, and through it humans were able to enter new territories by fashioning raw materials into protective and manipulative devices that would allow them to survive where they were not suited biologically. This did not place people above nature but thrust them into a different relationship with it.

One example of how human beings are a part of, and are dependent upon, nature is the fact that people, like all organisms, are a part of *food chains*. A food chain is a sequence of sources of energy, each source being dependent on another source. The sun is the major source of energy for plants, plants provide energy for *herbivores,* and herbivores are eaten by *carnivores* and *omnivores* (Figure 1-4).

The relationship of organisms in a food chain can be seen in the following example. At least one of the Great Lakes already is near "death" from industrial wastes. That is, if the pollution of the lake continues, it will not be able to support any

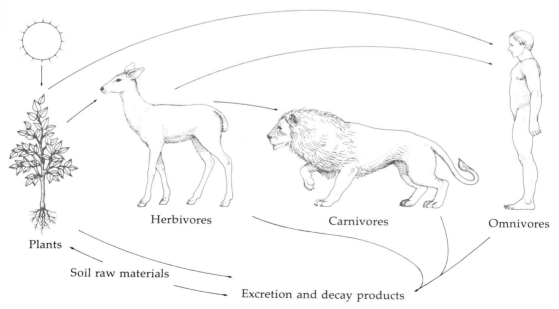

Herbivores   Carnivores   Omnivores

Plants

Soil raw materials

Excretion and decay products

Figure 1-4   Food chain. *The sun is the ultimate source of all food energy. From this base various food chains develop.*

plant or animal life.[10] The oceans are also being increasingly polluted, and if they were to "die," which appears to be a possibility, animal life would probably become extinct. It is the green plants that provide us with the oxygen we breathe. Seventy-one percent of the earth's surface is covered with water. If all the aquatic plants were to pass out of existence, so would all animal life.[11]

Plants are at the bottom of most food chains. That is, all animals ultimately depend on them, and not only for oxygen, but for sustenance. That hamburger you had for lunch could not have existed without the grass, corn, or other plant material the cow ate. The amount of plant material available will determine the number of cows and hence the amount of beef available for people. As the human population increases, it becomes increasingly difficult to feed everyone. Since there is little reason to believe that the problem can be solved technologically, population control appears to be the ultimate answer (Chapter 16).

Thus culture and biology, along with environment, have interacted with each other in the formation of humankind, resulting in a multidimensional entity. At the highest level of abstraction, people are cultural beings. But our potential for culture depends upon our existence as biological organisms; this distinction is shared with all animals and plants. Human biology is a result of the individual components that are the building blocks of the body. A person is made up of chemical substances; this characteristic is shared with all matter. On the lowest level of abstraction, a person's entire being, like all things in the universe, is subject to the physical laws of nature, such as the laws of gravity, thermodynamics, motion, and collision.

[10] Quincy Dadisman, "Not Quite Dead: The Pathology of Lake Erie," *Nation*, 214, no. 16 (17 April 1972), 492–496.

[11] Hearings before the Subcommittee on Oceans and Atmosphere, United States Senate, serial no. 92-49, 1972.

Myths about Humankind

We have been discussing several essential features of human beings, but many things about humans which are believed to be true actually are myths.

Myths about human antiquity Many believe that humans were formed last, after the stage had been set for them. According to the Bible, humanity was created on the sixth day and commanded to "subdue" the natural environment and the other living things. Even those people who have had some contact with evolutionary theory often believe that human beings were the last organism to evolve, being the end product of the previous mistakes and experiments of nature. These ideas are incorrect. Many kinds of animals have arisen after *Homo sapiens*. In fact, in the last 5,000 years our domestication of animals has produced many new breeds of animals. In addition, living peoples have as long an ancestry as any presently living animal; all animals ultimately derive from the cells that originated billions of years ago. Also, the group of animals to which humans belong, the primates, has been around longer than many other kinds of mammals, such as the rodents.

In a sarcastic mood you might describe the chimpanzee on the television screen as being your friend's relative. A common misconception is that people evolved from living apes. In reality the apes are our collateral relatives. They have a common ancestor with us in the distant past. They are *not* direct ancestors. One cannot evolve from a contemporary. Separate paths from a common ancestor probably developed before 15 million years ago (Chapter 14). As the human line developed, it diverged from that of the apes. As early as 250,000 years ago, the species *Homo sapiens* may have come into existence.

The myth of technology In the last century people have accomplished almost unbelievable technological feats. From the invention of the steamship to the development of the spaceship, humankind's mechanical genius has been displayed. A phone is picked up and through a thin, plastic-coated wire, conversation reaches people around the block or thousands of miles away. Television creates images on a glass screen, and soon, through holography (the projection of three-dimensional images by laser beams) a screen may not even be needed. This apparent technological mastery has led people to the quite incorrect and dangerous belief that technology can solve any and every problem the environment presents. All that is needed is enough time, effort, money, and knowhow.

But not everything is possible. For instance, unaided humans in their present form could not run a mile in one minute, or anywhere near it. That is believed to be biologically impossible.

Just as some things are biologically impossible, others are technologically infeasible or improbable. It is not likely that we will solve the world's food problem technologically. Even with the great advances in methods of food production, more people are starving today than ever before. This is partially because population is increasing faster than the research and innovations that compensate for such population growth.

Technology, for most people, is not the solution to loneliness or despair, nor will it alleviate hatred or prejudice. It can be a tool but not a total cure. In fact, the advanced technologies of modern peoples might ultimately end our existence, because if technological "progress" is not accompanied by appropriate social change and ecological responsibility, people may drown in the poisons of their own industrial wastes (Chapter 16).

The myth of plenty This leads us to the third myth, the idea that people can continue to increase in numbers forever. There are two main reasons why this is not true. First, there is a limited amount of certain essential resources that life depends on. For example, there is only a finite amount of solar energy that green plants can capture. This vegetation is the ultimate source of all animal food. Because of the limitation of solar energy, and because vegetation reproduces its bulk more slowly than animals, there is an absolute limit to the size of the population of any animal, including humans, for a particular environment (Figure 1-5).

The second reason that people cannot continue to increase forever is simply the lack of space. People cannot occupy every inch of the earth's surface without cutting off their food and water supplies. That wide-open land in the American Midwest must remain wide open. It is from here and from similar places that the enormous amount of food needed to feed each of the more than 200 million people in the United States comes. Wheat could not be grown in a coast-to-coast Manhattan.

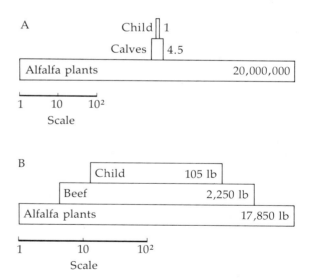

Figure 1-5 **Food pyramids.** *Pyramid A shows the number of plants required to support the number of calves needed to support one child in a hypothetical situation. Pyramid B shows the same thing in terms of the total weight.*

The myth of human superiority It was once thought that the sun revolved around the earth, that the earth was the center of the universe, and that humans were the highest form of life on earth. This *anthropocentricity,* which is comforting but scientifically useless, embodies the fourth myth. It is true that humans are capable of more conscious activities geared to modify the environment. Yet this is only one out of many criteria for superiority. For instance, the termites discussed earlier have been around longer than humans, and evolution has brought about solutions to their problems of starvation, internal conflict, and division of labor. Termite societies are highly organized and extremely efficient. These insects, which often are considered so lowly, also greatly outnumber us. Any of these characteristics could be taken as a measure of *their* superiority. Of course, the point is that superiority is relative to the criteria being used. If human beings are superior, it is only because we define ourselves as such.

How free are people? Growing out of the idea of human superiority is the belief that people control their own destiny, that they possess "free will." There is more variation in behavior between human groups and individuals than among other animals. This is due to the great diversity of learned behavioral patterns among humans. However, there are limitations to behavior. Free will is not so much "free" as it is confined. Every action that we take depends on our biological makeup, our culture, and the environment that surrounds us at the moment. On the biological level, for example, some people simply are not equipped to be the heavyweight boxing champion. On the cultural level, patterned, learned behavior creates habitual ways of thinking that inclines people to analyze experiences according to the particular standards of their culture. In other words, the choices made are conditioned or caused by previous events. The environment also

limits what you can and cannot do. You could not go skiing in the middle of the Mohave Desert.

The following chapters will provide more explanations of these and other myths. The proper understanding of humanity involves learning not only about what people are but also about what they are not.

Summary

People are both biological and cultural beings. Most animals adapt to their environments in terms of somatic changes and innate behavior. For some, such as the chimpanzee, learning plays an important role. However, with people, learned, patterned, transmittable behavior, which is defined as culture, is not only important but is a part of virtually all behavior except simple reflex actions.

Culture can be thought of in two ways. First, it is a means of adaptation, that is, a way of coping with the environment. Second, cultural behavior creates environments. The potential for cultural behavior has added the dimension of mind to that of body. The mind is the specific and unique internalization of the individual's cultural experience.

People are not biologically divergent from the rest of the animal kingdom. However, there are certain traits that are developed to their greatest degree in humans. We must realize that it is the complex of various traits that defines humanity, for people do not have an exclusive claim to any one trait. Each species has its own complex of characteristics.

One of the most important aspects of the human complex is the neural and laryngeal potential for speech. Humans also display habitual bipedalism. In addition, sexual receptivity is not closely controlled by hormonal cycles, and humans have low reproductive risk. People, like all animals and plants, are a part of food chains, and for this reason we cannot ignore our relationship with other organisms. Humans have great antiquity and today represent one of the most widely dispersed species.

There are many things that people are not. We are not capable of totally controlling nature through technology, and, indeed, much of our technology may be more destructive in the long run than constructive. The human population cannot continue to grow indefinitely. It is also incorrect to consider humans superior to all other creatures. All organisms have their specific complex of adaptations which serve them. Nor is it correct to think that human will is totally free. Humans, like all animals, have biological limitations. Even though the human mind frees people's actions from most innate behavior, it also locks them into habitual, patterned behavior.

WHAT IS ANTHROPOLOGY?

The anthropologist is an explorer in pursuit of answers to the questions: What is it to be human? and What is the nature of humankind? The word *anthropology* derives from the Greek *anthropos,* meaning "people," and *logos,* meaning "study." Therefore, anthropology is the study of people.

Concepts Common to All Branches of Anthropology

Anthropology is not the only discipline devoted to the study of people. But anthropology is a discipline with a broad range of interests and is distinguished by several basic principles and concepts. The culture concept, already discussed, is one unifying principle, as is the theory of evolution, which will be discussed throughout the text. In addition, the principles of holism, relativism, and comparison are central to all anthropological studies.

The principle of holism　The first and foremost principle of anthropology is that people must be understood in terms of their total being. This ap-

proach, called *holism,* assumes that in order to understand, for example, the political system of a people, their religious system, art, kinship, and so on also must be considered. It goes further than this. The anthropologist believes that the biological being and cultural being cannot be separated. Biology and culture are so mutually interdependent that to talk about one without the other is simplistic, except in a highly analytic and abstract sense. Yet, another factor must also fit into the pattern: the *natural environment.* Everything outside the biological organism and everything beyond the cultural innovations are part of the natural environment—the trees, climate, mountains and rivers, and all the plants and animals that live in association with people.

Consider the following analogy. Assume that each of the cultural behavior patterns is like individual pickup sticks. To these sticks are added another set, which are human biological characteristics. Still one more set—the environmental factors—is placed alongside the first two. Now all three sets of sticks are mixed up and thrown to the floor. Assume that they fall in such a way that if any one of them is picked up, almost all the others will move. Some will move violently; others will hardly budge, but almost all will be moved (Figure 1-6). This is admittedly a contrived analogy, but it illustrates the fact that people are both a collection and a result of many different interrelated factors.

The principle of relativism　Each human system, each culture, each society is what it is because of the combination of biological, cultural, and environmental factors. As with each independent throw of the combined pickup-stick sets, the above factors are combined differently for each system. The system can be viewed only in terms of the principles, background, frame of reference, and history that characterize it. This is the principle of *relativism.*

Relativism simply means that what is being

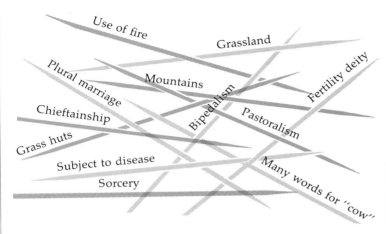

Use of fire
Grassland
Plural marriage
Mountains
Fertility deity
Bipedalism
Chieftainship
Pastoralism
Grass huts
Subject to disease
Many words for "cow"
Sorcery

Figure 1-6 Pickup-stick analogy. *Every element of a system has some relationship to every other element. If one of the elements is altered, changes will take place in other elements of the system.*

studied at the moment must be interpreted in terms of the system in which it is found. For instance, obesity might be considered beautiful among people who are constantly in fear of famine because to them obesity represents well-being. Anthropologists do not say that a particular trait is good or bad, right or wrong; this is the preoccupation of the moralist. Instead, the anthropologist investigates the form, structure, and function of characteristics and systems.

Form, structure, and function Behavior patterns and material objects have *form, structure,* and *function.* Humor can serve as an example. Humor takes different forms in different societies and, indeed, different forms in different social situations within the same society. What would be funny to an Ojibwa Indian might not be funny to a Navaho and could actually be insulting to an Australian aborigine.

The form of humor, together with the form of all other traits in the society and the way each trait influences and relates to the others, is the structure of the system. For example, the Ojibwa Indians (as well as many other societies throughout the world) differentiate between different

cousins, depending on whether those cousins are considered to be within the same or a different clan. This is one aspect of the form their kinship system takes. Humor is related to kinship. Among the Ojibwa one would never joke with a cousin of the opposite sex in the same clan. However, vigorous joking occurs between cousins of the opposite sex from different clans. The structure refers to the form of humor, kinship, and other factors and the relationships between them.

The way each element of the system contributes to the operation of the system as a whole is that element's function. For example, one of the functions of humor, as noted by anthropologist A. R. Radcliffe-Brown,[12] is to reduce tension between in-laws. Among the Ojibwa cousins in different clans are potential mates, and joking is geared toward breaking down barriers. So one function of joking is to promote the unity of the group.

The anthropologist is also interested in *process,* the interaction of elements in a biological or cultural system and how a change in the form,

[12] A. R. Radcliffe-Brown, *Structure and Function in Primitive Society* (New York: Free Press), 1965.

structure, or function of an element affects that of other elements. That is, biology and culture are seen as being dynamic. Among the Ojibwa, for instance, if cousin marriage ceased, the relationship of humor to kinship would be altered. However, how it would be altered would depend on the total cultural system. Similarly, if one biological characteristic of a population of organisms were altered—say, an increase in the acuteness of vision—other characteristics would be influenced —the other senses, coordination, methods of movement, and so on.

The idea that a human system must be viewed in terms of its milieu does not presuppose that there are no human universals. One of the general conclusions that anthropologists have come to is that people throughout the world are very similar to each other. To a large extent, what varies is life-style. The essence of humanity supersedes these details. However, it is only through a close examination of the specifics that the essence emerges.

The emphasis on comparison, contrast, and synthesis The main tasks of anthropologists, regardless of the subfield in which they are specializing, are to seek out, describe, order, analyze, and synthesize data on human nature and the various configurations that nature takes. They do this by careful study of the problem directly before them and then by comparison of their results with those of other researchers. All knowledge is interrelated, and the anthropologists' data and insights simply add to the growing reservoir of information from the social, natural, behavioral, and physical sciences, along with the humanities. Anthropologists look for universals by analyzing truly comparable similarities and differences and attempt to predict patterned similarities and differences by examining universals. Along with holism, then, a major methodological approach of anthropology is the emphasis on *comparison, contrast,* and *synthesis.*

The Branches of Anthropology

When you tell someone that you are an anthropologist, a usual reply is, "Have you dug up any bones lately?" or "Do you know Margaret Mead?" Anthropology is not all old bones and Margaret Mead. There are four main branches to the study of people: sociocultural anthropology, archaeology, linguistics, and physical anthropology (Figure 1-7). They are separate only in the sense that their emphasis (the specific area of human behavior being addressed) and methods are somewhat different. Their target is the same — humanity.

Sociocultural anthropology Sociocultural anthropology aims at understanding human social organization. Some anthropologists focus their study on social patterns and social interactions that occur within a society; they are called *social anthropologists.* A *society* can be defined as a group of interacting people who share a geographical region, a sense of common identity, and a common culture. The members of a society interact with each other with varying degrees of intensity. Whereas a society is an actual group of people, a culture is the learned behavioral patterns displayed by these people. The anthropologists that study these learned patterns of behavior are called *cultural anthropologists.*

Sociocultural anthropology can involve the investigation of the various ways that different peoples secure their food, decorate themselves and their homes and tools, and organize their systems of law, politics, economics, kinship, and religion. Methods of child rearing, curing the sick, avenging a wrong, and having fun are scrutinized. The responses humans make in adapting culturally and socially to the environment are studied by the sociocultural anthropologist.

The raw data are supplied by *ethnographies. Ethno* simply means "peoples" and is combined with a number of suffixes to produce similar words. An ethnography is a description of a so-

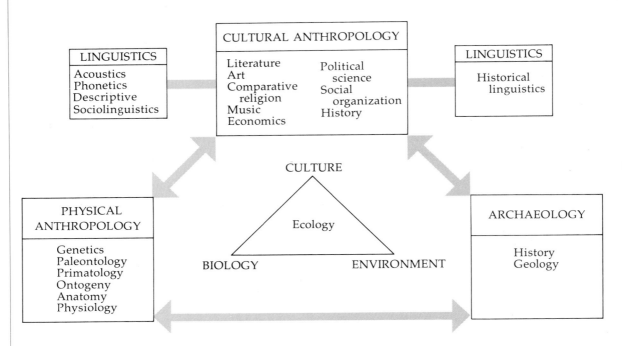

Figure 1-7   **The branches of anthropology.** *The interrelation of the branches of anthropology, with some of their major areas of interest and related fields.*

ciety or culture or a part of one. The *ethnographer* collects the data; the *ethnologist* analyzes, interprets, and compares these data.

While many social scientists collect data administering questionnaires or tests, the major method of data gathering for the ethnographer is *participant observation*. First, the ethnographer is a participant who attempts to "get into" a culture and, to a degree, to participate in its activities. Not a few anthropologists have been initiated into adulthood by the groups they have studied. Through all this, the anthropologist remains an observer attempting to retain a high degree of objectivity.

Social and cultural anthropology provide us with an insight into the extrasomatic nature of humankind. They show us how our common humanity takes various shapes in different places and circumstances. They investigate all aspects of human society and culture and include studies of human social relationships, social groups, political and economic organization, religious and family organization, the relation of culture to the individual, problems of culture change, music and the arts, and so on. From comparative studies of cultural similarities and differences, principles of human nature can be inferred.

Archaeology   Whereas ethnographers deal with living cultures, *archaeologists* reconstruct cultures of the past. They cannot enter a living culture and attempt to participate in its activities, but they can uncover a culture and try to picture it as it was.

Archaeologists are puzzle solvers. They carefully piece together the available data and attempt to reconstruct the culture from them. The data include all the aspects of the culture which can be determined from the manufactured remains, the artifacts from the site, and their context. Archaeologists use these artifacts as evidence of the adaptations made by the culture to the environment.

An *artifact* is a manufactured expression of a culture. This expression is a clue to the solution of the puzzle, for if archaeologists can discover what the artifact expresses, they gain an insight into the culture. For instance, the automobile may be considered an artifact of an industrial culture. The automobile is not merely a mode of transportation but also functions as a status symbol (various cars carry more or less status). If a future archaeologist were to uncover an automobile junkyard, the various forms of the automobile that would be found might be an important source of data in the reconstruction of the culture from which they came.

Artifacts are manifestations of behavior. That is, the types of materials discovered, the methods by which they were manufactured, and the arrangement and context in which they are found indicate something beyond the "where" and "when" of the culture. On the basis of this evidence the archaeologist develops hypotheses about the form, structure, function, and processes within the system of behavior that once existed. For help, the archaeologist calls upon the theories of ethnology, as well as sociology, economics, political science, and any other area of knowledge that will assist in a reconstruction.

Linguistics Another area of human research is *linguistics*. A person who simply speaks many languages is not necessarily a linguist in the anthropological sense of the word. The anthropological linguist examines the history, function, structure, and physiology of one of people's most definitive characteristics—language. Many linguists concentrate on the social and cultural contexts of language, that is, how the general social and cultural milieu acts to influence language and at the same time is reflected in language. For instance, the living conditions, types of jobs, and family organization of each social segment of a population lead to specific words, phrases, and even grammatical constructions that reflect these factors. Starting from the other direction, an analysis of language can tell a great deal about the social and cultural setting of a people.

Language, perhaps as much as any other phenomenon, has allowed people to develop into the complex cultural beings they are. Modern people without language would be an absurdity. Language is the means by which people communicate abstract thought. It is also the way one generation transmits its acquired knowledge to the next generation.

Physical anthropology Physical anthropology is *human biology*. In fact, in recent years the term *biological anthropology* has been used with increased frequency in place of physical anthropology. However, it is somewhat different in emphasis and approach from the human biology of zoologists. The difference lies in the mind of the anthropologist. Whereas the zoologist studying human populations may note that one population has a higher frequency of dark skin than another, then neatly describes this variation, and perhaps investigates the genetic mechanisms that led to the differentiation, the anthropologist also attempts to discover cultural conventions that may be keeping the dark-skinned population from interbreeding with the light one. For instance, cultural conventions involving concepts of beauty, class distinctions, kinship considerations, economic relationships, and so on all affect breeding patterns. In other words, the biological anthropologist takes note of the fact that culture both builds upon and modifies biology.

The scope of physical anthropology is broad indeed. Anything that involves human biological development is fair game for a research project or a theoretical conjecture. One of the main interests of the field has been in seeking an answer to the question: How did humans acquire their present form and behavior? Some have assumed that people always have been the way they are today. The anthropologist is convinced that human beings, like all plants and animals, have changed over time in response to changing conditions. So, one of the anthropologists' main aims is to find evidence for evolution and generate theories about it. Recently, the anthropologist's concern for evolution has focused on the principles of *genetics*. It is the genetic material of an animal that environmental forces work upon to create evolutionary change. Genetics also throws light on the relationship between biology and culture, medical problems, and the nature of individual and group differences (Chapters 3 to 6).

The concept of *race* has also been an intriguing concern of the anthropologist. In recent years, the study of *human variation* has discredited biased value judgments and superficial classifications of people based on a few outward characteristics. Again, genetics plays a major role. Through a description of the differences in the frequencies of various genes in different populations, studies of human variation can be made quantitatively objective (Chapters 7 and 8).

Primatology is another area of continuing research. The primatologist attempts to answer such questions as: What relationship do other living primates, such as the apes and monkeys, have to human beings? How can studies of their behavior aid us in understanding human behavior? Can an understanding of their place in nature lead to an understanding of ours? (Chapters 9 to 12).

One of the major focuses of physical anthropology is the study of *human evolution*. Comparative studies of the living primates, including people, can lead to a reconstruction of human evolutionary pathways. Since humans and chimpanzees, for example, share a common ancestry, they also share a great number of anatomical and physiological features. The study of *comparative anatomy* and *comparative molecular biology* provides one line of evidence for human evolution (Chapter 12).

Some physical anthropologists play it safe. They work with specimens that do not bite, yell, or squirm. Their subjects are long dead and often remain only as a disarticulated pile of bones. Actually, the anthropologist who specializes in *human paleontology* might occasionally find some intact skeletons, but at other times he or she might spend decades searching for human ancestors and turn up a few teeth of a humanlike creature who lived millions of years ago. The study of the fossil record has revealed a substantial metamorphosis in the human form. As will be seen, the story is still unfolding (Chapters 13 to 15).

Some anthropologists seek answers to such questions as: Why do some people mature sexually faster than others? Why do girls tend to grow faster than boys at first and then are surpassed by their male age-mates? Why do we age at all? Some trees are virtually immortal; is there anything we can do to prevent or delay death in humans? These and other similarly fascinating questions are being investigated by research into *human ontogeny*, that is, studies of growth and development (Chapters 8 and 12).

The science of *human ecology* is a special interest of physical anthropology. It is the study of the dynamic relationship that exists between humans and the environments in which they live. Ecological studies are dependent upon all the other fields of research mentioned. We hope that the data from human ecological research will help us understand and solve the problems that face humans as a species before people pass into the same extinction as hundreds of other organisms through time (Chapter 16).

CONCLUSION

At the onset it should be cautioned that there are no simplistic answers to questions raised in this chapter. The purpose of this book is to provide a basic understanding of humans, their development, and their place in nature. We cannot promise that all questions about people will be answered; in fact, we can promise that they will not. A great deal has been learned about human nature over the centuries, and especially in the last hundred years. Yet, anthropology is a dynamic subject. With each publication of a research project, it is probable that new information will be added to our knowledge of humanity. In other words, data needed to answer crucial questions about the human species are still being uncovered.

Why study anthropology? Anthropology provides empirical knowledge about the human condition. On one level, this simply serves to feed our curiosity about ourselves. However, anthropological studies also provide data useful to the fields of medicine, environmental maintenance, urban planning, education, and so forth. Anthropology also attempts to provide a profile of human potentials and limitations. We will attempt to give, in each part of this text, a fuller statement of the relevance of anthropology.

The text is divided into five parts. Part One, which includes this chapter and the next, provides a background for anthropology in general and physical anthropology in particular. The main theme of physical anthropology is human evolution and the biological nature of humankind. Part Two discusses the general theory of evolution and its specific application to humans. The study of human genetics and population genetics provides a background for understanding the mechanisms of the evolutionary process itself. The problems of human variation, introduced in Part Three, are discussed within the context of population genetics and evolutionary theory.

The remainder of the book deals with the reconstruction of the pathways of human evolution. Part Four reports on ideas and research in the area of primatology, including the natural history, behavior, and comparative anatomy of the living primates. Comparisons of contemporary forms enable the anthropologist to develop insights into the nature of human evolution and to reconstruct some of the events of this evolution. Part Five discusses the actual physical evidence of human evolution, that of the fossil record. The concluding chapter examines some of the consequences of people's past evolution for contemporary humans and surveys some ideas about our evolutionary future.

SUGGESTED READINGS

The readings listed for Chapters 1 and 2 are general in nature. References to information on specific topics that are mentioned in these introductory chapters will be given in the chapters that discuss those topics in more detail.

Brew, J. O. (ed.). *One Hundred Years of Anthropology.* Cambridge: Harvard Univ. Press, 1968. A series of articles by distinguished authors discussing the developments of the past hundred years in the various branches of anthropology.

Eiseley, L. *The Immense Journey.* New York: Vintage, 1946. An imaginative and insightful exploration of the history of the earth and of man.

Elliott, H. C. *The Evolution of the Human Brain.* New York: Scribner's, 1964. Excellent text on the human brain, with some interesting philosophical comments.

Honigmann, J. J. *The Development of Anthropological Ideas.* Homewood, Ill.: Dorsey, 1976. A detailed look at the development of cultural anthropology.

Kroeber, A. L., and C. Kluckhohn. *Culture: A Critical Review of Concepts and Definitions.* New York: Vintage, 1963. A summary of the various ways in which the culture concept has been used and defined.

Montagu, M. F. A. (ed.). *Culture: Man's Adaptive Dimension.* Oxford: Oxford Univ. Press, 1968. A series of essays dealing with culture as a means of adaptation.

Chapter Two
Prerequisites to the Development of an Evolutionary Theory

EARLY VIEWS ON THE ESSENCE OF HUMANS, NATURE, AND TIME

Ideas are formed, nurtured, and brought to maturity in the context of particular intellectual backgrounds. That is, the things we think, the relationships we see, and the very process of creativity are at least partially determined by our cultural environment. Similarly, the knowledge of any one time represents an accumulation of information and ideas. In this light, the theory of evolution was not developed by one person. It was part of a chain of intellectual events, each link being necessary to the continuity of the chain.

Although there were many variations in early ideas about the universe, in many instances they were opposite to those embodied in present evolutionary theory. These old ideas had to be challenged before a new concept of reality could arise.

First among the early views was the idea of human superiority. The earth was seen to occupy a place at the center of the universe, with all celestial bodies revolving around it. Humanity, in turn, was conceived of as the center of life on earth. God provided the animals and plants for people's use and fancy. This belief is termed *anthropocentricity*. Similarities between people and animals and between various animals were seen as reflecting the design of the Creator. Certain shapes and forms were pleasing to God, and so they were used as models.

Life was considered to have arisen out of the will of the Creator from nonlife. Some believed that the process of creation from nonliving materials continued even after the original six days of Genesis. The explanation for the appearance of maggots on meat, for example, was that the meat was possessed of the "spirit of life." The idea that life can be generated directly from nonliving material is called *spontaneous creation*. It was commonly thought that once a type of organism was created, its descendants remained in the exact same form, *immutable*, from generation to generation.

The original creation as described in Genesis was seen to have taken place a few thousand years before the Greek and Roman Empires. In fact, in 1650, Archbishop James Ussher of Armagh, Ireland, proposed that the earth came into being on the morning of 4004 B.C. Another churchman calculated this birth to have taken place at exactly 9 A.M. on October 23!

The concept of a spontaneously created and static life brought into being only 6,000 years ago is directly counter to modern evolutionary theory. The development of evolutionary theory depended on an increasing disbelief in the old ideas.

Questioning the Old Ideas

What a shock it must have been to European scholars of the sixteenth century when Nicolaus Copernicus (1473–1543) showed conclusively that the earth was not the center of the universe. It was not even the center of the solar system! This was but one of a series of revelations that were to bombard old ideas.

Expecting to fall off the edge of the earth a weary sea captain might have been both elated and confused at the greeting he received from an exotic people living on a shore that could not possibly exist. The age of exploration served to display variations in life not dreamed of before. In 1600, Europeans knew of 6,000 plants. One century later, they recognized 18,000 and by the beginning of the nineteenth century they knew of 50,000 types of plants. Although the precise number is debated, one source states that over 550,000 species of plants are recognized today.[1] Also, during the age of exploration, strange animals never mentioned in the Bible were seen by Europeans for the first time.

[1] T. E. Weier, C. R. Stocking, and M. G. Barbour, *Botany: An Introduction to Plant Biology* (New York: Wiley, 1974), p. 7.

What is the relationship between living things? Although all cultures classify plants and animals into some kind of scheme, it was not until the seventeenth and eighteenth centuries that comprehensive written classifications were made. The Swedish naturalist Carolus Linnaeus (1707–1778) succeeded in classifying every animal and plant known to him into a system of categories and subcategories. This type of classification is absolutely necessary for a scientific understanding of the relationship of one plant or animal to the next. Yet, at first it reinforced traditional ideas. Linnaeus saw each category as fixed, the result of divine creation (Chapter 9).

Linnaeus' scheme was to become important to modern biological sciences for many reasons. First, it imposed order upon nature's infinite variation. Linnaeus saw that structure and function could be used to group plants and animals into categories. The most specific groups included organisms that were very much alike, whereas the more general levels encompassed the specific groups, thereby representing a wider range of variation. Linnaeus said that the first order of science is to distinguish one thing from the other, and his classification helped do just that.

Second, although Linnaeus considered organisms to be immutable, paradoxically it was his classification that provided a means for "seeing" change and possible ancestral relationships. It was pondered that similar organisms might be related to common ancestry. Therefore, if two or more types had a common origin but were now somewhat different, evolution must have occurred. In fact, Linnaeus, who had been so emphatic about the idea of unchanging species, began in later life to question this concept of fixity. He had observed new "types" of plants resulting from crossbreeding and had decided that perhaps all living things did not result from divinely created pairs.

Third, Linnaeus included people in his classification. Although he did not contend that humans were related to other animals, his very placement of humans in this scheme was sure to raise the question.

Could nature be dynamic? The informed people of this period were intrigued with the rapidly increasing information brought to the fore by exploration. Not only did the number of known plants and animals increase enormously, but so did the number of kinds of people. Who were the American Indians, the Polynesians, the Africans? Were they human, or were they part human and part ape? Credible answers to these and other questions could not be supplied by traditional ideologies.

The effect of exploration in guiding people to new realities was intensified by the great revolutions of the eighteenth and nineteenth centuries. These revolutions included the technological changes in the industrial age and political upheavals, such as the French and American Revolutions. Technological and political developments which brought about major social changes created an atmosphere in which the ideas of immutability could be questioned. If people could change their social systems so rapidly, if human life could be so dynamic, then perhaps nature was also fluid. It was in the late eighteenth century that the first modern theories of organic evolution emerged.

Early evolutionary ideas Comte de Buffon (1707–1788), a contemporary of Linnaeus, proposed every major point that Darwin would later include in *The Origin of Species.* Buffon recognized the tendency of species to increase at a faster rate than their food supply and hence the struggle for survival. He noted the variations within species and speculated on methods of inheritance. He questioned spontaneous creation and also proposed that the earth was much older than 6,000 years. Buffon's importance was diminished by his lack of conciseness. He might

consciously have been vague and apologetic about his thoughts for fear of being considered a heretic.

Although Buffon, and others of the era, implied evolution in their writing, it was left to Jean Baptiste de Lamarck (1744–1829) to propose articulately a systematic theory of evolution as an explanation of organic diversity. Lamarck used the previously nonevolutionary idea that organisms could be ranked in a progressive order, with humans at the top. He envisioned evolution as a constant striving toward perfection. He believed that deviations from an exact progression were due to local adaptations to specific environments.

Lamarck is remembered by many for his explanation of the cause of these deviations. Again, using an idea that had been around for centuries, he proposed that an organism acquired new characteristics in its lifetime by virtue of using or not using different parts of its body and that these newly acquired characteristics could then be inherited by the individual's offspring. For instance, if an animal constantly had to stretch its neck to get at food in the branches of a tree, its neck might get longer. If the trees were to get taller, the animal might then have to stretch more, and again the neck would get longer. This was Lamarck's explanation of the giraffe. He believed that a trait, once acquired, would be passed on to the next generation.

Lamarck's importance lies in his proposal that life is dynamic and that there is a mechanism in nature which promotes ongoing change; however, the method of change he suggested is incorrect. Acquired characteristics are not transmitted to offspring. Someone who lifts weights and becomes a champion will not have a muscle-bound baby or even a child with any more propensity toward muscularity than if he had never worked out with weights.

Lamarck, like so many famous people of science, was a synthesizer. He combined previously existing notions (such as Linnaean classification and the idea of acquired characteristics) into a new system with new meaning. Although the details of his ideas are incorrect, his emphasis on change gave impetus to the thoughts of those investigators who would ultimately discover accurate explanations for the change he proposed.

What is the age of the earth? By the early nineteenth century, masses of new data had been gathered which threw doubt on traditional interpretations. Charles Lyell (1797–1875) synthesized this new information in a textbook, *Principles of Geology,* published in 1830. In it he popularized the theory of *uniformitarianism,*

Figure 2-1 Stratigraphy. *The Grand Canyon shows the various strata that have accumulated over millennia.*

Prerequisites to the Development of an Evolutionary Theory

which was a main prerequisite to the development of a credible evolutionary theory. The principle of uniformitarianism states that physical forces, such as wind, rain, heat, cold, moving water, and earthquakes, that are working today to alter the earth were also in force and working in the same way in former times. Therefore, "the present is the key to the past."

Lyell also realized that the processes of physical alteration of the earth as they operate today would require very long periods of time to form *strata,* layers of the earth (Figure 2-1). It therefore could be inferred that the large number and often great thicknesses of strata formed in the past must have taken a long time to develop. This

indicated an age of the earth many times greater than that of the Biblical chronology. In developing the theory of uniformitarianism, Lyell was also setting the stage for a theory of the evolution of the inorganic world.

In addition, Lyell studied fossil plants and animals embedded in the various layers. Through these and other similar investigations, it became obvious that not only was the earth extremely old but that life had existed in various forms, some now extinct, for hundreds of centuries. Lyell, himeslf, did not become convinced of the evolution of living things until later in his life; in his text *The Antiquity of Man* (1864), he supported Charles Darwin's theory of evolution.

Fossils and extinct forms of plants and animals had been known long before Lyell's time, and many valid interpretations had been made. However, as is often the case, the evidence was more frequently viewed in terms of the predispositions and special interests of the observer and was not analyzed critically. For instance, extinct animals were thought by many to be creatures "who did not make the Ark." After Lyell's systematic investigation, some scientists began at least to speculate on the idea of a more dynamic world. Yet, the notion of prehistoric people was still heresy. Were not all humans descendants of Adam and Eve?

Humans before Adam and Eve? The first person to make a systematic attempt to demonstrate that there must have been a prehistoric period was Jacques Boucher de Crèvecoeur de Perthes (1788–1868). While digging on the banks of the Somme River in southwestern France, he discovered that many of the stones were not made of the same material as the walls of the pit in which they were uncovered. In addition, the stones had obviously been shaped into specific forms. Other people had also observed these types of rocks and considered them to be "figured stones" of unknown origin or "thunder stones" cast to the

Figure 2-2 Thunder stones. *This is an example of a hand ax from the Lower Paleolithic of southwestern France.*

earth by God during thunderstorms. Boucher de Crèvecoeur de Perthes was convinced that they were made by ancient people (Figure 2-2). To back up this conviction, he collected what he thought was an immense amount of evidence to support his case. When he submitted his report in 1838 to various scientific societies, it was considered ridiculous. Not until twenty years later, a year before the publication of Darwin's *On the Origin of Species*, was his material accepted.

By the time of Darwin, the notions of anthropocentrism, immutability, and a date of 4004 B.C. for the earth's origin had been altered or reversed. For most of the scientific community, the final discrediting of spontaneous creation would have to wait until the time of Louis Pasteur.

How does life change? It was Charles Darwin (1809–1882) who proposed a comprehensive theory of organic evolution that accurately utilized the available evidence. Darwin had taken the post of naturalist on the H.M.S. *Beagle,* a ship commissioned to explore the globe. During the five-year voyage, Darwin noted that minute differences existed between the same basic kinds of animals in differing environments. He hypothesized that environmental forces acted to weed out those characteristics which were not as well suited to a particular situation as other characteristics. An example he used was that of the different bill shapes of finches.

Finches are songbirds, like sparrows, crossbills, and linnets. Darwin noted several species of finches which were unique to the Galápagos Islands. Within this group of birds were several variations in beak size (Figure 6-12). Darwin further observed that although some overlap in diet existed, the various types of birds ate basically different foods. The finches with powerful beaks could break open hard seeds which other finches could not. One variety of finch had a short, thick beak; its diet consisted mainly of leaves, buds,

blossoms, and fruits. Another finch had a long, straight beak and subsisted on nectar from the prickly pear cactus, as well as on other foods.[2]

Having evolved these different bill shapes, the different varieties of finches were able to take advantage of different habitats. Darwin believed that competition for specific habitats leads to diversity in animal and plant types. For example, the small-beaked birds could not compete for hard seeds with the birds having more powerful beaks. Unless the birds with smaller beaks possessed characteristics which would allow them to exploit a different segment of the environment, they might become extinct. Note that an animal does *not* evolve characteristics in order to survive, but must possess *in advance* characteristics that will allow it to survive (Chapter 6).

Darwin was not the only person developing a theory of evolution based on adaptation to the environment. As often happens in science, two people came up with basically the same conclusion simultaneously. As a matter of fact, in the summer of 1858, on receiving an essay from Alfred Russel Wallace (1823–1913), another famous naturalist with whom he had been corresponding, Darwin must have received a jolt. Wallace had come up with basically the same ideas that Darwin had worked on for two decades. Both men received credit for their work at a meeting of the Linnaean Society in 1858. However, Darwin published his book *On the Origin of Species* quickly after that in 1859 and has since received most of the credit for modern evolutionary theory, although Wallace deserved more credit than he is usually given.

Both men had read Thomas R. Malthus's (1766–1834) *Essay on the Principles of Population.* It appears that this essay, which stated that world population was growing at a faster rate than

---

[2] David Lack, *Darwin's Finches* (New York: Cambridge Univ. Press, 1947).

food production (remember, Buffon had also asserted this), implanted the idea of natural selection in the minds of both. Darwin and Wallace saw *natural selection* as the process by which individuals within a population that are better suited to the environment will survive at a greater frequency than those who are less well suited (Chapter 5). Whereas Malthus was concerned only with humans, Darwin and Wallace saw this process as being applicable to all life. The development of the theory of natural selection was Darwin's and Wallace's great contribution to the theory of organic evolution, which had been emerging from the work and ideas of many individuals.

Darwin's *Origin of Species,* along with later works, such as *The Descent of Man,* which attempted to demonstrate the common ancestry of humans and apes, irreversibly changed the scientific view of humankind and nature. It sparked some of the most vicious debates ever witnessed between scientists, on the one hand, and the general public, on the other.

Do organisms spontaneously arise from non-living material? At about the same time that Darwin was introducing his theory of evolution, Louis Pasteur (1822–1895) was disproving spontaneous creation. Remember the assertion that maggots spontaneously arise from meat. These maggots are the larvae of flies which have laid eggs in the decaying flesh. A similar situation occurs with any nutrient material exposed to the air. If flies do not contaminate the material, some other organism may.

It would seem a simple matter to prove that the nutrient does not generate the organisms. Simply put a sterilized food source in a sterilized and sealed container. If nothing grows, you have proved your point. This was done, but the proponents of spontaneous creation argued that the spirit of creation was prevented from entering the container and that the nutrient material was destroyed by sterilization. Pasteur designed an experiment that would answer these complaints. He made a flask with a swan-shaped neck. He then placed a boiled sugar solution, with yeast added, into the vessel. Even with the flask open, growth was prevented because the germ-laden dust was trapped in the bend of the neck. Next, he tipped the flask, drawing some of the dust collected in the bend into it. After the contaminated material was allowed to stand, it became clouded with microorganisms. This showed that boiling had not destroyed the supportive ability of the fluid. Pasteur had demonstrated that it was outside influences — insect eggs or microorganisms — not the dead material that gave rise to life.

Summary

Evolutionary theory has been shown to be a valid and reliable explanation of basic questions about life. Modern evolutionary theory grew out of a European intellectual climate that saw humans as the superior center of a world populated by spontaneously created organisms that did not change once created. Each of these ideas fell in the light of new knowledge gathered by hundreds of scholars, including Copernicus, Linnaeus, Buffon, Lamarck, Lyell, Boucher de Crèvecoeur de Perthes, Darwin, Wallace, and Pasteur.

It is now believed that the earth is about $4\frac{1}{2}$ billion years old and that life has existed for approximately $3\frac{1}{2}$ billion years. In this time, through natural processes, life has diversified and filled a multitude of environmental situations. Along the way, extinction was a common occurrence, as it continues to be.[3]

[3] More than fifty species of mammals and birds have become extinct in the last fifty years, many because of human hunting practices or other intrusions into their environments.

THE NATURE OF SCIENCE

The physicist investigating the relationship between time and space, the chemist exploring the properties of a new substance, the biologist probing the mysteries of the continuity of life, and the anthropologist searching for human origins share a common trait, curiosity. Not that nonscientists are not curious; most people possess this characteristic. The scientist, however, uses a specific method to delve into these enigmatic problems — the *scientific method*.

Unfortunately, science and its method are misunderstood. The multiplication of our knowledge in medicine and technology has led to the idea that science can cure all and explain all and that only enough time, money, and intelligence are needed. In truth, science cannot provide all answers. In fact, many phenomena are not even subject to scientific explanations.

On the other side of the coin, science has been attacked as a cause of most contemporary problems. It is said to be responsible for the depersonalization of the individual, for stripping creativity from human behavior, and for creating massive threats to the species through the development of nuclear power, insecticides, and polluting machinery. If we analyze the situation, we can see that it was not the original intent of the people who developed computers to debase humankind, nor was mass production proposed as a method to crush creativity. It is what society, policy makers especially, does with scientific achievements that makes them social or antisocial. There is nothing inherently good or bad about science.

The Many Aspects of Science

Just what is science? Here is where the dictionary fails, for science is not something that can be simply defined. It is an activity, a search, and a method of discovery which results in a body of knowledge.

Science is the activity of seeking out reliable explanations for phenomena. By ''reliable'' is meant *predictable*. Predictability does not mean assurance; it simply indicates in what percent of cases under a given set of conditions a particular event will occur.

Science is also a search for order. Nature does not categorize; people do. Through classifications, such as that of Linnaeus, systematic similarities and differences can be found. This displaying of ordered relationships allows for discoveries which might otherwise never be made.

The Scientific Method

Science is a method, and that method deserves some note here. Four basic elements precede the formation of a scientific statement: observation, question, hypothesis, and experiment. The fifth step, theory, is a goal.

Observation   Observation lies at the base of all human mental activity. An *observation* is any information received. In science the input must be *empirical,* that is, received through the senses, either directly or through extensions, such as telescopes and cloud chambers. The phenomenon being observed must be recurring. If something happens once, how can it be subjected to study? Observations have to be accurate, and this is not an easy task. There are always unknowns in the receiving of information. Is the receiver biased? Does the observer's social background make for observations that are a result of that background and not of the phenomenon? Is he or she colorblind or tone deaf, or does the observer have a sinus condition? Any of these factors could bias an observation. The end result of the scientific method depends on the validity of the initial observations, the original *data.*

Question After a set of observations is made, a *question* is asked: How did the phenomenon come to be? What is the difference between this and that? The question must be *relevant* and *testable*. "Relevant" simply means that it must have something to do with the observation. "Testable" means that the information must be susceptible to experimentation. The relevance and testability of a question are often not easy to ascertain. Sometimes we attempt an experiment, only to find that the thing or process being tested cannot be controlled, that there are too many variables, that evidence cannot be gathered, or that the phenomenon cannot be isolated.

Hypothesis Once a question is asked, a guess as to its answer is provided. This is the *hypothesis*. Since any particular question might have many possible answers, the guess made must be a good one or else the scientist will be testing questions all his or her life, never coming up with anything.

Many nonscientists share these first three features of the scientific method as working principles. It is not unusual to observe something, question it, and propose an answer. The fourth step, experimentation, separates science from conjecture.

Experimentation The *experiment* is a means of testing the *reliability* of a hypothesis. It provides evidence that will either add to the credibility of the hypothesis or disprove it. An experiment is a situation in which the scientist has control over the *variables* that are affecting a particular phenomenon. For instance, if one has formed the hypothesis "raising the temperature of a solution will decrease the amount of time that it takes for salt to dissolve in it," it must be possible to manipulate the variables of temperature and time. This, of course, might not be enough; other factors, such as pressure, volume, and the amount of salt added, might also have to be considered, along with the kind of solvent.

Control means more than just manipulation of variables. A controlled situation is one in which a comparison can be made between a specific situation and a second situation which differs in only one aspect from the first. The first situation is the control and the second the experiment. By comparing the results of the experiment and the control, we can measure the effect of the variable.

Because it can never be certain that all variables have been taken into consideration, a hypothesis can never be proved. If the experiment disproves it, for example, if temperature does not increase the solubility of salt, a new hypothesis can be generated on the basis of a reexamination of the original data and the experimental data. If the hypothesis is not disproved, the experimental data become evidence for its reliability. New experiments are performed, with the conditions being varied. If all the results support the hypothesis, its credibility continues to rise. Because a particular hypothesis can never be proved, experimentation on it can continue forever. Just one experiment could reveal a hidden variable that will either disprove or modify the original hypothesis. This hypothesis-experiment-hypothesis-experiment cycle is the self-corrective factor of science. The scientist realizes that the results are never final.

A hypothesis can be disproved on the basis of one set of experimental data. This does not mean that the results have to indicate an all-or-none effect. Consider the following: We hypothesize that drug X cures disease Y. Next, we administer the drug to 100 persons who have the disease, and 85 get better, while from a second group of 100 persons who have not received the drug, only 5 improve. The fact that the drug is not 100 percent efficient does not disprove the original hypothesis but modifies it to "85 percent of the people who are given drug X will be cured of disease Y." Now, as the new hypothesis is tested, the figure of 85 percent may remain constant or fluctuate with the new data. As experiments continue, indications appear of why some people are not curable by the drug.

Theory and law Science is cumulative. After hundreds of experiments have been done on a set of similar hypotheses with confirming results, a *theory* may be proposed. For instance, the hypothesis "if an apple is thrown into the air, it will return to the ground" could be shown to be reliable in every case that it is tested, under thousands of circumstances. Similar hypotheses about other objects likewise are accurate. As the evidence builds, a theory can be proposed: Everything that goes up must come down.

The difference between a hypothesis and a theory is that a hypothesis must be supported by evidence; a theory goes beyond evidence. By saying "*everything* that . . . ," cases which have not yet been tested can be included. In other words, a theory is based on a set of highly confirmed hypotheses and generalizes to conditions not yet tested. The longer a theory stands without being disproved, the greater the chances are that it will never be disproved. However, longstanding theories sometimes fall prey to new evidence which destroys them or adds corollaries.

When a theory is so reliable that it can be used to predict the outcome of events with apparent exemption from mistake, it might be termed a *law*. Laws are rare. There are few laws, simply because most phenomena have too many variables for us to be confident that statements generated about them will hold under all circumstances.

In sum, a hypothesis is a guess; a theory is a statement based on a set of highly confirmed guesses; and a law is a theory or set of theories whose predictive value appears to be precise. However, even a law is subject to disproof or modification. Perhaps in another galaxy Newton's law does not hold.

Science as a Creative Process

Science can be a creative process. The scientist must be keenly observant, possess a questioning mind, and ask unique, nonstereotyped questions. The scientist must be clever in the suggesting of possible answers to his or her own queries. Above all, he or she must be innovative in designing an experiment that will validly test the hypothesis. It is a mistake to believe that intuition and passion are absent from science. A hunch, along with persistence, has more than once led to a revolutionary discovery, as when Mary Leakey and her husband, L. S. B. Leakey, found evidence of early humans in an area they had been combing for twenty-eight years (Chapter 14).

The passion involved in the search for a new truth or simply a new fact can be as intense as that of the artist attempting to create a masterpiece. From Pasteur's swan-necked flask to modern methods of exploring primate behavior, the scientist displays an ability to see unique solutions to problems that most people do not even recognize as problems.

Science and Religion

The theologian deeply involved in an interpretation of scriptures, the bereaved individual looking to prayer for the reason for death, and the medicine man dancing for rain are putting their trust in traditional doctrines which, for the most part, they do not question. The biologist studying cell structure, the anthropologist studying death rituals, and the meteorologist investigating the weather rely on methods and techniques that are aimed at producing new information and validating or correcting old explanations, thus building a body of knowledge with which accurate predictions about natural occurrences can be made.

Science is the process of testing questions about the nature of empirical observations. The credibility of scientific conclusions is based on valid and reliable evidence; belief in religious doctrines is based on faith.

Scientists can only attempt to answer some questions; others cannot be subjected to the scientific method and are therefore not in the domain of empirical or objective research. For example, science cannot deal with the question of the existence of an omnipresent force. As discussed earlier, in order for an experiment to be carried out, a control must be possible. If a phenomenon is present always and everywhere, how can its absence be tested?

Scientists do not claim that their conclusions are absolute. They realize that their statements are only as good as the data they have and that new information may alter their concepts. A religious doctrine changes in response to personal interpretation and public opinion, which are not necessarily linked to new empirical facts. At any one time, a religious doctrine is often taken as being absolutely true, whereas at no time is a scientific statement considered totally and irrefutably correct.

Not only industrial peoples practice science, although it is only in modern societies since the 1600s that the scientific method has been consciously and consistently used. All people make conclusions on the basis of experimenting with observations. The phenomena that they can treat in this way make up their objective knowledge; the more mysterious facets of life are treated religiously or magically. For example, the Trobriand Islanders of the Pacific do two types of fishing: one in the shallow coastal pools and the other far out at sea. The first type is safe and is undertaken by men, women, and children. The second is filled with danger and the unknown. Men occasionally do not return from deep-sea fishing expeditions. Since shallow fishing is undertaken with regularity, time is spent making observations of fish behavior, and experiments are performed on how best to catch this prey. Nothing is done religiously or magically to protect the fishing party or to ensure a catch. The story is different with deep-sea fishing, in which elaborate rituals are performed in order to appease or appeal to the gods of the unpredictable seas.[4]

So, in conclusion, a scientific statement asserts the natural causality of phenomena. One thing happens because of preceding events that lead up to it. Things happen and conditions exist because of the physical, chemical, biological, behavioral, and/or cultural characteristics of the thing in question and the context in which it is found. Religious or magical statements assert causality beyond the natural. When natural causality cannot be determined or is not sought, spiritual causality is often assumed.

Summary

Science is the activity of seeking out reliable explanations for phenomena. Science is also the search for order and a method for discovery. The end result of the activity of science is a body of empirical knowledge that can be used to better understand the universe and to predict the processes, structure, form, and function of natural occurrences. The method of science provides a systematic way of investigation and includes observation, question formation, hypothesis formation, and experimentation. If an experiment disproves a hypothesis, a new hypothesis is tested. However, if a hypothesis is confirmed, it joins a body of knowledge which may lead to theory. A law is a theory or set of theories whose predictive value appears to be precise. All scientific statements are tentative. The progression from hypothesis to theory to law represents an increasing degree of reliability, but even laws can be disproved or modified on the basis of new evidence.

[4] B. K. Malinowski, in *Encyclopaedia of the Social Sciences* (New York: Macmillan, 1931), vol. 4, pp. 621–646.

It is because new evidence is always possible that a scientific statement can never be completely and without doubt proved.

Science is not a mere mechanical pursuit for collecting knowledge but involves creativity and the passion of discovery and accomplishment. Many breakthroughs, as well as more mundane discoveries, have resulted from a hunch followed by long years of persistence at validating it.

The scientist and the theologian are both interested in giving answers. However, the scientist proceeds by testing questions about the nature of empirical observation, whereas the theologian consults the philosophy of his or her particular religion and interprets the meaning of that philosophy for a particular situation. The scientific method cannot deal with those phenomena which are not testable, whereas religion and magic address themselves to anything that is of human concern. Scientific statements are never considered absolute, whereas at any one time religious doctrine often is. All people have a body of empirical (scientific) knowledge, but for the things they fear or cannot understand in an empirical way, religion and magic provide a measure of comfort and assurance.

SUGGESTED READINGS

Darwin, C. *On the Origin of Species.* New York: Modern Library, n.d.

Lyell, C. *Principles of Geology,* 3 vols. London: J. Murray, 1830–1833; New York: Johnson Reprint, 1969.

You might find glancing through these two classics interesting.

Bronowski, J. *The Ascent of Man.* Boston: Little, Brown, 1973. Gives a good idea of the intellectual climates of various periods. Chapter 9 deals with Darwin and Wallace.

Eiseley, L. C. *Darwin's Century: Evolution and the Men Who Discovered It.* Garden City, N.Y.: Doubleday, 1958.

Mason, S. F. *A History of the Sciences.* New York: Collier, 1962.

Schwartz, G., and Gishop, P. W. (eds.). *Moments of Discovery.* New York: Basic Books, 1958.

The four books mentioned above are a sample of the many volumes that have been written about the history of science.

Green, J. C. *The Death of Adam: Evolution and Its Impact on Western Thought.* Iowa City: Iowa State Univ. Press, 1959. A comprehensive and well-written exploration of the development of evolutionary theory.

Hempel, C. G. *Philosophy of Natural Science.* Englewood Cliffs, N.J.: Prentice-Hall, 1966. This book deals with the application of the scientific method to natural sciences.

Nagel, E. *The Structure of Science: Problems in the Logic of Scientific Explanation.* New York: Harcourt, Brace and World, 1961. A detailed and comprehensive look at scientific explanation.

PART TWO
THE MECHANISMS OF EVOLUTION

In 1859, Charles Darwin wrote: "The laws governing inheritance are for the most part unknown. No one can say why the same peculiarity in different individuals of the same species, or in different species, is sometimes inherited and sometimes not so; why the child often reverts in certain characters to its grandfather or grandmother or more remote ancestor; why a peculiarity is often transmitted from one sex to both sexes, or to one sex alone, more commonly but not exclusively to the like sex."[1]

Over 100 years later, science is able to answer many of the questions Darwin asked. Geneticists are not only able to explain much about the nature of inheritance but also have explored the physical and chemical nature of the genetic mechanism itself. In 1957, F. H. C. Crick, one of the pioneers in molecular genetics, wrote that "the nucleic acids are the blueprints—the molecules on which the Secret of Life, if we may speak of such a thing, is written. . . . It seems, according to our best present information, that they direct the manufacture of proteins and hold the key to the hereditary constitution of all living things."[2]

An understanding of the basic mechanisms of inheritance is essential to an understanding of evolution itself. The first two chapters in this part will present this basic material, followed by two chapters in which the concept of evolution is discussed.

[1] *On the Origin of Species* (New York: Modern Library, n.d.), p. 19.

[2] "Nucleic Acids," *Scientific American*, 197 (September 1957). Copyright © 1957 by Scientific American, Inc. All rights reserved.

Chapter Three
Human Genetics

The most accurate descriptions of evolutionary theory are those which are phrased in genetic terms. Evolution can be best understood in relation to the collective genetic makeup of interbreeding groups of organisms. These groups, called *reproductive populations*, are the primary evolutionary units.

There are other reasons for a concern with genetics. Human beings are both biological creatures and cultural beings. What we are physically is the result of both biological inheritance and the interaction of that inheritance with the environment. Although we adapt to our environment primarily in terms of cultural behavior, we are still animals. An understanding of people as animals is necessary for a complete understanding of people as cultural and social beings.

The study of human genetics is also of great concern to modern medicine. A large number of human diseases and abnormalities are of genetic origin. Many people with these abnormalities live reasonably normal lives; others are confined to medical or mental institutions. Parents who have given birth to a genetically defective child face the important questions: Should we have more children? Will our next child also be defective? Other people wonder: If I have a genetic abnormality, will it be passed on to my children? A tremendous amount of heartbreak and physical and financial hardship can be involved.

There are great social implications that develop directly from such questions as those asked above. Society must often assume the burden of the care of genetically handicapped individuals. Many people feel that persons with genetic problems, while living as normal a life as possible themselves, should not be permitted to reproduce. This is essentially a moral question that cannot be discussed intelligently without a knowledge of the genetic principles involved. A similar problem is that of therapeutic abortion when it can be demonstrated that the child within the womb does carry a genetic defect.

Another area of interest is the nature of individual differences. No two persons are exactly identical in appearance. What causes differences between individuals? Why are some people tall and others short, some smart and others not quite as smart? The causal factors are many. Some involve the cultural environment or the natural environment. Many differences are genetic, while the vast majority include the interaction of all these factors.

Still another important area of study is the nature of group differences. People living in the same social unit tend to look more alike than people living in different social units. No one can deny that, on the average, the English look different from Nigerians and Australian aborigines look different from Polynesians. Much of this difference is genetic. The nature of this variation, and the nature of human diversity in general, will be the subject of Part Three. An accurate understanding of human variation calls for an unemotional, empirical knowledge of the genetic nature of people and the mechanisms of differentiation. The misunderstanding of the nature of this variation has created much human suffering.

NINETEENTH-CENTURY STUDIES OF HEREDITY

Almost everyone would probably agree with the statement that children tend to resemble their parents. Peculiarities in physical traits often characterize family lines. The members of the Hapsburg dynasty of Europe often show a peculiarly narrow, undershot jaw along with a protruding underlip. Because of the high social status of this family, there are portraits going back to the fourteenth century showing the existence of this trait

from that time to the present (Figure 3-1). But to move from a simple and quite obvious statement about family resemblances to an actual determination of the genetic mechanisms involved is a long jump, which we hope to make in this chapter.

Early Notions of Human Heredity

One early attempt at explaining family similarities was called the *blending theory*. It implied that a child was a sort of human alloy, intermediate between paternal and maternal characteristics. This was an incorrect notion. Hereditary material maintains its integrity from generation to generation. It does not blend or mix.

Charles Darwin made an effort to explain inheritance. He believed that particles present in the body were influenced by activities of the organism. These particles traveled to the reproductive cells via the circulatory system. They modified the sex cells in such a way that the acquired characteristics of the individual organism could now be passed on to the next generation.

This concept of heredity, called *pangenesis,* like the blending theory, was wrong. Because of poor methodology, inappropriate materials, and incorrect hypotheses, others of Darwin's time went equally astray in their quest for an explanation of the transmission and differentiation of life.

Galton's study One of the most famous monographs on human heredity from the last century, Sir Francis Galton's (1822–1911) *Hereditary Genius* (1869), can serve as an example of an elaborate but erroneous attempt at a hereditary theory. Galton, a cousin of Charles Darwin, was interested in the nature of *intelligence,* or, to use Galton's term, *eminence.* That trait is still of great interest to students of human heredity, as witnessed by the great number of recent studies,

(a)

(b)

Figure 3-1 The Hapsburgs. (a) *Karl von Flämischer (c. 1515).* (b) *Archduke Karl von Teschen (1771–1847). Two members of the Hapsburg dynasty showing the inherited trait known as the Hapsburg jaw.*

especially those attempting to correlate intelligence with race (Chapter 8).

Galton defined eminence as the attainment of a position of influence or renown. The men he studied were scientists and scholars, statesmen, and members of the church. He calculated that while only about 1 person in 4,000 reaches eminence, its attainment is not random but concentrated in certain family lines. Galton studied hundreds of families of eminent men and noted that out of 100 men, 31 had eminent fathers, 41 had eminent brothers, and 48 had eminent sons.

Galton believed that the trait of eminence, or intelligence, was for the most part hereditary;

while he did not deny the influence of education and upbringing, he felt that the genetic factors were predominant.

Recent ideas about intelligence In more recent times intelligence has been defined in ways different from Galton's idea of eminence. But what is intelligence? We cannot discuss the genetics of a trait unless it is carefully defined. The *Encyclopedia of Human Behavior* defines intelligence as "general mental ability, especially the ability to make flexible use of memory, reasoning, and knowledge in learning and in confronting new situations and problems." But the statement continues: "There is no universal agreement on any single definition of intelligence, including the one just offered." And in the next paragraph it is stated: "Many psychologists have abandoned the attempt to give a formal definition of intelligence and offer a practical definition instead: intelligence is that which an intelligence test measures."[1] This is hardly satisfying to someone attempting to determine the precise mechanisms of the heredity of intelligence.

Today, intelligence is often seen as being reflected in IQ test scores. However, many scientists believe that this type of test has questionable validity. Factors such as general health, nutrition, motivation, socioeconomic status, and ethnic background all influence the score. Anthropologist Ashley Montagu has provided a strong argument (discussed in Chapter 16) that social environments, such as those of ghettos, can cause serious brain damage to children brought up in them.[2] The problem of race and intelligence will be discussed at length in Chapter 8.

The Work of Gregor Mendel

From the discussion of the problems involved in the study of the inheritance of intelligence, it should not be surprising that the breakthrough in the understanding of hereditary principles took place outside the area of human genetics. For a number of reasons, some of them implied above, humans are not good subjects for this type of scientific study. During the nineteenth century, many scientists turned their attention to small animals, such as mice, and to the plant world. In 1865 a monk named Gregor Mendel (1822–1884), while working with the common pea plant, first determined many of the principles of heredity.[3] Such discoveries originate in an atmosphere bombarded by new ideas, but they are often born in patient and solitary contemplation. Gregor Mendel's life represented an ideal situation for innovation. Although his discoveries remained unrecognized until the turn of the century, his studies stand today as a milestone in biological science.

Mendel began to develop his familiarity with nature on his father's small parcel of land in Silesia. At the age of twenty-one he began his theological studies, and eight years later he entered the University of Vienna. It was in Vienna that the great works of both past and contemporary scientists became known to him.

In 1854 he accepted a teaching post at the Brünn Modern School and remained there for fourteen years. It was during this time that he did his significant work on genetics. His experiments, which will be discussed in a moment, were beautifully contrived and controlled and represent an excellent example of the scientific method. However, in 1868 he was elected abbot of his monastery and had to give up his teaching position along with the great amount of time that had been available for conducting experiments. Although he thought that time would be available to resume his work once he was settled in his new job, this did not occur. The duties of his office were so great that he never again was able to carry out detailed experiments.

Mendel's work did not become generally

---

[1] R. M. Goldenson, *The Encyclopedia of Human Behavior* (New York: Doubleday, 1970), p. 1. Copyright 1970 by Doubleday and Company. Used with permission of the publisher.

[2] Ashley Montagu, "Sociogenic Brain Damage," *American Anthropologist*, 74 (1972), 1045–1061.

[3] Gregor Mendel, "Versuche über Pflanzen-Hybriden," *Verhandlungen des Naturforschenden Vereins Brünn*, 4 (1866), 3–47. Trans. in Curt Stern and Eva R. Sherwood (eds.), *The Origins of Genetics* (San Francisco: Freeman, 1966), pp. 1–48.

known until 1900, sixteen years after his death. In that year three scientists, Hugo De Vries of Holland, Karl Correns of Germany, and Erich Tschermak of Austria, independently rediscovered Mendel's principles.[4] Today, Gregor Mendel is credited with laying the foundation for the modern science of genetics.

Mendel's experiments Mendel realized that if the inheritance of a trait is to be understood, that trait must be carefully and precisely defined. The best traits are those which are either obviously present or completely absent rather than those which have intermediate values and must be measured on some type of scale. Mendel chose seven contrasting pairs of clearly defined characteristics of the common pea plant. They included flower color (red or white), stature (tall or dwarf), and shape of the ripe seed (smooth or wrinkled).

Mendel also observed each plant separately and kept the different generations apart. The results were quantified and expressed as ratios. He used as large a sample as possible to eliminate chance error. The edible pea was chosen only after several years of experimentation with many different plants.

In the first series of experiments, Mendel started with *true-breeding* plants. These are plants which have been bred only with plants of the same kind and show the same traits over many generations. Mendel cross-pollinated true-breeding plants which produced only red flowers with true-breeding plants which produced only white flowers. These plants made up the parental, or P_1, generation. The plants grown from the seeds produced by these parental plants made up the next generation, called the first filial, or F_1, gen-

eration. Mendel noted that plants of the F_1 generation produced only red flowers. No white flowers or flowers of intermediate color, such as pink, were observed. These plants are termed *hybrids*. The hybrid plant produces red flowers, as did one of the parental plants. The hybrid plant differs from the true-breeding parents in having one parent which produced flowers unlike its own, in this case white.

Mendel then permitted the hybrids to self-pollinate to produce the next generation, called F_2. In this generation he found that some plants showed red flowers while others showed white flowers. When he counted the number of plants showing each trait, he found that approximately three-fourths of the plants bore red flowers while one-fourth bore white flowers—a ratio of 3:1.

The F_1 hybrid plants bore red flowers only, although these plants had parents with white flowers. When the F_1 generation was self-pollinated, some plants with white flowers were produced. The trait which is seen in the hybrid is termed *dominant,* while the other, which is not seen and yet can be passed on in a later cross, is termed *recessive.* Mendel noted that red flowers, tallness, and smooth seeds were dominant features, while white flowers, dwarfness, and wrinkled seeds were recessive.

A model of genetic events "A *model* is a formulation that mimics a real-world phenomenon, and by means of which predictions can be made."[5] The model may be a diagrammatic representation of some phenomenon, a statistical description, or a mathematical formula. The pickup-stick analogy in Figure 1-6 is an example of a diagrammatic model. Looking at it, one can predict that a change in one element

[4] A. H. Sturtevant, *A History of Genetics* (New York: Harper & Row, 1965).

[5] E. P. Odum, *Fundamentals of Ecology,* 3d ed. (Philadelphia: Saunders, 1971), p. 3. (Italics ours.)

will affect all the other elements. However, for precise predictions to be made, models must be phrased in mathematical terms. For instance, the formula $A = \pi r^2$ allows us to predict exactly how a change in the radius of a circle will affect the area of that circle. Models act as summaries of the known characteristics of a phenomenon. They also provide a means of testing hypotheses about the phenomenon by measuring the effect of one element (variable) of the model on others.

Gregor Mendel was not aware of the physical or chemical realities of the hereditary mechanism, but he did develop a model to explain what he had observed. Mendel believed that in every plant the hereditary factors for each trait are paired. These hereditary factors are particulate; that is, they maintain their individuality by not mixing with one another.

Principle of segregation In the formation of sex cells—pollen and ova—the hereditary factors separate, forming sex cells which contain either one or the other factor. For example, they may contain the factor for red or white flower color, but not both. This is the principle of *segregation*. Thus, in the parental generation the red-flowered plant produces sex cells which carry the factor for red flowers only, while the white-flowered plant produces sex cells which carry the factor for white flowers only. The hybrid develops from the union of two sex cells, one carrying the unit for red color and one carrying the unit for white color. The hybrid therefore contains a pair of units. One member of the pair is for red color and the other is for white. Since the unit for red color is dominant, the flowers blooming on the hybrid plant are all red (Figure 3-2).

When the hybrid produces sex cells, the two units segregate, producing sex cells of two types. Half the sex cells carry the unit for red flowers, while the other half carry the unit for white flowers. When fertilization takes place, three dif-

ferent combinations may occur in the new plants. Some F_2 plants may inherit two units for red flowers, others may inherit two units for white flowers, and still others may inherit one unit for red flowers and one unit for white flowers. This last combination can occur in two ways: red-white or white-red. Since the red-red, red-white, white-red combinations result in red flowers, three out of every four plants will produce red flowers, while only one out of every four will produce white flowers.

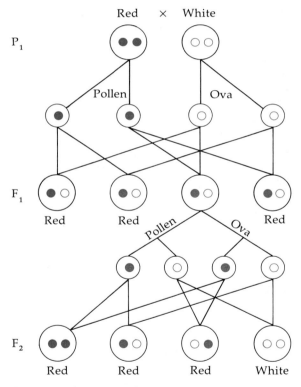

Figure 3-2 Segregation. *In the formation of sex cells, the hereditary factors separate, forming sex cells which contain either one or the other factor. Individual sex cells combine at fertilization, producing new combinations of hereditary units.*

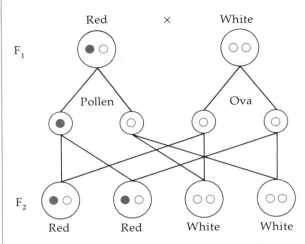

F₁

Red × White

Pollen   Ova

F₂

Red   Red   White   White

Figure 3-3   Black cross. *The hybrid red-flowered plant is crossed with the true-breeding white-flowered parent.*

To test his hypothesis, Mendel planned a new experiment. He predicted the results before beginning and managed to predict them correctly. He crossed an F₁ hybrid with a true-breeding,

white-flowered plant. This is known as a *back cross.* Figure 3-3 shows the results of this experiment.

Principle of independent assortment   Mendel next studied the simultaneous inheritance of more than one trait. For example, he crossed a plant of normal stature (tall) bearing red flowers with a dwarf plant bearing white flowers. The F₁ hybrid was a tall plant with red flowers. When the F₁ hybrids were crossed, four distinct types of offspring resulted: tall plants with red flowers, tall plants with white flowers, dwarf plants with red flowers, and dwarf plants with white flowers, with the frequencies of $9/16$, $3/16$, $3/16$, and $1/16$, respectively. The explanation for these results can be seen in Figure 3-4.

From these data Mendel formulated the principle of *independent assortment.* This principle states that the inheritance patterns of differing traits are independent of one another. Whether a plant is tall or dwarf is unrelated to whether that plant bears red or white flowers.

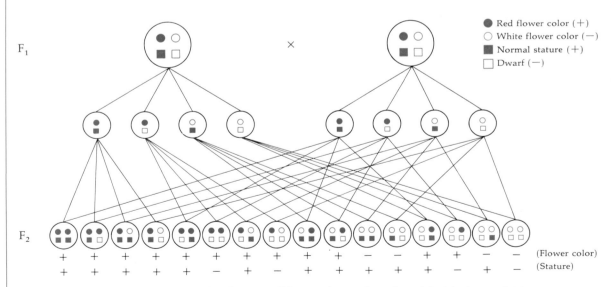

- ● Red flower color ($+$)
- ○ White flower color ($-$)
- ■ Normal stature ($+$)
- □ Dwarf ($-$)

F₁   ×

F₂

(Flower color)
(Stature)

Figure 3-4   Independent assortment. *The inheritance of flower color is independent of the inheritance of stature.*

Summary

A full understanding of the concept of evolution depends on a knowledge of heredity. Heredity is also important for ecological, medical, and social studies as well as for an understanding of individual and group differences. Early studies of heredity did not isolate the mechanisms of the transmission of life. Some, like Galton's study of intelligence, dealt with such complicated phenomena that the variables could not be isolated. Modern IQ test scores are influenced by factors of both natural and social environments and do not accurately measure inherited factors that may be involved with mental efficiency.

Because of the difficulty in studying genetics in humans, the first breakthrough came in the study of other organisms, such as the common pea plant. Armed with an expert knowledge of the scientific method, Gregor Mendel performed experiments which elegantly demonstrated suspected facts, revealed previously unknown principles, and set the stage for further discoveries. He was able to verify that a certain trait may express itself at the expense of another. The expressed trait is called dominant, the masked one recessive. He also discovered two major genetic principles. The first, the principle of segregation, states that the paired units of heredity within an organism separate, each unit going to different sex cells. The second, the principle of independent assortment, states that different traits are inherited independently of one another.

THE STUDY OF HUMAN GENETICS

Difficulties of Studying Human Heredity

The study of human heredity is many times more difficult than the study of heredity in pea plants, fruit flies, mice, or bacteria, which have yielded most of the basic principles of heredity. Although anthropologists have learned much from the type of experiment that was performed by Mendel, they are primarily interested in people.

The experimental method requires control over the object of experimentation. Yet, no scientist can control human matings. One might find a person with some interesting characteristics and would like to see what would happen if that person mated with a person with some different but equally interesting characteristics. Try and talk them into it! The study of human genetics must accept the matings that have already occurred.

In addition to the above problem, the human family is small. Mendel obtained his numerical ratios from counting hundreds of progeny. An accurate statistical conclusion demands an adequately large population size. If you were successful in talking a couple into producing children, your next step would be to convince them to have twenty. In addition, the length of the human generation is much too great to allow one investigator to follow the inheritance of a particular trait for more than two generations.

One of the major difficulties in studying human genetics is the choice of the right trait to study. The features that many people are interested in—skin color, intelligence, and so on—are greatly affected by the environment: skin color by sunlight and intelligence by factors such as diet and education. Also, many traits result from the interaction of multiple genetic factors. Many traits are difficult to measure and quantify. Until quite recently, when the use of sophisticated instruments came into use, skin color was difficult to measure accurately. Traits like stature can be measured by a tape measure, but what results is continuous variation. Instead of dealing with a series of discrete units, there is the problem of interpreting the hereditary mechanisms of a mating between a man 161 centimeters (6 feet 1 inch) and a woman 145 centimeters (5 feet 6 inches), in one case, and a man 163 centimeters (6 feet

2 inches) and a woman 136 centimeters (5 feet 2 inches) in another.

What is a trait? A person's observable or measurable characteristics make up the *phenotype*. The phenotype includes, among other things, the physical appearance, internal anatomy, and physiology of an individual.

In describing the phenotype of one individual, certain features, such as skin color, eye color, hair color and form, and general body build, can be observed. We can also measure such traits as stature, head circumference, nose width, and arm length. Such studies of the measurements of the human body make up the field of *anthropometry* (Chapter 7). Various physiological traits, such as the rate of glucose metabolism, can also be analyzed. Even the personality and intelligence can be investigated. The result of these examinations is a profile of the individual's total phenotype.

A trait is but one aspect of that phenotype—a particular hair form, an IQ score, a blood type. The phenotype results from the interaction of the individual's *genotype,* that is, the specific genetic constitution, and the environment. A trait can be the result of the interaction of many genetic and environmental factors.

The effects of the environment upon the phenotype If genetic mechanisms are to be understood, we must know the degree to which traits are determined by genes. One of the most difficult tasks of the geneticist is to discover the role of the environment in the development of a particular trait.

Many traits are determined genetically. Other traits are determined almost exclusively by the environment—a broken leg or a dyed head of hair. But most features are influenced by both genetic and environmental factors. Here it be-

comes the task of the investigator to determine the relative influence of genetic and environmental factors in the development of specific traits.

One method of estimating the environmental influence on a particular trait is by studying twins. Identical, or *monozygotic*, twins, which are derived from a single fertilized egg, or *zygote*, share identical genotypes. On the other hand, fraternal, or *dizygotic*, twins, are derived from separate zygotes; they have genotypes which differ to the same extent as those of brothers and sisters who are not twins. Monozygotic twins are always of the same sex, while dizygotic twins can be the same or different sexes.

Since monozygotic twins share the same heredity, it follows that differences in phenotypes between partners are due entirely to the effects of the environment. On the other hand, differences between dizygotic twin partners are due to both genetic and environmental factors. If the intratwin environments are the same between sets of monozygotic and dizygotic twins, we can estimate the importance of genetic versus environmental factors with respect to a given trait using twin data.

There exist several methods for making such an estimate. One is to locate one partner with a particular trait and see whether or not the other twin also has that trait. For example, in one study, in 19.6 percent of the monozygotic twins and 15.5 percent of same-sex dizygotic twins both partners had cardiovascular disease. One could conclude from these data that the genetic factor in the development of cardiovascular disease was relatively unimportant. But with respect to schizophrenia, the percentages were 44.4 percent for monozygotic twins and 12.1 percent for dizygotic twins. This leads us to the conclusion that there is a strong genetic factor in the development of schizophrenia. But since both partners had the trait in only 44.4 percent of the monozygotic twins and not in 100 percent, we must conclude that there still is a very strong environmental factor.[6]

Twin studies give indications of the relationship between heredity and environment, but these studies present problems. For instance, monozygotic twins tend to be treated more similarly by parents, friends, and teachers than dizygotic twins. Therefore, a similarity in a set of monozygotic twins' behavior might be due to their parallel treatment rather than to genetics. Also, the results of twin studies are valid only for the population from which the twins come. The results of studies of the same characteristics will vary in different populations.

Similarly, an estimate of the relationship between the genetic and environmental effects of a trait is valid only for the specific environment the estimate is made for. If the environment changes, this relationship may also change. For example, if monozygotic twins were both raised in the same environment, their stature would be similar. However, if one of a set of such twins were deprived of vitamin D while the other was not, the former's stature would be reduced because of bone deformations that would take place.

Mendelian Inheritance in Humans

It can be quite difficult to find human characteristics that are inherited in a simple Mendelian manner, but there are several traits which can be used to demonstrate these principles. One of these is the ability to taste the organic chemical *phenylthiocarbamide* (PTC). This ability is tested by having people chew a piece of paper soaked in a concentrated PTC solution. Some people experience a definite bitter taste; others find the paper has no taste.

The ability to taste PTC is an ideal trait for genetic study. It is extremely easy to determine a person's phenotype; just give that person a piece of treated paper to taste. Only two phenotypes exist for concentrated solutions: taster and nontaster. There are no problems of quantification and measurement. It appears that the ability to taste is not affected by the environment.

Genealogical studies show that a mating between a taster and either another taster or a nontaster may produce both taster and nontaster children but a mating between two nontasters produces nontaster children only. The explanation for the observed data is as follows: The genetic unit for a particular trait is called a *gene*. The gene for PTC tasting occurs in two forms. Alternate forms of a gene are termed *alleles*. The allele for tasting is dominant, while the allele for nontasting is recessive. The dominant allele is indicated by a capital letter, in this case, *T*, and the recessive allele by a lowercase letter, in this case, *t*.

A person with a pair of alleles for tasting (genotype *TT*) will be a taster, while a person with a pair of alleles for nontasting (genotype *tt*) will be a nontaster. These people are said to be *homozygous*, which means that they have two alleles of the same kind. The former is *homozygous dominant*, the latter *homozygous recessive*. The individual with the genotype *Tt* is said to be *heterozygous*, which means that there are two different alleles. Since the allele for tasting *T* is dominant, it is expressed in the phenotype, whereas the recessive allele *t* is not. The heterozygous individual is therefore a taster.

While tasters and nontasters cannot be mated in the same way as mice of various colors, couples of certain phenotypes can be located and their children studied. Three basic types of matings would be found: taster × taster, taster × non-

[6] B. Harvald and M. Hauge, "Hereditary Factors Elucidated by Twin Studies," in J. V. Neel, M. W. Shaw, and W. J. Schull (eds.), *Genetics and the Epidemiology of Chronic Diseases* (Washington: Public Health Service Publication No. 1163, 1965), 61–76.

Table 3-1 Possible Combinations and Offspring for a Trait with Two Alleles

Mating Type	Offspring		
	TT	Tt	tt
$TT \times TT$	1	0	0
$TT \times tt$	0	1	0
$TT \times Tt$	$1/2$	$1/2$	0
$Tt \times TT$	$1/2$	$1/2$	0
$Tt \times Tt$	$1/4$	$1/2$	$1/4$
$Tt \times tt$	0	$1/2$	$1/2$
$tt \times TT$	0	1	0
$tt \times Tt$	0	$1/2$	$1/2$
$tt \times tt$	0	0	1

taster, and nontaster × nontaster. But the tasters can be either homozygous (TT) or heterozygous (Tt). Table 3-1 shows all possible matings in terms of genotype and the expected proportions of possible offspring.

Independent assortment in humans   There are several other traits which can be used to demonstrate Mendelian inheritance in humans. For example, the ability to roll one's tongue longitudinally is inherited as a dominant. People who are homozygous recessive for this trait cannot perform this feat.

PTC tasting and tongue rolling can serve to illustrate independent assortment in people. We will examine the results of a mating between two individuals who are heterozygous for both traits. Using the letter R to represent the tongue-rolling gene, the mating can be expressed $TtRr \times TtRr$.

In the production of sex cells, the T and t segregate, as do the R and r. The segregation of the T and t is totally independent of the segregation of the R and r. Therefore, four kinds of sex cells will result. Some will carry the T and R. Others will carry the T and r, or the t and R, or the t and

r. The male sex cells, the *sperm*, and the female sex cells, the *ova*, combine at random. A TR sperm may fertilize a TR, Tr, tR, or tr ovum, or a Tr sperm may fertilize a TR, Tr, tR, or tr ovum. The same is true for the other two types of sperm. Table 3-2 shows the sixteen different combinations which can occur. When the phenotypes are worked out, it is noted that there are four possibilities: taster-roller, taster-nonroller, nontaster-roller, and nontaster-nonroller, which occur in the frequencies $9/16$, $3/16$, $3/16$, and $1/16$, respectively.

Deviations from the Mendelian Principles
This chapter has been dealing with the basic principles of genetics as worked out by Gregor Mendel. These principles can be demonstrated in all living organisms. But the inheritance of a great number of traits does not follow these basic patterns. In fact, examples of traits which are inherited in the basic Mendelian pattern are the exception rather than the rule. This is because the actual modes of inheritance are usually more complex.

Problems often arise in the interpretation of the inheritance pattern of a trait when that trait appears to be inherited differently in different family lines. This often is due to different genes occurring in each family line, although these genes are acting in a similar way.

Many genes often affect the same characteristic. For example, the inheritance of stature is said to be *polygenic*, that is, the result of the interaction of several genes, the exact number of genes being unknown. We will assume that the inheritance of stature is due to the interaction of just three genes (it is probably more than that) which have the same phenotypic effect, each of which occurs in two allelic forms. An extremely tall individual might have the genotype $A^1A^1B^1B^1C^1C^1$, while an extremely short person might

Table 3-2 Independent Assortment: Possible Genotypes and Phenotypes from a Mating between Two Individuals Heterozygous for Two Traits, PTC Tasting and Tongue Rolling*

		Offspring					
	TR		*Tr*		*tR*		*tr*
TR	*TTRR* taster-roller	*TTRr* taster-roller	*TtRR* taster-roller	*TtRr* taster-roller
Tr	*TTRr* taster-roller	*TTrr* taster-nonroller	*TtRr* taster-roller	*Ttrr* taster-nonroller
tR	*TtRR* taster-roller	*TtRr* taster-roller	*ttRR* nontaster-roller	*ttRr* nontaster-roller
tr	*TtRr* taster-roller	*Ttrr* taster-nonroller	*ttRr* nontaster-roller	*ttrr* nontaster-nonroller

Summary of Phenotypes	Probability of Phenotypes
9 taster-rollers	$^9/_{16}$
3 taster-nonrollers	$^3/_{16}$
3 nontaster-rollers	$^3/_{16}$
1 nontaster-nonroller	$^1/_{16}$

* The mating can be written in terms of their genotypes *TtRr* × *TtRr*. Each individual will produce four types of gametes, *TR, Tr, tR, tr*, in equal frequency.

be $A^2A^2B^2B^2C^2C^2$. If they mated and produced an offspring, that offspring would have the genotype $A^1A^2B^1B^2C^1C^2$ and would be intermediate in stature. The genotypes $A^1A^2B^1B^1C^1C^1$ and $A^1A^2B^1B^2C^2C^2$ would show still different statures.

The examples used in this chapter involve two alleles for each gene, one dominant, and one recessive. But other situations exist. First, there may be *multiple alleles* for any particular gene. In the *Duchenne type of muscular dystrophy* there are three alleles. The dominant allele results in a normal phenotype, but the abnormality is the result of the action of one of two recessive alleles. They differ in that one brings about a later onset of the disease, while the other brings about an earlier onset.

A second complication is *intermediate expression*. This is the situation in which a heterozygous genotype is associated with a phenotype which is intermediate between the two homozygous genotypes. For example, in the male the tenor and bass singing voices result from homozygous genotypes. The heterozygous individual is intermediate, a baritone. A third situation is *codominance*, in which in the heterozygous person both alleles are expressed. For example, the *hemoglobin* molecule, which serves to transport oxygen in the red blood cell, exists in several forms. One allele is responsible for the production of hemoglobin A, another for the production of hemoglobin S. A person homozygous for A will produce hemoglobin A. A person homozygous for S will produce hemoglobin S. But a person who is heterozygous will produce both hemoglobins.

The expression of an allele may be variable for several reasons, one of which is the existence of a *modifying gene*. This is a second gene which alters the expression of the first. In some pedigrees, *cataracts* (opacity of the eye lens) are inherited as a dominant, yet the type of cataract may vary according to which alleles of a second gene are present.

Whereas modifier genes affect the expression of other genes, *regulatory genes* can initiate or block the activity of other genes. They may be important in controlling the amount and timing of the production of various molecules of the body (Chapters 5, 6, 8, and 12). To date, little is known about gene regulation in organisms other than viruses and bacteria.[7]

A particular allele may be *incompletely penetrant*. This means that the allele is not always expressed in an individual possessing it. *Penetrance* may have a genetic basis in that the expression of the allele may be altered by a modifying gene. The environment also may play a role. For example, *diabetes* has a genetic basis, but whether or not an individual has the disease may depend upon other factors, such as diet.

The expression of many genes is influenced by the sex of the person. A *sex-limited* trait is one which is expressed in only one sex. For example, the genes controlling the development of a beard are found in both males and females but are usually expressed only in the male. A *sex-controlled* trait is one which is expressed differently in males and females. For example, *gout* is found in both sexes and appears to have a genetic basis. But the trait is incompletely penetrant. When the allele is present, it is expressed about 80 percent of the time in males but only about 12 percent of the time in females. This is why the disease is usually associated with males.[8]

Finally, a single allele may affect an entire series of traits. This is known as *pleiotropy*. For example, the allele for *sickle-cell anemia* in the homozygous condition results in such conditions as anemia, poor physical development, kidney damage, lung damage, and heart damage. Such a complex of associated features is known as a *syndrome*. Some others will be discussed in Chapter 4.

[7] J. A. Miller, "What Controls the Genes?" *Science News*, 110 (27 November 1976), 348–349.

[8] C. Stern, *Principles of Human Genetics*, 3d ed. (San Francisco: Freeman, 1973), p. 404.

Summary

Because of the lack of control over matings, the small size of families, the long generation span, the difficulties in determining what part of a trait is genetic as opposed to environmental, and problems of measurement and quantification, human beings have not been easy subjects for genetic research. However, there are traits which can be studied in people. A trait is one specific, observable, or measurable characteristic of the individual. Trait is synonymous with one meaning of the word phenotype. However, phenotype can also mean the sum of all traits. The environment can affect phenotype (both specific phenotype and the total phenotype). Studies of twins are one means of measuring how much of a trait is genetically determined and how much is environmentally determined.

Several genetic terms have been introduced in this section. A gene is the hereditary unit which controls or contributes to the control of a specific trait, such as eye color, PTC tasting, and tongue rolling. However, each trait can have different aspects, and each aspect is controlled by alternate forms of the gene called alleles. The type of alleles that an individual possesses for a specific gene is that individual's genotype. The term genotype can also apply to the totality of allelic pairs of an organism. If an individual has two of the same allele, the genotype for that particular gene is said to be homozygous. If the allele is dominant, the individual is homozygous dominant; if the allele is recessive, the individual is homozygous recessive. A combination of two different alleles of a gene is called heterozygous.

Mendel developed a series of principles, the principles of segregation and independent assortment, which serve to explain the inheritance of specific traits. But most traits are not inherited in a simple Mendelian manner. Deviations may be due to a variety of reasons, such as polygenic inheritance, multiple alleles, intermediate expression, codominance, modifying genes, incomplete penetrance, sex-limited and sex-controlled expressions, and pleiotropy. These situations do not invalidate Mendel's ideas but simply indicate the great complexity of the mechanisms of heredity.

MEDICAL GENETICS

About 2,300 inherited traits are now known for people. While this number is rapidly increasing, these traits represent the expression of only about 1 percent of the number of genes which have been estimated to exist in humans.[9] A large number of the known inherited traits are abnormalities. Today, the most active area of research in human genetics is medical genetics.

The Effect of Environment and Culture on the Fetus

One of the problems in the study of inherited abnormalities is the determination of the genetic factor as opposed to the environmental factor. It is known that such abnormalities as *phocomelia*, in which the limbs are not developed properly (Figure 3-5), and the *rubella syndrome*, which includes eye and heart defects, are environmentally caused. The first can result from the drug thalidomide, the second from the rubella virus, which causes German measles. The drug and virus are two among many *teratogenic agents*, factors which can cause abnormal development of the fetus. In addition, there are a number of defects, such as diabetes, which result from an interaction of the genotype and the environment.

Even before a baby is born, it is affected by

Figure 3-5 A child with phocomelia. *The environment can affect normal development. In this case the drug thalidomide, taken by the mother during early pregnancy to relieve nausea, interfered with the development of the fetus.*

the culture of its parents. For instance, the Australian aborigine child of the early 1960s would have had less chance of being born with phocomelia than a child in Germany. Drugs, such as thalidomide, which were in use at this time, were not available to the Australian aborigine parents. Similarly, the diet available to a people will affect the developing fetus's phenotype. For example, the people of a culture whose diet is low in calcium might have a relatively high frequency of children born with bone deformities.

Genetic Abnormalities

A number of abnormalities are primarily the result of the action of the genotype. Some of the better-known ones are listed in Table 3-3. They result from the inheritance of a simple recessive or dominant allele. Note that some are structural abnormalities, such as *dwarfism*, while others are errors in metabolism, such as *Tay-Sachs disease*. Some of these defects can be medically managed so that the affected individual may expect to live a reasonably normal life. Others cause

[9] V. McKusick, *Mendelian Inheritance in Man: Catalogs of Autosomal Dominant, Autosomal Recessive, and X-linked Phenotypes*, 4th ed. (Baltimore: Johns Hopkins Press, 1975). This volume contains an exhaustive list of human traits and abnormalities known and thought to have a genetic basis.

Table 3-3 Some Known Genetic Abnormalities

Condition	Inheritance*
Achondroplasia or chondrodystrophy: dwarfism of short-limb type	D
Albinism: little or no pigment in skin, hair, or eyes	R
Alkaptonuria: homogentisic acid excreted in urine, arthritis	R
Brachydactyly: short fingers and toes	D
Cataract: cloudiness of the lens	D, v
Diabetes mellitus: low glucose tolerance	R
Galactosemia: galactose not converted to glucose	R
Gout: abnormal uric acid metabolism	D, v
Hapsburg jaw: protruding chin, excessively long lower jaw	D
Huntington's chorea: progressive muscular spasm, disturbance of speech, dementia	D
Night blindness: congenital and stationary	D
Phenylketonuria: phenylpyruvic acid in urine, feeblemindedness	R
Polydactyly: extra fingers and/or toes	D, v
Retinoblastoma: tumor of the retina	D, v
Sickle-cell anemia: sickling of red blood cells when deprived of oxygen, fatal anemia	R
Tay-Sachs disease: blindness, motor and mental impairment, death in infancy or early childhood	R
Thalassemia: abnormal shapes of red blood cells when deprived of oxygen, fatal anemia	R

* D = dominant, R = recessive, v = incomplete penetrance and/or variable expressivity.

From Theodosius Dobzhansky, *Mankind Evolving* (New Haven and London: Yale Univ. Press, 1962), pp. 107–111. Used with permission of the Yale University Press.

serious mental and physical retardation, and many are *lethals,* causing premature death. The incidence of some selected genetic anomalies is given in Table 3-4.

Phenylketonuria A number of inherited abnormalities involve errors in metabolism. One of the best known of these is *phenylketonuria,*

Table 3-4 Incidence of Selected Genetic Abnormalities

Abnormality	Incidence	Population
PKU	4 per 100,000	United States
Tay-Sachs disease	12–23 per 100,000	Ashkenazi Jews
	17–26 per 10,000,000	U.S. non-Jews
Achondroplasia	1.1 per 10,000	Denmark
Albinism	5 per 100,000	Holland
	1 per 10,000	Ireland, Norway
Diabetes mellitus	1.1 per 100	United States
Galactosemia	1.4 per 100,000	England
	5.6 per 100,000	United States

Excerpted from Max Levitan and Ashley Montagu, *Textbook of Human Genetics,* pp. 644–645. Copyright © 1971 by Oxford University Press, Inc. Reprinted by permission.

(PKU). It is an example of an abnormality inherited as a recessive. PKU involves a mistake in the conversion of the amino acid *phenylalanine* to *tyrosine.* Amino acids are basic building blocks of proteins. (The biochemistry of this process will be dealt with in the next chapter.)

A child with PKU is unable to convert phenylalanine into tyrosine. Not only does this result in an inadequate supply of tyrosine, but the levels of phenylalanine build up in the blood. As this buildup progresses, the excess phenylalanine is broken down into alternate by-products which can be detected in the urine. These by-products usually cause, among other things, severe brain damage and mental retardation. This defect occurs in 4 per 100,000 live births in the United States and accounts for about 1 percent of all admissions to mental institutions.[10]

Studies of pedigrees PKU is known to be inherited. Studies of human genetics are after-the-fact studies. After the child with PKU has been

[10] R. Koch et al., "Phenylalaninemia and Phenylketonuria," in W. L. Nyham (ed.), *Heritable Disorders of Amino Acid Metabolism: Patterns of Clinical Expression and Genetic Variation* (New York: Wiley, 1974), pp. 109–140.

born, an attempt is made to reconstruct the matings which have already occurred. Such a reconstruction is called a *pedigree*.

In the pedigrees of Figures 3-6 and 3-7 the males are indicated by squares and the females by circles. Matings are indicated by horizontal lines, while descent is indicated by vertical lines. Individuals with the trait in question are noted in black. As you examine the pedigree in Figure 3-6, note that the trait is infrequent. In every case the parents of a PKU child are normal, since a PKU individual normally does not reproduce (but see page 56). Therefore, it can be concluded that the parents are heterozygous for the trait while the affected individual is homozygous recessive.

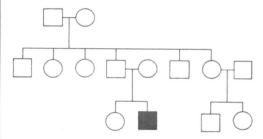

Figure 3-6   Pedigree of PKU. *PKU is inherited as a recessive trait.*

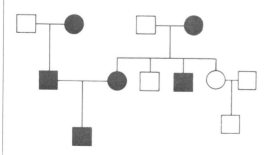

Figure 3-7   Pedigree of dwarfism. *This type of dwarfism is inherited as a dominant trait.*

Now let us compare this pedigree of a recessive trait with that of a dominant trait. Figure 3-7 is a pedigree of *chondrodystrophic dwarfism*. A chondrodystrophic dwarf is a person whose head and trunk are of normal size but whose limbs are quite short. This abnormality results from the inheritance of a dominant allele. Note in the pedigree that all dwarf children have at least one parent who is also a dwarf. Since the abnormality is the result of a dominant allele, it is expressed in both the homozygous dominant and the heterozygous individual. A homozygous dwarf will therefore have all dwarf children. Note that a mating between two normal persons produces normal children only.

You might think that a good way to identify the mode of inheritance from a pedigree is to look for the characteristic Mendelian proportions. But such proportions are rarely found. The size of the families is too small to provide a large enough sample. The data from several families can be pooled, but this requires specific mathematical procedures.

Does dominant mean "normal"?   Dominance and recessiveness have no necessary relationship to normality or abnormality. A dominant trait can be either normal or abnormal, as can a recessive trait. In the examples used so far, one abnormality, PKU, was recessive, while the other, chondrodystrophic dwarfism, was dominant. The reason most people are not dwarfs is that the frequency of the dominant allele is very low. Dominant alleles are not necessarily more frequent than recessive alleles, and both can be very common or very rare.

Variations such as different eye colors can be either dominant or recessive. Brown eyes are generally dominant over blue; neither condition, however, is any more "normal" than the other. In fact, the terms "normal" and "abnormal" are actually difficult to define. They are relative terms and often reflect the bias of the observer.

Genetic counseling When the parents of a PKU child learn that they are carriers, they often are greatly concerned whether to have another child or not. This can bring the parents to a *genetic counselor.* Genetic counseling units can now be found in a great number of medical centers throughout the United States. Persons having relatives with a genetic abnormality or possessing a genetic abnormality themselves are referred to these centers. The major questions asked are: Is the abnormality inherited? If it is, can an affected person be expected to live a reasonably normal life? If a person has a defect which is not lethal, or has a child, parent, or other relative with a defect, should that person have children?

The first question can be answered by detailed diagnostic testing and pedigree collecting. The second involves an expanding area of medical science. For example, children with PKU, if identified early enough, can expect to live fairly normal lives with medical treatment. In this case a special diet is required.

Perhaps one of the most important questions is: Should a person with a history of a genetic abnormality have children? A geneticist cannot answer this question. He can only provide the odds of a genetic disease with a known mode of inheritance appearing in the offspring of a couple whose family history is known sufficiently to make the necessary calculations. The actual decision must be made by the parents involved.

Predicting genetic events Genetic events are chance events. That is, if one of your parents is heterozygous for a particular gene, the question of which allele you will inherit can be answered in the same way as the question arising when you flip a coin: Will it land heads or tails? Therefore, let us begin with a consideration of coin flipping.

A coin is flipped. Assume that it will land either heads or tails. However, it cannot be said whether *this* particular flip will land heads or tails. What we can do is to list the possibilities and express in mathematical terms the probability of each possibility occurring.

An unbiased coin (one which does not have a tendency toward landing either heads or tails more than the other) when flipped will land either heads or tails; these are the only two possibilities. The probability of that coin landing one particular way, say, heads, is one of the two possibilities. These odds can be expressed in many ways: 50-50, 1:1, 0.5, or $\frac{1}{2}$. The limits of probability are 0 and 1. A probability of 0 indicates impossibility. A probability of 1 means certainty. Later on, it will prove easier to express probabilities in terms of a fraction or decimal.

Now, flip that coin a second time. Since the outcome of the first flip in no way influences the outcome of the second, again the probability of the coin landing heads is $\frac{1}{2}$. That is, there is no physical connection between the two events. Each flip of the coin is an independent event whose probability of landing heads is $\frac{1}{2}$. This is true whether we are dealing with the second, tenth, or hundredth flip of that coin.

Now, consider a slightly different question: What is the probability of flipping a coin twice in a row and landing heads both times? If you prefer, two coins can be flipped simultaneously. It makes no difference, since the situations are mathematically the same.

Now there are four possibilities instead of two: the coin could land heads both times or tails both times; heads the first and tails the second; or the reverse, tails the first and heads the second. These events can be summarized as follows: HH, TT, HT, TH. Here we are concerned with the probability of one out of the four possibilities taking place. Therefore the probability of the coin landing heads twice in a row is $\frac{1}{4}$. This is also true for the other three combinations. But if we ask, what are the odds of the coin landing heads once and tails once without the order being specified, then we must add up the two cases, HT and TH: $1/4 + 1/4 = 1/2$.

An alternative method of obtaining the above answer is to realize that the probability of the occurrence of two independent events is the product of the individual probabilities. Since the probability of landing heads in each case is $1/2$, the probability of landing heads twice is $1/2 \times 1/2 = 1/4$, three times is $1/2 \times 1/2 \times 1/2 = 1/8$, and so forth. This is equally valid for consecutive flips of the coin or simultaneous flips.

The application of probability theory to genetic events We now apply these concepts to genetic events. A return to the problem of PKU will serve as an example.

A couple's first child has PKU, and the parents are concerned about having a second child with the disease. The parents must be carriers of the recessive allele. But will the second child receive the recessive allele from both the father and the mother? This question cannot be answered, but an answer can be provided to the question: What is the probability of the second child having PKU? The birth of the second child is an independent event, totally unrelated to the first.

In order to have PKU, the child must inherit the recessive allele from *both* parents. From the father the child will receive either the dominant allele K or the recessive allele k. The probability of receiving the k is therefore $1/2$. This is also the case for the mother. To have PKU, the child must inherit a k from both parents. These are two independent events, since there is no link between the father's sperm and the mother's egg before fertilization. The probability of receiving a k from the father is $1/2$, and the probability of receiving a k from the mother is $1/2$. Therefore, the probability of receiving a k from both is $1/2 \times 1/2$, or $1/4$. That is the answer to our question. The

probability of any child of the couple being considered, whether the first, second, or fifth, having PKU is $1/4$. Knowing the odds, it is then up to the parents to make the decision.

This fraction, however, must not be misunderstood. It might be assumed that if the probability of having a PKU child is $1/4$, and you already have one, then the next three children might be expected to be normal. This does not work, for each child is a totally independent situation.

However, one may ask: What is the probability of having two children in a row with PKU? Here we simply multiply the individual probabilities, $1/4 \times 1/4$, to obtain the answer, $1/16$.

Slightly different is the case of chondrodystrophic dwarfism. Assume that a male dwarf is heterozygous for the trait, which is inherited as a dominant. We can make this assumption if we know that one of his parents is of normal stature. The dwarf consults a genetic counselor to find out the probability of having a dwarf child. His mate is normal.

To be a dwarf, the child must have at least one allele for dwarfism. The mother is normal, so the probability of receiving the allele for dwarfism from her is zero. The father is heterozygous for dwarfism. The child will therefore either receive the allele for dwarfism or the allele for normal from the father, a probability of $1/2$ for each. So, two types of offspring could result: one with a normal allele from the mother and a normal allele from the father, and one with a normal allele from the mother and an abnormal allele from the father. The chance of these two types is equal — a probability of $1/2$.

The role of the genetic counselor is simply to establish the nature of inheritance and to state the odds. The question of whether or not to go ahead and have children is not a scientific issue but a personal and perhaps a moral issue. It is also a social issue and, more subtly, an ecological one. These aspects of the problem will be discussed further in Chapter 5.

Control of Inherited Abnormalities

Medical science at this time cannot cure inherited abnormalities, but in many cases they can be controlled.

Although the allele for PKU cannot be medically changed into the normal form, the damaging effects of the disease can be arrested if the PKU child is identified as soon as possible. One method of identification involves the chemical detection of one of the by-products of the alternate breakdown of phenylalanine in the urine. But these products do not show up in the urine until the fifth or sixth week after birth. The best way of detecting the abnormality is the Guthrie blood test, which can reveal the disease by the fourth or fifth day of life. This test is required by law in many states.

In 1955 a method of preventing the damaging effects of PKU was developed: placing the baby on a diet low in phenylalanine. The baby is given a special formula and is later switched to low-phenylalanine foods, which include most fruits, vegetables, tapioca, and butter. By the age of five or six the child can be put on a normal diet. The child on this diet develops normally physically, although his or her IQ never goes as high as that of parents or siblings.[11]

Another approach to the problem is the identification of genetic abnormalities in the fetus. If the fetus is found to be defective, a therapeutic abortion can be performed if the parents so decide. The technique used is called *amniocentesis*. A sample of the *amniotic fluid*, the fluid surrounding the fetus, is taken. The cells in the fluid are of fetal origin. These cells can be cultured in the laboratory and tested for a variety of enzyme deficiencies. More than forty metabolic disorders can now be detected prenatally.

A third approach to the control of inherited abnormalities is the detection of carriers. More than fifty abnormalities can now be identified in the carrier, including PKU, Tay-Sachs disease, hemophilia, and cystic fibrosis. Detection is made possible by the fact that the carrier often shows some slight signs of the defect in question.

For example, carriers for PKU are discovered by means of a phenylalanine tolerance test in which the patient swallows a known amount of phenylalanine. Blood samples are taken at intervals following the intake, and the blood phenylalanine levels are determined. From the rate at which the blood phenylalanine levels fall, the carrier can be distinguished from the homozygous normal individual.[12]

To date, it is not possible to test everyone for every trait. Testing for carriers is done when a particular abnormality is found in a certain family line. Sometimes mass testing becomes practical when a high incidence of a particular trait is found within a specific segment of the population. Two examples are the testing for Tay-Sachs disease among Jews of Eastern European origin and for sickle-cell anemia among persons of African origin.

Summary

A large number of diseases have a hereditary component. Some are due primarily to the genotype, while others result from the interaction of the environment with the genotype.

The study of pedigrees can help to indicate whether a disease is inherited or due to environmental factors alone and whether the inheritance of an abnormality is dominant or recessive. Be-

---

[11] R. S. Paine, "Phenylketonuria," *Clinical Proceedings*, 20 (1964), 143–152.

[12] H. Harris, *The Principles of Human Biochemical Genetics*, (Amsterdam: North-Holland, 1970), pp. 171–172.

cause genetic events are chance events, their prediction is subject to the laws of probability. Thus, the genetic counselor can provide the odds of a genetic disease with a known mode of inheritance appearing in the offspring of a specific couple whose family history is well known.

At this time genetic diseases cannot be cured, but many can be controlled. Some, like PKU, can be medically controlled. In some cases where there is no method of arresting the disease, an affected fetus can be identified and aborted, or potential parents who are carriers can be identified and informed of the odds of producing an abnormal offspring.

A knowledge of the influence of the environment on genotypes and phenotypes can provide insights into the most advantageous activities to pursue or not pursue for the purpose of good health. For instance, knowing the effect that her activities can have on a developing fetus, an expectant mother can take the proper precautions, such as discussing diet and drugs with a doctor.

Genetics is important in understanding many diseases and why certain diseases affect certain populations more than others. Conversely, the study of these diseases may increase our knowledge of genetics. New genetic knowledge might then be used to further illuminate problems of evolutionary theory, ecology, and individual and group differences.

SUGGESTED READINGS

Baldwin, R. E. *Genetics*. New York: Wiley, 1973. A self-teaching program for general genetics, beginning with Mendel's experiments.

Bergsma, D. (ed.). *Birth Defects: Atlas and Compendium*. Baltimore: Williams & Wilkins for The National Foundation, March of Dimes, 1973. A series of one- or two-page articles on the known genetic abnormalities in humans, many illustrated. An excellent source book.

McKusick, V. A. *Human Genetics*, 2d ed. Englewood Cliffs, N.J.: Prentice-Hall, 1969. A basic survey of human genetics. Assumes some general background.

Moody, P. A. *Genetics of Man*, 2d ed. New York: Norton, 1975. A good basic text in human genetics.

Roberts, F. J. A. *An Introduction to Medical Genetics*. London: Oxford Univ. Press, 1970. Discusses the major principles of genetics with specific chapters on genetic abnormalities and prognoses.

Sootin, H. *Gregor Mendel: Father of the Science of Genetics*. New York: Vanguard, 1959. One of several biographies of Mendel.

Stern, C. *Principles of Human Genetics*, 3d ed. San Francisco: Freeman, 1973. A good, basic and complete textbook on human genetics.

Vegotsky, A., and C. A. White. *A Programmed Approach to Human Genetics*. New York: Wiley, 1974. A programmed text in human genetics.

Volpe, E. P. *Human Heredity and Birth Defects*. Indianapolis: Bobbs-Merrill, 1971. A well-written discussion of human heredity, emphasizing genetic abnormalities.

Winchester, A. M. *Human Genetics*. Columbus, Ohio: Merrill, 1971. A good, elementary, short introduction to human genetics.

Chapter Four

Cytogenetics and Molecular Genetics

When Gregor Mendel first worked out the basic principles of inheritance, he was not aware of the actual physical and chemical nature of the genetic mechanism. Around 1900, scientists began to examine the processes within the cell that determined the genotype of the organism. From such research came knowledge of the physical and chemical realities of heredity.

CYTOGENETICS

The branch of science which specializes in the biology of the cell is termed *cytology* from *cyto*, meaning "cell." The study of the hereditary mechanisms within the cell is called *cytogenetics*.

The Cell

The *cell* is the basic unit of all life. In fact, cells are the smallest units capable of performing all the functions which are collectively labeled as life. These are such things as taking in energy and excreting waste; using and storing energy; combining nutrients into substances for growth, repair, and development; adapting to new situations; and, perhaps the most important of all, reproducing new cells. It was the cell that the geneticists began to probe for the secrets of heredity and the location of the units of inheritance, the genes.

Besides the dynamics of cell activity, the great variety of different types of cells all have several other common characteristics. Cells are bounded by a *plasma membrane*, which allows for the entry and exit of certain substances but maintains the cell's integrity. A *nucleus* in the cell is contained within its own *nuclear membrane*. The material between the nuclear membrane and the cell membrane is called the *cytoplasm* (Figure 4-1).

The Chromosomes

When the cell begins to divide, long, ropelike structures become visible within the nucleus.

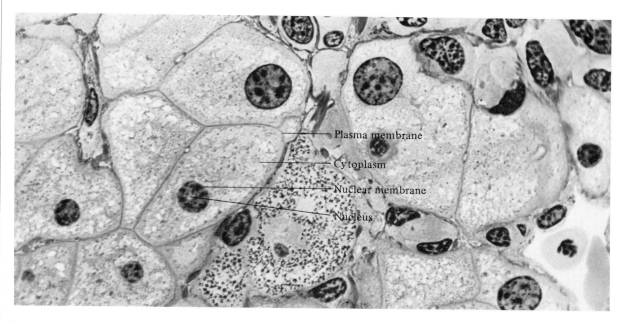

Figure 4-1   Typical animal cells. *These animal cells are seen under a microscope. The nuclei appear dark in this photograph because they have been stained with a purple dye.* [*Courtesy Carolina Biological Supply Company.*]

Because these structures stain very dark purple, they are called *chromosomes,* from *chroma,* meaning "color," and *soma,* meaning "body." Viewed under the microscope, a single chromosome is seen to consist of two strands, the *chromatids.* These chromatids are held together by a structure called the *centromere.*

The routine study of chromosomes has been made possible by a series of techniques developed since 1952. Figure 4-2 is a photograph of chromosomes prepared from a human blood sample. The chromosomes have been stained and dispersed over a large area so that the individual chromosomes can be identified.

Much information can be obtained from a photograph of chromosomes. First, the chromosomes can be counted. Different kinds of animals are characterized by specific chromosome numbers. For example, the fruit fly has eight,

the chimpanzee forty-eight, and humans forty-six.

After counting the chromosomes in the cell, it can be noted that not all chromosomes are alike. They differ greatly in relative size and in the position of the centromere. In some, the centromere is centered so that the "arms" of the chromosomes are equal. In others, the centromere is off center so that the arms are unequal. Thus it is possible to classify and identify chromosomes. Each chromosome in a photograph like Figure 4-2 can be cut out and arranged in a standardized way, known as a *karyotype* (Figure 4-3).

Looking at the karyotypes in Figure 4-3, we can see that all the chromosomes, with one exception, exist as pairs. The one exception is the *sex chromosomes* of the male. In the normal female there are two identical sex chromosomes,

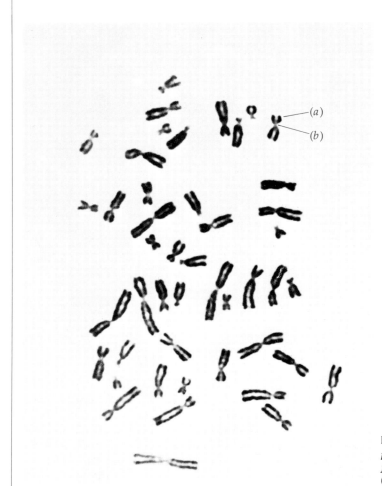

Figure 4-2 Human chromosomes. *This photograph was made of chromosomes obtained from a blood sample of a normal female. Note* (a) *the chromatid and* (b) *the centromere.*

called the X *chromosomes.* The male, however, has only one X chromosome, which pairs with a different type, the Y *chromosome.* In both sexes there are twenty-two pairs of nonsex chromosomes referred to as *autosomes.* These autosomal pairs are numbered from 1 to 22. In addition, all chromosomes are classified into seven major groups, A through G, on the basis of relative size and position of the centromere.

Because the members of a particular group are often so similar, they cannot always be paired without the use of special techniques. Differentiation of chromosome pairs within a group of similar appearing chromosomes can be accomplished by several methods such as giemsa staining, developed in 1970.[1] After a series of steps,

[1] S. R. Patril, S. Merrick, and H. A. Lubs, "Identification of Human Chromosomes with a Modified Giemsa Stain," *Science,* 173 (27 August 1971), 181–182; J. J. Yunis and O. Sanchez, "The G-banded Prophase Chromosomes of Man," *Humangenetik,* 27 (1974), 167–172.

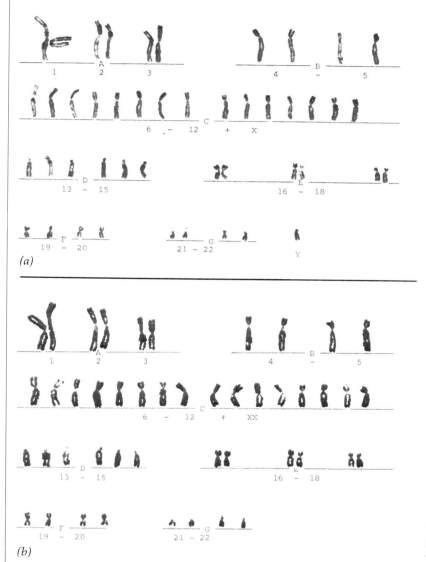

Figure 4-3 Human karyotypes.
Karyotypes of (a) a normal male and
(b) a normal female.

the chromosomes are stained, revealing their banded patterns. Since this pattern is distinctive for each chromosome pair, pairing within a group can easily be made (Figure 4-4).

Cell Division

The physical basis of Mendelian genetics becomes clear when the behavior of chromosomes during cell division is observed. There are two

21   22   Y

Figure 4-4 Giemsa-stained chromosomes. *Each chromosome pair can be distinguished by the distinctive banding patterns which result from the process known as giemsa staining. Here the human G- chromosomes (numbers 21, 22, and the Y chromosome) can be distinguished.*

basic forms of cell division, mitosis and meiosis. *Mitosis* is the means by which a one-celled organism divides into two new individuals. In a multicellular organism mitosis results in growth and the replacement of body cells. *Meiosis,* on the other hand, is specialized cell division resulting in the production of sex cells, or gametes.

Mitosis The events of mitosis follow each other in a continuous fashion. Various studies seem to indicate that in humans it takes thirty minutes to 1½ hours for one complete mitotic division.[2] The speed of division varies among different types of cells, as does the frequency of division. For example, some cells, such as skin cells, are constantly being replaced and divide often. On the other hand, nerve cells may stop dividing at birth or shortly thereafter. In order to make the events of this process clear, mitosis can be divided into a number of arbitrary phases based on certain landmark events.

Interphase is the time between the ending of

[2] J. L. Hamerton, *Human Cytogenetics* (New York: Academic, 1971), vol. 1, p. 56. The time is based upon studies of fibroblasts and lymphocytes in culture.

one mitotic division and the beginning of another. The chromosomes normally are not seen at this time. In the infrequent cases where they have been viewed, they appear as extremely thin, threadlike, faintly stained structures.

The cycle of mitosis begins with *prophase.* During prophase the chromosomes contract and readily take up the stain. They appear dark, short, and fat as the long, thin strands begin to coil. Soon the individual chromatids and the centromeres can be seen. On the outside of the nucleus two small bodies, the *centrioles,* become visible. The two centrioles move around until they are at opposite poles of the cell. The nuclear membrane has disappeared.

In *metaphase* a structure known as the *spindle* develops between the two centrioles. The spindle is a complex of fibers which extend from pole to pole and from the poles to the centromeres. The chromosomes move so that their centromeres line up on a plane, the *equatorial plane,* which is usually equidistant from the two poles of the spindle. The centromeres then divide. It is important to note that in metaphase of mitosis each chromosome acts independently, even members of the same pair.

During *anaphase,* the individual chromatids are pulled by the spindle fibers toward the two poles, forming two separate sets of forty-six chromatids. In the last phase, *telophase,* new nuclear membranes form as the chromosomes disappear from view. Then division of the cytoplasm takes place. There are now two new cells, each with a complement of forty-six chromosomes. However, each chromosome consists of a single chromatid. During the interphase which follows, each chromatid will replicate, producing chromosomes consisting of two chromatids. These events are summarized in Figure 4-5.

Meiosis Meiosis differs from mitosis in many ways. First, meiosis takes place only in specialized

The Mechanisms of Evolution

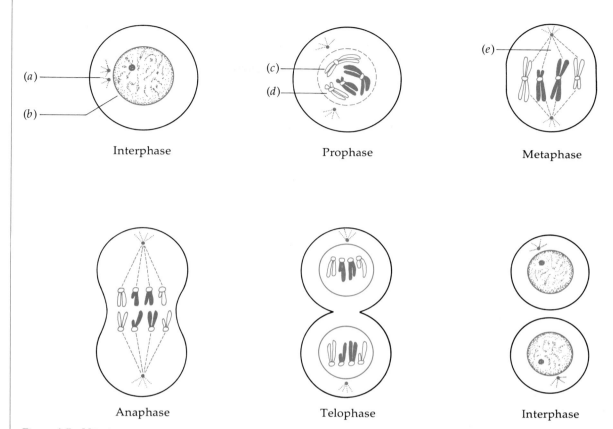

(a) ——
(b) ——

Interphase

(c) ——
(d) ——

Prophase

(e) ——

Metaphase

Anaphase

Telophase

Interphase

Figure 4-5   **Mitosis.** *Diagram of the events of mitosis in a hypothetical cell with four chromosomes. Features include (a) centrioles, (b) nuclear membrane, (c) chromatid, (d) centromere, (e) spindle. One member of each chromosome pair is white, the other colored. Note that members of a given pair move independently of each other.*

tissue in the testes of the male and the ovaries of the female. Meiotic division results in the production of gametes, *sperm* in the male and *ova* in the female.

One of the most significant features of meiosis is the reduction in chromosome number. If a sperm and ovum each contained 46 chromosomes, the cell resulting from the fertilization of an ovum by a sperm would have 92 chromosomes. In the next generation there would be 184 chromosomes, and so on. Instead, meiotic divi-

sion in humans results in gametes with 23 chromosomes each. So, when fertilization takes place, the number of chromosomes remains constant at 46.

Meiosis consists of two cycles ot division. In the male a complete meiotic cycle takes approximately seventy-four hours.[3] The prophase of the

[3] C. G. Heller and Y. Clermont, "Kinetics of the Germinal Epithelium in Man," *Recent Progress in Hormonal Research,* 20 (1964), 570.

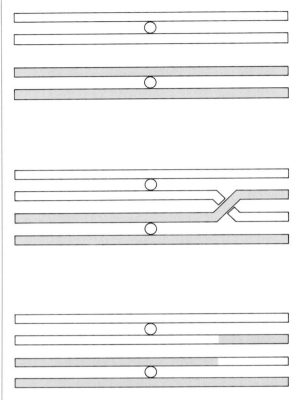

Figure 4-6   Crossing-over. *This phenomenon is shown in a highly diagrammatic fashion since the details of the actual process are not precisely known.*

time that *crossing-over* occurs. According to one theory, the homologous chromosomes come together, forming a *tetrad* of four chromatids. Crossing-over occurs as the result of breaks in a pair of chromatids and subsequent fusion of the broken homologous sections on opposite chromatids. The result is an interchange of chromosomal material between chromatids (Figure 4-6). The significance of crossing-over will be taken up later in this chapter.

In metaphase I of the male the paired chromosomes move toward the equatorial plane with the centromeres of each chromosome coming to lie on opposite sides of the equatorial plane. Note that, unlike the pattern in mitosis, the homologous chromosomes associate closely with one another in metaphase. In anaphase I the chromosomes separate and are pulled to opposite poles by the contracting spindle fibers. As they move toward the poles, each set becomes enclosed within a nuclear membrane during telophase I. Because the centromere has yet to divide, entire chromosomes, consisting of two chromatids, have moved to opposite poles. During telophase I the cytoplasm also divides, and the result is two cells with one set of twenty-three chromosomes each. This is the *haploid* condition, or the *n* number of chromosomes.

The second meiotic division of spermatogenesis is very much like mitosis except that it starts with the haploid number of chromosomes. The chromosomes line up on the equatorial plane, the centromeres divide, and the individual chromatids move to opposite ends of the cell as the cell membrane again pinches inward, creating two cells from each of the haploid cells. The end result is four cells where originally there was one. Figure 4-7 summarizes these events.

The first meiotic division differs in the female in that the spindle does not form across the center of the cell but off to one side. During cell division, one nucleus carries the bulk of the cytoplasm.

first meiotic division, prophase I, is quite long. The chromosomes become visible as they contract and thicken. At this point the chromosome is still single-stranded, but it will soon double. There are forty-six chromosomes. This is the *diploid* number, or the *2n* number. The *n* stands for the number of chromosomes in a sex cell. In humans, *n* equals twenty-three.

As prophase I continues, *homologous chromosomes* (that is, members of a pair) come together along their entire length. It is during this

This is also true of the second meiotic division. Thus a single large ovum and three very small cells, the *polar bodies,* are produced from the one original cell. The large ovum contains enough nutrients to supply the embryo until the embryo implants itself in the wall of the uterus.

Spermatogenesis, or sperm production, begins in the average American male at twelve to

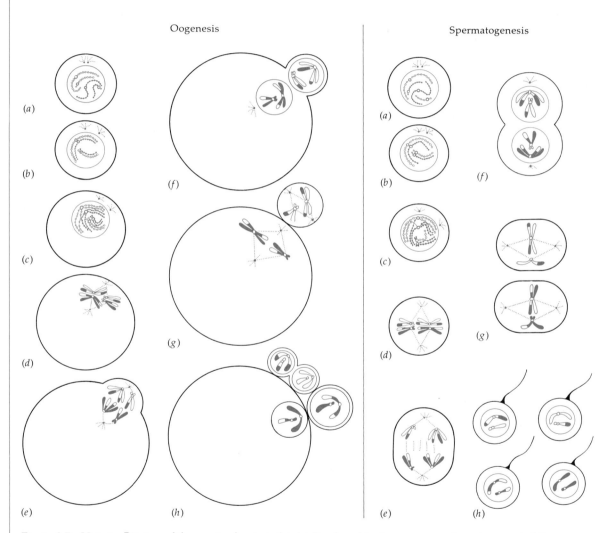

Figure 4-7   Meiosis. *Diagram of the events of meiosis. (a)–(c) Prophase I [note occurrence of crossing-over in (c)], (d) metaphase I, (e) anaphase I, (f) telophase I (note uneven division of cytoplasm in oogenesis and production of polar body), (g) metaphase II, (h) end of meiotic division.*

thirteen years of age and usually continues throughout life.[4] The male normally produces millions of sperm at any one time. *Oogenesis,* or ova production, is different. The beginnings of the first division of meiosis occur within the ovaries during fetal development between the fifth and seventh months after conception. These cells remain in metaphase until they are stimulated, beginning at puberty, by certain hormones to complete their development.

Oogenesis is cyclical. While the length of the cycle is often given as twenty-eight days, it is actually highly variable not only within the female population but also in the same female at different times of her life.[5] The cycle itself is under hormonal control. At the midpoint of the cycle, the ovum has matured and breaks through the wall of the ovary. This event is known as *ovulation.* In contrast to the great quantity of sperm produced by the male, the average human female usually produces only one ovum during each cycle.

Fertilization must take place within a few days after ovulation. In nonhuman mammals, sexual receptivity is related to the ovarian cycle. The female comes into *estrus,* the period of sexual receptivity, around the time of ovulation.[6] But

[4] The onset of spermatogenesis is variable, not only among individuals but also among the averages for different populations.

[5] In one study the median length of the cycle for American women between the ages of twenty and forty, calculated for each year, ranged from 26.2 to 27.9 days; 50 percent of the cycle lengths ranged from a low of 24.4 to a high of 30.6 days, while 90 percent ranged from a low of 21.8 to a high of 38.4 days. A. E. Treloar et al., "Variations of the Human Menstrual Cycle through Reproductive Life," *International Journal of Fertility,* 12 (1967), 77–126.

[6] The term *estrus* has two meanings. It can refer to the reproductive cycle in the mammalian female, or, as used here, it can refer to the period of sexual receptivity in the female, what is often referred to as *heat.*

unlike that in other mammals, sexuality in the human female is not periodic (Chapter 11).

Chromosomal Abnormalities

The processes of mitosis and meiosis are precise, yet errors do occur. Any alteration of the genetic material is called a *mutation.* A mutation can be an alteration of the genetic material on the molecular level (pages 96 to 100). Here we shall consider mutations on the chromosomal level, termed *chromosomal aberrations.* These are of two types, abnormal chromosome number and abnormal chromosome structure.

Abnormal chromosome number The most common errors of meiosis are those of *nondisjunction,* which lead to abnormal chromosome numbers in the second-generation cells. This occurs when instead of members of a chromosome pair moving to opposite poles, both chromosomes move to the same pole together. Thus, two second-generation cells are formed, one with twenty-two chromosomes and one with twenty-four. A gamete with the normal complement of twenty-three chromosomes which unites with a gamete with an abnormal number of chromosomes will produce a zygote, or fertilized egg, with either extra or missing chromosomes. For example, if a sperm with twenty-four chromosomes fertilizes an ovum with twenty-three, the zygote will have forty-seven chromosomes.

What phenotype is found in an individual developing from a zygote with an abnormal karyotype? Figure 4-8 shows a karyotype of an individual with forty-seven chromosomes, one too many. Since the extra chromosome is a number 21, a fairly small chromosome, a relatively small number of genes is involved. Figure 4-8 also shows a child with this karyotype. The condition is called *Down's syndrome* or *mongolism.*

Down's syndrome is characterized by a peculiarity in the eyefolds (which some seem to think resembles the Mongoloid eye, although it is different), short stature with stubby hands and feet, and congenital malformations of the heart and other organs. Perhaps the most significant feature is severe mental retardation.

Down's syndrome is not rare. It is found on the average of 1 in 668 live births.[7] But there is a close correlation between the probability of having such a child and the age of the mother. For a mother under twenty years of age, the risk of having a Down's child is only 1 in 2,300, but for mothers over forty-five years of age the risk is about 1 in 46.[8]

The increased risk of having a Down's child is related to the age of the mother but not the age of the father. While sperm are being constantly produced and individual sperm have relatively short life spans, the beginning of the first division of oogenesis takes place during fetal life. These immature ova remain in this early stage until division continues to maturation under normal influence. This completion of oogenesis can take place at any time between the onset of puberty until menopause. Thus the age of the ovum at the time of fertilization can vary widely. L. S. Penrose and G. F. Smith suggest that the older the ovum the greater the probability of some environmental factor or accident occurring, resulting in some interference with normal meiotic division.[9] This view has been supported by evidence from India, where a population living in an area with relatively high natural background radiation had a higher incidence of Down's syndrome than a

[7] J. L. Hamerton, *Human Cytogenetics* (New York: Academic, 1971), vol. 2, p. 200.

[8] Ibid., p. 201.

[9] L. S. Penrose and G. F. Smith, *Down's Anomaly* (Boston: Little, Brown, 1966).

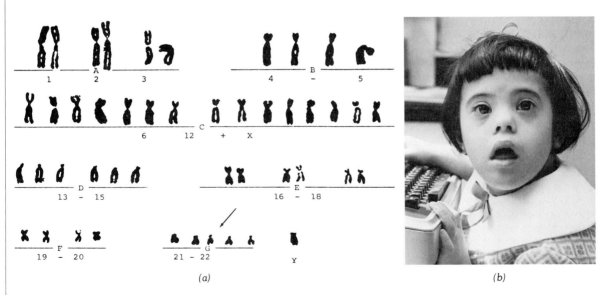

Figure 4-8 Down's syndrome. (a) *Karyotype of male with Down's syndrome. Note the extra chromosome 21.* (b) *Girl with Down's syndrome.*

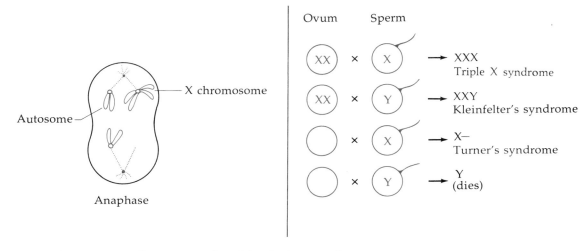

Figure 4-9 Nondisjunction. *Consequences of nondisjunction in oogenesis.*

control group living in a region lacking this high radiation level.[10]

Nondisjunction of the sex chromosomes More common than nondisjunction of autosomes are extra or missing sex chromosomes (Figure 4-9). A person with a sex chromosome count of XXY has *Klinefelter's syndrome* and is phenotypically a male. However, these individuals are characterized by underdeveloped external genitalia, sterility, sparse body hair, a tendency for long-leggedness, and often feminine breast development. These males may be mentally normal, but they show a higher incidence of mental disorders than normal males. Klinefelter's syndrome occurs about once in every 500 live male births.[11]

An individual with forty-five chromosomes and a sex chromosome count of X– has only one X chromosome yet is a female. This is *Turner's syndrome* (Figure 4-10a). The characteristics include short stature, low-set ears, broadly spaced breasts, female external sex organs but a small uterus and ovaries which appear only as a fibrous streak. This syndrome occurs in 1 out of every 2,200 live female births. Mental retardation is not involved.[12]

The phenotype of women possessing three X chromosomes is variable. Many appear perfectly normal and produce children, while others show mental retardation and sexual abnormalities. The triple X syndrome is found in approximately 1 out of every 833 live female births. Cases of XXXX and XXXXX are known but quite rare. They are usually associated with severe mental retardation and sexual abnormalities.[13]

Another abnormal sex chromosome count found in males is the XYY. These males appear to

[10] N. Kochupillai et al., "Down's Syndrome and Related Abnormalities in an Area of High Background Radiation in Coastal Kerala," *Nature*, 262 (1 July 1976), 60–61.

[11] Hamerton, op. cit., pp. 3–6.

[12] Ibid., pp. 68–80.

[13] E. H. R. Ford, *Human Chromosomes* (London: Academic, 1973), pp. 192–194.

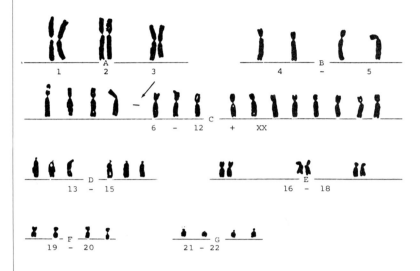

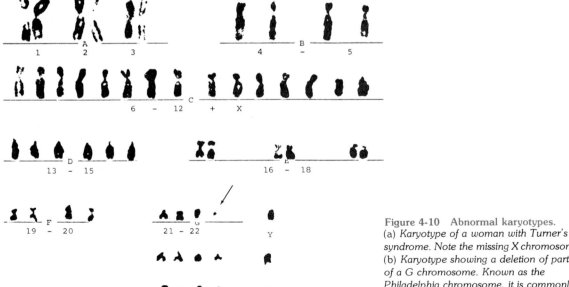

Figure 4-10 Abnormal karyotypes.
(a) *Karyotype of a woman with Turner's syndrome. Note the missing X chromosome.* (b) *Karyotype showing a deletion of part of a G chromosome. Known as the Philadelphia chromosome, it is commonly found in chronic myeloid leukemia patients.*

be phenotypically normal, although they tend to be above average in stature. XYY individuals are able to have children. Some lead normal lives, but others seem to show a tendency toward antisocial, aggressive behavior. It has been estimated that the incidence of XYY males in the total American "white" population is about 0.11 percent, but the incidence in mental and penal institutions is 2 percent.[14] However, we may not be dealing with tendencies toward criminal behavior as such. It has been suggested that the elevated crime rate in XYY individuals may represent a higher arrest rate due to a low intelligence level.[15]

Structural aberrations of chromosomes In addition to abnormal numbers of chromosomes

[14] E. B. Hook, "Behavioral Implications of the Human XYY Genotype," *Science*, 179 (12 January 1973), 139–150.

[15] H. A. White et al., "Criminality in XYY and XXY Men," *Science*, 193 (13 August 1976), 547–555.

due to nondisjunction, several types of structural abnormalities can occur. Structural aberrations are the result of breaks in the chromosome itself.

Deletion occurs when a chromosome itself breaks and a segment of it which is not attached to the spindle fails to be included in the second-generation cell. The genetic material on the deleted section is "lost." *Duplication* is the process whereby chromosome parts are repeated, that is, a section of a chromosome is repeated. *Inversion* occurs when parts of a chromosome break and reunite in a reversed order. No genetic material is lost or gained, but the position of the alleles involved is changed. *Translocation* is the process whereby segments of chromosomes become detached and reunited to other nonhomologous chromosomes. The causes of chromosome mutations will be discussed later in this chapter (Figures 4-10*b* and 4-11).

Abnormal chromosome numbers and structural aberrations account for a significant number of defects in newborns. It has been estimated that

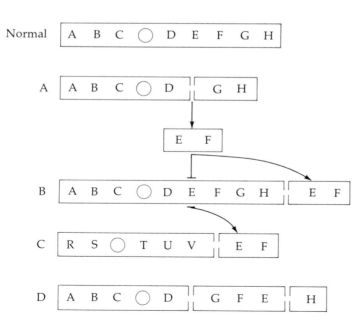

Figure 4-11 Chromosomal aberrations. (a) *Deletion*, (b) *duplication*, (c) *translocation*, (d) *inversion*.

about 1 percent of all children born have some chromosomal abnormality that can be identified.[16] A way of preventing what is very often a tragedy is to identify the abnormality before birth through amniocentesis (Chapter 3). From the fetal cells found in the amniotic fluid, karyotypes can be made. If chromosomal abnormalities are seen, the early fetus can be aborted. Amniocentesis is now routine in many hospitals in special situations, such as identification of Down's syndrome in fetuses of mothers over the age of forty.

Reexamining Mendelian Genetics

The details of cell division can help us understand Mendelian genetics. Mitosis is merely a copying of the genetic material, but in meiosis the physical reality of Mendel's principles of segregation and independent assortment can be observed.

Each individual cell contains two of each type of chromosome. One member of each pair is obtained from the mother and one from the father. When the individual then produces gametes, the paired chromosomes will separate during the first meiotic division. This is segregation. Therefore, each gamete will contain only one of each pair and, hence, only the alleles on those particular chromosomes.

As one meiotic division follows another, gamete after gamete is produced. Yet each individual gamete is unique, consisting of a particular set of chromosomes. One mechanism of meiosis that is responsible for the uniqueness of each gamete is *recombination*. As the twenty-three chromosomes line up in metaphase, they can recombine into several configurations, following the principle of independent assortment. In Figure 4-12 let us assume that the chromosomes with the dominant alleles are inherited from the

mother (*A, B*) while those with the recessive alleles are inherited from the father (*a, b*). Looking at two pairs, they can be oriented in two basic patterns: both paternal chromosomes can lie on one side and the maternal chromosomes on the other, or one of each on each side. From this, four types of gametes are produced, as shown in the figure. When all twenty-three chromosome pairs are considered, there are 8,324,608 possible combinations.

A child born from the union of a sperm with an ovum has four grandparents. The sperm contains the father's chromosomes, which were inherited from the father's parents. The same is

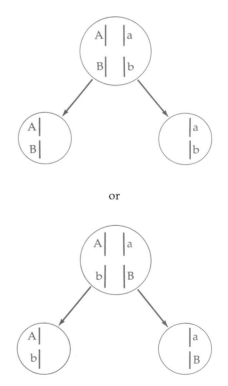

Figure 4-12 Recombination. *The chromosomes can orient themselves in two different ways, resulting in four distinct combinations of alleles.*

[16] W. M. Court Brown, *Human Population Cytogenetics* (New York: Wiley, 1967), p. 26.

true of the ovum with respect to the mother's parents. The child usually is considered to be descended equally from each of the four grandparents; and if one grandparent shows a special biological or even social characteristic, the child is said to be one-quarter of whatever that characteristic happens to be.

An examination of the process of meiosis shows that this is not true. When the chromosomes derived from the father's parents line up in metaphase of meiosis, they could line up so that the sperm contains a greater number of chromosomes from the father's mother than from the father's father. For example, of the twenty-three chromosomes inherited from the father, eleven may have been derived from the father's father but twelve from the father's mother. Thus, more genes are inherited from the grandmother than from the grandfather.

Another factor bringing about unique gametes is crossing-over. Chromosomes often are not inherited exactly as they existed in the parent. Crossing-over involves the exchange of genetic material between chromosomes inherited from the father and those inherited from the mother. The result is individual chromosomes containing genetic material from both parents.

Variation among gametes is the rule. The variations which result among living individuals form the basic raw material for the operation of natural selection (Chapters 5 and 6).

Linkage

Early studies of inheritance revealed the fact that Mendel's principle of independent assortment did not always work. It is true that traits carried on different chromosomes behave in the way he described, but if different genes are on the same chromosomes, they tend to remain together in the formation of gametes. It is interesting to note that some of the seven traits Mendel studied in the pea plant are located on the same chromosome, but in his experiments which demonstrated independent assortment, he chose by chance pairs of traits located on separate chromosomes.[17]

Genes on the same chromosome are said to be linked, and the phenomenon is called *linkage*. Theoretically, if two genes are linked, only two types of gametes are produced instead of the four predicted by the principle of independent assortment. In reality, crossing-over can occur, whereby alleles from homologous chromosomes are exchanged (Figure 4-13). The farther apart two genes are on a chromosome, the greater the chance that they will cross over. According to one theory, this is because there are more points between the genes at which the chromosome can break and then reunite.

Pedigree studies in various plants and animals have permitted the reconstruction of genetic maps. Genes which show linkage must reside on the same chromosome, and the relative number of recombinations resulting from crossing-over can be used to determine the relative distance separating genes on the chromosome. But these types of study require very large numbers of progeny and generations, which limits their usefulness in human genetics. However, new techniques have been developed to make the assignment of individual genes to specific chromosomes possible for humans.

Techniques for determining the location of specific genes on specific chromosomes involve hybrid cells containing both human and mouse chromosomes. Each of these cells contains a full set of forty mouse chromosomes but only some of the human set of chromosomes. Which human chromosomes are present varies from cell to cell.

[17] S. Blixt, "Why Didn't Gregor Mendel Find Linkage?" *Nature*, 256 (17 July 1975), 206.

Therefore, the presence or absence of specific human proteins can be correlated with the presence or absence of specific human chromosomes

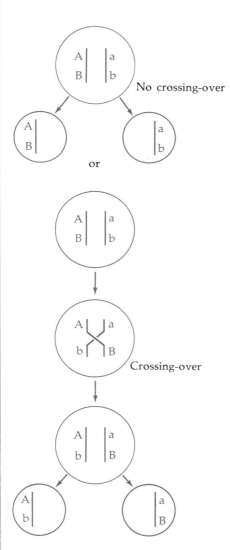

or

No crossing-over

Crossing-over

Figure 4-13   Linkage. *Genes located on the same chromosome will be inherited as a unit except when crossing-over occurs, bringing about new gene combinations.*

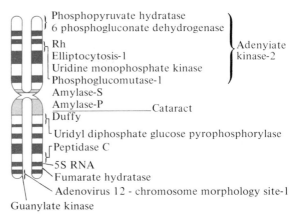

Phosphopyruvate hydratase
6 phosphogluconate dehydrogenase
Rh
Elliptocytosis-1
Uridine monophosphate kinase
Phosphoglucomutase-1
Amylase-S
Amylase-P
Duffy
Uridyl diphosphate glucose pyrophosphorylase
Peptidase C
5S RNA
Fumarate hydratase
Adenovirus 12 - chromosome morphology site-1
Guanylate kinase

Adenyiate kinase-2

Cataract

Figure 4-14   Gene map. *A map showing the location of some of the genes known to be carried on chromosome 1.*

in the hybrid cell.[18] As an example, seventeen genes have been located on chromosome number 1. These include the genes for one form of cataract, for the enzymes amylase and peptidase C, and the Rh and Duffy blood type systems.[19]

The new techniques of giemsa staining, described earlier, have permitted the mapping of genes on the chromosome. Missing portions of a chromosome, seen in terms of absent bands, can be correlated with the absence of a specific trait. Figure 4-14 shows a map of chromosome number 1.

Sex Linkage
The X and Y chromosomes are not homologous; each has genes unique to it. Genes on the Y

[18] F. H. Ruddle and R. S. Kucherlapati, "Hybrid Cells and Human Genes," *Scientific American,* 231 (July 1974), 36–44.

[19] V. A. McKusick and F. H. Ruddle, "The Status of the Gene Map of the Human Chromosomes," *Science,* 196 (22 April 1977), 390–405.

chromosome are said to be *Y-linked,* whereas genes on the X chromosome are said to be *X-linked.* Because of this nonhomogeneity, inheritance of traits carried on the X and Y chromosomes does not follow the simple Mendelian pattern.

Y linkage   A Y-linkage pattern of inheritance has been demonstrated for very few traits. The Y chromosome is small and probably carries few genes. Since male progeny inherit the Y chromosome, all males would inherit the Y-linked trait.

Y linkage, however, is difficult to distinguish from a sex-limited trait. These traits behave as if they were on the Y chromosome when actually they are carried on an autosome but expressed only in the male.

One trait thought by many geneticists to be determined by a Y-linked gene is that of long, stiff hairs on the rims of the ears. But this is not a clear-cut example, since the trait shows variable expression and is not expressed in some individuals for whom it would be predicted to occur.[20]

Recently a second trait was discovered which is determined by a gene on the Y chromosome. This is the *H-Y antigen,* a protein which researchers suggest is the basis for sex determination. It is possible that the production of the H-Y antigen, which would occur in XY and not XX individuals, may be involved in the development of undifferentiated embryonic sex organs into male sex organs.[21]

X linkage   The story is different with the X chromosome. A number of genes are known to

[20] C. Stern, W. R. Centerwall, and S. S. Sarkar, "New Data on the Problem of Y-Linkage of Hairy Pinnae," *The American Journal of Human Genetics,* 16 (1964), 455–471.

[21] S. S. Wachtel et al., "Expression of H-Y Antigen in Human Males with Two Y Chromosomes," *The New England Journal of Medicine,* 293 (20 November 1975), 1070–1072.

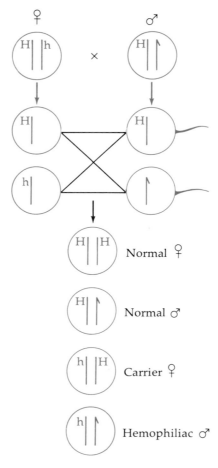

Figure 4-15   Inheritance of hemophilia. *The gene for hemophilia is located on the X chromosome but not on the Y, resulting in the X-linked pattern of inheritance.*

be distinctive to it. Actually, more is known about the X chromosome than any of the other chromosomes. The inheritance of X-linked traits is different from classical Mendelian inheritance. One such trait, hemophilia, will be used as an example.

Hemophilia is a recessive X-linked trait characterized by excessive bleeding due to a defect in the clotting mechanisms of the blood. Although there is now treatment for the disease which reduces its fatality, in the past hemophiliacs rarely lived past their early twenties.

It was noted early that males were the only apparent victims of the disease. It is now known that this is because the allele for hemophilia is carried on the X chromosome but not on the Y. Since the trait is recessive, a female would have to be homozygous for the recessive allele in order to have the disease. Because a male has only one X chromosome and a Y chromosome which does not carry the trait, he need have only one recessive allele for defective clotting to result (Figure 4-15).

Since the male child had to receive his Y chromosome from his father, his mother is the only parent who can transmit the disease to him. The statistical probability of a normal male, $X^H Y$, mating with a carrier female, $X^H X^h$, having a hemophiliac son is $1/2$. This is because all sons will inherit the Y chromosome from the father, but there is an equal chance that the mother will transmit the normal or abnormal allele. All daughters are statistically expected to be normal, since they must have received the normal X from the father. But one-half can be expected to be carriers because one-half the mother's X chromosomes are carrying the abnormal allele.

Can a woman be a hemophiliac? Until the early 1950s, no female hemophiliacs had been identified. It was assumed that $X^h X^h$ individuals either died before birth or at the onset of menstruation or that they were phenotypically normal and hence not distinguishable from $X^H X^H$ or $X^H X^h$ individuals. However, female hemophiliacs have now been discovered (Figure 4-16).[22] The reason their existence is so rare is that it is improbable that $X^h Y$ and $X^H X^h$ individuals will

[22] M. C. G. Israëls et al., "Hemophilia in the Female," *The Lancet*, 260, no. 6670 (30 June 1951), 1375–1380.

■ ● Hemophiliac
⊙ Definite carrier
⊘ Presumed carrier

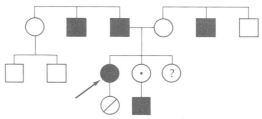

Figure 4-16   Pedigree of a female hemophiliac.

mate. Before the development of new medical procedures, matings between people with the above genotypes would have been limited because of the low probability of hemophiliac males living to reproductive age.

Recent treatment of hemophiliacs allows them to live somewhat normal lives. Since the disease is simply controlled and the defective allele is not "repaired," two concerns may be relevant in the future. First, there might be an overall increase in the frequency of the X^h allele; second, there may be an increase in the number of homozygous recessive females (see Chapter 5).

An example of the inheritance of hemophilia
During the nineteenth and twentieth centuries, hemophilia occurred with some frequency in the royal houses of Europe. The disease probably originated with Queen Victoria of England, because all the people involved are descended from her. Her father was normal, and there is no reason to believe that her mother was a carrier, so Victoria probably received a mutant allele from one of her parents. Of Queen Victoria's nine children, two daughters were carriers, one daughter was a possible carrier, and one son (Leopold) had the disease. These people and their children

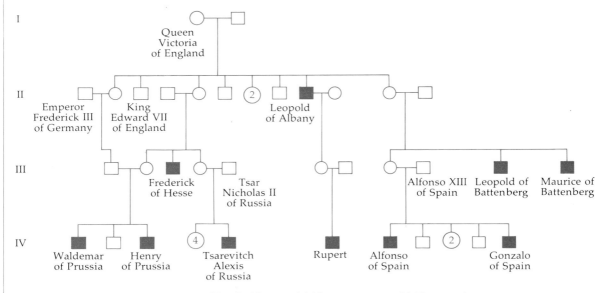

Figure 4-17 Queen Victoria's pedigree. *Not all of her grandchildren or great-grandchildren are shown.*

brought the disease into the royal families of England, Spain, Russia, and possibly Germany (Figure 4-17).

The most famous of these is Alix, granddaughter of Victoria, who married the future Czar of Russia, Nicholas II, and became known in Russia as Alexandra. She had four daughters and one son, Alexis, who was a hemophiliac. Historians have suggested that the preoccupation of Nicholas and Alexandra with their son's disease brought them under the control of Rasputin and hastened the overthrow of their government.

Hemophilia is perhaps the best known and most dramatic of the X-linked traits. However, many other characteristics are known to be inherited in a similar manner. Other genes known to be on the X chromosome are *red-green color blindness, congenital night blindness, Xg blood type, vitamin D–resistant rickets, glucose-6-phosphate-dehydrogenase deficiency,* and one form of *muscular dystrophy,* among others.

Summary

Stimulated by Mendel's work, early geneticists began to search for the physical reality of the gene. Their work led them to the cell and to those small bodies within the nucleus of the cell, the chromosomes.

Through special techniques, chromosomes can now be routinely observed through the microscope. Each chromosome consists of two strands, the chromatids, held together by the centromere. For a particular species there is usually a characteristic chromosome number. However, abnormalities in number and structure occur.

There are two basic forms of cell division. Mitosis is the division of body cells, while meiosis is the production of gametes—sperm and ova—in special body tissues. Detailed studies of the behavior of the chromosomes during cell division have provided a physical explanation for Mendelian genetics.

Deeper probing of the mechanisms of inheritance has shown that Mendel's principles do not always work. This is not because they are wrong but simply because the real hereditary mechanisms are very complex. For example, some traits are inherited on the sex chromosomes, so that their pattern of inheritance differs from the patterns determined by Mendel.

THE MOLECULAR BASIS OF HEREDITY

In the last section the behavior of chromosomes was studied as a means of explaining and expanding the observations of Mendel. But the chromosome is not the gene itself. This section will ask questions such as: What is the gene and how does it operate? To answer this question and others, it is necessary to turn to an examination of the chemical nature of the hereditary material.

All substances are composed of *atoms*, the basic building blocks of matter. Of the ninety-two kinds of atoms which occur in nature, four are found in great quantity in living organisms. These four are *carbon, hydrogen, oxygen,* and *nitrogen.* Others which play extremely important roles, but are less common, include *iron, potassium, sodium,* and *sulfur.*

Atoms can be joined together to form *molecules,* which can vary tremendously in size depending on the number of atoms involved. The molecules found in living organisms tend to be of great size because carbon atoms, which are usually the main constituent of such molecules, tend to form long chains. These chains can consist of hundreds or thousands of atoms, and often they include rings of five or six carbon atoms. Other types of atoms are attached to the carbon backbone.

Molecules of Life

Most of the molecules found in living organisms fall into four categories: carbohydrates, lipids, proteins, and nucleic acids. The *carbohydrates* include the sugars and starches. *Lipids* include the fats, oils, and waxes.

Some of the most important molecules of the body are *proteins.* An understanding of the protein molecule is essential in understanding the action of the genetic material. Proteins are long chains of basic units known as *amino acids.* All twenty basic amino acids share a common subunit, which contains nitrogen in addition to carbon, oxygen, and hydrogen. Attached to this subunit are various units ranging from a single hydrogen atom to a very complicated unit consisting of several carbon atoms.

The end of one amino acid can link up with an end of another, forming a *peptide bond.* Short chains of amino acids are called *polypeptides.* A protein is formed when several polypeptide chains join together.

In addition to simple chains of amino acids, many proteins are further complicated by other bonds. These bonds can involve sulfur and hydrogen and can lead to a folding, looping, or coiling of the protein molecule. The three-dimensional structure of proteins is important in determining how they function.

The complex and specific structure of the protein molecule is especially important for the role it plays as an *enzyme.* An enzyme is a molecule which makes a specific chemical reaction possible or speeds up reactions within cells but is itself not used up in the reaction. Enzymes control every chemical reaction within the body.

The Nucleic Acids

The largest molecules found in living organisms are the *nucleic acids.* The hereditary material that was discussed earlier is a nucleic acid.

Like the proteins, the nucleic acids are long chains of basic units. In this case the basic unit is called a *nucleotide.* The nucleotide itself is fairly complex, consisting of three lesser units. These are a five-carbon sugar, either *ribose* or *deoxy-*

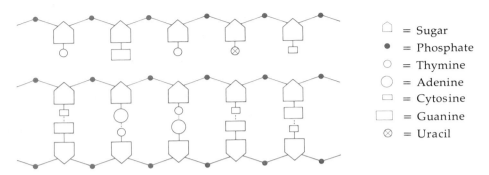

= Sugar
• = Phosphate
○ = Thymine
◯ = Adenine
▢ = Cytosine
▭ = Guanine
⊗ = Uracil

Figure 4-18   Structure of the nucleic acids. (a) *Short segment of the mRNA molecule*, (b) *short segment of the DNA molecule.*

ribose, a *phosphate* unit, and a *base*. The bases fall into two categories, *purines* and *pyrimidines*, both containing nitrogen. The purine consists of two connected rings of carbon and nitrogen atoms; the pyrimidine consists of a single ring.

The nucleic acid based upon the sugar ribose is called *ribonucleic acid* (RNA). The nucleotides which make up RNA contain the following bases: the purines *adenine* (A) and *guanine* (G) and the pyrimidines *uracil* (U) and *cytosine* (C). The nucleic acid based upon the sugar deoxyribose is called *deoxyribonucleic acid* (DNA). DNA also contains adenine, guanine, and cytosine, but in place of uracil is found the pyrimidine *thymine* (T) (Figure 4-18).

The DNA molecule   As with the proteins, the three-dimensional structure of the nucleic acids can be critical in understanding how the molecule works. Since the DNA molecule is the hereditary material itself, it will be considered in some detail.

The basic structure of DNA consists of a pair of extremely long polynucleotide chains composed of many nucleotide units lying parallel to one another. The units are linked in such a way that a backbone of sugar and phosphate units are formed with the bases sticking out. The chains are connected by attractions between the hydrogen

atoms of the two bases. Since the distance between the two chains must be constant, one of the two bases must be pyrimidine and the other a purine. Two pyrimidines would be too narrow and two purines too wide. In addition, because of the nature of the bonding, bonding can take place only between an adenine and a thymine and a cytosine and a guanine. These are said to be *complementary pairs*. In 1953 J. D. Watson and F. H. C. Crick proposed a model for the three-dimensional structure of DNA.[23] DNA consists of two long chains wound around each other forming a double helix, with a complete turn taking ten nucleotide units (Figure 4-19).

Replication of DNA   At the end of mitosis and meiosis, each chromosome is composed of a single chromatid which will eventually replicate itself to become double-stranded again. A chromatid is basically a single DNA molecule. In molecular terms, the DNA molecule has the ability to replicate itself to become two identical molecules.

[23] J. D. Watson and F. H. C. Crick, "Molecular Structure of Nucleic Acids: A Structure for Deoxyribose Nucleic Acid," *Nature*, 171 (1953), 737–738.

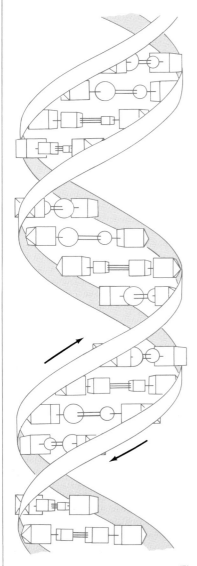

Figure 4-19 The DNA molecule. *The three-dimensional structure of the DNA molecule as determined by Watson and Crick.*

In replication, the bonds holding the complementary pairs together are broken and the molecule comes apart, with the bases sticking out from the sugar-phosphate backbone. Individual nucleotides of the four types (ultimately obtained from the digestion of food) are found in the nucleus, and the bases of these nucleotides become attracted to the exposed bases on the chain. Thus, a nucleotide with an adenine becomes attracted to a thymine, and so on. When the nucleotides are in place, they become bonded to one another (Figure 4-20).

The genetic code In order to function as the hereditary material, there must be a method by which information is stored in the DNA molecule. Remember, there are four bases which can be arranged in a number of ways. In the following

Table 4-1   The Genetic Code

Amino Acid	Codons*
Alanine	CGA, CGG, CGT, CGC
Arginine	GCA, GCG, GCT, GCC, TCT, TCC
Asparagine	TTA, TTG
Aspartic acid	CTA, CTG
Cysteine	ACA, ACG
Glutamic acid	CTT, CTC
Glutamine	GTT, GTC
Glycine	CCA, CCG, CCT, CCC
Histidine	GTA, GTG
Isoleucine	TAA, TAG, TAT
Leucine	AAT, AAC, GAA, GAG, GAT, GAC
Lysine	TTT, TTC
Methionine	TAC
Phenylalanine	AAA, AAG
Proline	GGA, GGG, GGT, GGC
Serine	AGA, AGG, AGT, AGC, TCA, TCG
Threonine	TGA, TGG, TGT, TGC
Tryptophan	ACC
Tyrosine	ATA, ATG
Valine	CAA, CAG, CAT, CAC

* The code is given in terms of the nucleotide sequence in the DNA molecule. In addition, there are specific codons signaling the beginning and end of a sequence.

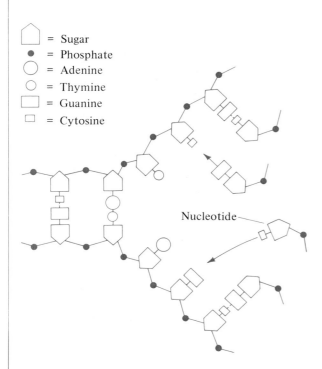

= Sugar
= Phosphate
= Adenine
= Thymine
= Guanine
= Cytosine

Nucleotide

Figure 4-20 Replication of the DNA molecule.

hypothetical example, the DNA backbone of sugar and phosphate units is indicated by a single line, the bases by letters on the line:

C T C G G A C A A A T A

What is coded in the above sequence are the amino acids. Each amino acid is determined by specific three-base units called *codons*. This code has been broken. Thus, CTC on the DNA molecule is the codon for glutamic acid, and GGA is proline (Table 4-1).

Messenger-RNA The blueprint for a specific protein is located in the DNA molecule within the nucleus of the cell. However, the actual production of proteins by the joining of specific amino acids in a specific sequence takes place elsewhere.

How is the information transmitted from the DNA in the nucleus to the site of protein manufacture?

The carrier of the information is *messenger-RNA*. This molecule copies the sequence of base pairs from the DNA molecule. A segment of DNA which contains the code for a particular polypeptide chain unwinds, thus leaving a series of bases on the DNA chain exposed. Nucleotide units of RNA are found in the nucleus. These units are attracted to the complementary bases on the DNA chain, with the adenine of the RNA being attracted to the thymine on the DNA, the guanine to the cytosine, the cytosine to the guanine, and the uracil of the RNA (remember, uracil replaces thymine) to the adenine on the DNA.

After the nucleotide units are in place, they link together and leave the DNA molecule as a unit. This chain of nucleotide units is called

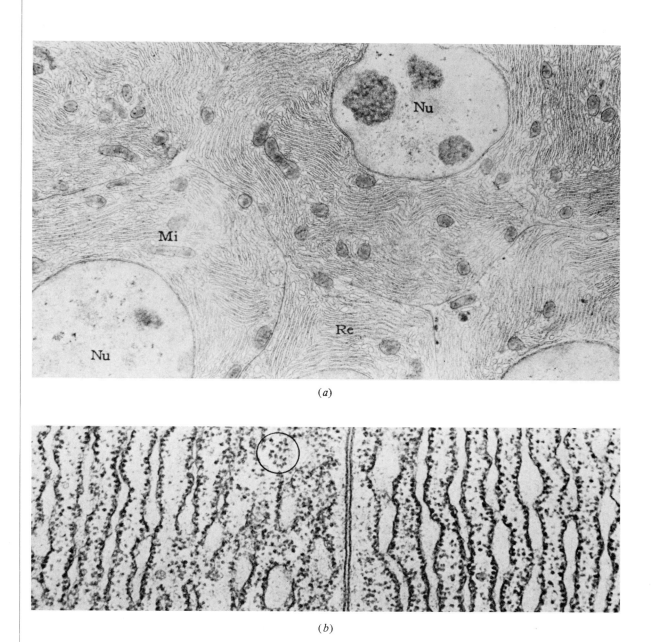

(a)

(b)

Figure 4-21 The site of protein synthesis. (a) *An electron microphotograph of pancreas cells showing the nucleus (Nu), mitochondria (Mi), and endoplasmic reticulum (Re), magnified 7,600 times. (b) A closeup (at 53,000 magnification) reveals the small particles called ribosomes attached to the endoplasmic reticulum. The ribosome is the site of protein synthesis.*

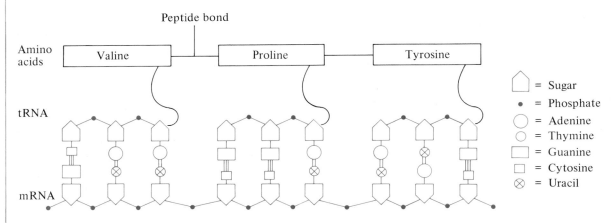

Figure 4-22   Protein synthesis in the ribosome.

messenger-RNA (mRNA). A molecule of RNA is considerably shorter than a molecule of DNA, since the mRNA contains the code of a single polypeptide chain only.

Protein synthesis   Under an electron microscope, a number of structures are found to exist in the cytoplasm (Figure 4-21). One such structure is the *endoplasmic reticulum,* a highly folded membrane. Attached to this membrane in many places are extremely small, spherical bodies known as the *ribosomes.* It is within the ribosome that protein synthesis takes place.

In the ribosome another form of RNA, called *transfer-RNA* (tRNA), is found. tRNA is extremely short, consisting in part of a series of three nucleotide units. The three bases involved form an anticode for a particular amino acid. That is, if the code on the mRNA is ACG, then the code on the tRNA consists of the complementary bases, UGC. Attached to the tRNA is the amino acid being coded.

The tRNA moves in and lines up opposite the appropriate codon on the mRNA molecule. For example, GUA is the code of valine on the mRNA. The tRNA which carries the amino acid

valine will have the base sequence CAU. After the amino acids are brought into their proper positions, they link together by means of peptide bonds and the polypeptide chain moves away from the mRNA and tRNA (Figure 4-22).

Genetic Abnormalities as Mistakes in Proteins
It is now known that a great number of genetic abnormalities result from abnormal protein molecules. Since the blueprints for proteins are located in the DNA molecule, it follows that these abnormal proteins are the result of an incorrect sequence of nucleotides in the DNA molecule itself. This can be demonstrated with respect to sickle-cell anemia and PKU.

The molecular structure of hemoglobin   Blood is a very complex material composed of a liquid and a solid portion. The solid portion consists of the *erythrocytes* (*red blood cells*), the *leukocytes* (*white blood cells*), and the *platelets.* The liquid portion is called *plasma.* The term *serum* refers to the plasma after the clotting material has settled out. Dissolved in the plasma is a wide variety of materials, including salts, sugars, fats, amino acids, and hormones, along with the important plasma proteins.

Packed into the erythrocytes are millions of molecules of the red pigment *hemoglobin*. Hemoglobin functions in transporting oxygen from the lungs to the body tissues and carbon dioxide from the body tissues back to the lungs.

Normal adult hemoglobin is *hemoglobin A* (HbA). The major constituent of the molecule is a large *globin* unit, to which are attached four *heme* groups. The latter are small iron-containing molecular units. The globin unit consists of four chains, two *alpha* and two *beta chains*. Each alpha chain consists of 141 amino acids, and each beta chain consists of 146.

Several other normal hemoglobins are known. *Hemoglobin A₂* is found in small amounts in adult human blood. HbF, or *fetal hemoglobin*, is found in the fetus but normally disappears within the first year after birth. These three hemoglobins differ somewhat in their abilities to carry oxygen.

Abnormal hemoglobins Perhaps the best-known of all the hemoglobin abnormalities is *hemoglobin S* (HbS), which is responsible for sickle-cell anemia. This disease is characterized by the physical distortion of the red blood cells into a sickle shape, which results in anemia, heart failure, kidney damage, and other serious physical ailments (Figure 4-23).

The genetics of sickle-cell anemia is relatively simple. The individual homozygous for HbA is normal, while the person homozygous for HbS has abnormal hemoglobin and the potential of

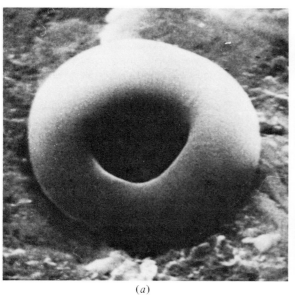

(a)

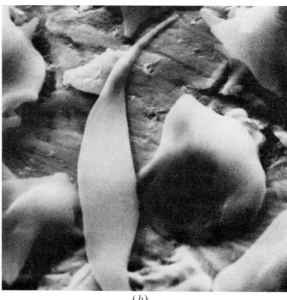

(b)

Figure 4-23 Normal and sickled erythrocytes. *The electron microscope reveals the distinctive shape of the* (a) *normal erythrocyte and the* (b) *sickled erythrocyte.*

Cytogenetics and Molecular Genetics

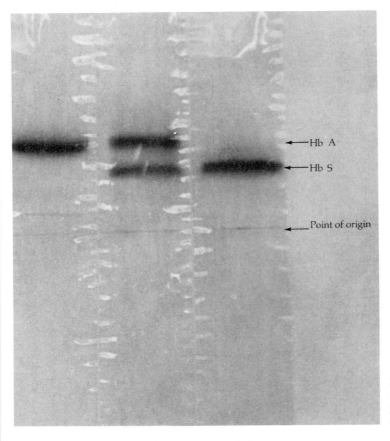

Hb A ←— Hb A

←— Hb S

←— Point of origin

Figure 4-24 Electrophoresis. *Charged hemoglobin molecules, placed initially at the point of origin, migrate differentially in an electric field.*

Hb A   HbAS   Hb S

developing the disease sickle-cell anemia. The heterozygous individual has a combination of normal and abnormal hemoglobin but very rarely has symptoms related to HbS. Such an individual is said to have the *sickle-cell trait*.

Identification of the individual heterozygous for sickle-cell anemia is relatively simple, and many methods now exist, including the use of *electrophoresis*. In this method a hemoglobin sample is placed in a solution containing atoms which carry electric charges. These, in turn, cause the proteins to develop electric charges of their own. The sample is then placed in an electric field, and the proteins migrate to one of the poles. The speed of travel depends on the weight of the molecule and the strength of the charge. The proteins are stopped before they reach the poles, and the relative position of the proteins can be used to identify them. Figure 4-24 shows the result of such a procedure.

The precise molecular structure of HbS has now been worked out. Remember that the hemoglobin molecule consists of four heme units and a globin. The globin, in turn, consists of a pair of alpha and a pair of beta chains. In HbS the alpha chains are normal. The defect is found in the beta chains. Out of the 146 amino acids in each of the beta chains, the sixth from one end is incorrect. Instead of glutamic acid, found in HbA, is the amino acid valine. The rest of each chain remains the same. If the codons for the two amino acids are studied, it can be seen that they differ in only one base pair. One code for glutamic acid is CTT, while one code for valine is CAT. There are 146 amino acids in the chain; a mistake in only one, brought about by a single mistake in the code, produces an abnormal hemoglobin with such drastic consequences.

A great number of other abnormal hemoglobins are known. Over thirty of them result from defects on the alpha chain, and over fifty involve the beta chain. All these result from a substitution of one amino acid for another at some point in the polypeptide chain. The substitution, in turn, results from some alteration of the genetic code.

The molecular basis of PKU   When you eat a piece of steak, you are ingesting protein. This protein is digested into its constituent amino acids in the digestive system. The amino acids then enter the bloodstream, to be transported to places in the body where they are needed. The body does two things with these amino acids. They can be used to build up new protein molecules, or

they can be metabolized (broken down) to provide energy and waste material.

The amino acids *phenylalanine* and *tyrosine* are very similar in structure. Phenylalanine in the body is either used as a unit in the manufacture of proteins or is converted into tyrosine. Tyrosine, in turn, can be broken down or can be further converted into a wide variety of molecules such as the hormones *adrenaline* and *thyroxine* and the skin pigment *melanin*.

Each step in the breakdown of tyrosine or in the conversion of phenylalanine or tyrosine into something else is controlled by a highly specific enzyme. The enzyme is a protein molecule, the structure of which is controlled by the genetic code in the DNA molecule.

PKU results from the presence of the incorrect form of the enzyme *phenylalanine hydroxylase* of the liver. This enzyme is responsible for the conversion of phenylalanine into tyrosine. If the enzyme is defective, it will not function, and the reaction will not take place. In this specific example phenylalanine will not be changed into tyrosine, resulting in a shortage of tyrosine in the body. But more significantly, phenylalanine begins to accumulate in the blood since phenylalanine cannot be broken down without first being converted into tyrosine. As phenylalanine levels rise in the blood, some of the excess phenylalanine begins to be converted by subsidiary reactions into a series of products such as

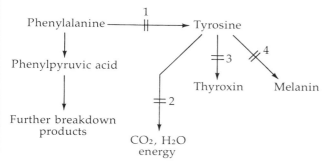

Figure 4-25   Metabolism of phenylalanine. *Abnormal enzymes will produce blockages in metabolism, resulting in various genetic abnormalities: (1) PKU, (2) alkaptonuria, (3) cretinism, (4) albinism.*

phenylpyruvic acid and phenylacetic acid. These products are found in the urine of the person with PKU (Figure 4-25). The high levels of these products in the blood do the damage which produces the symptoms of the disease. The control of PKU involves the detection of the enzyme abnormality as soon as possible after birth and the precise control of phenylalanine levels in the blood by regulation of the diet. While methods exist for detecting the carrier of PKU, they are not suitable for screening large populations.

A number of other genetically determined abnormalities are due to a defective enzyme. Daniel Bergsma lists seventy-five abnormalities where specific enzyme defects have been described. This list includes *albinism, alkaptonuria, galactosemia,* and *glucose-6-phosphate dehydrogenase deficiency.*[24] Remember that an enzyme is a protein molecule the structure of which is coded by a portion of DNA. An alteration of the genetic code can bring about an abnormality in protein structure resulting in a metabolic defect.

What Is a Gene?

We can examine this question in the light of studies of the structure and function of the hereditary material, the DNA molecule. The concept of the gene was originally developed as part of a model used to explain the mechanisms of heredity when the actual physical and chemical nature of the hereditary material was unknown.

"A gene is a segment of DNA recognizable by its specific function."[25] That function could be the coding of a particular protein or a major constituent of a protein, a polypeptide chain. Or, it

could be a regulatory function, that is, control of the activity of other genes. In the first situation, the 438 nucleotides which code for the structure of the hemoglobin beta chain can be thought of as a gene.

Blood-Type Systems

A tremendous number of proteins are found in blood. Some of these, such as hemoglobin, are essential to the body. Alterations of these molecules lead to abnormalities and death. Other proteins are not as critical. Some people may have them, others not. Often they occur in several alternate forms. These proteins are said to be *polymorphic,* from *poly,* meaning "many," and *morph,* "structure." Polymorphism refers to the presence of distinct forms within a population. The polymorphic situation makes these proteins very valuable in the study of human evolution and human variability.

Through blood transfusion and the occasional mixing of maternal and fetal blood at birth, proteins can be introduced into the blood of a person whose blood naturally lacks them. The body reacts to these foreign proteins by producing or mobilizing *antibodies,* whose role is to destroy or neutralize foreign substances which have entered the body. A protein which triggers the action of antibodies is known as an *antigen.* Antigen-antibody reactions are of great medical significance and help define differences in blood proteins which exist in humans.

The ABO blood-type system The best-known set of blood antigens is the *ABO blood-type system.* This system consists of two basic antigens, which are simply called antigens A and B. Other antigens in the system do exist, and the actual situation is much more complex than is presented here.

There are four phenotypes in the ABO system, depending on which antigens are present.

[24] D. Bergsma (ed.), *Birth Defects: Atlas and Compendium* (Baltimore: Williams & Wilkins for The National Foundation, March of Dimes, 1973), p. 908.

[25] W. F. Bodmer and L. L. Cavalli-Sforza, *Genetics, Evolution, and Man* (San Francisco: Freeman, 1976), p. 110.

Type A indicates the presence of antigen A, while type B shows the presence of antigen B. Type AB indicates the presence of both antigens, while type O indicates the absence of both antigens. The antigens themselves are large protein molecules found on the surface of the red blood cells.

The inheritance of ABO blood types is relatively simple, although three alleles (I^A, I^B, and i) are involved instead of two. Two of these alleles are dominant with respect to i: I^A results in the production of the A antigen and I^B in the production of the B antigen. In relationship to each other alleles I^A and I^B are said to be *codominant*, in that an $I^A I^B$ individual produces both antigens. The allele i is recessive and does not result in antigen production. The various genotypes and phenotypes are summarized in Table 4-2.

The ABO system is unusual in that the antibodies are present before exposure to the antigen. Thus, type A individuals have anti-B in the plasma, while type B individuals have anti-A in the plasma. Furthermore, an AB individual has neither, while an O individual has both antibodies (see Table 4-2).

Because of the presence of antibodies in the blood, blood transfusions can be risky if the blood is not accurately typed and administered. If, for example, type A blood is given to a type O individual, the anti-A present in the recipient's blood will agglutinate all the type A cells entering the recipient's body. The term *agglutination* refers to a clumping together of the red cells, forming small clots which may block blood vessels.

Table 4-2   Phenotypes and Genotypes of the ABO Blood-type System

Type	Antigen	Antibody	Genotype
A	A	Anti-B	$I^A I^A$, $I^A i$
B	B	Anti-A	$I^B I^B$, $I^B i$
O	—	Anti-A, anti-B	ii
AB	A,B	—	$I^A I^B$

Table 4-3   Results of Blood Transfusions*

Recipient	Donor			
	A	B	O	AB
A	—	+	(+)	+
B	+	—	(+)	+
O	+	+	—	+
AB	(+)	(+)	(+)	—

* + indicates heavy agglutination of donor's cells. (+) indicates no agglutination of donor's cells, but antibodies in donor's blood may cause some agglutination of recipient's cells. − indicates no agglutination of donor's cells.

Table 4-3 shows the consequences of various types of blood transfusion. Blood type O is often referred to as the universal donor. It is true that the entering O cells lack antigens of this system and therefore cannot be agglutinated, but it is also true that type O blood contains anti-A and anti-B, which can cause damage in an A, B, or AB recipient. However, such damage is minimal since the introduced antibodies become diluted and are rapidly absorbed by the body tissues. But the safest transfusions are between people of the same blood type.

The Rh system   Another major blood-type system, which is a great deal more complex than the ABO system, is the *Rh blood-type system*. In the United States and Europe most people have the Rh antigen. They are referred to as Rh-positive (Rh+). However, about 15 percent of the people in the population lack this antigen, which is inherited as a simple dominant.[26] These people are Rh-negative (Rh−).

Although Rh incompatibility can cause problems in transfusion, its greater interest lies as the cause of *erythroblastosis fetalis*, a *hemolytic*

[26] M. Levitan and A. Montagu, *Textbook of Human Genetics* (New York: Oxford Univ. Press, 1971), p. 217.

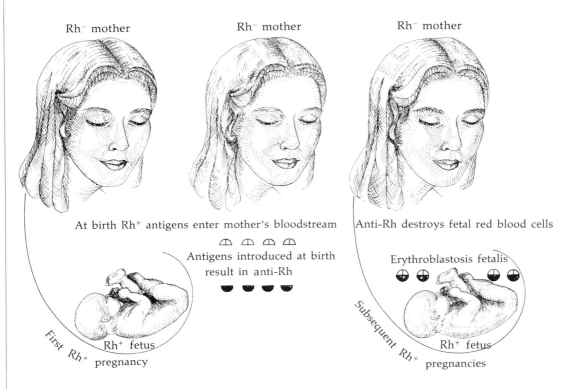

Rh⁻ mother   Rh⁻ mother   Rh⁻ mother

At birth Rh⁺ antigens enter mother's bloodstream   Anti-Rh destroys fetal red blood cells

Antigens introduced at birth result in anti-Rh   Erythroblastosis fetalis

First Rh⁺ pregnancy   Rh⁺ fetus   Subsequent Rh⁺ pregnancies   Rh⁺ fetus

Figure 4-26 Erythroblastosis fetalis.

(blood-cell-destroying) disease affecting 1 out of every 150 to 200 newborns. The problem results when an Rh-negative mother carries an Rh-positive fetus. At the moment of birth the Rh antigen in the fetal blood can mix with the maternal blood, causing in the mother the development of the antibody anti-Rh. Although the first few pregnancies usually do not present any dangers to the fetus, after this point the anti-Rh levels in the mother's blood are fairly high. The anti-Rh, which then comes into contact with the fetal bloodstream, can cause destruction of the fetal blood cells (Figure 4-26).

The Rh problem can be handled in two ways. Before delivery, the blood types of the parents can be determined. If the mother is Rh-negative and the father is Rh-positive, preparations can be made to completely replace the child's blood at birth by transfusion. Unfortunately, however, death often occurs before birth. Recently, an alternate method has been developed. Within seventy-two hours after each birth, the mother is given an injection of anti-Rh which suppresses her own production of the antibodies. Soon the injected antibodies disappear, leaving the mother's blood free of any anti-Rh and, therefore, safe for future pregnancies.[27] It is now also possible to transfuse the fetus while it is still in the uterus.

[27] C. A. Clarke, "The Prevention of 'Rhesus' Babies," *Scientific American*, 219 (November 1968), 46–52.

Other blood-type systems There are many other blood-type systems which are known for human blood. They include the *MNSs, Diego, P, Lutheran, Kell, Lewis, Duffy, Kidd, Auberger, Sutter,* and *Xg.* Each of these systems consists of a number of antigens. Because of this diversity of antigens, the probability of two persons having an identical combination of antigens is small. It also has been discovered that certain antigens and frequencies of antigens tend to be found in particular geographical regions. This will be discussed in Chapter 8.

Summary

Processes like inheritance can be understood on many levels. In the years after Mendel proposed his model for inheritance, scientists began investigating the chemical nature of genetic transmission. Through these examinations, it is known that the genetic material is a nucleic acid, DNA. DNA controls cell activities and hence determines inherited physical characteristics. DNA, which has the ability to replicate itself, is also the mechanism through which one generation passes its characteristics on to the next. The information contained in the DNA molecule is coded by the arrangement of base pairs. A small mistake in the arrangement can have extreme consequences. The information on the DNA molecule is transmitted by messenger-RNA to the ribosome, the site of protein manufacture, where transfer-RNA functions to bring the appropriate amino acids into position.

On the molecular level, a gene is a segment of the DNA molecule which codes a particular functioning protein or segment of a protein. Mutations arise when a random change is made in this code. The various alleles of a particular gene are simply slight variants in the code itself.

Blood studies have traditionally been important to anthropology because they provide a relatively easy way to study genetically controlled variability in human populations. A number of proteins in blood are present in some people and absent in others. The study of blood types and other biological systems has further expanded Mendelian genetics by, for instance, providing examples of traits with more than two alleles.

SUGGESTED READINGS

Beadle, G., and M. Beadle. *The Language of Life.* Garden City, N.Y.: Doubleday, 1966. An introductory text in genetics, with several chapters detailing the nature of DNA and protein synthesis.

Ford, E. H. R. *Human Chromosomes.* London: Academic, 1973. A basic introduction to human cytogenetics.

Garber, E. D. *Cytogenetics: An Introduction.* New York: McGraw-Hill, 1972. A well-illustrated and detailed introduction to general cytogenetics.

Hackett, E. *Blood.* New York: Saturday Review, 1973. A general discussion of blood, including the blood-type systems.

Hamerton, J. L. *Human Cytogenetics.* 2 vols. New York: Academic, 1971. A detailed discussion of human cytogenetics.

Harris, H. *The Principles of Human Biochemical Genetics.* Amsterdam: North-Holland, 1970. Deals with genetics on the biochemical level. Includes discussions of enzymes, protein synthesis, blood groups, and the genetic basis of metabolic abnormalities.

McKusick, V. A. *Human Genetics,* 2d ed. Englewood Cliffs, N.J.: Prentice-Hall, 1969. A basic survey of human genetics which assumes some general background in genetics. Excellent material on cytogenetics.

Stanbury, J. B., J. B. Wyngaarden, and D. S. Fredrickson. *The Metabolic Basis of Inherited Diseases,* 3d ed. New York: McGraw-Hill, 1972. Detailed and up-to-date discussions of inherited abnormalities in metabolism.

Stent, G. S. *Molecular Genetics: An Introductory Narrative.* San Francisco: Freeman, 1971. Detailed text on the nature of DNA and the functions of DNA within the cell.

Watson, J. D. *Molecular Biology of the Gene,* 3d ed. New York: Benjamin, 1976. Detailed discussion of DNA and gene structure by one of the discoverers of the structure of DNA.

Up to this point we have been mainly concerned with the mechanisms of heredity in the individual and in family groups. However, anthropological interest lies predominantly with evolution, and the individual is not the unit of evolution. It is true that people change over time. They get taller and heavier; perhaps their hair changes color, along with all those other things that are variously labeled growth, development, and decline. Yet, even though an individual today is not the same individual he or she will be tomorrow, that person is not evolving. Nor is the fact that people produce offspring different from themselves in itself evolution. For no two individuals, whether contemporaries or living at different times, or whether related or not, are exactly alike. Variation is not evolution. Evolution is change that can lead to the development of new kinds of populations, and the population is the unit of evolutionary change.

Chapter Five

Population Genetics

A MODEL OF POPULATION GENETICS

Populations

A population is a group of similar organisms. The unit of evolution is the *reproductive* or *Mendelian population*, which can be defined as a group of organisms potentially capable of successful reproduction.

Successful reproduction requires sexual behavior culminating in copulation, fertilization, normal development of the fetus, and offspring that are normal and healthy, capable of reproducing in turn. A number of conditions can prevent closely related populations from exchanging genes by preventing successful reproduction. One of the many ways this may occur is if the sexual behavior of the male, such as the mating dance of birds, fails to stimulate the female of a closely related population. Several forms of reproductive isolating mechanisms will be discussed in Chapter 6.

Of course, successful reproduction of a population requires a rate of reproduction sufficient to sustain the population. The number of individuals produced each generation must be great enough to compensate for deaths due to accident, predation, disease, etc. However, the rate of reproduction cannot be so great that the population will increase to the point where it can no longer be supported by its food sources or other elements in the environment. In other words, a successful reproductive rate is one that maintains a balance between population size and the potentials and limitations of the environment.

The largest natural population is the *species*, the members of which are potentially capable of successful reproduction among themselves but not with members of other species. Species can be broken down into smaller reproductive populations, which are to some degree, and often temporarily, isolated from one another (Chapter 6).

Phenotype of a population   Just as one can speak of the phenotype of an individual, it also is possible to speak of the phenotype of a whole population. Since a population is made up of varied individuals, such a description must be handled statistically. For example, the average stature of a population can be calculated and the variation from that average noted. It also is possible to calculate the percentage of blood type O, blue eyes, red hair, and so on, and emerge with a statistical profile.

As stated earlier, no two individuals are ever alike; the possible combination of alleles is staggering. However, the frequency of alleles in a population may remain relatively constant over many generations. What we have are individuals being formed out of a pool of genes that can be combined in an almost infinite number of ways. New combinations do not necessarily change the

frequencies of any gene in the next generation (Figure 5-1).

Genotype of a population   It also is possible to speak of the collective genotype of a population. This is known as the *gene pool*. The frequency of alleles in the gene pool can be calculated by formulas which will be discussed in a moment. Each

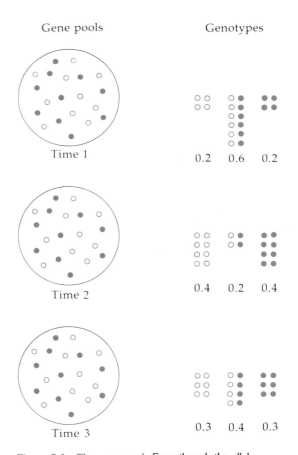

Figure 5-1   The gene pool. *Even though the allele frequencies remain constant, the genotype frequencies can differ through time.*

individual can be thought to contribute one cell to the gene pool. From these cells the genes can be extracted and tallied. It may be noted, for example, that if the alleles for PTC tasting in a population are tallied, 41.3 percent of them are dominant (T) and 58.7 percent are recessive (t). On further examination it might be found that 17.1 percent of the genotypes that emerge from the gene pool of PTC alleles are homozygous dominant, whereas 48.4 percent are heterozygous and 34.5 percent are homozygous recessive. The frequency of these genotypes makes up a statistical statement about the genotype of the population.

Genetic Equilibrium

Before discussing the mechanisms of evolution, evolution must first be defined. *Evolution* is change. *Biological evolution* can be defined as a change in the gene pool of a population. So, for example, if the frequency of the allele T changes from 41.3 percent to 42.1 percent, the population is said to have evolved.

A population is evolving if the frequencies of its alleles are changing; it is not evolving if these frequencies remain constant. This latter situation is termed *genetic equilibrium*. Since several factors can bring about frequency changes, it is best to begin with a consideration of genetic equilibrium and follow, one at a time, with a consideration of the factors which bring about change.

A model of genetic equilibrium In building a model of genetic equilibrium, we can simplify things by considering only one gene which occurs in two allelic forms, A and a, each with a frequency of ½. Brackets will be used to indicate "frequency of." Therefore, $[A] = \frac{1}{2}$, and $[a] = \frac{1}{2}$. If these are the only alleles for this gene, they must add up to 1, or unity: $[A] + [a] = \frac{1}{2} + \frac{1}{2} = 1$.

A model that will be proposed presents a hypothetical situation of no change. It is the fact that populations *do* change that makes the model important. By being able to specify under what conditions a static condition would exist, we can see, measure, and analyze change.

Certain conditions must be assumed for a population to remain in genetic equilibrium: (*1*) it must be assumed that mutation is not taking place; (*2*) the population must be infinitely large, so that change does not occur by chance; (*3*) mating must take place at random, that is, without any design or propensity of one type for another; (*4*) these matings must be equally fertile; that is, they must produce the same number of viable offspring. Deviation from equilibrium shows that one or a combination of these conditions is not being met.

If the frequencies of the alleles are each ½, what are the frequencies of the different individual genotypes? If $[A] = \frac{1}{2}$, it follows that $[AA] = \frac{1}{2} \times \frac{1}{2} = \frac{1}{4}$. So, one-fourth of the population will be homozygous dominant. To continue, $[Aa] = 2 \times \frac{1}{2} \times \frac{1}{2} = \frac{1}{2}$. Why the number 2? Because we are including two separate cases, Aa and aA. While the origin of the alleles differs in the two, the genotype is the same. Therefore, one-half of the population is heterozygous. Continuing, $[aa] = \frac{1}{2} \times \frac{1}{2} = \frac{1}{4}$. One-fourth of the population is homozygous recessive.

Now let the individuals within this population mate at random. The possible matings are $AA \times AA$, $AA \times Aa$, $AA \times aa$, $Aa \times Aa$, $Aa \times aa$, and $aa \times aa$. Three of the six types of mating can be accomplished in two ways. For example, $AA \times Aa$ could also be $Aa \times AA$. To simplify matters in each of these three cases, the two situations will be combined as one mating.

The next question which can be asked is: How frequent is each of the mating types? One simply multiplies the frequencies of each of the genotypes. So, for example, the frequency of the first type, $AA \times AA$ is $\frac{1}{4} \times \frac{1}{4} = \frac{1}{16}$. In the case where a mating type can be accomplished in two ways, the number 2 must be included. The frequencies of the mating types can be summarized as shown in Table 5-1. Note that the frequencies add up to 1.

The next step is to calculate the frequency of children produced. We are interested in seeing how the frequencies of the alleles change between generations. Table 5-2 is a series of calculations showing the contribution of each mating type to the next generation. The first case, $AA \times AA$, occurs one-sixteenth of the time and therefore produces one-sixteenth of all the offspring. Since all these offspring are AA, it can be said that this mating type contributes $^1/_{16}$ AA children to the next generation, as indicated in the AA column in Table 5-2. In the second case, $AA \times Aa$, which accounts for one-fourth of all matings, produces one-fourth of all the offspring. Of these offspring, one-half are AA and one-half

are Aa. Since $^1/_2$ of $^1/_4$ is $^1/_8$, $^1/_8$ is placed in the AA column and in the Aa column. The same procedure is followed for calculating the contributions of the other mating types. When the totals of the three genotypes produced in the next generation are added up, it is found that one-fourth are AA, one-half Aa, and one-fourth aa. In other words, the frequencies of the varying genotypes have remained unchanged from the previous generation. The population is therefore in genetic equilibrium.

The Hardy-Weinberg equilibrium The above calculations were first made independently by Godfrey Hardy and Wilhelm Weinberg in 1908 and are often referred to as the *Hardy-Weinberg equilibrium*. This equilibrium has been described above, using a specific case. But the concept also can be developed algebraically (Table 5-3). This results in the following general formula for the Hardy-Weinberg equilibrium:

$$p^2 + 2pq + q^2 = 1$$

where $p = [A]$ and $q = [a]$, from which it follows that:

$$[AA] = p^2 \qquad [Aa] = 2pq \qquad [aa] = q^2$$

The assumptions necessary for this formula have already been listed: no mutation, infinite population size, random mating, and equal fertility. These conditions can never hold true for any population. The Hardy-Weinberg formula defines a model which can be used to test hypotheses about gene pools and the evolutionary forces that work on them.

Using the Genetic-Equilibrium Model

While no population is actually in genetic equilibrium, some do come close. Initially, for the sake of illustration, a hypothetical population which is large in size will be used, along with a trait which does not play a role in mate selection or influence fertility or survival to any appreciable degree. We

Table 5-1

Mating Type	Frequency
$AA \times AA$	$^1/_4 \times {}^1/_4 = {}^1/_{16}$
$AA \times Aa$	$2 \times {}^1/_4 \times {}^1/_2 = {}^1/_4$
$AA \times aa$	$2 \times {}^1/_4 \times {}^1/_4 = {}^1/_8$
$Aa \times Aa$	$^1/_2 \times {}^1/_2 = {}^1/_4$
$Aa \times aa$	$2 \times {}^1/_2 \times {}^1/_4 = {}^1/_4$
$aa \times aa$	$^1/_4 \times {}^1/_4 = {}^1/_{16}$
Total	1

Table 5-2

Mating Type	Frequency	Offspring		
		AA	Aa	aa
$AA \times AA$	$^1/_{16}$	$^1/_{16}$		
$AA \times Aa$	$^1/_4$	$^1/_8$	$^1/_8$	
$AA \times aa$	$^1/_8$		$^1/_8$	
$Aa \times Aa$	$^1/_4$	$^1/_{16}$	$^1/_8$	$^1/_{16}$
$Aa \times aa$	$^1/_4$		$^1/_8$	$^1/_8$
$aa \times aa$	$^1/_{16}$			$^1/_{16}$
Total		$^1/_4$	$^1/_2$	$^1/_4$

Table 5-3

Allele	Frequency	Genotype	Frequency of Genotype in Population
A	p	AA	p^2
a	q	Aa	$2pq$
		aa	q^2

Offspring Resulting from Random Matings

Parents	Frequency of Mating Types	Frequency of Offspring		
		AA	Aa	aa
AA × AA	$p^2 \times p^2 = p^4$	p^4	—	—
AA × Aa	$2 \times p^2 \times 2pq = 4p^3q$	$2p^3q$	$2p^3q$	—
AA × aa	$2 \times p^2 \times q^2 = 2p^2q^2$	—	$2p^2q^2$	—
Aa × Aa	$2pq \times 2pq = 4p^2q^2$	p^2q^2	$2p^2q^2$	p^2q^2
Aa × aa	$2 \times 2pq \times q^2 = 4pq^3$	—	$2pq^3$	$2pq^3$
aa × aa	$q^2 \times q^2 = q^4$	—	—	q^4

$$[AA] = p^4 + 2p^3q + p^2q^2 = p^2(p^2 + 2pq + q^2) = p^2(1) = p^2$$
$$[Aa] = 2p^3q + 2p^2q^2 + 2p^2q^2 + 2pq^3 = 2pq(p^2 + pq + pq + q^2) = 2pq(1) = 2pq$$
$$[aa] = p^2q^2 + 2pq^3 + q^4 = q^2(p^2 + 2pq + q^2) = q^2(1) = q^2$$

will use as an example PTC tasting, discussed in Chapter 3.

PTC tasting In taking a random survey of a hypothetical population, it is found that out of 1,000 individuals tested, 640 are tasters and 360 are nontasters. What are the frequencies of the alleles T and t, and how many tasters are carriers of the recessive allele?

Since 360 out of 1,000 individuals are nontasters, and hence tt, the equation $q^2 = 0.36$ (q^2 being the proportion of homozygous recessive individuals and 0.36 being the decimal equivalent of 360/1,000) can be set up. If $q^2 = 0.36$, then $q = 0.6$ (0.6 being the square root of 0.36). If $q = 0.6$, it follows that p must equal 0.4 (since $p + q = 1$). Therefore, 40 percent of the alleles in the gene pool are the dominant T, while 60 percent are the recessive t. This may be surprising at first, since the majority of the individuals are

tasters, while the majority of the alleles are those for nontasting. This means that most of the recessive alleles must be found in the heterozygous condition and are therefore not phenotypically expressed.

What proportion of the population consists of heterozygous tasters (carriers)? The answer is $2pq$, or 48 percent ($2 \times 0.4 \times 0.6$). Only 16 percent ($p^2 = 0.4 \times 0.4$) are homozygous dominant tasters, and 36 percent are nontasters.

PKU Now let us turn to a consideration of the metabolic abnormality PKU. We will use data from England, where approximately 1 out of every 40,000 children born has this defect.[1] Sev-

[1] The incidence of PKU in England ranges between 2 and 6 per 100,000; 1/40,000 falls within this range. T. A. Munro, "Phenylketonuria: Data of 47 British Families," *Annals of Eugenics*, 14 (1947), 60–88.

eral questions may be asked: How frequent is the defective allele in the gene pool? What is the probability of an individual in the population being a carrier? What is the probability of two normal individuals mating at random having a child with PKU? This is not a case of genetic equilibrium, since the assumptions for genetic equilibrium are not being met. For example, until very recently, children with PKU did not grow up and reproduce. However, genetic equilibrium can be assumed, and the Hardy-Weinberg formula can be used to estimate the answer to these questions.

If the rate of the abnormality is 1 child out of 40,000, the frequency of the trait is 1/40,000, or 0.000025 (0.0025 percent). Therefore $[kk] = q^2 = 0.000025$. Then $q = 0.005$. This means that 0.5 percent of the gene pool consists of k, while 99.5 percent ($p = 0.995$) consists of the normal allele K.

What is the probability of being a carrier? The answer is $2pq$, which equals 0.00995 (2 × 0.995 × 0.005), which will be rounded off to 0.01. This means that approximately 1 percent of the population are carriers. This is 1 out of 100 individuals, which is a large number, especially when it is realized that only 1 out of 40,000 actually has the disease.

What is the probability of two persons mating at random having a PKU child? The probability of being a carrier is 0.01. The probability of two persons being carriers is 0.01 × 0.01, or 0.0001. If both are carriers, 1 out of 4 of their children is expected to have the defect. When 0.0001 (the probability of both being carriers) is multiplied by $1/4$ (the probability of two carriers having a PKU child), the answer is 0.000025, or 1/40,000.

It can be seen from the above that the population contains a large reservoir of deleterious alleles hidden in the heterozygous condition. In fact, it has been estimated that every person is carrying an average of three to five recessive alleles which in a homozygous condition would

lead to death or disablement.[2] The term *genetic load* refers to the totality of deleterious alleles in a population. The expression of this genetic load is responsible for certain natural abortions and abnormal conditions such as PKU.

Sex linkage It was demonstrated in the last chapter that an X-linked recessive genotype is more commonly expressed among males than females. Now a sex-linked trait will be considered in terms of population genetics.

A trait which is receiving considerable attention is called *glucose-6-phosphate dehydrogenase deficiency* or *G6PD deficiency*. This trait is characterized by the absence of the enzyme glucose-6-phosphate dehydrogenase in the red blood cells of homozygous recessive individuals. People with this trait develop severe anemia when their diet includes the fava bean or they are administered certain antimalarial drugs. In one study it was found that in a population of Israeli immigrants from Yemen, about 5 percent of the males showed this abnormality.[3]

The male has only one X chromosome and therefore only one allele for the trait. Therefore, $[X^g] = q = 0.05$. It follows that $[X^G] = p = 0.95$. When females are considered, the frequencies of the alleles remain the same, but note that there are three genotypes, as follows:

$$[X^G X^G] = p^2 = 0.95 \times 0.95 = 0.9025$$

$$[X^G X^g] = 2pq = 2 \times 0.95 \times 0.05 = 0.0950$$

and

$$[X^g X^g] = q^2 = 0.05 \times 0.05 = 0.0025$$

In other words, the female population consists of 90.25 percent homozygous normal individuals,

[2] L. L. Cavalli-Sforza, *The Genetics of Human Populations* (San Francisco: Freeman, 1971), p. 365.

[3] Ibid., p. 175.

9.5 percent carriers, and 0.25 percent with the trait (as compared with 5 percent among the males). The females have the same number of recessive alleles, but the majority of them are found in the carrier, where the effect of the allele is masked.

Demonstrating genetic equilibrium   The Hardy-Weinberg formula can also be used to demonstrate whether a population is in genetic equilibrium with respect to a particular trait. We can also gain some idea of the impact of the forces of evolutionary change upon the population. As an example, we can take a hypothetical population with the following genotypic frequencies: [AA] = 0.34, [Aa] = 0.46, and [aa] = 0.20. To find the frequency of A we add the frequency of the AA individuals, who contribute only A alleles to the gene pool, and one-half the frequency of the Aa individuals, since only one-half of their alleles are A. Therefore, $[A] = p = [AA] + \frac{1}{2}[Aa]$ = 0.34 + 0.23 = 0.57. Since $p = 0.57$, $q = 0.43$.

To determine whether this population is in genetic equilibrium with respect to this gene, we take the calculated allele frequencies and determine the expected frequencies of the genotypes. Thus, the expected frequencies are

$$AA = p^2 = (0.57)^2 = 0.325$$
$$[Aa] = 2pq = 2 \times 0.57 \times 0.43 = 0.490$$

and

$$[aa] = q^2 = (0.43)^2 = 0.185$$

When these figures are compared with the observed frequencies, they do not agree. The amount of disagreement between the expected and observed frequencies may or may not be statistically significant. Methods exist for determining significance, but they will not be discussed here. Therefore, our population is not in genetic equilibrium with respect to the gene.

Summary
The unit of evolution is the reproductive population. Such a population can be said, in statistical terms, to have both a phenotype and a genotype. The genotype of a population is referred to as the gene pool. As the frequencies of alleles within the gene pool change, the population evolves. Conversely, if the allele frequencies remain constant, the population does not evolve and is said to be in a state of genetic equilibrium. However, genetic equilibrium can only be a hypothetical state because the evolutionary forces of mutation, finite population size, nonrandom mating, and unequal fertility are always present and lead to change.

The Hardy-Weinberg formula allows the strength of evolutionary forces to be measured by allowing comparisons to be made between the hypothetical situation of no change and observed situations of change. Also, the formula can be used to calculate the frequencies of specific alleles and specific genotypes, such as carriers, within a population.

MECHANISMS OF EVOLUTIONARY CHANGE

In the model of a population in genetic equilibrium, the frequencies of the alleles in the gene pool remain constant. Such a population is not evolving. But in order to have genetic equilibrium, four requirements must be met. Since no natural population meets these requirements, it follows that all populations must be evolving. The mechanisms of evolutionary change are mutation, small population size, nonrandom mating, and differential fertility rates.

Mutations

A *mutation* is a mistake. It is any alteration in the genetic material, whether it is a change at a particular point on the DNA molecule (*point mutation*) or an aberration of the chromosome (Chapter 4). It must be realized that these errors are chance errors. A point mutation, for example, is a chance alteration of a single base in the DNA molecule.

What is the probability of such a chance alteration of the genetic code being advantageous to the organism? Imagine a Shakespearean sonnet being transcribed into Morse code. Suppose that in transcribing the sonnet, a dot was chosen at random and replaced with a dash. What is the probability that this change would improve the poem? Probably it would result in a misspelled word; it might even change the word, and hence, its meaning.

In a like manner, the probability that a chance alteration in the genetic code would be an improvement is very low. In fact, mutations are almost always deleterious to individual organisms. Most result in the death of the zygote or embryo. In addition, since a population is probably adapted to its environment, an individual who has a new mutation will in many cases reproduce fewer offspring in that environment than the other members of the population. Mutations which are advantageous, or at least neutral, are usually very subtle and are difficult to notice in the phenotype.

Whereas mutations are usually deleterious to individuals, they are necessary to the continued survival of a population. That is, the environment that a population is adapted to at one time may not be the same at another. Mutation within a population represents a potential to meet new conditions as they arise. Put another way, mutations are often not fit for the environments they originated in, but they might provide the needed variation to survive in a new environment. The individual is the guinea pig in nature's experiments to keep the population viable.

Mutations do not arise to fulfill a need. They arise with no design, no predetermined reason or purpose. In other words, they are random. However, mutation is the ultimate source of all variation within the gene pool. It creates variability rather than directly bringing about evolutionary change.

How do mutations occur? A mutation may occur *spontaneously,* that is, in response to the usual conditions within the body or the environment, or it may be *induced* by various agents. In both cases, some factor is actively causing the mutation to occur. But the exact cause for any specific mutation in most cases cannot be determined, although in experimental situations various agents can be shown to increase the frequency of the occurrence of mutations. Nor can the exact mechanisms by which mutations occur be demonstrated.

It is thought, however, that many point mutations result from mistakes in the replication of the DNA molecule. Thus, if in replication of the codon ATA (tyrosine) the incorrect complementary base were incorporated into the DNA molecule, the new codon might read AAA (phenylalanine), resulting in an amino acid substitution. Once the alteration had occurred, it would be the basis for the replication of additional DNA with the same error. We should point out that all but two amino acids are coded by more than one codon so that some mutations can be genetically neutral. For example, if a mutation changed the codon ATA and ATG, there would be no change in the amino acid indicated since both codons code for the same amino acid, in this case tyrosine.

The factors which initiate spontaneous mutations are for the most part still mysteries. It was once thought that background radiation from the general environment accounted for a large proportion of the observed spontaneous mutations. Most geneticists now believe that this is not true.[4] Naturally occurring chemicals and fluctuations in temperature may account for a proportion of

[4] C. Stern, *Principles of Human Genetics,* 3d ed. (San Francisco: Freeman, 1973), pp. 588–589.

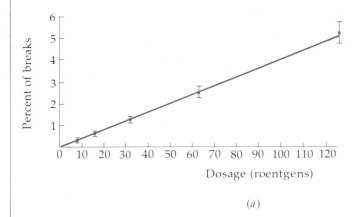

Dosage (roentgens)

(*a*)

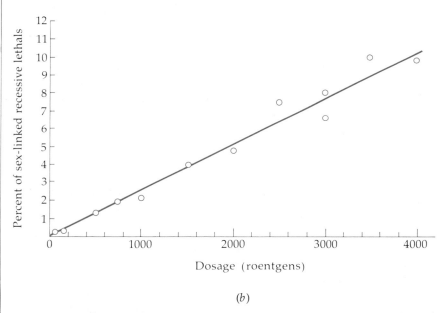

Dosage (roentgens)

(*b*)

Figure 5-2 Effects of radiation on the genetic material. (a) *X-ray dosage and frequency of induced chromosomal breaks in cells of a grasshopper.* (b) *X-ray dosage and frequency of sex-linked recessives induced in fruit fly spermatozoa.*

spontaneous mutations, with other factors not being known at this time.

The story is different for induced mutations. In 1927, H. J. Muller demonstrated that mutations could be induced in fruit flies by using x-rays.[5] In fact, the increase in the frequency of mutations was directly proportional to the increase in dosage of radiation (Figure 5-2). This discovery increased the awareness of the dangers of artificial radiation, such as from medical or occupational exposure, as well as from fallout. Although the U.S. Atomic Energy Commission has set what are considered to be safe levels of radiation, it can generally be stated that "all radiation absorbed by a person's gonads over and above the normal background radiation will increase the likelihood of his producing new mutations beyond the spontaneous rate."[6]

Certain chemicals added to foods, found in medicines or insecticides, or poured into the atmosphere or waters are known to cause mutations in bacteria. The effects of many of these agents on multicellular animals are not known. Some of these substances, although they may enter the animal, may be kept from the chromosomes by plasma and nuclear membranes. Since many substances that are commonly used are suspect, it is important that they be fully investigated. In addition, certain viruses are known to cause mutations.[7]

When mutations do occur, they may have no effect on the phenotype of the organism, for example, when the mutant allele is a recessive; or they can produce phenotypic alterations that range from extremely subtle to drastic. If mutations occur in somatic cells, cell death and abnormal development, including cancer, could possibly result. A single chance mutation taking place in a skin cell, for example, may have virtually no effect on the phenotype. But the same isolated mutation taking place in a sex cell may have a significant effect on the individual conceived from that sex cell. Such a mutation may result in potentially valuable characteristics, abnormal conditions, or even an inviable gamete.

Mutation rates How frequent are mutations? There are methods for estimating their rate. Although the mutation rates vary from trait to trait, most estimates for mutations that occur in sex cells are about 1 in 100,000 gametes per generation per gene (Table 5-4). When the large number of genes per gamete is considered, the probability of a particular gamete carrying at least one new mutation is about $1/2$. Since many of these new mutations are recessive, they probably will not bring about any problem in the immediate offspring.

Effects of Small Population Size

The model of genetic equilibrium is mathematical and assumes an infinitely large population. But natural populations are not infinitely large. Especially when we deal with small populations, we see changes in gene frequencies due to chance error.

Sampling error Political polls which predict the winners of elections can serve as an example of *sampling error*. Imagine it is election time, and you have been hired by one of the candidates to predict the winner. There are 100,000 eligible voters, but it is impossible to reach them all because of time and money limitations. So you decide to take a sample.

The first question is: How large must the sample be to represent the population adequately? If

[5] H. J. Muller, "Artificial Transmutation of the Gene," *Science,* 66 (1927), 84–87.

[6] M. Levitan and A. Montagu, *Textbook of Human Genetics* (New York: Oxford Univ. Press, 1971), p. 684.

[7] F. Vogel and G. Röhrborn (eds.), *Chemical Mutagenesis in Mammals and Man* (New York: Springer-Verlag, 1970).

Table 5-4 Some Estimated Spontaneous-Mutation Rates in Human Populations

Abnormality	Inheritance*	Estimated Mutation Rate (per million gametes per generation)	Population	Source†
Retinoblastoma	AD, v	6–7	German	1
Tay-Sachs disease	AR	11	Japanese	2
		4	European	2
Congenital total color blindness	AR	28	Japanese	2
		15	European	2
Albinism	AR	28	Japanese	2
		15	European	2
		33–70	Northern Irish	3
Hemophilia A	XR	13	North American	4
Hemophilia B	XR	0.5	North American	4

* AD = autosomal dominant; AR = autosomal recessive; XR = X-linked recessive; v = incomplete penetrance and/or variable expressivity.

† 1 = F. Vogel, "Neue Untersuchen zür Genetik des Retinoblastoms," *Zeitschrift für menschliche Vererbungs und Konstitutionslehre*, 34 (1957), 230, 234; 2 = J. V. Neel, et al., "The Incidence of Consanguineous Matings in Japan with Remarks on the Estimation of Comparative Gene Frequencies and the Expected Rate of Appearance of Induced Recessive Mutations," *American Journal of Human Genetics*, 1 (1949), 175–176; 3 = P. Froggart, "Albinism in Northern Ireland," *Annals of Human Genetics*, 24 (1960), 226–227, 231; 4 = I. Barrai, et al., "The Effects of Parental Age on Rates of Mutation for Hemophilia and Evidence of Differing Mutation Rates for Hemophilia A and B," *American Journal of Human Genetics*, 20 (1968), 195.

you take only 10 people, by pure chance they all might be voting for the same person. Maybe they are relatives and are the only ones voting for this candidate! If you take a sample of 100 individuals, the predictive value of the poll might be increased. But here, too, you must protect against bias by not polling 100 people who because of their ethnic background, financial situation, party affiliation, and so forth might be inclined toward one candidate, while other groups might be inclined toward another candidate. One way of achieving an unbiased sample is by randomly polling an adequate sized sample. The actual size of a representative sample depends on the variation within the population. There are statistical formulas which can be used to determine what sample size is needed to ensure that predictions will be within a desired level of accuracy.

As another example, suppose you wished to take a representative sample of the color of marking pens in a "population" of such pens. If the entire population were red, a sample of one would be sufficient. However, if there were ten colors in various frequencies, the sample would have to be large enough to include all the colors *and* reflect their relative numbers. Any deviation from this would be a sampling error.

One more, slightly different example can be used, flipping coins. Since the odds of landing heads are $1/2$, it would be expected that one-half of the flips will always be heads. So, if you flipped a coin 10 times you would expect 5 heads; 100 times, 50 heads; and 1,000 times, 500 heads. Yet if the coin is flipped the suggested number of times, the results might deviate from the predicted situation. If, for example, you flip the coin 10 times, you *might* end up with 5 heads; however, any number from 0 to 10 is possible. Furthermore, if you flip the coin 10 times over and over again, the number of heads will fluctuate from series to series (Table 5-5). If a large number of flips, say, 1,000 is done, you not only will come closer to the ideal probability of $1/2$ heads, but the fluctuations from one series to another will not be as dramatic (Table 5-6).

Genetic drift   As the genes in a gene pool are being passed from one generation to the next by the gametes, we are, in effect, taking a sample. Just as with a sample of voters, colored pens, or coins, all the possibilities may not be represented. If the gene pool is large, and hence the number of matings great, the odds are great that the new gene pool will be fairly representative of the old one. But if the gene pool is small, the new pool may deviate appreciably from the old. Such chance deviation in the frequency of alleles in a population is known as *genetic drift.*

Figure 5-3 plots the change of allele frequency through time as the result of genetic drift. Note that the fluctuations appear to be random and that when the allele frequency is high, there is a strong possibility that it will reach 100 percent, with the alternative allele disappearing from the population.

Founder principle   Another form of sampling error is called the *founder principle.* This occurs if there is a movement of a segment of a population to another area. The migrating group represents a sample of the original, larger population. The sample probably is not a random representation of the original group. It may be made up of members of certain family groups, for instance, whose gene frequencies vary considerably from the average of the original population. If the migrant population settles down in an uninhabited area or restricts mating to itself, it will become the founder population for the larger population which will develop from it (Figure 5-4).

The founder principle is significant in many situations. For instance, in a natural disaster, such as a flood or an epidemic, the surviving population may not be representative of the original population. Also, a colonizing group may differ markedly from the general population from which it comes. The English descendents in the United States, Australia, and South Africa, for example, differ from each other as well as from the "mother" population. Exploration and trade can provide another medium through which the founder principle may work. A group traveling through the world for one of these reasons may become stranded. Such an event occurred in 1789, when several members of the crew of the ship *Bounty*

Table 5-5   Sampling Error in a Set of Actual Trials

Possible Combinations for Ten Throws		Times Combination Thrown	
Heads	Tails	Number	%
10	0	0	0
9	1	0	0
8	2	3	3
7	3	7	8
6	4	23	26
5	5	23	26
4	6	13	15
3	7	12	14
2	8	5	7
1	9	1	1
0	10	0	0
		—	—
		87	100

Table 5-6   Population Size in a Set of Actual Trials

Number of Throws	Number Expected (heads)	Number Observed (heads)	Deviation from Expected, %
250	125	118	5.6
500	250	258	3.2
1,000	500	497	0.6

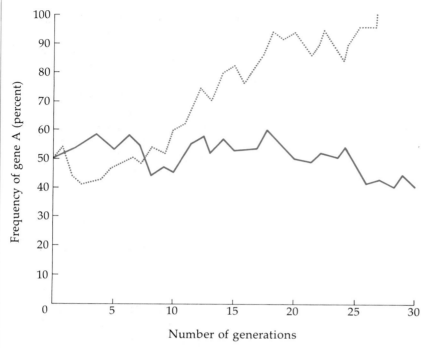

Figure 5-3 **Genetic drift.** *This diagram traces genetic drift in two hypothetical populations, beginning with an allele frequency of 50 percent. After thirty generations, one allele has reached a frequency of 100 percent while the other has dropped to 40 percent.*

mutineered. They settled on Pitcairn Island in the South Pacific and were trapped there. The mutineers, whose numbers were far too small to be representative of the British population, became the male ancestors of almost the entire modern population of Pitcairn.

Nonrandom Mating

The statistical model of genetic equilibrium calls for random mating.[8] If mating were truly random,

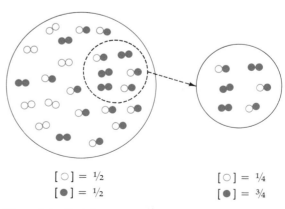

[○] = ½   [○] = ¼
[●] = ½   [●] = ¾

Figure 5-4 **Founder principle.** *The founders of the new population represent a nonrandom sample of the original population.*

[8] It should be pointed out that *marriage* and *mating* refer to different things. Marriage is a social relationship which may or may not involve mating, while mating is a sexual act which may or may not take place within a marriage relationship.

the probability of mating with anyone of the opposite sex would be the same. This is not the case. When you choose a mate, very definite factors determine that choice—factors such as physical appearance, education, socioeconomic status, religion, and geographical location.

There are two basic types of nonrandom mating which will be discussed here. The first is *consanguineous mating,* or mating between relatives; the second is *assortative mating,* which involves preference for or avoidance of certain people for physical and social reasons.

Consanguineous mating For most of American society mating between relatives is now rare. Yet, in some other societies, consanguineous mating is not only common but preferred.

In many societies there are cultural patterns of preferential marriage with a particular relative. *First cross-cousin preferential marriage* is one common type. In this system, the preferred marriage partner is your mother's brother's child or your father's sister's child, who are your first cousins. Yet, marriage may be prohibited between you and your mother's sister's or father's brother's child.

Cousin marriage is quite common in many parts of the world. Table 5-7 shows the incidence of first-cousin marriage in several societies.

Marriages also occur between second and third cousins, as well as between other types of relatives, such as uncle and niece. In fact, a preferential marriage that is considered quite repulsive to most Western societies, brother-sister marriage, was common for the royalty of several societies, including the Hawaiians and ancient Egyptians. Some scholars believe that Cleopatra was the offspring of a brother-sister marriage. Also, at one time she was married to her brother.

What are the effects of consanguineous matings on a gene pool? Let us look at an example which has been used by L. C. Dunn.[9] It has been determined in Sweden that the frequency of a recessive allele for Tay-Sachs disease is 0.005. This means that the number of individuals who are heterozygous for the trait is 1 percent of the total population. Therefore, the probability of two carriers mating is 0.01×0.01, or 0.0001. Since one-fourth of their offspring would have the trait, we conclude that the probability of two

[9] L. C. Dunn, *Heredity and Evolution in Human Populations,* rev. ed. (New York: Atheneum, 1965), pp. 125–126.

Table 5-7 Frequencies of Cousin Marriages

Population	Period	Number of Marriages (in sample)	% First-Cousin Marriages
United States, urban	1935–1950	8,000	0.05
Brazil, urban	1946–1956	1,172	0.42
Spain:			
Urban	1920–1957	12,570	0.59
Rural	1951–1958	814	4.67
Japan:			
Urban	1953	16,681	5.03
Rural	1950	414	16.40
India, rural	1957–1958	6,945	33.30

From: Curt Stern, *Principles of Genetics,* 3d ed. San Francisco: W. H. Freeman and Company. Copyright © 1973.

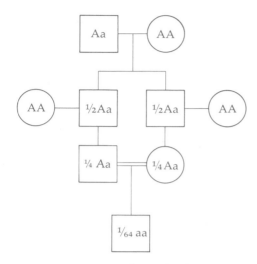

Figure 5-5 Cousin mating. *See explanation in text.*

persons mating at random and having a child with this abnormality would be 0.000025, or $1/40,000$, the observed frequency of the trait.

Now instead of two persons mating at random, suppose two first cousins mate whose common grandfather is a carrier. If the grandfather married a person who is homozygous normal, the probability of their offspring being a carrier would be $1/2$. The probability of getting carriers in the third generation, assuming that all people marrying into the family were homozygous normal, would be $1/2 \times 1/2$ or $1/4$. This is because matings between AA and Aa individuals would have a probability of $1/2$ for production of Aa offspring. However, since we know that the probability of the parents in the second generation being Aa is $1/2$, we must multiply $1/2 \times 1/2$, the individual probabilities of the two separate events. In the third generation each cousin has a $1/4$ probability of being a carrier. The probability of the cousins mating and both being carriers is $1/4 \times 1/4$ or $1/16$. The probability of these cousins having a child with Tay-Sachs disease is $1/16$ (the prob-

ability of the cousins both being carriers) $\times 1/4$ (the probability of two carriers producing a homozygous recessive child) which equals $1/64$ (see Figure 5-5).

In the above problem it was stated that the cousins' grandfather was a carrier. Of course, it is seldom known whether a particular ancestor was a carrier or not, but the probability of a common ancestor being a carrier can be calculated from gene-frequency data on the population in question. In this case the probability of two first cousins having a defective child is $1/3,200$, compared with $1/40,000$ if the mating was random.

Consanguineous matings tend to increase the probability of a homozygous recessive genotype. In the example above, the probability of producing a homozygous recessive individual is $12 1/2$ times greater if first cousins mate than it is with random mating. In fact, some recessive alleles are so rare that the probability of a carrier mating with another carrier at random is just about zero. But the probability of relatives within a family where the allele is known to exist carrying the same allele is much greater. Some recessive abnormalities are known only from inbred family groups.

The result of consanguineous matings in a population is a reduction in the number of heterozygous individuals and an increase in the number of homozygous individuals. If the homozygous recessive genotype is deleterious, the frequency of the abnormality will increase.

Not all inbreeding is the result of preferential marriage. In a small society it may be impossible to find a mate who is not a relative. Because of this, the effects of consanguineous marriages and genetic drift are often operating together in the same population, as will be seen in the following example.

The Amish The Amish are a series of small populations which have remained socially isolated for religious and cultural reasons. Today, there are more than 45,000 Amish, most of whom are found in Pennsylvania. The Amish are one of several religious isolates that are ideal for population studies. They are a strictly defined, closed group with good genealogical records, high nutritional and health standards, and good medical care. Almost all the Amish are at the same socioeconomic level, and they tend to have large families. They are rural, and most modern Amish families are found on the same land as their ancestors many generations back.[10]

Most of the Amish of Lancaster County, Pennsylvania, who are one of the populations called the Pennsylvania Dutch, are the descendents of about 200 pre-Revolutionary War ancestors who migrated to Pennsylvania from Europe between 1720 and 1770. This was the founder population. Because of the small population size, most available mates are related to some degree, although first-cousin marriages are prohibited.

The Amish represent the results of the founder effect, genetic drift, and consanguineous mating. In this population is found a fairly high frequency of some rather rare alleles, such as the one responsible for the Ellis–van Creveld syndrome.

The *Ellis-van Creveld syndrome* is characterized by dwarfism, extra fingers on the hand, and often congenital malformations of the heart. The syndrome is quite rare, with fewer than fifty cases being known outside the Amish. But among the small Amish population alone, forty-three definite cases are known. A great number of these individuals can trace their descent back to three common ancestors, one of whom was probably the carrier.

Many such isolates, like the Amish, have been studied by students of human evolution. Besides showing a higher incidence of several rare recessive traits, these populations also show allele frequencies for such traits as blood type which differ from the frequencies of the surrounding population. For example, among the Dunkers, a group of 3,500 individuals in Pennsylvania descended from German ancestors who migrated to America beginning in 1719, more than 44 percent are of blood type M, compared with the 29 percent blood type M found today in the general populations of the United States and West Germany.

Assortative mating　In the United States consanguineous matings are not common. However, mating is far from random. Deviation from random mating stems from the fact that Americans choose spouses by certain cultural conventions which they learn from contact with parents, friends, the mass media, and so on, and that out of all potential mates only some are "available." The term *assortative mating* means that certain phenotypes tend to mate more or less often than would be expected if matings were random.

Stature provides an interesting example of assortative mating. In American society it is quite common for the husband to be taller than the wife. The reverse is uncommon and is often the source of jokes when it occurs. What effect does this have on the gene pool?

Take two men, one 5 feet 8 inches (150 centimeters) (about the average adult male height in the United States) and the other 6 feet 2 inches (163 centimeters). If stature is a convention in mate selection, then the first man would be considering women 5 feet 8 inches (150 centimeters) or less, while the second man would be considering women 6 feet 2 inches (163 centimeters) or less. The second man has a greater population of women to choose from and might find it easier to find a wife than the first man. Likewise, a woman 6 feet (158 centimeters) tall may have difficulty

[10] A. McKusick, J. A. Hostetler, J. A. Egeland, and R. Eldridge, "The Distribution of Certain Genes in the Old Order Amish," *Cold Spring Harbor Symposium on Quantitative Biology*, 29 (1964), 99–114.

finding a mate, since she is "restricted" to men more than 6 feet (158 centimeters) tall. As a result, she may mate later and therefore have a shorter reproductive life and potentially fewer children.

Other important factors which determine mate selection include education and geography. Education is easy to document, and it appears that college-educated people generally prefer to marry other college-educated people. According to the results of one study, it is expected that a female college graduate would marry a male college graduate only 10.7 percent of the time if marriages were random; but actually such marriages take place 59.9 percent of the time.[11]

Geography is also important. Before you can marry someone, you must meet that person. People tend to meet and marry in the community in which they live (see page 157).

Besides showing preferences in choice of a mate, individuals also show avoidances. For example, mentally deficient people would not be selected as mates as frequently as mentally normal individuals.

Differential Fertility Rates

The model of genetic equilibrium assumes that all matings are equally fertile. But this is obviously not the case. Some couples have three children, others one, and still others no children at all. This means that the contribution to the gene pool of the succeeding generation varies from couple to couple.

V. A. McKusick presents some very interesting figures.[12] He estimates that more than one-half

[11] C. V. Kiser, "Assortative Mating by Educational Attainment in Relation to Fertility," *Eugenics Quarterly*, 15 (1968), 98–112.

[12] V. A. McKusick, *Human Genetics*, 2d ed. (Englewood Cliffs, N.J.: Prentice-Hall, 1969), p. 167.

of all zygotes never reproduce: 15 percent are lost before birth, 3 percent are stillborn, 2 percent are lost in the neonatal period, 3 percent die before maturity, 20 percent never marry, and 10 percent marry but remain childless.

Each zygote is a unique genotype, representing a unique assortment of alleles, a particular combination which will never occur again. Why do more than half of these fail to reproduce at all? Many are lost because of some inherited abnormality either before or after birth. Others never mate because they are placed in mental institutions. Some are killed in wars or accidents. Many mate but never have children because of a medical problem. And some do not mate or marry, or marry but have no children by choice.

Of the 47 percent of the original genetic combinations which do reproduce, reproductive rates vary. Some have only one child, others a dozen. What factors determine the differences in fertility? Some are medical, such as a blood-type incompatibility, but many are cultural. For instance, many couples today restrict their families to one or two children because of ecological concerns, while others believe that salvation lies in high fertility. The point is that the next generation is the result of the reproductive activities of only some of the individuals of the parental generation and that among those who are reproductively active, fertility varies.

What we have been talking about is *natural selection*, the heart of the theory of evolution. Natural selection is not simply "survival of the fittest" but the fact that certain individuals tend to have more offspring than other individuals and therefore make a greater contribution to the gene pool of the next generation. Factors which result in greater fertility, *if genetically determined*, will be passed on to the next generation with greater frequency. Factors which result in lowered fertility or higher mortality, such as a genetic abnormality, will tend to be eliminated.

Summary

Natural populations are not in genetic equilibrium. There are four mechanisms which bring about changes in allele frequency. Mutations, the ultimate source of genetic variability, provide one way in which the predicted frequencies deviate from the observed. Since mutations are usually deleterious to the individual, they rarely "catch on." Their importance lies in providing a potential to adapt to new situations.

Sampling error, in the forms of genetic drift and the founder principle, is another factor in evolutionary change. With genetic drift, by chance alone, not all alleles in a population will be represented proportionally in the next generation. The smaller the population, the more pronounced this effect. According to the founder principle, a new population established on the basis of a small sample of the original population may show distinctive gene frequencies. Again, the smaller the sample, the greater the potential deviation from the original group. Sampling error is in part responsible for much of the physical variation in different human populations.

The genetic-equilibrium model assumes random mating. However, individuals consciously choose mates for myriad reasons, for example, preferring to marry a relative in order to keep power and wealth within the family or wanting to mate with someone with green eyes for personal aesthetic reasons. Nonrandom mating leads to changes in gene frequencies from generation to generation.

Differential fertility, or natural selection, is a powerful force of evolutionary change. This topic will be a major focus of the next chapter.

As a final note, it should be emphasized that the mechanisms of evolution—mutation, drift, nonrandom mating, and natural selection—work *together* to create net change. For instance, natural selection would have nothing to "select" for or against if the variability provided by mutation were not present.

EUGENICS AND EUTHENICS

Knowledge of genetics is, and may increasingly become, a factor in future human evolution. Several basic problems which have been noted in this and previous chapters are being attacked by genetic researchers. They include the development of medical techniques to help genetically impaired persons live normal lives, methods of preventing such births in the first place, and ways of reducing the genetic load of populations. Geneticists are asking: Can we—by manipulating matings, fertility, and the hereditary material itself—improve the physical and mental condition of humans? These are the problems which make up the study of *eugenics*.

Eugenics

A recent political cartoon showed a scientist busily at work in a genetics research laboratory, totally unaware that the person to whom he was talking was being devoured by a grotesque monster supposedly resulting from the research. The caption read, "I give up, Charlie, what has six legs, four eyes and eats liquid nitrogen?"[13] This cartoon and others like it were responses to news of a new genetic technique involving *recombinant DNA*, which will be discussed shortly. This scientific development, first successful in 1973, has received more attention from the media and more scrutiny from scientists and government agencies than perhaps any other recent type of research. Research into recombinant DNA is one of many new areas of study which some day may play a major role in the treatment and cure of genetic disease and in other eugenic goals.

Science fiction, in the form of novels, short stories, and motion pictures, plus inaccurate reporting in popularized magazines, has created many misconceptions of what can and cannot be

[13] Mike Peters, *Dayton Daily News,* March 1977.

done eugenically.[14] However, many ideas and techniques which sounded like science fiction only a few short years ago are now on the threshold of reality. In this section we shall examine many ideas, not all of which are applicable to humans at this time.

Assortative mating   Eugenics includes the various methods which can improve the inherited qualities of a species. This idea is certainly not new. In fact, it predates genetic theory by thousands of years and has been applied successfully to animal breeding.

Plato, in *The Republic*, suggested that "the best of both sexes ought to be brought together as often as possible, and the worst as seldom as possible." What he had in mind was a type of assortative mating that would strengthen the population through discouraging reproduction of the "worst" people and encouraging reproduction of the "best." The problem, of course, is defining what is "best" and what is "worst."

The goals of modern eugenics can be accomplished by both negative and positive means. *Negative eugenics* involves the elimination of deleterious alleles from the gene pool. On the other hand, it is also possible to encourage the reproduction of people with desirable traits and thereby increase the frequency of these traits. This is called *positive eugenics*.

Negative and positive eugenics can be accomplished to some degree through the methods implied by Plato—preventing the breeding of certain types of people and encouraging that of others. For example, the inheritance of blue eyes is often like that of a recessive trait. Therefore, all

offspring of a blue-eyed couple usually would have blue eyes. If such matings were prevented, the number of blue-eyed children would decrease. If society placed total selection against blue eyes, not allowing any blue-eyed individuals to reproduce, in time the reservoir of the blue-eyed allele in heterozygous individuals would be depleted and the trait would disappear. Eye color is not an especially important trait and is used here for illustration only. However, the same principle could be used in the breeding of other traits inherited in the same way. Complications would arise with traits controlled by more than one gene.

Artificial insemination, fetal transplants, and test-tube babies   It has been suggested that the sperm and ova of the healthiest men and women and those who have specific potentials could be frozen and used repeatedly to produce offspring. This is partially achievable now with sperm. Through freezing sperm and using methods of artificial insemination, gametes can be deposited for later use.

The freezing of sperm is practical for men working in dangerous jobs. For example, since radiation can cause sterility and an increased mutation rate, these threats can be partially offset by storing sex cells in radiation-proof areas. This method might be used to protect not only individuals but also an entire population from the threat of nuclear accidents.

Storing sperm is a long way from creating specific types of people. Because of the amount of genetic variability within the billions of possible sperm from a single man, plus the variability of the mother's ova, in addition to environmental influences, all offspring produced by even one man would be significantly different from each other.

For a variety of reasons, some women cannot bear children. For instance, a woman's oviducts

---

[14] Topics relating to eugenics have been favorites of science fiction writers for decades. One classic is *Brave New World* by Aldous Huxley (New York: Harper and Row, 1946). Another title is *Time Enough for Love* by Robert Heinlein (New York: Putnam, 1973).

may be blocked, preventing the descent of the ovum into the uterus. Or her uterus may be too small to accommodate a fetus. In the first case, it has been proposed that an embryo be developed in a test tube by removing an ovum from the mother and artificially fertilizing it with the father's sperm. The ovum, fertilized outside the mother's body, would then be transferred from the test tube at the proper stage of development back into the mother from which the egg was originally taken. Or the embryo could be placed into a "substitute" mother, where it would develop to term and then be turned over to the mother who provided the sex cell. In the second case, an embryo could be removed from the mother and placed into a substitute mother to term.

In 1976, researchers removed an ovum from a human female and placed it in a laboratory dish. It was then fertilized by her husband's sperm. After about 4⅓ days of being cultured in the "test tube," the embryo was reimplanted in the mother. This embryo survived only thirteen weeks because it became implanted in the Fallopian tube rather than the uterus, but the fact that the process proceeded to this point seems to indicate that successful fertilizations outside the body and reimplantations resulting in live offspring may not be far off.[15]

In 1975, the first live primate birth from an embryo transplant occurred. Unlike the example above, in which the ovum was fertilized outside the body, this case involved the recovery of a naturally fertilized ovum from a female baboon and the transplanting of the zygote to another female. The procedure was rather complex, but in about 174 days a normal male was delivered to the substitute mother.[16]

While an embryo can develop normally in a test tube during the very early stages, breeding a human from conception to "birth" in a test tube lies far in the future.

Predetermining the sex of a child   Amniocentesis can be used to discover the sex of a human fetus. There has also been some success in predetermining sex in nonhuman mammals. This is not now possible in humans, although it appears to be theoretically possible.[17]

Predetermination of sex could have numerous social implications. There is a tendency in some societies to prefer children of one sex. If parents could determine the sex of their child, there might be an increase in the number of the preferred sex born and a decrease in the other. This could greatly alter the sex ratio and lead to the development of problems within the society. For example, in societies where monogamy (marriage between one man and one woman) is practiced, an increase in the proportion of one sex over the other would mean that a substantial number of one sex would remain unmarried.

Cloning   Another idea is to produce human clones. A *clone* is a group of asexually produced offspring. To produce a clone, a somatic (body) cell with the full diploid complement of chromosomes is used instead of a normal zygote. Each offspring which develops from such a somatic cell is genetically identical to the parent. A group of such identical offspring is referred to as a clone. In this way, an individual who is physically and mentally fit could be reproduced over and over.

Cloning has been done with plants. Many plants are not reproduced from seeds; indeed,

---

[15] P. C. Steptoe and R. G. Edwards, in press.

[16] D. C. Kraemer et al., "Baboon Infant Produced by Embryo Transfer," *Science*, 192 (18 June 1976), 1246–1247.

[17] R. L. Sinsheimer, "Genetic Engineering," *Engineering and Science*, 35, no. 7 (June 1972), 3–8.

many cultivated plants do not even form seeds. In these cases humans must intervene, removing and planting a section of the parent plant. This section then takes root, and a new plant develops. Cloning of animals would, of course, involve other methods such as removing the nucleus of a normally fertilized egg and substituting the nucleus of a somatic cell. The new individual would then have the identical genetic code of the donor. This has been accomplished with amphibians.[18] If this could be done with humans, thousands of people with some desired characteristic could be bred. But who would determine what is "desirable"?

Parthenogenesis Throughout history, women have claimed to become pregnant without participation of the male. These claims have always been passed over as ridiculous, which they probably are. However, it has been noted in certain animals that very rarely an unfertilized egg will develop into a fetus. This is called *parthenogenesis*. Ova have been stimulated in mammals, but only in the rabbit have living offspring developed.[19]

Since parthenogenesis involves the ovum only, and an ovum can have only an X chromosome, the offspring would have to be female. Also, the individual produced by parthenogenesis would not possess any genes that the mother did not have, except those which arose through mutation. All recent claims of parthenogenesis in humans that have been investigated have been shown false on genetic grounds.

The eugenic effects of parthenogenesis should be obvious. Hundreds of individuals would be produced from a woman deemed to be "superior" with the idea that like begets like. This is not now possible.

Artificial genes and recombinant DNA Some day it might be possible to alter human genetic material in order to eliminate or repair deleterious alleles and change certain alleles to more advantageous types. In this way a desired type of person could be produced.

In 1976, it was announced that a completely artificial gene, used to replace a defective gene in a virus, had been synthesized.[20] In very recent years, researchers have also been making advances in determining what "turns genes on and off," that is, how genes can produce their products at one time but not at others. To date, scientists have been able to affect the action of at least one gene in a bacterium.[21] The production of synthetic genes and regulation of gene action have been accomplished only in a virus and a bacterium, but the techniques could have revolutionary consequences if they are ever applicable to humans.

The recombinant DNA research involves the transferring of genes from one organism to another. At present, the work is confined to bacteria. The method is seen as a means of acquiring knowledge about the functioning of genes and cells in general. It could also increase our understanding of cancer and other diseases. Some scientists believe that bacteria could be created that could act as producers of needed chemicals such as hormones and antibodies. Another possible application would be to introduce genes into

---

[18] Ibid.

[19] P. A. Moody, *Genetics of Man,* 2d ed. (New York: Norton, 1975), p. 6.

[20] T. H. Maugh II, "The Artificial Gene: It's Synthesized and It Works in Cells," *Science,* 194 (1 October 1976), 44.

[21] "To Clone a Gene," *Scientific American,* 236 (January 1977), 47–49.

crops that do not fix nitrogen and hence eliminate the need for nitrogen fertilizers.

In 1974, some scientists began to believe that there were potentially great hazards in this type of research. Although no one envisioned the creation of a monster, it was thought that harmful bacteria could be created and perhaps "escape" through carelessness from the laboratory and threaten human life. Since 1974, scientists have set guidelines to regulate their own research, a unique event in the history of science. Local governments, the National Institutes of Health, the Department of Health, Education, and Welfare, as well as the Congress have all been dealing with the potential dangers of recombinant DNA research, as have other countries throughout the world.

The possible eugenic applications of recombinant DNA research would include on one level the altering or replacing of defective genes with normal ones. On a second level recombinant DNA might be used to introduce traits into humans. These traits, derived from other organisms or "synthetics," would drastically alter the phenotype, creating people with certain characteristics to order. Both of these applications of recombinant DNA are far from feasible now. However, if they ever become possible, especially if the ability to control regulatory genes, to synthesize genes, and to clone also became a reality for humans, the possibilities of altering human biology could be almost limitless and the potential consequences enormous.[22]

---

[22] For further information see C. Russel, "Biologists Draft Genetic Research Guidelines," *BioScience,* 25 (April 1975), 237–240; editorials and dialogues in *BioScience,* 26 (October 1976); N. Wade, "Recombinant DNA: A Critic Questions the Right to Free Inquiry," *Science,* 194 (15 October 1976), 303–306; and G. Grobstein, "Recombinant DNA Research: Beyond the NIH Guidelines," *Science,* 194 (10 December 1976), 1133–1135.

Eugenic Problems

Even if medical means of controlling genetic diseases were further developed, and if assortative mating methods of eugenics or the ideas mentioned above could be applied, the problems associated with eugenic goals are immense.

Dysgenic effects Should genetic diseases be cured or arrested? This is not the easy question it might appear to be. If a disease is eliminated by weeding out the alleles that cause it, this is a eugenic effect. A *eugenic effect* is an improvement in the gene pool. However, if the disease is simply controlled phenotypically, the genetic factor is propagated even further. This is a *dysgenic effect,* a tendency to increase the frequency of the disease.

As an example of the possible dysgenic effect of such control, let us look again at PKU. PKU individuals are now detected early, and early treatment is decreasing their mortality along with the trait of greatly lowered IQ. As a result, the chance of these persons producing offspring has increased. But as these homozygous recessive individuals reproduce, the frequency of the recessive allele increases. If the PKU individual mates with a homozygous normal person, all their offspring will be carriers. This means that the potential genetic load increases, and the allele becomes more widely distributed through the population.

The increase in the frequency of such an allele is not necessarily disadvantageous as long as there are medical facilities to handle the increasing number of defective individuals. The potential danger lies in the fact that if the methods of treatment become unavailable or ineffective, these persons, phenotypically normal but dependent upon the treatment, could once again develop all the symptoms of these abnormalities, just like all the newborn who possessed the trait.

It would appear that the safest way to handle

genetic diseases is to eliminate the lethal allele by altering the DNA molecule itself. Since this cannot be done at present, an alternative is to discourage people carrying a deleterious recessive from having children. If they do attempt to have children, abortions can be performed if amniocentesis proves the fetus to be defective.

It must be kept in mind, however, that even if persons who are homozygous recessive and heterozygous for a deleterious recessive trait were prevented from mating, it would be impossible to eliminate specific diseases totally. This is because of mutations which are always occurring. A percentage of any specific genetic defect showing up in a population is the result of mutation, not inheritance from parents. This still does not mean that carriers of severe genetic diseases should not be discouraged from having children. The reduction in frequency of the disease would be significant; it just would not be total.

Reduction of variability Another possible danger of eugenic attempts is the reduction of variability in a population. A major question is: What traits should be eliminated? Genetic abnormalities which lead to an early death, extremely low intelligence, and severe skeletal abnormalities will probably never have any advantages in future generations. But what about certain mild metabolic defects or blood disorders which could conceivably have beneficial effects if the environment should shift? Also, alleles which are deleterious in the homozygous state may confer adaptive advantage in the heterozygote.

A classic example of this situation is the relationship between sickle-cell anemia and malaria. Sickle-cell anemia is often a lethal trait, bringing about disability and early death. Yet the presence of this deleterious allele in the heterozygous individual brings about a resistance to malaria, a resistance also found in the homozygous recessive individual. There are many other examples of

alleles which, although disadvantageous in the homozygous recessive state, bring about a greater adaptation in the heterozygous than in the homozygous normal individual.

Imagine a situation whereby, using eugenic means, it is possible to reduce the frequency of the allele for sickle-cell anemia through detection of heterozygotes. This is a fine goal. But what if the techniques of control of malaria become ineffective? Then, because of the disappearance of the sickle-cell allele, the population would lack the protection from malaria conferred by this allele. This is not farfetched, since the major means of control of malaria is to destroy the disease-carrying mosquito with insecticides, such as DDT. Already there are large populations of mosquitos which, through a combination of mutation and natural selection, have developed immunities to DDT. If malaria became a threat again and the sickle-cell allele no longer existed, the population would be less fit in the new malarial environment than it was in the old one (Figure 5-6).

It is seen that, as the situation changes, what was advantageous (the sickle-cell trait) might become disadvantageous and conceivably advantageous again. Also, new diseases can arise, and if certain types of people are deleted from the population through eugenics, it might be those people who carried the immunity to the new disease.

In addition to the biological problems discussed above, there are other problems associated with eugenic attempts which are not simply technological but social and moral.

Racism The British, in exterminating the people of Tasmania, the Spanish and United States governments, in drastically reducing the number of North American Indians, and Hitler's attempts at genocide of the Jews are extreme examples of racism. *Racism* is the belief that cultural and social differences between people are in whole or in part the result of hereditary differences. Very often these differences are seen in terms of a supposed natural or inherent superiority of one group over another. In the instances mentioned, the group that considered itself superior eliminated or tried to eliminate the other.

Racism actually can be an application of eugenics. If a people in power decide that others are inferior or undesirable, they might in the guise of "improvement" practice negative eugenics against these people. But there is no evidence that any group is genetically inferior to others. All human groups have a common ancestry and a common gene pool. The physical differences that are observed between people are for the most part superficial adaptations to particular environments or the results of drift. Other differences are usually a matter of cultural tradition (see Chapters 7 and 8).

Elitism   Another potential danger of eugenics is the creation of a biological elite, that is, a caste of persons who, for their own purposes, manipulate the conception of other individuals. Soldiers, artists, or clerks could be bred to order. This *elitism* would be the ultimate in "big brotherism."

Can birth control affect genetics?   Since different social groups reproduce at varying rates, their contribution to the total human gene pool varies. If one group practices birth control and another does not, the former's genetic contribution to the general gene pool will decrease, assuming that both groups have the same reproductive risk for all other factors.

But population control is necessary. With the earth's decreasing resources and increasing pollution, people must seek just methods to curb population growth. Many minority groups believe that this would be tantamount to genocide against them. This fear is not totally unwarranted. If a majority group put stronger controls on the reproduction of other groups, the end result would be a decrease in these groups in proportion to the controlling group. However, if zero population growth is accomplished uniformly, there will be no net increase or decrease in any specific group.

Although some eugenic methods may be beneficial to the population as a whole, most are

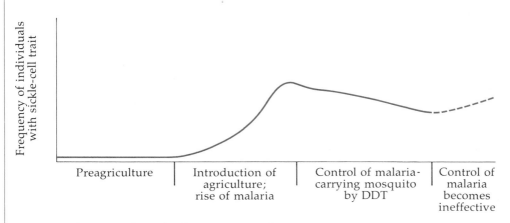

Figure 5-6   **Dynamic relationship between genes and environment.**

full of dangers. As we have shown, if variability is decreased and the genetic load is increased, a full eugenic program, when and if it became possible, might greatly weaken the human species.

Euthenics

Eugenics may be called genetic engineering, an attempt to artificially better the human species by the manipulation of inherited traits. *Euthenics* is environmental engineering, the alteration of the environment. Since the phenotype is determined in part by the environment, changes in the environment can greatly affect the biological nature of humans.

Euthenics began when the first humans learned to modify natural objects into tools. These tools could then be used to compensate for physical incapabilities of the species as a whole. Every technical or social·innovation which followed, such as domestication of plants and animals, development of metallurgy, and industrialization, contributed to creating an environment made by humans.

Euthenics has the tendency to equalize varying phenotypes within a specific group. The gun, for instance, was called the great equalizer in the early days of Western expansion. It allowed people of differing physical abilities to face each other on an equal basis. Such cultural innovations as clothing, shelter, markets, and modes of transportation permitted phenotypes to survive that could not do so otherwise.

The creation of a therapeutic environment has been one major euthenic feat of the last century. Through sanitation and medical advances, environments have been created which allow a larger variety of people to live longer, healthier, and in many cases happier lives. Many human ills are often cured by changing the environment rather than by changing the individual, as when a disease such as cholera is eliminated through proper methods of sanitation.

Dysthenic effects

A *dysthenic effect* is an alteration of the environment which tends to increase the frequency of disease and discomfort. Some attempts at improving the human condition through euthenics have backfired. The development of weapons which allowed the physically weak to stand up to the strong has also permitted maniacs to ravage peoples with their ideas of superiority and lust for power. The innovations of plant and animal domestication, which allowed for more stable food sources, contributed to the rise of the population to the point where more people now live under the threat of starvation than ever before. Urbanization, which provides protection to individuals, places to redistribute goods, and recreational resources, represents noise, dirt, and alienation for many. The industrialization and mass production which have raised the standard of living in some areas also have brought with them noise and air and water pollution which endanger the very survival of the human species.

Summary

Eugenics and euthenics are related and interdependent. For example, one way of reducing genetic disease is through euthenic means. Conversely, a dysthenic effect, such as increased radiation, might have dysgenic effects, such as the increase in mutations of abnormal traits.

Both eugenics and euthenics have their limitations and dangers. Much effort in these areas, especially euthenics, has gone astray. It would perhaps be wise if we attempted to gain insight into these processes by analyzing the mistakes of the past. Such mistakes, for example, the production of various types of pollution, could prove terminal if not counteracted quickly. However, increased knowledge of these problems might allow for truly eugenic and euthenic accomplishments in the future.

SUGGESTED READINGS

The following books contain good introductory discussions of population genetics:

Bodmer, W. F., and L. L. Cavalli-Sforza. *Genetics, Evolution, and Man.* San Francisco: Freeman, 1976.

Dobzhansky, T. *Genetics of the Evolutionary Process.* New York: Columbia Univ. Press, 1970.

Dunn, L. C. *Heredity and Evolution in Human Populations.* New York: Atheneum, 1970.

Volpe, E. P. *Understanding Evolution,* 3d ed. Dubuque: Brown, 1977.

The following contain articles on human population genetics:

Boyer, S. H. IV (ed.). *Papers on Human Genetics.* Englewood Cliffs, N.J.: Prentice-Hall, 1963.

Morris, L. N. (ed.). *Human Populations, Genetic Variation, and Evolution.* San Francisco: Chandler, 1971.

Chapter Six
Natural Selection and the Origin of Species

NATURAL SELECTION

Just as the physical world, the crust of the earth, and the planets and stars are constantly in flux, so are living things. Evolution is the process of continuous change.

Variation within the population is at the base of biological evolution. If all organisms were genetically identical, there could be no change in gene frequencies, only fluctuations in numbers of individuals or extinction. In reality, there is always variation within a population of organisms. In a relatively stable situation, organisms with characteristics that increase their efficiency at exploiting that situation will survive and reproduce at a greater frequency than organisms which lack the advantageous characteristics. If the situation changes, certain genotypes may be better equipped to survive in the changed condition and hence reproduce at a higher rate than other genotypes. Any differential in fertility is natural selection.

Variability of Populations

All populations display genetic variability. Some of this variability is clearly observable, such as color, size, and shape. Other differences are observable only through dissection or microscopic and biochemical analysis.

Humans as a variable species Humans are both polymorphic and polytypic. *Polymorphism* refers to the presence of several distinct forms with frequencies greater than 1 percent within a population. An example of this would be the presence of individuals with A, B, AB, and O blood types within a given population.

Many species, including *Homo sapiens*, can be said to be *polytypic*, that is, composed of several distinct populations. A local population in southern Africa is characterized by traits which serve to distinguish it from local populations in eastern Asia. Myths about physical variability have been one reason for mistrust and hatred throughout human history. The easiest differences to note are those which have been labeled "racial," that is, differences in skin color, hair type, facial characteristics, and body build (see Chapters 7 and 8).

It is easy to see variation in some phenotypic traits among human populations from different parts of the world. Even among siblings from a single family, there are differences in physical features, blood types, and even psychological patterns. Some of these differences are a function of sex and age. Others are influenced by the cultural or natural environment, while many, such as blood type, are totally genetic.

It can be asked: How many different kinds of individuals are possible? Ignoring for the moment identical twins and environmental factors, it has been calculated that there are about 10^{963} possible combinations of alleles in humans. This number is a 1 followed by 963 zeros. It is a number trillions of times larger than the total number of people who have ever inhabited the earth. To this can be added the effects of differing environments, which increase the variability even more. Because of exposure to differences in the environment, even identical twins differ from each other.

Mechanisms of variation As we noted in the last chapter, mutation is the ultimate source of all genetic variability. Mutations, which provide the raw material for the processes of evolution, have the potential to enter into new combinations with existing alleles.

Mutations provide new alleles, but variation can be provided in another way. Because of independent assortment and crossing-over, every time a zygote is formed, a new combination of alleles that never existed before and never will again is produced. Natural selection can work upon new mutations and recombinations of existing alleles.

Environment, Habitat, and Niche

The term *environment* refers to the complex of physical factors, such as the lay of the land, temperature, and rainfall, plus biological factors, such as vegetation and the various animal species external to the organism. The *gross environment* is a general description of a region, such as a tropical rain forest. But within the gross environment are a multitude of *microenvironments,* specific combinations of physical and biological factors. Various organisms adapt to specific microenvironments.

The term *habitat* refers to the place where a particular plant or animal lives. But more useful than the term *habitat* is the concept of ecological niche.

The term *niche* or *ecological niche* refers, first, to the specific microenvironment in which a particular species lives. This microenvironment is defined by rather specific physical and biological requirements. For example, a particular organism may require a certain species of tree to live upon and may occupy space only on the end branches of that tree. There may be a rainfall requirement, whereby the animal cannot survive if the habitat becomes too wet. In addition to these factors, the term niche also includes the anatomical, physiological, and behavioral methods by which the organism exploits physical space and its relationship to other organisms. Two animals occupying the same physical area, but one consuming leaves and the other fruits or one active at night and the other active during the day, would be occupying different niches (Figure 6-1). The "study of the

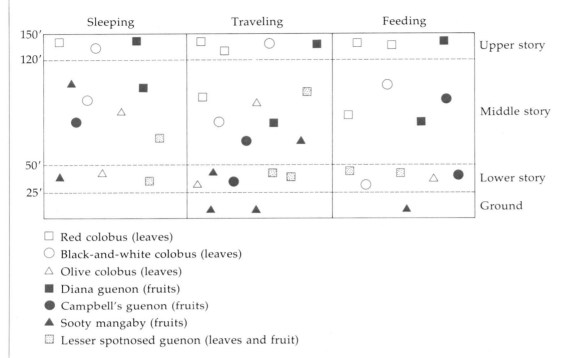

Figure 6-1 **Ecological niches.** *This chart shows the spatial distribution of seven species of African arboreal monkeys in relationship to three different activities. Differences in diet are also shown.*

relationship of organisms or groups of organisms to their environment" is the study of *ecology.*[1]

The Mechanisms of Natural Selection

Within a population, differences in mortality and fertility are found. Possessors of some genotypes live to reproduce and do so to varying degrees; possessors of other genotypes either die before reproductive age or live but do not reproduce. There are many reasons for failing to reproduce

[1] E. P. Odum, *Fundamentals of Ecology,* 3d ed. (Philadelphia: Saunders, 1971), p. 3.

in great numbers or at all. Some are environmental, but many are genetic.

Any factor which brings about differences in fertility or mortality is a *selective agent.* A selective agent places *selective pressure* upon certain individuals within the population which results in a change in the frequency of alleles in the next generation. This is evolution.

An example of selection in a population could be a smallpox epidemic. The selective agent is the smallpox virus. In this population some individuals will come down immediately with the disease and die. Others will get mild cases, while still others will not get the disease at all. Why? Factors such as exposure, hygiene, age, diet, and stress could play a major role, but it has been suggested that certain biochemical factors, such as ABO blood types, also play a role in determining who dies of smallpox.[2] The possessors of certain genotypes will have a high death rate, and their genes will not be transmitted to the next generation in great numbers. Those who survive will live to transmit their genes. Smallpox therefore can place selective pressure on the population which results in a new gene pool that is more resistant (better adapted) to the disease environment (Figure 6-2).

It must be noted here that natural selection acts upon the phenotype of the individual, and the phenotype is influenced by environmental factors. However, only that part of the phenotype which is determined by the genotype can be passed on to the next generation's gene pool.

It also should be pointed out that an environmental factor that may cause death but does not "select" one phenotype over another is not natural selection. That is, if an atomic bomb were dropped without warning on an area and everyone died, or if only a random sample of people who happened by chance to be in a sheltered area at the time survived, natural selection would not be taking place. On the other hand, if some people on the periphery of the bomb were biologically more resistant to the radiation than others and survived at a greater frequency, this would be an instance of natural selection.

Fitness Individuals or populations that have higher fertility and lower mortality rates than other individuals or populations in a particular environment are said to display a greater fitness to that environment. *Fitness* is a measure of how well a particular individual or group is adapted to the

[2] F. B. Livingstone, "National Selection, Disease and Ongoing Human Evolution, as Illustrated by the ABO Blood Groups," *Human Biology*, 32 (1960), 17–27.

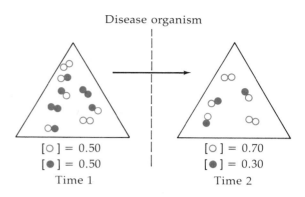

Figure 6-2 **Disease as a selective agent.** *Disease can bring about different survival rates among the processors of different genotypes, hence changing the allele frequencies in the gene pool.*

requirements imposed by the environment. Survival to reproductive age, successful mating, and fertility may be related to such factors as size and strength but often are not. Because of the protection that hemoglobin S provides against malaria, for example, an individual with the sickle-cell trait, although less healthy in ways not related to malaria than a person with normal hemoglobin, may be more fit in a malarial area (Chapter 5). Fitness also does not necessarily correspond to characteristics which a society values. A highly educated, wealthy good citizen who has no children has an effective fertility rate of zero.

Fitness varies with the situation. Since environments change and populations may shift into new niches, selective pressures are not always constant. For this reason, a trait which has a high fitness value in one niche may lose this fitness in another, whereas a trait with a low fitness value may gain greater fitness in a new niche.

Therefore, in general, natural selection tends to affect the frequency of alleles by eliminating alleles and allele combinations that are nonadaptive, that is, deleterious to a majority of those who carry them. Natural selection also tends to retain and increase the frequencies of alleles and allele combinations that are adaptive.

(a)

(b)

Figure 6-3 Industrial melanism. *A light and dark form of peppered moth as seen against* (a) *a light-colored and* (b) *a dark-colored tree trunk.*

An Example of Natural Selection in a Nonhuman Population

Natural selection is not some mystical or hypothetical force that exists only in the mathematical formulations of anthropologists and biologists. It can be seen in action.

A classic and clear-cut example of natural selection was provided by the British biologist H. B. D. Kettlewell on color changes in the peppered moth.[3] This example illustrates both how environments shift and how natural selection eliminates disadvantageous alleles while increasing the frequency of beneficial ones.

Before the industrial revolution, the English peppered moth lived on light, lichen-covered tree trunks. The moth's light-colored body with dark peppering on it effectively camouflaged it from predatory birds. However, within the moth population there was a mutant allele that produced individuals with a dark gray body. On the light-colored trees these mutants were easy prey for birds (Figure 6-3). Consequently, the birds, which represented a selective agent, eliminated the mutant alleles as fast as they arose. In other words, the dark moths had a very low fitness in this particular environment and represented less than 1 percent of the total population in 1848.

The industrial revolution caused the environment to change. Smoke from the factories killed the light lichens on nearby trees and darkened the tree trunks with soot. Now, the light-colored moths became more conspicuous and were eaten at a higher frequency than the dark moths. In other words, the fitness of the dark moths became greater, while that of the light moths decreased. Selective pressure was letting up on the dark moths while increasing against the light ones. By

[3] H. B. D. Kettlewell, "A Survey of the Frequencies of *Biston betulara* (L.) (Lep.) and Its Melanistic Forms in Great Britain," *Heredity*, 12 (1958), 51–72.

1898, around Manchester, the dark form made up 99 percent of the total moth population!

Here is a rapid environmental change due to human intervention. In the changed environment the light moth was no longer adapted to the environment, and so its mortality rate increased. At the same time, the dark-colored form became more adapted, its mortality decreased, and eventually it made up the majority of the population.

Darkening of the tree trunks did not take place all over England, however, and in some areas, populations of the light-colored form are still found. So, by the mechanism of natural selection, the development of two different forms of the same species in contrasting environments can be seen. In addition, with the implementation of smoke-control mechanisms the frequency of the light form of peppered moth is beginning to rise.[4]

The rapid change seen in the peppered moth resulted from a rather dramatic change in the environment brought about by human activity. Several other species of animals have adapted to changes in the environment brought about by industrialization in the same way. The change of allelic frequencies in industrial areas toward populations with darker coloration has been labeled *industrial melanism*. Before the evolution of humans and in environments not as greatly altered by human activity, changes also take place, but usually not as dramatically or as rapidly. Consequently, natural selection is usually a much slower and more subtle mechanism.

Natural Selection in Humans

Natural selection also is occurring in human beings. But because of the long period of time

[4] L. M. Cook and R. R. Askew, "Increasing Frequency of the Typical Form of the Peppered Moth in Manchester," *Nature*, 227 (12 September, 1970), 1155.

between generations, examples of selection in human populations are not easy to document except in the case of a lethal trait. Yet several studies have dealt with what might be real, but subtle, examples.

Selection against simple dominant and recessive alleles The least complicated cases of natural selection in humans are those involving total selection against a simple dominant abnormality which is completely penetrant and lethal. An example is *retinoblastoma*, a cancer of the retina of the eye in children. This abnormality is fatal unless the entire eye is removed. Since the trait is clear-cut, affects all individuals with the allele equally, and results in death before reproductive age, selection will eliminate the allele in the next generation. Since none of the individuals with the abnormality can reproduce (assuming surgery is not performed), the appearance of the trait in any generation will be due to new mutations.

Such an allele has a *selective coefficient s* of 1.00; selection is complete. The *relative fitness* (RF) of an individual with the allele is given by the formula RF = $1 - s$. The relative fitness in this case is 0; no offspring are produced by a person with a dominant lethal allele.

If selection is not complete, an abnormal dominant allele will tend to be eliminated, but more slowly. For example, if the selective coefficient is 0.50 and the relative fitness is 0.50, then persons with the trait would leave behind only one-half the number of offspring on the average than those without the trait, all other factors being equal. Thus, the number of persons with the trait, barring new mutations, would be cut by one-half in each generation.

Natural selection acts much more slowly against a recessive trait, since only the homozygous recessive individuals are eliminated. Since the allele will be carried by the heterozygous indi-

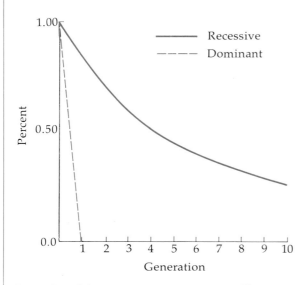

Figure 6-4 **Selection against rare genotypes.** *The rate at which frequencies of rare genotypes are reduced by natural selection. One line shows a dominant and the other a recessive abnormality. In both cases, the frequencies begin at 1 percent, and selection is complete. Assume no new mutations.*

viduals to the next generation, the allele will tend to be eliminated, but much more slowly than a dominant trait with the same fitness (Figure 6-4).

Natural selection and the ABO blood types Differences in blood-type frequencies are found in various populations. For example, 35.38 percent of a population in India were of blood type B; 33.21 percent were type O; 24.55 percent were type A; and 6.86 percent were type AB. This contrasts strongly with a Kwakiutl Indian population from British Columbia, Canada, where 67.74 percent were of type O and 32.27 percent type A. Types B and AB were totally absent.[5]

Why should these differences exist within and between populations? Likely explanations are random genetic drift and natural selection.

Because until relatively recent times all people existed in small groups, it can be easily hypothesized that differences develop from group to group because of genetic drift. Likewise, when a small group migrates from one population to establish a new population, it is expected that differences will develop because of the founder principle. This was pointed out in the last chapter for the MN blood system among the Dunkers. Current evidence suggests that natural selection may also play a role in the polymorphism of the ABO blood-type system. Here the selective pressures are small, and the changes they cause have developed over hundreds and thousands of years.

In Chapter 4 (pages 87 and 88) hemolytic disease involving the Rh blood-type system was discussed. It now appears that in some respects ABO incompatibilities might have a greater selective effect than Rh incompatibilities. Several investigators have noted that in situations where the mother is of blood type O and the fetus is of type A or B, hemolytic disease may develop in the newborn infant. Surveys of matings show that when the mother is type O and the father type A, fewer type A children are produced than when the mother is type A and the father type O.

The type O mother carries anti-A and anti-B in her blood. These antibodies often, but not always, cross over into the fetal blood system, where, if the fetus is of type A, damage may occur. In one study 12 percent of all the newborns were of type A_1 (a subtype of A) and B, with type O mothers; 0.5 percent of these newborns showed clinical symptoms of blood destruction.[6]

It is important to realize that fertility rates differ for different types of matings. On the aver-

[5] A. E. Mourant, A. C. Kopeć, and K. Domaniewska-Sobczak, *The Distribution of the Human Blood Groups and Other Polymorphisms*, 2d ed. (London: Oxford Univ. Press, 1976).

[6] H. Levene and R. E. Rosenfield, "ABO Incompatibility," in A. G. Steinberg (ed.), *Progress in Medical Genetics* (New York: Grune and Stratton, 1961), vol. 1, pp. 120–157.

age, for example, a mating between an O mother and an A father will produce fewer offspring than a mating between an A mother and an O father, and fewer of the former's children will be of blood type A. These differences in fertility can bring about subtle, but real, changes in allele frequencies over many generations.

Several diseases also appear to act as selective agents against certain blood types. In 1953 a significant correlation was discovered between cancer of the stomach and blood type A.[7] Type A also has been correlated with cancer of the pancreas and pernicious anemia. Blood type O has been linked to duodenal and stomach ulcers. In populations of European descent, the risk of developing a duodenal ulcer is 35 percent higher among persons of type O than among persons of the other three ABO blood types (Figure 6-5).[8]

Natural selection and sickle-cell anemia You have already been introduced to sickle-cell anemia, an abnormality which involves the inheritance of hemoglobin S. The genotype Hb^AHb^A results in the manufacture of HbA. The genotype Hb^SHb^S can produce a person with sickle-cell anemia, which usually causes death at an early age. The heterozygote Hb^AHb^S has blood containing both hemoglobins.

As would be expected, in many areas such as the United States natural selection is operating to eliminate the allele Hb^S since the fitness of the individual with sickle-cell anemia is effectively zero. But in many parts of Africa, southern Europe, and the Middle East, there are populations with very high Hb^S allele frequencies, as

[7] I. Aird, H. Bentall, and J. A. F. Roberts, "A Relationship between Cancer of Stomach and the ABO Blood Groups," *British Medical Journal* (1953), 799.

[8] J. Buettner-Janusch, "The Study of Natural Selection and the ABO (H) Blood Group System in Man," in G. E. Dole and R. L. Carniero (eds.), *Essays in the Science of Culture* (New York: Crowell, 1969), pp. 79–110.

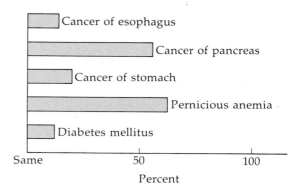

Figure 6-5 Natural selection and the ABO blood types. *The relatively greater risk, in percent, of blood type A individuals developing the diseases listed than type O individuals.*

high as approximately 0.20. This means that as many as 36 percent of the individuals in these populations have the sickle-cell trait or sickle-cell anemia. The high frequency for Hb^S is startling, especially when we remember that the frequency of the allele for PKU, also a deleterious recessive, is only 0.01 or less in all populations for which data are available. What factors are responsible for the high frequency of Hb^S?

The British geneticist Anthony Allison was one of the first to realize that the high frequencies of Hb^S are found in areas characterized by a high incidence of falciparum malaria.[9] The distribution of HbS (seen in Figure 6-7) correlates highly with that of malaria. This suggests that it is the heterozygote, with both HbA and HbS, who is relatively resistant to malaria and has a higher fitness than either homozygous type. This increased resistance has been validated.

Malaria involves parasites which reproduce in

[9] A. C. Allison, "Protection Afforded by Sickle-Cell Trait against Subtertian Malarial Infection," *British Medical Journal*, 1 (1954), 290–294. For further discussion, see F. B. Livingstone, listed in Suggested Readings.

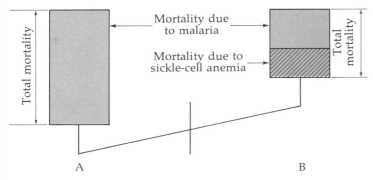

Figure 6-6 **Balanced polymorphism.** *The total death rate from malaria in a population lacking the sickle-cell allele (A) is greater than the total death rate from malaria and sickle-cell anemia in a population with the sickle-cell allele (B).*

part in the red blood cells and do not do well in the presence of HbS, probably due to an inadequate oxygen supply. The fitness of the anemic individual is low because of the effects of sickle-cell anemia. The fitness of the individual homozygous for HbA in malarial areas is lowered because of the high mortality due to malaria and the fact that malaria often leaves the victim sterile. The fitness of the heterozygote, however, is relatively high due to the lower mortality from malaria. It is the heterozygote who has the greatest probability of surviving, reproducing, and contributing the most genetic material to the next generation. Yet because the heterozygote produces a certain proportion of children with the disease, the death rate from sickle-cell anemia may be high in areas where the allele is plentiful.

People must adapt to their environment. Disease organisms are important environmental factors. It is believed that 10,000 years ago, malaria as it is known today did not exist in Africa. With the development of agriculture, a cultural change, came an opening of the forest and the creation of stagnant pools of water. In these pools the mosquitoes, which are the carriers of the malarial parasites, reproduce. As the rate of malaria increased, so did mortality. There are several possible fates for a population in a malarial environment. For instance, it may die off when the mortality rate is so great that the population is no

longer large enough to maintain itself, or a hidden and chance mechanism for survival might save it.

It seems that sickle-cell anemia already existed. Before the rise of malaria, the frequency of the allele Hb^S would have been kept low because of the low fitness of the anemic individual. But with the increase and spread of malaria, the fitness of the heterozygote became greater than the fitness of the homozygous $Hb^A Hb^A$ individual, and the frequency of the allele Hb^S rose. Today, the populations in these areas have achieved a balance whereby the combined mortality due to malaria and sickle-cell anemia is lower than the mortality due to malaria alone if sickle-cell allele did not exist. This situation, in which the heterozygous individual is best fit, is a form of *balanced polymorphism* (Figure 6-6).

Recently, some new factors have come to light. It has been found that in some parts of South and East Africa and the West Indies, where the frequency of the sickle-cell allele is high, people who are homozygous for sickle-cell anemia often show few or none of the expected symptoms.[10]

Some investigators have associated the absence of symptoms with dietary factors. About sixty plants contain *nitrilosides*, which are chemi-

[10] R. G. Houston, "Sickle Cell Anemia and Vitamin B₁₇: A Preventive Model," *American Laboratory*, 7 (1975), 51–63.

125

cals present in association with B-complex vitamins.[11] Nitrilosides are found in such foods as fruit seeds, bitter almonds, cassava, lima beans, millet, sorghum grains, and certain types of grasses. The nitrilosides act as antisickling agents, allowing blood cells that would otherwise be defective to function normally. Foods that contain these chemicals are major parts of the diet in areas where the symptoms of sickle-cell anemia would be expected to be high but are not. It also appears that nitrilosides in the diet are associated with reduced frequencies of certain types of cancer, hypertension, and coronary artery disease.[12]

In this light, sickle-cell anemia may not accurately be labeled a disease in areas with food sources rich in nitrilosides. "Rather, it may be understood as a naturally selected hemoglobin variant conferring the survival advantage of increased malaria resistance in its properly nourished, asymptomatic subjects."[13] This forms a good example of a relationship between genetics and environment, in this case diet and the presence of malaria.

One of the chemicals associated with nitrilosides that acts as an antisickling agent is called *cyanate.* Cyanate, in the form of sodium cyanate, has been considered as a treatment for sickle-cell anemia, preventing sickling episodes.[14] Unfortunately, the use of cyanates in treatment has dangerous side effects. In addition, dietary treatments in the United States have not proved successful.

Other diseases and malaria Several other genetic conditions are associated with the distribution of malaria. Some of them have been quite

[11] Ibid., p. 51.

[12] Ibid., pp. 58–62.

[13] Ibid., p. 60.

[14] A. Cerami and C. M. Peterson, "Cyanate and Sickle-Cell Disease," *Scientific American,* 232 (April 1975), 45–50.

conclusively shown to reduce the impact of malaria upon human populations, and others are suspected of performing this function. The picture is complicated by the fact that there is more than one type of malaria and differing genetic traits may protect the individual against different forms of the malarial parasite.

In northwestern sections of Africa an abnormal hemoglobin, *hemoglobin C,* overlaps the distribution of hemoglobin S. Perhaps these two hemoglobins protect against different types of malaria. A series of abnormalities referred to as the *thalassemias* differ from the abnormal hemoglobins in that the hemoglobins are normal but the amounts produced are less than normal. *Thalassemia major,* which occurs in the homozygous individual, can be severe and is often fatal, but *thalassemia minor,* which occurs in the heterozygous individual, is not severe and is believed to be associated with malarial resistance. Glucose-6-phosphate dehydrogenase deficiency, discussed earlier (page 95) has also been linked to malarial resistance. Figure 6-7 shows the distribution of some of these traits and malaria.

Summary
Variability is inherent in all populations. The human species is both polymorphic and polytypic, and it is upon this variability that natural selection operates.

Natural selection can be seen as differences in fertility rates among the variants within the population. Possessors of some genotypes live to reproduce to varying degrees, while others leave behind no offspring. Since the possessors of different genotypes produce differing numbers of offspring, their contribution to the next generation differs, bringing about changes in the gene pool. Individuals or populations with higher survival or fertility rates are said to be better fitted in the environment in which they live. But a genotype that is fit in one environment may lose some or all of its fitness in a new one. The converse is also true.

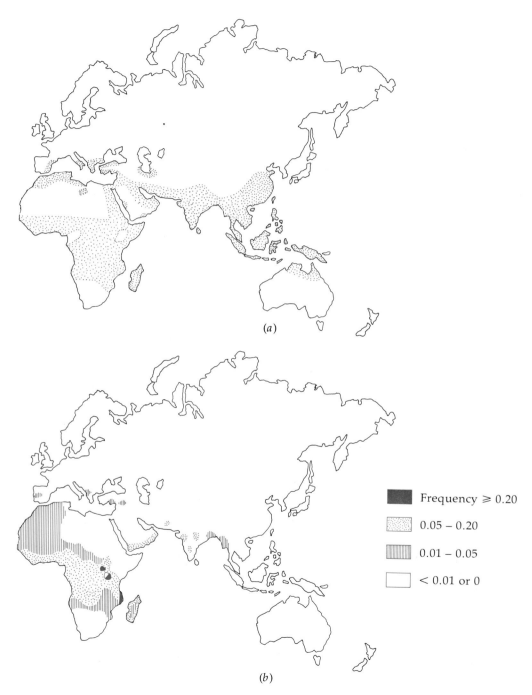

Figure 6-7 Distribution of *(a)* falciparum malaria, *(b)* hemoglobin S, *(c)* hemoglobins C and E, and *(d)* thalassemia in the Old World.

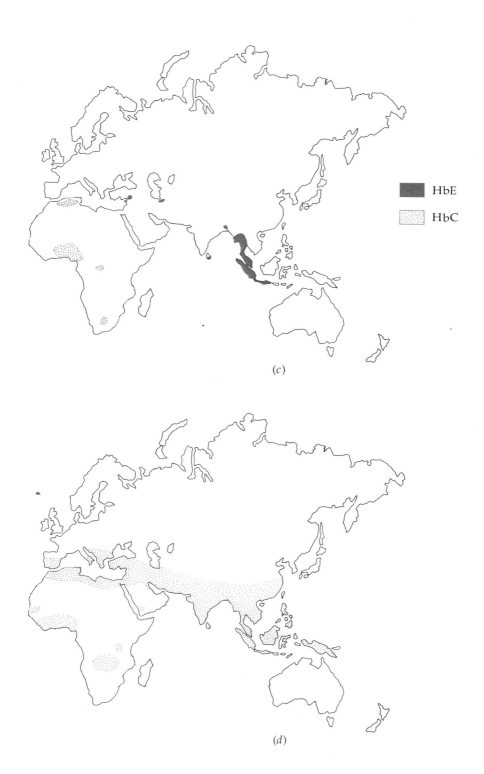

(c)

(d)

Selective pressure can operate against either a dominant or a recessive condition. In some cases, it can act against the heterozygous condition. When the heterozygote is most fit, the recessive allele is maintained at a higher than expected frequency.

Natural selection is (or was) involved in the establishment of all or most polymorphisms in living populations. Drift and the other mechanisms of evolution work with natural selection in distributing and redistributing different alleles and allele combinations and in altering gene frequencies.

THE ORIGIN OF SPECIES

Natural selection, genetic drift, and nonrandom mating, working upon the variation within a population, provide the force for continuous change in living populations. Major evolutionary changes can be seen as an accumulation of minute changes in the gene pool over long periods of time.

There are two ways of viewing evolutionary change. A species can become progressively more fit and adapted to an ecological niche which has changed little over time. This is termed *anagenesis* or linear evolution and leads to increasing specialization. Or related groups of plants or animals which have become isolated from one another may evolve into different types of organisms because of differing mutations, differing selective pressures, and so on. This process is called *cladogenesis* or branching evolution (Figure 6-8).

The population is the basic unit of evolutionary change. What are the mechanisms by which one population takes on a new identity? How could this planet have evolved from a sterile globe to a living earth with all the species of plants and animals existing today and in the past?

The Evolution of Subspecies

All natural populations of plants and animals have variation within them. Variation also can be found in or between segments of a population. For instance, within your community, your classroom, and your family there are obvious differences in physical appearance. These differences are compounded by less obvious differences in such traits as blood type and resistance to disease.

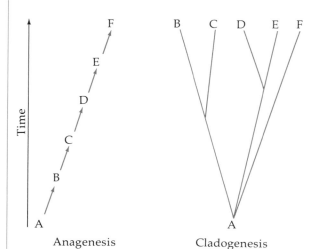

Anagenesis

Cladogenesis

Figure 6-8 Anagenesis and cladogenesis. *In anagenesis a species becomes progressively better fitted to an ecological niche which has changed little over time. In cladogenesis related populations evolve into different types of organisms.*

Population variation is a function of spatial distribution. The local population itself is termed a *deme*. A deme is the local group of organisms that live together, exploit the same habitat, and mate most frequently with one another. Individuals within the deme tend to resemble one another more closely than they do individuals of adjacent demes. A group of neighboring demes occupying similar habitats shows similar characteristics.

The development of differences between groups of demes results from a number of factors. Genetic drift and the founder principle may be involved. A particular mutation may occur in one group and not occur or not be transferred to another. Mating will be nonrandom, and patterns of mating may vary from one group to another. Most important, different groups occupy slightly different environmental situations.

Populations that occupy slightly different niches are subject to subtle differences in selective pressures. When these populations interbreed with lower frequency, distinct characteristics may develop. When significant differentiation between groups within a larger population has occurred, we say that *subspecies* or *races* have developed.

What constitutes a significant difference between populations? This is one of those questions which has no clear answer. Determining whether a species is made up of one more or less homogeneous group or whether it has 3, 25, or 200 subspecies depends on the criteria being used and therefore upon the problem or question being asked. Different scientists use different criteria, and there is not always agreement. For example, most might agree that two groups of animals within the same population that differ greatly with respect to size, coloration, and diet are different subspecies. However, if the groups differ only slightly in size and display few other differences, should they be called different subspecies? Of course, data on the degree of reproductive isolation may be useful here.

There is the additional problem of *continuous variation*. For instance, in California the yarrow plant varies in height according to the altitude at which it is found. It does not vary in distinct jumps but gradually decreases in height with increased altitude. This type of gradient is referred to as a *cline*. Clines also exist in human populations. For instance, blood type O reaches a frequency of about 75 percent in Western Europe and gradually decreases to the East, where it reaches about 50 percent in Russia.[15] The question becomes: Can one draw a line anywhere along the cline and say that on one side exists one subspecies and on the other a different subspecies? This problem will be considered in detail in Chapter 8.

Speciation

Races or subspecies are populations within the larger population, the species. These subspecific units can differ from each other in respect to several traits, yet they are at the same time interfertile. That is, they are capable of successful reproduction (see pages 90 and 91). The continuation of reproductive success is the result of occasional mating between adjacent groups, which to a degree counteracts the differences that develop between them.

When a member of one subspecies mates with a member of another subspecies of the same species, alleles are transferred from the one group to the other. If, for example, an advantageous mutation develops in group A, and if there are occasional matings between groups A and B, the mutation may be introduced into group B. The anthropologist speaks of *gene flow* as the movement of alleles from one group to another (Figure 6-9).

However, if intergroup matings are cut off, each subspecies may evolve separately. As an example, Figure 6-10 shows the distribution of

[15] Mourant, Kopeć, and Domaniewska-Sobczak, op. cit.

A B C

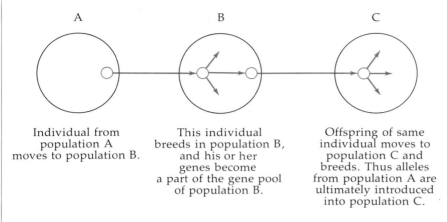

| Individual from population A moves to population B. | This individual breeds in population B, and his or her genes become a part of the gene pool of population B. | Offspring of same individual moves to population C and breeds. Thus alleles from population A are ultimately introduced into population C. |

Figure 6-9 Gene flow.

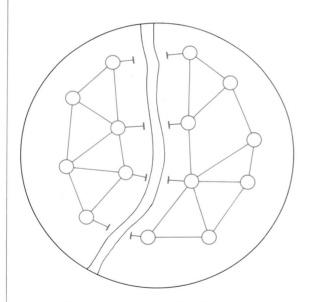

Figure 6-10 First step in speciation. *Geographic isolation of two groups of demes prevents gene flow between them. Small circles represent demes, and connecting lines between them represent gene flow.*

demes over a region. A river has changed its course, separating the population into two parts. The population's inability to swim prevents matings between the two demes. Gene flow has been effectively stopped. Genetic drift, as well as nonrandom mating, will occur differently in the two areas, and selective pressures may differ because of differences in the environments on each side of the river. In addition, mutations which may occur in one group may not occur in the other. All these factors result in changes in allelic frequencies between the two groups. If the differences in gene frequencies between the two groups become great enough, they will no longer be capable of successful reproduction with each other if the barrier is later removed. Thus the two groups may evolve into two distinct subspecies and then into two distinct species.

The role of geographical isolation *Geographical isolation* is a primary initiator of speciation in animals. Geographical isolation is the process by which members of a population become separated from a larger population through barriers, such as bodies of water, mountains, deserts, or any other terrain that prevents the interchange of genes between the separated populations. *Speciation* occurs when the separated populations acquire characteristics that prevent reproductive success between them even if the geographical barriers are lifted. Species which occupy mutually exclusive geographical areas are called *allopatric species.*

Speciation may result from spatial isolation, which is more subtle than major geographical barriers. An organism adapts to an ecological niche, and this niche may be very narrowly defined. Within a tropical forest, for example, the tops of trees present niches which may be quite different from the niches of the tree trunks or those of the ground. Speciation may result from spatial isolation within the same geographical region.

The role of temporal isolation   Populations extend not only through space but also through time. That is, a population that remains in one geographical area may acquire new mutations from generation to generation and may respond through adaptation to changing conditions that occur in that same area—in climates, terrain, extinction of some organisms and evolution of others, and so forth. Genetic alterations may build up over the generations so that the population many generations hence may be quite dissimilar genetically from the ancestral population.

A species is defined in terms of reproductive success. One species becomes two if the two subspecies are no longer capable of successful reproduction. However does this work over time? Population A evolved over a thousand generations into population B. Are they distinct species? They may look different, and these differences can be measured. However, we know from work with contemporary species that variation within a species can often be quite dramatic. Since it is

impossible to gather reproductive data on a prehistoric population, the definition of a species with respect to the past becomes very difficult and highly problematical, as will be seen in the chapters on fossil humans.

Paleontologists, who study past geological periods, break up a continuous progression, as seen in the fossil record, into species. Such continuous gradations are further examples of clines, and the species established by such a procedure are called *paleospecies.* This concept will be discussed further in Chapter 13.

Reproductive Isolating Mechanisms

Speciation is initiated by spatial or temporal isolation. However, once speciation has been accomplished, distinct species may come into contact within the same region. Such species are known as *sympatric species.* There are eight reproductive isolating mechanisms which serve to separate species living side by side.[16]

Ecological or *habitat isolation* is the condition in which two closely related populations are separated by what is often a slight difference in the niche they occupy. Some species are so closely adapted to extremely narrow niches that minor differences, such as variations in soil conditions, can effectively separate them, even when they are living next to each other.

Seasonal or *temporal isolation* occurs when the breeding seasons of two closely related populations do not exactly correspond. For example, a male from one species whose breeding season is in April will not mate with a female from another species whose breeding season is in June.

Sexual or *behavioral isolation* presents barriers to mating between individuals of closely re-

[16] Ernst Mayr, *Population, Species and Evolution* (Cambridge, Mass.: Belknap, 1970), pp. 55–65.

132

Figure 6-11 Mating behavior. *Part of the courtship dance of the wandering albatross.*

lated populations due to incompatibility in behavior. That is, one or both sexes of a species may initiate mating by some pattern of behavior which acts as a stimulus to the other sex of its species but not as a stimulus to the opposite sex in another closely related species. These stimuli might take the form of certain visual signals, such as the mating rituals of certain birds (Figure 6-11) or the light signals sent out by male fireflies. The member of the opposite sex responds only to the signal characteristics of its group. Auditory stimuli, such as calls, and chemical stimuli, such as the release of odoriferous substances, can also act as behavioral isolating mechanisms.

Mechanical isolation occurs because of an incompatibility in the structure of the male and female sex organs. In some cases copulation is attempted, but there is no transfer of sperm.

The ecological, seasonal, sexual, and mechanical reproductive isolating mechanisms discussed above may be called *premating mechanisms* in that the species do not exchange gametes. The mechanisms which follow are *postmating mechanisms*, since gametes are exchanged but either no offspring result or the off-

spring which do result are inviable, sterile, or have reduced fertility. Premating mechanisms are less wasteful than postmating mechanisms, since in the former, gametes are not consumed, while in the latter they are.

Gametic mortality is the process by which sperm are immobilized and destroyed before fertilization can take place. This may occur because antibodies in the genital tract of the female kill the sperm or because the sperm cannot penetrate the membrane of the egg.

Zygotic mortality is the situation in which fertilization occurs but development ceases soon after.

Hybrid inviability occurs when a mating between two species gives rise to a hybrid which is fertile but which nevertheless does not leave any offspring. This process is not well understood. However, the lack of success of the hybrid may depend on its inability to compete effectively with either kind of nonhybrid individual of the groups from which it is derived. In other words, it may not be as well adapted to the environment as the nonhybrid parents, or it may not be successful behaviorally in mating. These adaptive

The Mechanisms of Evolution

and behavioral limitations may prevent the production of progeny.

Hybrid sterility is said to occur when the hybrid of two species is sterile. The classic example is the hybrid of the horse and the donkey, the mule, which is incapable of reproduction.

Speciation in Genetic Terms

Why is isolation necessary for speciation to occur? The answer can be phrased in genetic terms. Isolation allows derived populations to develop in an undisturbed manner, without the flow of genes into the population from some other closely related population. In this way, the genetic material in the isolated population can be reconstituted, resulting in the development of one of the reproductive isolating mechanisms previously discussed. As long as there is significant gene flow between populations, these mechanisms cannot come into being.

The genetic reconstitution of separated populations As has been stressed, mutation, drift, nonrandom mating, and selection are the forces in speciation. But they operate to bring about speciation only in isolated populations. In an isolated population the chance that the *same* mutation will occur or that mutations will occur in the same sequence as in another isolated population is effectively zero. The different mutations will create different potential genotypes.

There is also an almost infinite number of ways in which recombination can occur. This is important since the same allele can have differing selective advantages in the context of different genotypes. Each isolated population consists of unique gene combinations. Also, varying gene combinations may have no difference in their selective values, but by chance new combinations may be established in the different populations.

In addition, it must be realized that no two habitats are identical; therefore, separate populations are exposed to different selective pressures. The genetic systems of the separated populations tend to adjust to the differing environments. In fact, they must or else become extinct. The new populations also represent different sectors of the parental population because of the founder principle. Therefore, they start off somewhat different from each other.

Regulatory genes and speciation In the early 1960s, two French scientists, François Jacob and Jacques Monod, proposed a model of genetic events that seems to account for evolutionary occurrences not explainable by other models.[17] They proposed the existence of two major classes of genes. The first type, called *structural genes,* codes for specific polypeptide chains that make up protein molecules such as hemoglobin and melanin. The second class is termed *regulatory genes.* They do not code for any structural or enzymatic features of the phenotype but control the activity of structural genes. Regulatory genes turn structural genes "on and off" and so control the time of production and quantity of polypeptide chains.

Although the precise mechanisms of regulatory genes are not known for most organisms, it appears that mutations in regulatory genes may be extremely important in speciation. A mutation in a regulatory gene would not affect the coding for a structural unit (polypeptide chain) but might change the timing of the production of that structural unit or block its production altogether. It now appears that the differences between closely related species might be due more to mutations in the regulation of structural genes than changes in the structural genes themselves. For example, researchers have found that, on the average, a

[17] F. Jacob and J. Monod, "Genetic Regulating Mechanisms in the Synthesis of Protein," *Journal of Molecular Biology,* 3 (1961).

group of forty-four human and chimpanzee proteins are 99 percent identical (Chapter 12)! Yet these organisms are anatomically quite dissimilar. Mary-Claire King and Allan C. Wilson believe that these differences as well as anatomical evolution in general are due mainly to changes in regulatory, not structural, genes.[18]

Ecology and Speciation

All animals can spread out into new geographical regions and occupy similar ecological niches which exist there. However, this capability varies from an extremely limited potential in some groups to an almost unlimited expansive ability in others. The major factors are the nature of the geographical barriers, the amount of change a group of organisms can tolerate, and the mode or modes of dispersal, the ability of the organism to "get around."

When a population enters a new region, it occupies niches similar to those it occupied in the original area. But the niches will not be identical because of minor environmental differences or because the niche may already be occupied by another species.

Competition When two populations occupy the same or parts of the same niche, they are said to be competing with one another. *Competition* does not necessarily mean that individuals belonging to the two species physically fight one another but simply that they eat the same food, seek out the same sleeping areas, are active at the same time of the day, and so forth.

When two populations are competing in the same niche, differences in anatomy, physiology,

or behavior may give one population the edge. For example, the population which is able to gain access to food at the expense of the other will be able to maintain itself in the niche. The other population will either die out, move, or — an important factor in speciation — adapt to another or a more restricted niche. Thus, if one population's diet includes fruits, leaves, and occasionally insects and another population's diet consists of fruits and leaves only, the first might increase its intake of insects and ultimately become primarily *insectivorous* in its habits.

Preadaptation Populations entering new geographical areas often will occupy niches or be forced to occupy niches not found in the original area. These populations will not be totally adapted to the new niches, since the selective pressures characteristic of these niches have not been operating on them. However, many populations, or individuals within the population, may have developed in the original habitat characteristics which prove to be adaptive in the new situation. The term *preadaptation* refers to the potential to adapt to a new niche. Organisms do not adapt because they need to but because by chance they have the potential to.

As already mentioned, a population's niche may change not only because of movement into new habitats but also because of changes in the environment within an area. Therefore, preadaptation is important even to species that remain in one locality. Because preadaptation is a chance event, extinction often occurs instead of survival in a new situation.

Ecologically specialized species A species is said to be *specialized* when its relationship to its environment is such that it can tolerate little change in that environment. Such a form may not be able to spread into new niches, even when the environmental conditions are similar, and may not be able to compete successfully with other

---

[18] M-C. King and A. C. Wilson, "Evolution at Two Levels in Humans and Chimpanzees," *Science,* 188 (11 April 1975), 107–116; and G. B. Kolata, "Evolution of DNA: Changes in Gene Regulation," *Science,* 189 (8 August 1975), 446–447.

populations. An example of an extremely specialized animal in terms of diet is the koala bear of Australia, whose diet consists almost exclusively of the leaves of the eucalyptus tree. The distribution and proliferation of this tree therefore determines the distribution of the animal. Any change in the tree population, due to a change in climate or in human use, for example, will affect the koala bear population directly.

Because a specialized species can tolerate little change in its ecological niche, its dispersal is limited. If a new population does become geographically isolated from the parental population and develops a specialized relationship with the new environment, not only the geographical barrier but also the ecological specialization will act as an isolating mechanism, preventing gene flow. Hence, speciation will occur.

Ecologically generalized species A *generalized species* is one that can survive in a variety of ecological niches. Humans are perhaps the most generalized of all species in that through our cultural ingenuity we can adapt to the extreme cold of the arctic environment by building appropriate shelters and tools and can also live in the hot, humid tropics or at high altitudes or in deep valleys. And now, with the development of life-support systems, we can live for extended periods under the sea and in outer space. This ability to move into a variety of environments has been responsible for our great dispersal over the earth and perhaps in the future will be responsible for our dispersal through the solar system.

Because of our lack of precise environmental requirements and cultural adaptiveness, geographical barriers have had little chance to effectively isolate "pockets" of human populations. Since gene flow has been continuous, speciation has not been able to occur among humans. People are, of course, not the only generalized animals. In fact, generalized and specialized must be considered to be relative terms. At one end we

have the extremely specialized koala bear and at the other the very generalized *Homo sapiens*. Within these limits are found varying degrees of generalization and specialization.

Specialized and generalized traits The concepts of generalization and specialization have been used here to refer to the relationship between the population as a whole and its niche. But these terms also can be used to label specific characteristics displayed by the members of the population.

Every trait can be considered separately with regard to its generalization or specialization. For instance, the human hand may be considered to be generalized in that it can be used for a number of purposes, whereas the foot may be considered specialized in that it is used for basically one thing. What is important here is that the relative specialization or generalization of a specific trait, such as diet, may be more important for survival than another trait. Also, as a general rule, the more specialized anatomical, physiological, or behavioral features an animal has, the more specialized the total phenotype will be.

Specialization can lead not only to speciation but also to evolutionary dead ends. The more specialized an animal becomes, the less likely it will be to move into new niches and hence the less chance for the isolation necessary for further speciation. Also, a species that becomes so specialized to a particular niche that it cannot tolerate change is in greater threat of extinction than a more generalized animal. If eucalyptus trees die out, so will koala bears. However, if one of the environments that humans live in becomes unlivable, we have others that will support us.

Rates of Speciation

The rates at which speciation occurs are difficult to ascertain. The fossil record is of little help. First, it is difficult or impossible to know when reproductive isolating mechanisms came into being. How is one to know from bones whether such things as differences in mating behavior or mating season were in force between two morphologically similar populations?

Second, even if these isolating mechanisms were potentially observable in the fossil record, they take place in too short a time for the points at which differentiation took place to even be noticed. That is, whereas reproductive isolating mechanisms might occur quickly, a fossil progression might be made up of forms that lived thousands of years apart.

Although rates of speciation cannot be measured effectively, we can infer that they are dependent on two main types of factors, *internal* and *external*. Internal factors include such things as point mutations, chromosome changes, and other genetic factors that may lead to reproductive isolating mechanisms. External factors include such things as the type and amount of barriers to gene flow and the types of new ecological niches available. It may be assumed that related populations that have a low mutation rate, live in a homogeneous environment without physical barriers, and are not under great selective pressure may remain basically the same and not develop sufficient differences for speciation. However, a high mutation rate, aided by a variety of selected pressures and different ecological niches and separation by geographic barriers, may provide the necessary conditions for rapid speciation. Both the above situations are extreme, and variations in any of the elements may have an effect on the rate of speciation.

Adaptive Radiation

Over time, species became adapted to their particular niches, although some became more highly adapted (specialized) than others (which are more generalized). A population within a particular niche tends to increase in size until the number of organisms comes into equilibrium with its environment. Yet population and other pressures sometimes force certain individuals to enter new habitats.

Entrance into new ecological niches depends upon many factors. First, there has to be physical access to the new niche. If a lowland animal is in a valley surrounded by high mountains, its chances for dispersal will be less than for a similar animal form occupying flatlands. The new niche most likely resembles the old, and indeed may overlap it considerably in many of its characteristics. Second, the individuals entering the new niche must be preadapted to it. Third, the new niche must either be unoccupied, or the entering individuals must be able to compete successfully with other species already existing in the new niche. However, it must not be assumed that populations seek and enter drastically different niches.

A generalized species is usually able to survive in a wide variety of habitats. Members may spread into new ecological niches to which they are preadapted and form new populations. Over time, these populations will take on distinctive characteristics as they become more closely adapted to their new niches. Subspecies will form and, ultimately in many cases, new species will emerge. This is especially true when a species enters an uninhabited environment or one in which competition basically does not exist (as in the example below), or when a species or group of species develops new anatomical or physiological adaptations which permit them to compete successfully in a variety of niches. Such a proliferation of new species is referred to as *adaptive radiation*.

One of the classic examples of adaptive radiation is the case of the finches of the Galápagos Islands, 600 miles (965 kilometers) off the coast of Ecuador. Darwin observed the many varieties of finches on the islands and proposed that natural selection was the force behind this variation.[19]

On the mainland of South America is found a single species of seed-eating ground finch, which is thought to be similar to the ancestral form of at least fourteen distinct species of finches on the Galápagos Islands. When the ancestral finches arrived on the islands, they were able to survive in the varied habitats available to them. This was possible because there was no competition for living space and food resources from other birds and because the finches were pre-adapted for survival in the new environments.

As time passed, finch populations began to adapt to local niches. Each differing ecological situation presented different selective pressures. In addition, the islands were far enough apart to minimize contact between the populations. As time went on, subspecies and, ultimately, species differences emerged. From the single ancestral population evolved a large number of distinct species. Some remain seed eaters, although beak size varies among these species. The large-beaked ground finches eat both large, hard seeds and smaller food. But the smaller-beaked birds must rely on the smaller and softer foods only. At the present time, the competition for food is not great, for the larger birds usually ignore the smaller seeds. If the larger birds were to compete with the smaller species, the more specialized small birds would very likely either become reduced in numbers or become extinct.

Finches with other beak forms also evolved. One with a straight beak feeds on the prickly pear cactus, utilizing the nectar and soft pulp. The vegetarian tree finch, with a parrot-like beak, eats leaves, fruits, and buds. Several finches are insectivorous (Figure 6-12). Perhaps the most interesting of the Galápagos finches is the woodpecker finch. This bird uses a cactus spine or twig to remove an insect from a crack or hole in the bark of trees. The bird habitually uses a tool in order to

[19] David Lack, *Darwin's Finches* (New York: Cambridge Univ. Press, 1947).

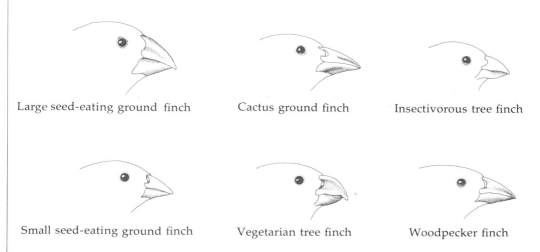

Large seed-eating ground finch   Cactus ground finch   Insectivorous tree finch

Small seed-eating ground finch   Vegetarian tree finch   Woodpecker finch

Figure 6-12 Darwin's finches. *The diverse bill forms represent adaptations to different niches, an example of an adaptive radiation.*

Figure 6-13 The woodpecker finch. *This bird uses and sometimes makes a tool in order to exploit an ecological niche.*

obtain its food supply and has even been observed altering twigs to the most efficient size or shape (Figure 6-13).[20]

Extinction

While evolution is constantly bringing about the development of new species, other species are disappearing. When pressures develop in an environment, natural selection does not always bring about new adaptations. In many cases, the organisms involved simply do not have the potential to adjust. They are too specialized and are not preadapted to the new situation. They then become *extinct*.

Extinction is not an unusual event. Extinctions of the past far outnumber the total number of species which are living today. Humans, through their technology, have brought about an increasing rate of extinction. The extinctions brought about by humans are not like those that

occur otherwise. There is usually competition between organisms over particular niches, wherein some of the competitors are displaced. But no large animal can compete successfully with *Homo sapiens* for any environment. (It is interesting to note that those organisms which do compete successfully with humans are small forms, such as mice, flies, and disease organisms.) Therefore, the give and take, the periods of adjustment and reestablishment of new balances, and the derivation of new types do not generally occur when people take over an environment.

Summary

The forces of natural selection operate upon the various demes within a species, bringing about changes in gene frequencies within the local gene pools. Since different demes occupy different habitats, selective pressures may differ from group to group. When these groups become to a degree reproductively isolated from other such groups, subspecies or races may develop. Cutting off gene flow between demes may produce changes in these populations which make successful reproduction between them impossible. Such elimina-

[20] K. R. L. Hall, "Tool-using Performances as Indicators of Behavioral Adaptability," *Current Anthropology* (December 1963), 483.

tion of gene flow is usually the result of spatial isolation. Over time, these populations may become distinct species.

Allopatric species occupy mutually exclusive geographical areas, while paleospecies occupy different time periods. Sympatric species may come into contact in the same area but are reproductively isolated from one another by one of the many isolating mechanisms.

Members of a species tend to spread out into new regions and occupy similar niches which can never be identical to the original ones. Certain individuals within the population may be preadapted to the new niche. When a population enters an area where there is a lack of competition or when a species or group of species develops new anatomical or physiological adaptations, speciation may be quite rapid, giving rise to what is referred to as adaptive radiation. However, if members of a species are not preadapted to a changed situation, extinction may result.

SUGGESTED READINGS

The following books contain introductory discussions of the principles of evolution:

Dobzhansky, T. *Genetics of the Evolutionary Process*. New York: Columbia Univ. Press, 1970.

Dunn, L. C. *Heredity and Evolution in Human Populations*. New York: Atheneum, 1970.

Mayr, E. *Populations, Species and Evolution*. Cambridge, Mass.: Belknap, 1970.

Moody, P. A. *Introduction to Evolution*, 3d ed. New York: Harper & Row, 1970.

Volpe, E. Peter. *Understanding Evolution*, 3d ed. Dubuque, Iowa: Brown, 1977.

Bejema, C. J. (ed.). *Natural Selection in Human Populations*. New York: Wiley, 1971. A collection of articles detailing studies of natural selection in man.

Livingstone, F. B. *Abnormal Hemoglobins in Human Populations*. Chicago: Aldine, 1967. A review of the different abnormal hemoglobins, plus tables of frequencies in various populations.

Odum, E. P. *Fundamentals of Ecology*, 3d ed. Philadelphia: Saunders, 1971. One of the best introductory textbooks in ecology.

PART THREE

THE NATURE OF
HUMAN VARIABILITY

"Group differences are one thing; how we perceive them and think about them is quite another. . . . Nothing that strikes our eyes or ears conveys its message directly to us. We always *select* and *interpret* our impressions of the surrounding world."[1]

Many times the differences we "see" between peoples are illusions brought about by culturally determined stereotypes. For example, the Dahomeans of West Africa are organized into different clans. Each clan is a group of people who trace their ancestry back to a legendary common ancestor. One Dahomean clan is said to have been created "when a peanut was magically transformed into a man who then mated with a poor woman who lived on roots. Dahomeans believe that the members of the Peanut clan lack the fine, smooth skin of other Dahomeans: 'It is rough like the shell of a peanut.' Further, the members of the Peanut clan are said to be recognizable on sight."[2]

Empirically this cannot be true. Members of each clan must marry outside their own clan, and, therefore, genetic isolates with radically different phenotypes cannot develop. Dahomeans know in advance who are members of the Peanut clan and perceive these individuals in the manner in which they have been taught.

This part will explore both nonscientific and scientific attempts at classifying human beings. The nature of human variability will then be examined from the perspective of modern genetic theory and growth and development studies.

[1] Reprinted by special permission from Gordon W. Allport, *The Nature of Prejudice*, 1954, Addison-Wesley Publishing Company, Inc., Reading, Mass.

[2] From *Anthropology: The Study of Man*, 4th ed., by E. Adamson Hoebel. Copyright 1972 by McGraw-Hill Book Company. Used with permission of McGraw-Hill Book Company.

Chapter Seven

The Classification of Human Groups

ATTEMPTS AT CLASSIFICATION

People are natural classifiers and see nature basically as being composed of types of things, not individual entities. If every individual rock, tree, or animal had a unique label attached to it, effective communication would not be possible. So people speak in categories and talk of igneous rocks, pine trees, and mammals.

Each group of people classifies the world around it. In any human group the question: What kinds of rocks, trees, or animals are there? will be answered. The categories expressed by the people do not necessarily describe the world as seen by objective science, and often include stereotypes (Figure 7-1). These classifications are part of specific cultural traditions and differ from group to group. Anthropologists refer to such classifications as *folk taxonomies*.

Categorization or classification is necessary in everyday communication as well as in science. Without the ability to generalize, conversation would be impossible, and laws and theories could not exist. But folk taxonomies do not always correspond to reality. When these inaccuracies apply to categorizations of people, they often mirror hatred and mistrust.

Folk Taxonomies of Race

In coping with the world, people visualize human variation in terms of categories. A simple type of classification is that in which a particular people will classify itself as "human" and everyone else as "less than human." For instance, the Navaho call themselves *diné*, which, roughly translated, is "The People." This label implies "a strong sense of difference and isolation from the rest of humanity."[1] This common type of conceptualization also could be found among the ancient Greeks, who divided humankind into two cate-

[1] Clyde Kluckhohn and Dorothea Leighton, *The Navaho*, rev. ed. (New York: Doubleday, 1962), p. 23.

(a)

(b)

(c)

Figure 7-1 Four American racial stereotypes. (a) *Jay Silverheels as Tonto in "The Lone Ranger,"* (b) *Warner Oland as "Charlie Chan," and* (c) *Hattie McDaniel and Vivian Leigh in "Gone with the Wind."*

gories, Greeks and barbarians. Some Greeks believed that these barbarians just made noises or babbled. Today we play a reversal on the Greeks with the saying, "It's all Greek to me."

Especially in urban centers, a person encounters daily a variety of people of different statures, skin colors, and facial features. If people at an American suburban shopping center were asked: What are the different types of people in the World? the most frequent answer would probably be Caucasoids, Mongoloids, and Negroids or perhaps, whites, blacks, Indians, and Orientals.

These classifications are examples of folk taxonomies which reflect how the average American sees human differences. Are they also reflections of reality? The answer is yes and no. These folk taxonomies do have a social reality in that many forms of behavior are determined by them. In a situation requiring interaction with another person the average American may behave differently depending on whether this other individual is "white" or "black" or "Oriental." But physical anthropologists deal primarily with biological reality, and here the folk taxonomies just do not reflect what we know about human variation.

The average American has never seen people from many areas, such as the Ainu, Australian aborigine, Negrito, Dravidian, Bushman, or Lapp (Figure 7-2). Most Americans have contact primarily with peoples from Europe, parts of Africa, Latin America, and parts of Asia, particularly Japan and China. A person who looks somewhat different from those normally encountered is forced into one of the existing categories. Thus, American soldiers during World War II often classified the Melanesians as "Negro," a categorization with no scientific foundation.

(a)

(b)

(c)

The Nature of Human Variability

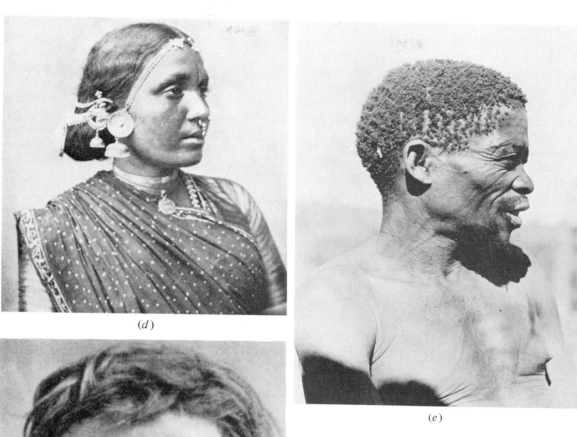

(d)

(e)

(f)

Figure 7-2 (a) Ainu, (b) Australian aborigine, (c) Negrito, (d) Dravidian, (e) Bushman, and (f) Lapp.

The Classification of Human Groups

Why Does Anthropology Need to Classify Human Variation?

"Races do not exist; classifications of mankind do."[2] Scientific classifications, like folk taxonomies, are attempts at dividing human beings into specific groups, but this is where the similarity should stop. Folk taxonomies are basically means by which individuals and societies classify and hence deal with those people who are being labeled as different. The classification serves a social purpose and is an end in itself. By setting itself off from others a people can rationalize its behavior toward other groups on the basis of the characteristics attributed to those groups. For instance, slavery can be justified by characterizing the enslaved people as inferior and not worthy or capable of anything but serving their masters. Genocide can be justified in a like manner.

Unlike folk taxonomies, a scientific classification is not an end in itself but a means to discover the processes that create the phenomenon being classified, that is, human variation. A scientific classification of human variation would be a model serving a function similar to that of other scientific models, such as the Hardy-Weinberg formula (Chapter 5). This formula was discussed as a method of determining and measuring the forces of evolution working on a population. A classification of human variability should be a tool for discovering the processes involved in creating genotypic and phenotypic variation between populations.

Folk taxonomies are usually based on ethnocentric ideas about the inherent differences in physical appearance and behavior between groups. Although some of these beliefs may be partially based on observations, most are based on mythology. For instance, the contention that a peanut was magically transformed into a man, who became the founder of the Dahomean Peanut clan (see Part Three opening) can probably be considered not to be an empirical fact. In contrast, the criteria used for scientific classification and explanation of human variation must be derived from empirical studies. That is, the attributing of different characteristics to different populations must be validated through the procedures of the scientific method (Chapter 2).

Attempts at Scientific Classification

Linnaeus, who was mentioned in Chapter 2, was perhaps the first person to apply systematic criteria in a uniform way in classifying humans. Linnaeus's contribution, the first scientific taxonomy of the living world, included people. Linnaeus labeled all humans *Homo sapiens*, from *Homo*, meaning "man," and *sapiens*, meaning "wise." He then divided the species into four groups based on the criteria of skin color and geographical location. These four categories are: *Homo sapiens Africanus negreus* (black), *Homo sapiens Americans rubescens* (red), *Homo sapiens Asiaticus fucus* (darkish), and *Homo sapiens Europeus albescens* (white).

Among scientists this classification did not stand the test of time. For one thing, it seemed to exclude many peoples. Where were the peoples of Oceania, India, and other areas to be placed? Also, could it legitimately be said that all peoples of Africa had the same skin color? North Africans were light-skinned, Bushmen are brownish-yellow, and Bantu are dark. While Linnaeus's general system of classification of plants and animals was readily adopted by the scientific community, his classification of people was not. However, his notion of four races is the one basically used by the general public of Europe and America.

[2] George A. Dorsey, "Race and Civilization," in Charles A. Beard (ed.), *Whither Mankind: A Panorama of Modern Civilization* (New York: Longmans, Green, 1928), p. 254.

Measuring human variation Nineteenth-century studies of variation were carried out largely by means of *anthropometry*, the study of the measurements of the body. The basic instruments of anthropometry are the metric tape, spreading caliper, sliding caliper, and anthropometer, shown being used in Figure 7-3.

With these and other instruments, thousands of measurements can be made on the human body. On the head alone, the circumference, length and breadth, several diagonals, distance between the eyes, and dimensions of the nose, lips, and ears can be measured and populations compared. One nineteenth-century scientist described more than 5,000 measures and indices that could be made on the skull alone.[3]

Nineteenth-century classification Johann Friedrich Blumenbach (1752–1840), thought of by some as the father of physical anthropology, was a German doctor who studied comparative human anatomy. On the basis of his studies he divided the human species into five "races": *Caucasian, Mongolian, Ethiopian, Malayan,* and *American.* The term *Ethiopian* was later changed to *Negro.*

Anders Retzius (1796–1860) noted that there was a great deal of variation within the five types proposed by Blumenbach. He decided that the shape of the head was an important criterion for classifying people and developed the cephalic index as a means of comparing populations. The *cephalic index* is the breadth of the head relative to the length, as given by the formula

$$\frac{\text{Head breadth}}{\text{Head length}} \times 100$$

[3] A. von Torok, *Grundzüge einer systematischen Kraniometric* (Stuttgart, 1890).

These early attempts set up two criteria as significant in the development of classifications: outward physical characteristics and geographic origin. Unfortunately, the mass of data collected on measurements and indices led to classifications that were descriptive in nature and did not explain the processes creating the observed variation. Today, attempts are made to link such differences to specific evolutionary forces, such as natural selection. New instruments that precisely measure skin color and calculate various physiological functions of the body, such as heat loss, have been developed. The quantity of various chemical constituents of the body can also be measured. Rates of growth and development can be determined.

Use of blood types in classification With the development of genetic theory, anthropologists began to doubt the use of the traditional criteria of classification. Skin color, they argued, was a poor criterion since its exact mechanism of inheritance is not known and it is strongly affected by the environment and culture. Partially for these reasons, some anthropologists turned to blood-type systems as a basis for classification. Blood type is easy to determine; in most cases blood typing can be done in the field. A given type is either present or absent, and blood type does not appear to be affected by the environment. In addition, the mechanisms of inheritance are, for the most part, known.

The criterion of blood type was used, for example, by William Boyd, who presents the following classification: (*1*) *Early European* (hypothetical, represented today only by the Basques), (*2*) *European* (Caucasoids), (*3*) *African* (Negroid), (*4*) *Asiatic* (Mongoloid), (*5*) *American Indian,* and (*6*) *Australoid.* The defining characteristics are blood-type frequencies. For instance, the European group is defined in terms of a high frequency of Rh-negative and A_2, one of the two major

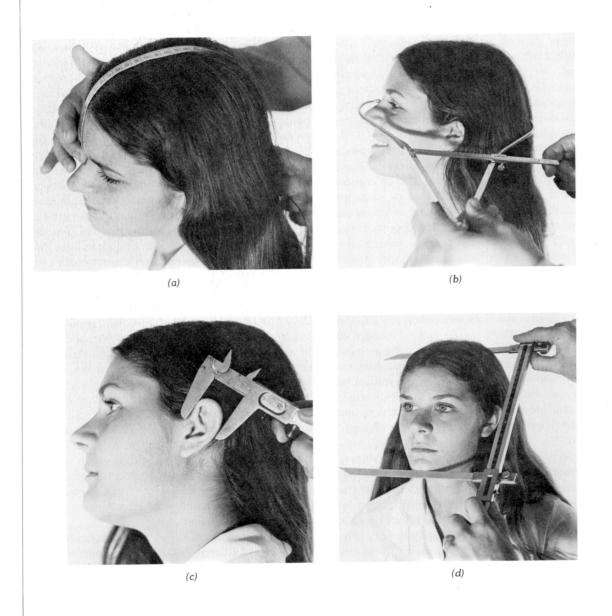

(a)

(b)

(c)

(d)

Figure 7-3   Anthropometric instruments. (a) *Metric tape,* (b) *spreading caliper,* (c) *sliding caliper,* (d) *anthropometer.*

The Nature of Human Variability

varieties of blood type A. The Asiatic, however, is characterized by little Rh-negative and A_2 but high frequencies of A_1 and a variety of Rh-positive, Rh^z.[4]

The basic problem with this method is that clearly defined categories do not always emerge. While it is possible to generalize for a large geographical area, specific groups often deviate from this generalization. For instance, most North American Indians show a high frequency of blood type O (Cherokee, 96 percent, Chippewa, 88 percent); however, the Blackfeet show an O frequency of about 25 percent.[5] On the other side of the coin, specific populations from different parts of the world can show similar blood-type frequencies. For example, the Atayal of Taiwan show 45.2 percent type O, 32.6 percent type A, 17.1 percent type B, and 5.1 percent type AB.[6] A group from Macedonia, Greece, shows frequencies of 45.2 percent type O, 32.3 percent type A, 19.3 percent type B, and 3.2 percent type AB, very similar to those of the Atayal.[7] Are we to say that the Blackfeet are not North American Indians because the frequency of their blood types deviates from those of most other North American Indians, and are we to place the Atayal and the Macedonians in the same group?

The distribution of blood types can be characterized by pockets of groups that show exceptions to general rules. It is then difficult to place these groups in the classification. Also, blood-frequency distributions are often clinal (see page 153). When clines exist, it becomes an arbitrary matter where they should be divided to create categories.

Classification and the fossil record   To many, there is a finite number of categories of people which corresponds to basic divisions which occurred in the remote past. One of the classifications which uses the fossil record is that of Carlton S. Coon, who divides the human species into five groups: *Australoids, Mongoloids, Caucasoids, Congoids* (dark-skinned Africans), and *Capoids* (the Bushmen and Hottentot).[8] Coon postulates that humankind separated into these five divisions before the evolution of *Homo sapiens*. To him the different fossils which have been uncovered represent early stages in this pre-*sapien* development. An early fossil found in Java is taken to be an early Australoid, whereas a fossil from Peking is considered to be an early Mongoloid, and so on.

In Chapter 15 we will discuss recent fossil evidence that links certain finds with contemporary populations. However, the problem with such links is that human variation does not follow clear-cut evolutionary lines. Gene flow between adjacent groups and migrations, coupled with changing selective pressures and new mutations, serves to confuse such lines. If there were a specific number of subspecies of humans in the past, they most likely would have evolved not into modern variants of a unified species but into separate species. This did not happen.

If the only remaining fossils from America were those of a professional basketball center, would it be correct to characterize the stature of the entire population by this individual? Fossil finds have been linked to living populations on

---

[4] W. C. Boyd, *Genetics and the Races of Man* (Boston: Little, Brown, 1956), p. 268.

[5] A. E. Mourant, A. C. Kopeć, and K. Domaniewska-Sobczak, *The Distribution of the Human Blood Groups and Other Polymorphisms,* 2d ed. (London: Oxford Univ. Press, 1976). Figures for North American Indians are for groups with no known, or minimal, gene flow from Europeans.

[6] Ibid.

[7] Ibid.

[8] C. S. Coon, *The Origin of Races* (New York: Knopf, 1962).

Table 7-1 Mean Cephalic Index Taken on Living Males
in Various Populations

Population	Mean Cephalic Index
Australians (Arnhem Island)	71.8
Kikuyu (Kenya)	76.0
Ituri Pygmies (Congo)	76.5
Ainu (Japan)	77.3
Sioux (central United States)	79.6
Japanese	80.8
Norwegians	81.0
Baluba (Congo)	81.6
Germans	82.5
Koreans	83.4
Hawaiians	84.0
Norwegian Lapps	85.0
Maya (Yucatán)	85.8
Montenegrins (Yugoslavia)	88.6

From G. A. Harrison, J. S. Weiner, J. M. Tanner, and N. A.
Barnicot, *Human Biology: An Introduction to Human Evolution,
Variation, and Growth* (New York and Oxford: Oxford Univ. Press,
1964), p. 209.

the basis of one characteristic, such as shape of the head. But one or a few specimens are not an adequate statistical sample and may not represent the ancient population from which they came.

In addition, since traits can differ independently of each other, a similarity in one characteristic may not mean a similarity in others. For example, the average cephalic indices of the Japanese and Norwegians are about the same (Table 7-1). If individuals from these populations were found by future anthropologists, would they be justified in grouping them together?

Because the selective pressures of the past were not the same as those of the present, and because of shifts in areas of a particular selective pressure, traits may have been clustered differently in the past than the present. Taken one step further, selective pressures of the present and future may tend to create similar characteristics in populations that are genetically divergent at present. For instance, diseases associated with urban centers, along with smog, noise, crowding, and so on, may create similar selective pressures in any urban area anywhere in the world. An anthropologist 50,000 years from now might have a hard time tracing evolutionary lines because of such parallel evolution.

Stanley Garn's classification One more attempt at classifying human variation, that of Stanley Garn,[9] deserves note. He carefully defines his terminology and speaks of geographical races, local races, and microraces.

His division of the species *Homo sapiens* into nine large *geographical races* is based on the observation that people living in the same large geographical area tend to resemble each other more closely than people in different geographical areas. This is a gross generalization with a great number of exceptions. It is significant that here geography alone is the major criterion for classification, not some arbitrarily chosen trait, such as skin color, blood type, or cephalic index. Since gene flow does take place more within a major geographical zone than between adjacent zones, populations in the same major geographical area will generally show some similar gene frequencies.

Garn's nine geographical human races are: (1) *Amerindian* (the inhabitants of North and South America), (2) *Asiatic*, (3) *Australian*, (4) *Melanesian* (peoples of New Guinea and nearby islands), (5) *Micronesian* (peoples of the islands of the northwest Pacific), (6) *Polynesian*, (7) *Indian*, (8) *African*, and (9) *European*.

Garn divides these large geographical races into a series of *local races*. There are two basic types of local races. Some are distinctive, partially isolated groups, usually remnants of once larger groups. Examples used by Garn include the Ainu and the Bushman. In addition to these small local

[9] S. M. Garn, *Human Races*, 2d ed. (Springfield, Ill.: Thomas, 1965), pp. 7–9.

races, there are local races of much larger proportion. Large local races are not as isolated, and there is a larger degree of gene flow between them. An example of this type of local race would be the northwestern Europeans.

Within larger local races is found considerable variation. If allele frequencies within the northwestern European local race are mapped, for example, constant changes in frequencies often are found as we travel in a particular direction. This is clinal variation (see page 153). Since there is considerable variation within a particular local race, Garn divides the local race into a number of units called microraces.

Microraces are arbitrary divisions of a large local race. Precise boundaries cannot be drawn, and specific individuals within one microrace may look more like members of another microrace than like each other. But one fact remains: people living in the same community tend to mate more frequently with one another than with individuals of other communities.

A main difficulty with Garn's classification is that it is basically static, that is, it defines fixed categories of peoples. In reality, human variation is dynamic. The shape of clines is constantly changing, and old partial isolates are broken down and new ones established.

Between 1845 and 1854, 3 million people migrated to the United States. Between 1800 and 1924, 36 million people entered the United States from such places as England, Italy, Germany, Spain, Russia, Portugal, and Sweden.[10] Some of these people formed partial isolates, such as Germans in Pennsylvania, Welsh in upper New York, or Scandinavians in Wisconsin and Minnesota.[11] Others mixed in greater but varying degrees with

peoples of different national origins. The point is that with each new migration the gene pool would be reconstituted, and hence a description of the people in a geographical area at one time may not hold at another time (Figure 7-4).

The Nature of Human Variation

The significance of one trait in relationship to another is a relative matter. An illustration will clarify this point. Skin color has always been considered important in judging a person's worth. This is one aspect of racism. Yet, how significant is skin color?

As will be discussed in Chapter 8, dark skin color might have some significance as protection from the harmful effects of ultraviolet radiation. Skin color also regulates vitamin D synthesis. However, let us assume that a person with light skin is critically injured and needs a blood transfusion. This person is taken to a small hospital which does not have a supply of blood on hand. There are two possible donors, one dark-skinned and one light-skinned. The injured person is blood type A and the light-skinned person is type B, whereas the dark-skinned person is blood type A. A transfusion using the light donor's blood might kill the patient because of blood-type incompatibility. The dark person's blood is compatible and might save the patient's life. Skin color and blood type are two independent traits, and their importance depends on the situation. Yet, in some areas the light person would refuse the blood of the dark person and vice versa, simply because of skin color.

The above discussions point to weaknesses in traditional methods of classifying human variation. These weaknesses can be summarized as follows. Arbitrary traits are often used to divide humankind into a finite number of groups. When one, two, or twenty traits are used in such classifications, the underlying assumption is that groups

[10] Emrys Jones, *Human Geography* (New York: Praeger, 1965), p. 75.

[11] Ibid., p. 77.

so classified will be different from each other in other traits not used in the classification. This is not necessarily true. If another set of traits were used, the classification might be different. *Homo sapiens* is a collection of thousands of characteristics, and isolating the variation between groups for a few does not explain the totality of similarities and differences or even a small portion of them. Also, when a trait shows continuous gradation, the point at which the cline is broken into two groups is arbitrary.

In addition, any classification of humans into a fixed set of categories makes little sense in light of the dynamic process that constitutes human variation. There simply are no stable or finite numbers of human groups. As mentioned in Chapter 5, all populations are evolving. Since it would be improbable that any two groups over a period of time would be changing in exactly the same manner, it can be concluded that groups are always changing in relationship to each other.

In order to partially solve these problems, we

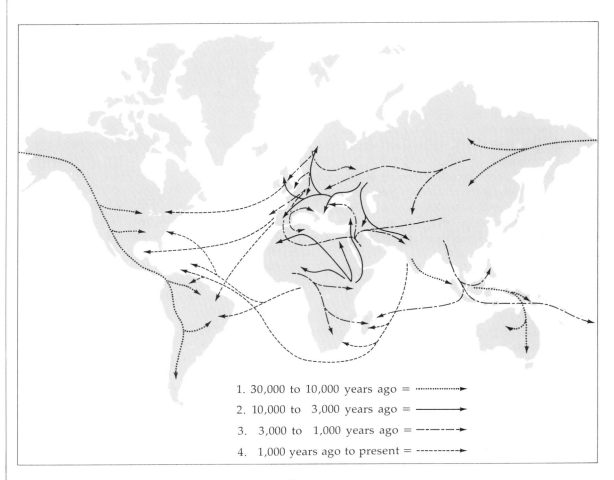

1. 30,000 to 10,000 years ago = ·················▶
2. 10,000 to 3,000 years ago = ⎯⎯⎯⎯▶
3. 3,000 to 1,000 years ago = ⎯·⎯·⎯▶
4. 1,000 years ago to present = ⎯ ⎯ ⎯ ⎯▶

Figure 7-4 Major movements of humans in the last 30,000 years.

The Nature of Human Variability

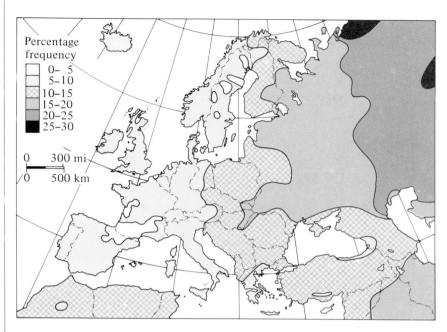

Figure 7-5   Distribution of blood type B in Europe. *This is an example of a basically clinal distribution.*

can consider human variation in terms of clinal and discontinuous variation. With *clinal distribution* a gradation of gene frequencies exists, as in the case of blood type B, shown in Figure 7-5. *Discontinuous variation* occurs if a particular allele or allele combination appears in high or low frequencies in various areas with little or no gradation between those areas, as with the frequency of red hair in the United Kingdom, illustrated in Figure 7-6.

These different types of distributions exist because of a complex interaction of all the factors of evolution. A cline characterized by a high frequency grading into a low frequency might be determined by a gradual change in some selective pressure. For instance, the decrease in intensity of ultraviolet radiation from around the equator to the middle latitudes may be the reason why

skin color in many cases goes from darker to lighter in this direction (Chapter 8). As the selective pressure changes, so might the distribution of the trait.

Discontinuous variation can occur, for instance, if a group travels from one area to another. In relation to skin color, dark-skinned peoples were brought into areas of lighter-skinned peoples through the institution of slavery. This created a nonclinal skin-color distribution in the Americas. Human variation is a complex matter which cannot be summarized by simple generalizations.

Many populations that resemble each other in one way differ in other respects. In order to illustrate this, we will use four characteristics and see how five populations compare in relationship to them.

Examining the data in Table 7-2, we can see

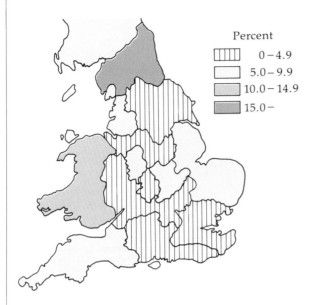

Percent

▥	0 – 4.9
▢	5.0 – 9.9
▨	10.0 – 14.9
▦	15.0 –

Figure 7-6   Distribution of red hair in the United Kingdom. *This is an example of discontinuous variation.*

Table 7-2   Comparison of Traits in Five Populations
(Data expressed in average percentages unless otherwise indicated)

Trait	Population				
	South American Indian	West African	English	Japanese	Greek
PTC nontasting*	1.2	2.7	31.5	7.1	
Blood type B†	0–5	15–20	5–10	20–25	10–15
Lactase deficiency‡	Up to 100	Up to 100	32	90	88
Sickle-cell trait and anemia§	Up to 16	Up to 34	0	0	Up to 32

* G. A. Harrison et al., *Human Biology* (New York: Oxford Univ. Press, 1964), p. 274.

† A. E. Mourant, A. C. Kopeć, and K. Domaniewska-Sobczak, *The Distribution of the Human Blood Groups and Other Polymorphisms*, 2d ed. (London: Oxford Univ. Press, 1976).

‡ Lactase deficiency is the inability to break down lactose, a major component of milk. This will be discussed in Chapter 8. Robert D. McCracken, "Lactase Deficiency: An Example of Dietary Evolution," *Current Anthropology*, 12 (1971), 479–517, and Norman Kretchmer, "Lactose and Lactase," *Scientific American*, 277 (1972), 76.

§ Frank B. Livingstone, *Abnormal Hemoglobins in Human Populations* (Chicago: Aldine, 1967), pp. 162–470.

that populations which are similar to each other in one trait can differ in others. West Africans are closest to South American Indians in relation to PTC nontasting and lactase deficiency, yet in relation to sickle-cell anemia they are closest to Greeks. If we arranged the five groups from lowest to highest frequency of blood type B, the following would result: South American Indian, English, Greek, West African, Japanese. In this characteristic West Africans are closest to Greeks and Japanese. In relation to sickle-cell anemia the English and Japanese are the same. If such a table were constructed 1,000 or 5,000 years from now, the relationship between populations in the five areas might be different.

When you have a number of characteristics for a variety of populations, the task of comparison becomes difficult. Statisticians have developed a method of combining a variety of information on one population into a single numerical value. This value for one population can then be compared to that of other populations and thus reflect overall variance between populations. The procedure for calculating these numbers is complex, and computers are used to facilitate the operation, called *multivariate analysis*.

SUMMARY

All cultures contain systems of classification of the world around them, known as folk taxonomies. The way people categorize human variation may have social reality but does not necessarily reflect biological reality. Scientific attempts to classify human groups have also been characterized by considerable difficulties, especially when they try to picture *Homo sapiens* as being divided into a limited number of distinctive groups.

A scientific classification should not be an end in itself but a means of discovering the factors that create variability. The various classification schemes discussed often arbitrarily choose some physical trait, such as skin color or blood-type frequencies, and attempt to divide humans into a small number of groups on the basis of this sole criterion. Such classifications can explain little of the totality of human variability. There are also other problems with traditional scientific attempts at classifying human variation.

Any description of the distribution of humans must take into account the dynamics of such a distribution. Plotting the continuous and discontinuous nature of traits allows for hypotheses to be generated on the forces that create those distributions. The observation of changes in the shape of clinal distributions and the establishing or breaking down of isolates provides a "natural laboratory" in which such hypotheses can be tested.

SUGGESTED READINGS

Alland, A., Jr. *Human Diversity*. Garden City, N.Y.: Anchor/Doubleday, 1973. A modern approach to human variation that centers on the idea that "race" is a social concept which is not biologically valid.

Kennedy, K. A. R. *Human Variation in Space and Time*. Dubuque, Iowa: Brown, 1976. A short and concise treatment of human variation.

Kuttner, R. E. (ed.). *Race and Modern Science*. New York: Social Science, 1967. Essays by biologists, anthropologists, sociologists, and physiologists.

Mead, M. (ed.). *Science and the Concept of Race*. New York: Columbia Univ. Press, 1968. Essays on race that resulted from a symposium held at the meetings of the American Association for the Advancement of Science in 1966.

Osborne, R. H. (ed.). *The Biological and Social Meaning of Race*. San Francisco: Freeman, 1971. A collection of essays that explores human variation from its biological and social perspectives, with an article on the history of racial classification.

Richardson, K., and D. Spears (eds.). *Race and Intelligence*. Baltimore: Pelican, 1972. Presents several sides of this controversial issue.

Chapter Eight
Human Variability

THE FORCES OF EVOLUTION AND GROUP VARIABILITY

A common dream, which has served as the plot of more than one novel, involves viewing or meeting an exact duplicate of oneself who lives in another place or time. This "second self" can be no more than illusory. For as we have already seen, genetic factors alone reduce the probability to all but zero that two people can be exactly the same.

While all individuals are different in phenotype (even identical twins show variation due to differences in their environment), we should also note that people who are living in the same community tend to resemble each other more closely than people who live in different communities.

The Mechanisms of Variability

The mechanisms involved in bringing about differences between organisms were discussed in earlier chapters. They will now be discussed specifically in terms of differences between human populations.

Mutation The ultimate source of variation is mutation. Mutation provides new alleles which can enter into unique combinations with existing alleles. However, the same mutation may not occur in all populations. Because of this, certain alleles can become established in one population but not in the next. Eventually, gene flow will introduce these alleles to adjacent populations.

Small population size Before people began to build cities, they habitually lived in small communities. The first urban centers arose about 5,000 years ago in Mesopotamia. The time from that date to the present represents less than 1 percent of human evolution. But the early cities were small by modern standards. One such city, Ur, had a population of about 20,000. Babylon, which existed about 3,700 years ago, contained approximately 85,000 people.[1]

Studies of contemporary hunting and gathering societies show that local bands often contain an average of only 25 persons, and Joseph B. Birdsell believes that this may have been generally true in the past.[2] The band is a large family group which moves around within a defined area. Among the Australian aborigines bands are then joined together into larger units, referred to as *tribes*. These tribes are not political units but simply groups of bands which share a common cultural tradition and speak the same dialect. The average tribal size in Australia is 500, with the majority of all marriages occurring within the tribe but not within a person's own band.[3] The remainder of the marriages take place with adjacent tribes. Since the number of children within such a reproductive unit is relatively large, the actual number of actively reproducing adults is quite small. Under these circumstances, genetic drift can be a major factor in bringing about group differences.

The founder effect also plays a large role in initiating variation between groups. The peopling of the New World, Australia, and Polynesia has involved the migration of small groups of individuals (becoming the founder populations) to new territories. This would account for much of the variability seen in these areas. The results of the founder effect continue today. Every displacement because of war (such as the Arab refugees in Israel or the Pakistani refugees in India) or because of natural disaster (such as earthquakes in the Andes) creates new founder populations.

Nonrandom mating One of the most important factors in the development of group differences is the fact that people tend to mate within their own local group. One study shows that in a small English village in 1861, virtually all spouses had lived in communities no farther apart than about 45 miles and that even a 10-foot-wide river acted as an efficient barrier to mating.[4] This is illustrated in Figure 8-1. Although modern means of transportation have increased mobility for some, William J. Goode has reported that within the last two decades more than half the urban marriages in the United States were between people living less than a mile from each other.[5]

In many societies, outsiders are considered less than human or at least not suitable for matrimony, and the majority of marriages occur within a closed community. Not only does this minimize gene flow, but it tends to fix certain minor traits, like "family resemblances," within the populations. Other factors can bring about genetic isolation. For example, inbreeding is the rule in many religious groups, such as the Amish of the United States and the Jewish ghetto of Rome, both of which have been the object of genetic study. Inbreeding can also occur in social groups defined on the basis of ethnic identification or wealth.

Stephen Birmingham has written several books about the life-style of the rich, including *The Right People*.[6] In this book he relates a story

[1] Frank M. McGraw and Dean L. Phelps, *The Rise of the City* (San Francisco: Field Education Publications, 1971).

[2] Joseph B. Birdsell, "Some Predictions for the Pleistocene Based on Equilibrium Systems among Recent Hunter-Gatherers," in Richard B. Lee and Irven DeVore (eds.), *Man the Hunter* (Chicago: Aldine, 1968), p. 235.

[3] Ibid., p. 232.

[4] C. F. Küchemann, A. J. Boyce, and G. H. Harrison, "A Demographic and Genetic Study of a Group of Oxfordshire Villages," *Human Biology*, 39 (1967), 251–276.

[5] William J. Goode, *The Family* (Englewood Cliffs, N.J.: Prentice-Hall, 1964), p. 34.

[6] Stephen Birmingham, *The Right People* (Boston: Little, Brown, 1968).

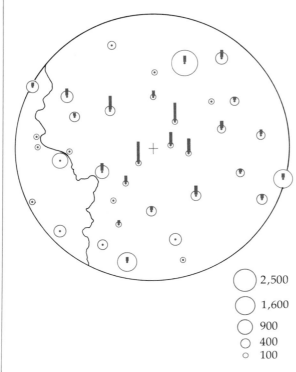

Figure 8-1 Nonrandom mating. *Contributions (solid bars) of surrounding villages to the breeding populations of Charlton, England, in 1861. The area of the circle centered on each village is proportional to the number of inhabitants in that village in 1861. The line on the left of the diagram represents the course of the River Cherwell.*

of a young lady from one of the wealthiest families of Philadelphia. Although she was beautiful and popular, she never married. It seems that she fell in love with a man "below" her in social class and not of her religion. Her father explained that it would be out of the question for her to marry him. She took her father's advice but never married anyone else. The point is that groups such as the very wealthy often maintain themselves through restricting marriage to those within a rather small circle. In one study of marriages in New Haven,

83 percent of the marriages were between people who were defined to be in the same or adjacent economic classes.[7] This can have effects similar to inbreeding among religious isolates, such as the Amish and the Jews of the Roman ghetto. The net result is the maintenance of specific characteristics within these groups, such as the Hapsburg jaw or hemophilia in Queen Victoria's descendents.

When inbreeding practices break down and people of one group begin mating with people from adjacent groups, the unique gene frequencies will begin to equalize. The forces of history continually have erected and broken down barriers to mating. Roman soldiers conquered most of Europe and North Africa, the French invaded England, the Spanish came to the New World, Asian merchants moved to Africa, and the United States received people from every area of the world. In every case, but to varying degrees, these movements of people meant gene flow; so groups are not static but are in a constant state of fluctuation.

Differential fertility (natural selection) Natural selection is another powerful force in creating differences in allele frequencies between groups. A particular trait may be beneficial in one area and disadvantageous in another. It was pointed out earlier how the sickle-cell allele may be maintained at high frequencies in areas where malaria is present and where dietary factors reduce its potential adverse effects (see Chapter 6) but eliminated in nonmalarial areas, where it not only has no advantage but can be deleterious.

The distribution of variability If a certain trait has selective advantage for a particular niche, its frequency will tend to be either maintained or in-

[7] Goode, op. cit.

creased. Through gene flow, such a trait or combination of traits may spread to new areas. Its spread will be controlled by the mobility of the members of the population dispersing the trait and the details of the selective forces for each area the trait enters. If the trait confers selective value, as many abnormal hemoglobins do in malarial environments, it may be established in similar environments. The frequency of a trait such as the sickle-cell trait is determined partially by the intensity of the malaria, partially by the diet, and partially by the degree of migration.[8]

The members carrying a trait into an area where it is less fit than other traits will produce fewer offspring, and the trait will not become established. Therefore, such a trait will be characterized by a cline in which high frequencies are found in areas where the trait is most advantageous and a decreasing frequency as the selective pressure against it increases.

Because of migrations, discontinuous selective pressures, and isolation, not all traits show clinal distributions. Some, such as the Ellis–van Creveld syndrome (Chapter 5) or red hair coloring in the United Kingdom (Chapter 7), are found predominantly in one or a few distant populations or are discontinuous within the same general area.

Distribution of Anatomical Traits

Anatomy refers to the study of body structure. From volumes of data concerning various aspects of the physical nature of the bodies of different *homoiothermic* (warm-blooded) animals (Chapter 9), scientists have come up with several rules. It must be emphasized from the start that these

[8] Frank B. Livingstone, "Gene Frequency Clines of the β Hemoglobin Locus in Various Human Populations and Their Simulation by Models Involving Differential Selection," *Human Biology*, 41 (1969), 223–235.

are *generalizations* derived from the data and that there are exceptions in each case.

One such generalization, known as *Golger's rule*, states that within the same species there is a tendency to find more heavily pigmented populations toward the equator and lighter populations away from it. *Bergmann's rule* refers to body size and states that within the same species, individuals (or subspecies) with less body bulk tend to be found near the equator, while those with greater bulk are found farther from it. *Allen's rule* states that members of the same species living near the equator tend to have more protruding body parts and longer limbs than individuals or subspecies farther away from the equator. In other words, these three rules describe clines in pigmentation, body bulk, and size and shape of extremities, respectively.

Many attempts have been made to validate these generalizations for people. This has been done with respect to skin color, as will be seen in the next section. Although there is correspondence to the rules in many instances, there are also many exceptions. These exceptions may be due mainly to the migration of many human groups over large areas and the mediation of various cultural factors between human biology and the environment.

The nature of skin color Labels that refer to skin color for various human populations are of all types. It is common to hear people being referred to as red, white, black, yellow, or brown. Yet, in spite of this apparent rainbow of humanity, for the most part only one main pigment, *melanin*, is responsible for human colorations. Skin color is also affected by hemoglobin in that the small blood vessels underlying the skin will give lighter-skinned people a pinkish cast and the larger the number of blood vessels the greater the influence of hemoglobin on skin color.

Melanin is produced in the outermost layers

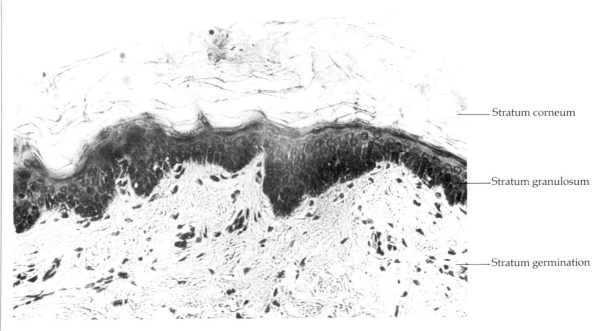

Figure 8-2   Human skin. *A photograph of the outermost layers of the skin (epidermis) as seen through the microscope. In this cross section of dark skin, the concentration of melanin can be seen in the stratum granulosum.*

of the skin, the *epidermis*. In the epidermis are specialized cells called *melanocytes,* which form melanin through a complex process (Figure 8-2). The melanocytes have several branchlike projections called *dendrites.* The function of the dendrites is to transport the melanin to higher layers of the epidermis. People with dark skin and people with light skin have, on the average, the same number of melanocytes in the same area of the body. What makes skin color different is the amount of melanin produced, the size of the melanin particles, and the location of the melanin in the skin.

The distribution of skin color   Today, because of mass movements, peoples with differing colors are distributed throughout the world. Also, interbreeding has always led to the introduction of genes for one kind of skin coloration into populations of basically different coloration, resulting in new skin-color values. However, before recent mass movements, dark skin color was found mainly near the equator, and skin color became lighter as the distance from the equator increased, much as we would expect from Golger's rule (see Figure 8-3).

Why should a darker skin color be found closer to the equator? In what way is dark skin adaptive to an equatorial climate? One hypothesis holds that dark skin provides protection against the harmful effects of ultraviolet radiation from the sun, which can cause sunburn and sunstroke and stimulate the development of skin cancers.[9]

[9] C. J. Witkop, Jr., "Albinism," *Natural History,* 84 (1975), 53.

A dark skin would cut down the amount of ultraviolet radiation which passes through the outer layers of the skin.

Another hypothesis links skin color with problems of vitamin D synthesis, which some feel is more significant than the harmful effects of ultraviolet radiation. Vitamin D is vital for calcium absorption from the intestine. Calcium, in turn, is necessary for normal bone development. The lack of this substance leads to bone diseases, such as rickets, while too much of it leads to calcification of the soft tissues of the body, a condition which can be fatal.

Although some vitamin D comes from digested food, most is manufactured within the human body. However, the biochemical reaction involved requires ultraviolet radiation. The hypothesis is that melanin exerts a regulatory force on vitamin D production by controlling the amount of ultraviolet radiation reaching those layers of the skin where vitamin D synthesis takes place. According to the hypothesis, the higher the concentration of melanin, the greater the protection from ultraviolet radiation.

The areas of most intense ultraviolet radiation are the grasslands and deserts of the equatorial region. Peoples of this region often have extremely dark skin, which always remains dark. This can be seen among the peoples of the grasslands of East Africa and the desert of northern Australia. Extremely dark pigmentation is not, however, characteristic of the indigenous tropical

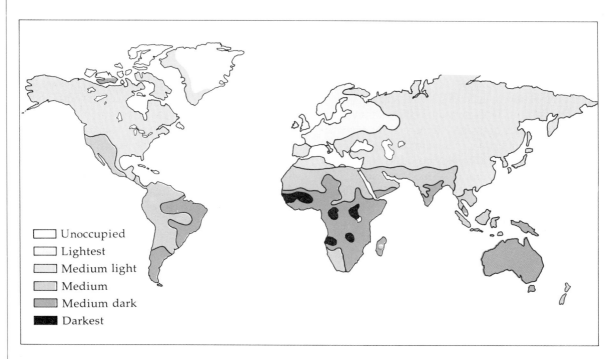

Figure 8-3 Distribution of human skin color before 1492. *Before the mass movements of people beginning in the sixteenth century, the distribution of skin color, in a general way, conformed to Golger's rule.*

forest dwellers, for whom heavy vegetation filters out much of the solar radiation. The Pygmies of the Congo Basin of Africa, for example, are lighter than the people who entered the forest some 2,000 years ago from the Cameroons, which lie northwest of the Congo.[10]

In the more temperate regions of the earth is found a skin which is capable of tanning under the influence of sunlight. According to the hypothesis, in order to prevent an overproduction of vitamin D during the summer, the skin tans to a darker color. During the winter, when solar radiation is at a low level, the lighter color maximizes the amount of ultraviolet radiation passing through the skin. In addition, a very definite gradient of skin color can be seen in traveling from south to north. For example, the skin color found in Italy is generally darker than that of Scandinavia. In the far northwest, such as in Great Britain, can be found skin which has lost its ability to tan.

Genetic and cultural factors for skin color   The exact genetic mechanisms of skin color are not known. It is agreed that polygenetic inheritance (Chapter 3) is involved. The well-known geneticist Theodosius Dobzhansky believes that "skin color differences between Negroes and whites . . . are due to joint action of several or many genes. Each of these genes would, by itself, change the pigmentation . . . by only a small amount. . . ."[11] How many genes, and the nature of their interaction, are debated. However, Curt Stern believes that three to four gene pairs may be involved in variations in skin color for Americans

with African ancestry, although this is a very tentative conclusion.[12]

Cultural factors may also affect skin color. For instance, light-skinned people who wear little clothing or make a practice of sunbathing will appear darker in the summer than genetically similar people who protect themselves from tanning. Suntan lotions also alter the color of the skin. Of course, darkened skin produced by exposure to ultraviolet radiation or tanning lotions will not be passed on to the next generation. However, if there is an advantage or disadvantage to the *process* of tanning, natural selection will increase or decrease the frequency of this trait.

Stature   Human populations vary greatly in average height. Extremes of height can be found in Africa, where Pygmies average less than 5 feet and male Nilotes of East Africa average more than 5 feet 10 inches. Values between these extremes are found distributed throughout the world.

Stature is the result of the interaction of environmental and genetic factors. It is known that people living under conditions of malnutrition are often shorter than those who enjoy a well-balanced diet. If nutrition is upgraded in an area, or if people migrate to areas where food supplies are better, they usually produce children taller than themselves. The average height of the Japanese increased about 2 inches since World War II, at least in part on the basis of new types and greater quantities of food.[13]

Environmental factors, such as diet and disease, account for the nongenetic components

[10] For a discussion of the hypothesis that skin pigment regulates skin vitamin D synthesis and the possible evolutionary significance of the hypothesis see R. M. Neer, "The Evolutionary Significance of Vitamin D, Skin Pigment, and Ultraviolet Light," *American Journal of Physical Anthropology*, 43 (1975), 409–416.

[11] Theodosius Dobzhansky, *Mankind Evolving* (New York: Bantam Books, 1962), p. 109.

[12] Curt Stern, "Model Estimates of the Number of Gene Pairs Involved in Pigmentation Variability of the Negro-American," *Human Heredity*, 20 (1970), 165–168.

[13] For a discussion of evolution and nutrition see W. A. Stini, "Evolutionary Implications of Changing Nutritional Patterns in Human Populations," *American Anthropologist*, 73 (1971), 1019–1030.

of stature. Pygmies living in the United States might produce children taller than themselves; however, they would produce very few candidates for a professional basketball team. On the other hand, a people who under good conditions have the genetic potential for tall stature but are subjected to an inadequate diet may produce children who will not realize that potential.

Natural selection and body build While drift, the founder effect, and nonrandom mating affect the average stature of a population, natural selection plays a major role. This is especially true if stature is considered together with weight and body build. Basically, climatic factors tend to create clines in body structure. Natural selection creates the maximum pressure in extreme conditions. That is, if people live in a climate that is mild for nine months of the year but frigid for three, they must obviously be adapted to the harsh conditions as well as the mild. In other words, a specific selective pressure may not be constant, but when it is intense, the population must be adapted to it. Each time an intense selective situation exists, those who survive will be the ones who produce the next generation. Hence, the population should become increasingly adapted to its local situation.

Like all mammals, humans must maintain their internal body temperature at a more or less constant level. Body size and build are to a large extent related to this function. In a cold environment, heat energy must be conserved, while in a warm climate, excess heat must be dispersed. Heat originates from metabolism and from absorption of solar radiation. It is dispersed primarily by evaporation, which is accomplished by perspiration and radiation.

The efficiency of radiation as a mechanism for heat loss is related to the ratio of surface area to body mass. The following example will show why this is so. Suppose you had two brass objects, a sphere and a cube, of identical weight.

You heat these objects to the same temperature, let them stand in the air, and then measure their temperature after a period of time. Which object cools faster? You will find that the cube cools faster because although the two objects have the same weight, the cube has more surface area from which the heat can radiate. In fact, a sphere has the smallest surface per unit weight of any three-dimensional shape.

While weight increases by the cube, surface area increases only by the square. Therefore, stocky individuals produce more heat than thin ones but have less surface area from which the heat can radiate. A more linear person will produce relatively less heat and have more surface area from which the heat can radiate. This minimizes heat production and maximizes heat dis-

Table 8-1 Ratio of Body Weight to Body Surface Area in Males*

Population	Medial Latitude	Ratio (kilograms per square meter)
China:		
North		36.02
Central		34.30
South		30.90
North Europe to North Africa:†		
Finland	65°N	38.23
Ireland	53°N	38.00
France	47°N	37.78
Italy	42½°N	37.15
Egypt (Siwah)	26°N	36.11
Arabs (Yemen)	15°N	36.10

* Women show ratios different from men's. This may be due to differences in the mechanisms of heat regulation between men and women. For example, the ratio for France (women) is 38.4, compared with 37.78 for men, as seen above.

† There is some discontinuous variation in the North Europe to North Africa range. For example, the ratio for Germany is 39.14, even though it is south of Finland.

Data from Eugene Schreider, "Variations morphologiques et différences climatiques," *Biométrie Humaine,* 6 (1971), 46–49. Used with permission of Dr. Schreider.

Figure 8-4 *(a)* An Eskimo and *(b)* Nilote.

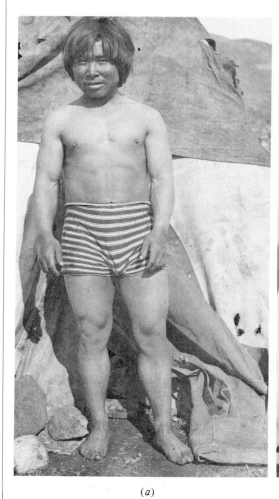

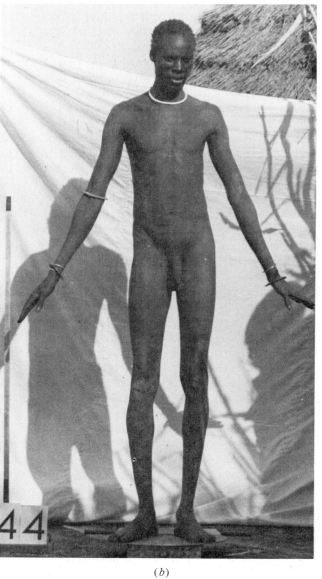

(*a*)

(*b*)

The Nature of Human Variability

persion. For this reason a clinal distribution for body build can be found in which relatively thin people tend to be found in equatorial regions, with stockier people in the more northern and southern regions (Table 8-1).

Since a sphere has the smallest surface area per unit weight, a short, stocky body would have a minimal surface area per unit weight. Thus, in order to minimize heat loss, people in arctic regions would be expected to be short and stocky, with short limbs. When the Eskimo's body build is examined, this in a general sense is indeed true (Figure 8-4). The Nilotes of East Africa show the opposite extreme. Figure 8-4 shows that they have long, linear trunks with very long arms and legs. This body shape provides a large surface area for radiation, especially from the arms, hands, and fingers.

Other anatomical traits We have chosen to talk about body build and skin color, but variability extends to all parts of the anatomy. Facial characteristics have been the subject of much study. Because the sense organs—the eyes, ears, nose, and mouth—are located on the face, this is the hardest part of the body to cover completely and still go about the daily routine. Even the Eskimo, hunting in an extremely cold environment, must expose part of the face to the bitter climate, at least some of the time. The face has had to adapt to environmental conditions, and some of the most notable differences among populations can be seen in the face and head.

Variations in the *nasal index* show a generally good correlation with climate. (The nasal index is a measure of the length of the nose relative to its breadth.) A nasal index of 100 means that the nose is as broad as it is long, whereas a nasal index of 50 means that the nose breadth is half the nose length. Both humidity and temperature are important factors in influencing the distribu-

tion of nose shapes. Such distributions are often clinal in nature. For instance, among groups of Eskimos and Australian aborigines studied by M. H. Wolpoff, the shape of the nose shows a distribution in which the narrowest noses occur in the coldest and driest climates.[14]

Hair form also differs from population to population. In fact, type of hair has been included in virtually all racial classifications. Variation in hair form depends on two factors. The first is the shape of the cross section of the hair shaft. Straight hair tends to be circular in cross section, while curly hair is more oval. The second factor is the thickness of the hair shaft. Thus, hair which is round in cross section and thick will be straight, whereas hair which is oval in cross section and thinner will be tightly and spirally curled.

Various adaptive explanations have been put forth for differences in hair form. Carlton Coon, Stanley Garn, and Joseph Birdsell postulate that woolly hair may provide insulation for the head in hot, dry areas.[15] This, like other hypotheses, is speculation. Because the original situations under which these variations in hair form arose might no longer exist, it may not be possible to accurately test hypotheses about this problem. Hair also varies from population to population in color and distribution on the body.

Earwax Even earwax comes in more than one variety. There are two distinct types, wet (waxy) and dry (flaky). Earwax is inherited in a simple Mendelian way. There are two alleles, the one producing the wet type being dominant over that

---

[14] M. H. Wolpoff, "Climatic Influence on the Skeletal Nasal Aperture," *American Journal of Physical Anthropology*, 29 (1968), 405–423.

[15] C. S. Coon, S. M. Garn, and J. B. Birdsell, *Races* (Chicago: Thomas, 1950).

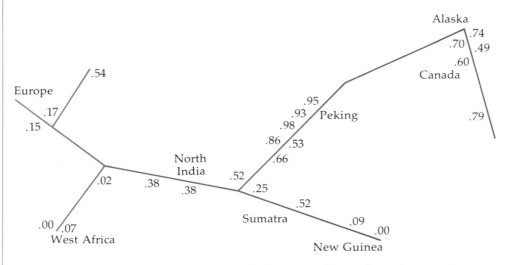

Figure 8-5 Earwax cline. *Various frequencies of the dry-earwax allele are shown. American data are for Indian populations.*

for dry. The dry allele reaches high frequencies among indigenous populations of Asia and American Indians but decreases in all directions away from this area (Figure 8-5). The wet allele has a high frequency in European populations, American populations derived from Europe and Africa, and African populations.[16]

What is responsible for the distribution of the types of earwax? Migration is one definite factor. For instance, American Indians show many genetic similarities to Asian populations, which supports the hypothesis that they are derived from such populations.[17] Various factors of natural selection also have been suggested as influencing the distribution of earwax types. These include differences in the effectiveness of the wet and dry types in relationship to resistance to ear diseases, correlations with humidity, and so on. However, at this time these hypotheses remain unvalidated.

Distribution of Blood Types

It has already been noted that there is considerable variation in the frequencies of particular blood types from population to population. Also, some specific blood antigens are characteristic of particular populations.

Figures 8-6 to 8-8 show the relative frequencies of the ABO blood-type alleles in several populations. Note that in some instances we find gradations in the frequencies of a particular allele from one area to the next; that is, clines exist. However, not all blood-group distributions are clinal.

[16] N. L. Petrakis, "Evidence for a Genetic Cline in Earwax Types in the Middle East and Southeast Asia," *American Journal of Physical Anthropology,* 35 (1971), 141–144.

[17] Ibid.

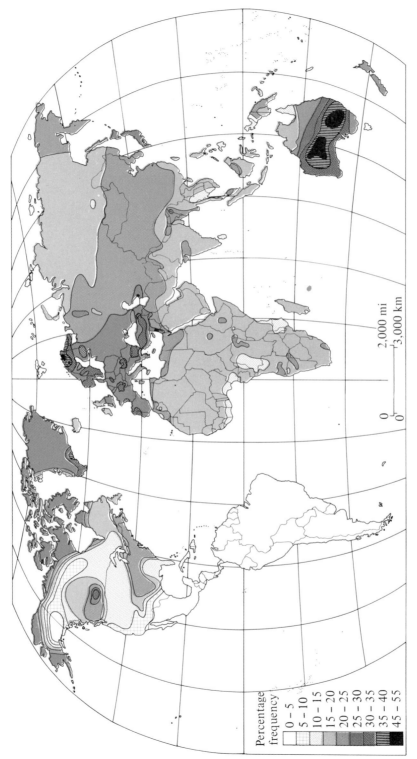

Figure 8-6 The distribution of the allele I^A in the aboriginal populations of the world.

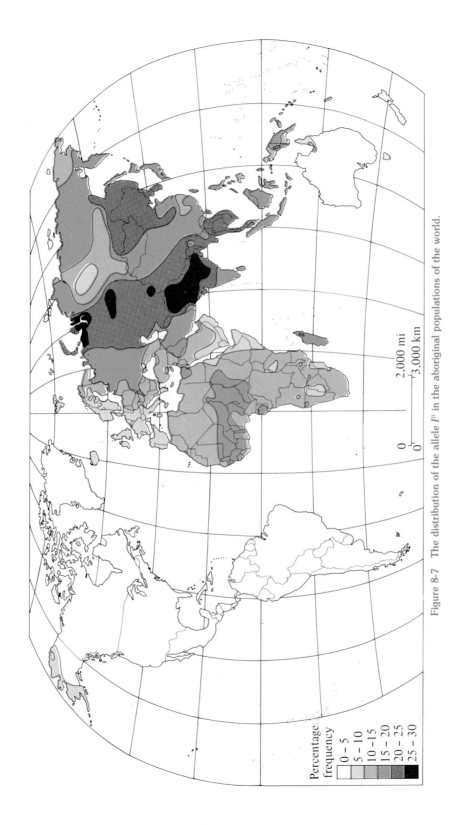

Figure 8-7 The distribution of the allele I^B in the aboriginal populations of the world.

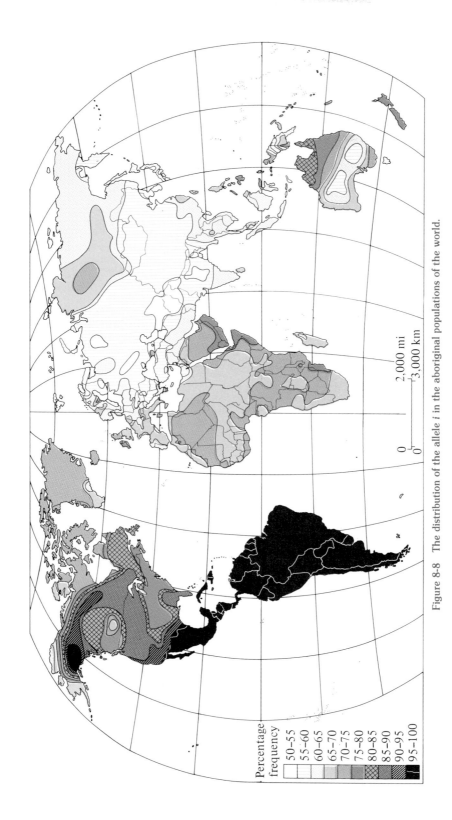

Figure 8-8 The distribution of the allele *i* in the aboriginal populations of the world.

Percentage
frequency

50–55
55–60
60–65
65–70
70–75
75–80
80–85
85–90
90–95
95–100

2,000 mi
3,000 km

As discussed in Chapter 6, selective pressures are operating on the ABO system. For example, it has been hypothesized that smallpox is more severe and mortality rates are higher among people of blood types A and AB than among people of types O and B. If this hypothesis is correct, smallpox, in areas where it is common, would tend to eliminate A and AB individuals, leaving O and B people to reproduce most of the next generation. Maybe this is why, in areas such as India, where smallpox was prevalent, B is the most common blood type.

An interesting distributional study is that for the Diego blood antigen. Table 8-2 shows that this antigen is restricted to Asiatics usually referred to as "Mongoloid" and to the aboriginal populations of the New World who are derived from the

Table 8-2 Frequencies (percent) of Diego-positive Phenotype in Various Populations

Population	Frequency of Diego-positive
Caingangs (Brazil)	45.8
Carajas (Brazil)	36.1
Caribs (Venezuela)	35.5
Maya Indians (Mexico)	17.6
Guahibos (Venezuela)	14.5
Japanese	12.3
Chippewas (Canada)	10.8
Koreans	6.1
Guajiros (Venezuela)	5.3
Apaches (United States)	4.1
Eskimos (Alaska)	0.8
Lapps (Norway)	0.0
Polynesians	0.0
Aborigines (Australia)	0.0
Whites (United States)	0.0
Asiatic Indians	0.0
Africans (Liberia, Ivory Coast)	0.0
Bushmen (South Africa)	0.0

From G. A. Harrison et al., *Human Biology* (New York: Oxford Univ. Press, 1964), p. 275.

Table 8-3 Frequencies (percent) of Blood Type Rh-negative of the Rh System for Several Populations*

Population	Location	Frequency of Rh-negative
Basques	Spain	28.5
Swiss	Safien and Valsertal	21.8
English	Nottinghamshire	18.1
Austrians	Vienna	17.1
Portuguese	Madeira	14.6
Italians	Florence	12.4
Arabs	Algeria	12.4
Swiss	Uri	11.2
Indians	Calcutta	8.0
Bantu	South Africa	4.9
Ethiopians	Ethiopia	4.2
Italians	Sassari, Sardinia	3.9
Japanese	Tokyo	0.4
Eskimos	Alaska	0.04
Australian aborigines	Australia	0.00
Fijians	Fiji	0.00
Koreans	Korea	0.00

* Persons who react negatively to anti-Rh_0 (anti-D). Data from A. E. Mourant, A. C. Kopeć, and K. Domaniewska-Sobczak, *The Distribution of the Human Blood Groups and Other Polymorphisms*, 2d ed. (London: Oxford Univ. Press, 1976).

"Mongoloid" peoples of Asia. It has been postulated that the "Mongoloids" are of fairly recent origin and that the Diego antigen is one of the characteristics of this group. The antigen was carried to the New World when the ancestors of the American Indians migrated across the Bering Strait. According to this hypothesis, it is not found in other adjacent populations because it is relatively new and simply has not moved into these other populations yet. Of course, selective factors cannot be ruled out.

There are other differences in other blood-type systems. Although research is being done, not as much is known about them. Tables 8-3 and 8-4 show the frequencies of Rh-negative and type M of the MN blood-type system.

Table 8-4 Frequencies (percent) of Blood Type M of the MN System for Several Populations

Population	Location	Frequency of Blood Type M
Navaho	New Mexico	84.5
Eskimos	East Greenland	83.5
Aleutian Eskimos	Alaska	71.8
Chamulas	Mexico	63.5
Yemenite Jews	Yemen	57.0
Finns	Eastern Finland	43.8
Hindus	India	42.7
Tutsi	Ruanda-Urundi	40.2
Chinese	Malaya	39.2
Basques	San Sebastian	34.6
American whites	New York City	30.1
Japanese	Japan	28.5
Germans	Württemberg	28.5
Sea Dyaks	Borneo	20.5
Ashanti	Ghana	15.0
Ainu	Japan	14.0
Fijians	Fiji	11.0
Australian aborigines	Queensland	2.4
Australian aborigines	New South Wales	0.0

Data from A. E. Mourant, A. C. Kopeć, and K. Domaniewska-Sobczak, *The Distribution of the Human Blood Groups and Other Polymorphisms*, 2d ed. (London: Oxford Univ. Press, 1976).

Variability in Frequency of Disease

Tay-Sachs disease involves the progressive degeneration of the central nervous system, leading to death in the first few years of life. Two-thirds of all cases in the United States are children of Jewish parents derived from Eastern Europe. The rate of this trait in this population is 1 per 3,000 births, compared with 1 per 160,000 births in the non-Jewish population. One out of every 27 Jews derived from Eastern Europe is a carrier, while only 1 out of every 200 non-Jews is a carrier. Examples of this type can be found in other populations. The question is: Why?

Certainly all the four basic mechanisms of evolutionary change are involved, with drift playing a major role. But geneticists are constantly looking for selective pressures which could account for these differences, and heterozygote advantage might be one of the mechanisms involved (Chapter 6). Sickle-cell anemia has already been discussed in this light. Because of the mechanism of heterozygote advantage or *balanced polymorphism* in the form of an adaptation to malarial environments, the allele responsible for the sickle-cell trait is found in high frequencies in these environments.

There are several inherited mechanisms which might provide an adaptation to malaria. *Hemoglobin C*, which may be a more recent abnormal hemoglobin, is today found in West Africa. Since the homozygous recessive condition is not lethal while sickle-cell anemia can be, this may be a more efficient system to cope with the problem. *Hemoglobin E* is associated with high-malaria areas of Asia. Similar mechanisms occurring in Europe, Asia, Indonesia, Melanesia, and Africa include *thalassemia* and *glucose-6-phosphate dehydrogenase deficiency* (Figure 6-7).

Balanced polymorphism may explain the high frequency of many deleterious alleles in specific populations. It has been suggested that this mechanism may be involved with the elevated frequencies of *cystic fibrosis, phenylketonuria, schizophrenia*, and others.[18] Because modern technology has alleviated the selective advantage of many balanced polymorphisms, it may be impossible to discover the nature of the former heterozygote advantage.

Color blindness For most people the world is a colorful one. However, there is a rare defect that causes a total inability to see color, and the world is then perceived as white and various

[18] Curt Stern, *Principles of Human Genetics*, 3d ed. (San Francisco: Freeman, 1973), pp. 739–740.

Table 8-5 Frequency of Color Blindness in Males of Various Populations

Population	Color-blind Males (%)
Belgians	8.6
Todas (India)	8.6
Hindus (India)	8.1
Norwegians	8.0
Scottish	7.8
Germans	7.5
Chinese	5.6
United States blacks	3.9
Mexicans	2.3
American Indians	2.0
Congolese	1.7

From G. A. Harrison et al., *Human Biology* (New York: Oxford Univ. Press, 1964), p. 282.

shades of gray. Much more common than this *total color blindness* is the inability to distinguish between shades of red and green. This involves a defect in the cones, the bodies in the eye that are sensitive to color. There are several types of *red-green color blindness*. The *deutan type* is an insensitivity to green, whereas the *protan type* is an insensitivity to red. Both types exist in a mild and a severe form.

It has been known for a long time that males have a much higher frequency of red-green color blindness than females. In the United States about 8 percent of the men have some type of red-green color blindness, while only 0.4 percent of the women do.[19] In other words, color blindness is twenty times higher in males. The reason for this is that it is an X-linked trait; a male will have the defect if he possesses only one allele for any type, but a female must have two. Color blindness is inherited in a manner similar to hemophilia, discussed in Chapter 4.

[19] A. M. Winchester, *Human Genetics* (Columbus, Ohio: Merrill, 1971), p. 73.

Selective pressures that might be working in relation to color blindness are unknown. The defect shows quite a bit of variation in different populations (Table 8-5). Generally, it has the lowest frequency in hunting and gathering societies, followed by farming societies, with the highest frequencies in industrial societies.

High frequencies of total color blindness are known to have been established by the founder principle. In one case a hurricane killed off most of the people of the island of Pingelop, in the South Pacific. Of the twenty survivors, a much higher percentage than in the original population must have carried the allele for total color blindness, because 6 percent of the people there today have the defect.[20] This compares with 0.003 percent in the population of the United States.

Resistance to disease   It has also been found that resistance to noninherited infectious diseases varies from population to population. This is probably due to the disease itself acting as a selective agent. Each succeeding generation is produced by individuals whose mortality in the face of disease is lower.

An example of this is the introduction of tuberculosis into the Qu'Appelle Valley Indian Reservation in Saskatchewan, Canada. Between 1881 and 1886 the general death rate rose from 40 per 1,000 to 127 per 1,000 people per year. The annual mortality rate from tuberculosis alone reached almost 10 percent. After three generations, however, the rate had dropped to 0.2 percent.[21] Tuberculosis had acted as a selective agent, eliminating those with a low resistance to

[20] Ibid., p. 158.

[21] R. G. Ferguson, *Studies in Tuberculosis* (Toronto: Univ. of Toronto Press, 1955), pp. 6–9.

the disease. Since those who were resistant remained to breed, the resistance of the population increased from generation to generation and mortality decreased until a stable relationship between the disease organism and the human host population was reached.

Distribution of Ontogenetic Variation

A miniscule zygote contains the genetic code for an entire organism. Cells that are derived from the zygote will differentiate into the various types of cells (such as liver, muscle, and nerve cells) which make up the individual. The interaction of the genetic code, the environment, and cultural factors will determine the rates and sequences of growth and development as well as the morphology and physiology of the individual at each point in the life cycle. These interacting factors will determine when the individual will take his or her first step, the age at which sexual development will occur, what height and weight the individual will have, and all other growth and developmental occurrences. The term *ontogeny* refers to the growth and development of an organism.

Growth begins with the fertilized ovum and can be defined as the "process of self-multiplication of living substance."[22] This growth is accomplished in three ways. The first is *hyperplasia*, which is an increase in the number of cells as a result of mitotic division (Chapter 4). The second is *hypertrophy*, which is an increase in the size of the cell. The third is *accretion*, which is an increase in intercellular materials. The term *development*, on the other hand, involves the "specialization and differentiation of cells into different functional units."[23] Thus, specialized tissues of different types develop from the group of generalized cells which make up the early embryo.

Individuals differ in their ontogenetic potentials and in their rates of growth and development. By potential ontogeny we mean the ultimate growth and development attainable for specific genotypes. The rate of growth and development is the "speed" at which ontogeny occurs. The phenotype is the result of the interplay of genetic, environmental, and cultural factors. The study of these various factors and how they interrelate to create ontogenetic variation has become an exciting area of research in physical anthropology.

Animals usually experience most of their growth and development early in life. For instance, at birth the brain of a rhesus monkey has already reached about 75 percent of its adult size. Humans, however, experience a prolonged period of growth and development. At birth our brains are less than 30 percent of their adult size (Figure 12-20). In most characteristics, it takes humans a greater percentage of their lives to reach the adult phase of development than for other animals (Figure 12-19). This long period of growth and development allows for a longer and greater influence of nongenetic factors on the individual. Since these nongenetic factors are highly variable from place to place and from time to time, various human groups tend to differ more from one another than various groups within the same species of other animals will. Also, as pointed out previously, the prolonged period of growth and development and the generally long life span in humans allow an extended period of learning and the development of cultural behavior (Chapter 1).

Within any given population there is a range of variation for any ontogenetic measure, such as age at *menarche* (the onset of first menstruation), spermatogenesis, tooth eruption, menopause, and so on. But the averages also differ between populations, as can be seen in Tables 8-6 and 8-7. The reasons for both individual and group variations

[22] R. M. Malina, *Growth and Development: The First Twenty Years in Man* (Minneapolis: Burgess, 1975), p. 1.

[23] Ibid.

Table 8-6 Median Age at Eruption of Permanent Upper Second Molars in Various Populations

Population	Median Age (years)
Pima Indians (United States)	11.4*
Zulu (South Africa)	11.7*
Hutu (Rwanda)	11.9†
Tutsi (Rwanda)	12.2†
English	12.3*
American whites	12.7*

* A. A. Dahlberg and R. M. Menegaz-Bock, "Emergence of the Permanent Teeth in Pima Indian Children: A Critical Analysis of Method and an Estimate of Population Parameters," *Journal of Dental Research* 37 (1958), 1123–1140.

† J. Hiernaux, *La Croissance des écoliers Rwandais* (Brussels: Outre-Mer, Royal Academy of Science, 1965).

Table 8-7 Median Age at Menarche (First Menstruation) in Several Populations

Population or Location	Median Age (years)
Wealthy Chinese (Hong Kong)	12.5*
Wroclaw (Poland)	12.6*
California (United States)	12.8*
Moscow (U.S.S.R.)	13.0*
Tel Aviv (Israel)	13.0†
Burma (urban)	13.2*
Oslo (Norway)	13.5*
Wealthy Ibo (Nigeria)	14.1*
Transkei Bantu (South Africa)	15.0*
Tutsi (Rwanda)	16.5‡
Hutu (Rwanda)	17.1‡
Bundi (New Guinea)	18.8*

* J. M. Tanner, "The Secular Trend Towards Earlier Physical Maturation," *Trans. Soc. Geneesk.*, 44 (1966), 524–538.

†A. Ber and C. Brociner, "Age of Puberty in Israeli Girls," *Fertility and Sterility*, 15 (1964), 640–647.

‡J. Hiernaux, *La Croissance des écoliers Rwandais* (Brussels: Outre-Mer, Royal Academy of Science, 1965).

in ontogeny, as well as any other phenotypic characteristic, are complex and involve both genetic factors and nongenetic (physical and cultural environmental) factors such as nutrition, disease, stress, and others. Although each factor may be discussed alone, it must be emphasized that it is the interaction of these factors that creates the total variation for any phenotypic characteristic. (In Chapter 3, pages 46 and 47, we discussed one method of estimating the relative influences of genetic and nongenetic factors for particular traits.)

The effects of genetics on growth and development At the moment of conception a new life has begun. The new individual starts out as a single cell, the zygote, which carries a unique combination of alleles. The specific combination of alleles of this particular organism will first of all mark it as a member of a specific species. A zygote resulting from the union of a human sperm and a human ovum will not develop into a chimpanzee. In addition, the genetic code will influence or determine many of the specifics of that individual's growth and development. Children born to

tall parents will have a higher probability of being tall than those born to short parents.[24] Children born to parents with, or carrying alleles for, various genetic diseases will have a greater probability of having those diseases or being carriers than children born to parents without them (Chapter 3). Genetic factors most likely have some effect on all phases of a person's ontogeny.

One of the genetic factors most important in influencing rates of growth and development as well as the adult phenotype is the inheritance of patterns of hormonal secretion. *Hormones* are complex molecules that regulate many bodily functions and processes. The hormone *somatotrophin,* or *growth hormone,* influences hyperplasia and to a lesser extent hypertrophy. Other

[24] R. M. Malina, A. B. Harper, and J. D. Holman, "Growth Status and Performance Relative to Parental Size," *Research Quarterly,* 41 (1970), 503–509.

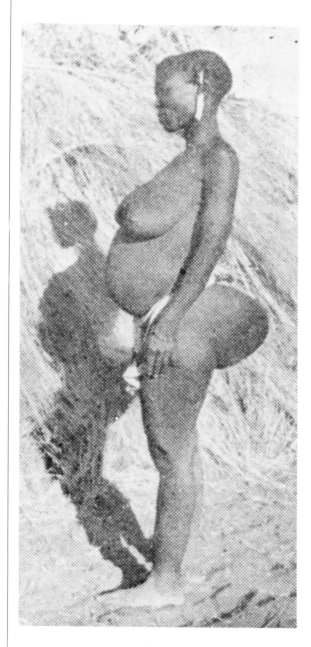

Figure 8-9 Steatopygia. *Steatopygia, a large amount of fat in the upper thighs and buttocks, occurs in Bushman and Hottentot populations.*

hormones, such as *thyroxin, insulin, testosterone, estrogens,* and *progesterone,* are important in skeletal, muscular, and sexual development. Hormonal secretions are also influenced by environmental factors such as diet. Since most hormones are proteins, a protein-deficient diet would affect their production, as would deficiencies in other nutrients needed for the productions of specific hormones. Also, cultural factors such as stress from athletic competition might stimulate the production of *adrenalin* and other hormones.

The genetic potential for some developmental features seem to be restricted to certain groups. One example of this is *steatopygia,* an unusually large amount of fat located in the upper thighs and buttocks (Figure 8-9). It is found among the Bushman and Hottentots of Africa. The function of steatopygia is not known, but the fact that only these groups display it, even though other peoples live in these and similar environments, seems to indicate that the potential for it is genetic.

The action of regulatory genes (Chapters 3 and 6) might be an important factor in growth and development. Regulatory genes turn structural genes "on and off." Therefore people with the same genotype with respect to a particular structural gene but with different regulatory genes for that structural gene may display different phenotypes. The difference in phenotype may be expressed as differences in rates of growth and maturation, as well as other processes. Like other aspects of inheritance, regulatory genes may be affected by the physical and cultural environments. Although the idea of regulatory genes has been around for some time, not much is known about their activity in most organisms, including humans. Research in this area has intensified recently, and the possible consequences of people being able to control human regulatory genes could be wide-ranging. If this could be done, growth and maturation could be controlled and perhaps even stopped at a "desired" stage (see Chapter 5).

The effect of nutrition on growth and development Every individual starts out with a specific genetic potential for growth and development. These potentials also differ from population to population. One factor that influences ontogeny to a great extent is the quality and quantity of the nutrients available and used.

Nutrients (food) are substances taken into the body (*ingested*) and ultimately used to sustain growth and development, to repair damage, to maintain vital processes, and to provide energy for bodily activities. There are several different classes of nutrients. In most human societies *carbohydrates* (sugars and starches), which make up a large proportion of cereal grains and root crops, are the primary sources of fuel for the energy needs of the body. Additional sources of energy are provided by *lipids* (fats, oils, and waxes), such as butter, margarine, and cooking oils; lipids are found also in meats, eggs, milk, cheeses, nuts, and other sources. The *fatty acids,* important building blocks of many molecules of the body, are energy sources as well. Body fats provide stored energy as well as insulation.

Proteins are the main structural elements of the body (Chapter 4). In addition, some hormones and all enzymes are proteins. Ingested proteins are broken up into amino acids, which are absorbed by the body. Amino acids are then used to construct new proteins. Excess protein can be used as a source of energy. If the amounts of carbohydrates and fats are not sufficient to provide the energy needs of the body, proteins will take up this function.

Vitamins are organic molecules (molecules with carbon backbones) that occur in foods and perform various specific and important functions. Most vitamins are not manufactured by the body. *Minerals* are inorganic chemicals such as calcium, magnesium, phosphorus, iron, iodine, and zinc, which participate in a great number of chemical reactions in an organism. Some are involved in

the formation of hard tissues such as bone and teeth, while others play vital roles in normal muscle and nerve activity. Another inorganic molecule, *water,* accounts for more than half of an average person's weight. Water plays an important part in all bodily processes. It is necessary for digestion, circulation, and lubrication of joints, to mention only a few.

If any of the essential nutrients are missing, are insufficient, or, in some cases, overabundant in the daily diet, specific abnormalities may occur. For example, a diet lacking calcium may lead to rickets, whereas one lacking sufficient vitamin A could retard growth, interfere with successful reproduction, contribute to blindness, and so forth. On the other hand, excessive lipids in the diet could lead to heart, respiratory, menstrual, and other health problems. Some specific dietary deficiencies and excesses and their relationship to diseases affecting growth and development are listed in Table 8-8.

In addition, some diets can prevent the symptoms of certain diseases from developing. We have already discussed the effects of nitrilosides in the diet as possibly preventing the sickling of red blood cells in people homozygous for hemoglobin S (Chapter 6) and the use of low-phenylalanine diets in preventing the development of symptoms associated with PKU (Chapter 3). Diet therapy is becoming recognized as important in the treatment of a wide range of diseases such as fevers and infections, diabetes, atherosclerosis, cardiac disease, diseases of the stomach and intestines, blood diseases, allergies, and so forth, as well as diseases of the musculoskeletal and nervous systems and various types of mental illnesses.[25]

Since the diets of different groups vary be-

[25] H. S. Michell, et al., *Copper's Nutrition in Health and Disease,* 15th ed. (Philadelphia: Lippincott, 1968), pp. 255–479.

Table 8-8 Examples of Dietary Deficiencies and Excesses and Their Relationship to Disease

Nutrient	Effect of Too Little	Effect of Excess
Lipids	Dermatitis,[a] slower overall growth	Cardiac problems, respiratory difficulties, elevated blood pressure, menstrual abnormalities, diabetes mellitus, detrimental effects on established diseases, and other problems
Protein	Kwashiorkor (growth retardation, edema, disorders of pigmentation of skin and hair, enlarged liver), marasmus (wasted, dull and dry hair, thin and wrinkled skin, stiffness of limbs, diarrhea, vomiting)	Perhaps lessened bone mineralization, leading to greater risk of bone fractures in older adults[b]
Vitamin A	Possible growth retardation, reproductive and lactational problems, cortisone[c] deficiencies, impairment of bone and teeth development, nerve damage, blindness	Loss of appetite, abnormal skin pigmentation, loss of hair, dry (itching) skin, pain in long bones, increase in general bone fragility
Vitamin D	Rickets (improper bone calcification resulting in pigeon chest, enlarged wrists and ankles, bowed legs and knock knees; severe and prolonged cases can result in a general stunting of growth)	Hypercalcemia (lack or loss of appetite, nausea, weight loss, polyuria,[d] constipation, azotemia,[e] and, rarely, mental retardation)
Vitamin C	Scurvy (restlessness, loss of appetite, general soreness to touch, sore mouth and gums with bleeding and loosening of teeth, petechial skin hemorrhages,[f] swelling of legs, and sometimes anemia)	No agreed-upon effect
Calcium and phosphorus	Growth retardation, bone abnormalities, and a very wide range of other effects	
Iron	Iron-deficiency anemia	
Iodine	Common goiter,[g] insufficient thyroxin (thyroid hormone)	
Water	Dehydration (can be fatal); inadequate water intake can affect every organ, process, and function of the body	

[a] Inflammation of the skin.

[b] R. B. Mazess and W. Mather, "Bone Mineral Content of North Alaskan Eskimos," *American Journal of Clinical Nutrition*, 27 (1974), 916–925.

[c] A hormone from the adrenal gland.

[d] The passage of a large quantity of urine.

[e] An excess of urea in the blood.

[f] Bleeding in the skin seen as a pinpoint, round, purplish red spot.

[g] An enlarged thyroid gland seen as a swelling in the neck.

From H. S. Mitchell, et al., *Cooper's Nutrition in Health and Disease*, 15th ed. (Philadelphia: Lippincott, 1968), pp. 25–46, 55–114, and 215–237 (except *b*).

Human Variability

cause of choice, custom, or availability of food, the growth and development of differing groups may differ on nutritional bases. For instance, a group with little protein in their diet may not attain the same average for stature as a genetically similar group with a diet high in protein. Or a group with a high degree of vitamin A deficiency may show an elevated frequency of blindness. Populations in Central America, parts of Brazil, Haiti, parts of Africa, Egypt, Vietnam, and several other regions show a high frequency of vitamin A–related blindness.[26]

The different ways different groups prepare food have an effect on nutrition. For example, overcooking of many foods causes vitamin loss, and if foods are cooked in water that is subsequently discarded, there will be mineral losses as well. Thus, the same amount and type of food will provide different nutrient value depending on the method of preparation. In addition, some factors might be unknowingly added to foods as a result of preparation, such as copper and iron from metal cooking vessels and arsenic and lead from glazed pottery vessels.[27]

Many other cultural variables may influence the nutritional value of food. Wild foods collected at different times of the year have different food values. Whether domestic food animals are fed grass, corn, fishmeal, soybean, or other feeds will affect their protein-fat ratios and hence the amount of these nutrients in the human diet. The injection of growth hormones and the ingestion of insecticides that occurs in the domestic animals of some cultures may add unwanted chemicals to the group's diet. Different groups ingest varying amounts of what might be called *antinutrients,*

substances that adversely affect the activity and quality of needed nutrients. For example, substances in tobacco smoke absorb vitamin C, and caffeines affect the functioning of the pancreas, which secretes digestive enzymes, among other functions. In addition, there are eight essential amino acids which must be present in the diet in the proper proportion. A deficiency of one essential amino acid is not compensated by an abundance in the others. Groups of people who have diets high in the total amount of protein but deficient in a specific essential amino acid are characterized by malnutrition. Methods of storing, preserving, packaging, and curing foods also affect their nutrient value.

Comparative nutritional studies are still in their infancy. Yet it is certain that variables in quantity and quality of food available or used in the environments of different groups, the presence or absence and the sophistication of nutritional therapy, and differences in methods of food collection, production, preparation, and storage will differentially affect growth and development of various groups. Hence, nutrition is a major factor in creating human variation.

The effects of circadian and other rhythms on growth and development A factor that influences many bodily functions and processes is the *circadian rhythm* of the individual. Circadian rhythm is the alternation between rest and activity as well as the periodic cycles that many chemical reactions go through in the body. Circadian means "about a day," and these rhythms coincide approximately with the day-night cycle. So, within a twenty-four-hour period specific chemical reactions will reach a high and low point of activity. Functions of the body, such as digestion and body temperature, are affected by such rhythms and are more efficient at different times of the day. Therefore, the times of the day when

[26] Ibid., p. 222.

[27] S. M. Garn, "Introduction to Symposium: Nutrition in Physical Anthropology," *Yearbook of Physical Anthropology, 1975,* 19 (1976), 155.

food is eaten are important nutritionally. Different groups vary in the number of meals and snacks they eat in a day and in the times of the day they eat. Thus 2,500 calories a day may have the effect of 2,000 calories a day, if ingested over a twenty-hour period, whereas 2,000 calories a day may act like 2,500 calories if concentrated into two to four nutritionally balanced meals. The number of meals and the distribution of nutrients over a twenty-four-hour period may be significant.[28] One reason is that all eight essential amino acids must be present at the same time for the conversion of the amino acids into proteins.

Body rhythms of shorter and longer duration than a day can also influence growth and development. Some shorter rhythms include those associated with heart and respiration rates, muscle-fiber firing, and brain waves. Among the longer body rhythms are the menstrual cycle and migration patterns. These rhythms, like circadian rhythms, can influence the functioning of other bodily processes, for example, digestion and hormonal secretions. Such effects could have significant affect on ontogeny.

The effect of nongenetic disease on growth and development   It has already been pointed out that the inheritance of genetic diseases and disease caused by nutritional imbalances can affect growth and development. In a like manner, diseases caused by fungi, bacteria, viruses, and parasites can influence ontogeny. Many areas of the world are exposed to high levels and varieties of nongenetic diseases in addition to malnutrition. Where this occurs the degenerative effects are multiplied.

Some environments are "healthier" than others. For instance, the habitat of the Aborigines

of the central Australian desert has only one species of parasitic intestinal roundworm and no species of either intestinal or blood parasitic protozoans (one-celled organisms). Yet, the Pygmies of central Africa share their environment with eleven species of parasitic worms and nine species of protozoan parasites.[29] It is difficult to establish the significance of this information since so many other factors are involved in bringing about variation between Australians and Pygmies. However, when a basically homogeneous population is studied, the effects of disease can be better understood. For example, a study of preschool Guatemalan children showed that the number of days ill with diarrheal disease was associated with growth retardation.[30] Although common childhood diseases like measles and chicken pox in reasonably well-nourished children have no significant or lasting effect on growth and development,[31] it seems likely that severe and prolonged nongenetic disease may be a factor that influences ontogeny. Therefore, at least some of the variation between human groups may be the result of these disease factors.

Other factors affecting growth and development   Earlier in this chapter we discussed Bergmann's and Allen's rules. The data seem to indicate that climate exerts selective pressures upon human populations, resulting in differences in body build and limb proportions. The genetic aspects of these differences have developed by

[28] Ibid., p. 155.

[29] F. L. Dunn, "Epidemiological Factors: Health and Disease in Hunter-Gatherers," in R. B. Lee and I. DeVore (eds.), *Man the Hunter* (Chicago: Aldine, 1968), p. 227.

[30] R. Martorell, et al., "Diarrheal Disease and Growth Retardation in Preschool Guatemalan Children," *American Journal of Physical Anthropology*, 43 (1975), 341–346.

[31] Malina, op. cit.

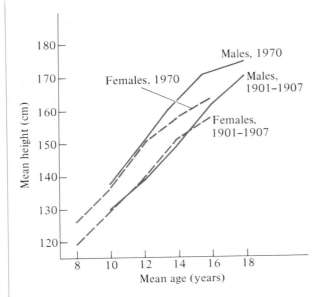

Figure 8-10 Secular trend. *This graph shows the mean height of white Australian males and females measured in 1901–1907 and 1970.*

natural selection over long periods of time. There is also evidence that variations in climate affect the growth and development of people who are genetically similar. However, it is difficult to determine whether a specific difference in ontogeny is due to climatic variation or to other factors. For example, American children reared in the tropics show a more linear physique than their counterparts raised in temperate zones.[32] Although this is suggestive of a climatic factor influencing ontogeny, many other variables could be involved.

Other factors can cause group differences in ontogeny. The amounts and types of pollutants in the water, soil, and air may have an effect (Chapter 16). Cultural modifications of the human body, to be discussed shortly, can bring about ontogenetic change. There also may be still undiscovered factors which affect growth and development.

The secular trend in growth and development
Occasionally you read a newspaper or magazine article that reports that people are getting larger each generation. Scientists have been aware of such phenomena for some time. It is true that "children are taller and heavier, age for age, and mature earlier than children of several generations ago. In addition, the ultimate height attained by adults is greater than that attained generations ago."[33] This tendency over the last hundred or so years for each succeeding generation to mature earlier and become on the average larger is referred to as the *secular trend*. The secular trend is not confined to one area of the world but has occurred throughout the world.[34] Based upon all

[32] Ibid., p. 48.

[33] Ibid., p. 49.

[34] H. V. Meredith, "Findings from Asia, Australia, Europe, and North America on Secular Change in Mean Height of Children, Youths, and Young Adults," *American Journal of Physical Anthropology*, 44 (1976), 315–326.

studies done, the secular change in human mean body height per decade in the twentieth century has been about 1.3 centimeters (0.5 inch) in late childhood (eight years old for girls and ten years old for boys), 1.9 centimeters (0.75 inch) at mid-adolescence (age twelve for females and age fourteen for males), and about 0.6 centimeters (0.25 inch) in early adulthood (Figure 8-10).[35]

Weight has also displayed a secular trend. In North America, one-, six-, and fifteen-year-old boys in 1960 weighed respectively about 1.6 kilograms (3.5 pounds), 2.7 kilograms (6 pounds), and fifteen kilograms (33 pounds) more than the same aged boys in 1880.[36] Other features of ontogeny, such as menarche, have also showed secular change.

What causes the secular trend? No one knows for sure. Some researchers believe that a general improvement in nutrition coupled with better sanitation and less tedious life styles, plus other social and environmental changes, have created the secular trend. Others are not convinced that the explanation has been found. This remains one of the more provocative questions to be answered by ontogenetic research.

Cultural Variation

People are cultural animals. They depend on learned as opposed to innate behavior and have been able to move into many environments because of their cultural inventiveness. Outer space and underwater exploration are examples of people's movement into environments for which they would not be suited without special cultural aids—space suits and diving gear. Nor would people be able to survive in an arctic environment without the cultural inventory of fire, adequate shelter, and waterproof clothing.

Different groups vary in their cultural inventories. They have different technologies, marriage patterns, religions, and economic practices as well as different concepts of nature, justice, and law, and so on almost indefinitely. Even body movements and patterns of thought are culturally tempered. Within a group, all these factors are integrated into a functional system, each element being related in some way to the others. The cultural system, in turn, is intimately related to the environment and to human biology. The relationship between the biology, environment, and culture of a specific group makes up its *ecosystem*, with cultural adaptations supplying much of the variability between different groups.

Cultural deformation of the body Different peoples have different concepts of beauty based on their cultural traditions. To achieve effects they consider to be aesthetically pleasing, many groups permanently alter the shape and structure of the body by artificial means. This alteration may also be carried out as a means of visually distinguishing individuals who have a different status, especially in groups where little clothing is worn. Various groups also give medical and religious justifications for body alterations. Examples of body alterations include circumcision, clitorodectomy, scarification, and tattooing in puberty and other ceremonies.

The face and head are especially subject to modifications. The Shipobo Indians of Peru, for instance, place a board on the soft foreheads of their infants to flatten the front of the skull. The Punan girls of Borneo slit their earlobes and put brass rings in them, which extends the lower part of the ear down to the shoulder. Other groups

[35] Ibid., pp. 321–322.

[36] H. V. Meredith, "Changes in the Stature and Body Weight of North American Boys during the Last 80 Years," in L. P. Lipsitt and C. C. Speker (eds.), *Advances in Child Development and Behavior* (New York: Academic Press, 1963), vol. 1, pp. 63–114.

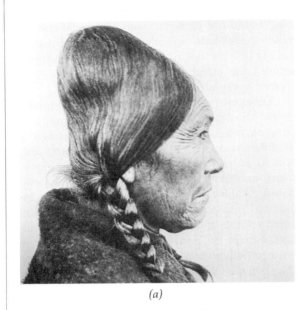

(a)

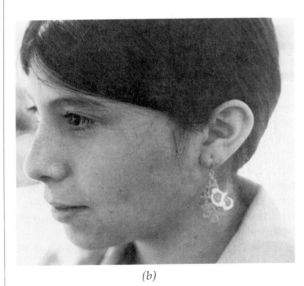

(b)

Figure 8-11 Deformation of the head. (a) *Woman from Koskimo (Kwakiutl) tribe, Vancouver Island. An example of head flattening.* (b) *American with pierced ears.*

throughout the world do other things to enhance their beauty, attain status, or become initiated. Several groups pierce the nasal septum, others slit the lips, and in the United States, many individuals pierce the earlobes, all to permit ornaments to be attached (Figure 8-11). Such practices as binding the feet, plastic surgery, silicone injections, hair and skin transplants, and many other surgical or cosmetic alterations of the body are practiced in various parts of the world. In describing the physical appearance of a group, anthropologists must know whether they are dealing with genetic and environmental characteristics or cultural modifications of some genetically determined trait.

The effect of culture on genetics Mutation rates can be increased by the use of x-ray machines and by atomic fallout, as well as a number of other cultural practices. Customs of inbreeding and outbreeding affect the gene pool. Migrations establish founding populations and lead to the reconstitution of invaded populations. Selective pressures are created by cultural practices, such as domestication, which was discussed in conjunction with sickle-cell anemia.

Milk and cultural selection With the exception of sea mammals of the Pacific basin, all mammal infants receive milk. Most northern Europeans and Americans of European ancestry have thought that milk is the solution to the world's nutritional problems. It now appears that not everyone needs milk or can even tolerate it. In fact, most adults cannot digest it. Most babies are able to break down *lactose* (milk sugar), one of the main elements of milk, because they possess sufficient quantities of *lactase*, an enzyme that accomplishes the breakdown process. However, in most populations of the world, after two to four

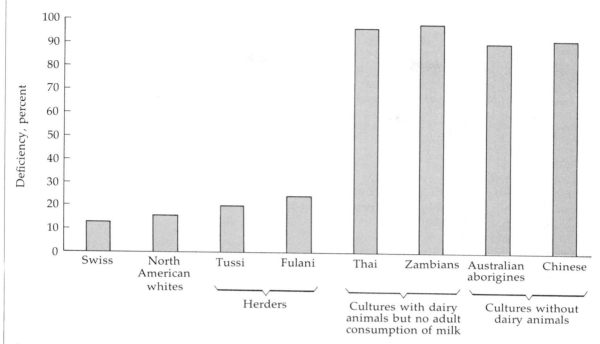

Figure 8-12 Lactase deficiency among adults in various populations.

years of age the amount of lactase in the individual becomes deficient and hence, there is little tolerance of milk (Figure 8-12). In these cases milk can cause "gastric distress, including stomach cramps, bloating, borborygmy, flatulence and diarrhea."[37]

Persons who can tolerate milk are those whose societies have a history of dairying. There is evidence that some individuals gain their tolerance because of "the mere presence of milk in the diet [which] suffices to stimulate lactase activity in the individual, perhaps by 'turning on'

genes that encode the synthesis of the enzyme."[38] However, this does not seem to be able to account for all individuals. It is likely that a mutation resulting in the ability to digest lactose was widespread in human populations. With hunters and gatherers there might not have been any selective advantage for adults to be able to drink milk. However, about 10,000 years ago dairying developed in some areas. Adults in societies using dairy products who could tolerate milk may have had a selective advantage over those who could not; in this way the mutant allele would increase

[37] Robert D. McCracken, "Lactase Deficiency: An Example of Dietary Evolution," *Current Anthropology*, 12 (1971), 481.

[38] Norman Kretchmer, "Lactose and Lactase," *Scientific American*, 227 (October 1972), 74.

in frequency. Although investigators have been careful to say that this is speculation,[39] it appears to explain the distribution of lactose-tolerant peoples among northern Europeans, pastoral tribes of Africa, and others for whom dairying has been important over a long period of time.

Summary

The four factors leading to evolutionary change are also responsible for the development of variation between populations. Mutations may result in new alleles in one population and not in another. The fact that people tend to marry within their own local community explains the development of genetically based "family resemblances" in these communities. The small population size of human groups for the vast majority of human history and the splintering off of even smaller segments of a group to form new populations indicate the significance of genetic drift and the founder principle as mechanisms for bringing about variation between groups. And finally, natural selection is also operating, for people are spread over a wide variety of environments with differing selective pressures. Human variation is often clinal in nature, that is, expressed as gradations. However, some traits appear almost exclusively within one or a few populations or show a distribution that is not clinal.

An important point to remember is that variation results from dynamic processes. There are no stable divisions of *Homo sapiens*. As social barriers are erected and broken down, patterns of gene frequencies change. As environmental conditions alter, selective pressures shift. New mutations are always occurring.

Humans differ in their anatomy, physiology,

---

[39] Ibid., 78.

ontogeny, and culture. Except for culture, which is by definition learned, all these factors can have a genetic component. In many instances the environment also plays a powerful role in creating variation. In fact, it would be more accurate to say that human morphology (form) and behavior are products of the dynamic interaction between cultural, biological, and environmental variables. Because the relationship between these factors is dynamic, the differences between human groups are in a constant state of flux. For any particular trait, two groups may become more or less similar to each other at different times, depending on the particular situations.

RACE AS A SOCIAL PROBLEM

The simplistic division of humankind into a limited number of races, such as Caucasoid, Negroid, and Mongoloid, is considered inaccurate by anthropologists today. However, the general population still uses this type of classification, and such categories play important roles in the daily relationships of people and their analyses of "racial" situations. It is important to note that these common terms refer to social stereotypes of humans, not biological classifications. In this section, widely held beliefs about human differences will be explored in the light of objective science.

Race and Intelligence

There is presently no valid or reliable way to test intelligence, although pioneer research is going on in this field at the present time. During most of the twentieth century, intelligence has been equated with an IQ score. The problem has been that such scores are highly biased.

An IQ test uses symbols developed within the particular culture that administers the test. For example, an American middle-class individual may think that the question shown in Figure 8-13 is a perfectly logical thing to ask anyone. Yet, on closer examination, it becomes obvious that making the correct choice in the time given depends on previous experience. If this question were given to Australian aborigines, for example, or others who had little or no contact with concepts of two-dimensional geometry, they would probably miss it because of their lack of experience with the things pictured.

Verbal exams are equally biased. In one of these, a battery of questions is asked, such as: Who wrote *Faust?* The answer to this, Goethe (Gounod wrote the opera), might be more familiar to children who emigrated from Germany or who have German parents. Or, it might be known to a high school student who has taken World Literature as opposed to one who has taken English Literature. Going one step further, the middle-class teenager who does not have to work after school to help support his family may spend some leisure time reading, whereas a person from a poor family who must work may have no time or motivation for it. On this same test, by the way, is the question: What is ethnology? Ethnology is a branch of anthropology, and the answer given for this entry conforms to none of the modern anthropological definitions of this term.[40] In other words, an incorrect response might be marked correct! The point is that these tests are biased toward middle-class experiences, and in some cases the answers required by the testers are imprecise. An even more serious criticism is that what the tests are testing for is not clear (Chapter 3).

In the light of the above, it is easier to see why blacks in the United States tend to score, on the average, about twelve points lower than

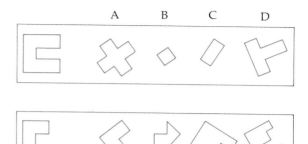

Figure 8-13   Intelligence testing. *This is an example of a test for the measurement of spatial ability. The subject is asked to mark the drawing which will make a complete square of the first figure. Speed is important. This type of test would be extremely difficult for a member of a society in which geometric shapes are not utilized to the same degree as in American society.*

whites on standard IQ tests. These tests are designed for the white, middle-class experience and embody questions that are considered important to this group of people. In fact, such commonly used tests as the Stanford-Binet were standardized by using white subjects only, "with no explanation about this on the part of the authors."[41] There is an emphasis on mathematical manipulation, a subject that middle-class children usually are exposed to early in life. Their parents often have been to college, and many of these children have had early preschool experience as well. In lower socioeconomic communities the parents often have had to go to work early in life, and few have gone to college. Mathematical logic is both less important and less attainable to them. Existing educational systems are often not valued be-

[40] M. L. Moerman, "Ethnology, the Dictionary, and IQ," *Anthropology Newsletter*, 16 (May 1975), 24.

[41] J. Ryan, "IQ, the Illusion of Objectivity," in K. Richardson and D. Spears (eds.), *Race and Intelligence* (Baltimore: Pelican, 1972), p. 53.

cause they are not seen as helpful in job preparation or in providing social mobility, and the children often do not attend preschool. Vocabulary and other dialect differences exist between social classes, ethnic groups, and regions of the country. Lowered IQ scores often reflect a lack of understanding of the question because of the way in which it is worded.

As more blacks, Mexican-Americans, and other ethnic-group members attain middle-income status, it is becoming clear that IQ scores are correlated not with skin color but with the pocketbook and style of living. When people from minority groups buy educational toys for their children, take them on trips, send them to good preschools, and provide a home atmosphere conducive to scholastic achievements, their IQ scores do not deviate significantly from those of whites in the same situation. In other words, IQ scores are a gauge of the degree of white middle-class standards and conditions present in a group.

Race and Cultural Capabilities

Some believe that the nonwhite races are incapable of developing civilizations. The term *civilization* is like the term *culture*. Everyone has a different conception of what it is. It is beyond the scope of this text to discuss the various schools of thought on the subject. Instead, let us define it in terms of the common elements in most recent definitions. Civilization usually implies technological complexities, such as a large number and variety of artifacts and a body of "scientific" knowledge. But, more important, it implies complex social arrangements, such as occupational specialization, centralized governments, religious and political hierarchies, social classes, and codes of law and conduct. In civilizations the individual becomes subject to regulations of a "state," whereas in noncivilizations the family (including extensions of the family, such as clans) is the single most important regulating agent (see Chapter 16).

Civilization arose in areas where there was a maximum of trade and movements of people. This provided for the diffusion of artifacts and ideas. Because innovation is basically a recombination of things existing in a society into new forms, as the number of elements increase in a society, the rate of innovation goes up. The cart could not have been invented if the wheel did not already exist.

Civilizations did not originate in central Africa because the terrain was not suitable for quick movements of people or goods. The rivers of this area are not navigable because of great fault systems which create waterfalls along their courses. This, plus hot, humid climate, dense vegetation, and endemic disease, not innate inferiority, hampered the early development of civilization in the Congo. Yet, in areas of Africa where these conditions do not exist, early civilizations did arise and spread into the forest areas. The empires of Ghana, Kanem-Bornu, Mali, and Songhai rose to greatness, their goods being traded throughout the world. The people involved were not members of the "white race."

Are There "Pure Races"?

The assertion that some races are "purer" than others, which Hitler used to justify the killing of millions of people, is not validated by the data. People are spread over an extremely large area, and physical variation exists in all directions without extensive discontinuities. Through gene flow and migration or invasion, all areas of the world are constantly interchanging genes. This may be an extremely slow process, as in the case of the

Australian aborigine, or a very dynamic process, as in Europe.

The "racial" picture is a changing one. Since no two people are alike through time and space, the same is true of human groups. If we move back in time 50,000 years, the people inhabiting the earth would not fall into the groupings or clinal patterns of today. Even today, certain groups, such as the Ainu and Bushman, are changing, primarily by intermarriage with other groups; and new groups are emerging. Those Americans labeled as black are in many ways dissimilar to the African populations from which the slaves came. During the days of slavery, interracial matings were common. In fact, famous white American men had children by black women. For example, some historians believe that Thomas Jefferson had several such children.[42]

It has been estimated that today dark-skinned Americans contain about 20 percent white alleles,[43] although some estimates go as high as 30 percent. This can be seen in the statistics on such traits as lactase deficiency. The blacks brought to America came from such groups as the Yoruba and Ibo peoples of West Africa. Both groups display close to 100 percent lactase deficiency, whereas American blacks are only 70 percent lactase deficient, partially because of the flow of white northern European genes into this population.[44] In addition, a limited number of American Indian genes have entered the gene pools, which are predominantly derived from Africa and Europe. On the other side of the coin, the groups in the United States generally classified as white have a certain frequency of genes within their gene pools derived from African, American Indian, Japanese, and other non-European sources. As emphasized throughout Chapters 7 and 8, human gene pools are always being reconstituted; there are no stable divisions of Homo sapiens.

Some Other Racial Myths

Some have contended that one race is "sexier" than another or has body movements different from others. These are basically or completely the results of differing cultural traditions, not different genetic makeup.

Race and sex The idea that some whites hold about blacks being sexier is an example of the "grass is greener on the other side" logic. Because of historical circumstances, such as the breaking up of the family during slavery, black women often had a succession of "husbands." Also, black men in impoverished conditions often gained self-esteem by bragging about sexual exploits. This is mistaken by racists as being a biologically stronger drive for sexual activity when it is a social and cultural adaptation to low status in American society.[45]

Also, there have been sociocultural values strongly discouraging blacks and whites as well as members of other socially defined groups from overtly expressing or showing any romantic or sexual interest in each other. This has been especially true between black men and white women. The function of this has been to maintain rigid

[42] F. H. M. Brodie, *Thomas Jefferson: An Intimate History* (New York: Norton, 1974). See especially sections on Sally Hemings and her offspring.

[43] T. E. Reed, "Caucasian Genes in American Negroes," *Science*, 165 (1969), 762–768.

[44] Kretchmer, op. cit., pp. 77–78.

[45] E. Liebow, *Tally's Corner* (Boston: Little, Brown, 1967), pp. 137–160, 208–231.

social status systems, and one consequence has been the denying of any sexual attraction between black men and white women. Any such denial can lead to fantasizing.

Race and motor and posturing habits Motor habits, habitual ways of moving, have often been said to differ among races. These are, in fact, habits based upon learned behavior. For instance, the hand movements which Italians often use when talking are motor patterns which are learned as a part of the cultural tradition of their society. The one-legged stance of the Nilote (they often support themselves with a spear or stick and stand on one leg for hours) and the characteristic walk of the traditional Japanese female in her kimono represent cultural, not biological, patterns. Habitual motor or posturing patterns can affect biology, as when some peoples habitually sit on their ankles and thereby alter the shape of the ankles. However, this is an acquired characteristic which is not genetically passed on to the next generation.

Are some groups closer to the apes? This question will be answered more fully in the chapters on paleoanthropology. Humans and the great apes had a common ancestor perhaps some 15 million years ago. This common ancestor, by the way, was not an ape in the modern sense. All people are part of the same large population, sharing the same gene pool and the same prehuman ancestry. No segment of the human population is any closer to the ape than any other.

Summary

Remember the example of the white person needing a blood transfusion and getting it from a black. Most people do not divide humankind according to blood type. For one thing, blood type is not an obvious or easily noted characteristic, such as skin color.

People are socially classified into "races" which do not correspond to the biological facts. Folk taxonomies of race are frequently linked to ideas of superiority and inferiority. They serve as justification for the socioeconomic stratification that benefits the ruling group. It is easier to subject a group to harsh and unjust treatment if you can say that they do not share a common ancestry with you and if they are portrayed as being inferior.

While anthropologists have become more realistic about the nature of human variability, the general public still uses the more simplistic division of humankind into a small number of stereotyped "races." This section has discussed the problems which concern race as a social category. Race has often been correlated with differences in intelligence, cultural capabilities, sex and motor habits, and so on. Upon examination, these differences either are not supported by the data or are the result of cultural situations.

SUGGESTED READINGS

Alland, A., Jr. *Human Diversity*. Garden City, N.Y.: Anchor/Doubleday, 1973. A modern approach to human variation that centers on the idea that "race" is a social concept which is not biologically valid.

Kuttner, R. E. (ed.). *Race and Modern Science*. New York: Social Science, 1967. Essays by biologists, anthropologists, sociologists, and physiologists.

Mead, M. (ed.). *Science and the Concept of Race*. New York: Columbia Univ. Press, 1968. Essays on race that resulted from a symposium held at the meetings of the American Association for the Advancement of Science in 1966.

Osborne, R. H. (ed.). *The Biological and Social Meaning of Race*. San Francisco: Freeman, 1971. A collection of essays that explores human variation from its biological and social perspectives, with an article on the history of racial classification.

Richardson, K., and D. Spears (eds.). *Race and Intelligence.* Baltimore: Pelican, 1972. Presents several sides of this controversial issue.

Little, M. A., and E. B. Morren, Jr. *Ecology, Energetics, and Human Variability.* Dubuque, Iowa: Brown, 1976.

Stini, W. A. *Ecology and Human Adaptation.* Dubuque, Iowa: Brown, 1975.

Underwood, J. H. *Biocultural Interactions and Human Variation.* Dubuque, Iowa: Brown, 1975.

These three books, part of the Elements of Anthropology Series, deal with various aspects of human variation.

PART FOUR
OUR CLOSEST RELATIVES

At a meeting of the British Association for the Advancement of Science in 1860, a confrontation took place between the famous biologist Thomas H. Huxley and Bishop Wilberforce. In an attempt to discredit Huxley's support of the evolutionary theory, Bishop Wilberforce asked Huxley whether it was through his grandfather or his grandmother that he claimed descent from a monkey. Huxley replied, "If . . . the question is put to me would I rather have a miserable ape for a grandfather or a man highly endowed by nature and possessing great means and influence and yet who employs those faculties and that influence for the mere purpose of introducing ridicule into a grave scientific discussion — I unhesitatingly affirm my preference for the ape." The Bishop's wife, upon hearing the gist of Huxley's remarks, exclaimed, "Descended from the apes! My dear, let us hope that it is not true, but if it is, let us pray that it will not become generally known."[1]

Of course, modern people are not descended from modern apes. However, it is now well established that modern people and modern apes have a distant common ancestor. This part will deal with the facts that can be learned about human nature and human evolution from an examination of the nature of our closest relatives — the living primates.

[1] Ashley Montagu, in Introduction to Thomas H. Huxley, *Man's Place in Nature* (Ann Arbor: Univ. of Michigan Press, 1959).

People are animals. They are part of a great diversity of living things, all of which share certain basic traits. Within the depths of the cell, biochemical mechanisms are remarkably similar wherever they are found. Yet, upon this base, life has developed into a bewildering variety of forms which we try to understand.

TAXONOMY

All human societies attempt to order their world. To understand the nature of living things and their diversity, classification into a manageable number of groups, which can then be related to one another, must be accomplished.

All peoples have systems of classification. Folk taxonomies of human races were examined in Chapter 7. The scientist, too, is involved with the development of classificatory schemes, since ordering is the first step in science. If the scientific methodology is to be used, the units of study must be precisely defined and related to one another. A system of ordering data is *classification,* and the theory of classification is known as *taxonomy.*

Linnaeus' Classification

The most significant attempt to order the living world was that of the Swedish biologist Carolus Linnaeus (1707–1778). Although fundamental differences exist in terms of theory, the system developed by Linnaeus is the basis of the system used in modern taxonomy.[1]

To Linnaeus, the basic unit of classification was the *species.* However, he considered the species a unit of creation, unchanging and distinct through time. His task was to define all the species

Chapter Nine
People's Place in Nature

---

[1] Carolus Linnaeus (Karl von Linné), *Systema Naturae,* 10th ed., published in 1758, is used as the basis for the form of the modern system of classification.

known to him (he listed 4,235 species of animals) and to classify them.

Binomial nomenclature   Linnaeus realized that a given animal was known by different names in different parts of the world and, indeed, often by several names in the same country. He decided that it would be best to invent new Latin names, since Latin was not only the language of science but also unchanging and politically neutral.

The system developed by Linnaeus is known as a *binomial nomenclature* because each species is known by two names. For example, Linnaeus gave humans the name *Homo sapiens.* The term *Homo* is the generic name, or name of the *genus* to which people belong. A genus is a group of similar species. This name is always capitalized, and no two *genera* (plural for genus) in the animal kingdom can have the same name. The second name is the specific name, which is never capitalized. It must always appear in association with the generic name. Thus, humans belong to the genus *Homo* and the species *Homo sapiens.*

Classification of species   The characteristics of each animal species, according to Linnaeus, were the result of creation and a reflection of the divine plan. Variations within the species did exist, but the reasons for this variation were not understood and thus were considered irrelevant. The taxonomist was not interested in variability, but in the basic divine blueprint, or *archetype,* of that particular species.

Linnaeus noticed that some animals were more alike than others. No one can doubt that monkeys resemble humans quite closely and that humans resemble dogs more than they do fish. Scientists of the eighteenth century believed that these relationships were a reflection of the divine blueprint and that perhaps the monkey was created to look like people for our entertainment or as some type of moral lesson. To study the similarities between animal forms and to classify them on this basis was to reveal this divine plan.

Archetypes are found on different levels. Each species is represented by an archetype. However, humans, monkeys, and apes share a number of features, and so were placed by Linnaeus into a common group, the primates. An archetype was considered to exist for the primates. It was simply a less specific blueprint than the archetype for the species. Taken one step further, humans, monkeys, dogs, horses, and others were placed into an even larger group, the mammals. Here again there is an archetype with more generalized specifications.

The Basis of Modern Taxonomy

The species is no longer thought of as a fixed unit of creation. As defined in Chapter 5, the species is a population whose members can successfully reproduce among themselves but not with members of other populations. Biologists today consider the species to be a dynamic unit, constantly changing through time and space. A species at one point in time may be quite different from its descendants millions of years later, and segments of a species may develop into subspecies and finally into separate species. Species are not defined on the basis of physical similarities per se but on the criterion of reproductive success.

The Taxonomic Hierarchy

The classification of higher units is based on similarities and evidence of evolutionary relationships. There are a series of taxonomic levels in the present system of classification. The seven basic levels are the *kingdom, phylum, class, order, family, genus,* and *species.* The species is the basic unit. The genus represents a group of species with not too remote a common ancestor, populations which in the recent past were merely subspecies of the same larger population. The next level in the taxonomic hierarchy, the family, represents a group of closely related genera, and so forth. Each higher level is defined on the basis of a greater number of generalized characteristics.

Humans belong to the species *Homo sapiens* and the genus *Homo.* Although the genus *Homo* contains only one living species, there was at least one other now extinct species, *Homo erectus.* The genus *Homo* belongs to the family Hominidae, which also includes the genera *Australopithecus* and *Ramapithecus.* The latter two exist only in the fossil record. The family Hominidae belongs to the order Primates, which includes, besides *Homo sapiens,* the monkeys, apes, and prosimians. The order Primates, in turn, belongs to the class Mammalia, also including dogs, cattle, whales, elephants, and anteaters, for example. The class Mammalia belongs to the phylum Chordata, which includes, in addition to the mammals, the birds, reptiles, amphibians, and fish. And, finally, the chordates belong to the kingdom Animalia, which includes all animal forms. These categories will be described later in this chapter and in Chapter 10.

The seven taxonomic levels, however, are not enough for a complete and satisfactory classification. The prefixes *super-, sub-,* and *infra-* can

Table 9-1   The Classification of *Homo sapiens*

KINGDOM: Animalia
  PHYLUM: Chordata
    SUBPHYLUM: Vertebrata
      CLASS: Mammalia
        SUBCLASS: Theria
          INFRACLASS: Eutheria
            ORDER: Primates
              SUBORDER: Anthropoidea
                SUPERFAMILY: Hominoidea
                  FAMILY: Hominidae
                    GENUS: *Homo*
                      SPECIES: *Homo sapiens*

also be used to create additional levels. Thus, there can be a superfamily, suborder, infraclass, and so on. Table 9-1 presents a detailed classification of the species *Homo sapiens.*

Determining Evolutionary Relationships

Just as Linnaeus recognized similarities between animals, the modern biologist realizes that some animal species are more closely related to one another than to other species. However, unlike Linnaeus, the modern biologist sees these similarities in an evolutionary light. Determination of evolutionary relationships is the key to the construction of systems of biological classification.

Homologies   Many resemblances between animals are fortuitous or the results of convergent evolution (see next page), but in the determination of evolutionary relationships the taxonomist is concerned with similarities due to inheritance from a common ancestor. Such similarities are known as *homologies.*

To understand the significance of homologous structures, we must point out that once a new structure has evolved, the probability of its evolving back into the exact thing from which it came is infinitely small. It can, however, disappear or evolve further into something else.

New structures do not simply appear from nowhere but represent a development from a pre-existing structure. Figure 9-1 shows the forelimb structures of a series of vertebrates. Externally, these forelimbs are quite different and serve different functions: manipulating objects, running, flying, and swimming. Yet, all are derived from the same basic structure found in a common ancestral form. While the whale flipper reminds one of a fish fin, upon dissection the derivation of the flipper becomes obvious: it is an elaboration of the basic structure of the forelimb of a four-footed land vertebrate.

While the forelimbs shown in Figure 9-1 are homologous, they do not serve the same function. Structures which do function in a similar manner are said to be *analogus,* but not all analogous structures are homologous. The wing of the butterfly may serve the same function as the wing of a bird, but the two are not homologous.

Homologous structures may serve such completely different functions that they are known to be homologous only from detailed anatomical study and evidence from the fossil record. For example, in people the incus, a bone of the middle ear, is derived from the same source as the jawbone of a shark. This is an example of *transformation.* This term refers to radical changes in *morphology* (anatomical structure). Yet even when morphology is transformed, evolutionary relationships can be determined through detailed anatomical, embryological, and paleontological studies.

Convergent evolution In determining the relationship of one animal to another, we cannot simply count up and tabulate the number of similarities. Figure 9-2 shows a North American wolf, a Tasmanian wolf, and a whale. If a biologist had to classify these animals on the basis of their evolutionary relationships, what criteria would be used?

A comparison of the North American and Tasmanian wolves shows a similarity in body size and shape, type of dentition, and eating habits. But there are great differences as well. The North American wolf and the whale are both placental mammals, that is, they both nourish the fetus through a placenta until birth (see page 208). The Tasmanian wolf is a marsupial, or pouched mammal, like the kangaroo. The complex method of fetal nourishment is more indicative of a close evolutionary relationship than size and shape, which are often the result of independent evolu-

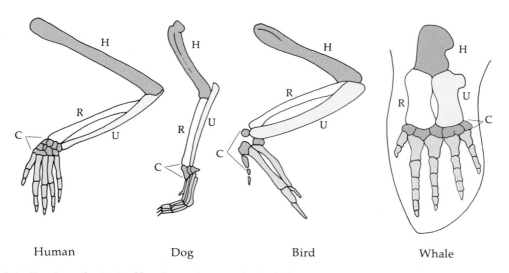

Figure 9-1 Vertebrate forelimbs. *Homologous bones in the forelimbs of four vertebrates: (H) humerus, (U) ulna, (R) radius, (C) carpals. Homologies are similarities resulting from the inheritance from a common ancestor.*

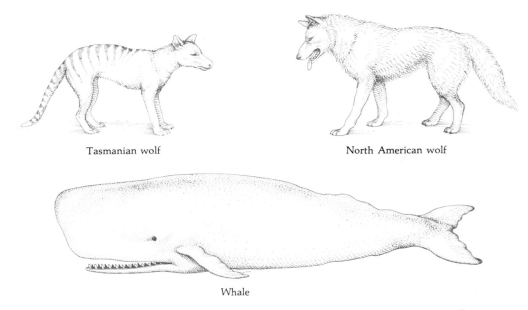

Tasmanian wolf

North American wolf

Whale

Figure 9-2 Convergent evolution. *The similarities between the Tasmanian and the North American wolf result from convergent evolution. Actually, the North American wolf is more closely related to the whale.*

tion because of similar selective pressures. The development of similar forms in divergent evolutionary lines is termed *convergent evolution.*

Parallel evolution Parallel evolution is the situation in which two evolutionary lines derived from a common ancestry develop in much the same way through the centuries, paralleling each other in their adaptations. A good example is the Old and New World monkeys. Derived from a common primate ancestor which was not a monkey more than 25 million years ago, they have independently developed a number of similar features, so that most people think of the two groups as being the same. Yet, as will be seen in the next chapter, there are a number of basic differences between them.

Reconstructing evolutionary relationships A good classification scheme depends upon accurate determination of evolutionary relationships between animals. There are two basic methods of determining these relationships. One is the fossil record, but as will be seen in Chapter 13, this record is far from complete and not easy to interpret. Another method is that of comparative studies of contemporary forms. Closely related forms show a large number of homologies and evidence of a common origin in their anatomy, ontogeny, and physiology. This will be the topic of Chapter 12.

Summary

In 1758, Linnaeus published the tenth edition of his classification of the living world known to him, the form of which is used today. All living organisms were given a binomial name, and forms were placed in groups based upon observed similarities. Species were seen as unchanging, divinely created units represented by archetypes, or divine blueprints. Similar-looking animals were placed in categories based upon increasingly general archetypes.

Modern taxonomists think of the species as a dynamic unit defined in terms of reproductive success. Recent classificatory schemes are built on the basis of evolutionary relationships between the species being classified. These evolutionary relationships are based, in part, upon the determination of homologies, structures which show a similar origin.

PEOPLE AND THE ANIMAL WORLD

The Animal Kingdom

The first step in the classification of organisms is to divide them into large, basic units known as kingdoms. It was once thought that all organisms could be placed into either the plant or the animal kingdom, but today taxonomists realize that a large number of forms, such as the bacteria and viruses, do not fit neatly into these two groupings. The differing views on the number of kingdoms do not really concern us here, since humans clearly belong to the kingdom Animalia.

Animals differ from plants in a number of ways. Animals are incapable of synthesizing food from inorganic materials but must derive their food by consuming other organisms. Most animals are highly mobile and possess contracting fibers, such as muscles. Animals are composed of a great number of specialized kinds of cells. Most animals respond quickly to changes in their environment, since they possess nerves, muscles, and special sensing organs.

The animal kingdom can be divided into a number of units known as phyla. Each phylum represents a basic body plan within the animal kingdom. The number of phyla listed varies from author to author, but the total number is usually more than eighteen. However, most familiar animals belong to the nine phyla illustrated in Figure 9-3.

The Phylum Chordata

Humans belong to the phylum Chordata. The *chordates* include such forms as the tunicates, fish, amphibians, reptiles, birds, and mammals.

The phylum Chordata shares many features with other phyla. As an example, chordates can be compared with the phylum Arthropoda. Figure 9-4 shows a diagram of a grasshopper, representing an arthropod, and *Amphioxus,* a small, ocean-dwelling form without a spine, representing a chordate. Both are *bilaterally symmetrical;* that is, they can be cut down the middle to form two halves which are basically mirror images of each other. Both have a head and a tail. The two forms also have digestive systems with openings at both ends. But there are also differences.

One of the major features of the chordates is the presence of an internal skeleton and, most important, the skeletal element known as the *notochord.* The notochord is a cartilaginous rod that runs along the back of the animal. In all chordates the notochord is present in the embryonic stage. In the grasshopper the skeleton is external, and no notochord is present.

Lying on top of the notochord (*dorsal* to the notochord) is the nerve cord. In the chordates, the nerve cord is single and hollow. In the arthropods, the nerve cord is double and solid and is located on the *ventral,* or bottom, side of the animal.

198

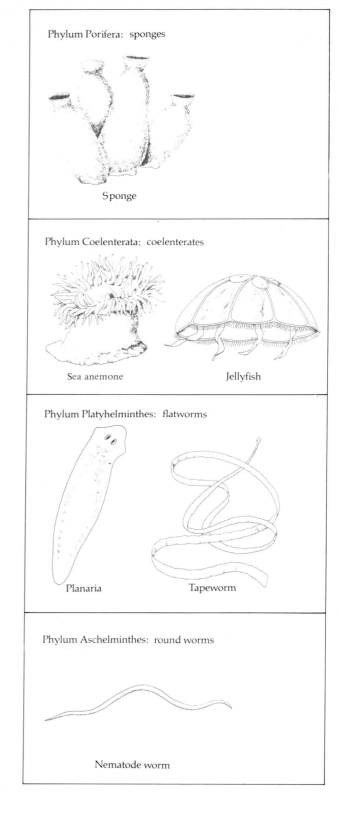

Phylum Porifera: sponges

Sponge

Phylum Coelenterata: coelenterates

Sea anemone   Jellyfish

Phylum Platyhelminthes: flatworms

Planaria   Tapeworm

Phylum Aschelminthes: round worms

Nematode worm

Figure 9-3 The animal kingdom. *The kingdom Animalia can be divided into over twenty major divisions called phyla. Each phylum represents a major body plan. The nine major phyla are pictured here.*

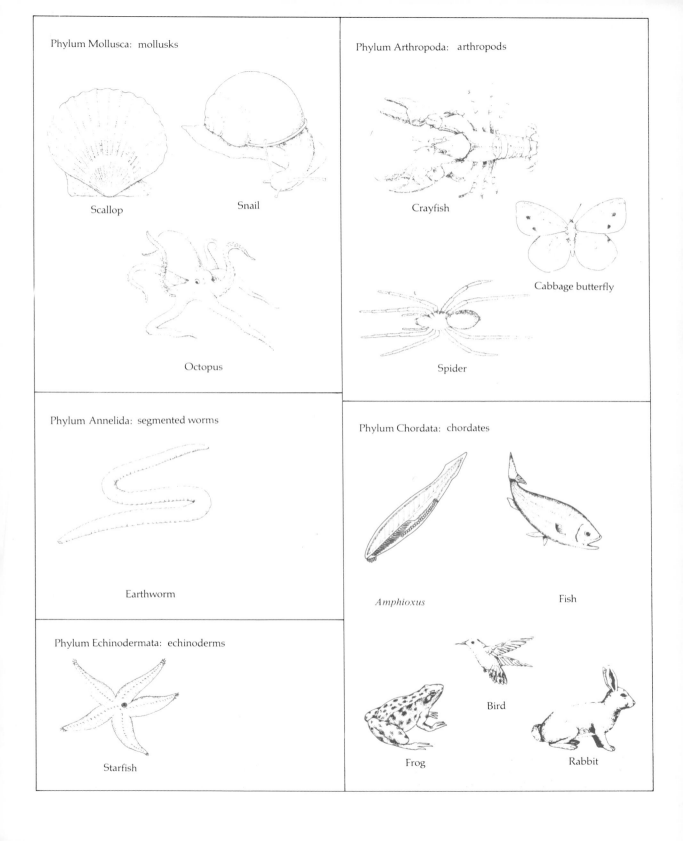

Phylum Mollusca: mollusks

Scallop

Snail

Octopus

Phylum Arthropoda: arthropods

Crayfish

Cabbage butterfly

Spider

Phylum Annelida: segmented worms

Earthworm

Phylum Chordata: chordates

Amphioxus

Fish

Bird

Frog

Rabbit

Phylum Echinodermata: echinoderms

Starfish

In addition, all chordates have *gill slits* at some time in their life history. Although gills do not really develop in people, structures which appear in the human embryo are thought by some embryologists to be *gill pouches*. Arthropods, such as the grasshoppers, supply air to the tissues through a series of tubes, while others, such as the crayfish, have feathery gills but no gill slits.

At the time when fossils became abundant in the earth's crust, most of the animal phyla were already established. According to the well-known paleontologist Alfred S. Romer, the earliest chor-

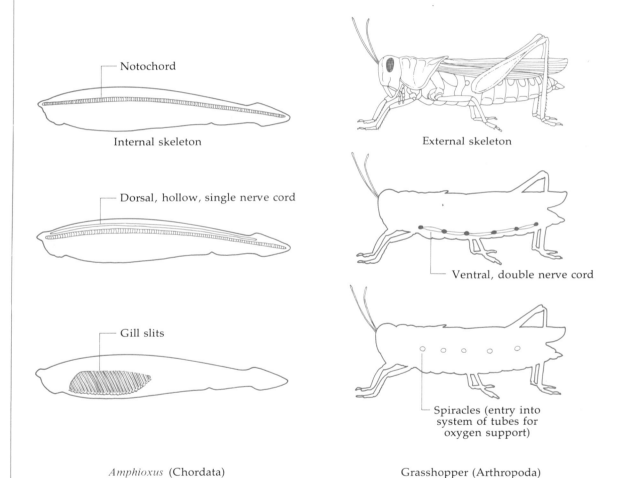

Internal skeleton — Notochord

External skeleton

Dorsal, hollow, single nerve cord

Ventral, double nerve cord

Gill slits

Spiracles (entry into system of tubes for oxygen support)

Amphioxus (Chordata)

Grasshopper (Arthropoda)

Figure 9-4   The phyla Chordata and Arthropoda. *The three major characteristics of the phylum Chordata are shown here and contrasted with those of the phylum Arthropoda.*

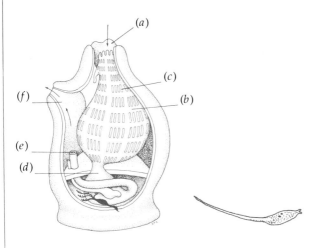

Figure 9-5   A filter feeder. *Adult tunicate with body wall cut away to show internal organs: (a) mouth, (b) wall of pharynx, which is perforated by numerous gill slits, (c) gill slit, (d) stomach, (e) anus, (f) exhalant siphon. The free-swimming larval stage is also shown (not to scale).*

dates were similar to living *pterobranchs*.[2] The pterobranch is a tiny, very rare animal. The adult, which is permanently attached to the sea floor, uses its many "arms" to bring small food particles into its mouth. From the pterobranch ancestor the *filter feeders* developed. These animals evolved gill slits to filter out the food particles from the water. Figure 9-5 shows a modern filter feeder, a *tunicate*. Currents are set up in the water by tiny, hairlike structures called *cilia*. Water enters through an opening and passes through the gill slits, which strain out the food particles. The water then passes out through a second opening. Many tunicates, commonly called *sea squirts*, are still found today.

Although the adult tunicate hardly looks like a chordate, the tunicate *larva* is a very typical chordate. While the adult is *sessile* (permanently attached), the larvae are highly mobile. These larvae contain all the diagnostic features of the chordates. After finding a suitable location, the larva undergoes a metamorphosis and becomes transformed into the adult form.

The development of free-swimming adult forms may have occurred by *paedomorphosis*. In paedomorphosis the larval form becomes capable of reproduction and an adult in its own right without undergoing metamorphosis. The modern chordate *Amphioxus* may be reminiscent of the early free-swimming chordates. From such a form biologists believe the earliest vertebrates evolved (Figure 9-6).

The Vertebrates

The early *vertebrates* were similar in many ways to *Amphioxus*, but in place of a notochord, a true *vertebral column, or spine,* had developed. Like the early chordates, the early vertebrates were filter feeders. Lacking jaws, they swam with an open mouth, forcing water into the mouth and out through the gills, filtering out the food particles. Vertebrates ultimately developed bone in place of cartilage, and many early forms were covered by bony plates. Today, the jawless vertebrates, the *agnathans*, are represented by the highly specialized *lamprey* and *hagfish*.

[2] A. S. Romer, "Major Steps in Vertebrate Evolution," *Science*, 158 (29 December 1967), 1629–1637.

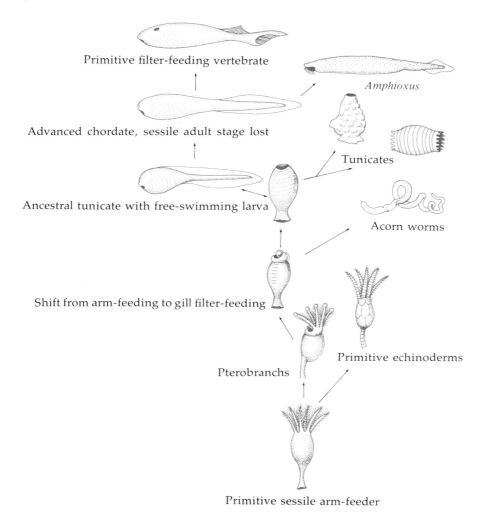

Figure 9-6   Vertebrate evolution. *A reconstruction of the evolutionary events leading to the development of the earliest vertebrates.*

The origin of jaws   One of the major events in vertebrate evolution was the development of jaws. New structures do not simply arise from nothing but are modifications of preexisting structures. The agnathans possessed skeletal elements, the *gill bars*, which supported the gill slits. In the early fish, the first gill bars enlarged to become a primitive jaw (Figure 9-7).

Jaws enabled the vertebrates to become more aggressive and to prey on each other. Filter feeding had restricted them to very small food particles. Especially in fresh water, jawed fish now

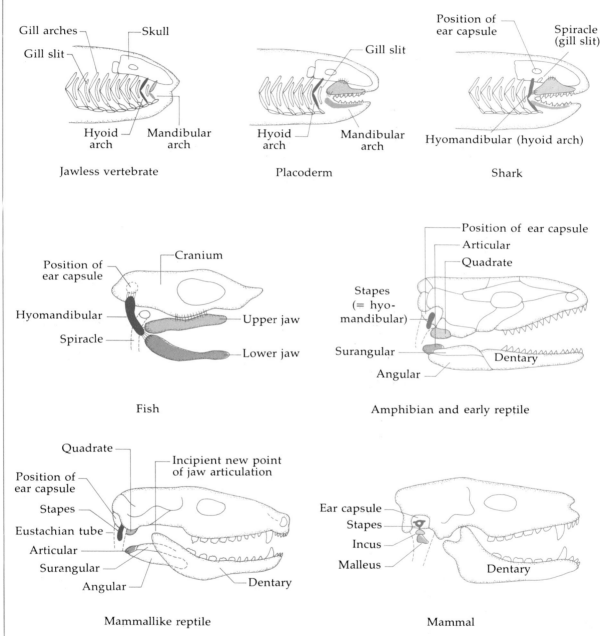

Figure 9-7 The evolution of the jaw and middle-ear bones. *Note the many examples of homologies. For example, the malleus of the mammal is homologous to the articular bone of the lower jaw in the amphibian and early reptile.*

proliferated. The fossil record shows an adaptive radiation of jawed fish some 400 million years ago. The earliest jawed fish were the *placoderms,* which became extinct. In salt water the *chondrichthyans* (cartilaginous fish), which are represented today by the *sharks* and *rays,* developed. In freshwater streams and lakes developed the bony fish, the *osteichthyans.* From this latter group the land vertebrates ultimately evolved.

The origin of land vertebrates One of the early groups of osteichthyans were the *crossopterygians,* a relatively small group, which gave rise to the land vertebrates. The crossopterygians were freshwater forms and were adapted to drought conditions, which were common at the time. Periodically lakes and streams would dry up or become small ponds of stagnant water. Crossopterygians had evolved lungs for supplementing their oxygen supply in oxygen-deficient water.

The origin of land vertebrates also depended on the evolution of legs. Unlike the fish of today, the crossopterygians had bony elements in their fins. The constant drying up of lakes and streams gave a local selective advantage to these early fish, which could move overland from one pond to the next. By 345 million years ago, the first land vertebrates, the *amphibians,* had arisen. By this time, the crossopterygians were almost extinct. Although they were thought to be completely extinct for some 75 million years, the first of several crossopterygians was caught off the east coast of South Africa in the 1930s.[3]

It must be emphasized that land vertebrates did not arise because there was opportunity on land. No fish ever lifted its head out of the water, surveyed the land, and decided that since the land was devoid of competition and food was plentiful, it would then evolve lungs and limbs.

These organs, which made life on land possible, evolved as adaptations to aid the fish in *water* under drought conditions. Yet, by chance, the animal also became preadapted to a life on land.

Amphibians and reptiles The earliest land vertebrates were the amphibians. Amphibians, however, were tied to the water. Most needed to keep their skins moist, especially to aid in breathing through the skin, and all had to lay their eggs in water. This prevented an extensive exploitation of the land environments.

A life spent totally on land was made possible by changes in the breathing apparatus, which increased the efficiency of the lungs, and by the *amniote egg* (Figure 9-8). The amniote egg, an egg with a shell, probably first developed as a method of protecting eggs in water. Once it had developed, reproduction on land became possible.

Since the embryo in an amniote egg develops within a shell, fertilization must be internal and must take place before the shell is formed. Within the egg, several membranes develop from the

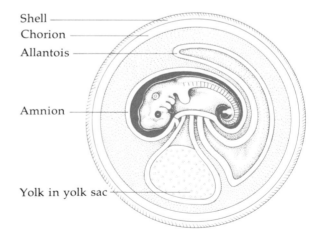

Shell
Chorion
Allantois

Amnion

Yolk in yolk sac

Figure 9-8 The amniote egg. *This type of egg could be laid on land.*

[3] K. S. Thomson, "Secrets of the Coelacanth," *Natural History,* 82 (February 1973), 58–65.

embryonic tissue. The embryo is contained within a fluid-filled *amnion,* which develops from the embryo's side. A second membrane develops from the amnion. This is the *chorion,* which lies just beneath the shell and acts as a surface for oxygen absorption. Growing out of the embryo's digestive tract are the *yolk sac,* which is filled in reptiles and birds with yolk, and the *allantois,* where waste material is deposited.

With the development of limbs, lungs, and the amniote egg, the vertebrates became independent of water. The earliest true land vertebrates were the *reptiles,* which some 300 million years ago began to spread out over the land. From this radiation developed the dinosaurs and modern reptiles, as well as the birds and mammals.

The origin of the mammals   The reptilian group from which the mammals ultimately emerged, the *synapsids,* appears very early in the reptilian radiation. These early reptiles were not reptilian in the sense of the modern snake or lizard, but from the beginning they showed marked mammalian features. Throughout the Age of Reptiles, when the dinosaurs "ruled" the earth, various members of the groups known as the *mammallike reptiles* were evolving a series of features which came to characterize the mammals.

The Mammals

A lizard sleeps through the cold desert night in an underground shelter. With the warmth of the sun, it emerges into the daylight and suns itself until it at last is ready to perform the activities of the day. Yet, when the desert sun is high, the lizard must seek shelter, for it cannot function in its fierce heat.

The activity of the reptiles is closely correlated with the environment. They are said to be *cold-blooded,* or *poikilothermal,* because their body temperature fluctuates with the temperature outside the body, not because the blood is necessarily cold. When the temperature falls, the animal becomes sluggish and may cease moving altogether. When the temperature is high, it must seek shelter or die. Even its eating habits are characterized by limited spurts of activity. Its food, which it swallows whole, must then rest in its digestive system while it is slowly broken down by the digestive juices.

Perhaps the most significant trait which separates the mammals from the reptiles and most other animals is the mammal's ability to maintain a constant level of activity in the face of fluctuations in the external environment. As a result, mammals are able to function at night or in a wide variety of environments, from the desert to the arctic. Many of the features which are considered characteristic of mammals are related to this basic trait.

Homoiothermy   Mammals are said to be *warm-blooded,* or *homoiothermal.* Homoiothermy refers to the body's ability to maintain a relatively constant temperature while the temperature outside the body fluctuates (Figure 9-9).[4] This is more of a problem for land animals than for aquatic forms, whose environment is characterized by a relatively constant temperature. The various biochemical reactions of the body are most efficient at certain temperatures. Maintenance of a constant body temperature permits both greater biochemical efficiency and a constant level of activity during the waking hours.

Maintenance of a constant body temperature involves a complex of interrelated features, such as the development of regulating mechanisms in the brain, fur, or hair which forms a layer of insulation, and sweat glands to permit cooling of the body if necessary. In addition, a reliable and fairly large intake of food is required. The snake eats perhaps once every other week. It simply swal-

[4] Birds are also homoiothermal.

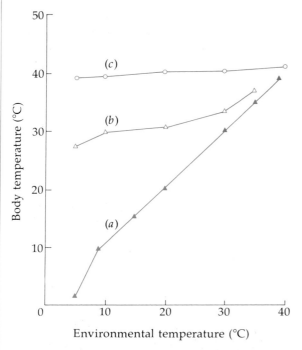

Figure 9-9 Homoiothermy. *Relationship between body temperature and environmental temperature in a reptile and mammals; (a) a lizard* (Cyclodus), *(b) an egg-laying mammal* (echidna), *and (c) a placental mammal* (cat).

lows its food whole and permits the animal in its stomach to dissolve slowly in the digestive juices, bone and fur being excreted. The mammals do not swallow an animal whole.

Mammals are characterized by *heterodont dentition,* the regional differentiation of teeth. Unlike the reptile, whose teeth are all simple, pointed structures, mammals have evolved a number of different types of teeth which serve the different functions of tearing, piercing, and chewing (Figure 9-10).

The lower teeth of the mammals are embedded in a single bone, the *mandible,* a solid structure able to take the stresses of chewing. The

reptilian lower jaw is composed of several bones (Figure 9-10). Mammals have only two sets of teeth, the baby, or milk, teeth and the permanent teeth. Reptilian teeth are constantly replaced. The saliva of mammals includes the digestive enzyme *ptyalin,* which begins the digestive pro-

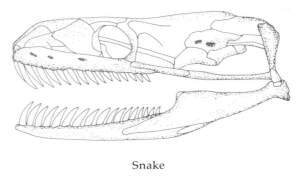

Snake

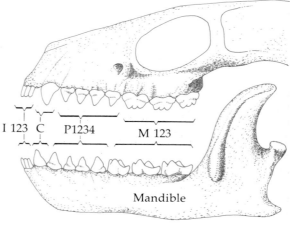

Mammal

Figure 9-10 Mammalian jaws and teeth. *The jaws and teeth of a mammal are compared to those of a reptile (a snake). The mammal pictured is a hypothetical generalized placental mammal. I: incisors, C: canines, P: premolars, M: molars.*

cess in the mouth. Thus, the mammalian body is assured of a constant flow of well-chewed and partially digested food needed to maintain the constant body temperature characteristic of the group.[5]

Many other anatomical features in mammals aid in adapting to terrestrial environments. These include the *diaphragm*, which ensures a more efficient intake of air; *the hard palate*, which separates the nasal from the oral cavity, permitting the animal to breathe and chew at the same time; and the *four-chambered heart*, which allows efficient separation of oxygenated from deoxygenated blood.

Mammalian reproduction The amniote egg, which could be laid on land, developed with the reptiles. In order to maintain their populations, reptiles laid eggs in great number; however, the eggs were given minimal care.

One of the important aspects of mammalian reproduction is that the offspring develop inside the mother and are not exposed as eggs to the environment. This ensures a higher survival rate for the fetus and means that fewer young need be produced to maintain the population.

As important as anatomical and physiological changes are behavioral changes. Mammalian infants do not have to obtain their own food but take milk from their mother's *mammary glands*. This results in a sure supply of food, permitting a higher survival rate. Equally important is the care given the young by the mother and often by the father. With some mammals, adults other than the parents can be involved in infant care. Humans, of course, would be an example. Unlike the reptilian young, who often never see their parents, mammalian young develop a close bond with their mother. This bond not only functions to protect the offspring but makes the transmission of learned behavioral patterns possible.

Mammalian behavior Adaptation is often thought of exclusively in terms of anatomy and physiology. But animals also adapt to their niches in terms of behavior. The complex behavioral patterns of the social insects, such as the termites, serve as a good example (see Chapter 1). Mammals also adapt to their niches to a large extent by behavior. In contrast to insect behavior, which is basically innate, much of mammalian behavior is learned. Behavioral adaptations can thereby change rapidly with changing environmental pressures, even within a single generation. Important in creating the potential for behavioral adaptation are improvements in the nervous system, including elaboration of the brain.

Classification of the mammals The phylum Chordata includes the subphylum Vertebrata, which accounts for most of the animals within the phylum. There are seven living classes of vertebrates: the jawless vertebrates, the sharks and rays, the bony fish, the amphibians, the reptiles, the birds, and the mammals. The mammals make up the class Mammalia.

The class Mammalia is divided into three groups corresponding to the three major types of mammals. First, the class is divided into two subclasses. The subclass Prototheria consists of the egg-laying mammals, while all others belong to the subclass Theria.

The *prototherian* mammals, also known as *monotremes*, include only two living forms, the *platypus* and the *echidna* (Figure 9-11). These animals lay eggs and also produce milk. In most ways they possess both reptilian and mammalian characteristics, and some taxonomists consider them to be mammallike reptiles. But the modern

---

[5] The constant body temperature of different species of mammals varies somewhat. For humans it averages about 37.4°C (98.6°F), for a mouse 36.5°C (97.7°F), and for a horse 37.7°C (99.8°F).

Figure 9-11   The echidna
*(Tachyglossus aculeatus). An
example of a prototherian mammal.*

Table 9-2   Classification of the Mammals with Examples

CLASS: Mammalia
  SUBCLASS: Prototheria
    ORDER: Monotremata (platypuses, echidnas)
  SUBCLASS: Theria
   INFRACLASS: Metatheria
    ORDER: Marsupialia (kangaroos, opossums)
   INFRACLASS: Eutheria
    ORDER: Insectivora (shrews, hedgehogs, moles)
    ORDER: Chiroptera (bats)
    ORDER: Lagomorpha (rabbits)
    ORDER: Rodentia (mice, beavers, squirrels)
    ORDER: Cetacea (whales, porpoises)
    ORDER: Carnivora (bears, lions, dogs, seals)
    ORDER: Proboscida (elephants)
    ORDER: Perissodactyla (horses, tapirs, rhinoceroses)
    ORDER: Artiodactyla (cattle, deer, pigs, hippopotamuses)
    ORDER: Edentata (sloths, armadillos)
    ORDER: Pholidota (pangolins)
    ORDER: Tubulidentata (aardvarks)
    ORDER: Hyracoidea (hyraxes)
    ORDER: Sirenia (sea cows)
    ORDER: Dermoptera (flying lemurs)
    ORDER: Primates (lemurs, tarsiers, monkeys, apes, humans)

mammals did not evolve from prototherianlike ancestors. Modern mammals represent a branch of the mammalian class which evolved a number of distinctive traits after the monotremes had branched off the mammalian evolutionary line.

The *therian* mammals can be divided into two infraclasses. The infraclass Metatheria consists of the *marsupials,* or pouched mammals (Figure 9-12). Most of them live in Australia, although the opossums are a well-known North American group. They differ from other mammals in many ways but most importantly in the method of reproduction. Metatherian offspring are born while they are still fetuses. The fetus then crawls into the mother's pouch, where development is completed.

The remainder of the mammals, and by far the larger number, belong to the infraclass Eutheria. These are the *placental mammals,* whose young remain inside the mother, nourished by the placenta, until an advanced state of development. The *placenta* is an organ which develops from fetal membranes. It penetrates the lining of the uterus, where the placental blood vessels come into close contact with the mother's blood. Oxygen, nutrients, and other substances pass from the mother's bloodstream into that of the fetus. Waste material passes in the opposite direction.

Today there are sixteen orders of placental mammals (see Table 9-2). Humans belong to the order Primates, which is the subject of the next three chapters.

Summary

People belong to the animal kingdom. This large group of organisms is divided into several phyla, representing basic body plans. The phylum Chordata, which encompasses all vertebrates, including humans, is characterized by a notochord, dorsal hollow nerve cord, and gills. Biologists have hypothesized that, by the processes of paedomorphosis, the larva of an early chordate form developed into the earliest vertebrates. In

Figure 9-12   Matchie's tree kangaroo *(Dendrolagus matschiei)*. *An example of a metatherian mammal, or marsupial.*

the vertebrates, the notochord is replaced by a vertebral column.

One group of early vertebrates, the crossopterygians, gave rise, through the refinement of lungs and limbs, to the first land vertebrates, the amphibians. With the evolution of the amniote egg, reproduction was no longer tied to the water. This evolutionary development resulted in the great reptilian radiation, which included a line of mammallike reptiles; these, through a long evolutionary history, ultimately gave rise to mammals.

The mammals comprise a class of chordates. They are characterized by homoiothermy, heterodont dentition, mammary glands, and complex patterns of behavior involving learned behavioral patterns. The mammals have radiated into a large number of orders. Included in one of these orders, the order Primates, are people.

SUGGESTED READINGS

Mayr, E. *Principles of Systematic Zoology,* New York: McGraw-Hill, 1969.

Simpson, G. G. *Principles of Animal Taxonomy,* New York: Columbia Univ. Press, 1961.

These two books might be considered the major sources of the basic principles of taxonomy. They contain discussions of the various problems of animal classification.

Romer, A. S. *The Vertebrate Story,* 4th ed. Chicago: Univ. of Chicago Press, 1959.

Romer, A. S. *The Vertebrate Body,* 3d ed. Philadelphia: Saunders, 1962.

Excellent discussions of vertebrate and mammalian evolution.

Mammals are an extremely varied group. They occupy ecological niches in the water, on the ground, beneath the ground (groundhogs, for example), in the air (bats), and in trees. Mammals include the largest animal ever to live (the blue whale), along with many extremely small forms, such as the shrews. Here we will be concerned with the order Primates of the class Mammalia.

Humans are primates and share features with the other members of the order. Comparisons of people with other primates aid in the investigation of the form, structure, and function of human biology and behavior. Humans and the other living primates evolved from an early common ancestor. Since some of the features of this early form have been retained in the various primate species, careful comparative studies of behavior, anatomy, ontogeny, and physiology permit anthropologists to infer some of the steps in the evolution of *Homo sapiens*.

Chapter Ten
The Living Primates

THE PRIMATE ORDER

There exist today sixteen orders of placental mammals. Mammals, in their adaptive radiation, have come to occupy a great variety of niches. All but one order can be defined on the basis of some specific adaptation. The members of the order Chiroptera, the bats, are characterized by their ability to fly, members of the order Carnivora by their meat-eating habits. Only when we come to the order Primates do serious problems of definition arise.

Primate Adaptations

The definition of the order Primates is difficult, since the primates are not characterized by any one distinctive trait. This was noted by the British anatomist Sir Wilfred LeGros Clark, who pointed out that, unlike other mammalian orders, which are defined in terms of some major adaptation, the primates are characterized by their *adaptability*. They are noted for their generalized anatomy and their variability and flexibility in locomotion and behavior.[1]

To understand the primates, we must first realize that the adaptability characteristic of this order is actually a response to the *arboreal environment*. Almost all primates live in trees. Even the more terrestrial forms, such as the baboons, readily take to the trees. People may be the only exception, but even with them the potential to climb is well developed. In fact, children from many cultures enjoy playing in trees.

The arboreal environment differs significantly from the terrestrial one. Trees provide a three-dimensional environment with holes, and in moving through the trees the animal is moving not only forward and backward, left and right, but also up and down. The arboreal environment also is unpredictable, since when an animal leaps to a branch it may break. Adolph Schultz noted that in a study of one of the apes, the gibbon, 31 percent of a set of 260 adult skeletons showed at least one healed fracture.[2]

Characteristics of the Primates

The major difficulty in discussing primate characteristics is the variability of the group. In other words, not all primates exhibit the same complex of features. Clark speaks of primate *trends* which are developed to a greater or lesser degree in the various primate species.[3]

Because some primates show fewer char-

[1] W. E. LeGros Clark, *The Antecedents of Man*, 3d ed. (Chicago: Quadrangle Books, 1971), pp. 41–43.

[2] A. H. Schultz, *The Life of Primates* (New York: Universe Books, 1969), p. 194.

[3] Clark, op. cit.

acteristics of the "ideal" primate complex than others, it is possible to rank-order the living species according to how closely they conform to the ideal. Such a sequence might list in ascending order the tree shrew, lemur, tarsier, New World monkey, Old World monkey, chimpanzee, and *Homo sapiens*. This implies an evolutionary sequence and, to some, the *incorrect* idea that humans have evolved directly from this sequence of modern forms (Figure 10-1). Of course, a species cannot be descended from its contemporary. Some modern forms may possess specific characteristics which were present in populations ancestral to the hominids. These forms may share a common ancestry with humans. But it must also be remembered that the modern nonhuman primates are end products of long evolutionary sequences, just as people are; thus, they cannot be human ancestors. These trends do indicate the relative time distance from a common ancestor. So, for instance, chimpanzees and people have a more recent common ancestor than monkeys and people, but monkeys and humans have a more recent common ancestor than tarsiers and people, and so on.

Movement in the trees Moving about through the trees, primates have retained a rather generalized anatomy for locomotion. This point will be discussed in considerable detail in Chapter 12, but here it should be noted that most mammalian groups are characterized by a number of specializations with respect to movement.

The forelimb structure of the primates corresponds well to the generalized limb structure of early placental ancestors (see Figure 12-3). Note the presence of the *clavicle* (collarbone), the two separate bones in the lower arm, and the five fingers (*pentadactylism*). This arrangement permits a great degree of flexibility in the shoulder, forearm, and hand, an asset when moving through the trees.

The horse represents a more specialized

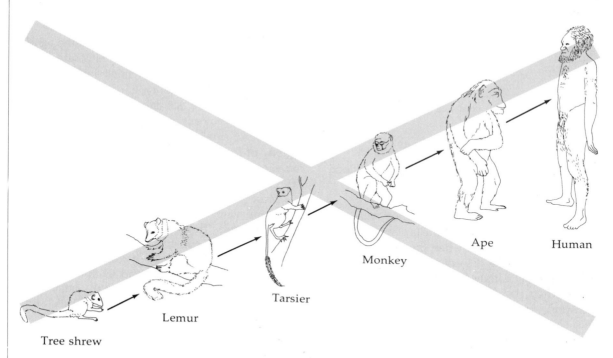

Figure 10-1 Evolutionary trends. *Since members of the order Primates show to differing degrees the development of the primate "evolutionary trends," the living primates often are arranged in a hierarchical manner as shown, implying that humans have evolved from these modern forms. This is an incorrect idea. In addition, the tree shrew, once classified as a primate, is now classified by most anthropologists as an insectivore.*

mammal. It has been adapted for high-speed running over hard ground, a means of locomotion which results in a great amount of jarring. But this manner of movement does not necessitate any real degree of flexibility in the forelimb. The horse does not need to pick up objects or to raise its forelimb over its head. As a result, many elements of the skeleton have been lost. The clavicle has disappeared, along with flexibility in the shoulder. The two bones of the lower arm have fused, and the five fingers have been reduced to one (see Figure 12-3). The primates have maintained the more flexible skeleton, and with it a wide range of locomotor patterns.

Movement in arboreal niches is facilitated by the ability to grasp. A monkey walking along a branch is grasping that branch. This requires mobile digits, along with a divergent and in many forms an opposable thumb. This mobility also has become important in the primate's ability to manipulate objects.

A squirrel scampers up a tree by digging its claws into the bark. As the primate moves up a tree, it is grasping the trunk. In most primates the claw has evolved into the *nail* (Figure 10-2). At the same time, the tips of the fingers in primates have *tactile pads*, which not only act as friction pads in grasping but also convey information

Claw   Nail

Figure 10-2   Nail versus claw. *The nail is homologous to the outer layer of the claw.*

about the environment by means of a refined sense of touch.

The senses   Among terrestrial mammals, the *olfactory* sense, or sense of smell, plays a crucial role. Hunters realize that when they approach an animal like a gazelle, the animal is not apt to see them, especially if they freeze when it is looking up. But they had better stalk that animal from downwind.

Smells are relatively unimportant in the trees. Most odors tend to hug the ground, and the wind blowing through the trees would eliminate their usefulness. Also, the sense of smell does not give an arboreal animal the type of information it needs, such as the exact direction and distance of one branch from another. Thus, in the primates the sense of smell has diminished. The olfactory regions of the brain have been reduced, and the muzzle or snout has become smaller (Figure 10-3).

Most mammals see only a two-dimensional black and white field and depend more on the olfactory sense. Through sight, these animals are aware of movement, but they cannot pick out and judge detail, especially of stationary objects. Most primates see in color and in three dimensions. Color vision helps distinguish detail, for close colors may blend together in black and

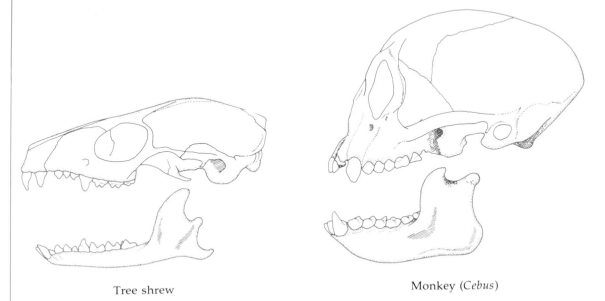

Tree shrew   Monkey (*Cebus*)

Figure 10-3   The primate face. *The facial skeleton of a monkey compared with that of a tree shrew. Note the reduction of the olfactory apparatus and the relatively flat facial skeleton of the monkey.*

white; and stationary objects stand out in a three-dimensional field. Such vision developed as a response to the selective pressures of the arboreal environment, where precise information of direction and distance is crucial.

Once developed, this vision provided the primates with more detailed information about the nature of their environment than any other mammalian form. A great deal of what we consider primate intelligence may be due to the primate's great awareness of the environment.

The eye itself is enlarged, and changes have occurred within its structure. The *retina* contains the cells which are sensitive to light. These cells are of two types, *rods* and *cones*. The cones, while not as sensitive to intensity of light as the rods, sense color and possess a higher degree of discrimination. In the central area of the retina is the *macula,* an area consisting of cones only, and within this macula is the *fovea,* a depression which contains a single layer of cones with no overlapping blood vessels. This is the area of greatest visual acuity, permitting fine visual discrimination in the primate eye (Figure 10-4).

Most primate eyes are encased in bony eye sockets, a feature not found in other mammalian skulls. The eye socket is not found in most of the lower primates, although these forms do have a bony ring which completely encircles the eye (Figure 10-5).

The eyes have rotated to the front of the face, permitting three-dimensional, *stereoscopic vision.* This type of vision also is made possible by a realignment of the optic nerves, as shown in Figure 10-6.

Primates are highly social animals, and vision plays a key role in primate communication (see Chapter 11). Unlike dogs, who smell one another on meeting, primates communicate largely through visual stimuli, although vocalizations also play important roles. For example, body postures and facial expressions are frequently used. Facial expression is made possible in many primates by

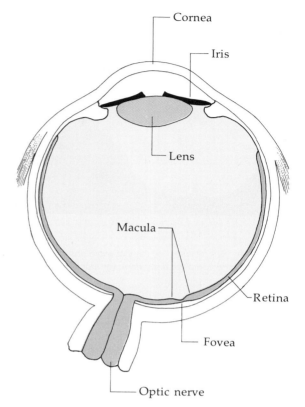

Figure 10-4   The primate eye. *A diagrammatic cross section of the human eye.*

the differentiation of the muscles of the face, which in other mammals exist as a relatively undifferentiated muscle sheet. Also, unlike other mammals, many primates have an upper lip which is not attached to the upper gum. This permits a wide range of gestures, including the kiss.

Not all anthropologists agree with the hypothesis that the characteristic features of primates developed primarily as an adaptation to locomotion in the trees. Matt Cartmill notes the excellent arboreal abilities of the arboreal rodents

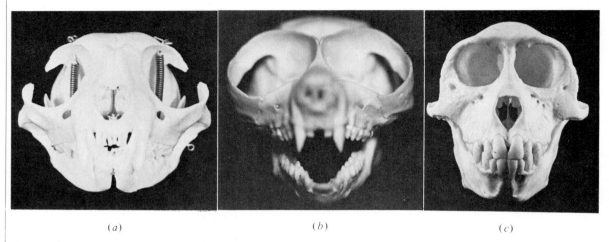

Figure 10-5   The eye socket. (a) *Cat (note absence of eye socket); (b) slender loris (while eye socket is absent, the eye is surrounded by a complete bony ring); (c) monkey (shows eye socket) (not to same scale).*

and marsupials, many of which lack the primate-like features for arborealism. He further notes that some primatelike specializations, especially the grasping feet and hands, are found in other groups such as some arboreal marsupials. These animals are insectivorous, as are many of the prosimians or "lower primates." Since the pri-

mate order probably evolved from the Insec-tivora, Cartmill postulates that the differentiation of the order Primates was based primarily upon the development of arboreal insect predation and that the basic primate features are an adaptation to this way of life. Thus the grasping foot enables the animal to catch an insect with its hands while

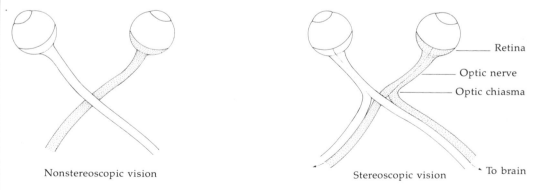

Figure 10-6   Stereoscopic vision. *With stereoscopic vision optic fibers from the same side of each eye go to the same side of the brain.*

holding on to the branch with its feet, and the development of stereoscopic vision would enable the animal to spot small insects moving through the leaves and branches.[4]

Other primate features Dentition will be discussed in detail in Chapter 12, but it should be mentioned here that primate dentition is characterized by a decrease in the number of teeth compared with the ancestral placental mammal. This ancestral form had forty-four teeth, but most higher primates, including humans, have only thirty-two. More important is the fact that primate teeth are relatively simple in structure, especially when compared with such forms as those of the grazing animals or carnivores.

Primates have evolved a more efficient form of reproduction. The primate placenta differs from that of the other placental mammals. In most mammals the blood vessels of the fetus and those of the mother come into close contact, but nutrients and other substances must pass through two vessel walls from the maternal to the fetal bloodstream. In the *hemochorial placenta*, found in most primates, the fetal blood vessels penetrate the lining of the uterus. The uterus undergoes changes to become a spongy, blood-filled mass. As a result, the fetal blood vessels are surrounded by the maternal blood, and materials pass through only a single vessel wall in moving from one blood system to the other (Figure 10-7).

Primates are also known for their great intelligence, related in part to their great awareness of the environment plus the ability to manipulate this environment. Nonhuman primates normally do exceptionally well on various psychological tests. The primate brain is large in relation to the size of the body, and those areas which control complex behavioral patterns are well developed. This permits a great degree of behavioral flexibility.

Much primate adaptability is the result of be-

[4] M. Cartmill, "Pads and Claws in Arboreal Locomotion," in F. A. Jenkins, Jr. (ed.), *Primate Locomotion* (New York: Academic, 1974), pp. 85–115; and M. Cartmill, "Rethinking Primate Origins," *Science* 184 (26 April 1974), 436–443.

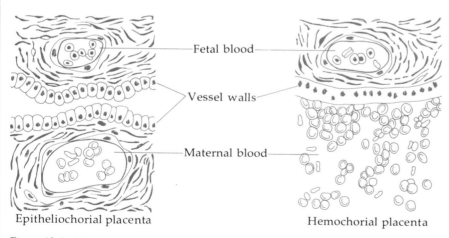

Epitheliochorial placenta   Hemochorial placenta

Figure 10-7 Hemochorial placenta. *The hemochorial placenta, as found in humans, compared with the epitheliochorial placenta, as found in lemurs.*

havioral adaptations which are learned. Most primates live in large social units and have a long childhood period, factors which facilitate learning. The social behavior of the primates is the topic of the next chapter.

Summary

The order Primates consists of forms characterized by their lack of specialization and their adaptability. This adaptability is due in large part to the nature of the arboreal environment. Primate characteristics have to be thought of more in terms of evolutionary trends than in terms of specializations. Among the important features of primates in general are the presence of a generalized limb structure and five fingers per limb; locomotor flexibility; nails and tactile pads on digits; reduction of the sense of smell and elaboration of the sense of vision, with stereoscopic color vision; the hemochorial placenta; great intelligence; and a large brain.

THE LIVING PRIMATES

This section surveys the various species of living primates. The survey is quite generalized, and many points are discussed in greater detail in Chapters 11 and 12.

Primate Taxonomy

Over 200 species of primates have been described. These species are classified into eleven families, as shown in Table 10-1. Primate taxonomy, like taxonomy generally, is open to considerable debate. A species has been defined in terms of reproductive success, yet reproductive data are seldom available. In addition, since the classification of species into higher categories is not based upon easily definable criteria which can be mechanically applied, there has been considerable argument over the exact details of the classification of the order. Our purpose here is not to enter into these debates but simply to recognize their existence. The classification given in Table 10-1 is not the only one possible, and specialists will argue many points. In the following survey of the living primates, the unit of discussion is the family.

The Prosimians

The primates can be divided into two major divisions, or suborders. One suborder is the Prosimii, the lower primates. These forms usually lack sev-

Table 10-1   Classification of the Living Primates

ORDER: Primates
  SUBORDER: Prosimii
    INFRAORDER: Lemuriformes
      SUPERFAMILY: Lemuroidea
        FAMILY: Lemuridae (lemurs)
        FAMILY: Indriidae (indris, avahis, sifakas)
      SUPERFAMILY: Daubentonioidea
        FAMILY: Daubentoniidae (aye-ayes)
    INFRAORDER: Lorisiformes
      FAMILY: Lorisidae (lorises, galagos)
    INFRAORDER: Tarsiiformes
      FAMILY: Tarsiidae (tarsiers)
  SUBORDER: Anthropoidea
    SUPERFAMILY: Ceboidea
      FAMILY: Callithricidae (marmosets, tamarins)
      FAMILY: Cebidae (squirrel, spider, howler, capuchin monkeys)
    SUPERFAMILY: Cercopithecoidea
      FAMILY: Cercopithecidae (guenons, mangabeys, baboons, macaques, langurs)
    SUPERFAMILY: Hominoidea
      FAMILY: Hylobatidae (gibbons, siamangs)
      FAMILY: Pongidae (orangutans, chimpanzees, gorillas)
      FAMILY: Hominidae (humans)

After J. R. Napier and P. H. Napier, *A Handbook of the Living Primates* (New York: Academic, 1967), pp. 343–354.

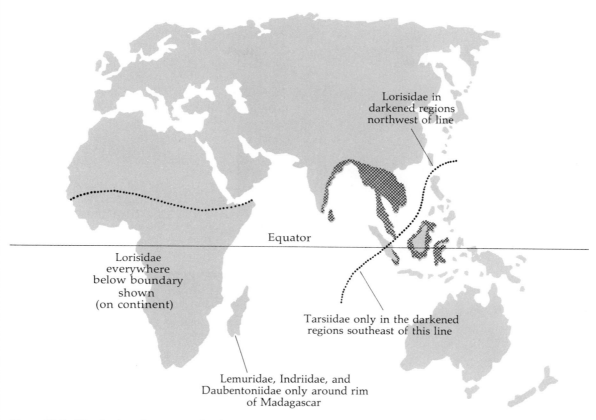

Figure 10-8 Distribution of prosimian families.

eral features which have been listed as characteristic of the order. While it is easy to think of the prosimians as ancestral forms, it must be kept in mind that they are modern and highly specialized. Figure 10-8 shows the distribution of the prosimian families.

The tree shrews While we have chosen not to include the family Tupaiidae, the tree shrews, in the classification of the primates, the exact status of this group has been the subject of much debate

and some primatologists consider the form to be a primate. They are most unprimate in appearance (Figure 10-9a), as suggested by the family name, which is derived from a Malayan word meaning "squirrel."

Primatologists who include the tree shrews in the Primate order point out the relatively well-developed eye and visual area of the brain. Although this form does not demonstrate three-dimensional vision, vision is acute. Clark and others also have pointed to the many similarities

(a)

Figure 10-9 *(a)* Tree shrew, *Tupaia glis;*
(b) ring-tailed lemur, *Lemur catta.*

(b)

between the tree shrews and members of the family Lemuridae, to be described shortly.[5] But recent detailed studies of the anatomy, physiology, and behavior of this animal place it more clearly into the order Insectivora.[6]

Nevertheless, discussion of the tree shrew is important to anthropology. First, it serves to remind us that neat taxonomic categories do not exist in nature and that classification schemes are attempts to impose order on an extremely complex and dynamic system. Second, the tree shrew serves to give us some general idea of what the earliest primate may have been like. However, this is not to suggest that the primates evolved from tree shrews, since modern tree shrews are highly evolved contemporary forms.

The Madagascar prosimians Three closely related families of primates, the Lemuridae, Indriidae, and Daubentoniidae, live on the island of Madagascar (Malagasy Republic) off the southeast coast of Africa. It is believed that the early ancestors of these forms found their way to the island, where, isolated from the more advanced monkeys, they underwent an adaptive radiation into a variety of forms.

The family Lemuridae includes the *lemurs* (Figure 10-9*b*). While most are nocturnal and solitary, the *ring-tailed lemur*, perhaps the best known, is *diurnal* and lives in large social units.[7] The eyes of the lemur are located on the front of the head, but it is uncertain whether they see in three dimensions. The ring-tailed lemur's sense of smell is well developed. When disturbed, it will often rub its anal region against a tree, a behavior known as *scent marking* and related to territoriality. The ring-tailed lemur male possesses a specialized gland on his forearm which is used in scent marking. The lemurs also possess a *dental comb* and nails on all digits except the second toe, where a claw for grooming has been retained. Their diet consists primarily of fruits, with some leaves and flowers.

The family Indriidae includes the *indri, avahi,* and *sifaka*. These are the most monkeylike of all the prosimians and in many ways represent a case of parallel evolution. They are basically arboreal, and with their long legs they are able to leap great distances.

The family Daubentoniidae consists of the *aye-aye*. The aye-aye, which is today almost extinct, once was considered to be a rodent but its primate status is no longer disputed. Its main distinguishing feature is the two large, chisellike teeth in the front of the jaws. The hand is characterized by a long, thin middle finger. The aye-aye is nocturnal and during the night uses its front teeth to tear open the outer layers of bamboo or the bark of trees to get at the insects inside, which it then plucks out with the elongated finger.

The family Lorisidae The *lorises* are small animals which have survived competition with the monkeys in Asia and Africa because of their nocturnal habits. The family can be divided into two subfamilies. The subfamily Lorisinae contains forms which walk along branches very slowly and deliberately, hand over hand. They have a very

[5] Clark, op. cit.

[6] L. Van Valen, "Tree Shrews, Primates, and Fossils," *Evolution,* 19 (1965), 147; C. B. G. Campbell, "The Relationships of the Tree Shrews: The Evidence of the Nervous System," *Evolution,* 20 (1966), 276–281; W. P. Luckett, "Evidence for the Phylogenetic Relationships of Tree Shrews (Family Tupaiidae) Based on the Placenta and Foetal Membranes," *Journal of Reproduction and Fertility,* Supplement 6 (1969), 419–433; and R. D. Martin, "Reproduction and Ontogeny in Tree Shrews (*Tupaia belangeri*) with Reference to Their General Behaviour and Taxonomic Relationships," *Zeitschrift für Tierpsychologie,* 25 (1968), 409–495, 505–532.

[7] Animals which are active during the day are said to be diurnal, while those active at night are *nocturnal.*

Figure 10-10 *(a)* Slow loris, *Nycticebus coucang;* *(b)* Mindanao tarsier, *Tarsius syrichta carbonarious.*

(a)

(b)

powerful grip, which is enhanced by the reduction of the index finger to a mere bump. Like the lemurs, they have a dental comb and a grooming claw on their second toe. The lorises are found as solitary animals or in pairs. Their diet is varied, consisting of fruits, leaves, seeds, birds and birds' eggs, lizards, and insects. The Asiatic members of the subfamily are the *slender loris* and *slow loris* (Figure 10-10a). The African members are the *potto* and *angwantibo.*

The subfamily Galaginae includes *galagos,* some of which are known as *bush babies.* They are nocturnal and insectivorous. These primates are characterized by their leaping ability, which is facilitated by their much elongated legs. In one study, the small *Galago senegalensis,* with a center of gravity perhaps 3¾ centimeters (1½ inches) off the ground, leaped vertically in the air 2¼ meters (7 feet 4¾ inches).[8] This leaping ability enables the animal to move quickly through the branches searching for and catching insects.

The family Tarsiidae It was once thought that early *tarsiers* were ancestral to the higher primates. Today, paleontologists believe that tarsiers represent an ancient, specialized primate family. Modern tarsiers, which today are the most advanced of the prosimians, are extremely small, with very long tails. Their legs are long, and their very name is derived from the long tarsal, or ankle, bones, which enable them to leap long distances. Their eyes have become so large that they cannot be moved by the eye muscles, which

[8] E. C. B. Hall-Craggs, "An Analysis of the Jump of the Lesser Galago (*Galago senegalensis*)," *Journal of Zoology,* 147 (1965), 20–29.

have become degenerate. Instead, the animal is capable of turning its head almost 180 degrees to look behind itself (Figure 10-10b).

The tarsiers possess many advanced features compared with other prosimians. For example, they have an incomplete eye socket and lack the dental comb seen in the other prosimians. They are strictly nocturnal, are usually found in pairs, and feed on insects and lizards. Tarsiers are native to Southeast Asia and do not do well in captivity.

Anthropoidea

The second major division of the order Primates is the suborder Anthropoidea, which includes the monkeys, apes, and humans.

The monkeys As we mentioned in the previous chapter, the monkeys of the New World and those of the Old World represent two different groups (Figure 10-11). The common ancestor probably was not a monkey, and the similar features of the two modern groups represent a case of parallel evolution. The New World and Old World monkeys differ from each other in a number of ways.

One way of immediately distinguishing the New World from the Old World monkeys is by the form of the nose. The Old World forms have what is termed a *catarrhine nose*, in which the nostrils are separated by a narrow nasal septum and open downward. This nose form also characterizes humans and the apes. The *platyrrhine nose* of the New World monkeys consists of nostrils usually separated by a very broad nasal septum and opening sideways (Figure 10-12). Another key distinction is in the number of teeth. The New World monkeys have three premolars

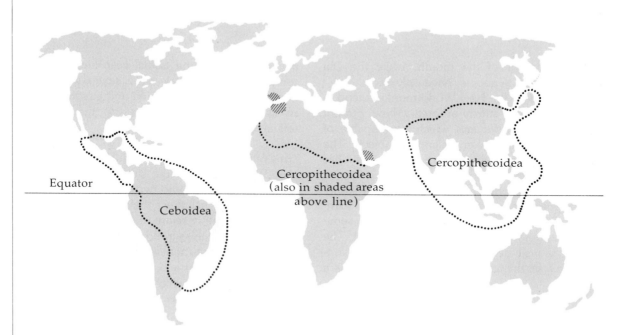

Figure 10-11 Distribution of the monkeys.

(a)   (b)

Figure 10-12 Nose forms among monkeys. (a) *A platyrrhine nose (hairy saki,* Pithecia monachus*); (b) a catarrhine nose (Hamlyn's guenon,* Cercopithecus hamlyni*).*

in each quarter of the mouth, while the Old World forms, like people, have only two.

In addition, the New World monkeys tend to be small and are strictly arboreal. Many, but not all, have *prehensile tails* which are capable of hanging onto and even picking up objects. The thumb is nonopposable, and in some forms it has disappeared.

The Old World monkeys tend to be somewhat larger, although some small forms do exist. Some Old World monkeys have become semiterrestrial, and none have a prehensile tail. The thumb is well developed and to a degree opposable.[9] In the anal region of the animal is a

pair of callouses, the *ischial callosities.* Also, in some species the female has a *sexual skin* which often turns bright pink or red and in some forms swells when the animal is in *estrus,* the period of sexual receptivity (Figure 10-13).

The New World monkeys   The monkeys of the New World make up the superfamily Ceboidea and can be divided into two families. The family Callithricidae includes the *marmosets* and *tamarins* and other related forms (Figure 10-14). In many ways this group represents the most primitive of all the monkeys. They lack the ability for facial expression and have claws on all digits except the big toe, which has a nail. The thumb is nonopposable. The members of this group usually produce twins at birth. The father carries the infants and transfers them to the mother for feeding.

[9] Although here too one form, the colobus, has no thumb.

Most of the New World forms belong to the family Cebidae. The *cebids* are divided into five subfamilies. The subfamily Cebinae includes the small *squirrel monkey* (Figure 10-15a) and the well-known *capuchin,* which is the common organ-grinder monkey. The squirrel monkey has been observed in bands of as many as 500 individuals. The subfamily Aotinae includes the *douroucolis,* or *night monkey,* the only completely nocturnal monkey, as well as the *titis.* In contrast to the squirrel monkey, the night monkey lives primarily in a social unit consisting of a male and a female and their young. The subfamily Pithecinae includes the *sakis* (Figure 10-12a) and *uakaris,* the latter being bald-headed forms whose naked faces are often a bright pink.

The last two subfamilies are characterized by the presence of the prehensile tail. The Alouattinae consist of the *howler monkeys* (Figure 10-15b). These are primarily leaf eaters, with a

Figure 10-13 Ischial callosities and sexual skin. *A female chacma baboon,* Papio ursinus, *showing swelling of the sexual skin. Underneath the swelling on the left can be seen part of the ischial callosity.*

Figure 10-14 Marmosets. *The pygmy marmoset,* Cebuella pygmaea.

highly specialized larynx which is responsible for their characteristic call. The *spider* and *woolly monkeys* are in the subfamily Atelinae. The social unit of the spider monkey varies in size from a family group to a troop of more than 100 individuals. The animals are of various coat colors and are noted for their prehensile tails, which serve as a third hand; they do not have thumbs. The bulk of their diet consists of fruits and nuts.

Because of the fairly remote relationship of the ceboids to humans, they have not been studied as extensively as the Old World forms. Today, however, interest is mounting; and data on these forms, especially on their social behavior, are becoming increasingly available.

The Old World monkeys The Old World monkeys constitute a large number of species spread over Africa and Asia, with one small group in Europe. The superfamily Cercopithecoidea consists of the single family Cercopithecidae, which, in turn, is divided into two subfamilies. The subfamily Cercopithecinae includes both Asiatic and African forms and the one European group on the Rock of Gibraltar. Members of this subfamily are *omnivorous* and possess *cheek pouches* (pouches which open into the mouth and are used for temporary food storage), and many are semiterrestrial.

Most of the arboreal and some semiterrestrial monkeys of Africa are the *guenons* (Figure

(a)

Figure 10-15 New World monkeys. (a) *Squirrel monkeys*, Saimiri sciureus; (b) *red howler monkey*, Alouatta seniculus.

(b)

(a)

Figure 10-16 Old World monkeys. *Representatives of the subfamily Cercopithecinae:* (a) *Barbary "ape" macaque,* Macaca sylvanus; (b) *gelada,* Theropithecus gelada.

(b)

(a)

(b)

Figure 10-17   Old World monkeys. *Representatives of the subfamily Colobinae:* (a) *common langur, Napal,* Presbytis entellus; (b) *Kikuyu colobus monkey,* Colobus polykomos kikuyuensis.

10-12*b*) and the *mangabeys.* There are twenty-three species of mangabeys, which are found throughout Africa in rain forest, woodland, and savanna habitats. The large, ground-dwelling monkeys of the savanna are the *baboons.* One species, the *Hamadryas baboon,* lives in the semi-desert regions of southern Ethiopia and spends the night sleeping on cliffs rather than in trees. The baboons are often referred to as the "dog-faced monkeys" because of the presence of a well-pronounced muzzle (Figure 10-13). Associated with the muzzle are large, formidable teeth,

especially in the adult males. The social behavior of one of the baboon species is described in Chapter 11. Also found in Africa are the *patas monkey, drills,* and *mandrills,* and the *geladas* (Figure 10-16*b*).

The Asiatic representatives of the Cercopithecinae are the *macaques* (Figure 10-16*a*). The twelve species of macaques are found in a great diversity of habitats, including tropical rain forest and semideserts. In Japan, the macaques survive winter snows. The only European monkey is a macaque living on the Rock of Gibraltar. The

The Living Primates

diet of the macaques is quite varied and includes, besides fruits, roots, and other vegetable material, insects and shellfish.

The other subfamily, the Colobinae, also is found in both Africa and Asia. The members of this subfamily differ from those of the Cercopithecinae in that they lack cheek pouches and can eat mature leaves. The ability to digest leaves is due to the presence of a complex saccated stomach, in which bacterial action is able to break down the cellulose of the leaves.

The major group of Colobinae in Asia is the langurs, comprising fourteen species (Figure 10-17a). They are found in the Himalayas up to an elevation of 3,650 meters (12,000 feet) as well as in very dry zones, where, unlike other monkeys, they can survive, due to their ability to digest dry, mature leaves. The langurs of India have been extensively studied. The African representatives of the Colobinae are the *colobus monkeys* or *guerezas* (Figure 10-17b).

The family Hylobatidae   The last three primate families belong to the superfamily Hominoidea. The family Hylobatidae includes apes of Southeast Asia, the *gibbons* and *siamangs*, which are sometimes referred to as the *lesser apes* (Figure 10-18).

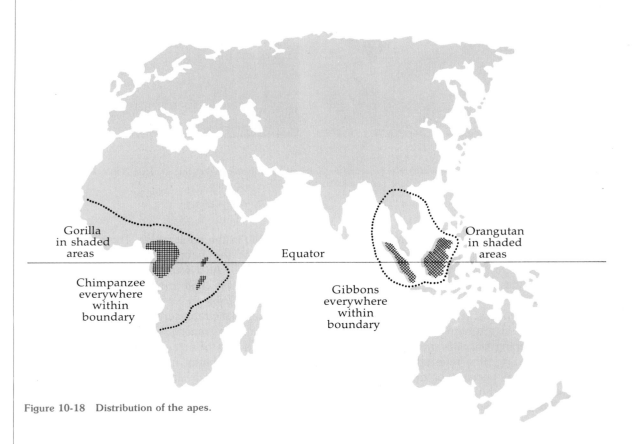

Figure 10-18   Distribution of the apes.

(a)

Figure 10-19 The family Hylobatidae. This family includes the lesser apes: (a) white-handed gibbon, Hylobates lar lar; (b) island siamang, Symphalangus syndactylus.

(b)

Figure 10-20   The family Pongidae. *This family includes the great apes:* (a) *orangutan,* Pongo pygmaeus; (b) *chimpanzee,* Pan troglodytes; (c) *pygmy chimpanzee,* Pan paniscus; (d) *lowland gorilla,* Gorilla gorilla *(on page 234).*

(a)

(b)

(c)

(d)

The gibbons are small animals, weighing some 6 kilograms (13 pounds) (Figure 10-19a). They have short, compact bodies with exceedingly long arms, an adaptation for *brachiation,* hand-over-hand locomotion along a branch. They are the classic brachiators among all primates and are primarily arboreal. Their diet consists basically of fruits, but they also consume leaves and buds, birds' eggs and young birds, and insects.

Unlike most primates, the gibbons live in small family groups consisting of a mature pair with several young. Each group occupies a distinct territory which is defended by loud vocal displays by the male. While they tend to sleep near the center of their territory—where, unlike the other apes, they do not build nests—they travel during the day near the boundaries, where contact with other groups is common.

The *siamangs,* found in Sumatra and the Malay peninsula, are similar to the gibbons but are larger and have longer arms (Figure 10-19b). They are characterized by an air sac under the chin which inflates when vocalizing.

The family Pongidae The Pongidae include the *great apes.* The Asiatic great ape is the *orangutan,* which is found today only on the islands of Sumatra and Borneo (Figure 10-20a). They are quiet, slow-moving animals; and even though they are quite large, they are primarily arboreal. They are completely vegetarian.

The social groupings of the orangutan are unstable. Often, mated pairs or just mothers with infants travel together. Groups of adolescents and solitary males also are seen. There is a great degree of *sexual dimorphism;* that is, great differences exist in anatomy between the sexes. The males are large, weighing more than 68 kilograms (150 pounds); the females often weigh only half as much. The males of the Borneo subspecies develop large pouches under the chin and flanges

of flesh on the cheeks. These physical features are not found in the female.

The largest living primate is the *gorilla* of Africa (Figure 10-20d). There are two major groups: the lowland gorilla of West Africa and the highland gorilla of East Africa. The former is the type normally seen in zoos, but the highland gorilla has been the subject of several recent studies in the wild. A great amount of erroneous material has been written about the gorillas. In the wild, they are strictly vegetarian animals that live a rather peaceful existence, knowing no enemy save humans.

Gorillas are basically terrestrial, but they construct nests, often in trees, for sleeping. Their size prevents them, especially the adult males, from moving easily through the trees. On the ground, gorillas walk on all four limbs, but instead of placing their palms flat on the ground, they walk on their knuckles like the chimpanzee.

The best-known apes are the *chimpanzees.* Although the orangutan and gorilla are probably equal to the chimpanzee in intelligence, the smaller and more easily manageable chimpanzees are easier for scientists to work with, and hence there is more information on them. There are two species of chimpanzee, the *common chimpanzee,* found north of the Congo (Zaire) River (Figure 10-20b), and the rare *pygmy chimpanzee,* found south of the Congo River (Figure 10-20c).

Sociable and curious animals, chimpanzees are much more active than gorillas. They live in rather flexible social groups, as contrasted with most nonhuman primates. Like gorillas, chimpanzees build nests in trees and are knuckle walkers. They have been studied extensively in the wild, and their behavior will be discussed in some detail in the next chapter.

The family Hominidae The family Hominidae contains only one living species, *Homo sapiens.* In many ways this species represents the most complete development of the primate complex discussed earlier in this chapter. Humans have the most highly developed brain and the most flexible hands of all primates.

Unlike the other primates, humans have lost much of their locomotor flexibility. While still able to climb trees, they are essentially habitually erect, terrestrial bipeds. This pattern of posture and locomotion is not unique to *Homo sapiens,* but only this species among all primates has become specialized for it. While the human skeleton is still basically apelike in the upper sections, from the pelvis down, especially in the feet, it has become specialized for bipedal walking and running.

Humans are omnivorous, yet animal flesh is considered superior to plant material and meat eating plays a significant role in almost all human societies. The only other primates that have been known to kill and eat other mammals are baboons and chimpanzees, which do so infrequently compared with the practice of humans.

Humans have the longest *gestation period* of any primate and produce the most helpless infants. The period of infant dependency is very long, and adult status is often not reached until the second decade of life. This long childhood period provides the opportunity for the development of complex patterns of learned behavior. Indeed, this is *Homo sapiens'* most significant

distinction: the dependence upon culture for adapting to the environment.

Summary

This section has introduced the various primate groups in anticipation of the comparative studies which follow. The order Primates is divided into two suborders. The first, Prosimii, includes the lemurs, lorises, and tarsiers, forms which do not possess all the features that characterize the other suborder. The second suborder, the Anthropoidea, includes the New and Old World monkeys, apes, and humans.

SUGGESTED READINGS

Eimerl, S., and I. DeVore. *The Primates.* New York: Time-Life, 1965. A good general introduction to the primates.

Jolly, A. *The Evolution of Primate Behavior.* New York: Macmillan, 1972. Although this book is primarily concerned with behavior, there are excellent introductory chapters on the primates in general.

Napier, J. R., and P. H. Napier. *A Handbook of Living Primates.* New York: Academic, 1967. A detailed listing of all primate genera, with excellent photographs. Also includes discussions of primate taxonomy, comparative anatomy, and ecology.

Reynolds, V. *The Apes.* New York: Dutton, 1967. A detailed discussion of the various ape species.

Discussions of adaptation usually involve analyses of anatomical structures. Yet animals adapt to their ecological niches largely in terms of behavior. This is illustrated by the social insects, whose complex behavioral patterns are basic to their survival. These behavioral patterns are determined by the genetic code, as are aspects of their anatomy and physiology.

Primates also adapt by means of behavior. However, unlike insect behavior, a large part of primate behavioral patterns is learned rather than innate. Because much primate behavior is learned and hence variable, problems arise about the validity of generalizations drawn from a limited number of studies. Behavioral patterns differ not only from species to species but also from group to group within the same species. Nevertheless, the study of primate behavior is essential to a complete understanding of the primate complex. The contrast between nonhuman primate behavior and human behavior may serve to make one aware of the nature of humankind.

Chapter Eleven
Primate Behavior

STUDIES OF PRIMATE BEHAVIOR

Early studies of living primates were concerned primarily with anatomy. Increasingly, attention has been given to naturalistic behavior; and today, studies of primate behavior make up a dominant subject area within the field of *primatology*.

Early behavioral studies were conducted primarily with *zoo populations*. Data from these studies led to a number of erroneous conclusions. Today it is realized that these data reflect the unnatural and overcrowded conditions in the cage. When a zoo population is given adequate space and a good food supply and is kept in natural social groupings, its behavior is very similar to that of wild populations.

Several recent studies have compared wild populations with caged populations of the same species.[1] T. Rowell writes, "The same units of social behavior were observed in both wild and caged populations, and no behaviour patterns were seen in one and not the other." However, she notes that the intensity of social interaction is much greater in the caged populations.[2]

Perhaps the most valid type of study is a field project in which the observer spends enough time with a *natural population* of animals to recognize individuals. This also results in the animals' becoming familiar with the observer, permitting close observation. The major difficulty here is the tremendous number of hours necessary to make contact and the low yield of information per hour. Some major field studies include those of the baboon by Irven DeVore and Sherwood Washburn, of the chimpanzee by Jane Goodall, of the langur by Phyllis Dolhinow, of the mountain gorilla by George Schaller, and the early studies of the gibbon and howler monkey by C. R. Carpenter.[3]

Increasingly popular are studies of *provisionized colonies*. These are groups of primates which have become accustomed to humans because of the establishment of feeding stations. The group will travel to the feeding station daily, permitting close observation of individuals and collection of census data, such as births and deaths. Studies away from the feeding stations are facilitated by the primate group's tolerance of people. The yield of data is greater than with the standard field study, and new observers can be introduced into the research situation quite readily. Provisionized colonies include those of the Japanese macaque at Takasakiyama and the rhesus macaque on Santiago Island.[4]

While the natural populations and provisionized colonies are the most frequently studied situations, mention should be made of *artificial colonies* found at many universities and research stations. These are attempts to reconstruct a natural situation within the confines of captivity, permitting detailed study by large numbers of individuals. There are also *laboratory studies* which involve manipulation of the animals in a laboratory situation and which are conducted primarily by psychologists.

The purpose of this chapter is not to survey all studies of primate behavior or to make gross generalizations but to give the reader an idea of the nature of such studies and to point to some of the findings that have led to a better understanding of human beings. Two specific studies will be discussed, that of the baboon by DeVore and Washburn and that of the chimpanzee by Goodall. The baboon has been chosen because it is a semiterrestrial primate inhabiting an en-

[1] L. Klein and D. Klein, "Aspects of Social Behavior in a Colony of Spider Monkeys," in J. Lucas (ed.), *International Zoo Yearbook* (London: Zoological Society of London, 1971), vol. 11, pp. 175–181; H. Kummer and O. Kurt, "A Comparison of Social Behavior in Captive and Wild Hamadryas Baboons," in H. Vagtborg (ed.), *The Baboon in Medical Research* (Austin: Univ. of Texas Press, 1965), pp. 65–80; T. Rowell, "A Quantitative Comparison of the Behaviour of a Wild and a Caged Baboon Group," *Animal Behavior*, 15 (1967), 499–509.

[2] Rowell, op. cit., 499, 501.

[3] I. DeVore and K. R. L. Hall, "Baboon Ecology," K. R. L. Hall and I. DeVore, "Baboon Social Behavior," and J. Goodall, "Chimpanzees of the Gombe Reserve," in I. DeVore (ed.), *Primate Behavior: Field Studies of Monkeys and Apes* (New York: Holt, 1965), pp. 20–52, 53–110; P. Dolhinow, "The North Indian Langur," in P. J. Dolhinow (ed.), *Primate Patterns* (New York: Holt, 1972), pp. 181–238; G. Schaller, *The Mountain Gorilla: Ecology and Behavior* (Chicago: Univ. of Chicago Press, 1963); C. R. Carpenter, *Naturalistic Behavior of Nonhuman Primates* (University Park, Pa.: Pennsylvania State Univ. Press, 1964).

[4] K. Imanishi, "Social Behavior in Japanese Monkeys, *Macaca fuscata*," and C. B. Koford, "Group Relations in an Island Colony of Rhesus Monkeys," in C. H. Southwick (ed.), *Primate Social Behavior* (New York: Van Nostrand Reinhold, 1963), pp. 68–81, 136–152.

vironment not unlike that of early hominids. The chimpanzee's behavior is explored because it is our closest living relative.

The Social Behavior of the Savanna Baboon

The ecology of the savanna baboon has been likened by many anthropologists to that of the early hominids. John E. Pfeiffer writes:

The more we know about the range of adaptations to open woodlands . . . the better we will understand the behavior of the first hominids, who depended increasingly on their ability to cope with such terrain. Going one step further, our ancestors gradually moved out of open woodlands into still more open grassy savanna lands, and the impact of that change can be appreciated more fully by considering how other primates have adapted to similar conditions.[5]

Baboons range throughout large areas of Africa and represent the major monkey form which has become adapted to a largely terrestrial life. The study of DeVore and Washburn in Kenya, in 1959 and 1960, deals with the savanna (grassland) baboon of East Africa.[6]

The baboon troop   All baboons live within a social unit called a *troop*. Animals live their entire lives within the troop into which they were born, although occasionally a male may transfer his affiliation. The baboon troop varies in size from 9 to 185 individuals, the usual number being between 30 and 45.

While a baboon troop remains within a fixed boundary, the *home range*, distinct defended territories do not exist. The significance of terri-

torial defense has been overemphasized, especially in the popular literature. A fixed area and boundaries do exist, as illustrated by the inability of an observer to drive a troop across these boundaries. But boundaries are never defended, and the home ranges of neighboring troops often overlap extensively. When more than one troop occupies sections of overlapping area, they will tend to avoid contact. When contact between baboon troops is unavoidable, such as around a water hole during the dry season, either several troops will mingle freely and drink side by side or the smaller troops will simply give way to the larger.

The home range is that area in which the troop spends the majority of its time. The size of the home range varies from 2 to $15\frac{1}{2}$ square miles, depending upon the size of the troop and the concentration of food. Within the home range are certain *core areas*. These may contain a concentration of food, a water hole, a good resting area, or, most important, sleeping trees. These core areas are used exclusively by a single troop, which will spend more than 90 percent of its time within the two or three core areas existing within its home range (Figure 11-1).

The savanna is basically a dry grassland with scattered groups of trees. Although food is easily found, the baboon must obtain this food on the open plain, where danger from predators poses a real threat. The location of sleeping trees is extremely important for protection during the sleeping hours, and the troop must reach the safety of these trees by nightfall. During the day the troop depends upon the collective protection of the large males and relies to some extent on the alarm calls of other animals to warn them of the proximity of carnivores. Healthy animals rarely fall prey to predators.

The basic food of the baboon is grass, which makes up about 90 percent of the diet during the dry season. This is supplemented by other vegetable matter, such as seeds, flowers, and fruits.

[5] J. E. Pfeiffer, *The Emergence of Man*, 2d ed. (New York: Harper, 1972), p. 283. Used with permission.

[6] DeVore and Hall, op. cit., and Hall and DeVore, op. cit.

Boundary of Nairobi Park

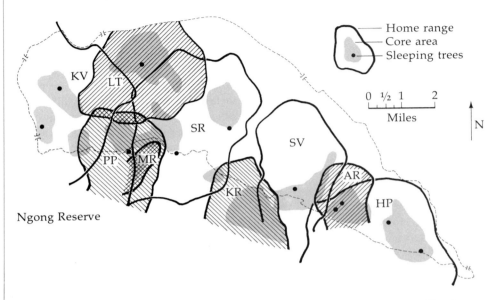

Figure 11-1 Troop distribution. *Home ranges and core areas of nine baboon troops in Nairobi Park, Kenya. The troops vary in size from twelve to eighty-seven individuals, with home ranges varying from slightly over 2 to 15½ square miles.*

Insects and some small reptiles are consumed, and eating of mammalian flesh has been reported.

The feeding habits of the baboon were studied by Robert S. O. Harding in 1970 to 1971.[7] The percent of feeding time spent by the adult males in procuring and eating various food types were grasses, 79.9; fruits, seeds, and flowers, 18.1; and animal protein, 2.0. In 1,032 hours of observation, Harding observed 47 vertebrates being killed and eaten. The animals killed included infant Thomson's gazelles, various antelopes, and hares. Most of the killing was done by

adult males, who, on occasion, seemed to search deliberately for prey. The high-ranking males dominated these meat-eating activities, and the meat was never voluntarily shared.

Structure of the baboon troop Within the baboon troop, several distinct classes of individuals can be identified. These are the adult males, adult females, subadult males, juveniles, and infants.

The adult males play especially important roles in baboon social life, for when foraging in the open, the entire troop is dependent upon them for protection. Troop defense is related to collective defensive behavior by the adult males. The male is much larger than the female and possesses much longer canine teeth, which are

[7] R. S. O. Harding, "Meat-Eating and Hunting in Baboons," in R. H. Tuttle (ed.), *Socioecology and Psychology of Primates* (The Hague: Mouton, 1975), pp. 245–257.

deadly weapons even against the most powerful carnivores. This difference in size and structure between males and females is referred to as *sexual dimorphism.* The baboons show a much greater degree of sexual dimorphism than most other species of monkeys.

Figure 11-2 diagrams a typical baboon troop moving through the savanna. The largest, most dominant males are in the center of the troop, protecting the juveniles and the females, especially the females with young infants. Surrounding the troop are the less dominant males and subadult males, which act as the first line of defense. In the presence of a predator, the adult males will form a line of defense between the source of danger and the rest of the troop, permitting the troop to gain the safety of the trees. Few carnivores will bother to approach a line of alerted adult males.

The adult males themselves are arranged in a *dominance hierarchy.* While this hierarchy is usually thought of as being strictly linear, the rela-

tive ranks of the lower ranking males are not always sharply defined. It is also possible for a pair of males to form an alliance which permits the pair to occupy a position in the system at a higher level than each could alone. The main significance of this arrangement seems to be that it permits the existence of several aggressive adult males within the same troop.

The most dominant males are usually in good physical condition, but this is apparently not the most important factor in determining rank. The major factor may be personality, especially such traits as confidence and aggressiveness and, most important, the ability to attract the support of other males. The most dominant males also seem to be the offspring of the most dominant females. The presence of a high-ranking mother permits a male child to intimidate other animals higher in rank than the child but lower in rank than the mother, who is quick to back up her child in a conflict situation.

Once formed, the hierarchy is extremely

Figure 11-2 A baboon troop moving through the savanna. *When a troop is moving through the savanna, the dominant adult males are found in the center of the troop, along with females with small infants and older infants. A group of young juveniles is seen below the center and older juveniles above. Other adult males and females lead and bring up the rear. Two estrus females (dark hindquarters) are in consort with adult males.*

Figure 11-3   Threat gesture. *The canine display.*

stable, although changes do occur, especially as members grow old and die. Young males entering the system simply cannot challenge the most dominant male for his position, for he will be supported by other dominant males. Some dominant males are able to maintain their high rank even after they have become old and weak, with their canines worn down to the gums.

Physical aggression is rare. Most aggression is expressed in terms of gesture rather than in actual fighting. Threat gestures include staring, raising the eyebrow so as to expose the distinctively colored eyelid, slapping the ground, or jerking the head back and forth. When you next visit the zoo and observe a baboon male "yawning," do not feel that he is bored. He is actually displaying his canines as a threat gesture directed toward the observer (Figure 11-3).

The dominance system operates in a variety of situations. A dominant male receives preference over choice food, such as meat, and over estrus females. A subordinate will give up his sitting place to a more dominant male (*displacement*). A subordinate male approaching a more dominant male will present his anal region to him (*presenting*), and often will be *mounted* by him. The observer uses data on such factors as displacement, presenting, and mounting to gain a picture of the dominance system within the troop.

It should be noted here that the rigid dominance hierarchy of the baboons is not necessarily characteristic of all monkey societies. A clear-cut dominance pattern is adaptive in the dangerous situations the baboons encounter on the open plain. In more arboreal forms the system is not as rigid, and dominance cues are more subtle.

Females also form a dominance hierarchy, but the relative position of the female may vary throughout the year depending on whether she is in estrus or is associated with a young infant. These changes are related, in part, to the interest of the male in estrus females and the great tolerance of males for young infants. Thus females in either situation find themselves in closer proximity to the dominant males, thus elevating their social rank in the troop. In addition, other females show great interest in newborns and will present to or groom the mother in an attempt to come into close association with the child.

Sexual relationships   The estrus cycle of the baboon is about thirty-five days long and is clearly indicated by the swelling of the sexual skin. As the swelling enlarges, the female becomes receptive to the advances of the males; the swelling, in turn, serves as a signal to the male that the female is indeed receptive.

Early sexual advances are made by the more subordinate males and are short in duration. As the female approaches the time of ovulation, she attracts the attention of the dominant males. The male and female will form a *consort pair* and remain together for several hours to several days. Since the dominant males are copulating around the time of ovulation, they will father the majority of the young.

The baboon child The newborn baboon becomes a focal point of troop interest. Females will present to the mother in order to be able to inspect the infant, but the mother is at first reluctant to release the clinging child. As the mother moves, the child clings to her underside, and at rest it is groomed constantly. The close proximity of a female to an infant is tolerated by the males, and she will stay very close to them, especially when moving through the savanna (Figure 11-4).

After the first month, the baboon child begins to experiment with riding on its mother's back.

The infant may move away from the mother for very short distances, but it still attempts to remain in sight of her. Other troop members, even the adult males, are very tolerant of the infants, who often will crawl over them or even play on them.

Between the fourth and sixth month of life, the color of the infant's coat changes from black to light brown. The infant now rides jockey style on its mother's back, begins to eat solid foods, and moves away from the mother for short periods to play with other young monkeys. The mother is more relaxed as the child moves away from her.

As the infant grows, it begins to associate more with its peers and less with its mother. From the eleventh to the fifteenth month, the child is weaned and begins to spend the majority of its time with its *play group*.

Figure 11-4 **Mother with child.** *Mother, with infant riding on her back, in close proximity to an adult male.*

Juveniles (age two to four) are quite independent of their mothers, although females will spend a great deal of time with their mothers. During the early part of this stage the play group is of greatest importance; but as the animal becomes older, this relationship begins to change. The older juvenile female leaves the play group and joins the clusters of grooming females. The older juvenile male is tolerated less and less by the adult males.

The female rapidly enters the adult stage and soon begins to bear offspring. She enters a dominance hierarchy which is not as rigid as that of the males. The relative position of the female fluctuates, depending on the stage of her sexual cycle and the presence of offspring. Female-female relationships are often expressed in terms of *grooming* activity. Grooming occupies several hours a day as the animals use their fingers to part the hairs, looking for debris. Grooming not only keeps the fur clean but is also a gesture of affection. Grooming is especially common between mothers and offspring, adult females, and estrus females and males. When the troop is at rest, the females settle down in *grooming clusters,* probably composed of several closely related females and their young.

Group cohesion   The baboon troop represents a type of social organization which is common among monkeys but infrequent among other mammals. The troop is not held together by herding on the part of the males.[8] The members of the troop appear to want to be together; and consequently, it is difficult to force a member to leave a troop or to introduce a new member into it.

Early researchers of primate behavior believed that it was the sexual attraction between the males and females which provided the major cohesive bond. But the female is receptive for only a few weeks of the year. Phyllis Jay, in her study of the Indian langur, estimates that the average female langur is pregnant for 25 percent of her adult life, nurses and protects a dependent infant for 33 percent of her adult life, and is engaged in weaning for 20 percent of her adult life. Sexual activity is suspended during pregnancy and lactation. When the female is not pregnant or lactating, receptivity is regulated by the estrus cycle. The typical female langur is therefore sexually receptive for less than 1 percent of her total adult life.[9] This is generally true of most monkey species. In addition, many monkeys mate only during certain months of the year, so that for a great part of the year no sexual activity takes place.

Group cohesion appears to be based on the attraction of the troop members to three categories of individuals: the dominant males, infants, and old females. At rest, the dominant males are surrounded by females and young who seem to be attracted to their presence. This is especially true of very young animals and mothers of newborns. Infants also become focal points of troop interest. When a newborn appears in a troop, the female members will attempt to look at and handle it and will show great attention to the mother. Finally, lengthy studies of the rhesus and Japanese macaques have demonstrated a bond which exists between mothers and their adult daughters. A basic subunit within the troop appears to be an old female with her grown daughters and their respective children.

Before leaving the subject of the monkey troop, we must emphasize that behavioral pat-

[8] The male Hamadryas baboon does herd his females by biting them on the neck if they stray too far. Here the social organization is quite different from that of the savanna baboon. See H. Kummer, *Social Organization of Hamadryas Baboons* (Chicago: Univ. of Chicago Press, 1968), pp. 36–37.

[9] P. Jay, "The Common Langur of North India," in I. DeVore (ed.), *Primate Behavior: Field Studies of Monkeys and Apes* (New York: Holt, 1965), pp. 233, 239–240.

terns differ greatly from species to species and even from population to population within a species. The above discussion should be taken not as a description of monkey behavior in general, but as a summary of the behavior of a specific population of savanna baboons.

The Social Behavior of the Chimpanzee

The following is based upon the field work of Jane Goodall, beginning in 1960.[10] The study was conducted on a semiisolated group of chimpanzees of the Gombe Stream Reserve in Uganda. Although chimpanzees normally inhabit dense forest, the more open forest of the reserve made for easier observation.

The chimpanzee social unit is an ever-changing association of individuals. These groups may be subunits of a larger, more definitive community; but animals, especially males, from adjoining areas frequently travel back and forth through the area.

The largest social group to congregate at any one time numbered twenty-three individuals, but this was unusual. The typical group numbers between three and six animals. The basic groups are of several kinds. The most frequent type consists of adult males and females with young. Other types of groups consist of females with young (Figure 11-5), mature or adolescent males with immature or adolescent females, all males, or solitary males. The composition of the group changes frequently; and when two groups meet, individuals will often change their association. The mother-infant bond is the only really stable unit; even when it is older, the offspring will frequently travel with its mother.

The chimpanzee is largely arboreal. Its food is found primarily in trees, and about 50 to 70

[10] J. van Lawick-Goodall, *In the Shadow of Man* (Boston: Houghton Mifflin, 1971), and Goodall, op. cit.

Figure 11-5 Chimpanzee social unit. *Fifi (left), a chimpanzee in Africa's Gombe Stream Game Reserve, nuzzles her brother, Flint, while their mother Flo holds the baby.*

percent of the day is spent feeding or resting in trees. The animals sleep in trees, building new nests each night. Yet, most traveling between trees is done on the ground. Chimpanzees travel many miles each day, the length and direction of travel depending on the availability of food.

The chimpanzee diet is basically vegetarian. It includes fruits, leaves, seeds, and bark. In addition, occasional insects, such as ants and termites, are consumed. The hunting and eating of meat have also been observed. Six to seven hours each day are spent actively feeding.

The termite stick The method used by the chimpanzee in feeding upon termites is of special interest to the student of human evolution, for

Figure 11-6 The termite stick. *A five-year-old chimpanzee uses a tool she made herself by stripping down a blade of grass to fish for insects in a termite mound.*

the chimpanzee manufactures and uses a tool for this purpose. At one time, anthropologists defined humans as *the* toolmaking animal; this definition must now be revised, since chimpanzees and other animals have been observed deliberately manufacturing tools.

Termite feeding becomes an important activity at the beginning of the rainy season. For a period of as long as nine weeks, chimpanzees spend one or two hours each day feeding on termites. This is the time when the termites grow wings in order to leave the termite hill to found new colonies. Passages within the hill are extended to the surface and sealed over while the termites await good flying conditions.

The chimpanzee scrapes away the thin seal over one of these passages. It then takes a *termite stick* and pokes it down the hole. After a moment, the tool is withdrawn with the termites hanging on, ready to be licked off by the chimp (Figure 11-6).

The termite stick is manufactured from a grass stalk, twig, or vine and is usually less than 12 inches long. A twig too long to use is broken to the right length. A leafy twig or vine is stripped of its leaves before it is used. Some care is given to the choice of material and nature of the tool.

Young chimpanzees do not appear to be interested in catching termites. Goodall reports that while a mother chimpanzee will spend hours termiting, the youngsters become impatient and often attempt to get her to leave. The art of termiting and termite-stick making is learned. When young chimpanzees first begin to show an interest in such activity, they will make termite sticks incorrectly and will have difficulty inserting the stick in the hole and pulling it out without losing the termites which are hanging on. Through watching their mothers the young chimpanzees learn, but some are better students than others and are able to make better tools.

Goodall describes other examples of tool manufacture. For example, a chimpanzee will make a sponge by chewing a leaf, which is then used to sponge up water. In addition, many natural objects are used as tools: sticks as clubs, rocks which are thrown, and leaf towels. But while chimpanzees, like people, do make tools in the wild, their inventory of tools does not even begin to approach the complexity of human technology or degree of dependence upon tools for survival.

Chimpanzees as hunters Unlike most primates, chimpanzees eat meat. Chimpanzees have been observed killing and eating young bushbucks, bushpigs, baboons, and young and adult monkeys, such as the red colobus monkey (Figure 11-7). The chimpanzee may simply surprise an

Figure 11-7 Chimpanzee eating meat. *Adult male chimpanzee (hair wet from rainstorm) dismantles and eats from a juvenile baboon carcass.*

animal in the undergrowth and kill and eat it. However, chimpanzees also deliberately hunt animals for food.

The decision to hunt is often triggered by the distress call of a young baboon, and an accidental kill is often the trigger for more purposeful activity. Hunting is most often a male activity, and several males will cooperate in trapping the ani-mal. The prey is killed by slamming it against a tree or the ground, or its skull is crushed between the teeth of the captor.

After the kill, other chimpanzees will arrive to share the meat and form temporary groupings, which can be called *sharing clusters*. Most members of the cluster eat some of the prey. The time spent in eating the meat has been observed to vary from one hour and forty minutes to more than nine hours.[11]

Some individuals, especially subadults and adult females, simply pick up pieces of meat which have been dropped by other individuals. Other animals tear off a piece of meat which is being consumed by another animal, usually a female. But often a particular animal will request meat by the characteristic gesture of holding a hand, open and palm up, under the possessor's chin. This is accompanied by characteristic vocalizations. The request may be made by any chimpanzee and is more often ignored than rewarded.[12]

The head is the choicest part of the animal by chimpanzee standards, and they will enlarge the foramen magnum, the large hole at the base of the skull, with their teeth and fingers in order to get at the brain. (As will be seen in Chapter 14, this also was done by early hominids.) The soft tissue is eaten together with leaves.

Social relationships among the chimpanzees
Individual social interactions between males can be described by the terms *dominance* and *submission*. Clear-cut dominance interactions have been observed, as when one animal moves out of the way of a more dominant one. However, a rigid dominance hierarchy, such as that found among the baboons, does not exist. This observation is consistent with the fluid nature of chimpanzee group composition.

Goodall describes dominance interactions between two males as follows. If two males go after the same fruit, the subordinate male holds back. More important, if a dominant male shows signs of aggression, the subordinate male responds with gestures of submission. These gestures include reaching out to touch the dominant animal and crouching.

Much chimpanzee aggression takes the form of gesture and display. One animal can achieve dominance over the others by the fierceness of his display activity. One such male, Mike, rose from the bottom of the ladder to the top by incorporating into his display some of Goodall's kerosene cans, which he would hurl in front of him as he charged the other males. The other males would get out of Mike's way quickly and respond with a submissive gesture.[13]

The female reproductive cycle is indicated in the chimpanzee by the periodic swelling of the sexual skin. The female may initiate sexual contact, but generally this results from male courtship displays. For about a minute, the male will leap into a tree and swing from branch to branch with the hair of his head, shoulders, and arms erect. As the male approaches the female, she crouches down in front of him. Consort pairs are not formed, and mating is quite promiscuous. On one occasion, Goodall reports that seven males mounted one female in succession.[14]

The mother-infant bond is extremely close, and mothers and their offspring travel together even after the offspring is fully grown. At first, the infant is totally dependent upon its mother and is constantly held and carried by her. Later the infant will sit upright on her back and will begin to move away from her. Mothers frequently play with their babies, who also play with other young and adult animals. Like human mothers, chimpanzee mothers vary in their patience and abilities. The following extract from Goodall's *In the Shadow of Man* illustrates the point.

[11] G. Teleki, "The Omnivorous Chimpanzees," *Scientific American*, 228 (January 1973), 32–42; G. Teleki, *The Predatory Behavior of Wild Chimpanzees* (Lewisburg, Pa.: Bucknell Univ. Press, 1973).

[12] Ibid.

[13] van Lawick-Goodall, op. cit., pp. 112–115.

[14] Ibid., p. 84.

Most of the mother chimpanzees we have watched were helpful when their small babies nuzzled about searching for a nipple. Flo had normally supported Flint so that suckling was easy for him throughout a feed, even when he was six months old. Melissa also had tried, though often she had bungled things and held Goblin too high so that his searching lips nuzzled through the hair of her shoulder or neck. But Passion usually ignored Pom's whimpers completely; if she couldn't find the nipple by herself it was just bad luck. If Pom happened to be suckling when Passion wanted to move off, she seldom waited until the infant had finished her meal; she just got up and went, and Pom, clinging for once under her mother, struggled to keep the nipple in her mouth as long as she could before she was relentlessly pushed up onto Passion's back. As a result of her mother's lack of solicitude, Pom seldom managed to suckle for more than two minutes at a time before she was interrupted by Passion, and often it was much less. Most infants during their first year suckle for about three minutes once an hour. Pom probably made up for her shorter feeds by suckling more frequently.[15]

After the child stops riding on its mother's back, the juvenile chimpanzee associates more frequently with a play group. Play activity becomes less important when puberty is reached, and the animals begin to enter adult life.

Other Forms of Primate Social Behavior

The social behavior of the savanna baboon and chimpanzee are of special interest to anthropologists, but they should not be thought of as typical of primates. Primates show a great range of social structures, and, in fact, none can really be

thought of as being typical. Even within the same species or genus we find a variety of social strategies which are correlated, in part, with the specific ecological situation of the population. For example, the forest-dwelling baboons lack the rigid and intense dominance hierarchies found on the open plains.

Basic patterns of social interaction are quite variable. Many nocturnal primates, such as the galagos and mouse lemur, have been described as semisolitary. While feeding alone, they do associate for other activities. Males tend to have definite defended territories, within which are found the smaller territories of the females. However, the females associate with one another and are often found sleeping together in the same nest.

Some primates, such as the gibbon and siamang, live as mated pairs or small family groups. Living within rather small ranges, they tend to be demonstrative in their territorial behavior. Other primates live in groups consisting of several adult males and females. These groups vary greatly in size. Within some, the dominance hierarchy is well developed, in others it is weak. In a few large groups, such as the Hamadryas baboon, the basic subunit within the troop is a small harem consisting of an adult male, two or more adult females, and their young.

Summary

Generalizations about primate behavior are difficult to make. Since much primate behavior is learned, great differences are found not only between differing species but also between differing groups within the same species.

The baboon has been described not because it represents a "typical" monkey group, if there is such a thing, but because early hominids evolved in an environment very similar to that of the savanna baboon. Of special interest in baboon studies is the nature of the baboon's use of space,

---

[15] J. van Lawick-Goodall, *In the Shadow of Man* (Boston: Houghton Mifflin, 1971), p. 149. Used with permission.

which differs from the concept of defended territories often described in the popular literature. The male dominance hierarchy functions for the protection of the troop in a dangerous environment on the plains. Group cohesion results not from herding activities on the part of the males or continuing sexual interest but from interest in and ties with the dominant males, infants, and older females.

The situation among the chimpanzees contrasts in many ways with that of the baboons. Chimpanzee group composition and structure are more flexible, and individual behavior is more variable. Goodall's study of the chimpanzee has also provided us with knowledge of toolmaking and group hunting, features which up to the time of her studies were considered to be (among the primates) uniquely human.

HUMAN BEHAVIOR IN PERSPECTIVE

Many anthropologists have studied the structure of primate society for clues to the origins of human society. The assumption has been that human society was derived from social systems similar to those of the living monkeys and apes. Yet, the social systems of modern primates also have developed through the centuries and do not necessarily represent ancestral or more primitive conditions. But comparative studies of all behavioral systems, including that of humans, can provide us with new insights as to the limits and possibilities of behavior.

Most of humankind today lives in agricultural or industrial societies. Yet agriculture is a recent human development, probably no older than 10,000 years, and industrialism is the product of the last few centuries. For the vast majority of human history, people have been hunters and gatherers of wild foods. The evolutionary forces responsible for making our species what it is were working primarily on hunting and

gathering hominids. Therefore, anthropologists turn to living hunting and gathering societies when comparisons are being made with other animal groups.

Today hunters and gatherers make up about 0.0001 percent of humankind.[16] They are usually found in marginal areas, where agriculture is not practical, such as in the arctic or desert regions. Most of these societies already have been influenced by neighboring agricultural and industrial peoples. Figure 11-8 shows the location of the hunting and gathering societies which have been studied by anthropologists within the past 100 years. These will provide the data for our comparisons.

The Human Band

The basic social unit of hunting and gathering peoples is the band. The band is sometimes a distinct unit consisting of about thirty-five to fifty members. But bands can be much larger, and band membership in a number of cases is quite variable. Some large bands will fragment into smaller units during that time of the year when food is scarce.

The structure of the human band Like the monkey troop, the human band consists of a number of adult males and females, juveniles, and infants. But here the similarity ends, for in the human band most of the adults are involved in exclusive male-female relationships based upon the social concept termed marriage. Such permanent or semipermanent male-female bonding between adults does not occur in other primate groups. For example, the gibbon social unit consists of a single male and female with their immature offspring, but a third adult is normally not

[16] R. B. Lee and I. DeVore (eds.), *Man the Hunter* (Chicago: Aldine, 1968), p. i.

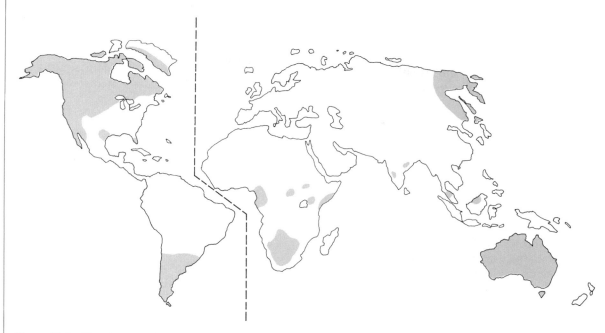

Figure 11-8 Distribution of hunters and gatherers. *Hunting and gathering societies which have been studied by anthropologists in the past 100 years.*

tolerated.[17] The larger sleeping groups of the Hamadryas baboon are fragmented into small, single, male-centered harem groups which will seek out food as a unit.[18] But within the human band, several male-female partnerships coexist.

Among the many factors related to permanent male-female bonding is the fact that human sexuality is not regulated to any great extent by the hormonal systems of the body. Human females do not exhibit a period of estrus but are potentially receptive at all phases of their repro-

ductive cycle. This may be related to the development of bonds of cooperation among the males of the band and the lessening of male-male competition over estrus females. Since all females are potentially receptive, males do not need to compete for the few females in the band who are near the time of ovulation. Specific factors regulating receptivity and male interest are usually cultural.

In the monkey troop there is an absence of food sharing. Except for infant nursing, each animal obtains its own food supply, and males and females are basically equal in their abilities to procure food. However, the males tend to monopolize choice foods which are in short supply.

Chimpanzees occasionally share food, but it is interesting to note that among chimpanzees it

[17] C. R. Carpenter, "A Field Study in Siam of the Behavior and Social Relations of the Gibbon (*Hylobates lar*)," in Carpenter, op. cit., pp. 209–211.

[18] Kummer, op. cit.

252

is meat which is shared. Hunting is also a male enterprise.

Food sharing is a major feature of the human group. The male and female are not equal in terms of their contribution to the food supply. The male is primarily a hunter, although he also engages in fishing and some gathering. The female, who is responsible for the care of the infant, gathers wild vegetable food, although she may also fish or aid in the hunt in various ways. Among most hunters and gatherers the female contributes the bulk of the food supply, but the hunter provides a highly valued food, meat.[19] The male and female have come to complement each other, and together they provide a balanced diet which is shared with the offspring and elders (who can make up as much as half the band). Sharing acts as an effective method of "social security" and goes beyond the immediate family to include all members of the band. The hunter who is having bad luck can obtain meat from a successful hunter, who will be repaid if the tables turn. Those too old to hunt not only will be supported by the younger people but are valued for their advice and knowledge.

In the human group, sharing goes well beyond food. Tools, weapons, and labor often become communal in nature. Most important, knowledge is shared. If a hunter discovers a new method of trapping an animal or a better way to make a tool, he will not keep it secret. To the hunter and gatherer, the more knowledge and skill each member of the group has, the greater the potential for survival. The sharing of knowledge is the basis for all technological advancement.

Dominance seems to be a recurrent feature of male-male social relationships among nonhuman primates, but in the human band the typical nature of male-male relationships is basically egalitarian. Although there are exceptions, hunting and gathering societies are characterized by cooperation, necessary for successful hunting, and the absence of strict hierarchical systems. Power hierarchies and class systems are not inherent in human society.

Relations within and between bands The monkey troop is essentially an inbreeding unit. Animals born into a particular troop remain with that troop for their entire lives, although a male may occasionally change group affiliation. All matings take place within the troop. Matings between siblings are theoretically possible.

Data from primate studies show that the incidence of mother-son matings is extremely low. For example, within a group of Japanese macaques studied for about twenty years, not a single case of mating between a mother and her offspring was recorded. Within a group of rhesus macaques, only two mother-son matings were observed out of 106 total matings.[20] This inhibition of mother-son mating may be due to the dominance of mothers over their offspring.

Attitudes toward incest differ among human groups. Brother-sister marriage occurred in upper-class Hawaiian society, as well as in Egypt and Peru. Yet, this is unthinkable to most Americans and is considered illegal.

There has been much discussion on the origins of the incest taboo. David F. Aberle et al. discuss its origins in the context of the mating patterns of other animals. They note that in mammals and birds "restrictions of inbreeding . . . are found among the larger, longer-lived, slower-maturing, and more intelligent animals."[21] In such

[19] Lee and DeVore, op. cit., pp. 30–48.

[20] D. S. Sade, "Inhibition of Son-Mother Mating among Free-Ranging Rhesus Monkeys," *Animals and Man*, 12 (1968), 18–38.

[21] D. F. Aberle et al., "The Incest Taboo and the Mating Patterns of Animals," *American Anthropologist*, 65 (1963), 260.

mammalian groups, inbreeding within the family is prevented by *intergenerational competition* whereby the young are forced out of the group when they reach sexual maturity. However, this would not be functional in people, since young humans reach a point at which they are capable of taking care of themselves several years after reaching sexual maturity. This pattern is probably related to the length of time required for the necessary transmission of cultural patterns for survival. "The incest taboo is a cultural phenomenon, and we must therefore assume that it emerged concomitantly with, or subsequent to, the beginnings of culture."[22]

The human band consists of a group of married and unmarried males and females. Mating is quite flexible in human groups. It is always permitted between husband and wife. However, depending on the culture, various premarital and extramarital relationships are often either promoted or else occur even though overtly restricted.

The human group is outbreeding. When seeking a wife, the male in many societies must find a woman in a neighboring band. The woman usually leaves the band of her birth and moves into the band of her husband. As with most human behavior, other variations do exist, but this is the most frequent type.

The result of outbreeding is that each person has relatives in adjacent bands. Frequently a man's wife and mother will have family in other bands while his sisters and daughters will move to other bands upon marriage. Thus, important social and economic relationships are formed between these bands. Kinship is the basic means of social organization, with the relationships of the family extended throughout the society.

The degree of territoriality among hunters and gatherers varies. However, in many parts of

the world, an area of land is not considered to be owned by a particular group, although tradition often places such locations as particular water holes and sacred areas in the realm of a group. In the case of a water hole, other groups will give the courtesy of asking permission to use it, and this permission is seldom refused. Warfare as we know it in farming and industrial societies does not occur among hunters and gatherers. However, formalized skirmishes or feuds do occur. The motivation for these is usually a belief that a death in one group was caused by the sorcery of a member of another. The victim's group may engage the suspected sorcerer's group and kill or injure one or a few people for revenge. Even this type of killing is completely foreign to some peoples.

Hominids as Hunters

Humans are omnivorous, eating both plants and animals. The significance of meat eating varies from society to society. Wholly vegetarian societies are products of civilization, a very recent development in human history.

Predatory activity is rare in primates. Many primates consume insects and small reptiles and birds, but only three primates have been observed eating mammalian flesh—baboons, chimpanzees, and humans. Although baboons and chimpanzees deliberately hunt, in terms of the total diet and social behavior, hunting is a minor activity.

Humans are hunters, although hunting as an economic activity has become relatively unimportant in many agricultural and civilized societies. But humans were hunters during the greatest part of their evolution, and the nature of human society must be understood in these terms. Students of human behavior have become greatly interested in the behavior of the social carnivores, for they exhibit similarities to human groups not shown by the monkeys and apes.

---

[22] Ibid., 262.

The social behavior of wild dogs Several studies have been made of the wild dog in East Africa.[23] Wild dogs live in packs which contain an average of five to seven adults with more adult males than adult females. These packs range over large areas following the migratory herds which are their prey.

The pack usually hunts at dusk and dawn. A herd of animals such as the gazelle, the most frequent prey, is stalked. When the herd becomes aware of the pack and begins to flee, the pack begins the chase. The leader chooses the prey, usually the slowest animal, and the rest of the pack follows its lead. Even if another potential victim crosses the path of a pack member, it will continue to chase the victim chosen by the leader. Members of the pack cut off the prey when it changes its course, thus forming a cooperative unit.

The chase usually lasts from three to five minutes, covering 1 to 2 miles. By the time the prey is overtaken, it is exhausted and often stunned. The animal is immediately killed, and the body is literally torn apart. The meat is swallowed in large pieces within a very short time. Over 85 percent of the chases end with success.

Among wild dogs the females form a linear hierarchy during the breeding season. Although there is usually a dominant male, in general, males are not ranked. Normally, only the dominant male and dominant female mate. The dominant female will prevent other females from mating through aggressive behavior, and if another female should give birth, these pups will be killed.

Therefore, usually only a single litter of six or seven pups is produced. The pups are left in a den which serves as a home base when the pack goes hunting, at least for the three-month period before the pups are old enough to follow the migratory herds. When the pack goes hunting, a guard, which may be either a male or female, is left behind. When the pack returns from the hunt with pieces of unchewed meat in their stomachs, much of the meat is disgorged in response to a characteristic begging gesture. Thus the guard and the pups are able to share in the kill (Figure 11-9). It has been suggested that producing only one litter per pack minimizes the time which must be spent in the vicinity of a den.[24]

Hominids as meat eaters George Schaller and Gordon Lowther maintain that the forms which social systems take are determined to a large extent by ecological conditions.[25] Simply because humans are closely related to the chimpanzees in a biological sense, it does not follow that the social behavior of the chimpanzee is an accurate model upon which a picture of early hominid behavior can be based. Unlike the chimpanzee, hominids are basically omnivorous hunters and meat eaters, and in a number of respects human society bears closer resemblance to the social carnivores—the lions, tigers, wild dogs, etc.—than to the apes.

As chimpanzees move through their territory, they construct a new nest each night in a different sleeping tree. The infant sleeps with its mother in her nest. Wild dogs with pups establish a home base to which they return after each hunt. The young are left with an adult at this home base. Human hunters and gatherers also establish

[23] R. D. Estes and J. Goddard, "Prey Selection and Hunting Behavior of the African Wild Dog," *Journal of Wildlife Management,* 31 (1967), 52–70; W. Kühme, "Communal Food Distribution and Division of Labor in African Wild Dogs," *Nature,* 205 (30 January 1965), 443–444; D. G. Kleiman and J. F. Eisenberg, "Comparisons of Canid and Felid Social Systems from an Evolutionary Perspective," *Animal Behavior,* 21 (1973), 637–659.

[24] Kleiman and Eisenberg, op. cit.

[25] G. B. Schaller and G. R. Lowther, "The Relevance of Carnivore Behavior to the Study of Early Hominids," *Southwestern Journal of Anthropology* 25 (1969), 307–341.

home bases. From these bases they move out to hunt or collect vegetable food, returning each evening. Mothers or other adults remain with the young children and sometimes take them a short distance from the camp when they gather vegetable food. These home bases are moved periodically, but normally a specific camp serves as a home base for several months. Unlike a group of wild dogs, a human group is likely to have infants around at all times of the year.

A factor related to food sharing is that meat is highly portable. It would be difficult for a herbivore to transport a quantity of grass or, for that matter, for a chimpanzee to transport a large amount of leaves or fruit. But meat, which is pound for pound higher in nutritional value than vegetable food, can be transported with little difficulty. A chimpanzee can carry a dead monkey in its hand, or a carcass can be dragged along the ground. Wild dogs transport meat in their stomachs. Humans can simply fling a carcass over their backs or cut it up into several large pieces. Unlike other primates, humans can also manufacture containers, such as baskets, for the transport of vegetable food.

Among wild dogs the guards can be either

Figure 11-9   Wild dogs, Tanzania. *Female (not the mother) regurgitates meat to pups.*

male or female, for both sexes hunt. People, with their helpless infants, have developed a *sexual division of labor* by which, basically, the male hunts and the female gathers vegetable food and dries the meat to reduce weight. Still, the basic pattern is that a segment of the group hunts and brings meat to a home base, where it is shared with other adults and children.

Cooperation on the hunt and the lack of a dominance hierarchy characterize human societies. Efficient hunting demands cooperation, and a dominance system is not consistent with sharing patterns. Among the baboons, meat is monopolized by the dominant males. Chimpanzees, however, not only cooperate in hunting but often share the kill. Wild dogs, although showing a dominance hierarchy with respect to mating, cooperate in hunting and also share food. Usually dominance systems do not develop within human hunting and gathering groups. Leadership patterns do appear, but they are based primarily upon skill. The leader usually has no coercive power, simply the power that comes from respect.

Human hunting techniques The dog pack stalks a herd and then chases down the prey. Human hunting techniques are quite different. While humans can run down small animals, such as young gazelles, the basic method of human hunting is to get close to an animal and to wound it in some way. Only rarely is an animal killed outright. It may take several hours or even several days to catch up with the fleeing and wounded prey. Unlike the carnivores, humans can keep up a steady pace, walking for most of the day, covering many miles, as they follow the wounded animal. Of course, people also can construct a variety of traps so that they need not even be present at the moment an animal is caught. Wounding, butchering, and sometimes transporting meat all involve the use of tools.

Communication

The linguist Benjamin Lee Whorf, in his book *Language, Thought and Reality,* claims, "Speech is the best show man puts on."[26] Indeed, anthropologists consider language to be such an important aspect of our nature that an entire branch of anthropology, *linguistics,* is devoted to its description and analysis. The understanding of linguistic behavior is important to the anthropologist's understanding of human adaptations and adaptability.

Language is but one means of communication. *Communication* is a very general term. In its broadest application, it simply means that some stimulus or message is transmitted and received. Communication means different things to different disciplines, and the term is used by the physicist, mathematician, engineer, and behavioral scientist. We are concerned with its usage in relation to animal life. In this context, communication means that one animal transmits information to another animal. This information could simply convey the presence of the animal, or it could mean such things as dominance, fear, hunger, or sexual receptiveness. Communication does not necessarily imply thought. As neurological complexity evolves, so do the methods, mechanisms, and potentials of communication.

Language *Language* is a complex form of communication and was defined by Edward Sapir, often called the father of American linguistics, as "a purely human and noninstinctive method of communicating ideas, emotions, and desires by means of a system of voluntarily produced sym-

---

[26] B. L. Whorf, *Language, Thought and Reality: Selected Writings of Benjamin Lee Whorf,* John B. Carroll (ed.) (Cambridge, Mass., and New York: Technology Press and Wiley, 1956), p. 249.

bols."[27] A *symbol* is something—a word, a picture, a situation—that represents something else that is distant in time and space from the symbol. This concept was discussed in Chapter 1.

Methods of primate communication Social animals are constantly communicating with one another. Even the spatial positions they assume in relation to one another can be forms of communication. Peter Marler has summarized four ways in which primates communicate: through olfactory, tactile, visual, and auditory signals.[28]

Compared with other mammals, the primates tend toward a reduction in the olfactory sense. The sense of smell is much more important to prosimians and New World monkeys than to Old World monkeys and apes. Some prosimians, such as the ring-tailed lemur, have specialized skin glands that excrete odoriferous substances. This material, along with urine and feces, is used by the animal in marking off territory. Many of the New World monkeys use the olfactory sense also and, like prosimians, have permanent scent glands.

The sense of smell is less predominant in Old World monkeys and apes. Yet male rhesus monkeys, for example, recognize an estrus female by specific odors originating in the vagina. The great emphasis on deodorants and perfumes indicates the role played by olfactory signals in human communication.

The tactile sense is also important in primates. Primates spend long periods of time touching one another. Grooming activity, for example, functions not only to remove dirt and parasites from the fur but communicates affection as well. Grooming is especially seen among the females, between a female and her infant, and between a male and an estrus female. In addition, the close physical contact between a mother and her infant is essential for normal child development.[29]

Of great importance to primates is visual communication. Positioning of animals in relationship to one another conveys information about dominance, feeding, sexual behavior, and attitude. The general body posture can signal tension or relaxation, for example. Motivational researchers have concluded that a political candidate, newscaster, or other person talking to large groups should stand slightly sideways rather than face directly ahead. The latter condition supposedly is taken as a "dominance" display and is said to make an audience nervous.

In addition to the positioning of the body, facial gestures are used extensively among primates to convey information. Various examples of gestures were discussed in relation to the baboon.

Vocal communication One thing is certain: primates, including people, do not have to open their mouths to communicate a wide range of information. But anyone who has been to a zoo and has heard the vocalizations of the siamangs and other primates or, for that matter, anyone who has visited a schoolyard, knows that primates not only vocalize but are quite noisy. Some arboreal monkeys and apes are among the loudest and most vocal of mammals.

Many primate sounds are, however, nonvocal. For instance, the gorilla will beat his chest, shake branches, or strike the ground to com-

[27] Edward Sapir, *Language* (New York: Harcourt/Harvest Books, 1921), p. 8.

[28] P. Marler, "Communication in Monkeys and Apes," in DeVore, op. cit., pp. 544–584.

[29] W. A. Mason, "The Social Development of Monkeys and Apes," in DeVore, op. cit., pp. 514–543.

municate frustration. Likewise, a bit of silence is often as meaningful as noise itself and often indicates danger.

Nonhuman primates produce a number of vocalized sounds. In prosimians and some monkeys, these sounds tend to be discrete. But the anthropoids tend to produce calls that grade into each other, forming a *call system*. Because of this blending, it is hard to estimate the number of *calls,* or specific messages, produced. Marler estimates that the number of signals averages between ten and fifteen for most species.[30]

Although there is a great deal of variation from one species to another in the meaning of different sounds, some generalizations can be made. Barking sounds are often used as alarm signals by gorillas, chimpanzees, baboons, rhesus monkeys, and langurs. Screeching and screaming sounds often signal distress, while growling indicates annoyance. Different types of grunts produced while moving around seem to function to maintain contact between the animals in a group. Sounds can be produced by one animal which direct the attention of another toward a specific object, convey quantitative information, specify a particular type of behavior that should be used, or initiate a whole sequence of related behaviors. Primates also have a great ability to inform one another about their moods at particular moments through subtle changes in their vocalizations.

Human language Other animals, especially primates, share many of the features of human language. However, there are several characteristics of language that are, as far as we know, unique or developed to a higher degree in humans. The calls of nonhuman primates are limited. The monkey or ape in the wild does not invent new calls for new situations.

[30] Marler, loc. cit., p. 558.

Human language is both *open* and *discrete.* Openness is the quality of being able to coin new labels for new concepts and objects. The hunter and gatherer who sees an airplane for the first time can attach a designation to it, just as a scientist who discovers a new phenomenon can give it a name. Words in a language represent discrete entities or experiences. The gibbon who is content one moment and frightened the next will simply grade one call into the next. The human conversing in language can say, "I am content" or "I am frightened." These are distinct messages that do not blend with one another.

Language is also characterized by *duality of patterning.* This means that a finite number of sounds can be combined into an almost infinite number of meaningful units, which in turn can be combined into an almost infinite number of phrases, sentences, paragraphs, and so on.

The discrete units of a language are *arbitrary.* That is, a word, for example, has no real connection to the thing it refers to. There is nothing about a pen that is suggested by the sound "pen." If we all agreed, it could be called a "table." Even though the potential for sound formation is innate, the meanings of the arbitrary elements of a language must be learned.

One of the most important and useful things about human language is *displacement.* Displacement is the ability to communicate about things at times other than the present, and to talk and think about things not directly in front of the speaker. It is this characteristic of language that makes learning from the past, as well as planning for the future, possible. It is to a large degree responsible for creativity, imagination, and illusion.

The characteristics of language discussed above, termed *design features,* have been intensively studied by the linguist Charles F. Hockett. These design features, as well as several not mentioned above, are summarized in Table 11-1.

Table 11-1   Design Features of Language

DF 1 Vocal-auditory channel	DF 10 Displacement (we can talk about things that are remote in space, time, or both from the site of the communicative transaction)
DF 2 Broadcast transmission and directional reception	
DF 3 Rapid fading (the sound of speech does not hover in the air)	DF 11 Openness (new linguistic messages are coined freely and easily, and, in context, are usually understood)
DF 4 Interchangeability (adult members of any speech community are interchangeably transmitters and receivers of linguistic signals)	DF 12 Tradition (the conventions of any one human language are passed down by teaching and learning, not through the germ plasm)
DF 5 Complete feedback (the speaker hears everything relevant to what he says)	
DF 6 Specialization (the direct-energetic consequences of linguistic signals are biologically unimportant; only the triggering consequences are important)	DF 13 Duality of patterning (every language has a patterning in terms of arbitrary but stable meaningless signal elements and also a patterning in terms of minimum meaningful arrangements of those elements)
DF 7 Semanticity (linguistic signals function to correlate and organize the life of a community because there are associative ties between signal elements and features in the world; in short, some linguistic forms have denotations)	DF 14 Prevarication (we can say things that are false or meaningless)
DF 8 Arbitrariness (the relation between a meaningful element in a language and its denotation is independent of any physical or geometrical resemblance between the two)	DF 15 Reflexiveness (in a language, we can communicate about the very system in which we are communicating)
DF 9 Discreteness (the possible messages in any language constitute a discrete repertoire rather than a continuous one)	DF 16 Learnability (a speaker of a language can learn another language)

Reprinted with permission of Macmillan Publishing Co., Inc., from Alison Jolly, *The Evolution of Primate Behavior*, p. 322. Copyright © 1972 by Alison Jolly. Table after C. F. Hockett and S. A. Altmann, ''A Note on Design Features,'' in *Animal Communication*, edited by T. A. Sebeok, Indiana Univ. Press, Bloomington, 1968, pp. 61–72, by permission of Indiana University Press; and P. Marler, ''Animals and Man: Communication and Its Development,'' in *Communication*, edited by J. D. Roslansky, North-Holland, Amsterdam, 1969, pp. 23–62, by permission of North-Holland Publishing Co. and P. Marler.

Symbolic Behavior in Chimpanzees

As research on primates continues, the uniqueness of humankind diminishes. With the realization that chimpanzees make tools, language has become the one characteristic thought of as unique to humans. But now several chimpanzees, including Washoe and Sarah, have cast doubt even on the exclusiveness of this characteristic.

For almost half a century, researchers have been attempting to teach chimpanzees language. Chimpanzees have been taught to understand more than a hundred words, and in the 1940s a chimpanzee named Vicki, after years of training, was with difficulty and lack of clarity able to say three words: *mamma, papa,* and *cup.*[31]

We now realize that the chimpanzee is not equipped to produce human sounds, and so systems of nonvocal communication, which nevertheless have the other design features of language, have been tried in experimental situations with a great deal of success. The chimpanzee Washoe has been taught to use the American Sign Language for the Deaf, and Sarah has been taught to use arbitrarily shaped plastic forms that represent words.

Washoe In the American Sign Language for the Deaf (Ameslan), different positions of the hand correspond to different words. The language is arbitrary, that is, the hand positions are not produced automatically but must be learned. The positions can be combined to form sentences, and different words can appear at different places in different sentences. Hence, Ameslan is characterized by duality of patterning. It is also an open system in that there is a potential to invent new "words" by a new hand configuration.

At the age of seven, Washoe could use 175 words. She had learned her first sign at about fifteen months and had acquired a vocabulary of some 50 words at the age of about three and a half. The fact that she could learn individual signs and use them in the proper context is interesting in itself. What is more significant is that she could invent both sentences and words. For instance, at two she combined the signs for "come-gimme" and "sweet." She had never seen the signs combined in this way; and this sentence, plus her invention of signs, meant that she

was capable of using an open system of communication (Figure 11-10).[32]

In relation to the invention of words, the Gardners, who worked with her, relate the following story. The Gardners did not know the sign for bib, and so invented one, wiping the mouth with the open hand.

One evening at dinner time, a human companion was holding up a bib and asking her to name it. Washoe tried "come-gimme" and "please," but did not seem to be able to remember the bib sign that we had taught her. Then, she did something very interesting. With the index fingers of both hands she drew an outline of a bib on her chest — starting from behind her neck where a bib should be tied, moving her index fingers down along the outer edge of her chest, and bringing them together again just above her navel.

We could see that Washoe's invented sign for "bib" was at least as good as ours, and both were inventions. At the next meeting of the human participants in the project, we discussed the possibility of adopting Washoe's invention as an alternative to ours, but decided against it. The purpose of the project was, after all, to see if Washoe could learn a human system of two-way communication, and not to see if human beings could learn a system devised by an infant chimpanzee. We continued to insist on the "napkin-wipe" sign for bibs, until this became a reliable item in Washoe's repertoire. Five months later, when we were presenting films on Washoe's signing to fluent signers at the California School for the Deaf in Berkeley, we learned that drawing

[31] K. J. Hayes and C. Hayes, "The Intellectual Development of a Home-raised Chimpanzee," *Proceedings of the American Philosophical Society,* 95 (1951), 105–109.

[32] B. T. Gardner and R. A. Gardner, "Two-Way Communication with an Infant Chimpanzee," in A. M. Schrier and F. Stollnitz (eds.), *Behavior of Nonhuman Primates* (New York: Academic, 1971), vol. 4, pp. 117–184.

Figure 11-10 Washoe. *Washoe using the Ameslan sign for "sweet" to name a lollipop.*

an outline of a bib on the chest with both index fingers is the correct sign for "bib."[33]

It is known that apes can recognize themselves in mirrors, while monkeys and other animals see the image as that of another animal. But until Washoe, this evidence was indirect (see Chapter 1). Washoe was gazing into a mirror one day and was asked by a trainer (trainers and other humans never talked in human language in Washoe's presence but always used the sign language and made chimpanzeelike noises), "Who is that?" Washoe gave the signs for "Me, Washoe."[34]

Sarah Sarah, another chimpanzee, using plastic shapes, is able to form sentences, answer ques-

[33] Ibid., p. 139. Used with permission of Academic Press and the authors.

[34] van Lawick-Goodall, op. cit., p. 250.

(a)

(b)

(c)

(d)

Figure 11-11 Chimp-to-chimp communication. *In this sequence two young males, Booee (right) and Bruno (left), communicate using Ameslan. Booee is requesting some fruit slices from Bruno: (a) "you"; (b) "feed"; (c) "Booee (his name sign)"; (d) Bruno gives Booee the fruit.*

tions, and describe the properties of objects.[35] She is able to "say" if something is the same or different. Thus, when shown two apples, she picks up the plastic form for "same," but if shown an apple and a banana, she chooses the form meaning "different." She is able to answer such questions as, "What is the same as . . .?" and to use the form meaning "name of" to construct a proper sentence in response to the question, "What is the name of . . .?" She is also able to perform the correct behavior when shown the sequence of plastic forms meaning, "Sarah put apple in pail and banana in dish." Sarah has also learned to use the conditional expressed by the words "if" and "then."

By 1972, Sarah had learned to use about 130 "words" and her level of correct usage was about 75 to 80 percent. There is evidence that she can think in "language," since she is able to understand words when the referent—that is, the thing the plastic form represents—is absent. Washoe also seems able to do this with the sign language. This would then be displacement and symbolic thought. The research with Washoe and Sarah indicates that chimpanzees at least have a rudimentary potential for an open, arbitrary, symbolic, learned system of communication that is characterized by duality of patterning and displacement.

In 1970, Washoe was moved to the Institute for Primate Studies, in Norman, Oklahoma. Here, Roger Fouts has trained other chimpanzees in the use of Ameslan. An especially interesting question is whether Washoe will transmit her knowledge of Ameslan to any children she may have. Already evidence is emerging that chimpanzees will communicate with one another using the sign language (Figure 11-11).[36]

Chimpanzees are learning symbolic systems of communications in admittedly artificial situations, yet such experiments are providing new and important insights into primate potentials and the evolution of human language. The fact that chimpanzees must initially be taught "language" by humans perhaps permits us, at least for the present, to maintain Edward Sapir's statement that language "is a purely human" characteristic.

On the other hand, it is entirely possible that the chimpanzee and other apes have a natural language of their own. Roger Fouts writes: "It is conceivable that chimpanzees may have a language of their own—if we can ever find a universally agreed upon definition of language, and if we are clever enough to make the appropriate observations."[37]

Protoculture

Humans have been described as the cultural animal, adapting to various niches largely by cultural means. *Culture* represents a body of behavioral patterns which are learned and passed down from generation to generation. (See Chapter 1 for a full definition of culture.) Primatologists are becoming increasingly aware of the fact that not only are nonhuman primates capable of adapting to certain new situations in terms of learned behavior, but many behavioral patterns are passed down from generation to generation as a type of social heredity. Those who feel that the transmission of learned behavior is common among these forms believe that primates, especially apes, do

[35] D. Premack, "Language in Chimpanzee?" *Science,* 172 (21 May 1971), 822; A. J. Premack and D. Premack, "Teaching Language to an Ape," *Scientific American,* 227 (October 1972), 92–99.

[36] R. S. Fouts, "Capacities for Language in Great Apes," in R. H. Ruttle (ed.), *Socioecology and Psychology of Primates* (The Hague: Mouton, 1975), pp. 371–390.

[37] Ibid., p. 373.

have a *protoculture;* that is, they are characterized by the simplest, most basic aspects of culture.

Protoculture in monkeys Some of the best data on the degree to which learned behavior is developed in nonhuman primates come from studies of the Japanese macaque. Over thirty troops have been intensively studied, some since the 1950s. J. E. Frisch has summarized these studies.[38]

Many behavioral patterns in the macaque are certainly genetically determined. Laboratory studies, in which animals have been reared away from the troop or reared by a human substitute mother, have shown that certain vocalizations and dominance gestures occur in the isolated monkey. Since the animal had no contact with the natural mother or troop, such similarities between isolated and troop-reared behavior must be interpreted as being genetically determined.

On the other hand, many behavioral patterns are apparently learned. One infant raised with its natural mother never learned to use its cheek pouches for food simply because its mother never used hers. Later the animal was placed in a cage with another monkey. This second monkey would rush to the food and place much of it in his cheek pouch, leaving little for the first. Very quickly, however, the original animal learned the proper use of the pouch.[39]

In the actual troop, because of the long-term studies, many introductions and changes have been observed in troop behavior as a result of natural or human-introduced events. At Takasakiyama, Japan, the death of the dominant male resulted in changes in troop behavior when a new male assumed the top rank. This occurred in a provisionized troop which regularly visited the feeding area. Under the old leader, the arrival time at the feeding ground would vary from day to day between 6 A.M. and 5 P.M. When the new leader took control, the arrival time was more restricted, mainly between 11 A.M. and 5 P.M.[40]

Human-induced changes have included the introduction of new types of food. The Japanese macaque does not eat everything available in its natural environment and does not always accept the introduction of new foods. Candy was accepted readily by the infants, who generally show a greater amount of exploratory activity than adults. However, even after several years, candy was not accepted by the entire troop. On the other hand, the introduction of wheat was immediately accepted by the dominant males and spread throughout the entire troop in only four hours.

Some of the best examples of behavioral changes have occurred on Koshima Island, Japan. One of the first of these was ocean swimming. When the troop was first studied, swimming rarely occurred. Then one day, one animal went for a swim after food, and within a short period of time, swimming was a very common activity.

The primatologists introduced sweet potatoes as a food. Normally, macaques rub dirt off food with their hands. One day a young female took her sweet potato to a stream and washed it. The value of this would appear to be its greater efficiency in dirt removal. Soon the pattern of sweet potato washing spread to the other members of her play group, then to the mothers of these young monkeys. Four years later, 80 to 90 percent of the troop were washing sweet potatoes (Figure 11-12a).

Later some monkeys began to wash their

[38] J. E. Frisch, ''Individual Behavior and Intertroop Variability in Japanese Macaques,'' in P. C. Jay (ed.), *Primates: Studies in Adaptation and Variability* (New York: Holt, 1968), pp. 243–252.

[39] Ibid., pp. 244–245.

[40] Ibid., p. 248.

sweet potatoes in salt water, the salt probably improving the flavor. Often the sweet potatoes would be carried some distance to the shore. In carrying sweet potatoes, the animals moved bipedally; hence, erect bipedalism has become a more frequent locomotor pattern of this troop on land (Figure 11-12b).[41]

This later development is of interest to students of human evolution. The earliest hominids developed erect bipedalism as a dominant form of locomotion. There was not necessarily a sudden shift to erect bipedalism, but a slow increase in the frequency of this mode of locomotion in response to some environmental factor. Anthropologists are not quite sure what this environmental change was, although the replacement of tropical forest by grasslands has been suggested.

On Koshima Island the investigators saw the increased use of this locomotor pattern in response to a new learned behavioral pattern, washing sweet potatoes in salt water. It is conceivable that if a behavioral pattern like this had some selective advantage, animals biologically more capable of bipedalism might contribute more genes to the gene pool of the next generation. At any rate, the behavioral changes in the Japanese macaque at least suggest how changes in the frequency of an anatomical trait might result from a change in a behavioral pattern.

Protoculture in chimpanzees Protocultural behavior is also present in the chimpanzee. Some of this learned behavior was discussed earlier in relation to young chimps learning to use termite sticks and the use of human-made objects in obtaining status. In addition, young chimps learn a great deal about chimpanzee society in their play groups. For instance, they learn who are the dominant adult females by the actions that are

(a)

(b)

Figure 11-12   The Japanese macaque. (a) *Sweet potato washing;* (b) *bipedal transport of sweet potato to ocean for washing.*

[41] Ibid., p. 249.

taken against them if they get into a fight with another youngster. Chimpanzee females also appear to learn how to be efficient mothers from watching their own mothers and taking care of their siblings. For instance, Goodall reports how a young female who took care of her orphaned brother seemed to be a more experienced mother when she had her first offspring than other first-time mothers.[42]

The point of this discussion is that the beginning of cultural behavior can be seen in monkey and ape societies. Continuing investigations into these phenomena can aid the physical anthropologist in understanding the possible ways in which culture developed in ourselves.

Summary

Perhaps most anthropologists would agree that members of our species are the only living organisms with the capability of asking the question: What am I? In the search for the answers to the question, anthropologists are carefully studying the behavior of closely related animal forms. While we would like to think of ourselves as something unique in the universe, continuing studies are leading us to the conclusion that the features which characterize *Homo sapiens* are in themselves not unique. What is unique is the degree of development and the complexity of many of these features.

The social structure of humans is similar in many ways to that of primate social groups, while in many other aspects it resembles that of the social carnivores. Among the features developed to a greater extent in ourselves than in any other primate group are long-term male-female relationships within a large social unit, lack of hormonal control over sexuality, sharing of food and other resources, sexual division of labor, cooperation and egalitarianism, and organization based upon kinship.

Parallels can be recognized between hunting in humans and social carnivores, such as the wild dogs of Africa, but humans differ in many ways. Rather than using the method of hunting whereby the prey is simply run down, humans wound their prey and then track it until it is found. The most notable feature of human hunting is the dependence upon tools for wounding, trapping, butchering, and transporting the meat.

Language is thought of as a uniquely human characteristic. Compared with the call systems of other primates, human language does show some distinctive features. But experimental work on chimpanzees, especially with Washoe and Sarah, has raised the question of what the linguistic abilities of the chimpanzee really are; research has been accelerated in this area.

Research into primate behavior has shown that many of these animals, especially monkeys and apes, have a protocultural ability. The study of the ways in which behavior is learned and transmitted in nonhuman primates will, we hope, aid in an understanding of the development and nature of culture in *Homo sapiens*.

[42] van Lawick-Goodall, op. cit., pp. 261–262.

SUGGESTED READINGS

Jolly, A. *The Evolution of Primate Behavior*. New York: Macmillan, 1972. Perhaps one of the best general discussions of all aspects of primate behavior.

Kummer, H. *Primate Societies: Group Techniques of Ecological Adaptations*. Chicago: Aldine, 1971. A discussion of primate behavior, with a special interest in ecology. Many of the examples used are based upon the author's fieldwork among the Hamadryas baboons.

Rowell, T. *The Social Behaviour of Monkeys*. Baltimore: Penguin, 1972. A discussion of the various aspects of monkey behavior.

DeVore, I. (ed.). *Primate Behavior: Field Studies of Monkeys and Apes.* New York: Holt, 1965.

Dolhinow, P. (ed.). *Primate Patterns.* New York: Holt, 1972.

Jay, P. C. (ed.). *Primates: Studies in Adaptation and Variability.* New York: Holt, 1968.

The above three books are readers in primate behavior.

Schaller, G. *The Year of the Gorilla.* Chicago: Univ. of Chicago Press, 1964.

van Lawick-Goodall, J. *In the Shadow of Man.* Boston: Houghton Mifflin, 1971.

The above two studies were written for the nontechnical audience and include discussions of the worker's experience in the field.

Chapter Twelve

The Comparative Anatomy, Ontogeny, and Molecular Biology of the Living Primates

Since living humans, apes, monkeys, and prosimians have all evolved from similar sources, they share a number of characteristics. Yet each primate species displays in its form and behavior the results of its specific evolutionary history. Comparative studies of anatomy, ontogeny, and molecular biology of the living primates provide data on the evolutionary relationships which exist between them and clues by which we can reconstruct the process of human evolution.

COMPARATIVE ANATOMY

The mechanisms of the evolutionary process have been worked out in considerable detail, yet knowledge of human evolution specifically is still in a formative stage. This is to be expected. Areas of knowledge such as mathematics, chemistry, and physics have been developed over hundreds of years. The modern study of evolution began only in the last half of the nineteenth century.

It is not surprising that the current literature is full of disagreements. This does not mean, however, that the evolutionary concept is incorrect. As Ernst Mayr tells us:

It must be stressed, for the benefit of nonevolutionists, that none of the arguments going on in these areas touch upon the basic principles of the [evolutionary] theory. It is the application of the theory that is sometimes controversial, not the theory itself.[1]

Evidence of our evolutionary past lies in the fossil record, but, as we will see in the next chapters, the fossil record is incomplete and a number of basic problems of interpretation exist. Com-

[1] E. Mayr, *Populations, Species and Evolution* (Cambridge, Mass.: Belknap, 1970), p. 7.

parative anatomy, ontogeny, and molecular biology of living forms provide data which can be used in conjunction with the fossil record to reconstruct the course of human evolution. Many of these data are based upon the realization that new anatomical structures do not suddenly arise from nowhere but represent the slow modification of preexisting structures. In the discussion of taxonomy in Chapter 9, we saw how homologous structures help us determine evolutionary relationships. Careful comparative studies attempt to establish these homologies, which not only display evolutionary relationships but also help in reconstructing the evolutionary events of the past.

An anatomical structure represents part of an adaptive complex and can be understood only in terms of that complex. Here the main task is to present information which will help reconstruct evolutionary relationships and events. The structures and features involved will be discussed within the context of their functions, which can be related to the behavior of the animal. It is important to realize from the beginning that anatomical changes develop within the context of behavioral changes, and new behavioral patterns often provide the selective pressures for evolutionary development.

It often is difficult to judge which anatomical changes are of greatest significance. In this chapter, the discussion of comparative anatomy will center on complexes which are considered by most anthropologists to be pivotal in the origin and development of the hominids: locomotion, manipulation, mastication, and mental processes.

Comparative Anatomy of Locomotion

Comparative studies of locomotion have been of great interest because many anthropologists believe that locomotor changes were largely responsible for the initial differentiation of the hominid line from the pongid line. Humans are erect bipeds. Humans are not the only erect bipeds in the animal kingdom, nor are they the only primate capable of this method of locomotion. But unlike other primates, the hominids are characterized by a dependence upon this mode of locomotion and have evolved a number of anatomical changes which have made efficient and habitual erect bipedalism possible.

Locomotor patterns among primates The order Primates is characterized by a great flexibility in locomotor patterns. Most mammalian orders are characterized by specializations in locomotion, as seen in such forms as the bats, whales and porpoises, and the hooved animals. But consistent with primate adaptability in general, most primates have retained a rather large repertoire of locomotor behaviors.

A number of locomotor patterns can be distinguished among primates. These have been classified by the Napiers; they distinguish four basic patterns, which are defined in terms of the functions of the forelimbs and hindlimbs. These four basic patterns are vertical clinging and leaping, quadrupedalism, brachiation, and bipedalism.[2]

It must be emphasized that this or any classification of locomotor behavior is based on dominant patterns. The primates are highly flexible forms, and any one species will show a wide variety of locomotor patterns. Table 12-1 is a list of such patterns as seen in one group of chimpanzees. In addition, the categories listed by the Napiers represent arbitrary divisions on a continuum; many primate species exhibit patterns which are intermediate to those described.

[2] J. R. Napier and P. H. Napier, *A Handbook of the Living Primates* (New York: Academic, 1967), pp. 385–391.

Vertical clinging and leaping (Figure 12-1a) has only recently been recognized as a basic pattern within the primate order. As the term indicates, the animal resting on a branch is normally clinging to the branch, keeping its body in a vertical, or *orthgrade*, position. In moving from one branch to another, it leaps, landing vertically on a second branch. On the ground, these animals move by hopping or bipedally.

Vertical clinging and leaping is the dominant locomotor pattern among several prosimians, such as the tarsier, galago, and sifaka. Napier believes that this type of locomotion is basic in the primate order and that forms displaying it were ancestral to the modern quadrupedal monkeys.[3] If this is the case, orthograde posture is also basic in the order.

[3] J. R. Napier and A. C. Walker. "Vertical Clinging and Leaping: A Newly Recognized Category of Locomotor Behaviour of Primates," *Folia Primatologia*, 6 (1967), 204–219.

In *quadrupedalism* the animal moves on all four limbs with the body held parallel to the ground, a posture known as *pronograde*. Several forms of quadrupedalism are recognized by the Napiers. The *slow-climbing* primates, such as the potto and loris, move along a branch in a slow, cautious manner. There is no leaping or running. On the other hand, *branch running and walking* is a form of quadrupedalism in which the primate will climb, jump, and leap among the branches and walk and run along the branches on all four limbs. The forelimbs and/or hindlimbs are used to grasp the branch. This form is characteristic of many of the lemurs and New World monkeys, such as the marmosets, squirrel monkeys, and capuchins, and one Old World group, the guenons.

Many Old World monkeys are more terrestrial in habits. Included here are the macaques, baboons, and patas monkeys. The *ground running and walking* type of locomotion does not in-

Table 12-1 Locomotor Patterns in the Chimpanzee

Name	Frequency	Ground or Trees	Distance Covered
Quadrupedal walk	Common	Both	Any
Quadrupedal run	Common	Both	Any
Rapid run	Common	Ground	30 feet
Gallop	Occasional	Ground	30+ feet
Vertical climb	Common	Trees	10–100 feet
Bipedal walk	Rare	Ground	Maximum seen, 9 paces
Bipedal walk on legs with use of arms	Occasional	Trees	15 feet
Ground leap	Occasional	Ground	6 feet
Vertical leap	Rare	Trees	30-foot leaps
Swing	Occasional	Trees	10 feet
Brachiation	Common	Trees	20 feet

Adapted from Vernon Reynolds and Frances Reynolds, "Chimpanzees of the Budongo Forest," in I. DeVore (ed.), *Primate Behavior: Field Studies of Monkeys and Apes.* Copyright © 1965 by Holt, Rinehart & Winston, Inc. Used by permission of Holt, Rinehart & Winston, Inc.

volve grasping with the hand. In the trees, these animals will branch walk and leap.

The term *brachiation* refers to a pattern in which the hands and arms are used as main organs of locomotion. Brachiation is properly used to describe the locomotor patterns of such forms as the gibbon, which will be discussed below. But in describing two additional types of quadrupedalism, the Napiers use the term *semibrachiation* to indicate the extensive use of the hands to suspend and propel the body in forms that are otherwise quadrupedal. In the *New World semibrachiation* type, as seen in the howler, spider, and woolly monkeys, the prehensile tail is used extensively, in addition to the hands (Figure 12-1b). In the *Old World semibrachiation* type, hand-over-hand locomotion is seldom seen, but leaping is common, with the arms extended out to grasp a branch. Examples of this latter type are the colobus and langurs. It is interesting that the black-and-white colobus monkey of Africa and the spider monkey of Central and South America, both semibrachiators, are thumbless. In these forms the elongated fingers act as a hook by which the animal can suspend itself from a branch.

In *true brachiation* the body is propelled by arm swinging. The body is suspended from above, and the animal moves through the branches hand over hand. This is the locomotor pattern of the gibbon and siamang (Figure 12-1c).

True brachiation and semibrachiation are parts of a larger behavioral complex which can be termed *suspensory behavior*. A gibbon, for example, will suspend itself by one arm from a branch for up to twenty minutes at a time. This type of behavior will take up to half of the animal's waking hours. In this position the gibbon collects with its free arm various fruits, berries, buds, and flowers. These items often grow on the ends of branches it would be impossible for a quadrupedal primate to reach since the end

of the branch would not support the animal's weight.[4]

While the great apes may occasionally show true brachiation, especially in young animals, the most typical locomotor behavior differs from that of the gibbons and siamang. The orangutans can be classified as *modified brachiators*, as they use their hindlimbs a great deal in suspensory activities. When arboreal, they move from tree to tree without descending to the ground. However, some orangutans spend some time on the ground.

Detailed studies of ape locomotion and anatomy have led Russel H. Tuttle to believe that the locomotor behavior of the African apes is best described as *knuckle walking* instead of modified brachiation (Figure 12-1d).[5] The chimpanzee and gorilla move from tree to tree on the ground, where they are essentially semierect quadrupeds, supporting the upper part of their bodies on the knuckles of their hands, as opposed to using the palms, like other primates. In knuckle walking, the fingers are flexed and the animal places his weight on special knuckle pads, which lie on the backs of the fingers. However, this is not the pattern in the orangutan, which usually walks on its palms or on the side of its fists.

The Napiers use the term *bipedalism* to refer to human *erect bipedalism*. Upright posture and walking on two hindlimbs are seen to a greater or lesser extent throughout the primate order, but only in the hominids is this the habitual mode of locomotion. A major area of interest in anthro-

---

[4] R. Tuttle, "Functional and Evolutionary Biology of Hylobatid Hands and Feet," in D. M. Rumbaugh (ed.), *Gibbon and Siamang* (Basel: Karger, 1972), vol. 1, pp. 136–206; C. R. Carpenter and N. M. Durham, "A Preliminary Description of Suspensory Behavior in Nonhuman Primates," *Proceedings of the Second International Congress of Primatology*, *Atlanta* (Basel: Karger, 1969), 2, 147–154.

[5] R. H. Tuttle, "Knuckle-Walking and the Problem of Human Origin," *Science*, 166 (21 November 1969), 953–961.

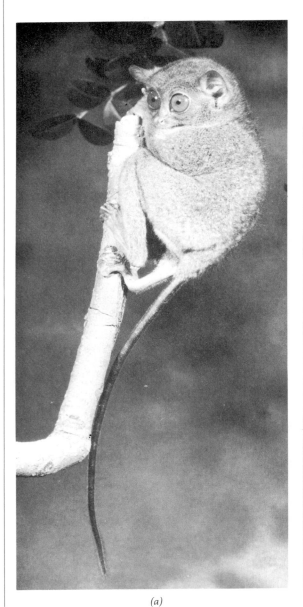

Figure 12-1 Primate locomotor patterns. (a) *Vertical clinging and leaping (tarsier)*; (b) *semibrachiation (spider monkey)*; (c) *brachiation (siamang)*; (d) *knuckle walking (chimpanzee)*.

(a)

(b)

(c)

(d)

The Comparative Anatomy, Ontogeny, and Molecular Biology of the Living Primates

pology is the origin of human bipedalism. Since humans and the chimpanzee are closely related in an evolutionary sense, studies of ape locomotion have been pursued in order to help solve this problem. There is a great deal of disagreement. Sherwood Washburn postulates that the hominids developed from a knuckle-walking stage;[6] that is, the hominid and pongid lines diverged at that point in pongid evolution where the ancestral form had developed a knuckle-walking pattern of locomotion. Tuttle sees no evidence for this and believes that the ancestors of the hominids probably engaged in some sort of *suspensory posturing,* using their hands and arms to suspend themselves from branches. However, this was not brachiation as seen in the modern gibbon.[7]

Studies of the comparative anatomy of locomotion One of the major aims of comparative anatomy is the reconstruction of the pathway of human evolution. Questions about the locomotor history of humans can be answered, in part, by detailed studies of that part of the skeleton, musculature, and nervous system involved in locomotor activity. If the human pattern evolved from a pongid pattern, evidence should be found by comparing the organs of ape and human locomotion. While similarities may result from *convergence,* the existence of a great number of detailed similarities is usually taken to indicate a common origin. In the reconstruction of a hypothetical common ancestor on the basis of similarities in modern apes and humans, specialized adaptations in these modern forms become evident. The following is intended not as a complete survey of the comparative evidence but as a discussion of the method of comparative anatomy and some of the basic conclusions which have been obtained.

The mammalian skeleton Figure 12-2 shows a tree shrew skeleton, which is used here to represent a rather generalized mammalian skeleton. The names of the important bones are indicated, and this diagram should be referred to during the following discussion.

The axis of the skeleton consists of the *spine,* or *vertebral column,* with the skull at one end. Attached to the spine are the *ribs,* which attach opposite the spine to the *sternum.* The spine itself consists of a series of interlocking *vertebrae,* which have different forms in various sections of the spine. The organs of locomotion, the forelimbs and hindlimbs, are attached to the spine through the *shoulder girdle* and the *pelvis.*

The shoulder girdle consists of two bones, the *clavicle* (collarbone) and the *scapula* (shoulder blade). The clavicle attaches to the upper part of the sternum and tends to place the forelimbs out to the side of the body. The articulations (joinings) of the clavicle with the scapula and the scapula with the *humerus* (single bone that constitutes the upper arm) are very close together, providing for a double-jointed structure in the shoulder. It is this double-jointed structure that permits a high degree of movement and flexibility in the shoulder. The upper arm, consisting of the humerus, articulates with the scapula as a ball in a socket, again permitting a wide range of movement. The lower arm consists of a pair of bones, the *ulna* and the *radius.* The radius articulates with the humerus in such a way that it can rotate around an axis. In so doing, the lower arm rotates. In humans, the lower arm can rotate 180 degrees, moving from a palms-up to a palms-down position. The wrist consists of eight bones, the *carpals.* The palm region of the hand consists of five

[6] S. L. Washburn, "The Study of Human Evolution," in P. Dolhinow and V. M. Sarich (eds.), *Background for Man* (Boston: Little, Brown, 1971), pp. 82–87.

[7] R. H. Tuttle, "Knuckle-Walking and the Evolution of Hominid Hands," *American Journal of Physical Anthropology,* 26 (1967), 171–206.

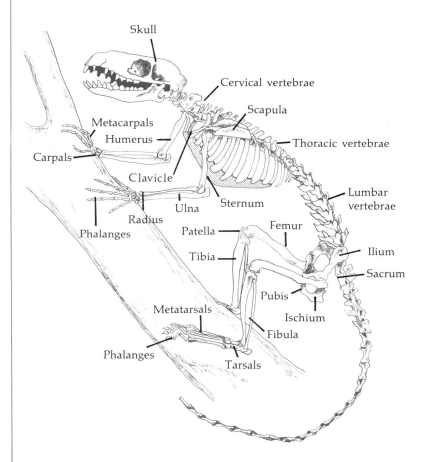

Figure 12-2 Skeleton of the tree shrew.

bones, the *metacarpals*, and the fingers of the *phalanges*, two in the thumb and three in each finger.

The hindlimbs are attached to the spine by means of the pelvis. The pelvis itself is composed of three units: a pair of *innominate bones* and a section of the spine known as the *sacrum*. Each innominate bone in the adult consists of regions which correspond to what were three separate bones in the child. These bones fuse together by the time of puberty to form a single bone. The three regions are the *ilium*, *ischium*, and *pubis*. The bone of the upper leg is the *femur*, and those

of the lower leg are the *tibia* and *fibula*. The ankle consists of seven bones, the *tarsals;* the arch of the foot of five bones, the *metatarsals;* and the toes of the *phalanges*, two in the big toe and three in each of the others.

Variations of the basic mammalian skeleton
The skeleton has been greatly modified in many mammalian orders. For example, the horse skeleton has been modified for high-speed running. In this type of locomotion there is constant jarring of the body, and great forces are transmitted through the limbs to the body. In the horse the

The Comparative Anatomy, Ontogeny, and Molecular Biology of the Living Primates

clavicle has been lost, so that the scapula attaches directly to the rib cage by muscles and forces generated by running are absorbed by these muscles. Of course, flexibility in the shoulder has been lost, but a plains grass-eating animal really has little need to lift its forelimb over its head. In addition, the ulna and radius of the forelimb have become fused together, and four of the five digits on each limb have been lost. The remaining digit has been modified into a hoof (Figure 12-3).

Figure 12-3 Limb skeleton of a horse and a human. *While the forelimb of the horse has been highly specialized for running on hard ground, the primate forelimb has remained relatively generalized. Note the fusion of the radius and ulna and the loss of four of the five digits in the horse.*

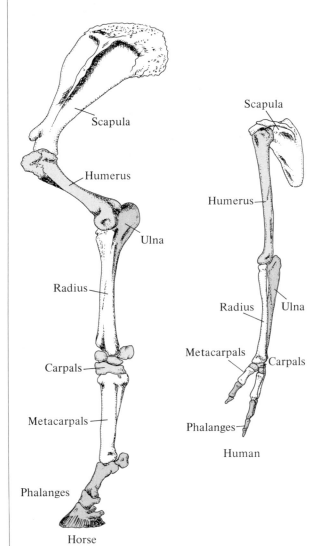

The primate skeleton   The primates, for the most part, have retained a basically generalized skeleton and have enhanced its flexibility. All primates have retained the clavicle, and most are able to rotate their forearms. With a few exceptions, the five fingers have been retained.

While it is possible to spend much time discussing the skeleton of the various primate species, our interest here lies in the hominids and in understanding human evolution. Therefore, we will discuss those aspects of the anatomy pertinent to these goals.

The trunk and shoulder girdle   In most mammals, including the monkeys, the body is carried parallel to the ground. The spine forms an arch supported by the limbs. The trunk tends to be rather long and narrow. The hominoids (which include both humans and apes) are characterized by a relatively short trunk, which includes a fewer number of vertebrae in this region of the spine. Unlike the monkey's, the hominoid back does not play any important role in locomotion, and the pongid body tends to be carried semivertically to the ground, with the human body being completely erect. The back muscles of the hominoids are fairly small, and the spine is relatively inflexible.

The relative position of the shoulder girdle and humerus can be seen in Figure 12-4. In the monkey, the scapula lies on the side of the body, and the head of the humerus points backward. In the hominoid, the long clavicles place the arms well to the side of the body. The clavicles extend backward, so that the scapula lies on the back and the head of the humerus points inward. The socket of the scapula is shallower in the hominoid, permitting a greater degree of rotation of the humerus. These changes permit the hominoid arm to be held directly overhead, as when an ape is suspending himself from an overhead branch. In addition, the hominoids are able to rotate the forearm approximately 180 degrees, compared with the monkey, which can rotate the forearm

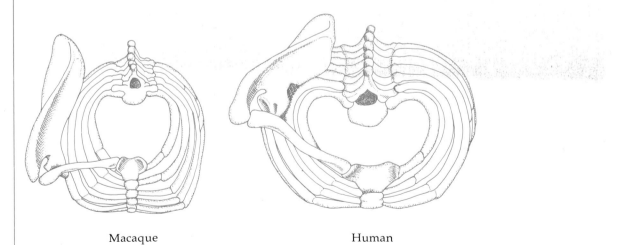

Macaque   Human

Figure 12-4   Cross section of trunk. *Note the differences in the shape of the rib cage and the relative positions of the clavicle and scapula.*

only about 90 degrees. Thus, humans can chin themselves with palms either toward the body or away from it.

These are only a few of the many characteristics common to the apes and hominids in the shoulder and arm. These features are adaptations to suspensory behavior. They indicate that the hominids possessed an ancestor adapted to arboreal locomotion which involved the use of the hands. This was not the true brachiation of the modern gibbon but simply an early development which emphasized the use of the arms in locomotion. Some term this *prebrachiation*. The evidence also points clearly to a close evolutionary tie between ourselves and the apes, especially the African apes.

The arms tend to be fairly long in both humans and the apes. In the macaques, the combined length of the humerus and radius is approximately 83 percent of the length of the trunk, but in humans and the gorilla this figure is 113 percent. However, there are great differences between humans and the apes in the relative proportions of the arms and legs.

The ratios of the arms to the legs can be given by the *intermembral index*, defined as

$$\frac{\text{Length of humerus} + \text{length of radius}}{\text{Length of femur} + \text{length of tibia}} \times 100$$

A resulting index of 100 means that the arms and legs (excluding the hand and foot) are of equal length. An index over 100 would indicate longer arms than legs, while an index under 100 would mean that the legs were longer.

Table 12-2 lists some representative intermembral indices. The quadrupedal monkeys tend to have indices from 70 to a little over 100. The brachiators and knuckle walkers have indices above 100, which indicates their long arms. The

Table 12-2   Intermembral Indices of Representative Primates

Primate	Index*	Dominant Locomotor Pattern
Tarsier	55	Vertical clinging and leaping
Galago	62	Vertical clinging and leaping
Sifaka	64	Vertical clinging and leaping
Human	70	Erect bipedalism
Lemur	70	Quadrupedalism, branch running and walking type
Capuchin	81	Quadrupedalism, branch running and walking type
Guenon	84	Quadrupedalism, branch running and walking type
Macaque	89	Quadrupedalism, ground running and walking type
Loris	92	Quadrupedalism, slow climbing type
Baboon	95	Quadrupedalism, ground running and walking type
Spider monkey	105	Quadrupedalism, New World semibrachiation type
Chimpanzee	107	Knuckle walking
Gorilla	117	Knuckle walking
Gibbon	129	Brachiation
Orangutan	144	Modified brachiation
Siamang	148	Brachiation

* Average for sample. Data taken from J. R. Napier and P. H. Napier, *A Handbook of Living Primates* (London: Academic, 1967), pp. 393–395. Used with permission of Academic Press and J. R. Napier. Human index taken from A. H. Schultz, "Proportions of Long Bones in Man and Apes," *Human Biology*, 9 (1937), 281–328.

vertical clingers and leapers, as well as the hominids, are characterized by long legs, for leaping in the first case and for bipedal progression in the second.

The pelvis and legs In general, the skeleton of the human trunk and upper limbs is similar to that of a prebrachiator. But humans lack the specializations which mark the adaptations to true brachiation. Adaptations to erect bipedalism in the hominids have taken place primarily in the pelvis, leg, and foot.

A chimpanzee occasionally will assume an upright stance. But for the ape the major problem is maintaining a balance of the trunk, for in an upright position the center of gravity is shifted in front of the pelvis and legs; the ape must therefore bend the leg at the knee, which results in a rather awkward and inefficient form of bipedalism.

A number of changes have occurred in the human skeleton, resulting in a balance of the trunk over the pelvis. The ilium of the pelvis has become short and broad, providing the surfaces necessary for the attachment of muscles involved in erect bipedalism. With the changes in shape and position of the ilium, the sacrum comes to lie in a new position. Since the sacrum is a part of the spine, the spine has had to take on a series of curves in order to keep the trunk upright and balanced over the pelvis. In humans, the sacrum lies closer to the point of articulation between the femur and the pelvis. As a result, the weight of the trunk is transmitted more directly to the legs (Figures 12-5 and 12-6).

The new position of the sacrum also creates a complete bony ring through which the birth canal must pass. In the chimpanzee, for example, the articulation of the sacrum to the innominate bones and the pelvis to the femur are farther apart than in humans. This means that the birth canal has a bony roof at one point and a bony floor at another. In humans, the bony roof has moved over the bony floor, creating a complete bony ring through which the head of the child must pass at

Figure 12-5 The pelvis and trunk.

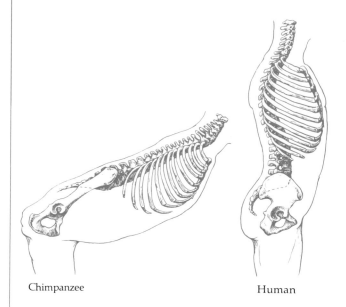

Chimpanzee

Human

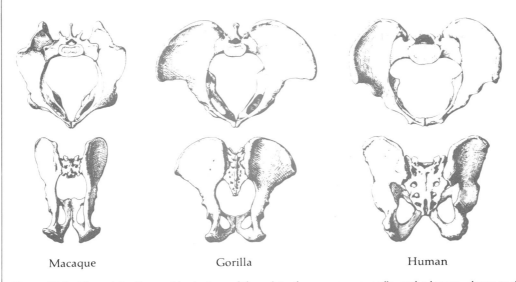

| Macaque | Gorilla | Human |

Figure 12-6 The pelvis. *Top and back views of the pelvis of a macaque, a gorilla, and a human, drawn to the same size.*

birth. However, the human infant's skull is very soft, allowing for a certain amount of compression as the child passes through the birth canal and a great deal of growth after birth.

Other animals' brains are almost completely developed at birth. For instance, the rhesus monkey at birth has a brain that is approximately three-fourths its adult size, whereas the human newborn has a brain less than 30 percent of the size it will ultimately attain. The human brain is premature at birth and will not attain its adult functional status until about puberty. This has the effect of making the child depend on others for a long time. It is during this extended period that learning and mental abilities are developed.[8]

The reconstruction of the pelvis in human evolution has brought about the reorganization of the muscles involved in movements of the leg.

[8] A. Montagu, "Sociogenic Brain Damage," *American Anthropologist*, 74 (1972), 1050.

In the hominoids there are three muscles of interest, the *gluteus maximus, gluteus medius,* and *gluteus minimus.* In the ape, all three act as *extensors,* extending the leg at the hip. In the chimpanzee, the gluteus medius is the largest of the three. In hominids, changes in the structure and orientation of the ilium have resulted in the repositioning of the gluteus medius and gluteus minimus. These muscles act as *abductors,* moving the body away from the midline, and also rotate the thigh laterally at the hip joint. These muscles are responsible for keeping the trunk in a stable upright position during walking. The gluteus maximus has become a very large muscle and acts as a major extensor of the leg in running and climbing (Figure 12-7).

Many changes also have occurred in the human leg and foot. The foot shows perhaps the greatest changes and is among the most specialized of human features. In other primates, the big toe is well developed and is capable of movements to the side of the foot. The animal can grasp

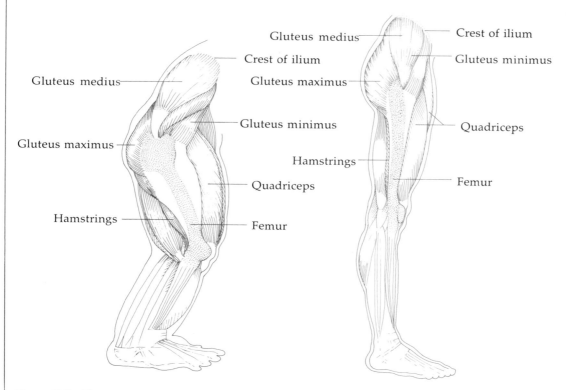

Figure 12-7 The gluteal musculature in a chimpanzee and a human.

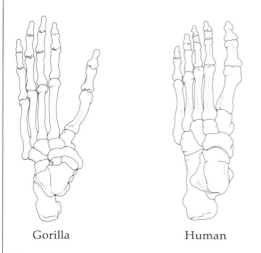

Gorilla   Human

Figure 12-8 The foot skeletons of a gorilla and a human.

with its foot; and in walking, the body weight in the monkey is borne between the first and second toes. The human foot is fairly inflexible, and an arch has developed. The toes are short, including the big toe, which is incapable of extensive sideways movement or grasping (Figure 12-8). In walking, the heel hits the ground first, and the push of the stepoff is on the big toe itself.

Comparative Anatomy of the Hand

The hand serves a number of functions. In most primates it is an organ of locomotion used in vertical clinging and leaping, in quadrupedalism, or in brachiation. The use of the hand or front paw for movement is a general characteristic of most mammalian forms. But in the primate order there is the additional development of the hand as an organ for manipulation. In most forms, the loco-motor function dominates the manipulative function. However, in humans, who normally use only their lower limbs in getting from one place to another, the hands are freed for purely manipulative activity.

In the tree shrew, movements of the hand are limited. The animal can draw its fingers toward its palm, but not enough to permit the easy grasping of an object by a single hand. The basic trend in the evolution of the primate hand has been toward a greater flexibility in the fingers, permitting the grasping and manipulating of objects.

In most prosimians and New World monkeys the fingers can be drawn back against the palm of the hand, permitting the grasping of branches and other objects. But this movement is limited. In these forms, movement of the thumb is re-

stricted to the joint between the metacarpal and first phalanges, as well as between phalanges.

(a)

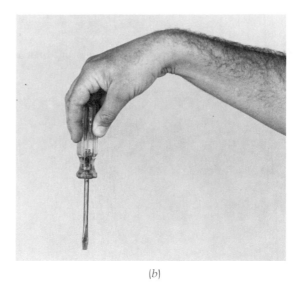

(b)

Figure 12-10 Human hand showing (a) power grip and (b) precision grip.

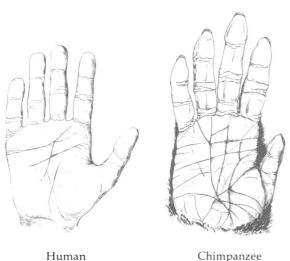

Human   Chimpanzee

Figure 12-9 The hands of a chimpanzee and a human.

In the Old World monkeys, apes, and humans, the development of a saddle configuration in the joint between the carpal and metacarpal permits the thumb to be directly opposed to the other fingers. Humans differ primarily in the degree of movement possible at this joint and the fact that the human thumb can oppose the fingers so that the fleshy tip of the thumb comes into direct contact with the fleshy tips of the fingers — all the fingers (Figure 12-9). In the apes, the fingers are elongated, and the metacarpals and phalanges are curved as an adaptation for brachiation and knuckle walking. In humans, these bones are straight.

The hand is capable of two major types of grips. In the *power grip,* an object is held between the fingers and the palm, with the thumb reinforcing the fingers. In this position, much force can be applied. All primates are capable of the power grip. The *precision grip* is used when an object is held between one or more fingers with the thumb fully opposed to the fingertips. Very delicate movements can be executed in this position. Humans have developed the precision grip to a degree not found in other primates (Figure 12-10).

Comparative Anatomy of the Head

The total structure of the head reflects several factors, such as the position of the head on the spine, the relative significance and the structure of the sense organs, the nature of the diet, and the development of the brain.

Position of the head on the spine Figure 12-11D shows the skull of a cat, along with several primate skulls, seen from the underside. On each skull is a large hole, the *foramen magnum,* through which the spinal cord enters and merges with the brain. On either side of the foramen magnum are two rounded surfaces, the *occipital condyles.* These condyles fit into a pair of depressions on the top of the uppermost vertebra. This is how the skull articulates with the spine.

The occipital condyles on the cat skull are located far to the rear of the skull. This animal is pronograde. The skull attaches directly on the front of the spine, where powerful muscles are needed to keep the head up. The muscles involved are the *nuchal muscles,* which, in such animals as the cat, can be relatively large. In the cat, a flange, known as the *nuchal crest,* has formed on the back section of the skull. It provides additional surface area for the attachment of the nuchal musculature. In the gorilla, the massive facial skeleton weights the head so that powerful nuchal muscles are needed; hence the presence of a dominant nuchal crest.

The apes are characterized by some degree of orthograde posturing; consequently, the occipital condyles have moved forward on the underside of the skull, to articulate better with the top of the spine in the vertical position. In humans, the condyles can be seen to have moved to a position almost directly in the center of the underside of the skull. With the reduction of the facial skeleton and the enlargement of the brain case, both to be discussed shortly, the skull has achieved a good balance on the top of the spine. Note the absence of a nuchal crest.

The sense organs The senses of hearing, tasting, smell, and sight are all located in the head. Changes in the relative importance of the olfactory and visual senses are reflected in the skull.

The primates are characterized by a general reduction of the sense of smell, hence a reduction of the snout as seen in the skull. This results in a general flattening of the face, although in many forms the massiveness of the teeth and jaw results in a *prognathism,* or jutting forward, of the jaw, as seen in the baboon or gorilla skull.

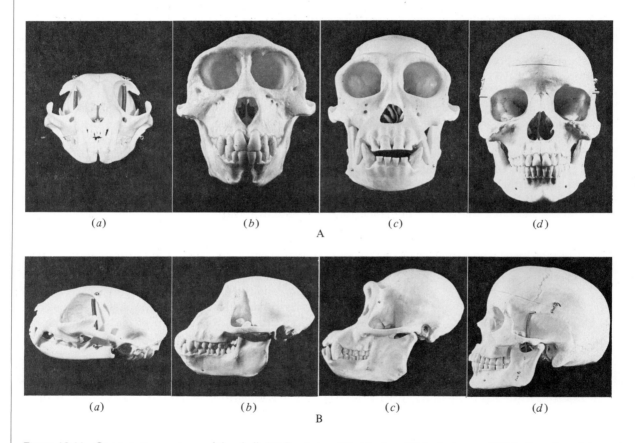

Figure 12-11 Comparative anatomy of the skull. (A) *Front view,* (B) *side view,* (C) *back view, and* (D) *bottom view of the skulls of a* (a) *cat,* (b) *rhesus macaque,* (c) *chimpanzee, and* (d) *human. (Not to scale.)*

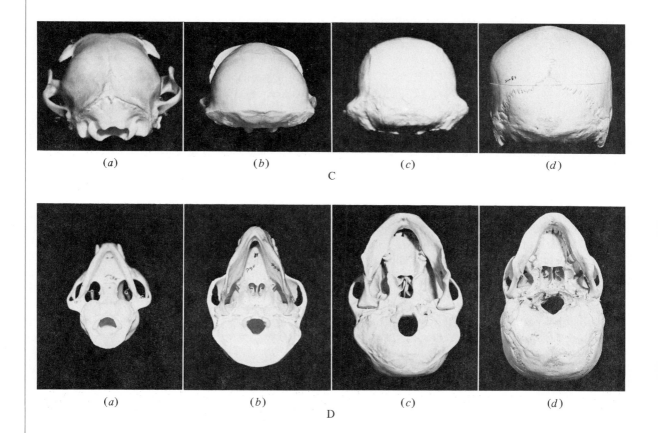

C

(a)   (b)   (c)   (d)

D

(a)   (b)   (c)   (d)

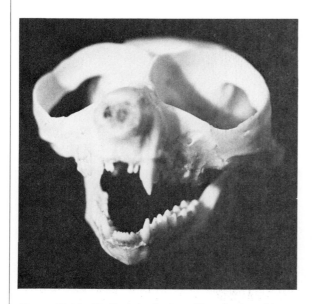

Figure 12-12 Skull of slender loris. *Note the ring of bone around the eye and the lack of an eye socket.*

The development of the primate eye is noted in the position of the eyes in the head. The eyes have come to be located on the front of the head instead of off to the side, allowing for stereoscopic vision. The eye of the higher primates lies in a complete bony socket. The eye socket of the tarsier is only partially complete, while that of the other prosimians is the least developed of the primates and is characterized only by a bony ring (Figure 12-12).

The teeth The teeth are of great importance in evolutionary studies because they are very sensitive to dietary and environmental changes. Some parts of the anatomy are quite conservative in their evolution, but enough differences in teeth patterns may develop to distinguish two closely related species whose *postcranial* skeletons (the skeleton behind the head) are identical. In addition, because of their durability, teeth may be the

only parts of the body preserved in the fossil record.

As was seen in Chapter 9, mammalian dentition is characterized by heterodonty. This refers to the regional differentiation of teeth into a number of types, namely, the *incisors, canines, premolars,* and *molars* (see Figure 9-10).

In the generalized mammal forty-four teeth can be counted. In each quarter of the mouth there are three incisors, one canine, four premolars, and three molars. This is indicated by the *dental formula* $\frac{3.1.4.3}{3.1.4.3}$. The top series gives the number of each tooth type in half the upper jaw, and the bottom series represents half the lower jaw (Table 12-3).

The general trend in primate evolution has been the retention of a fairly simple tooth structure and the loss of a number of the original teeth. However, this tooth loss has not progressed to the degree that it has in a number of other mammalian orders. The dental formulas for the prosimians show great irregularities. All the Ceboidea are characterized by three premolars per quad-

Table 12-3 Dental Formulas of Living Primates

Primate	Dental Formula	Total Number of Teeth
Lemur	$\frac{2.1.3.3}{2.1.3.3}$	36
Indri	$\frac{2.1.2.3}{1.1.2.3}$	30
Aye-aye	$\frac{1.0.1.3}{1.0.0.3}$	18
Marmoset	$\frac{2.1.3.2}{2.1.3.2}$	32
New World monkey	$\frac{2.1.3.3}{2.1.3.3}$	36
Old World monkey, ape, and human	$\frac{2.1.2.3}{2.1.2.3}$	32

rant, but of these, the cebids have retained three molars and the marmosets only two. All the Old World monkeys, apes, and humans have thirty-two teeth and the dental formula $\frac{2.1.2.3}{2.1.2.3}$. In apes and humans there is the possibility of further reduction in the dental formula when one or more of the third molars (wisdom teeth) do not develop at all in some individuals. Also, in people it is not uncommon for the jaw to be too small to accommodate the third molars even if they are present, requiring surgical removal.

Within the primate order, the incisor tends to be a broad cutting type of tooth with a rather simple structure. But in many primate forms it has become greatly enlarged. The canine serves many functions, such as grasping, ripping, and tearing food, as well as defense and antagonistic display. Canines of the Anthropoidea tend to be much larger in males than in females, an example of sexual dimorphism. For example, canines are highly developed in the terrestrial baboon, acting as a weapon in troop defense. The canine is a simple pointed tooth, very much like the canine of the ancestral mammal.

The premolars, or *bicuspids* in dental terminology, are simple teeth with two *cusps,* or points. In many mammals and some primates, the premolar has developed additional cusps so as to become more molarlike, but this has not occurred in the hominoids. The molars are the most complex in structure, due to the formation of several cusps. The structure of cusps and *cuspules* (minor cusps), ridges, and valleys makes the molars highly useful to the anthropologist in identifying species.

Pongid dentition Figure 12-13 shows the upper jaw of a chimpanzee. Note the broad, spatulalike incisors across the broad front of the jaw and the large, projecting canines. When the animal closes its mouth, the canines interlock, each fitting into a space, or *diastema*, in the opposite jaw. Note that in the upper jaw the diastema is in front of the canine, while in the lower jaw it is behind the canine. Thus, in chewing, the chimpanzee cannot use the more rotary motion characteristic of hominids.

The first lower premolar in the ape is also specialized, for the canine in the upper jaw shears directly in front of it. This premolar is larger than the others and presents a cutting edge for the canine. This is known as a *sectorial* premolar. The cheek teeth, the premolars and molars, are arranged in two straight rows which parallel each other, though they often converge toward the back of the jaw.

The basic structure of the molars in humans and the chimpanzee is the same. The upper molar contains four cusps and the lower molar five cusps. The arrangement of the five cusps and the grooves between them suggests a Y, and the arrangement is often referred to as the *Y-5 pattern.* This contrasts with the molar structure in the monkey, whose lower molar consists of four cusps with a small constriction separating them into two pairs.

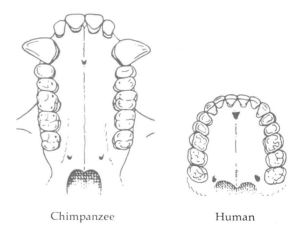

Chimpanzee   Human

Figure 12-13 Dentition of a chimpanzee and a human. *Drawings of the upper jaws of a chimpanzee and a human.*

Hominid dentition   The main trend in the evolution of hominid dentition has been the reduction in the size of the teeth. When viewed from the side, all the teeth are at the same level. The canine is not projecting, and the first lower premolar is not sectorial.

As can be seen in Figure 12-13, the teeth are arranged in a curved dental arcade with no diastema. The reduction of the teeth may be related to the development of tool use and a more meat-oriented diet. The large canine, for example, is used by the apes in breaking open hard fruits. Humans would use a chopping tool in the same situation. It has been further suggested that a major function of the large projecting canine is for antagonistic display. With the development of the cooperative hunting society in humans, such displays no longer occurred. Also, for defense, humans use weapons instead of canines.

It must be remembered that use and disuse of a structure during a lifetime does not directly affect the evolution of that structure. The reduction of the canine represents a shift in frequencies from the alleles that produce larger canines to those which produce smaller ones. That is, mutations were originally responsible for creating a range of variation in canine size. When the large canine lost its selective advantage to the use of tools, the smaller canines may have gained some selective advantage; and through time, the frequency of large canines gradually decreased. Drift and assortative mating could also have been important factors in establishing the new type of dentition.

Clifford Jolly has proposed an interesting idea on the evolution of hominid dentition. He notes a number of similarities between the dental structure of the gelada and humans. The similarities include relatively small and vertically implanted incisors, reduced canines, and large cheek teeth. These features in the gelada appear to be related to its diet, which consists of grasses and hard seeds. The early hominids may have consumed a number of small, hard food items, and the similarities between modern geladas and humans may be because their respective ancestors had similar diets.[9] This idea will be discussed further in Chapter 14.

The jaws and facial skeleton   The human jaw has also decreased in size. Since the jaw contains the teeth, smaller teeth would result in smaller jaws. Also, in chewing, humans do not need to exert as much pressure on food as the ape, since human food is usually cut up or in some way processed into smaller pieces and is easier to chew. In time, of course, fire was used to cook meat, thus tenderizing it.

In the chimpanzee, the forces generated by the jaw in eating are great, and the curved front section of the mandible has been reinforced internally by a buttress, the *simian shelf*. This shelf rarely occurs in the hominids. Recent hominids have developed a weak external buttress, the *chin*.

The muscles which operate the jaw have also changed in the course of human evolution, becoming, for the most part, smaller. For example, the *temporalis* muscle arises on the jaw and inserts on the side of the skull. In the gorilla this muscle is very large, while the brain case is relatively small. Since the temporalis attaches to the brain case, this massive muscle would not have enough room on a smooth-surfaced, small brain case. So a large flange, the *sagittal crest*, develops across the top of the skull which provides the surface area necessary for muscle attachment.

Also related to the size of the jaw is the development of *brow ridges*. Many feel that the brow ridges protect the eye. Why, then, do modern peoples lack brow ridges or develop very small

---

[9] C. J. Jolly, "The Seed Eaters: A New Model of Hominid Differentiation Based on a Baboon Analogy," *Man,* 5 (1970), 5–26.

ones? The brow ridge acts to reinforce the skull and absorb the forces generated by the process of chewing. Thus, animals with large jaws have large brow ridges, and those with small jaws have small brow ridges.

The brain case   The brain is housed in the brain case, which consists of two bone layers. The outer layer is smooth, but the inner layer roughly follows the contours of the brain itself. A webbed, bony structure exists between the two layers; at points where the layers are far apart, air spaces, or *sinuses*, develop.

In studies of fossil hominids the term *cranial capacity* is always mentioned. Cranial capacity is the volume of the brain case, *not* the size of the brain (Table 12-4). Although the two are close, it must be remembered that the brain itself is covered by tissue, nerves, and blood vessels, and so its volume is always less than that of the cranium.

A problem in paleontological studies is that measurements of cranial capacity are often made on incomplete brain cases. Also, there are wide variations within each species. So, while we can say that the average cranial capacity of modern humans is 1,345 cubic centimeters, the nonpathological range runs from about 900 to more than 2,000 cubic centimeters. Also, within each

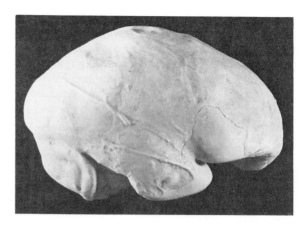

Figure 12-14   An endocranial cast. *An endocranial cast of* Homo erectus, *a fossil hominid from Choukoutien, China.*

species and within the nonpathological range of variation, there seems to be no correlation between brain size and intelligence. Even between species, the structure and physiology of the brain are more important than the size.

Since the inside of the brain case does conform roughly to the outside surface of the brain, it can be used to infer some information about the brain itself. Often a plaster cast is made of the inside of a cranium of a fossil find. This results in an *endocranial cast*, like the one in Figure 12-14. From such a cast the relative proportion of the lobes of the brain and other information can be inferred. However, it must be remembered that this is not a fossil brain, but simply a cast of the inside of the brain case.

Comparative Anatomy of the Brain

The major element of the nervous system in the primitive vertebrate was the single, hollow nerve cord. At the front end of the cord, the primitive brain developed. Here were located the sense organs, and information gathered by these struc-

Table 12-4   Cranial Capacities of the Living Hominoidea

Primate	Average Cranial Capacity (cubic centimeters)
Gibbon	102
Chimpanzee	399
Orangutan	434
Gorilla	535
Homo sapiens	1,345

From P. V. Tobias, "The Distribution of Cranial Capacity Values among Living Hominoids," *Proceedings of the Third International Congress of Primatology, Zurich, 1970* (Basel: Karger, 1971), vol. 1, 18–35.

tures was fed into the brain, which then produced some type of response. The primitive vertebrate brain was made up of three swellings in the hollow nerve cord associated with a thickening of walls. These three swellings, the *forebrain, midbrain,* and *hindbrain,* established the basic structure of all vertebrate brains, including that of the primates.

The evolution of the mammalian brain   In the earliest vertebrates, differentiation of each of the three divisions of the brain already had taken place. The forebrain was composed of three sections, the *thalamus, cerebral hemispheres,* and *olfactory bulbs* (Figure 12-15). The midbrain also developed special structures, including the *optic lobes.* The *cerebellum* developed as a large swelling on the hindbrain, with the thick lower portion becoming the *medulla oblongata.* These are only the major features of the early vertebrate brain, for many other structures were also developing.

In the early vertebrates the *cerebrum,* consisting of the paired cerebral hemispheres of the forebrain, were smooth swellings. They were associated primarily with the sense of smell. In the early reptiles, this portion of the forebrain enlarged; and although it was still associated with smell, a new area appeared. This new section of the brain was the *neocortex,* a gray covering on the cerebrum, involved with such things as the association and coordination of various impulses coming from the sense organs and other areas of the brain.

In the early mammals, the area of the cerebrum associated with smell remained important, but the neocortex began to expand and to be separated from the rest of the cortex by a groove. Soon the new area became the major part of the covering, or *cortex,* of the cerebrum. In the mammalian class, this part of the brain has expanded in size, and in many forms it has developed *convolutions* on the surface which function to increase the surface area and therefore the number of cells in this area. As this part of the brain expanded, many of the functions that previously were controlled by other sections of the brain came to be associated with the cerebral

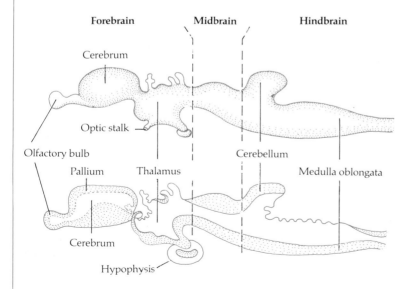

Figure 12-15   The vertebrate brain. *A generalized and schematized representation of the vertebrate brain. The lower figure is a longitudinal section showing differences in the thickness of the brain wall.*

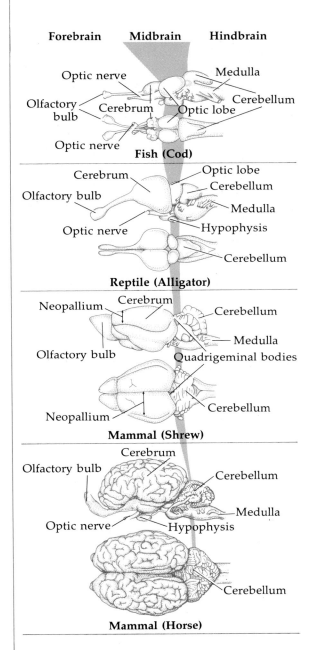

| Forebrain | Midbrain | Hindbrain |

Fish (Cod)

Optic nerve
Medulla
Olfactory bulb
Cerebrum
Optic lobe
Cerebellum
Optic nerve

Reptile (Alligator)

Cerebrum
Optic lobe
Olfactory bulb
Cerebellum
Medulla
Optic nerve
Hypophysis
Cerebellum

Mammal (Shrew)

Neopallium
Cerebrum
Cerebellum
Olfactory bulb
Medulla
Quadrigeminal bodies
Neopallium
Cerebellum

Mammal (Horse)

Cerebrum
Olfactory bulb
Cerebellum
Optic nerve
Medulla
Hypophysis
Cerebellum

Figure 12-16   Comparisons of vertebrate brains. *Side and top view of four vertebrate brains. Note the expansion of the forebrain in the mammals.*

cortex. For example, in mammals visual stimuli are received by the cerebral cortex rather than by the optic lobes of the midbrain. Vertebrate brains are compared in Figure 12-16.

The evolution of the primate brain   The evolution of the primate brain has been characterized by a general increase in size relative to body size. As the size of the body increases, so does the size of the various parts of the body including the brain, but not all body parts increase in size at the same rate. As the general body size increases, some parts of the body, such as the brain, increase at a faster rate. Thus, in many large animals, the brain is relatively larger than in closely related smaller species. This concept is referred to as *allometric growth.* Humans are large primates, but the increase in the size of the human brain through time is greater than can be explained by allometric growth and may be related in some way to an increasing intelligence.

The increase in brain size over and beyond that explainable by an increase in general body size can be measured by the *encephalization quotient.*[10] Several examples of this measure are given in Table 12-5. Note the tremendous difference between humans and other primates.

The neocortex is greatly expanded in the higher primates and has come to cover the entire cerebrum. The many convolutions have greatly increased its surface area. As a result of this expansion, the cerebral cortex in humans completely covers the olfactory lobes and the midbrain. Areas of the brain concerned with the sense

[10] The derivation and discussion of the encephalization quotient can be found in H. J. Jerison, *Evolution of the Brain and Intelligence* (New York: Academic, 1973).

Table 12-5 Encephalization Quotient (EQ) in Some Primates

Primate	EQ
Tarsier	1.29
Spider monkey	2.33
Rhesus macaque	2.09
Hamadryas baboon	2.35
Gibbon	2.74
Orangutan (male)	1.63
Gorilla (male)	1.53
Chimpanzee (male)	2.48
Human (male)	7.79

Data taken from H. J. Jerison, *Evolution of the Brain and Intelligence* (New York: Academic, 1973).

of smell have undergone reduction, while areas associated with vision and the sense of touch have become elaborated.

Different areas of the cerebral cortex are associated with differing functions (Figure 12-17). It is possible to map the areas on the surface of the cerebrum associated with vision, hearing, and so forth. In the course of primate evolution, these areas have become more clearly defined, so that in the higher primates they can easily be differentiated.

The cerebrum consists of several lobes. The *occipital lobes* have increased in size and have extended backward to practically cover the rest

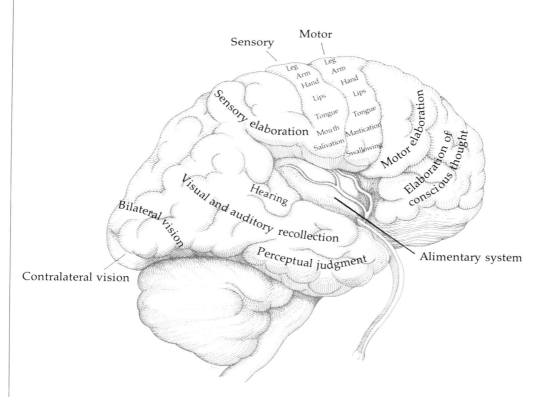

Figure 12-17 Some functions of the cerebral cortex.

of the brain. The *temporal lobes* and the *frontal lobes* also have enlarged.

Association and the cerebral cortex Several areas of the cerebral cortex have greatly expanded in the human brain. Of course, the human brain, in relative size, is the largest among primates and the most richly convoluted. A great deal of this enlargement has occurred with the frontal lobes, which are responsible for the vertical forehead so characteristic of modern humans.

The development of toolmaking, language, and other human features has affected the development of the brain. The cortical areas associated with hand coordination are about three times as extensive as in the ape brain, and the expansion of the areas concerned with language is even greater.

Sections of the cerebral cortex have been labeled the *silent areas*. Unlike other areas of the brain, electrical stimulation of the silent areas (which include parts of the frontal, occipital, and temporal lobes) produces little or no emotional or motor response. These areas increase in extent from the lower vertebrates and are major elements of the human brain.

Although there are still many unknowns in the research into these areas, it does appear that they aid in reasoning, curiosity, imagination, creativity, and basically all the higher mental activities. Neurologist H. Chandler Elliott believes that "our human neocortex, sensory, motor, and thinking is the New World of mind."[11]

The cerebral cortex allows for a level of complex behavior, which we might call intelligence, that is best developed in humans. As well as affecting individual intelligence, the cortex allows for *social intelligence*. That is, the knowledge and images that originate in an individual's brain can

[11] H. Chandler Elliott, *The Shape of Intelligence* (New York: Scribner's, 1969), p. 226.

be transferred by language (and in the last 5,000 years, writing) to the brains of others. The knowledge of an entire society, which is always greater than the knowledge of any one individual, can be drawn on to meet crises. This is one major factor that differentiates ourselves from other species.

Summary
Comparative anatomy reveals the structures that result from common ancestry and hence provides evidence of evolutionary relationships. The study of anatomy also yields data on the functioning of anatomical structures and their possible roles in adaptation.

Four main anatomical complexes are considered to be central in human evolution: locomotion, manipulation, mastication, and mental processes. In keeping with the primates' general trait of adaptability, we find great flexibility in primate locomotor patterns. Although one particular type of locomotion might be dominant for a specific species, the primate, unlike most animals, often varies its mode of locomotion depending on the situation. A chimpanzee, for instance, uses a modified method of brachiation in the trees but on the ground moves by knuckle walking. The type of locomotor pattern from which human bipedalism developed is still debated.

The hand is perhaps one of the most remarkable anatomical structures. In most primates it functions in locomotion as well as in manipulation. Human bipedalism has freed the hands from use in transporting the body; at the same time, the hands have developed into highly generalized structures capable of a wide range of tasks, including toolmaking, carrying objects, and generally altering the environment.

Studies of comparative anatomy of the teeth and jaws reveal that a rather simple tooth structure has been maintained. Although tooth reduction has not progressed as much as in some other mammals, the number of teeth does tend to be reduced through the primate line, and the jaw becomes smaller.

The brain progressively enlarges and develops in the cortical areas through the primate line. The human neocortex makes possible higher mental activities; and in association with other features, such as bipedalism and manual dexterity, it allows for social intelligence as well as individual intelligence. It is this social intelligence that allows humans as a species to interact with the environment. This interaction can be advantageous, for example, in the general increase in comfort and living standards that technology can bring, or devastating, as evidenced by pollution, war, and depletion of resources.

COMPARATIVE ONTOGENY

There is a famous and somewhat formidable saying, at least in biological circles, "Ontogeny recapitulates phylogeny." This means that *ontogeny,* the development of the individual, repeats the *phylogeny,* the evolutionary development of the species. Early *embryologists* saw in the developing embryo and fetus a history of the evolutionary stages of the species. For example, the human fetus develops a tail and even structures which are considered to be gill pouches. In fact, the early fetus of a human is practically indistinguishable from that of other vertebrates (Figure 12-18).

The fetus, of course, does not literally pass through the evolutionary stages of the species. It is just that the early stages of development are conservative and have changed little over time. Most specializations occur later in fetal development, and many are the result of alteration in growth patterns. Adolph Schultz remarks:

All evolutionary innovations acquired by adults are primarily due to some alteration in at least one of the complicated details of growth and de-

velopment. Specializations, therefore, do not become fully marked as a rule until rather late in development, just as they were not yet present in the earlier evolutionary stages of the species.[12]

The Comparative Ontogeny of the Living Primates

Figure 12-19 shows the relative length of the various subdivisions of growth and development in several primate forms. The life of an individual can be divided into several phases. The *prenatal* period lasts from conception to birth and is followed by the *infantile* period, which lasts from birth to the eruption of the first permanent teeth. Next is the *juvenile* period, which lasts from the eruption of the first to the eruption of the last permanent teeth. This is followed by the *adult* period.

The prenatal period The process of development before birth is known as *gestation.* It is important to distinguish between the nature of gestation and the speed of the gestational process. One of the major evolutionary trends in the primate order has been the prolongation of gestation. Table 12-6 notes the number of days for gestation in several primates.

In addition to the lengthened prenatal period, the human fetus is characterized by a more rapid rate of growth. For example, the orangutan fetus grows at an average rate of 5.7 grams per day, while that of the human fetus is about 12.5 grams per day.[13] Because the placenta develops sooner in humans, rapid growth begins soon after conception and remains rapid throughout the gestation process.

[12] A. Schultz, *The Life of Primates* (New York: Universe, 1969), p. 145.

[13] B. Campbell, *Human Evolution* (Chicago: Aldine, 1966), p. 247.

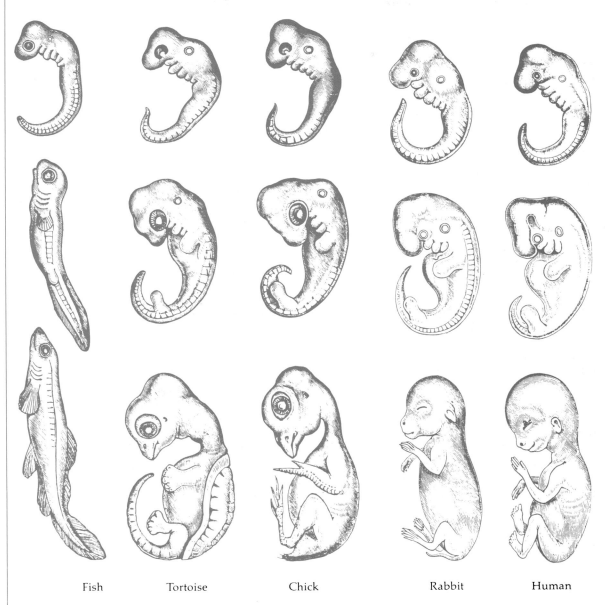

| Fish | Tortoise | Chick | Rabbit | Human |

Figure 12-18 Comparative embryology. *A comparison of vertebrate embryos at corresponding stages of development.*

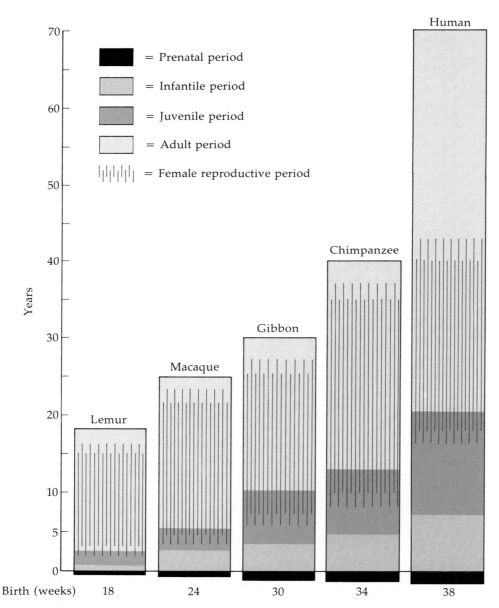

Figure 12-19 The life cycles of primates.

Yet, although the rate of growth is more rapid in humans, the human is born at a more immature stage of development than any other primate. The human infant at birth is virtually helpless. It cannot see well, cannot cling to its mother, and does not develop the ability to walk for almost a year or more. There appears to have been a stretching out of the stages of development of *Homo sapiens,* a prolongation of the state of immaturity. This immaturity at birth is largely related to the evolution of erect bipedalism and a large brain. Changes which have occurred in the structure of the spine and pelvis in the evolution of erect bipedalism have created a bony ring through which pass the birth canal and the head of the newborn infant, discussed earlier in this chapter. As a result, a greater proportion of the growth of the human brain occurs after birth compared with brain growth in other primates (Figure 12-20). Therefore, the infant is born at a much earlier stage of development.

Table 12-6   Length of Gestation in Primates

Primate	Gestation Period (days)
Lemur	120–135
Slender loris	160–174
Marmoset	142–150
Spider monkey	139
Squirrel monkey	165–170
Guenon	150–210
Macaque	162–186
Langur	196
Baboon	164–186
Orangutan	240–270
Gorilla	270
Chimpanzee	216–260
Humans	266

From A. G. Hendrick and M. L. Houstion, "Gestation," in E. S. E. Hafez (ed.), *Comparative Reproduction of Nonhuman Primates,* 1971. Used with permission of Charles C Thomas, Publisher, Springfield, Ill.

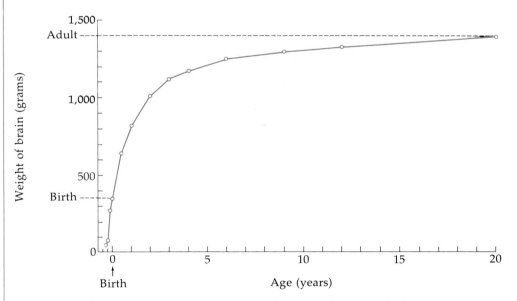

Figure 12-20   Growth of the human brain. *Note that the major period of growth of the human brain occurs after birth.*

The infantile and juvenile periods Just as the gestation process has been prolonged, so have the infantile and juvenile periods. The infantile period is characterized by a general helplessness on the part of the child. Survival of the infant depends upon effective parental care. Human children are usually born one at a time, and births are usually spaced several years apart. This results in a much reduced reproductive potential. Adolph Schultz has calculated the theoretical reproductive potential of several primates. A pair of chimpanzees producing one offspring per year with a sex ratio of one male to one female would result in a population of 408 individuals after 45 years. This compares with a figure of only 64 individuals with humans.[14] Yet this low reproductive potential is correlated with a low reproductive risk. The probability of any given human infant surviving to reproduce is greater than with an infant of any other primate species.

The prolongation of childhood in humans and the intensive care given the children by the parents and other members of society provide the opportunity for the acquisition of a large amount of learned behavior and ultimately the development of culture as an adaptive mechanism. In human societies, puberty arrives late, and even then there are many years following puberty before the individual becomes a fully integrated adult member of the society.

The adult period Along with a lengthened childhood period is a lengthened lifespan in general. Also of great importance is the fact that the human female lives long after her reproductive life is over, a unique situation among animals. There are two reasons why a postreproductive

existence would be of adaptive value. First, because of the lengthened childhood period, a mother who bears her last child at the end of her reproductive life still plays an important role in protecting and caring for that child for over a dozen years. Second, in a population which depends upon learned behavioral patterns for its adaptation, the cumulative knowledge of elders can be of great significance to the survival of the group.

Summary

Ontogeny refers to the growth and development of the individual. A major trend in primate evolution is a lengthening of the major stages in the life cycle, such as gestation, childhood, and total lifespan. The lengthening of these periods, especially that of childhood, permits the acquisition and transmission of many learned behavioral patterns. This trend culminates in the development of human culture.

COMPARATIVE MOLECULAR BIOLOGY

The studies of comparative anatomy have aided greatly in our understanding of evolution. Yet there are problems. It is difficult to describe structural similarities and differences in a statistical manner because of the lack of well-defined and discrete anatomical units. Also, any anatomical structure is affected by the environment, and it is often impossible to determine how much of the trait is genetically determined. In addition, there is the problem of distinguishing between homologies and the results of convergence.

Many anthropologists have turned to detailed studies of protein molecules. Protein structure, as discussed in Chapter 4, is directly related to the structure of DNA in that the sequence of amino acids in the protein is a direct indication of the base sequence in DNA. While some studies have

[14] A. Schultz, "The Number of Young at Birth and the Number of Nipples in Primates," *American Journal of Physical Anthropology*, 6 (1948), 1–23.

been made on the DNA molecule itself, most work has been done on protein molecules.

In the case of sickle-cell anemia, the appearance of the abnormal hemoglobin S resulted from a single amino acid substitution, a reflection of a single base change in the DNA molecule controlling the beta-chain synthesis (Chapter 4). However, not all such substitutions produce abnormalities. In the course of evolutionary development, occasional substitutions will occur which produce either no undesirable changes or, rarely, an improvement. Thus, in the divergence of two lines, which begin with a common protein structure, successive substitutions will occur, resulting after a time in two proteins with similar yet differing structures. The amino acid sequence of the same type of protein in a series of related species can be compared. Those with the more recent common ancestor should show the greatest similarities in the amino acid sequence; that is, they should show the fewest number of amino acid substitutions.

There is a growing literature on this subject, including studies on the DNA molecule itself and on comparative karyotypes, as well as many studies on protein molecules. Here only three studies will be discussed: cytochrome c, hemoglobin, and serum albumins.

Studies of Cytochrome c

Cytochrome c is an ancient protein associated with every living cell which uses oxygen in metabolism. It is found in all multicellular animals and plants and in most one-celled forms. The structure of the cytochrome c molecule is remarkably similar from yeast to humans. The molecule itself consists of 104 amino acids, plus a heme group, although in some forms a few extra amino acids are added onto the chain.

Richard E. Dickerson notes that differences in the amino acid sequence are most frequent in certain areas of the chain, while other areas are identical in all forms.[15] These latter areas appear to be the functional ones, so that alterations in the amino acid sequence in these areas would greatly alter the functioning of the protein. Alterations in other areas probably would not have as noticeable an effect and so would be preserved.

When the amino acid sequences of the various forms of cytochrome c are compared, it is noted that the sequence for humans and the chimpanzee are identical, while that of the rhesus macaque differs in only two amino acids. Other orders of mammals show similar differences. For instance, the cytochrome c of the pig, cow, and sheep are identical, but they differ from that of the horse in three amino acids. When human cytochrome c is compared to that of other orders of mammals, the following results: human differs from horse cytochrome c in twelve amino acids, from rabbit cytochrome c in eleven amino acids, and from dog cytochrome c in ten amino acids.[16] Amino acid differences generally conform to the evolutionary relationships seen in the fossil record and to studies of comparative anatomy.

Further comparisons show that mammalian and bird cytochrome c differ in ten to fifteen amino acids; mammalian and bird differ from tuna in seventeen to twenty-one amino acids; and vertebrate differs from yeast in forty-three to forty-eight acids.[17]

Studies of Hemoglobin

Cytochrome c indicates evolutionary relationships between major groups. But comparisons between

[15] R. E. Dickerson, "The Structure and History of an Ancient Protein," *Scientific American*, 226 (April 1972), 58–72.

[16] E. L. Smith and E. Margoliash, "Evolution of Cytochrome c," *Federation Proceedings*, 23 (1964), 1243–1247.

[17] Ibid.

more closely related species, such as those within the primate order, are best considered with a more recently evolved protein, such as hemoglobin. The structure of the hemoglobin molecule has been described in Chapter 4. Here the structure of human hemoglobin will be compared with that of other forms.

The determination of the precise amino acid sequence for hemoglobin is a costly and time-consuming process. One method of estimating differences in amino acid sequences is to break up a protein into a series of smaller units, called *polypeptides*. This is accomplished by utilizing certain enzymes which break the chain at specific amino acids. The general nature of these polypeptides can then be examined using a form of *electrophoresis* (see Chapter 4). In the study by Robert L. Hill and John Buettner-Janusch,[18] the alpha chain was broken into ten polypeptides. Table 12-7 shows the number of polypeptides

[18] R. L. Hill and J. Buettner-Janusch, "Evolution of Hemoglobin," *Federation Proceedings*, 23 (1964), 1236–1242.

Table 12-7 Ratio of Polypeptides of Hemoglobin Which Differ from Analogous Human Polypeptides to Total Number of Polypeptides Observed

Primate	Alpha Chain	Beta Chain
Gibbon	$0/10$	$1/12$
Rhesus macaque	$0/10$	$2/12$
Baboon	$3/10$	$8/11$
Squirrel monkey	$0/10$	$1/11$
Uakari	$0/10$	$2/11$
Galago	$2/10$	$3/10$
Sifaka	$2/10$	$6/10$
Ring-tailed lemur	$5/10$	$6/10$
Tree shrew	$7/10$	$6/9$

Modified from Robert L. Hill and John Buettner-Janusch, "Evolution of Hemoglobin," *Federation Proceedings*, 23, 1237, 1964. Used with permission of the Federation of American Societies for Experimental Biology and Dr. Robert L. Hill.

from various alpha chains which differ from those of human hemoglobin. Note that differences in the alpha chains are few and the number of differing polypeptides corresponds in a general way to the distance of the evolutionary relationships that have been reconstructed by other methods. The baboon appears to be an exception.

The beta chain appears to be more variable, and the number of actual polypeptides obtained differs from group to group. Yet again, with the exception of the baboon, the similarities to human hemoglobin are greatest in forms which are thought to be evolutionarily closest to ourselves on the basis of other data.

Studies of Serum Albumins

The serum albumins are single chains of about 570 amino acids found in all land vertebrates. Since time and cost did not permit the determination of the exact amino acid sequence, Vincent Sarich developed the following technique.[19]

He took a sample of purified serum albumin from his blood, along with samples from other primates. The samples were then injected into rabbits, which responded by manufacturing antibodies against the foreign protein. The antibodies from the rabbits were used as the test reagent, since the antibody reflected the structure of the injected protein.

The antiserums which developed from the injection of human serum albumin reacted strongly to human serum albumin. However, the reaction to chimpanzee serum albumin was less, and to the rhesus monkey serum albumin less still. The strong reaction between the antiserums and the serums from which the antiserums were derived was said to indicate an *immunological distance*

[19] V. Sarich, "A Molecular Approach to the Question of Human Origins," in P. Dolhinow and V. Sarich (eds.), *Background for Man* (Boston: Little, Brown, 1971), pp. 60–81.

(ID) of zero. Therefore the ID between one human and another is 0. The weakest ID is about 200. Antiserums were developed for serum albumin samples from humans, chimpanzee, rhesus monkey, and spider monkey, which were then tested against the serum albumins from these four forms. The results are listed in Table 12-8. The smaller the ID, the closer the evolutionary relationship. Figure 12-21 shows an evolutionary scheme based upon data of this type.

Sarich went further than simply indicating evolutionary relationships by placing a time factor for the ID unit. He postulates that the substitution of amino acids is a constant, and from comparative data he states that 1.67 ID units represents 1 million years of separation. Thus, the point of hominid-pongid divergence would be

Table 12-8 Immunological Distance Separating Primate Pairs

Pair	ID
Human–chimpanzee	7
Human–rhesus macaque	32
Human–spider monkey	58
Chimpanzee–rhesus macaque	30
Chimpanzee–spider monkey	56
Rhesus macaque–spider monkey	56

Adapted from Vincent Sarich, "A Molecular Approach to the Question of Human Origins," in P. Dolhinow and V. Sarich (eds.), *Background for Man* (Boston: Little, Brown, 1971), p. 66.

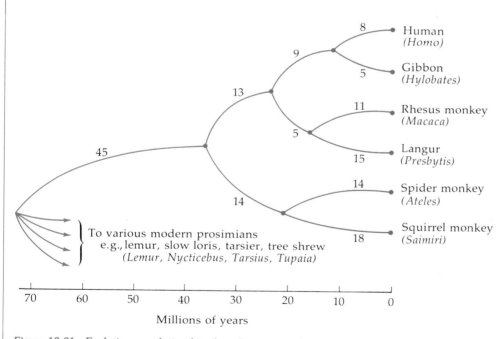

Figure 12-21 Evolutionary relationships based on serum albumin studies. *The evolutionary relationships shown on this chart are based upon Vincent M. Sarich's studies with serum albumin. The numbers refer to immunological distance.*

The Comparative Anatomy, Ontogeny, and Molecular Biology of the Living Primates

placed at a little more than 4 million years ago. As will be pointed out later, this is not consistent with the fossil record, and Sarich's method of calibration has been criticized on the basis that his assumptions about the rates of change in serum albumin are incorrect,[20] but this does not detract from the basic method as a means of determining evolutionary relationships.

Interpreting the Molecular Data

One rather surprising observation which can be made about this type of data is the extremely minor differences between human and chimpanzee proteins. The nature of such differences can be seen in Table 12-9. From these data we see that 99 percent of the human and chimpanzee polypeptides studied are identical. Studies of the human and chimpanzee DNA molecules show a difference of only about 1.1 percent.[21]

The differences in structural genes (Chapter 6) between *Homo sapiens* and the living chimpanzees are extremely minor. These differences are of the same order of magnitude as differences between similar-appearing, very closely related species. Yet the anatomical and behavioral differences between the two animals are substantial. It has been suggested that most of the changes which have taken place in hominid evolution are based upon changes in regulatory or modifier genes (Chapters 3, 6, and 8) and upon the relative positions of the genes on the chromosomes, rather than on mutations of structural genes.[22]

Another interesting aspect of the recent studies on regulatory genes is the new life it has given to an old concept. This hypothesis is called either the *fetalization* or *neoteny hypothesis*. The idea of neoteny was proposed by the Dutch anatomist Louis Bolk in the 1920s. The hypothesis states that humans are characterized by infantilization, that is, we have carried fetal or infant characteristics of the apes into adulthood. Bolk said that a human adult is a primate fetus that has become sexually mature (see Chapter 9, paedomorphosis). He presented twenty features that humans and fetal apes and monkeys share such as a rounded, bulbous cranium, small jaw, and an unrotated nonopposable big toe.[23] The recent work on regulatory genes has convinced some

Table 12-9 Differences in the Amino Acid Sequences of Human and Chimpanzee Proteins

Protein	Number of Amino Acid Differences	Number of Amino Acids in Protein
Fibrinopeptides A and B	0	30
Cytochrome c	0	104
Lysozyme	0*	130
Hemoglobin		
Alpha chain	0	141
Beta chain	0	146
Myoglobin	1	153
Carbonic anhydrase	3*	264
Serum albumin	6*	580
Transferrin	8*	647

* Approximation based on methods other than analysis of known amino acid sequences.
Adapted from M-C. King and A. C. Wilson, "Evolution at Two Levels in Humans and Chimpanzees," *Science*, 188 (11 April 1975), 108.

[20] C. Owen Lovejoy et al., "Primate Phylogeny and Immunological Distance," *Science*, 176 (19 May 1972), 803–805; H. M. Katzen and G. H. Vlahakes, V. Sarich, and A. C. Wilson, "Generation Time and Genomic Evolution in Primates," *Science*, 179 (16 March 1973), 1144–1147.

[21] M-C. King and A. C. Wilson, "Evolution at Two Levels in Humans and Chimpanzees," *Science*, 188 (11 April 1975), 107–116.

[22] Ibid.

[23] G. B. Kolata, "Evolution of DNA: Changes in Gene Regulation," *Science*, 189 (8 August 1975), 447.

scientists, such as Stephen Jay Gould, that Bolk was essentially correct. Gould believes that "changes in gene regulation . . . retarded developmental changes by retarding the sequence of gene expression in humans more than in apes and enabled human beings and apes to evolve from a common ancestor without substantial changes in structural genes."[24] Gould believes that the adaptive advantage of neoteny is a prolongation of the time to accumulate learned behavior.[25]

Restructuring the Taxonomic Chart

These studies, plus many others, have brought about suggestions for reconstructing the taxonomy of the primates. They have demonstrated the very close relationship between humans and the African apes, the chimpanzees, and the gorillas. It has been suggested that these three living forms be placed in a single family, Hominidae, while the orangutan be kept in the Pongidae. Physiological comparisons have also shown the remoteness of the gibbon, which should be placed in an entirely separate family or even superfamily. This latter idea is supported by the fossil data.

It must be emphasized here that in establishing evolutionary relationships, many lines of evidence are used. The fossil record, which will be discussed in the next three chapters, is the most direct method, but comparative studies of living species also yield important data. The different methods act as checks on each other. If comparative physiology yields a result that contradicts the evidence from comparative anatomy, the investigator must reexamine both methods for errors and perhaps look to other lines of evidence,

[24] Ibid.

[25] Ibid.

such as fossils or comparative ontogeny. By such checking and confirming, all methods become more refined and accurate.

Summary

In recent years, detailed biochemical studies of protein molecules have added a valuable perspective to evolutionary studies. By a comparison of protein molecules from various living species, it is possible to estimate the biochemical closeness of these species. This has been taken as an indication of evolutionary relationships. The evidence from such studies is basically consistent with the general outline presented by the fossil record and comparative anatomy. However, there are inconsistencies; and since biochemical comparisons are relatively new, we must wait until techniques are perfected and data are reanalyzed to determine the reliability of these studies. Also, it appears that some of the underlying assumptions may be incorrect, especially in relation to estimating evolutionary time intervals. These assumptions are being evaluated by many researchers at the present time.

Fossil evidence is direct evidence of evolution. It, along with comparative anatomy, molecular biology, and ontogeny, as well as natural selection seen in action, gives a remarkably clear general picture of the development and changes that have taken place in the living world.

SUGGESTED READINGS

Napier, J. R., and P. H. Napier. *A Handbook of Living Primates.* New York: Academic, 1967. Aside from the cataloging of the living primates, this book contains several summary chapters on various aspects of comparative anatomy.

Clark, W. E. LeGros, *The Antecedents of Man.* Edinburgh: Edinburgh Univ. Press, 1959. Perhaps the most complete general introduction to comparative anatomy of the primates.

PART FIVE

THE STORY OF HUMAN EVOLUTION

Theodosius Dobzhansky writes: "Evolution is change. Mankind has evolved; it is evolving; if it endures, it will continue to evolve. Human evolution has biological and cultural components. Man's biological evolution changes his nature; cultural evolution changes his nurture."[1]

The story of our past evolution, although incomplete since many of the passages are missing, can be read from the bones that ancient hominids have left behind. This story is a continually unfolding one. The fact that new discoveries are constantly being made and that debate often rages over the meaning of finds makes the study of the human past one of the most intriguing areas of human research. This part is concerned with the nature of the fossil record, what it can and cannot tell us about primate evolution. The last chapter examines humankind's continuing evolution and the prospects for future occupancy of the planet.

[1] Theodosius Dobzhansky, *Mankind Evolving* (New Haven: Yale Univ. Press, 1962), p. 23. Used with permission.

Chapter Thirteen
The Record of the Past

Confucius wrote, "Study the past, if you would divine the future." Through the ages, people have pondered their history. The anthropologist is interested in the past for what it will reveal about the nature and development of humans as biological, social, and cultural beings. The anthropologist believes, somewhat as Confucius did, that a knowledge of the events leading to the present human condition may be an important tool in coping with the problems that confront us.

Modern investigations of the history of the earth are based upon the principle of *uniformitarianism* (Chapter 2). This principle states that the forces which are working to create geological changes today are the same forces as those working in the past. This concept allows us not only to reconstruct the past but also to use our knowledge to foresee the consequences of our actions in the future. The past also illuminates the present. For instance, an understanding of the evolution of differences between human populations can help put contemporary racial problems into an objective perspective.

The past reflects a type of biological immortality. Life begets life; and through the processes of reproduction, the present becomes a slightly modified reconstruction of the immediate past. But there is still another type of immortality — that of the fossilized remains of an organism. It is through the preservation of body parts that the *paleontologist* and the physical anthropologist can see into the past and attempt to reconstruct the history of life.

FOSSILS AND THEIR INTERPRETATION

A *fossil* is the remains or trace of any ancient organism. Fossils have interested people for thousands of years. In fact, prehistoric societies may have attached magical or religious significance to fossils, since fossils have been found in archaeological sites containing the bones of early hominids who themselves are known only by the bones they left behind.

The Greeks and Romans not only knew of fossils but made some accurate assumptions about what they meant. For instance, about 500 B.C. some believed that fossil fish represented the ancestors of all life. However, during the Middle Ages most knowledge and theory about fossils was lost and replaced with other ideas. Fossils were considered remnants of attempts at special creation, objects that had fallen from the heavens, and even devices of the devil.

In the fifteenth century Leonardo da Vinci wrote, "The mountains where there are shells were formerly shores beaten by waves, and since then they have been elevated to the heights we see today." From this time on, debate has raged over the true meaning of geological formations and the fossils found in them. Only in the last few hundred years have scholars agreed that fossils are the remains of ancient organisms and that they can tell us a great deal about the history of life.

The Requirements for Fossilization

The "immortality" of the body is limited. Most organisms have left no trace of their existence, their dead bodies having been absorbed into the soil or eaten by other organisms. In order for an organism to be preserved, a number of conditions usually must be met. First, most organisms that have been preserved have had hard parts, such as bones, teeth, and shells. However, under ideal conditions an organism with only soft parts may be preserved by leaving a cast of its body. Second, the organism must not be destroyed immediately by other organisms or by the action of climatic or geological forces. Third, the organism must be protected immediately from decaying. This usually takes the form of rapid burial, which also protects the organism from being totally destroyed.

The vast majority of fossil remains occur in the form of mineralized bone (Figure 13-1a). As the bone lies in the ground, the organic matter in the bone is replaced by minerals. Yet, under certain conditions, other forms of preservation do occur.

Organisms or their traces can be preserved by being frozen in ice, like some mammoths in Siberia and Alaska. In some hot, dry regions, the organism quickly dehydrates. The result is a mummy whose soft parts remain. The American Southwest has yielded many fossils formed in this way, including a 2,000-year-old Indian woman whose skin still clings to her bones. Some organisms have been preserved in natural deposits of wax or asphalt. Some have been reduced to a carbon film. This film, while often as thin as tissue paper, can reveal in two dimensions fine details of anatomy.

Traces of ancient life forms also may be found as *molds* or *casts* (Figure 13-1b). The former is a cavity left in firm sediment by the decayed body of an organism. Nothing of the organism itself is left. This mold, if filled with some substance, becomes a cast that reflects the shape of the fossil. Tracks and burrows of animals have been preserved this way (Figure 13-1c). Materials ingested and excreted by animals also can be preserved and tell us much about the diet of the animal. But these forms of preservation rarely are found in the primate fossil record. Ancient hominids are best known by their fossilized bones.

Biases in the Fossil Record

In spite of the number of ways an organism can be fossilized, only a surprisingly small fraction of the individuals that have ever lived become preserved. With respect to fossil hominids, from the excavations at Omo, an East African early hominid site, Anna K. Behrensmeyer estimates that only 0.004 percent of the number of individuals which

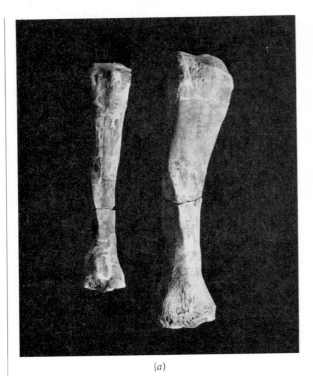

(a)

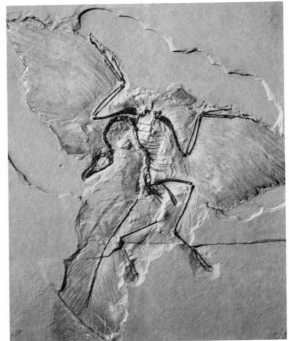

(b)

Figure 13-1 Fossils. *The remains of prehistoric life may take the form of* (a) *fossilized bone (limb bones of* Baluchterium), (b) *cast (Archeopteryx), and (c) tracks (dinosaur).*

once lived are represented in the fossil record.[1] Some entire groups of organisms are not represented at all. Usually one or more factors disrupt the conditions necessary for preservation.

Differential preservation   Whether a particular organism is preserved or not often depends on the part of the world in which that organism lives. Forms living in hot, humid, tropical areas often are not preserved because decay usually sets in before the body can be buried. On the other

[1] A. K. Behrensmeyer, "Taphonomy and Paleoecology in the Hominid Fossil Record," *Yearbook of Physical Anthropology 1975* (Washington: American Association of Physical Anthropologists, 1976), pp. 36–50.

(c)

hand, a hot, dry desert may yield a great number of fossils. The result is that paleontologists lack knowledge of many species which once inhabited tropical zones, while in many desert regions the fossils uncovered represent a good sample of the animals which once lived there. It already has been noted that soft-bodied organisms are not as readily preserved as those with hard parts, and therefore many species of soft-bodied organisms remain unknown.

The chance for preservation also is affected by the particular habitat occupied by the organism. In highland areas, erosion may destroy fossils before they can be discovered. Arboreal animals are not preserved as frequently as those living on the ground because an animal dying in the trees tends to remain exposed to the elements and rapidly decays. Flying animals are also poorly represented in the fossil record. On the other hand, aquatic forms are more frequently preserved because they fall to the ocean or lake floor at death and can be quickly covered by sediments. It can generally be said that each habitat differs in the conditions it offers for fossilization.

Once an organism dies, it is seldom buried immediately. Many things can occur from the time of death to the time of burial and the beginnings of the process of fossilization. Initially, predators and scavengers dismember the body, and many bones may be destroyed by chewing. The body, or parts of the body, may be carried some distance, as when a leopard drags a carcass up into a tree to protect it from competing hyenas. Once the bones are disarticulated, they are subject to weathering processes effected by temperature, wind, and rain. Light bones and bones with large surface areas, such as ribs, scapulae, and vertebrae, weather quickly. Hence, the majority of fossil remains consist of relatively dense bones, especially jaws and teeth. Bones are often swept into streams and rivers and may be transported great distances. The lighter bones move quickly near the surface while the heavier bones are trans-

ported at a much slower rate and therefore do not travel as far. The point of ultimate burial and fossilization may be hundreds of miles from the place of death, and the remains may be incorporated into a geologic environment totally different from the environment in which the organism once lived and died.[2]

Sampling error in the fossil record　The fossil record is a sample of organisms that once lived. But because of the problems of preservation discussed above, the sample is biased. Interpretations of the fossil record must take this fact into account (Figure 13-2).

One important bias is the fact that the frequency of fossil specimens does not necessarily reflect their true numerical relation to one another. Birds, for example, are not preserved as frequently as mammals, and so the fossil record shows a scarcity of bird forms when in reality they may have been a predominant life form in a particular area at a specific time. Primates, being arboreal animals, also are not preserved as frequently as terrestrial forms.

In addition, some genera, families, and even orders are better represented than others. A given taxon might be known only by certain of its species, such as lowland species which are more likely to be preserved, while highland species may not have been fossilized because of destruction of fossil beds by erosion.

Another factor in sampling is that of accessibility of sites. Some areas, such as southwestern France, have been extensively explored. Other areas, such as parts of Africa and Asia, remain untouched. There are the twin problems of physical accessibility and money. Excavation in areas away from urban centers can be costly in terms of transportation and labor.

[2] Ibid.

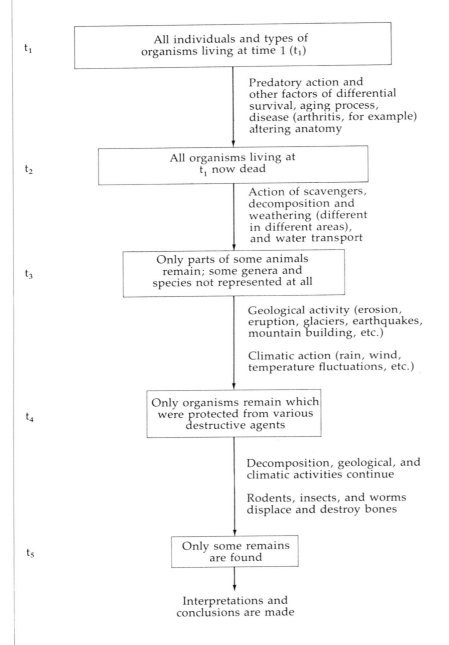

t_1 All individuals and types of organisms living at time 1 (t_1)

Predatory action and other factors of differential survival, aging process, disease (arthritis, for example) altering anatomy

t_2 All organisms living at t_1 now dead

Action of scavengers, decomposition and weathering (different in different areas), and water transport

t_3 Only parts of some animals remain; some genera and species not represented at all

Geological activity (erosion, eruption, glaciers, earthquakes, mountain building, etc.)

Climatic action (rain, wind, temperature fluctuations, etc.)

t_4 Only organisms remain which were protected from various destructive agents

Decomposition, geological, and climatic activities continue

Rodents, insects, and worms displace and destroy bones

t_5 Only some remains are found

Interpretations and conclusions are made

Figure 13-2 Sampling error inherent in the interpretation of the fossil record.

The Story of Human Evolution

An even more serious question is: What does the fossil represent? Since fossilization is a chance phenomenon and represents a sample of individuals of a given species, how reliable is the fossil record as a sample? To put it another way, is an individual fossil representative of the average member of the species, or is it a deviant? The probability is that any given fossil is representative of the species, since the majority of a given population is typical. But many unrepresentative fossils are also known, and there is the additional problem of having only a few representatives of a species that itself might have been extremely variable.

An example of this would be the case of the Neandertals,[3] who lived between 35,000 and 100,000 years ago. One of the early complete skeletons discovered was that of La Chapelle-aux-Saints from France. This skeleton has been used as the prototype of the Neandertals and is the one most often pictured in books. From this skeleton emerges a concept of a form with an unusual posture, hunched over and bowlegged, with massive brow ridges and bestial features (Figure 13-3).

But the specimen from La Chapelle-aux-Saints is not an average Neandertal. It is the skeleton of an old man suffering from an advanced case of arthritis of the spine! And if a series of Neandertals is compared, this particular individual appears to be one of the least modern in appearance. Actually, a more representative Neandertal would lack many of these exaggerated features. In fact, the term *Neandertal* is only a general designation and represents a group of hominids that show a great deal of intraspecific variation (Figure 15-8).

[3] The original spelling was Neanderthal, but early in this century Germany changed the spelling to Neandertal. The pronunciation is the same for both. The new spelling is becoming predominant in the anthropological literature.

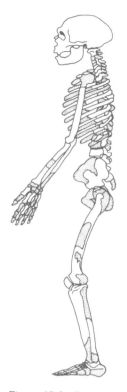

Figure 13-3 Reconstruction of La Chapelle-aux-Saints.

Gaps in fossil progressions It is often possible to follow the evolutionary history of a kind of organism for millions of years, only to encounter a period characterized by a lack of fossils which, in turn, is followed by the reemergence of that or a somewhat more evolved form in the fossil record. Such gaps are common, as will be seen in subsequent chapters.

Gaps in the fossil record result from a number of causes. For one thing, organisms do not necessarily stay in the same niche. As the species moves into a new niche, the probability of fossilization may change. Although the population seems to have disappeared, in reality it simply may not have been preserved during that period of time. Or perhaps the fossils do exist but have yet to be found.

Another factor bringing about gaps in the fossil record is a change in sedimentation. *Sedimentation* is the deposition of materials carried in water, wind, or glaciers. Most fossils are found in sedimentary deposits. If sedimentation ceases in a particular area, preservation may also cease and an apparent gap in the fossil record results. Subsequent erosion may destroy sedimentary beds which have been laid down.

What Can Fossils Tell Us?

The fossil record is like a puzzle, with many pieces missing and still others distorted. Yet a picture,

Figure 13-4   Flesh reconstruction. *A flesh reconstruction of* Homo erectus *from Choukoutien, China.*

even though incomplete, does emerge. Often the image of the past is only an outline; sometimes it is a well-documented history.

With a few exceptions, the fossil record consists of skeletal remains. However, from the skeleton, much can be inferred about the body. For example, areas of muscle attachment can be seen on the surface of bone, often as ridges or roughened areas. From this information, the shape, size, and function of various muscles can be reconstructed. This is of great importance when reconstructing locomotor patterns, for instance. Once the musculature has been reconstructed, it is possible to get some idea of what the organism might have looked like by placing a skin over the musculature (Figure 13-4). The fossil record, however, gives no indication of the color of the skin or the amount of hair on the body.

The relative size of the eye socket, nasal cavities, and hearing apparatus can tell us a great deal about what senses were most important in the fossil form. The development of vision in the primates can be seen in the development of the eye socket and the frontal position of the eye on the skull.

Although brains are never fossilized,[4] some inferences about brain size can be made from the brain case, as discussed in Chapter 12. Some idea of the gross structure of the brain can be gained from examination of the inside surface of the brain case, which conforms to the general size and shape of the brain. Grooves, representing arteries, are also seen (Figure 12-14). While such factors as intelligence, the development of culture, and the presence or absence of speech have been inferred from such data, one must always view these conclusions with a great deal of caution.

[4] Brain material may be preserved in a desiccated or frozen specimen, but such instances are infrequent and involve recent individuals.

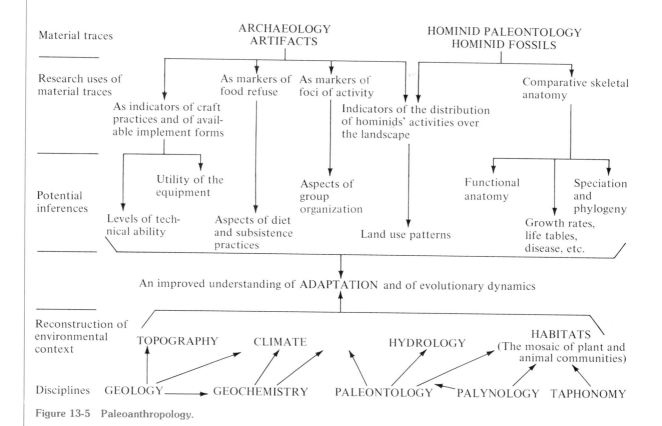

Figure 13-5 Paleoanthropology.

Patterns of growth and development are mirrored in the fossil record when one discovers a sequence of remains representing individuals of different ages. Data on life expectancies and population structure can also be derived from this material. For example, the age at death can be estimated from tooth eruption and wear patterns on teeth. *Paleopathology* deals with the investigation of injuries and disease in prehistoric populations. For example, arthritis and dental caries have been observed in Neandertals.

In addition to information about the individual and the species, the presence of fossil remains of animals in association with human remains, the remains of human activity, and the geological context can tell us much about the living patterns and ecological relations of the early hominids. Figure 13-5 shows the interrelationships of various types of data and interpretations which can be used to build a picture of the early hominids. The hominid fossils and the *artifacts*, the material remains of human behavior, are the primary data used in the reconstruction of technology, subsistence activities and diet, land-use patterns, and even, to a limited extent, group social structure. *Paleoanthropology*, the study of prehistoric hominids, combines with other disciplines, such as geology, *paleontology* (the study of fossils), *palynology* (the study of fossil pollen), and *taphonomy* (the study of burial and the process of fossilization) to reconstruct the environment in which the hominids functioned.[5]

Of course, the most important information anthropologists derive from the fossil record is evidence of evolutionary processes. For it is in the fossil record that the actual remains of the early forms are found.

A Note on the History of Excavation

The story of the discovery of specific fossils will be discussed in the next two chapters. But this is a good point at which to comment on the nature of excavation in human paleontology.

Although the actual fossil remains are of great importance, of equal importance is the *context* in which they are found. Data on the exact placement of the fossil within the site and the nature of the deposit are necessary if precise dating is to be made. In addition, the association of the fossil with the remains of other animals, plants, and tools provides data which can be used in cultural and ecological reconstructions.

Early excavations were not carefully controlled. This is not a condemnation of early workers but simply a realization of the state of excavation technology. Thus, for a great number of critical fossils, especially those discovered before the 1950s, many of the data needed for precise dating and cultural and ecological studies were either never recovered or were destroyed.

Another difficulty with the early discoveries was the failure to collect precise information about the fossils themselves, especially quantitative information. Again, this was largely because the questions asked today were not being asked when the material was originally recovered, and therefore no one thought of recording these necessary data. Thus, in using early data in a research project, this can be a major obstacle. When schemes of human evolution based upon the fossil record are discussed, these difficulties must be kept in mind.

Taxonomy and the Fossil Record

George Gaylord Simpson writes:

Men and all recent and fossil organisms pertinent to their affinities are animals, and the appropriate language for discussing their classification and relationships is that of animal taxonomy. . . . It is notorious that hominid nomenclature, particularly, has become chaotic.[6]

Much of the confusion on interpretation of the fossil record is the result of the incorrect usage of scientific nomenclature. Prerequisite to any discussion of the fossil record is a discussion of the problems of taxonomy and fossils.

The species concept in the fossil record Fossil taxonomy has been one of the most provocative areas in paleoanthropology. With each new find, a new debate begins over its placement in the evolutionary scheme. One of the major aspects of this problem is the definition of the species when applied to the fossil record. Since the definition of species for living populations is based upon the criterion of reproductive success (Chapter 6), the difficulties of applying this concept to the fossil material are obvious.

---

[5] G. L. Isaac, "Early Hominids in Action: A Commentary on the Contribution of Archaeology to Understanding the Fossil Record in East Africa," *Yearbook of Physical Anthropology 1975* (Washington: American Association of Physical Anthropologists, 1976), pp. 19–35.

[6] G. G. Simpson, "The Meaning of Taxonomic Statement," in S. C. Washburn (ed.), Classification and Human Evolution, *Viking Fund Publications in Anthropology*, no. 37 (1963), 4–5.

There are two schools of thought concerning the definition of species in the fossil record, diametrically opposed to each other in philosophical outlook. The *typological* viewpoint embodies the ancient philosophy developed by Plato that basic variation of a type is illusory; only fixed ideal types are real. The concept of the *archetype* was introduced in the discussion of taxonomy in Chapter 9. Thus, two fossils which differ from each other in certain respects represent two types, hence two different species.

An example of the typological viewpoint would be the naming of the fossil primate *"Kenyapithecus wickeri"* from East Africa. Before the discovery of this fossil, a species of early hominid, *Ramapithecus punjabicus,* from India, had been described. Following the typological point of view, L. S. B. Leakey placed the discovery from East Africa not only in a separate species but in a separate genus on the grounds that differences did exist between the two fossils and that they came from different parts of the world (Chapter 14).

The typological viewpoint has dominated human paleontology for what are probably psychological reasons more than anything else. The discovery of a new fossil is a highly emotional experience, and a new find becomes more significant if it can be said to represent a new species rather than simply another specimen of an already known species.

The *populationist* viewpoint is that only individuals have reality, while it is the type that is illusory. More precisely, the populationist argues that since no two individuals are exactly alike, variation underlies all existence. In this light, the populationist would consider *"K. wickeri"* and *R. punjabicus* to be species of the same genus, *Ramapithecus,* or variants of a single species, *R. punjabicus.* Some would argue that there is no more difference between these two forms than between individuals of a living species. Elwyn Simons writes:

In 1962, Leakey unfortunately coined a new genus and species for the East African primate maxilla, "Kenyapithecus wickeri." His diagnosis and description of this taxon exactly characterize the two Indian maxillae of Ramapithecus. . . .[7]

We can consider another example of the populationist viewpoint. If the heights of four individuals are 5 feet 1 inch, 5 feet 3 inches, 5 feet 5 inches, and 5 feet 7 inches, the average height will be 5 feet 4 inches. Not only do individuals in the sample vary 3 inches on either side of the average, but in this case no one individual is average. According to this reasoning, variation in fossil finds can be explained as divergence from a statistical average. If this deviation is no greater than that which might be found within a related living species, the populationist feels no reason to separate the finds into different taxonomic categories.

To illustrate this point, Figure 13-6 shows a series of skulls. Note the great amount of variation. How many species are represented here? In this case, they are all modern gorillas. Yet a series of hominid fossils which shows as much variation or less would be broken up by a great many paleoanthropologists into a number of distinct genera and species. This is why the typologists are often referred to as *splitters,* while the populationists are referred to as *lumpers.*

Paleospecies   The populationist taxonomic philosophy is gradually becoming dominant in the field of human paleontology, as are population genetics and theory in general. However, although most people appear to support the populationist viewpoint, its actual application to the data is lagging.

---

[7] E. L. Simons, *Primate Evolution* (New York: Macmillan, 1972), p. 268.

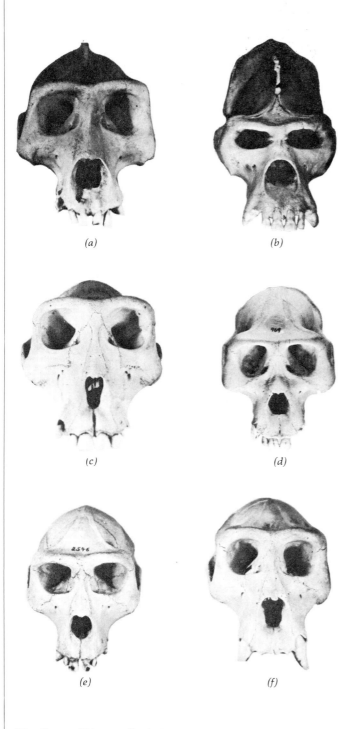

Figure 13-6 Intraspecific variation. *A series of six skulls, all members of the same species,* Gorilla gorilla. *Note the degree of variation:* (b) *and* (f) *are males,* (a) *and* (c) *are probably males, and* (d) *and* (e) *are probably females.*

(a)

(b)

(c)

(d)

(e)

(f)

317

How can species be defined for the fossil record? First, it must be reiterated that all taxonomic categories, with the exception of the living species, are arbitrary. Living species are defined in the objective terms of reproductive isolation. The larger units, such as genus, family, and order, classify species together on the basis of varying criteria.

Reproductive isolating mechanisms cannot be seen in the fossil record, nor can gene frequencies. At best, geographical isolation can be inferred in some situations. In dealing with the fossil record, the taxonomist is restricted to an analysis of morphological variation, and, as has been already noted, variation within a species can be great.

Many anthropologists have concluded that since the species concept as applied to living forms is based upon reproductive criteria, and since such data are not available in the fossil record, the species concept cannot be legitimately applied to fossil forms. Instead, we must speak of the *paleospecies*, a taxonomic category which resembles the species but is defined in terms of morphological variation rather than in terms of genetic isolation and reproductive success. A paleospecies is seen as a group of similar fossils whose range of morphological variation does not exceed the range of variation of a closely related living species. Determination of a paleospecies requires detailed statistical analysis of both the fossil series and the living species being used for comparison.

Reasons for variability in the fossil record The fossil record is an incomplete history of evolutionary change. Many of the differences seen in the fossil record represent the emergence of new species and higher taxonomic groups. But much of the variation which often is interpreted as interspecific actually is intraspecific.

One form of intraspecific variation is age and sex differences. Figure 13-7 shows the skulls of an infant and an adult chimpanzee. Note, for example, the absence of a prominent brow ridge and the generally more "human" appearance of the child's skull. One must be extremely careful when using anything other than adult material in interpretation.

Sexual dimorphism was discussed with reference to the baboon, where the structure of the male differed noticeably from that of the female. Anatomically, the male baboon is larger than the female, with longer canines. The sex of an adult

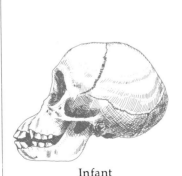
Infant

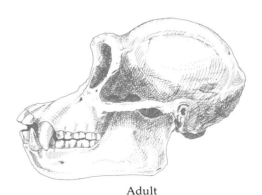
Adult

Figure 13-7 Age differences in chimpanzee skulls. *The skulls of an infant and an adult chimpanzee.*

baboon is therefore easily determined. On the other hand, a form like the gibbon shows little sexual dimorphism; and unless the female is nursing a child, the male and female cannot be distinguished at a distance. It is possible that early hominid forms showed a greater degree of sexual dimorphism than *Homo sapiens* does today.

Most variation within a species is due to the simple fact that (as was seen in the discussion of genetics) no two individuals are phenotypically identical; therefore, one cannot expect any two fossils to be exactly the same. Consider, for example, the tremendous variation within the species *Homo sapiens* with respect to such things as stature, body build, and cranial capacity.

An example of such variation is found in a study by R. B. Eckhardt, who determined that the range of variation in tooth dimensions within a living population of captive chimpanzees (*Pan troglodytes*) often exceeded the range of variation found among fossil apes which had been divided into several species.[8] For example, among the fossil apes, the length of the lower first premolar averaged 10.52 millimeters, with a range of variation from 7.92 to 13.12 millimeters. The average for the living chimpanzee population was 10.80 millimeters, ranging between 7.70 and 13.90 millimeters. Yet, as is clear from reproductive data, the living common chimpanzees make up a single species.

Cladogenesis and anagenesis There are two situations which are seen in the fossil record. One is the divergence of two evolutionary lines from a common ancestor, with each line adapting to different niches and hence becoming reproductively isolated. This situation is known as *cladogenesis*. But in the fossil record it is possible to

[8] R. B. Eckhardt, "Population Genetics and Human Origins," *Scientific American*, 226 (January 1972), 101.

follow the progressive adaptation of a single evolutionary line, a situation known as *anagenesis*. In this case, the population becomes increasingly specialized to a niche that has remained fairly constant through time. It is an arbitrary matter where the line is divided (Chapter 6).

Consider an evolutionary line undergoing anagenesis. The populations at the two extremes may be sufficiently different in structure to warrant separate species distinction. But where on the line are the two species to be separated? In reality, gaps in the fossil record usually provide convenient, arbitrary breaking points; but when fossils are found later which fill in the gaps, the situation must be reevaluated.

Summary

The remains and traces of ancient organisms make up the fossil record. Yet this record is far from being a complete history of life on earth. Only an extremely small proportion of the individuals that once lived have become fossilized, and some species are totally unknown as fossils. Effective fossilization usually depends on having hard parts, such as bones or shells, and being buried immediately after death. The work of predators and scavengers and the weathering effects of rain, heat, cold, and wind often serve to destroy most or all of an organism before final burial takes place.

Because of the nature of fossilization, the fossil record is a biased sample of the totality of life which once existed. Fossilization is more apt to occur in some areas, such as at the bottom of lakes, than others, such as tropical rain forests. Aquatic animals are preserved much more frequently than those living in terrestrial environments. Also, some parts of the world have been more thoroughly explored for fossils than others. A major problem of sampling is the realization that a fossil is a single individual. Is that individual typical of the species, or does it represent a deviant from the norm?

Fossils provide a great deal of information if studied carefully. From skeletal remains, the musculature can be reconstructed, and from the musculature one can get a good idea about the physical appearance of the animal. The brain case can tell us much about the brain. Series of remains of differing ages provide information about growth and development, and careful studies can even provide information concerning injury and disease. Also of great importance are the associated remains of animals, artifacts, and the geologic context, which provide a means of reconstructing the ecological relationships and even, to some extent, the behavior of prehistoric populations.

One of the biggest problems in paleoanthropology is the application of taxonomic principles to the fossil record. There are two major theoretical orientations. The typologist distinguishes species on the basis of morphological differences, while the populationist thinks more in terms of variable reproductive populations. In any case, the species concept as defined in terms of reproductive success cannot be applied to the fossil record. Instead, one must talk in terms of the paleospecies, defined in terms of morphological similarities and differences.

GEOLOGICAL TIME

It is somewhat paradoxical that in order to learn more about the earth, scientists have investigated the nature of the moon. Both bodies, along with the sun and the other planets, are thought to have been formed at about the same time. Because the crust of the moon has not undergone as much alteration as that of the earth, the examination of moon rocks may give a better estimate of the age of the earth than an examination of the earth

itself. This estimate now stands at about 4½ billion years.[9]

When people believed that the earth was only about 6,000 years old (see Chapter 2), evolutionary theory in both the biological and the geological sense was impossible to formulate. Evolution requires an extremely long time span. For instance, a conservative estimate separates the first members of the genus *Homo* from modern human populations by a minimum of 50,000 generations.

Because the concept of time is so central to human paleontology, it is important to understand the long periods of time involved. We can equate time with distance and say that the history of the earth is represented by a highway stretching from New York to Los Angeles. If New York represents 4½ billion years ago and Los Angeles is the present time, then as we travel from New York to Los Angeles, the first forms of life would appear in Indianapolis, but the first animal life would not arise until Phoenix, Arizona. The first primates would develop at about Disneyland, and hominids would be developing on the shore of the Pacific Ocean.

Absolute and Relative Dates

Two types of dates can be distinguished: absolute and relative. *Absolute dates* refer to specific points in time and are noted on specific calendrical systems. Calendrical systems are based upon natural recurring units of time, such as the year, and note the number of such units which have preceded or elapsed with reference to a specific point in time. For instance, *On the Origin of Species* was published in 1859. This date is based on the Gregorian calendar and refers to 1,859 revolu-

---

[9] J. E. Sanders, A. H. Anderson, Jr., and R. Carola, *Physical Geology* (New York: Harper's College Press, 1976), p. 13.

tions of the earth around the sun since the traditional date of the birth of Christ. The same book could be said to have been published in 5620, the date according to the Hebrew calendar, or in 1276, the date according to the Muslim calendar. In the first case the date is relative to the biblical origin of the world and in the second to the flight of Mohammed.

An absolute date is very often given as 115 years ago or 115 B.P., where B.P. stands for "before the present." The problem with this type of designation is that one must know the year in which the date was determined. For example, if a date is determined to be 780 B.P. in 1950, it would have to be changed to 800 B.P. in 1970, and so on. Many anthropologists today use 1950 as the reference point for all B.P. dates.

Absolute dates in paleontology are often given in the following form: 500 B.P. ± 50 years. The "plus or minus 50 years" does not represent an error factor but is a probability statement which is necessary when certain types of determinations are used. This probability is expressed as a *standard deviation*. A standard deviation of 50 years, for example, would mean that the probability of the real date's falling between 450 and 550 years is 67 percent. The probability of the real date's falling between two standard deviations, in our example of between 600 and 400 B.P., is 95 percent.

A *relative date* is not fixed to any calendrical system but simply specifies that one thing is older or younger than another. From a statement that Jack is older than Sue or even that Jack is ten years older than Sue, it is not known how old either is. The designations "older than," "younger than," or "of greater antiquity than" are relative dates. Of course, if two things are dated absolutely, then their relative dates are automatically known.

Often the paleoanthropologist must use both absolute and relative dates together. For example, if two fossils are dated at 30,000 ± 250 and 30,150 ± 250 B.P., respectively, the most probable real dates would overlap (29,750–30,250 B.P. and 29,900–30,400 B.P.), and so one cannot tell for sure which is older. A relative dating technique would solve the problem.

Absolute Dating Methods

There are a number of dating methods which give what is defined as an absolute date. Some, such as tree-ring dating (which is based on the annual rings of trees), have existed for a long time. However, the development of *radiometric* methods based upon the nature of radioactive substances has brought about a complete revision of our ideas about the age of the earth and the fossils it contains.

All radioactive materials are unstable. Their nuclei are constantly losing particles. This loss, called *radioactive decay*, proceeds at a constant rate for each radioactive element but varies from element to element. The *half-life* is the time in which half the atoms of a radioactive substance have decayed into new atoms.

Radiometric dating   The first radiometric dating method to be developed is the one based upon carbon 14, often referred to as *radiocarbon dating*. All living organisms contain large amounts of carbon. Carbon and other elements exist as atoms of differing *atomic weights*. These variants of an element are termed *isotopes*. The most common form of carbon is the stable atom with an atomic weight of 12, carbon 12. However, all living things contain a small amount of the radioactive isotope carbon 14, which has a half-life of 5,730 years.

Carbon 14 is formed in the upper atmosphere by the bombardment of nitrogen by cosmic radiation. This carbon 14 combines with oxygen to form carbon dioxide, which is then incorporated into plants by photosynthesis and into animals by ingesting plants or other animals. As long as the organism is alive, the amount of carbon 14 entering the body equals the amount lost by radioactive decay. When the organism dies, no new carbon 14 atoms are incorporated into the body, and those atoms present at death continue to decay. By measuring the amount of carbon 14 relative to the amount of carbon 12 in the sample, one can arrive at an absolute date. This method can be used to date any organic material including, but not limited to, bone, teeth, shell, charcoal, wood, and pollen. Radiocarbon dating can be used for material from the past 50,000 years. Beyond 50,000 years there is not enough carbon 14 left in the sample to be detected and measured reliably.

New methods, such as *potassium-argon dating*, are of value since they deal with isotopes of much longer half-lives. Potassium 40 has a half-life of 1.3 billion years. Thus, potassium-argon dating can be used to date the age of the earth and has been used extensively for calibrating the geologic time scale. Some researchers believe that potassium-argon dating can be used for dates as recent as 2,500 B.P.

Potassium-argon dating is based upon the radioactive decay of potassium 40. Only 11.2 percent of potassium 40 decays into argon 40, a gas which accumulates within certain rocks. Potassium is a fairly common constituent of rocks, but

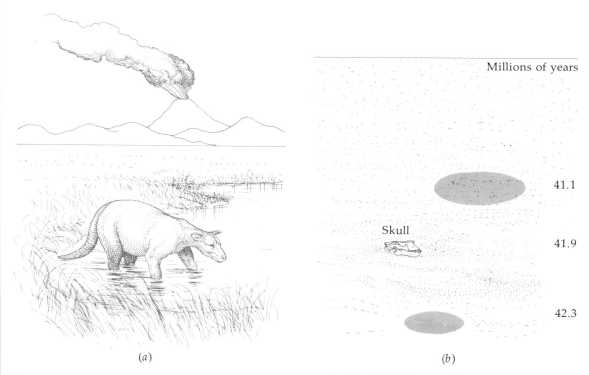

Millions of years

41.1

Skull

41.9

42.3

(a) (b)

Figure 13-8   Potassium-argon dating. (a) *Hypothetical live animal.* (b) *After death, the animal becomes incorporated into a sedimentary bed (lake deposit). Periodic volcanic eruptions have resulted in the creation of volcanic lenses in this bed. This volcanic material can be dated by the potassium-argon technique. The age of the fossil is determined from its context in relationship to the volcanic lenses.*

the method can only be used on rocks and minerals with a high enough potassium content. Under very high temperatures, such as those associated with volcanic activity, the argon gas is expelled. When the material cools and solidifies, it contains a certain amount of potassium 40 but no argon 40. As time goes on, the amount of potassium 40 decreases while the amount of argon 40 increases. These amounts are used in the calculation of the absolute date. This method is limited, with few exceptions, to volcanic ash falls and lava flows. It is seldom used to date an actual object, but is used to date artifacts and fossilized bones with respect to their placement in relationship to volcanic layers in the surrounding material (Figure 13-8). This method has been employed at Olduvai Gorge, a famous early-hominid site, where the presence of former volcanic activity has meant that many layers of volcanic material are incorporated into the sedimentary strata.

Amino acid racemization Many organic molecules, such as the amino acids, occur in two forms, identical in structure except for being mirror images of each other. The form usually found in living organisms is the L-amino acid. The L refers to *levo-*, which indicates the fact that a specified portion of the molecule extends to the left. The other form is the D-amino acid. The D refers to *dextro-*, which means that a specified portion of the molecule extends to the right. When an organism dies, the L-amino acids slowly turn into the D-amino acids. This process is known as *racemization.*

Each amino acid is associated with a characteristic speed of racemization at a given temperature. For example, in aspartic acid, the ratio of the D to the L form reaches 0.333 at 20°C in about 15,000 to 20,000 years. This time factor makes aspartic acid racemization especially useful for the period from 5,000 to 70,000 years ago, thus overlapping the range of radiocarbon dating.

Ratios of D- to L-aspartic acid can be compared to radiocarbon dates of the same fossil, thus permitting the various ratios to be calibrated with respect to known dates. Once calibrated, the method can be used to date material older than that which can be dated by carbon 14. Another advantage of this method is that much less of the fossil material is needed for a determination than for radiocarbon determinations. Other amino acids with different racemization speeds can be used to date even more ancient material.[10]

Not all paleontologists accept this new method as being accurate. There are a number of variables which can affect the racemization speed. The most significant variable is temperature. Because of this factor, ratios which have been calibrated by carbon 14 dates are valid only for a specific geographic area. In addition, the consistency of temperatures over long periods of time should be demonstrated. This method is still being developed, and the question of its accuracy still needs to be answered.[11]

Relative Dating Methods
The methods described below can yield only relative dates. They are used to place fossils in the proper time relationship to one another.

Stratigraphy *Stratigraphy* is the investigation of the composition of the layers of the earth and their relationship to each other. The main principle applied to such studies is the *principle of*

[10] J. L. Bada and R. Protsch, "Racemization Reaction of Aspartic Acid and Its Use in Dating Fossil Bones," *Proceedings of the National Academy of Sciences,* 70 (1973), 1331–1334; and J. L. Bada, R. A. Schroeder, and G. F. Carter, "New Evidence for the Antiquity of Man in North America Deduced from Aspartic Acid Racemization," *Science,* 184 (17 May 1974), 791–793.

[11] M. L. Bender, "Reliability of Amino Acid Racemisation Dating and Palaeotemperature Analysis on Bones," *Nature,* 252 (29 November 1974), 378–379.

superposition. Simply stated, this means that under stable conditions, layers, or *strata*, on the bottom of a deposit are older than the ones on top. This is because the atmosphere, through wind and corrosive activities, and bodies of water, through their movements, erode away dust, rock, and sediment, which are then deposited on top of materials deposited earlier. Since the composition and nature of these materials differ at different time periods, the various layers can often be visually identified. Areas like the Grand Canyon of Arizona graphically illustrate the process of stratigraphic successions (Figure 2-1).

As noted above, the principle of superposition has one of its simplest applications in the method known as stratigraphy. As material is laid down, newer material forms on top of the older. Therefore, as a site is excavated, progressively older remains are encountered as one digs deeper. In general, the object which is buried deeper in the ground is older than one which is located closer to the surface. Hence, fossils and cultural remains can be dated relatively on the basis of their position in a deposit (Figure 13-9).

In practice, stratigraphic sequences are not easy to interpret. Neat layers are not always present, and intrusions, such as a burial, can place a more recent fossil at the same level with much older material. Careful analysis of the soil can often reveal such intrusions. Earthquakes, volcanic eruptions, and other cataclysmic events can also alter stratigraphic sequences.

Fluorine dating   Special methods have been developed to test whether or not objects in a site are contemporary. As bones and teeth lie in the ground, they absorb fluorine and other minerals from the groundwater. On the other hand, the nitrogen content of the bones decreases as the material gets older. The amount of minerals absorbed and the amount of nitrogen lost can be used to calculate the relative chronology of the material in the site. But since the rates of absorption and loss depend on the specific nature of the groundwater, these methods can be used only for fossils found in the same area. The most frequent application of these methods is in determining whether two bones found together are indeed of equal age. If a human skull, for example, is found next to a mammoth rib, showing that they are of the same age would indicate that people lived at the same time as the mammoths.

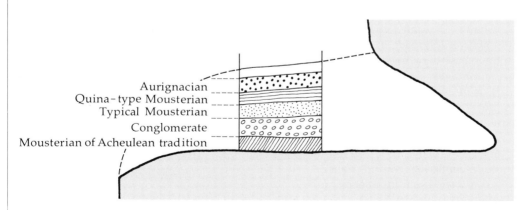

Figure 13-9   Stratigraphy. *A stratigraphic cross section of the upper shelter at Le Moustier, France. Various cultural manifestations are identified as well as a sterile layer, the conglomerate.*

Aurignacian
Quina-type Mousterian
Typical Mousterian
Conglomerate
Mousterian of Acheulean tradition

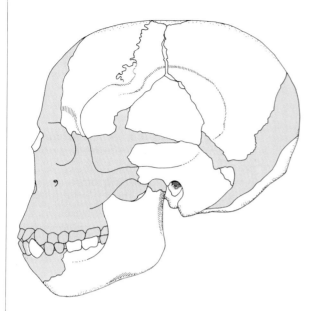

Figure 13-10 A reconstruction of the Piltdown skull. *The colored areas have been reconstructed.*

Otherwise, the skull could be interpreted as an intrusion into a lower level by means of burial.

A famous application of the fluorine dating method revealed one of the most elaborate hoaxes ever conceived. As Darwin's theory became acceptable, the search for "missing links" began. In 1912, Charles Dawson found a skull which became known as *Piltdown man*. It appeared to have a brain case very much like that of a modern person, but a lower jaw like that of an ape (Figure 13-10). Here was the missing link!

In the years that followed, other transitional forms were found which differed considerably from Piltdown. While Piltdown showed a large, developed brain associated with a modified apelike jaw, the more recently discovered transitional forms showed a small brain in association with essentially human teeth and jaws.

Finally, in 1953, it was announced that the Piltdown skull was fraudulent. When the brain case was subjected to fluorine analysis, it was found to contain only about 20 percent of the fluorine contained in the animal bones discovered in association with it. Hence, the Piltdown brain case was more recent than the estimates made on the basis of stratigraphic evidence. In addition, fluorine analysis revealed that the jaw did not belong to the rest of the skull. Although the brain case was a real fossil of fairly recent date, the jaw was a modification of the jaw of a modern orangutan! The culprit who had masterminded the hoax had filed down the canine teeth and stained the bones to make them appear to be of the same age as that of the animals which were "seeded" in the site.[12]

The Geological Time Scale

In many parts of the world, large sections of stratigraphic sequences are exposed. The layers are of various colors and are composed of different types of material representing the diverse environmental and geological conditions which existed at the time the layers were laid down. These facts are the basis of the geological time scale.

In addition to the contrasting geological features of the various strata, the fossil content also differs. In the late eighteenth century, an English geologist, William Smith (1769–1839), noted that particular combinations of fossil animals and plants occurred together in certain sedimentary rock formations. He realized that if these combinations of fossil species were found in areas other than the original, the periods in which the sedimentary layers were laid down in the two areas must be approximately the same. Therefore, strata from one area could be correlated with strata from another.

In this way, certain fossils or combinations

[12] J. S. Weiner, *The Piltdown Forgery* (Oxford: Oxford Univ. Press, 1955).

of fossils become markers for particular periods of time. Certain key fossils are known as *index fossils*. An index fossil is a species which has a very wide geographical distribution but which existed for a relatively short period of time, either becoming extinct or evolving into something else. The appearance of an index fossil in a particular stratum immediately provides the investigator with a relative date for that stratum. If the index fossil is dated absolutely, any other fossil found in association with it is given an approximate calendric date.

Geologic time The history of the earth as it is revealed in the stratigraphic record has been divided by geologists into a hierarchy of units. These are the *era*, *period*, and *epoch*.

Three of the eras are characterized by abundant fossils. Each is defined by major physical disturbances, such as times of extensive mountain building. The eras are also delineated by the type of plant and animal life they contained. The general outline of this scale is seen in Table 13-1. Basically, the farther back in time we go, the more difficult it becomes to determine the events that

Table 13-1   The Geological Time Scale

Era	Period	Epoch	Beginning Date (in millions of years)*	Comment
Cenozoic	Quaternary†	Recent	0.01	First domestication of plants and animals
		Pleistocene	1.8	Includes the Ice Ages
	Tertiary†	Pliocene	5.2	First hominids
		Miocene	24	
		Oligocene	38	First anthropoids
		Eocene	54	Mammals, birds, and insects dominate land
		Paleocene	65	Prosimian radiation
Mesozoic	Cretaceous		145	First prosimians; dinosaurs become extinct at end of period
	Jurassic		190	First mammals and birds
	Triassic		225	First dinosaurs
Paleozoic	Permian		280	Adaptive radiation of reptiles
	Carboniferous		345	First reptiles, amphibians abundant, adaptive radiation of insects
	Devonian		395	First amphibians and insects, fish abundant
	Silurian		430	Early fish
	Ordovician		500	First vertebrates
	Cambrian		570	Marine invertebrates
	Prepaleozoic (Precambrian)‡			

* These dates are approximate and vary somewhat, depending on the criteria used to determine them. Dates in this table are taken from J. E. Sanders, A. H. Anderson, Jr., and R. Carola, *Physical Geology* (New York: Harper's, 1976), p. 13.

† Many geologists and paleontologists today divide the Cenozoic into the Paleogene, which includes the Paleocene, Eocene, and Oligocene, and the Neogene, which includes the Miocene, Pliocene, Pleistocene, and Recent.

‡ The origin of the earth has been dated at 4,500 million years ago. The first life is thought to have developed 3,500 million years ago. The first abundant fossils appear at the beginning of the Cambrian, 570 million years ago.

occurred, since more recent events have tended to obliterate signs of earlier events. The time before the beginning of the Paleozoic we will simply refer to as the Precambrian.

Each era is divided into periods, and periods into epochs. Periods and epochs, like eras, are defined in terms of geological events and fossil forms. For example, the beginning of the Cenozoic is marked by the elevation and drying up of several inland seas. The Cenozoic is also called the Age of Mammals because it represents the time of the adaptive radiation of mammals into the numerous and various ecological niches they occupy today.

At the boundary of the two periods of the Cenozoic, the Tertiary and Quaternary, there occurred terrestrial uplifts, the gradual cooling of climates, and an increase in the number of mammals. Each period of the Cenozoic is divided into epochs. In anthropology, the Cenozoic era and its periods and epochs are of major concern since it was during this time that the primates, and ultimately *Homo sapiens,* evolved.

The Paleocene epoch The first period of the Cenozoic era is the Tertiary, and the first epoch of the Tertiary is the Paleocene. The first mammals had developed in the Mesozoic era, but it was not until the Paleocene that they began their major adaptive radiation. At the beginning of this epoch, the mammals found new opportunities for diversification into the ecological niches left vacant by the now extinct dinosaurs. Although no modern mammalian families came into being during this epoch, the ancestors of modern families were present.

In the Paleocene, mountains were raised to new heights and the climates were warm. The plant life was similar to modern flora. There were great hardwood forests and grassy plains. It was within this setting that the early primates began to develop. If this environment had been different, selective pressures would have been different and primates as we now know them might never have come into being.

In discussing the evolution of life in the first part of the Cenozoic we must realize that the con-

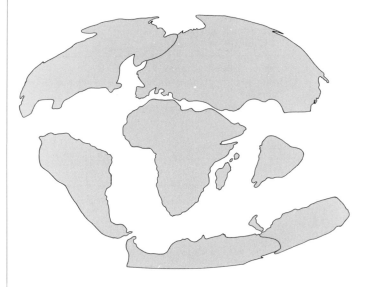

Figure 13-11 The world at the beginning of the Cenozoic. *This map shows the relative position of the continents 65 million years ago.*

tinents were not in their present positions. The concept of *plate tectonics* deals with the idea that the surface of the earth is divided into a series of large plates, which move in relation to one another. Each plate contains a continental mass. Figure 13-11 shows the position of the continents at the beginning of the Cenozoic, 65 million years ago. By Miocene times, the continents were more or less in their present position.

The Eocene epoch Nearly all the modern orders of mammals were present by the Eocene. Early primates, the prosimians, were widespread and showed many of the adaptations that were described as part of the primate complex (Chapter 10). The environment was wetter and warmer than that of the previous epoch. Forests were extensive, seas covered southern Europe and northern Africa, and lakes formed in the Western Hemisphere.

The Oligocene epoch In the Oligocene are found the remains of the earliest known monkeys and apes. Many of these finds come from what is now the Egyptian desert. In the Oligocene, this area was a tropical rain forest traversed by many rivers. Throughout the Cenozoic era, climates shifted and geological features changed, providing numerous adaptive challenges to the life of the era.

The Miocene epoch The Miocene was a mild and wet epoch. It was during the Miocene that the apes developed into a number of species and occupied large areas of Africa, Europe, and Asia. The earliest hominids come from this epoch. In the Miocene, about 16 to 17 million years ago, the Afro-Arabian tectonic plate collided with the Asian plate. As a result, Africa became connected to Asia and a large number of Asiatic animal forms entered the African continent. This was also a time of great volcanic activity and mountain building, resulting in a mosaic of habitats. The climatic changes brought about by the emerging mountains resulted in the development of localized grasslands as the forest slowly decreased in area.

The Pliocene epoch In the Pliocene, climates became cooler and still more varied. Especially in the Americas, mountain building continued. Mammals reached their high point in variety and size.

The Pleistocene epoch All but the last 10,000 years of the Quaternary period is occupied by the Pleistocene, which began 1.8 million years ago. This epoch includes the ice ages. This was a time of fluctuations in the earth's geology and climate. The Sierras uplifted; sea levels rose and fell. Great ice sheets, called glaciers, formed and melted; their massive weight caused depressions on the land and, over time, affected animal migrations. It was a time of the rise of many giant mammals, such as the giant ground sloths, mammoths, and mastodons, and the saber-toothed cat, and also the time of their extinction. During the Pleistocene, hominids had become efficient hunters, and it is now believed that they were, directly in some cases and indirectly in others, responsible for the extinction of many of these mammals.

Summary

The interpretation of the fossil record demands accurate dating of fossils. Absolute dating techniques include many based upon the nature of radioactive elements. Carbon 14 is the best known, but it can be used only for relatively recent material that was once living. Potassium-argon dating, based upon an element with a much longer half-life than carbon 14, can be used to revise the geological time scale itself.

Relative dating provides information on the time positions of fossils in terms of which are older or younger. The most common forms of relative dating are based upon the principle of superposition, which states that lower strata in a deposit are older than those above. Stratigraphy, a basic dating method of archaeology, is based upon this principle. One major difficulty with these methods is the possibility of newer material intruding into older material via burial or cataclysms. Methods like fluorine analysis can help establish whether two bones are contemporary or not.

The history of the earth is divided, in terms of geological and paleontological events, into three eras. Each era is divided into periods, which, in turn, are divided into epochs. The Cenozoic era is the Age of Mammals, which can be discussed in terms of its many subdivisions.

SUGGESTED READINGS

Bishop, W. W., and Miller, J. A. (eds.). *Calibration of Hominoid Evolution: Recent Advances in Isotopic and Other Dating Methods Applicable to the Origin of Man*. Edinburgh: Scottish Academic, 1972.

Butzer, K. W. *Environment and Archeology: An Ecological Approach to Prehistory*, 2d ed. Chicago: Aldine, 1971.

Michael, H. N., and E. K. Ralph (eds.). *Dating Techniques for the Archaeologist*. Cambridge, Mass.: Massachusetts Institute of Technology, 1971.

Oakley, K. *Frameworks for Dating Fossil Man*. Chicago: Aldine, 1964.

Zeuner, F. E. *Dating the Past: An Introduction to Geochronology*, 4th ed. New York: Hafner, 1958.

All these books give a good coverage of various dating methods and provide data on the time periods they deal with.

Colbert, E. H. *Wandering Lands and Animals*. New York: Dutton, 1973.

Sullivan, W. *Continents in Motion*. New York: McGraw-Hill, 1974.

These two books deal with plate tectonics and its relationship to the evolution of the vertebrates.

McAlester, A. L. *The History of Life*. Englewood Cliffs, N.J.: Prentice-Hall, 1968. A brief survey of the evolutionary developments of the various geological time periods from the origins of life to the emergence of *Homo sapiens*.

McCown, T. D., and A. R. K. Kennedy (eds.). *Climbing Man's Family Tree: A Collection of Major Writings on Human Phylogeny, 1699–1971*. Englewood Cliffs, N.J.: Prentice-Hall, 1972. Interesting essays that show how methods of collecting fossil data and interpreting these data have changed over the past three centuries.

Raup, D. M., and S. M. Stanley. *Principles of Paleontology*. San Francisco: Freeman, 1971. One of a number of good introductory books on paleontology. It includes sections on the description and classification (taxonomy) of fossils as well as sections dealing with the uses of paleontological data.

Chapter Fourteen
Primate Evolution before *Homo*

Natural occurrences usually do not proceed in well-defined stages with distinct beginnings and endings. Recently this fact has been made clear with attempts to legalize abortion. When is the zygote developed to the point of being labeled an individual? Is it the moment of fertilization, or is it when the hands, eyes, heart, lungs, or some other structures have been formed? Perhaps it is only at birth that this mass of protoplasm can be considered a new individual. In fact, some cultures do not consider infants to be human, and should an infant die, there is little or no mourning. This is because the infant had not yet begun to display the types of cultural behavior that would identify it with its group, nor had it contributed to the functioning of the society.

Empirically, it can be said that development from conception to death is continuous. Rates of growth and decline certainly differ from time to time, but the processes of life between conception and death are all dependent on antecedent events, and any attempt to divide life into specific stages must be based on arbitrary markers.

As with the life of an individual, the history of an evolutionary line also is continuous, with no well-defined breaks. In some cases, rates of evolutionary change greatly increase, and because of constant selective pressure an entire complex of traits, such as the primate complex of characteristics, develops quickly in relation to geological time. Major "jumps" in the development of a trait or complex of traits are often referred to as *quantum evolution*. Quantum changes do reflect rapid evolutionary change. However, what appears to be quantum evolution is often an illusion caused by gaps in the fossil record. At any rate, it is difficult to say when the first of some type of organism appears, and it is almost as difficult to ascertain the relationship of one fossil find to another since so much of the fossil record is missing. Nevertheless, the general picture of primate evolution is fairly clear, thanks to the meticulous collecting and analysis of fossil primates in recent years.

NONHUMAN FOSSIL PRIMATES

The earliest part of the primate fossil record is scanty, but by the Paleocene and Eocene epochs it becomes well documented, only to become sparse again in the Oligocene. It is very likely that the earliest prosimians were derived from the early insectivores of the Cretaceous period and were as similar in appearance to rodents and insectivores as to present-day prosimians. The first primates that are known from skeletal remains already display in their limb structure an arboreal adaptation, but many also had forward-projecting incisors, which indicates an adaptation for husking seeds and fruits, as in rodents.

The earliest primate comes from Cretaceous times, which was before the beginning of the Cenozoic. A single tooth is known from Cretaceous beds of Montana, beds which also contain the remains of one of the later dinosaur species. Other remains are known from the Paleocene. Although this creature, named *Purgatorius*, lived in what is now North America, we must remember the relative position of North America with respect to Europe in late Cretaceous times (Figure 13-11). Although much can be learned from a single tooth, it would be a little bold to draw major conclusions on the basis of such evidence. Although *Purgatorius* had a molar similar in some respects to that of later primates, it greatly resembles the insectivores. Its exact position in the story of primate evolution remains unknown.[1]

The Fossil Prosimians

The prosimians were abundant during the Paleocene and Eocene, being represented by more than sixty known genera. The best-known of the Paleocene fossils belong to the family Plesiadapidae, discovered in both the New and Old Worlds. The genus *Plesiadapis* is one of the best-preserved early Tertiary primates, with remains known from northern France and Colorado.

The Paleocene fossils are placed into the order Primates on the basis of details of dental and cranial anatomy. Actually, *Plesiadapis* resembles a rather generalized mammal with many features of the insectivores.

Plesiadapis does not display many of the traits of the primate complex (Chapter 10). For example, there is no eye socket in the skull and, unlike the eye in modern prosimians who also lack an eye socket, the eye is not surrounded by a bony ring. The facial skeleton is relatively large when compared with the size of the brain case. Perhaps the most distinctive feature of *Plesiadapis* is its dentition. The Plesiadapidae evolved large, procumbent incisors similar to those of modern rodents. The order Rodentia had yet to evolve in Paleocene and early Eocene times, and the rodentlike niches were occupied by the Plesiadapidae. Along with the enlarged incisors we find the reduction or absence of a canine and a large diastema separating the incisors from the premolars (Figure 14-1). From the postcranial remains it is thought that the locomotor pattern of *Plesiadapis* resembled that of the modern gray squirrel, including the use of claws on all digits. All in all the skeleton was very generalized, and although arboreal in habit, the animal had not yet developed those features associated with primate arboreal locomotion.[2]

Among the best-known primate fossils of the Eocene are members of the family Adapidae. Members of this family closely resemble the modern lemurs, and while they may not be direct an-

[1] L. Van Valen and R. E. Sloan, "The Earliest Primates," *Science*, 150 (5 November 1965), 734–745.

[2] E. L. Simons, *Primate Evolution* (New York: Macmillan, 1972), pp. 110–112.

cestors to the lemurs, they are probably close to the lemur evolutionary line. Their brain case is larger relative to the facial skeleton than in *Plesiadapis*, and studies of the brain case show an enlargement of the frontal portion of the brain which controls complex behavior. A complete bony ring encircles the eye, and the forward position of the eyes results in overlapping fields of vision. Nails are present on fingers and toes, and the several relatively complete skeletons show adaptations for leaping and grasping behavior.[3] This family can be divided into two subfamilies, one containing the European fossils including *Adapis*, and the other including the North American fossils, such as *Notharctus* and *Smilodectes* (Figure 14-2).

Lemurs are not found in the rather well-known fossil record of Africa. However, extinct lorises are known, such as *Progalago* of the East

African Miocene. This form shows a dental comb and a vertical clinging-and-leaping locomotor pattern similar to that of the modern galagos.[4]

While fossil lemurs have not been found in Africa, the great similarity between the fossil lorises from the African continent and the fossil lemurs from the island of Madagascar should be noted. It is believed that the ancestral lemurs reached the island from the African mainland by rafting across the Mozambique Channel. Even today natural rafts of tangled vegetation form in the large rivers which flow into the Indian Ocean.

[3] Ibid., pp. 124–139.

[4] W. E. LeGros Clark and D. P. Thomas, "The Miocene Lemuroids of East Africa," *British Museum of Natural History, Fossil Mammals of Africa*, 1 (1952), 1–117; G. G. Simpson, "The Tertiary Lorisiform Primates of Africa," *Bulletin of the Museum of Comparative Zoology*, 136 (1967), 39–61; and A. Walker, "Postcranial Remains of the Miocene Lorisidae of East Africa," *American Journal of Physical Anthropology*, 33 (1970), 249–261.

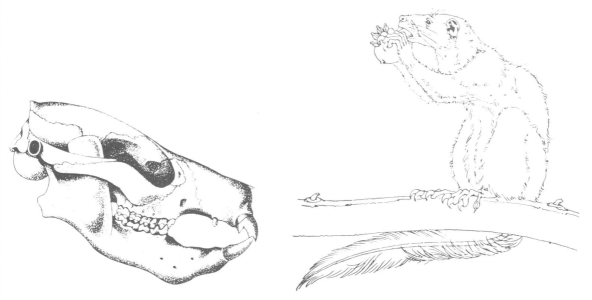

Figure 14-1 *Plesiadapis. This member of the family Plesiadapidae is known from the Paleocene.*

Although today the island is separated from the mainland by 400 kilometers (248 miles), it is believed that this separation was only about 80 kilometers (50 miles) in early Eocene times.[5] Some fourteen species of lemuroids from Madagascar are now known to be extinct. Many were contemporary with human occupation of the island, and it is suspected that most of these extinctions were probably due to human activity. In general, these extinct forms were larger than those living today. The largest form, *Megaladapis edwardsi*, was the size of a fair-sized calf.[6]

[5] A. Walker, "The Dissemination and Segregation of Early Primates in Relation to Continental Configuration," in W. W. Bishop and J. A. Miller (eds.), *Calibration of Hominoid Evolution* (Edinburgh: Scottish Academic Press, 1972), pp. 195–218.

[6] A. Walker, "Patterns of Extinction Among the Subfossil Madagascan Lemuroids," in P. S. Martin and H. E. Wright (eds.), *Pleistocene Extinctions* (New Haven: Yale Univ. Press, 1967), pp. 425–432.

Tarsierlike primates existed as long ago as 55 million years. The oldest skull showing relatively modern primate features belongs to the tarsierlike Anaptomorphidae of the early Eocene of Wyoming and Colorado. But members of the family Tarsiidae were already present in middle Eocene times. One of the best-known finds, represented by several skulls found in France, is *Necrolemur*. Many of the skulls are in an excellent state of preservation.

The name *Necrolemur* is one of the many confusing designations that often are applied to both living and fossil taxa. The name implies that it is similar to the lemurs when in fact it is considered by many to be in the family Tarsiidae. However, once a name is given to a taxon, it cannot be changed simply because it later becomes inappropriate. Having more than one name for a species in the literature has led to much confusion.

Although *Necrolemur* is probably not the direct ancestor of modern tarsiers, it does bear a

Figure 14-2 *Smilodectes. A lemurlike prosimian from the Eocene.*

Figure 14-3 *Necrolemur*. Necrolemur's *possible appearance is seen in this drawing by E. L. Simons.*

close resemblance to them (Figure 14-3). It has large eyes, judging from the orbits, and a rounded head and might have moved in a way similar to that of the modern tarsiers. Its brain seems more developed than that of *Smilodectus*, and its snout is more reduced. It appears to have been well adapted for life in the Middle Eocene forests.[7]

Almost all knowledge of the early prosimians comes from Europe and North America. Very little is known about their development in Asia and nothing at all in Africa. Perhaps it was in Africa that forms contemporary with *Smilodectus* and *Necrolemur* were evolving into the modern prosimians. One thing is certain. From the Oligocene on, fossil prosimians become scarce.

Many prosimian species which had developed rodentlike adaptations became extinct with the rise of the rodents. However, other early prosimian forms probably gave rise to more efficient monkeys and apes. The monkeys and apes were better able to exploit the prosimian niches, causing the demise of the prosimians from which they developed. During the Eocene epoch, perhaps in

Asia and more likely in Africa, early monkeys and apes were evolving, for at the beginning of the Oligocene there were already a number and variety of anthropoids.

The Fossil Monkeys

Although there are some differences of opinion, it is most likely that the New World monkeys (Ceboidea) and the Old World monkeys (Cercopithecoidea) evolved independently from different prosimian ancestors.[8] All fossil representatives of the superfamily Ceboidea are found in the New World. Relatively few fossil ceboids are known, and none of these seem to be ancestral to any modern species. The oldest New World fossil monkey is *Branisella* from the early Oligocene of Bolivia.[9] This form shows both prosimian and anthropoid characteristics. Other Tertiary forms have been found in Argentina and Colombia and a fossil from the recent past is known from Jamaica.

Fossil Cercopithecoids are relatively scarce in the Tertiary of the Old World. At the same time fossil apes are fairly well known, which suggests that the radiation of the Old World monkeys took place later in the Pliocene. A fragmentary mandible from Burma, described in 1927, dates from the late Eocene.[10] Although its taxonomic placement is uncertain, it does show some affinities to

[7] Simons, op. cit., pp. 164–165.

[8] For a hypothesis of African origin of the ceboids see R. Hoffstetter, ''Relationships, Origins, and History of the Ceboid Monkeys and Caviomorph Rodents: A Modern Interpretation,'' in T. Dobzhansky et al. (eds.), *Evolutionary Biology* (New York: Appleton Century Crofts, 1972), vol. 6, pp. 323–347.

[9] M. R. Hoffstetter, ''Un Primate de l'Oligocène inférieur Sud-Américain: *Branisella boliviana* gen. et sp. nov.,'' *Comptes Rendus de L'Académie des Sciences, Séries D, Paris,* 269 (1969), 434–437.

[10] G. E. Pilgrim, ''A *Sivapithecus* Palate and Other Primate Fossils from India,'' *Palaeontologia indica,* 14 (1927), 1–26.

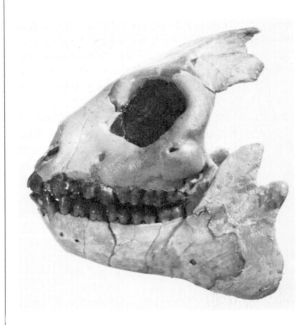

the early cercopithecoids. Oligocene and Miocene monkeys have been found only in Africa. Since European and Asiatic sites from this period are well known, we may conclude that the Old World monkeys are African in origin and later migrated to Europe and Asia.[11]

All the Oligocene cercopithecoid fossils come from a single site, the Fayum of Egypt. In Oligocene times the Fayum was a tropical forest bordering on the Mediterranean. The dense forests, swamps, and rivers were the homes of rodents, crocodiles, rhinoceros-sized herbivores, miniature ancestors of the elephants, and numerous species of primates (Table 14-1). Over the centuries the Mediterranean has retreated about 100 miles north of the Fayum, and the once lush tropical forest is now a desert with little plant or animal life.

Figure 14-4 *Apidium. A reconstruction of* Apidium, *an Oligocene monkey from Egypt.*

[11] E. L. Simons, "The Deployment and History of Old World Monkeys (Cercopithecidae, Primates)," in J. R. Napier and P. H. Napier (eds.), *Old World Monkeys: Evolution, Systematics and Behavior* (New York: Academic, 1970), pp. 97–137.

Table 14-1   Fossils from the Fayum, Egypt (Oligocene)

Species	Superfamily	Family	Level[a]
Parapithecus fraasi[b]	Cercopithecoidea	Parapithecidae	U
P. grangeri[b]	Cercopithecoidea	Parapithecidae	U
Apidium phiomense[c]	Cercopithecoidea	Parapithecidae	U
A. moustafai[c]	Cercopithecoidea	Parapithecidae	M
Aeolopithecus chirobates[d]	Hominoidea	Hylobatidae	U
Oligopithecus savagei[e]	Hominoidea	Pongidae (D?)[f]	L
Propliopithecus haeckeli[g]	Hominoidea	Pongidae (D)	M
Aegyptopithecus zeuxis[h]	Hominoidea	Pongidae (D)	U

[a] L = lower, M = middle, U = upper.

[b] Monkey form, related to *Apidium*.

[c] Monkey form, ancestral to *Oreopithecus*.

[d] Gibbon form.

[e] Oldest Fayum species: shows many prosimian features; may be early dryopithecine ape.

[f] D = Dryopithecinae.

[g] Perhaps an early dryopithecine, ancestral to *Aegyptopithecus*.

[h] Dryopithecine ape.

The Fayum has been the site of numerous expeditions, but the greatest number of fossils have been collected by a team of Yale paleontologists under the direction of Elwyn L. Simons.[12] The Fayum has yielded what are probably some of the oldest fossil remains of monkeylike forms, *Apidium* and *Parapithecus*.[13] These two genera, each with two species, make up the now extinct subfamily Parapithecinae within the Cercopithecoidea. *Apidium* is very well represented at the Fayum with a large number of cranial and postcranial remains. These were relatively small monkeys with short faces and relatively short canines (Figure 14-4). The hind feet of *Apidium* appear to be adapted for springing. *Parapithecus* is quite similar.

Old World monkeys are known from the Miocene of East Africa. Finds from Napak, Uganda, dated by potassium-argon at 19 million years old, show the presence of features charac-

[12] E. L. Simons, "The Earliest Apes," *Scientific American*, 217 (June 1967), 28–35.

[13] E. L. Simons, "Two New Primate Species from the African Oligocene," *Postilla*, 64 (1962), 1–12.

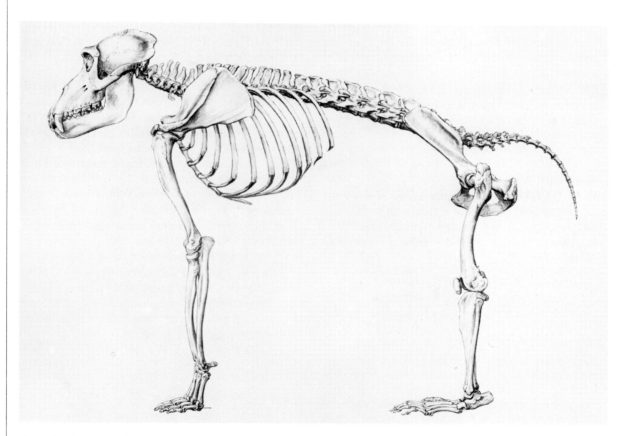

Figure 14-5 *Theropithecus. A reconstruction of the skeleton of the extinct giant species of gelada from Olduvai Gorge.*

teristic of both subfamilies of Old World monkeys, the omnivorous Cercopithecinae and the leaf-eating Colobinae. This suggests that the separation of these two evolutionary lines probably took place later than 19 million years ago.[14] *Victoriapithecus*, dated by potassium-argon at 18 million years old, was recovered on Rusinga Island in Lake Victoria, Kenya.[15] Analysis of the ulna suggests that this form was a semiterrestrial quadruped. Another Miocene monkey is known from Egypt.

By Pliocene times we see the presence of both Old World subfamilies. A large number of Colobinae are known from Europe, Asia, and Africa. Among the relatively abundant remains from the Pleistocene are the ancestors of several of the modern Cercopithecinae, such as the baboons and geladas. One extinct member of the modern genus *Theropithecus*, the geladas, from Olduvai Gorge, was about the size of a gorilla and may have been the largest monkey species that ever lived (Figure 14-5).[16]

The Fossil Apes

The apes are fairly well represented in the fossil record. In fact, during the Miocene the apes may well have been the predominant primate form, surpassing in number the monkeys in the Old World.

The fossil gibbons The family Hylobatidae, which includes the living gibbons and siamang, appears to have a lengthy evolutionary history. The oldest known hylobatid is probably *Aeolopithecus*, discovered by Elwyn L. Simons in 1964 in the Fayum.[17] A windstorm the evening before had blown off the top layer of soil, exposing the bones. The fossils are named after Aeolus, the Greek god of wind.

Hylobatids were quite common in the Miocene and Pliocene. The five species of *Pliopithecus* ranged in East Africa, Europe, and Asia. Their appearance in Asia preceded the appearance of monkeys in Asia. *Limnopithecus* of the East African Miocene is at or near the evolutionary line leading to the modern gibbons. Analysis of a fossil humerus shows an early adaptation for suspensory behavior.

Aegyptopithecus The oldest definitely known pongid dates from the late Oligocene. An earlier form, *Propliopithecus*, may also be related to the pongid evolutionary line (Table 14-1). This Oligocene form is *Aegyptopithecus* from the Fayum of Egypt. Although the first fossil remains of this creature were discovered in 1906, today we are lucky to be able to study a fairly complete skull discovered in 1966 (Figure 14-6).[18] The fossil bed from which the skull came was once a gallery forest with trees 100 feet high. There appears to have been no savanna or other type of open country in this area 28 million years ago, when *Aegyptopithecus* was presumably alive.

Aegyptopithecus is one of the best transitional forms found in the primate fossil record. It has characteristics of the prosimians, monkeys, and apes. For instance, it has a long snout reminiscent

[14] D. Pilbeam and A. Walker, "Fossil Monkeys from the Miocene of Napak, North-East Uganda," *Nature*, 220 (16 November 1968), 657–660.

[15] G. H. R. von Koenigswald, "Miocene Cercopithecoidea and Oreopithecoidea from Miocene of East Africa," *Fossil Vertebrates of Africa*, 1 (1969), 39–52.

[16] C. J. Jolly, "The Classification and Natural History of *Theropithecus* (*Simopithecus*) Baboons of the African Pleistocene," *Bulletin of the British Museum of Natural History, Geological Series*, vol. 22, no. 1 (1972).

[17] Simons, *Primate Evolution*, pp. 215–216.

[18] E. L. Simons, "New Fossil Ape from Egypt and the Initial Differentiation of the Hominoidea," *Nature*, 205 (9 January 1965), 135–139.

of that of the lemur, along with a relatively small brain case. It may have had a tail, like prosimians and monkeys but unlike modern apes. Yet its dentition and the form of its eye sockets indicate an affinity to the hominoid line. For example, details of the teeth and jaw structure are similar to those of the Miocene and Pliocene ancestors of the modern apes.

The locomotor behavior of *Aegyptopithecus* is known from the analysis of a fossil ulna. This ulna most closely resembles that of the howler monkey.[19] This in no way suggests genetic affinities with this monkey but indicates similarities in locomotor adaptations. The howler monkey is strictly arboreal and adapted for suspensory behavior. However, the howler also possesses a prehensile tail, an organ which was probably not a part of the anatomy of *Aegyptopithecus*.

Many paleontologists believe that *Aegyptopithecus* is on or near the evolutionary line leading to the great apes. The relationship of the Hominidae and Pongidae at this time is not known. If the branching of these two families took place later than the Oligocene, then *Aegyptopithecus* may represent a common ancestor of humans and apes.

Dryopithecus The subfamily Dryopithecinae (family Pongidae) includes a diverse group of Miocene and Pliocene apes, some of which may be ancestral to the modern gorilla, chimpanzee, orangutan, and possibly the hominids. In the more than 100 years during which dryopithecine remains have been discovered, more than 500 finds have been made, many being given distinctive scientific names. The result has been a confusing and inaccurate taxonomy that reflects few of the real relationships between the dryopithe-

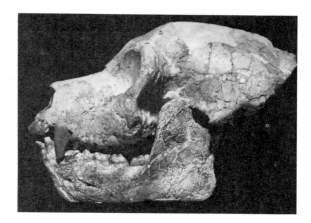

Figure 14-6 *Aegyptopithecus. The reconstructed skull of this Oligocene hominoid.*

cine fossils themselves or the fossils which preceded and followed them in time. Elwyn Simons and David Pilbeam have imposed some order on the vast array of discoveries.[20] After careful analysis of all known Tertiary ape forms, they decided that only two genera were justified, *Dryopithecus* and *Gigantopithecus*, the latter to be discussed in the next section.

Dryopithecus lived in the Miocene. Fossil remains of this genus have been dated between 23 and 14 million years ago. The early forms are found in Africa, but following the development of a land connection between Africa and Asia in the Middle Miocene (Chapter 13), they appear in Europe and Asia. Their habitats included both dense rain forests and more open areas, such as wooded savannas. The sizes of these species varied from that of a gibbon to larger than a gorilla (Table 14-2).

[19] J. G. Fleagle, E. L. Simons, and G. C. Conroy, "Ape Limb Bones from the Oligocene of Egypt," *Science,* 189 (11 July 1975), 135–137.

[20] E. L. Simons and D. R. Pilbeam, "Preliminary Revision of the Dryopithecinae (Pongidae, Anthropoidea)," *Folia Primatologia,* 3 (1965), 81–152.

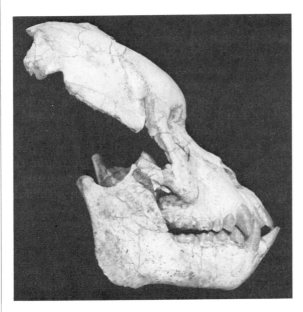

Figure 14-7 *Dryopithecus africanus. The skull of* D. africanus *found in 1948 in Kenya.*

Dryopithecus shared many features of modern apes, yet there are differences as well. The incisors are relatively small, and the incisors and canines are more vertically implanted than in modern apes. As a result, the relative width of the jaw between the canines is less than in modern apes, resulting in a more V-shaped dental arcade. Although hundreds of teeth and jaws are known, there is only one skull, that of *D. africanus* from Rusinga Island, Kenya (Figure 14-7). Analyses of postcranial material show that *Dryopithecus* was basically a generalized arboreal quadruped showing the beginning of the development of specialization for brachiation.

One of the African species, *D. major,* shows a dentition adapted for chewing tough plant foods, which suggests a relationship to the modern gorilla, and David Pilbeam actually hypothesizes that *D. major* is directly ancestral to the gorilla. Another African species, *D. africanus,* may have been ancestral to the modern chimpanzee.

Table 14-2   Miocene Radiation of the Pongidae (genus *Dryopithecus*)

Subgenus*	Species†	Size‡	Location
Dryopithecus (Middle to Late Miocene)	*D. fontani*	Medium	Europe
	D. laietanus	Small	Europe, Asia
Sivapithecus (Middle to Late Miocene)	*D. indicus*	Large	Asia
	D. sivalensis	Medium	Asia, Africa
Proconsul (Early to Middle Miocene)	*D. africanus*	Small	Africa
	D. nyanzae	Medium	Africa
	D. major	Large	Africa
Rangwapithecus (Early to Middle Miocene)	*D. gordon*	Small	Africa
	D. vancouveringi	Small	Africa

* A subgenus is a division of a genus. Species within a genus can be subdivided into groups of species based on the closeness of their evolutionary ties.

† Many paleoanthropologists believe that some of these species are actually subspecies. If so, the total number of species would be reduced.

‡ It has been estimated that these forms were approximately the size of the following modern forms: small: gibbon or pygmy chimpanzee; medium: chimpanzee; large: gorilla.

D. sivalensis, from India, has been proposed as a possible ancestor to the orangutan.

Many paleoanthropologists believe that the common ancestral form of the hominid and pongid lines was an early dryopithecine. Pilbeam writes:

The pongid species ancestral to the hominids is as yet unknown or unrecognized, although probably when it is known it will be classified as a dryopithecine. . . . The hominids seem to have diverged from the ancestors of the other apes at least 10 million and probably 15 million years ago.[21]

[21] Pilbeam, op. cit., p. 46.

Gigantopithecus The name *Gigantopithecus* implies a giant ape. Although there is disagreement about its actual size, *Gigantopithecus* has been estimated to stand 8 to 9 feet tall and to have weighed as much as 600 pounds.[22]

Gigantopithecus blacki was first discovered by Ralph von Koenigswald in 1935 in a Chinese pharmacy in Hong Kong, where fossilized teeth were used as medical ingredients. In the late 1950s and early 1960s three mandibles and over a thousand teeth were discovered in caves in Kwangsi Province, in southern China. These re-

[22] E. L. Simons and P. C. Ettel, "Gigantopithecus," *Scientific American*, 222 (January 1970), 76–85.

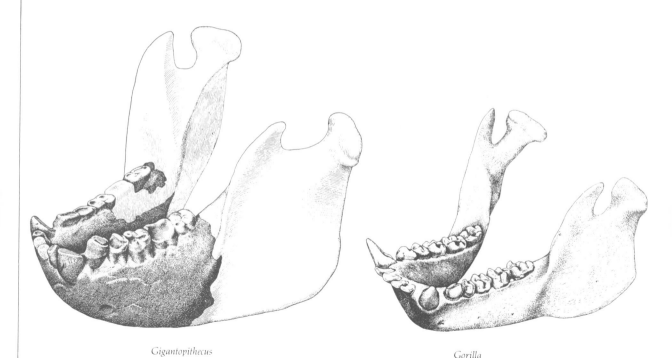

Gigantopithecus

Gorilla

Figure 14-8 *Gigantopithecus. A jaw of* Gigantopithecus, *with missing portions reconstructed, compared with the jaw of a male mountain gorilla.*

mains date from the middle of the Pleistocene, about 750,000 to 500,000 years ago. At that time the habitat was one of mixed forest and grassland. In 1968, the fossil remains of an earlier form was discovered in northern India and named *G. bilaspurensis*. This mandible dates from the middle Pliocene, 5 to 9 million years ago. It is associated with a mixed open-woodland and savanna habitat.

The jaw and teeth of *Gigantopithecus* bear some resemblance to those of the Hominidae. These hominidlike features include relatively small and vertically implanted incisors, reduced canines, and relatively flat grinding surfaces on the molars (Figure 14-8). These features have led some paleoanthropologists to suggest that there is a close relationship to the hominids and that *G. bilaspurensis* is ancestral to the later hominid forms while *G. blacki* is a late survival of a distinct evolutionary line.[23]

However, the more likely theory suggests that *Gigantopithecus* represents a diverging evolutionary line of apelike forms related to *Dryopithecus*. If this is the case, how are the hominidlike features explained? Similarities in anatomy can be explained on the basis of genetic relationship or upon similarities in adaptation. Clifford J. Jolly has commented upon the great similarities of the modern gelada to the hominids (Table 14-3).[24] These similarities are obviously not the result of a close evolutionary tie. The gelada lives in a grassland and is basically a terrestrial animal (Figure 10-16). The gelada eats primarily small and hard materials such as seeds and grasses, what Jolly

refers to as "small-object feeding." The reduction of the incisors and canines and enlargement of the molars may be related to the importance of the latter in grinding tough food material. In addition, the facial skeleton of the gelada has shortened, resulting in a more vertical arrangement of the chewing muscles, which produces a greater force for grinding.

It is also interesting to note that the gelada feeds sitting down, maintaining the trunk in a vertical position. Changes have occurred in the shape of the base of the skull, providing for a better balance of the skull on the spine. When moving, the gelada shuffles along on its bottom or walks bipedally for short distances. It also has evolved a shortened index finger and a well-developed thumb, permitting the fine-precision grip needed for picking up such small food items as seeds.

Like Pilbeam, many paleoanthropologists feel that *Gigantopithecus* represents an adaptation to small-object feeding.[25] While possessing many hominidlike features, its dental anatomy is still that of an apelike form with dentition adapted to powerful crushing activity. Pilbeam believes that *G. bilaspurensis* evolved from the earlier *D. indicus* and evolved into the later *G. blacki*, whose extinction may well have been due to human activity.

Oreopithecus Before we consider the early hominids, another divergent form must be mentioned. This is *Oreopithecus*, which lived about 14 million years ago in Europe and East Africa. First discovered in 1872, a nearly complete skeleton was discovered in 1958 in Italy. There has been considerable debate over the status of this primate. Opinions about its status have ranged from monkey, ape, and even a hominid. Elwyn

[23] R. B. Eckardt, "Population Genetics and Human Origins," *Scientific American*, 226 (January 1972), 94–103; and D. W. Frayer, "*Gigantopithecus* and Its Relationship to *Australopithecus*," *American Journal of Physical Anthropology*, 39 (1973), 413–426.

[24] C. J. Jolly, "The Seed Eaters: A New Model of Hominid Differentiation Based on a Baboon Analogy," *Man*, 5 (1970), 5–26.

[25] D. R. Pilbeam, "*Gigantopithecus* and the Origins of the Hominidae," *Nature*, 225 (7 February 1970), 516–519.

Table 14-3   The Small-Object Feeding Complex as Seen in the Gelada

Feature	Hominid	Gelada	Baboon
Relatively small incisors	+	+	−
Relatively small canines	+	+	−
Canine incisorlike	+	−	−
Front lower premolar bicuspid	+	−	−
Molar crowns more parallel-sided	+	−	−
Molars and premolars crowded	+	+	−
Molars and premolars with thick enamel	+	−	−
Eruption of canine early relative to eruption of molars	+	+	−
Rapid wear of molars as seen in a front-to-rear wear gradient	+	+	−
Ascending ramus of mandible vertical	+	+	−
Body of mandible very robust in molar region	+	+	−
Dental arcade parabolic	+	−	−
Well-developed opposability of thumb	+	+	−

+ = present; − = absent.

Adapted from C. J. Jolly, "The Seed Eaters: A New Model of Hominid Differentiation Based on a Baboon Analogy," *Man,* 5 (1970), 5–26.

Simons believes that *Oreopithecus* is a branch of the Cercopithecoidea which has evolved independently in the direction of the apes. In fact, Simons sees great similarities between *Oreopithecus* and *Apidium* from the Oligocene of Egypt.[26] The fact that this form lived in a swamp forest and that the skeleton shows the presence of long arms and curved fingers suggests that *Oreopithecus* was adapted to suspensory behavior.

Summary

The primate fossil record gives us a general picture of primate evolution, although a great number of gaps exist. The earliest primate, *Purgatorius,* evolved from insectivore stock before or during the Cretaceous. The Paleocene and Eocene saw an adaptive radiation of prosimian forms, some being lemurlike and others tarsierlike in nature. It is believed that from some Eocene prosimian the higher primates developed.

Oligocene fossil beds are rare. The only major Old World site from this period is the Fayum of Egypt. This site has yielded the remains of early monkeys and apes. *Aegyptopithecus* was probably a hominoid form which gave rise to the later apes and perhaps to the hominids. There is also fossil evidence of the independent evolution of the ceboid monkeys in the New World.

Monkey fossils are relatively rare in the well-known sites of the Miocene. Hylobatids and apes of the genus *Dryopithecus,* however, were very common. This genus probably includes the ancestor of the modern chimpanzee and gorilla. Perhaps an early dryopithecine form gave rise to the hominids. Besides these forms, two divergent genera were also present, *Gigantopithecus* and *Oreopithecus.* Table 14-4 summarizes the taxonomy of the living and fossil hominoids.

[26] Simons, *Primate Evolution,* pp. 262–265.

Table 14-4   Classification of the Living and Extinct Hominoidea*

SUPERFAMILY: Hominoidea
  FAMILY: Hylobatidae
    SUBFAMILY: Pliopithecinae†
      GENUS: *Pliopithecus*†
      GENUS: *Limnopithecus*†
      GENUS: *Aeolopithecus*†
    SUBFAMILY: Hylobatinae
      GENUS: *Hylobates*
      GENUS: *Symphalangus*
  FAMILY: Pongidae
    SUBFAMILY: Dryopithecinae†
      GENUS: *Dryopithecus*†
      GENUS: *Aegyptopithecus*†
    SUBFAMILY: Gigantopithecinae†
      GENUS: *Gigantopithecus*†
    SUBFAMILY: Ponginae
      GENUS: *Pan*
      GENUS: *Gorilla*
      GENUS: *Pongo*
  FAMILY: Hominidae
      GENUS: *Ramapithecus*†
      GENUS: *Australopithecus*†
      GENUS: *Homo*

* *Oreopithecus* perhaps is best placed in a separate superfamily, Oreopithecoidea, and *Oligopithecus* from the Fayum Oligocene may be placed in the subfamily Dryopithecinae.
† Extinct.

THE FOSSIL EVIDENCE FOR HOMINID EVOLUTION

It is difficult to discuss the hominid fossils of the Miocene, Pliocene, and the first half of the Pleistocene and almost impossible to arrive at any definite conclusions. The past fifteen or so years have witnessed a dramatic increase in paleontological fieldwork. This has resulted in the recovery of many new fossils that have greatly extended our knowledge of prehistoric populations far back in time and far afield in space. The great variety of hominid remains, refined dating techniques, and the recovery of associated cultural material have shattered many long-held concepts and interpretations.

Today, paleoanthropologists are engaged in debate over the significance and interpretation of these finds, and the resolution of these debates remains in the future. It is very tempting to select a single interpretation and present it as proved fact. Certainly this would make the task of the student much easier. But this would be dishonest. Therefore, although we will organize the information around a basic theme, it must be kept in mind that these interpretations are highly tentative.

It is the nature of science that we must collect and carefully analyze all data and from these data proceed to construct hypotheses (Chapter 2). But new data will always come to light, and new analyses must be attempted. Thus, we must constantly construct new hypotheses as we slowly progress toward a reasonably accurate understanding of our evolutionary history. As Bernard Campbell phrased it:

If our science is to progress at all, new data will prove every hypothesis to be wrong, and will require that every hypothesis be revised. The successive preparation and publication of such hypotheses is part of the necessary means by which science moves on from one approximation to another, each better and more accurate than the last.[27]

The oldest known member of the family Hominidae is *Ramapithecus* from Fort Ternan, Kenya, dated at 14 million years old. Similar material from India may also be this old. Not all paleoanthropologists agree that *Ramapithecus* is indeed a hominid, but most feel today that this

[27] B. Campbell, ''A New Taxonomy of Fossil Man,'' *Yearbook of Physical Anthropology 1973* (Washington: American Association of Physical Anthropologists, 1974), 195.

genus is an excellent candidate for hominid status and may well be an early ancestor of *Homo sapiens.* The remains of *Ramapithecus* are known from about 14 to 9 million years ago. Unfortunately, there is almost a total absence of fossil material between 9 and 5½ million years ago. But beginning at 3 million years ago, a fairly large number of fossil hominids are known.

The hominid material from the Pliocene and first half of the Pleistocene shows a highly variable anatomy, and this accounts in large part for the great problems and diversity of interpretation. However, a consensus is emerging that two major evolutionary lines of hominids were present during this period. The relationship between these two lineages is unknown, and it is impossible at this time to suggest a specific common ancestor, although they probably ultimately evolved from *Ramapithecus* or some similar form. But by 3 million years ago, and perhaps earlier, the presence of these two hominid lineages becomes apparent. One, the genus *Australopithecus,* first appears in the fossil record about 5½ million years ago, only to disappear some 4½ million years later. While the other genus, *Homo,* is definitely recognized after 3 million years ago, there is evidence for its presence before that time. *Australopithecus* and *Homo* were then contemporary for almost 2 million years. Eventually, *Homo* alone is found, and over a period of about 1 million years after the last of *Australopithecus, Homo* evolved into humankind of today.

While we cannot always discuss one genus without reference to the others, the evolution of the genus *Homo* will be left to Chapter 15. This section, then, will deal with the nature and history of the genera *Ramapithecus* and *Australopithecus.*

Ramapithecus

The earliest hominid known belongs to the genus *Ramapithecus* from Fort Ternan, Kenya, dated at

14 million years old.[28] Just before the publication of this find, Elwyn Simons had reanalyzed a fossil discovered in India in 1934 and named *R. punjabicus.*[29] G. Edward Lewis, in 1934, thought that these remains were the most hominid of the dryopithecines, but this concept ran counter to the opinion of the more influential paleoanthropologists of the time. It was not until Simons analyzed the material in the early 1960s that this form became accepted by many as a member of the family Hominidae.

Today, a fair number of *Ramapithecus* fossils are known, although almost all this material consists of teeth, jaws, and a small portion of the lower face. The fossils range between 14 and 9 million years old. The oldest finds are those from Fort Ternan, Kenya, and the material analyzed by Simons, from the Siwalik Hills of northern India. More recently discovered fossils come from Pakistan, China, Greece, and Hungary. It is difficult to say exactly how many different species are represented, with opinions ranging from a single species to two or more.

The dates for *Ramapithecus* are extremely interesting. In Chapter 13 we noted that during the Miocene the Afro-Arabian plate collided with the Asian plate, forming, among other things, a land connection between Africa and Asia. This event took place 17 to 16 million years ago, earlier than the earliest known *Ramapithecus.* The early members of this genus are known from both India and East Africa. Where then is the homeland of the Hominidae? Although many feel that the hominids evolved in Africa, it is very possible that the center of early hominid evolution lay in Asia, with

[28] L. S. B. Leakey, "A New Lower Pliocene Fossil Primate from Kenya," *Annals and Magazine of Natural History,* London, 13 (1962), 689–696.

[29] E. L. Simons, "The Phylectic Position of *Ramapithecus,*" *Postilla,* 57 (1961), 1–9; G. E. Lewis, "Preliminary Notice of New Man-like Apes from India," *American Journal of Science,* 27 (1934), 161–179.

Figure 14-9 *Ramapithecus. A partial upper jaw is shown articulated with a partial lower jaw. Both are from Fort Teman, Kenya, but are not from the same individual.*

the migration of early hominid forms to Africa after the development of a land connection. At present all we can say is that either is possible.

In its total morphological pattern, *Ramapithecus* resembles the later hominids. A list of *Ramapithecus* features would closely resemble the list of hominid features given in Table 14-3, except that practically all we know of *Ramapithecus* are teeth, jaws, and a small portion of the lower face (Figures 14-9 and 14-10). There are two important differences, however. The dental arcade of *Ramapithecus* does not curve inward toward the back but is divergent. A similar divergent pattern already has been noted for the Miocene dryopithecines. Second, the lower front premolar is *semisectorial*, that is, intermediate between the sectorial premolar of the dryopithecines and the nonsectorial, bicuspid premolar of the later hom-

inids. However, the basic dental pattern, with its curved dental arcade and reduced incisors and canines, is essentially hominid. There is little reason not to consider *Ramapithecus* an early member of the Hominidae, a possible ancestor to *Australopithecus* and *Homo*.

The hominid status of *Ramapithecus* must be inferred from dental and jaw remains. There is little direct evidence of toolmaking or erect bipedalism. Only one *possible* stone tool of this antiquity has ever been found.[30] Postcranial skeletal material has only recently been described and consists of a poorly preserved juvenile radius.[31] Yet, some paleoanthropologists point out that apes use their projecting canines for ripping, tearing, hold, and defense. They would argue that a form with reduced canines might substitute tools for teeth for these functions and an efficient toolmaker probably would be an erect biped, with the hands free for tool usage. However, there is no substantial evidence to support this idea, and the reduction of the canine may not be related to tool manufacture at all, as we shall see in the next section.

The Origins of the Hominidae

Many theories have been proposed to explain the origin of the family Hominidae. Most of these theories note that the Miocene was a time which saw the reduction in the expanse of forest and the development of grassland regions and postulate that early hominid adaptations represent an adaptation to the grassland habitat. As mentioned above, some people feel that the development of hominid dental characteristics is directly related to the development of toolmaking and erect bipedalism. But these ideas do not really explain how this came about.

[30] L. S. B. Leakey, "Bone Smashing by Late Miocene Hominidae," *Nature*, 218 (11 May 1968), 528–530.

[31] D. R. Pilbeam, personal communication.

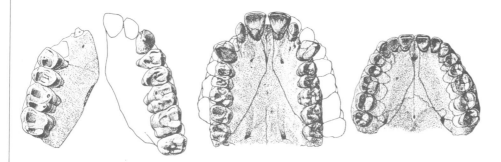

Figure 14-10 *Ramapithecus. The upper jaw of* Ramapithecus *is shown on the left. An outline of the* Ramapithecus *jaw is shown superimposed on the upper jaw of an orangutan (center) and a human (right).*

Many paleoanthropologists feel that the evolution of the characteristic hominid dentition may be a reflection of dietary adaptations. They note the great number of hominidlike features found in the gelada, discussed earlier and summarized in Table 14-3.[32] Gail Kennedy notes that the early *Ramapithecus* is found in sites associated with forest environments, not grassland environments.[33] *Ramapithecus* probably lived side by side with *Dryopithecus* and actually may have evolved from an early *Dryopithecus* species. At Fort Ternan, Kenya, *Ramapithecus* is associated with three species of *Dryopithecus* and many other forest-dwelling animals. As the result of competition between these closely related primate forms, each species became more highly adapted to a specific, relatively narrow niche. *Ramapithecus* may then have evolved through adaptation to a diet of seeds and grasses, a rather atypical diet for an ape. This is the same type of diet which in the gelada accounts for many of the hominidlike features. This same dietary factor may have been working in the early *Ramapithecus*, giving rise to the typical hominid dental and cranial pattern. Only later did *Ramapithecus* begin to exploit more and more the grassland habitats, especially as the forested regions were being progressively replaced by the savanna.

Australopithecus

The only Early Pliocene hominid fossil is that of *Australopithecus*, which consists of a piece of mandible from Lothagam, Kenya, dated at 5½ million years old.[34] The next oldest hominid remains do not appear until just after 4 million years ago, and by 3 million years ago the hominids become well documented in fossil record.

By 3 million years ago it becomes evident that two major evolutionary lines exist, although there is considerable confusion over the placement of many specific finds and the handling of the variability within each evolutionary lineage. One of these lines is the genus *Australopithecus*, perhaps best viewed as a series of forms which continued the exploitation of the seed and grass diet on the savanna. The other lineage, the genus

[32] Jolly, op. cit.

[33] G. E. Kennedy, *Paleoanthropology* (New York: McGraw-Hill, 1978).

[34] B. Patterson et al., "Geology and Fauna of a New Pliocene Locality in North-western Kenya," *Nature*, 226 (6 June 1970), 918–921.

Homo, very likely represents the development of new adaptations such as that of hunting and meat eating. The history of the genus *Homo* will be the topic of the next chapter. This section will deal with the australopiths.

The South African australopiths   In 1924, the best-known fossil form was Neandertal. The remains from Java (Chapter 15) were the oldest known hominids. In that year, fossil material was delivered to Raymond A. Dart of Johannesburg, South Africa. The area around Johannesburg is a limestone region riddled with caves, many of the more ancient ones filled in. The blasting activities of quarry workers on a limestone cliff formation brought to light a number of fossil forms. One piece showed what appeared to be a natural endocranial cast.

The material which fills the caves in this region, called a *bone breccia,* consists of masses of bone which have been cemented together with the calcium carbonate dissolved out of the limestone. It took Dart seventy-three days to work the skull out of the limestone matrix and a total of four years to separate the mandible from the rest of the skull. Dart published his find in 1925 and named the skull *Australopithecus africanus,* from *Australo-,* meaning "southern," and *pithecus,* meaning "ape."[35] This is an unfortunate label since the material today is considered unquestionably hominid.

The original *Australopithecus* was the remains of a child. It consisted of part of a mandible, facial skeleton, and a natural endocranial cast. The teeth in the mandible consisted of a set of milk teeth, along with the first permanent molar. From this evidence, the age of death was estimated at five or six years. Dart referred to the find as the Taung baby, named after the cave in which it was discovered (Figure 14-11).

Dart saw in *A. africanus* the characterics of a true hominid. At the time of discovery, he considered it to be the most primitive of humankind's known ancestors. While many considered the find to be more like that of a chimpanzee or a gorilla, Dart persisted in his contention that it was a bipedal, humanlike creature. The years have proved him correct.

The teeth of the Taung baby are very similar to those of a modern child. The foramen magnum is located underneath the skull pointing downward, a clear indication of the position of the head atop the spine. *Australopithecus* was an erect biped.

In the more than five decades since Dart's discovery, the remains of *Australopithecus* have become well known. But today the taxonomic position of this fossil, the only recovered hominid fossil from Taung, is unclear, underlining the difficulty of making taxonomic determinations on

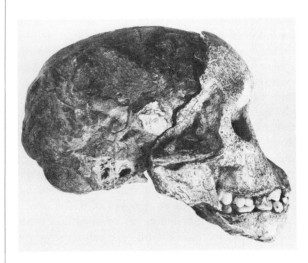

Figure 14-11   Taung baby. *The mandibular fragment, facial skeleton, and natural endocranial cast of* Australopithecus *found at Taung, South Africa, in 1924.*

[35] R. A. Dart, "Australopithecus africanus, the Man-Ape of South Africa," *Nature,* 115 (1925), 195; R. A. Dart, "Recollections of a Reluctant Anthropologist," *Journal of Human Evolution,* 2 (1973), 417–427.

juvenile material. The cave itself no longer exists, having been destroyed by human activity. While once considered to be a very ancient cave, it actually might have been quite recent, dated at less than 900,000 years ago, and the Taung specimen may represent one of the last surviving members of the genus *Australopithecus.*[36]

Following Dart's discovery, several other caves were investigated. Three important caves were close to one another in the Sterkfontein Valley—Sterkfontein, Swartkrans, and Kromdraai (Figure 14-12). In the 1930s Robert Broom excavated Sterkfontein, where he found the first examples of adult australopiths. These individuals were small and light in build and are often referred to as the *gracile* forms (Figure 14-13). However, the dentition shows a variability which may suggest a greater degree of *sexual dimorphism* than found in modern humans.

The australopiths found at Swartkrans and Kromdraai were different. They were larger and heavier than the gracile. forms and possessed large teeth and powerful jaw musculature. They are referred to as the *robust* forms (Figure 14-14). Swartkrans has been restudied by C. K. Brain, beginning in 1965; by 1970 he had recovered more than 11,000 bone fragments including 17 recognizable hominid fossils.[37] The anatomy of the australopiths will be described shortly.

The fifth South African site is located several hundred miles north of the Sterkfontein Valley. This site, Makapansgat, contains additional material of the gracile form.

The dating of the South African sites is of critical importance in the reconstruction of the evolutionary history of the australopiths. Unfortunately, the absence of suitable material precludes the use of radiometric dating. A recent attempt at dating on the basis of geological data has resulted in the following dates: Makapansgat,

[36] T. C. Partridge, "Geomorphological Dating of Cave Openings at Makapansgat, Sterkfontein, Swartkrans and Taung," *Nature,* 246 (9 November 1973), 75–79; K. W. Butzer, "Paleoecology of South African Australopithecines: Taung Revisited," *Current Anthropology,* 15 (1974), 367–382.

[37] C. K. Brain, "New Finds at the Swartkrans Australopithecine Site," *Nature,* 225 (21 March 1970), 1112–1119.

Figure 14-12 Map of *Australopithecus* sites.

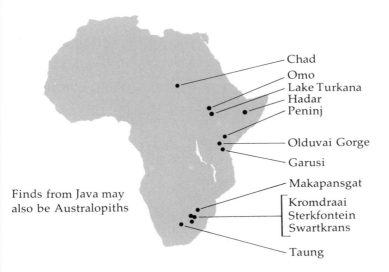

Chad
Omo
Lake Turkana
Hadar
Peninj

Olduvai Gorge

Garusi

Makapansgat

Kromdraai
Sterkfontein
Swartkrans

Taung

Finds from Java may also be Australopiths

Figure 14-13 A gracile australopith from South Africa. *Sts 5 from Sterkfontein.*

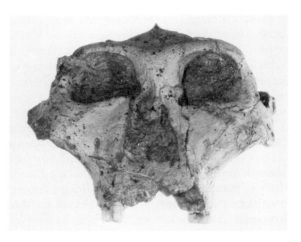

Figure 14-14 A robust australopith from South Africa. *SK 48 from Swartkrans.*

Figure 14-15 Olduvai Gorge, Tanzania.

3.7 million years ago; Sterkfontein, 3.3 million years ago; Swartkrans, 2.6 million years ago.[38] These dates represent the time when the caves were first opened, which makes them the oldest possible dates for the fossils found in the caves. Although these dates have been criticized, in general they are consistent with the dates for the East African australopiths.

The East African australopiths One of the most important sites in East Africa is Olduvai Gorge. This gorge, some 13 miles long and 150 to 250 feet deep, cuts into the Serengeti Plain of Tanzania, revealing geological beds which are the remains of ancient lakes and streams existing almost 2 million years ago (Figure 14-15). Olduvai Gorge is an extremely important site; here are found not only the bones of around 50 hominids but also the remains of the animals they ate and the tools they made. All these have been sealed as living floors, so that the spatial relationships of the various objects have been preserved. A *living floor* represents what was once the surface of the land. All bones and tools remain as they were either placed or dropped. A second important factor is that prehistoric volcanic activity provided abundant material for the application of radiometric dating techniques (Chapter 13). The *Australopithecus* remains are found in Bed I and the lower section of Bed II, dated by potassium-argon between 1.9 and 1.1 million years.

Louis S. B. Leakey began work in Olduvai Gorge in 1931, but although discoveries of animal fossils and archaeological remains were made early, the first significant hominid material did not appear until 1959. In 1959, Mary Leakey, Louis' wife, a noted paleoanthropologist, found an almost complete skull minus the mandible.[39] It

dates from 1.75 million years ago. First named *"Zinjanthropus boisei,"* this find can be seen as a superrobust australopith (Figure 14-16).

A major controversy was sparked by the announcement in 1964 of the discovery of a new species from Olduvai Gorge, named *"Homo habilis."*[40] This juvenile brain case was found in the same site as *"Zinjanthropus"* but is dated at 1.85 million years old. Other examples of both forms have been found at Olduvai, and many paleoanthropologists consider *"Homo habilis"* a gracile australopith.

In 1967 a number of paleoanthropologists began exploration of the Omo Valley of southern Ethiopia, just north of Lake Turkana (formerly Lake Rudolf). The fossil-bearing sediments are extensive, and in the future Omo should yield a number of important finds. To date both the

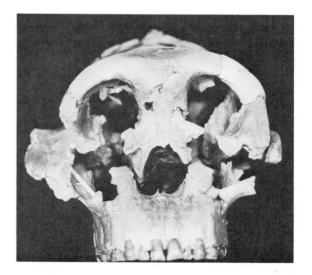

Figure 14-16 *"Zinjanthropus boisei."* A superrobust Australopithecus *from Olduvai Gorge.*

[38] Partridge, op. cit.

[39] L. S. B. Leakey, "A New Fossil Skull from Olduvai," *Nature,* 184 (15 August 1959), 491–493.

[40] L. S. B. Leakey et al., "A New Species of the Genus *Homo* from Olduvai Gorge," *Nature,* 202 (4 April 1964), 7–9.

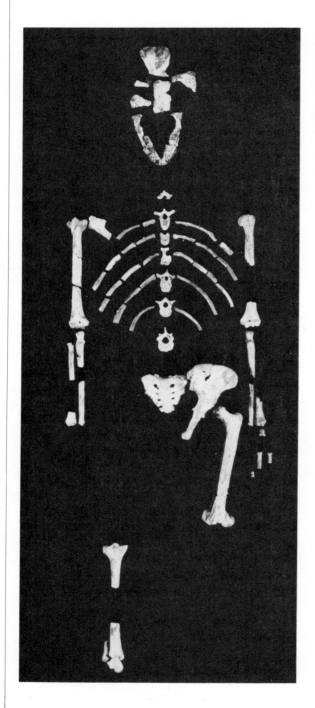

Figure 14-17 *"Lucy." A female gracile australopith skeleton from Hadar, Ethiopia.*

robust and gracile forms have been found, the sites being dated between approximately 3.3 and 0.8 million years.[41] Archaeological material found at Omo dates back to 2½ million years ago.

The work at Hadar was begun in 1973. Hadar is located in the Afar depression in eastern Ethiopia. The material is dated from 2 to 4 million years old.[42] Both the gracile and robust australopiths are present. Undoubtedly the most exciting find is AL 288, nicknamed Lucy. The preservation at Hadar is excellent, and this is seen in Lucy, an australopith skeleton. Although the skeleton is not complete, this is the first opportunity anyone has had to study various cranial and postcranial remains known to be from the same individual. Lucy is probably a female gracile form (Figure 14-17).

A very significant series of sites has been found in the East Lake Turkana region of north-

[41] F. C. Howell, "Remains of Hominidae from Pliocene/Pleistocene Formations in the Lower Omo Basin, Ethiopia," *Nature*, 223 (20 September 1969), 1234–1239.

[42] D. C. Johanson and M. Taieb, "Plio-Pleistocene Hominid Discoveries in Hadar, Ethiopia," *Nature*, 260 (25 March 1976), 293–297.

Figure 14-18 **The morphology of *Australopithecus* skulls** *(opposite page). A comparison of (A) gracile and (B) robust forms. Note the following features: (a) low forehead, (b) poorly developed brow ridges, (c) large facial skeleton and concave facial contour, (d) large mandible, (e) nasalfrontal suture upside-down V, (f) development of sagittal crest in robust form, (g) widest point low on brain case, (h) notable postorbital constriction, (i) flaring zygomatic arches, (j) relatively large molars and premolars, and (k) relatively small canines. For comparison of* Australopithecus *and* Homo *see Table 15-1 and Figure 15-1.*

A

B

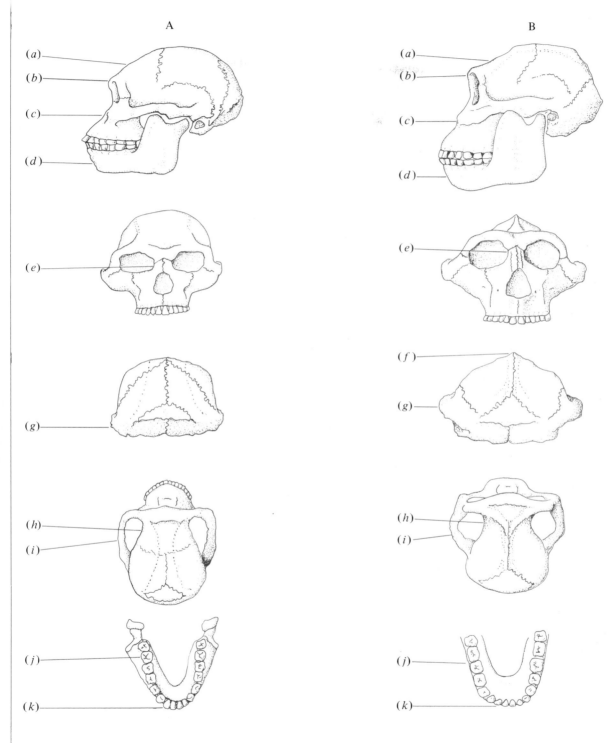

(a)
(b)
(c)
(d)

(e)

(g)

(h)
(i)

(j)
(k)

(a)
(b)
(c)
(d)

(e)

(f)
(g)

(h)
(i)

(j)
(k)

Primate Evolution before Homo

ern Kenya. This region has been studied by Richard Leakey since 1969, and over 120 hominid fossils have been recovered so far. The area is from 3 to 1 million years old and contains a number of excellent archaeological sites.[43] The major importance of Lake Turkana is that here we have undoubted proof that *Australopithecus* and *Homo* were contemporary. We will look at this evidence in Chapter 15 (but see Figure 15-1).

The morphology of the australopiths The genera *Australopithecus* and *Homo* are both members of the family Hominidae and hence share the general features of the family, but there are a number of characteristics which distinguish them. The basic features of *Australopithecus* are summarized in Figure 14-18.

[43] R. E. F. Leakey, "New Hominid Remains and Early Artefacts from Northern Kenya," *Nature,* 226 (18 April 1970), 223–224; "Further Evidence of Lower Pleistocene Hominids from Lake Rudolf, North Kenya," *Nature,* 231 (28 May 1971), 241–245; "Further Evidence of Lower Pleistocene Hominids from East Rudolf, North Kenya, 1971," *Nature,* 237 (2 June 1972), 264–269; "Further Evidence of Lower Pleistocene Hominids from East Rudolf, North Kenya, 1972," *Nature,* 242 (16 March 1973), 170–173.

The bones of the australopith skull are relatively thin. The cranial capacities usually range between 442 and 530 cubic centimeters. The brain case lacks the high vertical forehead of *H. sapiens* and the high roundness of the skull vault. From the back, the widest point of the skull is quite low on the brain case. The suture between the nasal and frontal bones has the shape of an upside-down V. The brow ridges are poorly developed, and behind the brow ridges is a notable *postorbital constriction,* seen in top view as a constriction immediately behind the brow ridges. The facial skeleton is large relative to the size of the brain case, often assuming a concave or dish-shaped contour. The jaw is relatively large, as are the jaw muscles. This is reflected in the development of a sagittal crest in some individuals and the expansion and flaring of the zygomatic arches. The molars and premolars are relatively large, while the canines are small relative to the premolars.

A number of postcranial bones are known. The pelvis is bowl-shaped and shortened from top to bottom, similar in basic structure to the pelvis of *H. sapiens* (Figure 14-19). Evidence from pelvic, leg, and foot bones leaves no doubt that *Australopithecus* was an erect biped. In fact, some

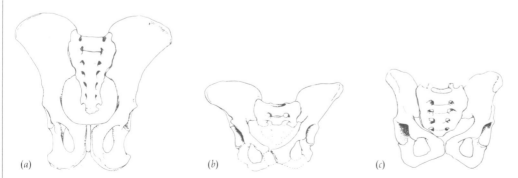

Figure 14-19 Australopith pelvis. *The pelvis of* (b) Australopithecus africanus *compared with the pelvis of* (a) *a modern chimpanzee and* (c) *a modern human.*

353

investigators feel that the locomotor pattern of *Australopithecus* is virtually indistinguishable from modern human bipedalism.[44]

We have already noted the presence in australopith sites of at least two major forms, the gracile and robust form, including the super-robust. These two forms are compared in Figure 14-18. The gracile form is small and light, with an estimated stature of 145 centimeters (4 feet 9 inches).[45] Its estimated cranial capacity is 442 cubic centimeters.[46] The facial skeleton is small, but the jaws are large in proportion to the rest of the skull. The dish-shaped profile is obvious.

The robust form is larger and more heavily built. Its estimated stature is 153 centimeters (5 feet), and the average cranial capacity is 530 cubic centimeters.[47] The heavier jaw of the robust form is associated with very large molars and premolars but relatively small incisors and canines. The massiveness of the jaw musculature is seen in the frequent development of a sagittal crest.

Many authors refer to the australopiths as ape-men. However, as is clear from the above description, there is really nothing apelike about the australopiths. It is true that the australopiths lack many of the features of *H. sapiens,* but features such as small cranial capacity should not be thought of as apelike characteristics but simply as archaic human features.

The significance of Australopithecus There exists a great variation in anatomy within the genus *Australopithecus*. In fact, this variability is rather impressive. Although we have talked in terms of two basic forms, gracile and robust, the actual fossils do not sort out into two neat categories. This variation has been explained on the basis of generic or species differences, subspecies or geographic variation, sexual dimorphism, and dietary differences. Some people think that there is only a single highly variable species, while others see several distinct evolutionary lineages. At this point it is impossible to come to a definite conclusion, and so perhaps it is best to think simply in terms of a single highly variable genus.

One of the major areas of discussion in anthropology involves the identification of that evolutionary line which led directly to *Homo* and eventually to *H. sapiens*. Since it now appears that *Australopithecus* and *Homo* were contemporary, many paleontologists feel that *Australopithecus* could not be ancestral to *Homo* but was simply a part of the general Miocene hominoid radiation or perhaps an early hominid radiation. Of course, *Australopithecus* goes back much further in time than *Homo*, and there is no reason not to hypothesize that *Homo* represents a branch developing from an early australopith. Thus, *Australopithecus* may still have a place in our family tree.

Earlier we looked at the possibility that *Ramapithecus* represents a hominoid adaptation to a seed and grass diet, eventually occupying the grassland habitat. Gail Kennedy thinks of *Australopithecus* as a continuation of this general adaptation, the most robust forms becoming highly specialized for small-object feeding and the gracile forms more closely approximating the ancestral condition.[48] At the same time, early members of the genus *Homo* were developing new dietary behaviors, becoming progressively

---

[44] C. O. Lovejoy et al., "The Gait of *Australopithecus,*" *American Journal of Physical Anthropology*, 38 (1973), 757–780.

[45] H. M. McHenry, "How Large Were the Australopithecines?" *American Journal of Physical Anthropology*, 40 (1974), 329–340.

[46] R. L. Holloway, "New Endocranial Values for the Australopithecines," *Nature*, 227 (11 July 1970), 199–200.

[47] Ibid., and McHenry, op. cit.

[48] Kennedy, op. cit.

more omnivorous and more centered on hunting and meat eating.

In contrast to these differences between the two genera it is interesting to note the great degree of parallelism in both evolutionary lines. Both show similar dental patterns, expansion of the brain, and development of habitual erect bipedalism, and there is evidence that both lineages manufactured tools and ate meat. Therefore, perhaps we should consider these features as being basic characteristics of hominid adaptation.

We must constantly keep in mind that these traits did not develop independently but in association with each other in what might be called a *feedback system.* That is, one trait influences the others, but those others, in turn, influence the first; so all the associated traits develop as a complex. For example, an upright posture affects the shape and function of the cerebellum, which controls coordination of muscular activity. Bipedalism also frees the hands for use in activities other than locomotion. If toolmaking has selective value, changes in the cerebellum and the freeing of the hands from locomotion would enhance toolmaking activities. Thus, greater coordination activities of the cerebellum and more perfected bipedalism would also have a selective advantage. Therefore, the evolution of erect bipedalism, motor coordination, and tool manufacture would develop together as a complex, along with such factors as creative intelligence and motivation.

When such complex feedback systems occur, the evolutionary record often shows a jump in the form and functioning of members of an evolutionary line, that is, quantum evolution. This may explain the very rapid divergence of the hominid line from the ancestral dryopithecine forms.

The behavior of Australopithecus   While the fossil record consists of skeletal remains, we must always keep in mind that anatomy evolves in response to behavioral changes (Chapter 12). The

development of such hominid features as the reduction in size of the canine and changes in the ilium of the pelvis are reflections of such behavioral patterns as bipedal locomotion, meat eating, and toolmaking.

We can infer some behaviors from anatomy. The postcranial remains give evidence of a developed erect bipedalism. Toolmaking depends, in part, upon the manipulative abilities of the hand. Hand bones have been found, and while they are basically human, they show many features which are intermediate between modern humans and chimpanzees. The phalanges are more curved in *Australopithecus* than in *Homo sapiens,* and the thumb is probably somewhat shorter. The hand probably was capable of a strong power grip, but it is not certain whether it was capable of delicate operations.

Were these hands capable of taking a piece of stone and altering the stone into a tool? Direct evidence of toolmaking is present in the archaeological record, but since *Australopithecus* and *Homo* are often found in the same sites, it is difficult to say for sure which form made the tools. But many animals *use* objects in the environment; a few, including the chimpanzee, *make* a limited number of crude tools, such as the termite stick described in Chapter 11. On this basis, *Australopithecus* most likely had some toolmaking ability. When Dart first presented his *A. africanus* as a hominid, many people rejected this classification on the ground that hominids were toolmaking forms and the Taung baby was not associated with evidence of toolmaking.

Dart disagreed. He noted the presence of many broken bones in the deposit and concluded that they were the result of deliberate toolmaking activity using bone material. He termed this an *osteodontokeratic culture,* from *osteo,* meaning "bone," *donto,* meaning "tooth," and *keratic,* meaning "horn" (keratin is a main constituent of horn). A femur was believed to have been used as a club, a broken long bone as a sharp cutting

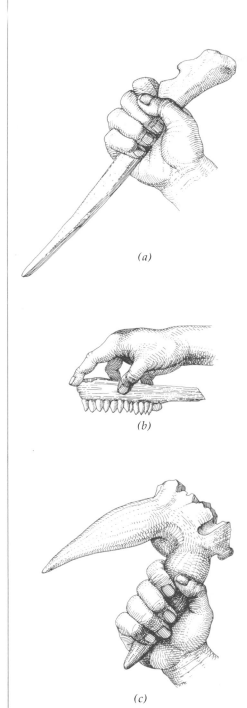

(a)

(b)

(c)

Figure 14-20 Osteodontokeratic tools. *Bone, tooth, and horn material from Makapansgat and their possible use:* (a) *an antelope ulna used as a dagger;* (b) *part of a small antelope mandible used as a knife blade;* (c) *horn cores and portion of cranium of fossil reedbuck.*

edge, a piece of mandible as a tooth scraper, and so forth (Figure 14-20).[49]

C. K. Brain has a different interpretation of the bones in the South African caves. He notes that the cave at Swartkrans was at one time an underground cavern connected to the surface by a vertical shaft. Because of a concentration of moisture, trees would be found in the region of the shaft, in an otherwise relatively treeless area. Leopards are known to drag their prey into trees where the carcass would be relatively safe from other carnivores. The remains of the prey animal would find their way down the shaft into the cave itself. This would account for the relative lack of postcranial remains, which would be destroyed to a large extent by the activity of chewing. *Australopithecus* would be among the prey species hunted.[50]

Today we know of stone tools which have been recovered from the South African caves. The tools found at Swartkrans include choppers, bifaces, cleavers, scrapers, flakes, and others, and are very similar to tools from Olduvai Gorge, discussed in the next chapter.[51] Perhaps these tools were made by *Australopithecus*.

The development of toolmaking reflects increasing mental abilities. Expansion of the brain and changes in its structure are characteristic of

[49] R. A. Dart, "The Osteodontokeratic Culture of *Australopithecus*," *Transvaal Museum Memoir* No. 10, Transvaal Museum, Pretoria, 1957.

[50] C. K. Brain, "New Finds at the Swartkrans Australopithecine Site," *Nature,* 225 (21 March 1950), 1112–1119.

[51] M. D. Leakey, "Stone Artefacts from Swartkrans," *Nature,* 225 (28 March 1970), 1222–1225.

the early hominids. We have seen that the cranial capacities of *Australopithecus* tend to average 442 cubic centimeters for the gracile forms and 530 cubic centimeters for the robust forms. But it is difficult, if not impossible, to correlate cranial capacity with ability and intelligence, except in the grossest sense (Chapter 12). Sir Wilfrid E. LeGros Clark writes:

But the fact is that, though we know the australo-pithecine brain was quantitatively small, we know nothing of its qualitative functions except from the indirect evidence of some of the endocranial casts that the gray matter of the cerebral cortex was quite complexly convoluted. .The mere mass of the brain is not so important for assessing intellectual abilities as the organization of its intrinsic structure. Even in Homo sapiens *the extremes of cranial capacity in individuals range from 900 cc or even less, to almost 2000 cc without in every case any evident difference in intelligence.*[52]

A further problem concerns the accuracy of these estimates of cranial capacity. Most of the fossil brain cases are fragmented when discovered, and often large pieces are missing and must be reconstructed. While this can be done with great precision in a number of cases, in others the determination of cranial volume is simply an educated guess.

There are several factors which influence cranial capacity. Within a given species, sexual dimorphism, which is thought to be a more significant factor in these early populations than in later ones, could result in different cranial capacities for males than for females. The individual's age is another important factor in cranial size. In modern humans, the brain continues to grow well into the twenties. Differences in cranial size

in the fossil record could in some cases be due to the age of the individual at death. Some of the increase in cranial capacity through this time period may correlate with the general increase in body size, although cranial volume increases faster than body size.

Studies of endocranial casts do show some gross features in the australopith brain. There appears to be an enlargement of the cerebellum relative to the rest of the brain when compared with cerebellum development in the apes. This might indicate the development of a fine control over movements, both locomotor and manipulative, which would be prerequisite for successful tool manufacture. Another area of expansion is in the parietal association area. This is of great interest since this is the area of the brain concerned with speech. Pilbeam sees no reason not to believe that the australopiths were capable of some type of rudimentary linguistic behavior.[53]

Summary

The earliest known hominid is *Ramapithecus* from East Africa, Europe, and Asia, which lived between 14 and 9 million years ago. Although primarily teeth, jaw fragments, and a little of the lower face are known, *Ramapithecus* closely conforms to the general picture of the family Hominidae. Most likely the early hominids evolved from an early dryopithecine as an adaptation for small-object feeding. While this probably first developed in forest areas, where the early hominids were sympatric with the early apes, adaptation for this seed and grass diet permitted *Ramapithecus* to expand its range onto the developing savanna grasslands.

The oldest known member of the genus *Australopithecus* dates from 5½ million years ago,

---

[52] W. E. LeGros Clark, *Man-Apes or Ape-Men?: The Story of Discoveries in Africa* (New York: Holt, 1967), p. 115.

[53] Pilbeam, op. cit., p. 191.

but members of this group are best known from 3 million years on. It is becoming clear that many australopiths were contemporary with the genus *Homo*. The first australopith was discovered in 1924 in South Africa. Since that time a number of remains have been found in South Africa and in East Africa at such sites as Olduvai Gorge, Omo, Hadar, and Lake Turkana. Although we can speak of a gracile and a robust form of *Australopithecus*, the genus is highly variable and the finds do not sort out into two separate groups. While showing a definite hominid pattern, *Australopithecus* is characterized by large molars and premolars with relatively small incisors and canines. These teeth are associated with a rather heavy jaw and large jaw muscles, and in some forms a sagittal crest develops. This can be seen as further adaptation to the seed and grass diet. Postcranially, *Australopithecus* was an erect biped whose locomotor abilities were similar to our own. Therefore, we can best think of the australopiths as part of a general hominid radiation, early forms of which may have given rise to the genus *Homo*.

SUGGESTED READINGS

Clark, W. E. LeGros. *Man-Apes or Ape-Men?: The Story of Discoveries in Africa.* New York: Holt, 1967. A discussion of the australopith finds of Africa.

Dart, R. A. *Adventures with the Missing Link.* New York: Viking, 1959. Dart's autobiographical account of his work with the australopiths of South Africa.

Day, M. *Guide to Fossil Man: A Handbook of Human Palaeontology.* Cleveland: World, 1965. Phenice, T. W. *Hominid Fossils: An Illustrated Key.* Dubuque, Iowa: Brown, 1972. Handbooks listing individual fossils, along with pertinent information about each.

Edey, M. A. *The Emergence of Man: The Missing Link.* New York: Time-Life, 1972. Part of The Emergence of Man series, a well-illustrated and up-to-date survey of the australopiths and related subjects.

Howells, W. (ed.). *Ideas on Human Evolution: Selected Essays 1949–1961.* New York: Atheneum, 1967. A collection of classic essays on human evolution.

Isaac, G. L., and E. R. McCown (eds.). *Human Origins: Louis Leakey and the East African Evidence.* Menlo Park, Calif.: Benjamin, 1976. A collection of important articles by Tobias, Brain, Isaac, Howell, R. Leakey, M. Leakey, Day, and others.

Leakey, L. S. B., Jack Prost, and Stephanie Prost (eds.). *Adam or Ape.* Cambridge, Mass.: Schenkman, 1971. A collection of articles, several of historical interest and many fairly recent.

Pfeiffer, J. E. *The Emergence of Man,* 2d ed. New York: Harper & Row, 1972. A beautifully written yet authoritative account of human evolution.

Pilbeam, D. R. *The Ascent of Man: An Introduction to Human Evolution.* New York: Macmillan, 1972. A survey of the Pleistocene fossil material, with an emphasis on the australopiths.

Simons, E. L. *Primate Evolution: An Introduction to Man's Place in Nature.* New York: Macmillan, 1972. A comprehensive and well-illustrated survey of the Tertiary fossil primates written by perhaps the best authority on this subject.

Tattersall, I. *The Evolutionary Significance of Ramapithecus.* Minneapolis: Burgess, 1975. A short book discussing the history of discovery, morphology, and significance of *Ramapithecus*.

Chapter Fifteen
The Evolution of the Genus *Homo*

In many respects the gracile form of *Australopithecus* could be a likely candidate for the direct ancestor of the genus *Homo*. Yet a number of paleoanthropologists, such as the late Louis Leakey, have felt that this may not be the case. They believe that the genus *Homo* itself has had an evolutionary history going back millions of years. Leakey realized that the best evidence to support this idea would be the remains of *Australopithecus* and *Homo* found together at the same level in the same site. In 1964, Louis Leakey reported the discovery of a hominid at Olduvai Gorge which he felt belonged to *Homo* and further to a new species, *"Homo habilis."*[1] This fossil was dated at 1.85 million years old and was found in the same site and at roughly the same level as the 1959 superrobust australopith skull.

Today, some paleoanthropologists believe that *"H. habilis"* is the early ancestral species of the genus *Homo*, which evolved independently from the australopiths. But others see *"H. habilis"* as a late australopith or an early *H. erectus*, a species to be described shortly. Still others see the individual fossils which make up *"H. habilis"* as a heterogeneous group with some individuals belonging to *Australopithecus* and others to *Homo*.

Leaving the problem of *"H. habilis"* aside, the evidence for the presence of *Homo* in the Pliocene and early Pleistocene is growing, and, as we shall see shortly, it is becoming apparent that the two hominid genera were indeed contemporary, at least for a time. Of course, this does not rule out the possibility that the earliest members of the genus *Homo* could have evolved from a still earlier form of *Australopithecus*.

[1] L. S. B. Leakey, P. V. Tobias, and J. R. Napier, "A New Species of the Genus *Homo* from Olduvai Gorge," *Nature*, 202 (4 April 1964), 7–9.

THE EARLY EVIDENCE OF THE GENUS *HOMO*

The last several years have seen a tremendous amount of excavation and the recovery of a great number of fossil hominids. One observation that has emerged from these new data is that the hominids of the Pliocene and early Pleistocene were extremely variable. But when most specialists examine this material, they divide these early hominids into two morphological groups, members of the genus *Australopithecus* and the genus *Homo*.

In actual practice the distinction between these two genera is not always clear-cut, and opinion often varies over the assignment of any one particular fossil. One major problem has been that although there appeared to be two distinct evolutionary lines, they had never been found together in the same site. Such an occurrence would be the best possible proof that they were indeed contemporary. In 1976 such evidence was at last published. The site was located at Lake Turkana, where the remains of a robust australopith were found in the same level in the same site as the remains of what is unquestionably a member of the genus *Homo*.[2] The finds are dated at 1.3 to 1.6 million years old, and the *Homo* skull might easily belong to the species *H. erectus* (Figure 15-1).

The Morphology of the Genus *Homo*

Homo and *Australopithecus* are both members of the family Hominidae and therefore share a large number of features. How then do these two genera differ?

We can use the two specimens from Lake Turkana, pictured in Figure 15-1, to illustrate the essential differences between the two genera. Perhaps the major differences lie in the dentition. While the dentition of early *Homo* shows the relative sizes of the incisors, canines, premolars, and molars to be as it is in modern humans, the incisors and canines are reduced and the premolars and molars expanded in *Australopithecus*. These dental features are related to the massiveness and muscular development of the australopith jaws, which in turn relate to the flaring of the zygomatic arches and, in some forms, the development of a sagittal crest. The dentition of *Homo* is smaller, and this is related to a smaller jaw, reduced zygomatic arches, and the lack of crest development on the brain case. The cranial capacity of early *Homo* is definitely larger than *Australopithecus*, and the facial skeleton of the former is very much reduced. These and other distinctions are summarized in Table 15-1.

A number of postcranial bones and bone fragments are known from this early period. The majority of these bones represent the lower limbs, the femur being the most commonly recovered bone. Bones of the trunk, shoulder girdle, and pelvis are rarely seen. Two basic anatomical patterns can be identified, an *Australopithecus* and a *Homo* pattern. The differences between the two morphological patterns are basically differences in proportions and details of structure and will not be listed here.[3] However, Michael Day concludes: "Although both forms are regarded as upright bipeds, there is not yet enough evidence to determine fine differences in stance and gait between these two forms."[4]

[2] R. E. F. Leakey and A. C. Walker, "*Australopithecus, Homo erectus* and the Single Species Hypothesis," *Nature*, 261 (17 June 1976), 572–574.

[3] See M. H. Day, "Hominid Postcranial Remains from the East Rudolf Succession: A Review," in Y. Coppens et al. (eds.), *Earliest Man and Environments in the Lake Rudolf Basin* (Chicago: Univ. of Chicago Press, 1976), pp. 507–521; and A. Walker, "New *Australopithecus* Femora from East Rudolf, Kenya," *Journal of Human Evolution*, 2 (1973), 545–555.

[4] Day, op. cit., p. 518.

The Early *Homo* Fossils

Evidence of the presence of the genus *Homo* in the Pliocene and early Pleistocene has come from a number of sites in East Africa. The oldest known evidence may date from 3.35 to 3.75 million years ago and consists of a number of teeth and mandibles recovered by Mary Leakey from Laetolil in Tanzania.[5]

At Hadar, Ethiopia, the evidence strongly suggests that *Homo* was present 3 to 2 million years ago and perhaps earlier. Fossil remains from this area include both robust and gracile australopiths along with forms which show a great resemblance to *H. erectus* from Java.[6] *Homo* was

[5] M. D. Leakey et al., "Fossil Hominids from the Laetolil Beds," *Nature,* 262 (5 August 1976), 460–466.

[6] D. C. Johanson and M. Taieb, "Plio-Pleistocene Hominid Discoveries in Hadar, Ethiopia," *Nature,* 260 (25 March 1976), 293–297.

also present at Lake Turkana between 3 to 2 million years ago.[7] As previously discussed, the remains of *Homo* and *Australopithecus* were recovered from the same level at the same site at Lake Turkana but represented a more recent period. In addition, other examples of *Homo* have been found in the Omo Basin and Olduvai Gorge. These sites are located on the map in Figure 14-13.

The Culture of Early *Homo*

As discussed in Chapter 12, there is a close relationship between anatomy and behavior. Human adaptations are to a large extent behavioral, and the anatomical specializations of humankind are a reflection of such behavioral characteristics as

[7] Leakey and Walker, op. cit.

Table 15-1   The Genera *Australopithecus* and *Homo* Compared

Australopithecus	*Homo*
Cranial capacity 440–530 cubic centimeters	Cranial capacity 750–2,300 cubic centimeters
Bones of brain case thin	Bones of brain case very thick to thin
Crests may develop on brain case	Crests never develop on brain case
Point of maximum width of brain case near bottom	Point of maximum width of brain case bottom to top
Marked postorbital constriction	Moderate to slight postorbital constriction
Brow ridges not developed	Large to slight brow ridges
Facial skeleton large relative to size of brain case	Facial skeleton small relative to size of brain case
Facial skeleton often dish-shaped	Facial skeleton never dish-shaped
Suture between nasal and frontal bones upside-down V	Suture between nasal and frontal bones horizontal
Flaring of zygomatic arches	Zygomatic arches not flared
Incisors and canine relatively small; premolars and molars relatively large	Relative size of incisors, canines, premolars, and molars as in modern humans; canine slightly larger
Jaw more massive	Jaw less massive; chin may develop

Figure 15-1   *Australopithecus and Homo* compared *(opposite page). Side, front, and top views of* (a) *robust* Australopithecus *(KNM-ER 406) and* (b) Homo *(KNM-ER 3733) from Lake Turkana, not to same scale. These finds represent the first direct evidence of* Australopithecus *and* Homo *living at the same time in the same place.*

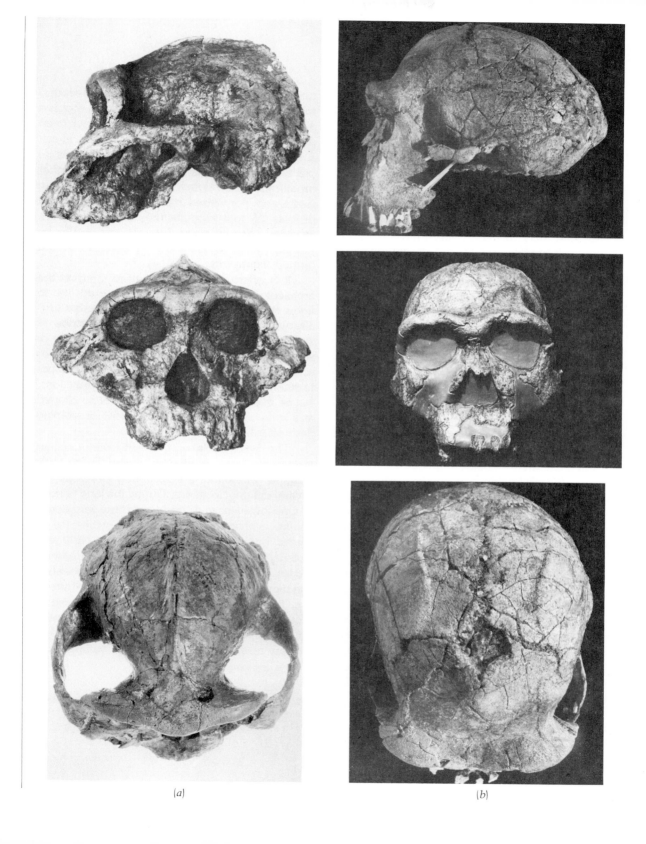

(a)   (b)

erect bipedalism and toolmaking. Some evidence of the behavior of the early members of the genus *Homo* can be seen in the archaeological material from the Pliocene and early Pleistocene. The study of this material is as important to the understanding of human evolution as the study of the structure of the fossil hominids themselves.

If both *Australopithecus* and *Homo* are present in the Pliocene and early Pleistocene, which one made the tools which have been recovered? It has been shown that *Australopithecus* probably did manufacture some tools, and given the toolmaking abilities of modern chimpanzees this should not seem surprising (Chapters 11 and 14). We may hypothesize that the differentiation of the two genera most likely lay in the progressive development of hunting and toolmaking in *Homo*. From this it follows that the bulk of the archaeological material recovered most likely represents the activities of *Homo*. The presence of an australopith in such a context may indicate that the relationship between *Homo* and *Australopithecus* was essentially antagonistic.

There are a number of terms which are used in describing archaeological material. Any physical remains of human activity are termed *artifacts*. An artifact which appears to have been created for a specific function is a *tool*. A *site* is any location where artifacts are found, and all the artifacts from a given site make up an *assemblage*. An assemblage is usually broken down into a series of *industries*, each containing all the artifacts made from the same basic type of material. Thus we can speak of a *lithic*, or *stone, industry* and a *bone industry* in the early sites. Because stone material is preserved better than others, most sites contain only a lithic industry, but we must constantly keep in mind that all hominids probably utilized bone, wood, and other perishable materials as tools.

Mary Leakey, in describing the material from Olduvai Gorge which makes up the Oldowan cul-

ture, divides the artifacts into three categories, tools, *utilized material,* and *debitage*.[8] A tool has already been defined. While a tool may have been deliberately manufactured in a certain way to suit a specific purpose, utilized material consists of pieces of stone which are used without further modification or *retouch*. Debitage refers to the waste and nonutilized material produced in the process of tool manufacture. In addition, unmodified, natural rocks brought into a site by human agency which show no signs of use are termed *manuports*.

It is often extremely difficult to interpret the archaeological record. Ideally we would like to know the functions of each artifact type, but usually we must be content merely to describe its shape or to place the tool in one of a number of standardized categories such as chopper or scraper. But the archaeologist must be careful not to interpret these categories as proved functions, for, as an example, a scraper may have functioned as a knife rather than as an instrument for scraping flesh off a hide.

The basic tools of this early period occur throughout large geographic areas. These tools were so simple that they probably developed in several different locations. During the long periods of time involved, and considering how very slowly culture evolved, similar tool types were able to spread out over great expanses. The early artifacts lack the standardization of the later assemblages and, at most, each category represents a variation on a basic theme. As we go from site to site, this variability can easily be seen. Some of these differences represent development over time or differences in the type of stone used as the raw material. Most importantly, variation be-

[8] M. D. Leakey, *Olduvai Gorge,* vol. 3, *Excavations in Beds I and II, 1960–1963* (Cambridge: Cambridge Univ. Press, 1971), pp. 3–8.

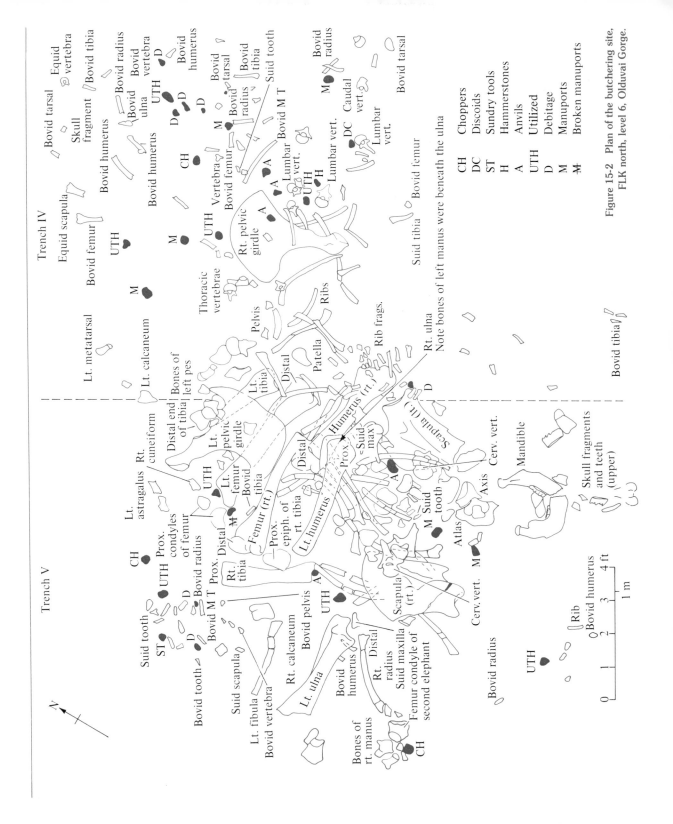

Figure 15-2 Plan of the butchering site, FLK north, level 6, Olduvai Gorge.

tween assemblages represents differences in behaviors. We would expect to find a different collection of artifacts at a butchering site than at a site where stone tools were actually manufactured.

Early stone tools discovered at Lake Turkana probably predate 2.6 million years. Artifacts from the Omo Basin also date from this same time. After 2.6 million years ago sites become more common, and each site contains a greater variety of material.

The Oldowan culture   Perhaps the best-known early archaeological assemblages are those of Olduvai Gorge, which make up the *Oldowan culture* and which have been described by Mary Leakey.[9] A typical type of site is the butchering

[9] Ibid.

site, such as Level 6 of site FLK, in Upper Bed I at Olduvai (Figure 15-2). This site contains the disarticulated remains of *Deinotherium*, an extinct form of elephant. Of course, it is not known whether the hominids actually hunted and killed the animal or whether it was simply found and then scavenged. All of the 123 recovered artifacts were associated with the elephant. Only five of the artifacts can be classified as tools. Most of these tools are choppers, which are very characteristic of the Oldowan culture.

A chopper is a *core tool*. A core is a nodule of rock from which pieces or *flakes* are removed. The individual flakes can be further retouched into *flake tools* while the remaining core can be fashioned into a core tool. A chopper is made from a cobble with a cutting edge created by flaking on one or sometimes two ends. The edge itself is often jagged but quite effective in butchering animals.

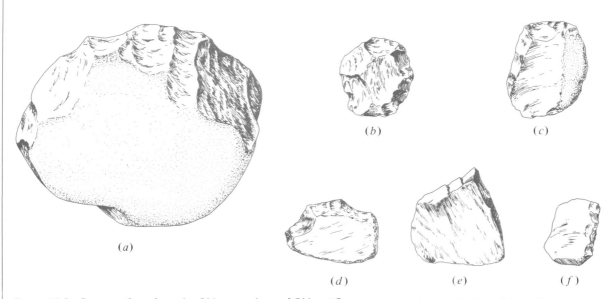

(a)

(b)   *(c)*

(d)   *(e)*   *(f)*

Figure 15-3   Stone artifacts from the Oldowan culture of Olduvai Gorge. (a) *Side chopper*, (b) *discoid*, (c) *end scraper*, (d) *side scraper*, (e) *burin*, (f) *utilized flake*.

365

Figure 15-4   Plan of the stone circle, site DK, Olduvai Gorge.

The DK site from Bed I is older than 1.75 million years. Like most sites of this period, the DK site was located close to water, and a large number of crocodile bones have been found. Other bones include those of extinct forms of tortoise, cattle, pigs, elephants, hippopotamus, horse, and giraffe, animals which must have played some role in the early hominid diet.

The DK lithic industry includes a number of tools, among them various forms of choppers (Table 15-2 and Figure 15-3). Other tool types include *scrapers*, flakes with a scraping edge on the end or side, and *burins*, special tools with thick points. Utilized material includes *anvils*, *hammer stones*, and utilized flakes.

One of the most interesting features at Olduvai Gorge is the stone circle of the DK site. This circle is about 12 to 14 feet in diameter and is formed of loosely piled basalt up to just under 1 foot high. Associated small piles of stones may have been supports for branches while the circle itself may have been a base to support a brush living structure (Figure 15-4). If this is indeed a hut of some type, this stone circle may well represent the earliest known human habitation.

Table 15-2   Lithic Industry from DK, Olduvai Gorge

	Number	%	Number	%
Tools:			154	12.9
Choppers	47	3.9		
Scrapers	30	2.5		
Burins	3	0.3		
Others	74	6.2		
Utilized material:			187	15.6
Anvils	3	0.3		
Hammer stones	48	4.0		
Flakes	37	3.1		
Others	99	8.3		
Debitage			857	71.5

Data from M. D. Leakey, *Olduvai Gorge*, vol. 3, *Excavations in Beds I and II, 1960–1963* (Cambridge: Cambridge Univ. Press, 1971), p. 39.

Summary

The earliest evidence of the genus *Homo* in the fossil record may come from Laetolil, Tanzania, and dates between 4 and 3 million years ago. *Homo* is definitely present prior to 2 million years ago at Hadar and Lake Turkana, and slightly later at Omo and Olduvai Gorge. Some of these more recent forms may belong to the genus *H. erectus*.

The genus *Homo* differs from *Australopithecus* in many ways. *Homo* is characterized by a cranial capacity between 750 and 2,300 cubic centimeters, relatively small facial skeleton, and many other features, summarized in Table 15-1. The cultures of these early forms are known in the archaeological remains from East Africa. Perhaps one of the more important archaeological sites is Olduvai Gorge, where evidence of a possible habitation structure has been found and dated at about 2 million years old.

HOMO ERECTUS

Until the 1960s, the fossil record of the family Hominidae was spotty. This last decade has seen the discovery of a great number of highly significant finds. But most research has centered on the hominid remains which date from the Pliocene and early Pleistocene, and very little has been done on the more recent periods, which are the subject of this section.

Most of the finds which exist for these later periods have been known for a long time, but unfortunately they were excavated under conditions which today would be considered unsatisfactory. One of the major problems has been that of dating. Where possible, modern methods have been applied; they show that many of the original dates were very far off. Several reexaminations of the old dates are still in progress, so interpretation of the relationships between known fossils is often extremely difficult.

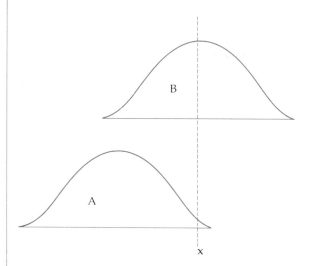

Figure 15-5 Morphological variation in two fossil populations. *Morphologically, skull X might belong to either population, as an average member of population B or as a nonrepresentative member of population A.*

Table 15-3 Divisions of the Pleistocene

Time (years ago)	Climatic Phase (Europe)	Division of Pleistocene
The present		Post-Pleistocene (Recent)
10,000		
100,000	Würm Glaciation	
	Riss-Würm (Third) Interglacial	Upper Pleistocene
200,000		
	Riss Glaciation	
	Mindel-Riss (second) Interglacial	Middle Pleistocene
	Mindel Glaciation	
750,000		
	Günz-Mindel (First) Interglacial	
	Günz Glaciation	Lower Pleistocene
	Villafranchian	
1,800,000		

Accurate dating becomes critical for this period because of the great variability in morphology. To illustrate this point, two populations at two different times are pictured in Figure 15-5. As can be seen, it is quite possible to have two skulls which are morphologically similar and date from different periods, yet have two quite different skulls that date from the same period. Because of the existence of what appear to be archaic and modern forms at the same time, and even as part of the same population, it becomes impossible to line up the fossil material in a correct evolutionary sequence purely on the basis of morphology. Instead they must be arranged strictly according to chronology.

Divisions of the Pleistocene

As was seen in Chapter 13, the Pleistocene is the segment of geological time beginning about 1.8 million years ago and lasting until 10,000 years ago. The last 10,000 years of the earth's history is referred to as the *Recent epoch* or *Post-Pleistocene*.

It was during the latter half of the Pleistocene that the great continental glaciers formed and advanced southward, melted, and retreated northward. This ebb and flow of glacial ice is usually divided into four great advances, or *glacials*, separated by three *interglacials*. Each glacial was, in reality, an extremely complex geological phenomenon with a number of major and minor advances and retreats.

The Pleistocene can be divided into a Lower, Middle, and Upper phase, as seen in Table 15-3. This section will deal with the species *H. erectus*, whose remains have been found during Lower and Middle Pleistocene times.

The Morphology of *Homo erectus*

The cranial capacity of *H. erectus* varies from 750 to over 1,300 cubic centimeters, well within the range of variation of modern *H. sapiens*. Yet the shape of the skull is distinctive. The forehead is shallow and slopes backward from very prominent brow ridges. Behind the brow ridge is a postorbital construction, more pronounced than in modern humans but not as developed as in the australopiths. The occipital region of the brain case is quite angular, and when seen from the rear, its widest point is very low. The bones of the brain case are very thick compared with those of the australopiths and the later *H. sapiens*. The facial skeleton is relatively large and projecting, but not dish-shaped as in *Australopithecus*. The teeth are relatively larger with respect to the size of the skull than in modern forms. Some early finds show a slightly projecting canine with a small diastema in the upper jaw. Although differences do exist in the postcranial bones of *H. erectus* and *H. sapiens*, these differences are relatively minor. Both species probably showed an identical or very similar form of erect bipedalism. The skeletal remains of *H. erectus* suggest an average stature between 132 and 145 centimeters (5 and 5½ feet) and an estimated average weight of 53 kilograms (117 pounds).[10] Many of these features are summarized in Figure 15-6.

[10] D. Pilbeam and S. J. Gould, "Size and Scaling in Human Evolution," *Science*, 186 (6 December 1974), 892–901.

The Discoveries of *Homo erectus*

The earliest discoveries of *H. erectus* were made in the 1890s. As each new find appeared, it was placed in a new species and often in a new genus as well. Some of the generic names were "*Pithecanthropus*," "*Sinanthropus*," and "*Atlanthropus*." Most paleoanthropologists today consider all these forms to be variants of the single species *H. erectus*, although the genus name "*Pithecanthropus*" is still occasionally used and some refer to the members of this species by the general term *pithecanthropines*.

Homo erectus from Africa   As we saw at the beginning of this chapter, the genus *Homo* may go back in time almost 4 million years. While it may be premature to place these early finds in the species *H. erectus*, members of this species known from Hadar, Lake Turkana, and Omo probably are earlier than 2 million years ago. The specimen from Lake Turkana (Figure 15-1) dates from 1.3 to 1.6 million years ago and was found in direct association with *Australopithecus*.

There are a number of later *H. erectus* finds in Africa. Fragmentary finds are known from North Africa, more specifically from Ternifine, Algeria, and Sidi Abderrahman and Rabat, Morocco. There are a couple of *H. erectus* specimens from Olduvai Gorge. The so-called *Chellean Man* was discovered in 1960 and is notable

Figure 15-6   A comparison of the skulls of (*A*) *Homo erectus* and (*B*) modern *Homo sapiens (opposite page)*.

H. erectus	Modern H. sapiens
(a) *Sloping forehead*	*Vertical forehead*
(b) *Prominent brow ridges*	*Brow ridges slight or absent*
(c) *Relatively large facial skeleton*	*Relatively small facial skeleton*
(d) *Angular occipital*	*Rounded occipital*
(e) *Relatively large teeth*	*Relatively small teeth*
(f) *Large mandible*	*Small mandible*
(g) *Horizontal nasal-frontal suture*	*Nasal-frontal suture upside-down* V
(h) *Widest point low on brain case*	*Widest point high on brain case*
(i) *Pronounced postorbital constriction*	*Slight postorbital constriction*

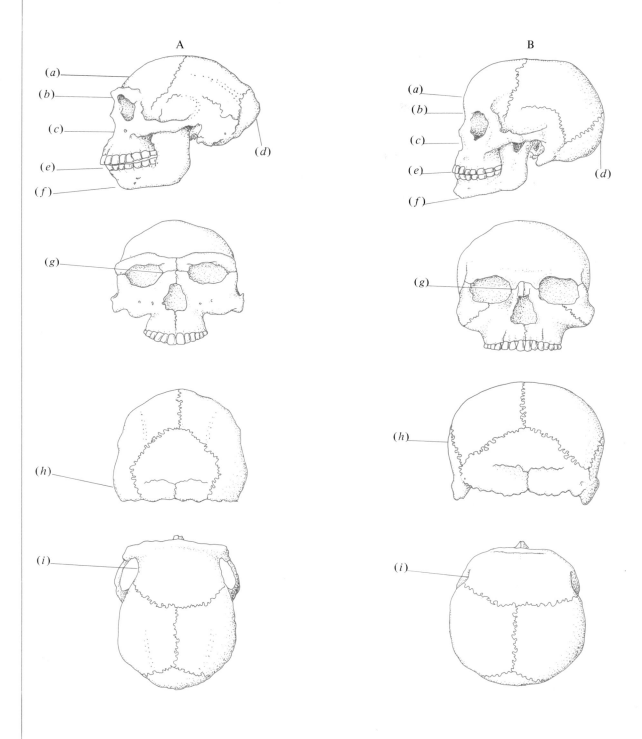

A

(a)
(b)
(c)
(d)
(e)
(f)
(g)
(h)
(i)

B

(a)
(b)
(c)
(d)
(e)
(f)
(g)
(h)
(i)

The Evolution of the Genus Homo

(a)

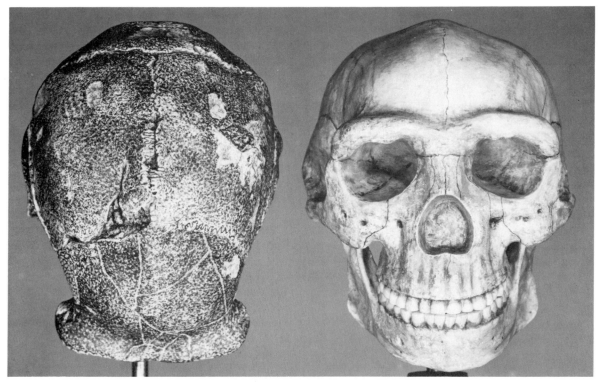

(b)   (c)

for its massive brow ridges, the largest of any known hominid skull. A small fragment is known from Kanam, Kenya.

The presence of *H. erectus* in South Africa is not clear. A mandible, first named *"Telanthropus capensis,"* has been considered by some to be a *H. erectus*, but this view has not been accepted by everyone. There is a more recent claim, but this material still must be evaluated.[11]

Homo erectus *from Asia*   In the last century a Dutch anatomist, Eugene Dubois, was convinced that Asia was the place of human origin. He traveled to the Dutch East Indies (now Indonesia) and in 1891 discovered a brain case at Trinil, in eastern Java. A year later he found a femur which demonstrated that this hominid walked bipedally, hence the original name, *"Pithecanthropus erectus."* The original brain case had an estimated cranial capacity of 850 cubic centimeters. The bones were very thick with a projecting, angular occipital and very large brow ridges. The femur was basically modern.

Dubois recovered more specimens in the 1890s, and others were excavated by von Koenigswald in the 1930s. The specimens consisted of skulls, mandibles, and femurs, without associated archaeological material, and came from two geological beds. The older Djetis Bed may be as old as 2 million years, and the younger Trinil Bed dates from 1 million to less than 500,000 years ago. Possible australopiths were found in the older Djetis Bed, which would make this the only evidence of the australopiths known outside of Africa.

[11] R. J. Clarke, F. Clark Howell, and C. K. Brain, "More Evidence of an Advanced Hominid at Swartkrans," *Nature*, 225 (28 March 1970), 1219–1222.

Figure 15-7   H. erectus from Choukoutien, China (opposite page). (a) *Side view of male skull*; (b) *top view, reconstructed skull*; (c) *front view, reconstructed skull.*

In 1927 a molar tooth was discovered in a cave near the village of Choukoutien, near Peking, China. This tooth was placed in a new species, *"Sinanthropus pekinensis."* The next ten years saw the recovery of over a dozen skulls and almost 150 teeth. These fossils disappeared at the time of the Japanese invasion of China and, except for a single specimen, all we have today are meticulous descriptions and excellent casts. Since the war, some additional material has been excavated.

The material from Choukoutien is significant because we are dealing with a population rather than a single isolated individual. The population shows a degree of variability and sexual dimorphism greater than that found among modern peoples. The cranial capacities range between 850 and 1300 cubic centimeters (Figure 15-7). Dating of this material is extremely difficult, but it has been suggested that *H. erectus* from Choukoutien may be as recent as 300,000 years. The fossils were found in an archaeological context with the remains of butchered animals, fire, and stone tools.

An earlier *H. erectus* from China was discovered in 1963 and 1964 in Lantian County, Shensi Province. The mandible and parts of a cranium, from different individuals, are quite similar to the remains from Java.

Homo erectus *from Europe*   The earliest hominids to have occupied Europe were probably *H. erectus*. The earliest evidence of this occupation comes from archaeological sites dated at less than 1 million years old. Early fossil remains have been found in Germany and Hungary, possibly dating from 700,000 and 400,000 years ago. The Mauer jaw, discovered near Heidelberg in 1907, is robust, yet the teeth are relatively small and resemble the later *H. sapiens* in many ways. The Vértesszöllös occipital from Budapest, Hungary, is rather large and modern in appearance.

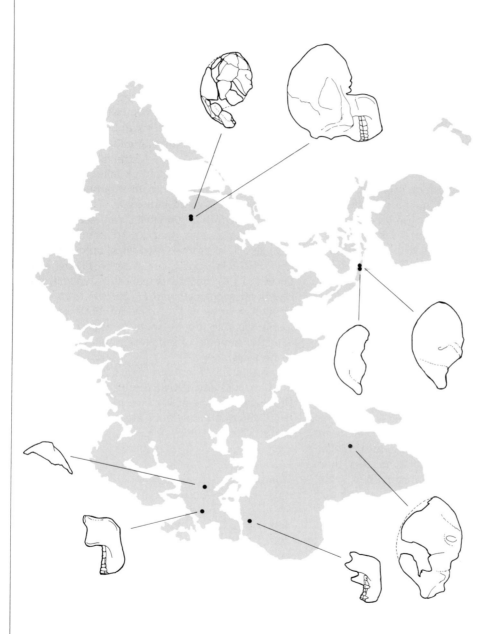

Figure 15-8 Variation and distribution of *Homo erectus.* (a) *Skull XI, Choukoutien, China;* (b) *Skull XII, Choukoutien, China;* (c) *Pithecanthropus erectus II, Java;* (d) *Pithecanthropus erectus, Java;* (e) *Chellean Man, Olduvai Gorge, Tanzania;* (f) *Ternifine II, Algeria;* (g) *Heidelberg, Germany;* (h) *Vértesszöllös, Hungary.*

373

There are two other finds which have really not been extensively studied. Although somewhat modern in appearance, their early date would tend to place them in *H. erectus*. These are the finds from Petralona, Greece, and Přezletice, Czechoslovakia.

Many of the finds discussed above are placed on the map in Figure 15-8. It can be seen that there is much variation among the *H. erectus* finds, but this variation can be explained in several ways. First, the finds represent a very small sample of all the individuals who once lived, and many areas are represented by only a single specimen. Second, since the material spans over 1 million years, the earlier individuals would be expected to differ from the later ones. And third, much of the variation is no doubt the result of geographical distance, which brought about variability in much the same manner as variation develops among modern populations. In addi-

tion, some of the variation could be due to the differences in age and sex of the individuals represented.

The Culture of *Homo erectus*

While the fossil remains of *H. erectus* are scanty, the same period during which they occur is well represented in the archaeological record. There appear to be two distinct cultural traditions. The artifacts found in Java and China and elsewhere in Asia are crudely made, especially when compared with the material in Africa, Europe, and western Asia. This primitiveness may be partly the result of the absence of suitable raw material. The artifacts from Choukoutien include large choppers quite like the more advanced Oldowan tools. But in Europe, North Africa, and southwest Asia as far east as Pakistan, there developed the well-known hand-ax tradition (Figure 15-9).

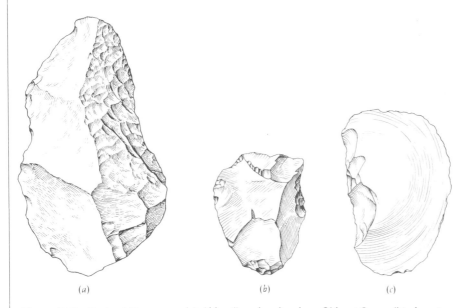

Figure 15-9 Tools of *H. erectus*. (a) *Abbevillean hand ax from Olduvai Gorge*, (b) *chopping tool from Choukoutien*, (c) *cleaverlike tool from Choukoutien*.

The Acheulean tradition The culture of *H. erectus* represents the latter part of the Lower Paleolithic, with the most dominant cultural manifestation being labeled the *Acheulean*. One of the highly diagnostic tool types of this period is the *hand ax*. It is produced by striking a nodule, or core, of flint or similar material with either a *hammer stone* or a *bone hammer,* thus removing a flake. The nodule is turned over and over so that flakes are removed from all sides. The resulting hand ax is an all-purpose tool that can be used for butchering an animal, preparing wood, cracking bones, digging for roots, and many other uses (Figure 2-2).

Throughout this period, the development of finer and finer technological control evident in the manufacturing of hand axes can be traced. The earlier forms were produced with hammer stones. The flakes removed were large and irregular, producing a rather ragged cutting edge. Later, the use of the bone hammer produced smaller and more regular flakes, resulting in a fairly straight cutting edge.

While hand axes are considered to be the major tool type, they make up only a small percentage of all the tool types from archaeological sites of this period. In fact, some sites lack hand axes altogether. Cores were also transformed into hammers and choppers, while the flakes were made into a variety of tools, such as scrapers, awls, and knives.

It should be kept in mind that differential preservation results in a very uneven representation of the entire tool inventory. The record is primarily of the stone artifacts. In reality, wood, bark, bone, antler, hides, sinew, and other materials were probably also used, and they may even have been more important than stone. But such tools are rare in the archaeological record.

The first use of fire From the presence of hearths, it appears that *H. erectus* was the first user of fire. The oldest-known hearths may be those at Escale, in southern France, which date at 750,000 years ago.[12] While fire may have been used for cooking (charred bones have been found), it served a number of other important functions. *H. erectus* probably used fire for warmth. They existed in some fairly cold climates, having spread outward from the more tropical zones where they originated. It may have been impossible for humans, basically tropical animals, to have inhabited the temperate zones without the aid of fire. In addition, fire could have provided a source of light and could have acted as a gathering point for the group, increasing social solidarity and ritualism.

Fire also probably functioned in hunting. Studies of charred soil behind areas where kills were made indicate that fires were set in order to run frightened animals into bogs, over cliffs, or simply toward waiting hunters.

Habitations The site of Terra Amata, in the city of Nice in southern France, was excavated in 1966. This site, once a part of the beach, is dated at approximately 400,000 years ago. In this site was found evidence of a number of dwellings. The floors are oval. The first one discovered measures 20 by 40 feet. From a study of the postholes, hearths, and the placement of stones, it has been suggested that the hut was made of saplings or branches.[13] *H. erectus* probably made use of a variety of dwellings.

The hunt *H. erectus* was an efficient big-game hunter whose hunting and gathering adaptations probably were not much different from those of *H. sapiens* hunters and gatherers. Alan Mann tells us:

[12] Henry DeLumley, "A Paleolithic Camp at Nice," *Scientific American,* 221 (May 1969), 42–50.

[13] Ibid.

The number of bones at Choukoutien and the number and size of animals at Torralba/Ambrona [Spain] indicate that the hominids of the Middle Pleistocene were accomplished hunters. Present evidence suggests that H. erectus differed from Australopithecus in the kind of hunting being carried out. Australopithecus probably did not hunt large animals to any great extent whereas the presence of at least twenty elephants at Ambrona and the bones of literally thousands of cevids at Choukoutien testify to the skill of H. erectus.[14]

The site of Terra Amata yielded evidence of hunting activity. Here were found the remains of the red deer, elephant, wild boar, ibex, rhinoceros, and wild ox, along with those of birds, turtles, rabbits, rodents of various kinds, and marine resources, such as oysters, limpets, mussels, and fish.[15]

At Ambrona, F. Clark Howell has excavated a hunting camp of *H. erectus*.[16] He has recovered the bones of the now extinct mammoth *Elephas antiquus*, along with smaller elephant species, deer, horse, and aurochs. No bones of *Homo* have been uncovered, however. The smaller animals were found dismembered and the bones scattered over the site. But many of the bones of the large mammoth were left intact as the meat was stripped off.

In association with the animal bones were more than 100 stone tools. Howell believes that a couple of *H. erectus* bands joined in running the animals into what was then boggy marshland. A fire was set behind the animals, which were then driven into the bog. Once the elephants became stuck in the soft ground, the hunters simply waited until they became exhausted from their fruitless struggle to free themselves. Then with wood spears and stone tools, they butchered their prey.

Hunting and the human brain Humans were basically modern from the neck down over 1 million years ago. In the period after this, the brain continued its development into its modern configuration. The absolute size of the brain probably is not as important as its morphology. There is reason to believe that big-game hunting, so characteristic of *H. erectus,* tremendously affected the development of the brain.

Hunting is no simple matter. Unlike the carnivores, people do not run down their prey but must stalk or build some type of trap; often they must follow a wounded animal for many miles, sometimes over a period of many days. This takes planning. The direction of the wind, possible routes of escape, methods of wounding the animal, the tracking of the wounded animal, and the kill and transport of the meat home must be well thought out. The proper tools and weapons must be made and, more important, must be used correctly. Driving animals off cliffs required coordinated group effort.

The dangers of the hunt and the skills needed to carry it out created selective pressures for both greater memory and increased ability to use memory in higher thought. John E. Pfeiffer has speculated on some of the types of development of the brain that might have occurred as the result of the pressures of the hunt.[17]

Pfeiffer notes that hunting is an efficient way of getting food, and those individuals or groups which evolved in the direction of increased ability

[14] A. Mann, "Homo erectus," in P. Dolhinow and V. M. Sarich (eds.), *Background for Man* (Boston: Little, Brown, 1971), p. 175. Used with permission.

[15] DeLumley, op. cit.

[16] Ibid., 78–86.

[17] J. E. Pfeiffer, *The Emergence of Man*, 2d ed. (New York: Harper & Row, 1972), pp. 163–164.

in this activity would have had an advantage over others. The hunter whose brain was able to remember experiences before reacting to a situation had the edge. Thus, natural selection resulted in the enlargement of the frontal areas of the brain, where higher mental activities take place, along with the temporal lobes, where speech is controlled.

In addition, human hunters range over more territory in the process of hunting than most other animals. The hunter comes across more varied situations which must be dealt with. So, again, selection would favor individuals who were more capable of storing and analyzing large amounts of diverse information.

Ritual activity   F. Clark Howell sees evidence of ritual activity at Torralba and Ambrona. One find was that of a single animal whose left side only was found lying in a semiarticulated position. The cranium and pelvis had been removed, but, contrary to usual practice, the long bones were not cracked open to obtain the marrow. Another find consisted of a tusk and five long bones lying in a straight line near the rest of the skeleton (Figure 15-10). These unnatural arrangements of bones may reflect some ritual activity.[18]

[18] Editors of Time-Life Books, *The Emergence of Man: The First Men* (New York: Time-Life, 1973), p. 82.

Figure 15-10   **Mammoth remains.** *A tusk and long bones were found in Spain arranged in a way which suggests ritual activity.*

Cannibalism There is good evidence that *H. erectus* occasionally ate one another. Many of the human long bones have been fractured and split. Five skulls from China have had the foramen magnum enlarged so that the brain could be removed.

E. Adamson Hoebel lists three motives for cannibalism in contemporary cultures that have been studied.[19] The first is *ritualistic;* the captor attempts to gain the victim's power by eating a part of that person. The second is termed *gustatory* cannibalism, in that people eat other people because they think they taste good. The third, called *survival cannibalism,* occurs in cases of stress, as when people who normally would be repulsed by cannibalism eat human flesh when faced with starvation. Of course, the reasons for this practice by *H. erectus* will probably always remain speculative.

Summary

The genus *Homo* can be divided into two species, *H. erectus* and *H. sapiens.* The skull of *H. erectus* differs from that of *H. sapiens* in the thickness of the bones, shallow forehead, prominent brow ridges, and angular occipital. Yet postcranially, the skeleton of *H. erectus* is not significantly different from that of *H. sapiens.*

Homo erectus is known from many sites in Africa, Asia, and Europe. African forms have been found at Hadar, Lake Turkana, Omo, Olduvai Gorge, two sites in Morocco, a site in Algeria, and possibly in South Africa. The first members of this species to be discovered were on the island of Java. A number of specimens were recovered from Choukoutien, China, and older fossils are known from Lantian in northern China. *Homo erectus* appears much later in Europe, and material is known from Germany, Hungary, Czechoslovakia, and Greece. Much of this material, although old, resembles the later *H. sapiens.*

While the physical remains of *H. erectus* are relatively scarce, cultural remains have been found in a great number of archaeological sites. This includes evidence of the use of fire, habitations, big-game hunting, ritual activity, and cannibalism.

THE EVOLUTION OF *HOMO SAPIENS*

The end of the middle Pleistocene saw the earliest members of the species *H. sapiens.* The dividing line between *H. erectus* and *H. sapiens* is not clear-cut, but many people consider it to be around 275,000 years ago. It is possible to divide *H. sapiens* into three temporal phases, the early *H. sapiens,* the Neandertals, and the modern *H. sapiens.*

The Early *Homo sapiens*

Between 450,000 and 250,000 years ago humans appeared with features that were rapidly moving in the direction of modern forms. *H. erectus* specimens, such as the Heidelberg mandible and the occipital bone from Vértesszölös, foreshadow later populations. During this time, increases in cranial capacity and changes in brain structure continued. Lagging somewhat behind changes in the brain case was a reduction in the size of the facial skeleton. The teeth and jaw became smaller and the skull more rounded.

The dividing line between *H. erectus* and *H. sapiens* is not very sharp. The oldest material assigned to *H. sapiens* exhibits many features of *H. erectus.* These fossils date from about 200,000 years ago. The Swanscombe find consists of an occipital, discovered in 1935, a left parietal, discovered in 1936, and the right parietal, belonging to the same individual, discovered twenty years

[19] E. A. Hoebel, *Anthropology: The Study of Man,* 4th ed. (New York: McGraw-Hill, 1972), p. 147.

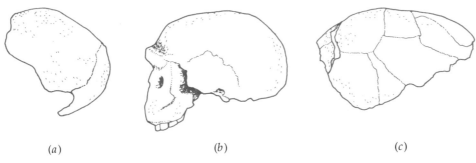

(a) (b) (c)

Figure 15-11   Transitional skulls. (a) *Swanscombe, England;* (b) *Steinheim, Germany;* (c) *Ehringsdorf, Germany.*

later. The skull comes from a site in England which is associated with an Acheulean tool assemblage. The Steinheim fossil, from Germany, discovered in 1933, is more complete and includes part of the facial skeleton. Both fossils show great similarities to one another.

Fossils found at Arago and Montmaurin in France have also been dated to the time of Swanscombe and Steinheim. The Arago finds were made in 1971 and consist of a partial skull with much of the facial skeleton present, two mandibles, and teeth. The find from Montmaurin, recovered in 1949, consists of a fragmentary jaw.

Swanscombe and Steinheim appear to be intermediate between the H. erectus forms and the later Neandertals. T. W. Phenice believes that Steinheim:

> . . . fits well into an expected range for H. erectus though it might also be [a] morphological intermediate between H. erectus and the Neandertals. Critical comparisons of the lateral view of Steinheim and the [Peking] skull series, for example, show that the only significant difference between [the two] lies in the occipital region.[20]

The Steinheim's cranial capacity is between 1,150 and 1,175 cubic centimeters (Figure 15-11).

A group of fossils from later in the Riss-Würm Interglacial show many advances. These represent a stage between Steinheim and Swanscombe and the Neandertals of the last glaciation. They include Ehringsdorf, from Germany, Saccopastore, from Italy, and Fontechevade, from France (Figure 15-11).

The fragments of the skull from Fontechevade are entirely within the range of variation of modern H. sapiens, as is the large cranial capacity of 1,460 cubic centimeters. Many see in this skull a form which is more modern in appearance yet older in time than the later Neandertal forms. Pilbeam believes that Fontechevade simply "represents part of the range of variation of archaic men living in Europe and adjacent areas at the time."[21] The major problem of interpretation of this period is the great scarcity of material.

Neandertals

The "cavemen" of cartoons and caricatures are based on early conceptions of what Neandertals looked like. Through the accident of discovery,

[20] T. W. Phenice, *Hominid Fossils: An Illustrated Key* (Dubuque, Iowa: Brown, 1972), p. 139.

[21] Pilbeam, op. cit., p. 178.

379

Table 15-4   Some Western European Neandertals (70,000 to 35,000 Years Ago)

Fossil Designation	Area Found	Comment
Neandertal	Germany	Found in 1856 and named after the Neander Valley, where discovered; shows usual Neandertal features
Spy I, II	Belgium	Anatomically similar to Neandertal Valley remains, found in association with Mousterian tools
La Chapelle-aux-Saints	France	Became the prototype of Neandertal; this was unfortunate since it was a pathological specimen
Gibraltar	Gibraltar	Actually the first fossil found of the kind later to be called Neandertal (1848)

Neandertals became the first known fossil representatives of prehistoric peoples. In 1848 a skull, which received little systematic examination, was discovered on Gibraltar. However, it was the second Neandertal find, made eight years later in the Neander Valley near Düsseldorf, Germany, which began a controversy that persists to the present.

The people of the Victorian age were totally unprepared to accept this archaic human form as one of their ancestors. At the time of its discovery, Darwin's *Origin of Species* was three years in the future, and none of the fossil forms mentioned in the preceding discussions had been discovered. The thought that this primitive-looking creature could have been a relative of modern people was repugnant to all but a few scholars. The alternatives offered were incredible. One Englishman considered it to be a "half-crazed, half-idiotic [type of man] with murderous propensities. . . ." Others considered it to be a freak, a stupid Roman legionnaire, or a victim of water on the brain!

In the years that followed, new discoveries were made. Today, Neandertal remains of over 150 individuals have been collected.

The term *Neandertal* in a strict sense is used to describe a series of finds from western Europe dating from the early part of the last glacial, about 70,000 years ago, to the rise of modern peoples, between 35,000 and 40,000 years ago. These are often referred to as the *classic Neandertals* (see

Table 15-4). The terms *progressive Neandertals, Neandertal collaterals, Neandertaloids, tropical Neandertals, Asiatic Neandertals, African Neandertals,* and *"false" Neandertals* have been used to refer to hominid remains from areas other than western Europe, dating from 100,000 years ago, and often earlier, to the rise of modern peoples (see Table 15-5).

The western European Neandertals   It is one of the great misfortunes of paleoanthropology that one of the earliest reasonably complete skeletons of a Neandertal was that of La Chapelle-aux-Saints, found in 1908. The bones, discovered as part of a burial, were sent to Paris, where the entire skeleton was reconstructed (Figure 15-12).

Marcellin Boule and Henri V. Vallois have described the La Chapelle-aux-Saints specimen as follows:

We are impressed by its bestial appearance or rather by the general effect of its simian [apelike] characters. The brain-box, elongated in form, is much depressed; the orbital arches are enormous; the forehead is very receding; the occipital region very projecting and much depressed; the face is long and projects forwards; the orbits are enormous; the nose, separated from the forehead by a deep depression, is short and broad; owing to the prolongation of the malar bones, the upper

The Evolution of the Genus Homo

jaw forms a kind of a muzzle; the lower jaw is strong and thick; the chin is rudimentary.[22]

Analysis of the postcranial remains led these scholars to conclude: "In general, the ordinary, normal carriage of Neandertal Man must then have differed in some degree from our own" (Figure 13-3).[23]

The above description was published in 1957, several years after it was discovered that the fossil from La Chapelle-aux-Saints was that of an old man with a severe case of arthritis of the jaw, spine, and possibly the legs.[24] In addition, this

[22] M. Boule and H. V. Vallois, *Fossil Men* (New York: Dryden, 1957), p. 214. Reprinted with permission of Holt, Rinehart and Winston, Inc.

[23] Ibid., p. 242.

[24] W. L. Straus, Jr., and A. J. E. Cave, "III. Pathology and the Posture of Neandertal Man," *The Quarterly Review of Biology,* 32 (1957), 348–363.

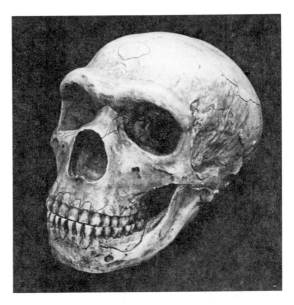

Figure 15-12   Cast of skull from La Chapelle-aux-Saints.

Table 15-5   Some Contemporaries and Near-Contemporaries of the Western European Neandertals

Fossil Designation	Area Found	Comment
Šipka	Czechoslovakia	A child with massive jaw and large teeth like the western European Neandertals, but having a chin
Tabūn	Israel	A male and female from the cave of Tabūn on Mount Carmel; female specimen lacks an occipital bun
Skhūl	Israel	Eleven skeletons from the cave of Skhūl on Mount Carmel; some resemble western European Neandertals; others resemble more modern populations
Amud	Israel	Five skeletons which show both Neandertal and modern characteristics
Shanidar	Iraq	Some of the seven skeletons reveal pelvic anomalies; they have more rounded brain cases than western European Neandertals; one individual buried with flowers
Haua Ftean	Libya	Two fossils very similar to western European Neandertals
Rhodesian (Broken Hill)	Zambia	While it resembles the western European Neandertals in many ways, this form is extremely robust and perhaps is the most extreme development of this period

find is not representative and appears rather extreme by Neandertal standards. Yet, this one individual has been considered by many as the prototype of the classic Neandertal.

The anatomy of western European Neandertals
Although Neandertals of western Europe were not the bestial creatures Boule and Vallois described, their remains do show distinctive features. Initially, it should be pointed out that most of these characteristics fall within the range of normal variation for modern peoples; so by calling them distinctive features we mean that they occur more often in Neandertal populations than in modern ones.

Western European Neandertals show a greater curvature of the femur than found in most modern humans. Also, the end of the tibia closest to the knee is sometimes bent backward. This last characteristic may not actually be the result of genetics but of the habit of resting in a squatting position. This feature does occur in high frequency among modern people who habitually squat.[25] However, unlike the early portrayals of Neandertal as being bent over and bowlegged, their posture and walk probably were not significantly different from the posture and walk of modern peoples.

Parts of the clavicle, humerus, radius, ulna, and hand bones tend to be more robust in Neandertals than in modern peoples. On the basis of this Kenneth A. R. Kennedy summarizes what the western European Neandertals might have looked like from the neck down:

We perceive a body build that was short, stocky, and muscular. Stature may have been just over five feet for males whose average weight has been estimated at about 160 pounds. The extremities of the body were short and trunks were relatively long and heavy.[26]

The skulls of the western European Neandertals are more distinctive than the postcranial skeleton. The skull is long with a prominent brow ridge over the eyes. The brow ridge arches above the eye sockets, the latter being further apart than in modern *H. sapiens*. The forehead is low and the occipital region is bun-shaped. The skull also tends to bulge at the sides.

Western European Neandertals and human evolution The past use of extreme forms, such as that of La Chapelle-aux-Saints, led many to believe that Neandertals represent a divergent line of human evolution which is not ancestral to more modern peoples. Many consider the Neandertals to belong to a separate species, *"H. neandertalensis."*

This hypothesis is based upon the presence of forms in Europe which differ more from modern humans than forms outside Europe (but there are exceptions) and the idea that forms which some see as more modern, such as Steinheim and Fontechevade, preceded them. According to some investigators, Neandertal developed as an adaptation to the extremely cold climates of Europe as a population genetically isolated by the ice sheets from the rest of the inhabited world. Furthermore, modern peoples, having developed outside of Europe, moved in with their superior technology and exterminated the Neandertals. Evidence for this includes the apparently sudden replacement of the Neandertal cultural material in Europe.

However, there are many difficulties with this hypothesis. First, western Europe was never totally cut off from the rest of the world; and even if it had been, the amount of time the population

[25] K. A. R. Kennedy, *Neandertal Man* (Minneapolis: Burgess, 1975), pp. 38–39.

[26] Ibid., p. 39.

would have been isolated might not have been great enough for speciation to have occurred. Second, forms as extreme as those found in Europe also are found outside of Europe. In fact, the skull often referred to as Rhodesian, from southern Africa, is in many respects more extreme in development than even that of La Chapelle-aux-Saints. Third, the specimen from La Chapelle-aux-Saints, when compared to other finds, is not representative but is rather robust, even by Neandertal standards. Fourth, the replacement of cultural materials is not as sudden as many believe. The cultures of the more modern forms shared a number of features with the Neandertal cultural manifestations. Fifth, the existence of more modern-looking forms antedating the Neandertals has been questioned. The pre-Neandertal material is very scanty, and these forms may be less modern in appearance than the individuals and fragments discovered have led many to believe.

Today, most paleoanthropologists consider Neandertal to be a major stage of human evolution, a subspecies of *H. sapiens*, *H. sapiens neandertalensis*. While Neandertals did possess many features which at least statistically distinguish them from modern peoples, if Neandertals were to appear on the streets today, groomed and clothed as people are today, probably no one would think anything was particularly strange about them.

The progressive Neandertals The Neandertal material outside of western Europe has been labeled by some as progressive because it is seen as being less extreme than such forms as that from La Chapelle-aux-Saints. Actually, this is not entirely true, since the find from Rhodesia shows a very extreme form indeed, and there are other exceptions.

Figure 15-13 shows the distribution and names of some of the better-known fossils from the Riss-Würm Interglacial until about the middle of Würm glaciation (150,000 to 35,000 years ago). As new finds have been made, it has become evident that peoples living during this time displayed a great deal of variability and that the designations *classic* and *progressive* are somewhat simplistic. The earliest Neandertals found were simply the most extreme. Later discoveries show that forms existed which were more like modern forms. The more extreme forms and the more modern forms existed side by side and are often found in the same site (see Tables 15-4 and 15-5). Thus it must be concluded that the population of this time was quite variable.

An example of this variability is found in the research of Dorothy Garrod.[27] Working on Mount Carmel in Israel, she found populations that displayed a surprising range of variation. In the lower levels of a cave called Tabūn, she found a specimen that reflected the essential features of Steinheim. Above it were individuals showing more modern characteristics in association with others which showed a mixture of more modern and Neandertal features. At another site on Mount Carmel, Skhūl, some 10,000 years more recent than Tabūn, a sample of eleven individuals revealed a population very modern in some aspects but retaining some Neandertal characteristics (Figure 15-14).

Many hypotheses have been proposed to account for this variability. As mentioned, some see the classic forms as an adaptation to an extremely cold environment and the variability as local adaptations to a variety of environmental niches. Others see population movements as the causal factors in the development of variable populations such as those of Mount Carmel. Still others see the development of small, isolated hunting groups as the basic factor. They argue that the type of hunting characteristic at this time resulted in a restricted breeding population. Fac-

[27] Pilbeam, op. cit., p. 184.

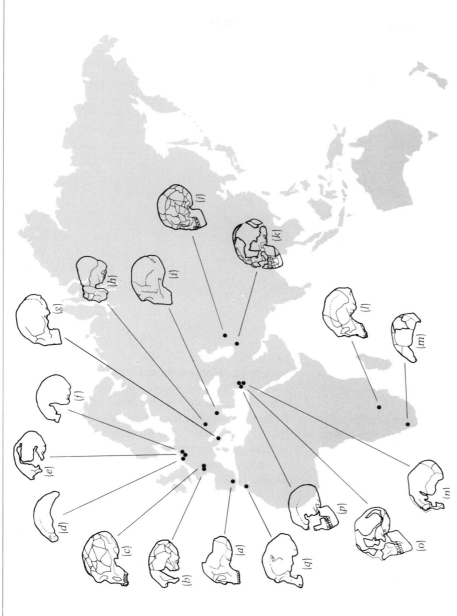

Figure 15-13 Variation and distribution of *Homo sapiens* dating from 150,000 to 35,000 years ago. (a) Gibraltar; (b) La Quina, France; (c) La Ferrassie, France; (d) Neandertal, Germany; (e) Spy I, Belgium; (f) Spy II, Belgium; (g) Monte Circeo, Italy; (h) Krapina, Yugoslavia; (i) Petralona, Greece; (j) Teschik Tasch Child, Uzbekistan, USSR; (k) Shanidar I, Iraq; (l) Rhodesian, Broken Hill, South Africa; (m) Saldanha, South Africa; (n) Skhūl IX, Israel; (o) Skhūl IV, Israel; (p) Tabūn, Israel; (q) Jebel Irhoud, Morocco.

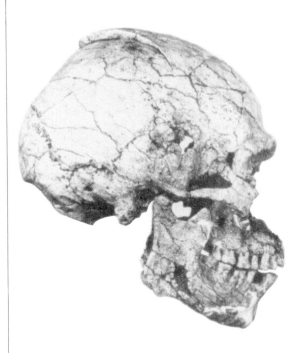

Figure 15-14   Skull V, Skhūl, Mount Carmel, Israel.

tors such as genetic drift would account for much of the variability in this case.

The disappearance of the Neandertals Between 35,000 and 40,000 years ago, the classic Neandertal individuals disappeared from the fossil record. Some believe that Neandertal was wiped out by the migrations of the more advanced modern forms, *H. sapiens sapiens;* yet many anthropologists feel that Neandertal populations gave rise to modern peoples.

David S. Brose and Milford H. Wolpoff see a continuous development of Neandertals to *H. sapiens sapiens.*[28] They point out that the

[28] D. S. Brose and M. H. Wolpoff, "Early Upper Paleolithic Man and Late Middle Paleolithic Tools," *American Anthropologist,* 73 (1971), 1156–1194.

modern populations do not overlap the Neandertal ones. The most recent Neandertal forms date from about 40,000 years ago, while the older modern forms date from about 26,000 years ago. They further note that in sites where there are continuous sequences spanning the period, the sequence shows a gradual transition in cultural remains from those characteristic of Neandertals to those characteristic of modern *H. sapiens.* A gradual transition of humans from Neandertal to modern forms has been noted throughout the Old World.

Brose and Wolpoff note the gradual increase in the number of specialized tools over all-purpose tools during the period and postulate that the more efficient technology which developed by the end of the Neandertal period reduced the selective pressures favoring large incisors and canines, which were used in holding objects.[29] C. Loring Brace notes the tremendous amount of wear on the Neandertal's teeth, which he feels resulted from their use in holding objects. He compares this to the way Eskimos use their teeth for softening leather. With a reduction in tooth size comes a reduction of the facial skeleton and a reorganization of the skull into the *H. sapiens* pattern.[30]

Sally R. Binford suggests that differences in demographic patterns related to the size of the breeding population may have been a major factor in the disappearance of the Neandertals.[31] Neandertal hunted a variety of game, probably concentrating on isolated animals. Toward the end of the Neandertal period, humans began to concentrate on herd animals, usually only a few species. This form of hunting is more efficient if carried out by large groups and, in turn, can support larger populations. Thus, the size of the breeding population increases, bringing about a reduction in the significance of genetic drift.

The Culture of the Neandertals

The cultural remains of this period make up the *Middle Paleolithic*. The cultural tradition associated most frequently with Neandertals is the *Mousterian*, named after the cave of Le Moustier in France. Just as the skeletal remains of the Neandertals reflect a wide range of morphological variation, the cultural material indicates variability in tool types as well. Also, it is with the Neandertals that the first concrete evidence of a concern with the supernatural emerges.

---

[29] Ibid., 1175–1176.

[30] C. L. Brace, "The Fate of the 'Classic' Neandertals: A Consideration of Hominid Catastrophism," *Current Anthropology*, 5 (1964), 3–43.

[31] S. R. Binford, "Early Upper Pleistocene Adaptations in the Levant," *American Anthropologist*, 70 (1968), 707–717.

The tools of Neandertals Stone, bone, wood, and shell, as well as hides and other animal parts, made up the materials used in Neandertal's inventory of tools, as had been the case for the species that preceded him. The Mousterian cultural tradition represents the continuation and refinement of the Acheulean tradition, an ultimate deemphasis of the hand ax, and an increase in the number and variety of flake tools. For example, in some early Neandertal sites, hand axes make up as much as 40 percent of the stone tools, whereas in later assemblages they drop to less than 8 percent.

The sites of the Middle Paleolithic show great variability in tool types and their frequencies (Figure 15-15). Several different lithic industries can be defined. This variability has been explained by some in terms of differing cultural traditions and movements of populations.

The Binfords have interpreted this variability in another way.[32] They note that human behavior is patterned in space. That is, different human activities take place in different places, and different human activities are associated with different tool types. Thus, the activities taking place in a classroom differ from those taking place in the cafeteria, office, or library. Tools associated with the classroom might include chalk and erasers, maps, and bulletin boards, while those associated with the cafeteria include plates and eating utensils.

The Binfords see the Mousterian as a single cultural tradition, with the different kinds of sites associated with different activities. For example, the typical Mousterian may represent butchering activities (Figure 15-15), while the Mousterian of Acheulean tradition may represent the activity of bone and wood manufacture.

---

[32] L. R. Binford and S. R. Binford, "A Preliminary Analysis of Functional Variability in the Mousterian of Levallois Facies," in J. D. Clark and F. C. Howell (eds.), *Recent Studies in Paleoanthropology* (Washington: Anthropological Association, 1966), pp. 238–295.

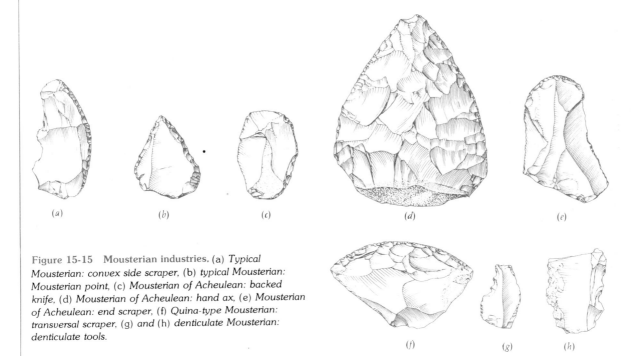

Figure 15-15 Mousterian industries. (a) *Typical Mousterian: convex side scraper*, (b) *typical Mousterian: Mousterian point*, (c) *Mousterian of Acheulean: backed knife*, (d) *Mousterian of Acheulean: hand ax*, (e) *Mousterian of Acheulean: end scraper*, (f) *Quina-type Mousterian: transversal scraper*, (g) *and* (h) *denticulate Mousterian: denticulate tools.*

Bone tools predominate in such Mousterian sites as that at Pin Hole Cave in England.[33] James Kitching believes that bone tools were used for a variety of purposes: ripping, hammering, cutting, skinning, digging, and hide preparation. Concave parts of the skeleton, such as hip sockets and skulls, were used as bowls, cups, scoops, and perhaps storage containers. Neandertals probably used wood and other materials that have deteriorated with time.

Were Neandertals "cavemen"? Caves are among the best places where fossils can be found. In many areas, there is less alteration between

[33] J. W. Kitching, *Bone, Tooth and Horn Tools of Paleolithic Man* (Manchester: Manchester Univ. Press, 1963).

wetting and drying in caves than in open sites, and hence less chance of rapid deterioration. Because of the buildup of garbage and the flaking off of material from the roof which then settles on the floor, caves often provide the researcher with a well-preserved stratigraphy of cultural remains. Because preservation is somewhat better in caves than in open sites, caves have been extensively investigated for signs of humans, and most Neandertal sites have been found in this context.

Humans are not by nature cave-dwelling animals. Caves are dark, often damp, and quite uncomfortable for humans. People did inhabit the mouths of caves, but not the deep interiors. Most often what are called caves are not caves at all, but *rock shelters*, or rock overhangs. Neandertals also may have spent a great deal of their time in open-air sites, which have not been preserved with as great a frequency as cave sites. This is an example of how differential preservation influences the data.

However, open-air sites are known; among the most famous is one at Moldova, in western Russia. Here, mammoth bones made up the support for animal hides that created a house with an inside area 18 feet in diameter. Fifteen hearths have been found in the floor of this ancient home.[34]

Some groups of Neandertals probably were more settled than others. Like modern hunters and gatherers, most groups moved from time to time in search of new sources of food and better weather conditions. While on the move and when staying in one place for a short time, they would probably have made huts and windbreaks out of grass, leaves, and sticks. These structures would not be preserved in the archaeological record.

Could Neandertals talk? The popular concept of Neandertal as a brutish creature capable of only limited communication through grunting and gestures is probably totally incorrect. However, in 1971 Philip Lieberman and Edmund S. Crelin argued that Neandertals were not capable of fully articulate human speech. This conclusion was based upon their reconstruction of the larynx from La Chapelle-aux-Saints.[35]

Lieberman and Crelin's hypothesis has been criticized for at least four major reasons. First, the accuracy of the reconstruction of the larynx has been questioned.[36] Second, it has been shown

that modern people who display the same anatomical features that Lieberman and Crelin believe would have prevented Neandertals from articulate speech are completely capable of human speech.[37] Third, studies of the endocranial cast suggest the neurological development necessary for speech.[38] And, finally, the Neandertals developed such a complex culture that it is almost inconceivable that they did not have a complex form of communication. Such communication would have been needed to organize hunts, to pass on technical knowledge from person to person and from generation to generation, and to develop religious concepts and the arts.

Thus we conclude that the Neandertals probably had the same or close to the same capabilities for language as modern peoples. In fact, it is most probable that *H. erectus* and, perhaps to a lesser extent, the australopiths, had systems of communication that were similar to modern language.

Neandertals as philosophers While paleoanthropologists can reconstruct diet and technology with a great deal of confidence, the reconstruction of religion and philosophy is a great deal more conjectural. From the rich finds of Neandertal cultures some generalities can be made about their philosophy of life, but they must remain generalities.

As far as is known, Neandertals were the first to systematically and ritually bury their dead (Figure 15-16). In one cave, an adolescent boy was carefully buried in a sleeping position. He rested on his right side, knees bent, and head positioned on his forearm. In his grave were stone tools and animal remains that may have been meant to aid him in a supposed next world. There also might

[34] C. S. Chard, *Man in Prehistory* (New York: McGraw-Hill, 1969), pp. 120–121.

[35] P. Lieberman and E. S. Crelin, "On the Speech of Neanderthal Man," *Linguistic Inquiry,* 2 (1971), 203–222.

[36] D. Falk, "Comparative Anatomy of the Larynx in Man and the Chimpanzee: Implications for Language in Neanderthals," *American Journal of Physical Anthropology,* 43 (1975), 123–132.

[37] M. LeMay, "The Language Capability of Neanderthal Man," *American Journal of Physical Anthropology,* 42 (1975), 9–14.

[38] Ibid.

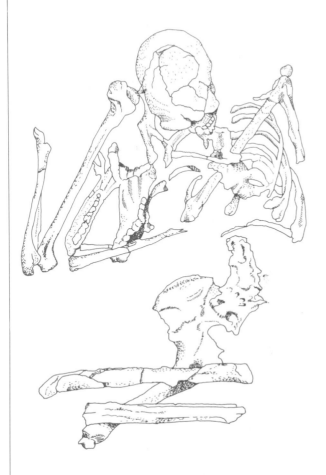

Figure 15-16 Neandertal burial. *An adult male burial from Mount Carmel. The body was buried with jawbones of a great wild boar.*

have been family cemeteries; one site has revealed closely spaced graves of a small infant, three children, and two adults.[39]

A possible bear cult of the Neandertals has puzzled investigators for years. The very fact that these people hunted the gigantic cave bear presents the first mystery. It stood more than 8 feet tall, had long and deadly claws, and perhaps a disposition to match. There were many other less

[39] Pfeiffer, op. cit., p. 189.

dangerous prey that could have been hunted, and it does not appear that they had to hunt the bear to survive. It is most probable that the bear had either some religious or magical meaning associated with it or that to kill it represented a test of manhood. Evidence that more than diet was involved comes from Drachenloch, Switzerland. Here was found a subterranean vault lined with stones and containing the skulls of several cave bears. At the same site was the skull of one bear with the leg bone of another bear stuck through its cheek. The skull was resting on the bones of a third bear. Other sites have revealed evidence of ritualistic practices involving the cave bear.[40]

The data have led some paleoanthropologists to the conclusion that Neandertals had an awareness of the uniqueness of each individual and the importance of the individual to society and of society to the individual. The burial of the dead emphasized both the worth of the individual and a preparation for a next life. The burial together of families, or at least members of a group, indicates relationships strong enough for people who were together during life to wish to remain together at death and in the afterworld.[41] Cult rituals today reinforce group solidarity by providing a common goal and communal activities. They also provide a united way for society to face the fears of the unknown. Perhaps similar functions were in force with the Neandertals.

From La Chapelle-aux-Saints comes further evidence of the value put on the individual. The skeleton found here, discussed earlier, was crippled with arthritis and probably could not have provided for himself. He was also between forty and fifty years of age when he died, an old man for a people whose average life expectancy was about thirty to thirty-five years. It appears that the individual was thought important enough for such a nonproductive and perhaps even burdensome person as he was to be kept alive.[42]

A further example of this comes from Shanidar Cave in Iraq. Shanidar I was a male who was about forty years old when he died. Aside from arthritis and blindness of the left eye, his right arm, clavicle, and scapula had never fully grown. The unusually great amount of wear on his front teeth suggests that the teeth were used for grasping in place of the right arm. In addition, analysis of the skull shows that the top right side was damaged and healed before his death. Such an individual would be of little value to the community; yet, he lived to a relatively old age.[43]

Summary

Neandertals and their contemporaries are among the best-known forms in the fossil record due in large part to their practice of burial. This large number of individuals demonstrates a great morphological variability which some paleoanthropologists see as variants of a single widespread population. However, other investigators see this variability as evidence of distinct populations, even separate subspecies or species.

The western European Neandertal form is usually seen in terms of La Chapelle-aux-Saints. This individual, however, is pathological, and its use as a prototype has led to the erroneous picture of Neandertal as a less than human form unrelated to modern peoples. Actually, although the western European Neandertals show a statistically distinctive cluster of characteristics, if Neandertals were alive today they would not be considered unusual and would probably be placed within the range of normal variation of modern *H. sapiens*.

A number of fossils are known outside western Europe for this same period of time. These are from Eastern Europe, Asia, Southwest Asia, and Africa. Some, like those from South Africa, are as specialized as those from western Europe, while others show a larger number of modern features. There is no reason to believe that these Upper Pleistocene forms were not directly ancestral to modern *H. sapiens*.

[40] F. C. Howell (ed.), *Early Man* (New York: Time-Life, 1965), pp. 126–127.

[41] Pfeiffer, op. cit., pp. 183–194.

[42] Howell, op. cit., p. 130.

[43] R. S. Solecki, *Shanidar: The First Flower People* (New York: Knopf, 1971), pp. 195–196.

The culture of the Neandertals in Europe is usually termed the Mousterian. The various Mousterian sites show a great deal of variability, which has been interpreted in a number of ways. The Binfords believe that this variation represents differences in activity rather than differences in cultural traditions.

It is during the Neandertal period, the Middle Paleolithic, that paleoanthropologists have come across the first burials, which, along with burial goods, indicate some belief in an afterlife. Evidence of a cave bear cult also exists. Of great interest is the idea that Neandertal had an awareness of the uniqueness of the individual, and several individuals have been found whose pathological conditions would make them less than fully participating members of the community.

HOMO SAPIENS OF THE LATE UPPER PLEISTOCENE

The late upper Pleistocene covers the latter half of the Würm glaciation, between 10,000 and 35,000 years ago, a period which makes up the *Upper Paleolithic* of the cultural historian. By 35,000 years ago, modern peoples, *H. sapiens sapiens,* had come to dominate the scene (Figure 15-17). But modern forms did not appear abruptly, for, as already discussed, forms showing modern features can be found in antecedent populations. However, in the Upper Paleolithic, cultural manifestations as elaborate as or even more elaborate than many contemporary ones developed.

The human remains from the Upper Paleolithic show much variability. Many anthropologists have attempted to equate specific Upper Paleolithic populations with specific modern populations (Chapter 7). There are many problems associated with such attempts. First, populations are constantly changing, and even an isolated population would change in terms of average physical features over the centuries. However, gene flow is the rule, and the result of the gene flow would be even greater change. A skull found 5,000 years ago which looked similar to skulls known from a modern population would not necessarily be an ancestor of the modern population. Second, migration brings about changes in the gene pool in any given locality. Gross morphological similarities do not necessarily indicate genetic relationship.

Fossil *Homo sapiens sapiens*

Due to the recent age of the material and the practice of burial, numerous hominid finds from this period are known from throughout the world.

Asia The earliest known *H. sapiens sapiens* is from Niah Cave, in North Borneo, and has been carbon 14–dated at about 40,000 years ago. Don R. Brothwell says that it resembles the Tasmanians, who became extinct in recent times.[44] This correlation is especially questionable, since it is made on the basis of *one* skull and part of the face of a teenaged youth.

Many of the finds from Southeast Asia have been said to resemble the modern Australian aborigine. It was during the Upper Pleistocene that humans entered Australia. The Wadjak skulls from Java, discovered in 1890, show large brow ridges, a receding forehead, a deep nasal root, and large teeth.

Many finds have been made in China. Perhaps the best known is a series of skulls from the Upper Cave of Choukoutien. Three of the skulls are fairly complete. They are all modern but are interesting in that each one is different in many

[44] D. R. Brothwell, "Upper Pleistocene Human Skull from Niah Caves, Sarawak," *Sarawak Museum Journal,* 9 (1961), 323.

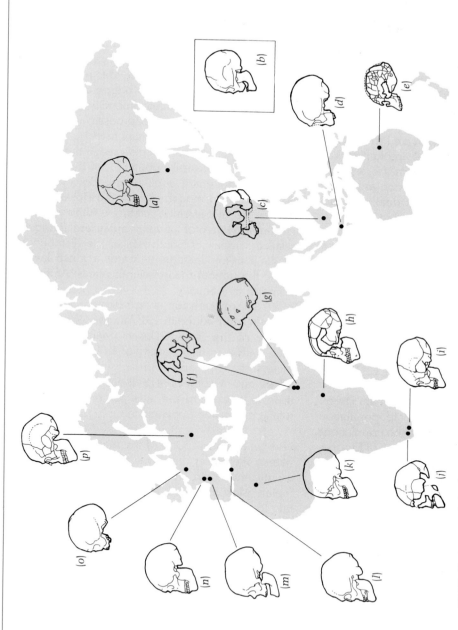

Figure 15-17 Variation and distribution of *Homo sapiens sapiens*. (a) Choukoutien, Upper Cave 101, China; (b) Tepexpan, Mexico; (c) Niah Cave, Borneo; (d) Wadjak, Java; (e) Talgai, Australia; (f) Omo, Ethiopia; (g) Omo, Ethiopia; (h) Lothagam Hill, Kenya; (i) Fish Hoek, South Africa; (j) Cape Flats, Cape Peninsula, South Africa; (k) Asselar, Sahara Desert; (l) Afalou, Algeria; (m) Cro-Magnon, France; (n) Combe Capelle, France; (o) Oberkassel, Germany; (p) Predmost, Czechoslovakia.

respects, a good example of intrapopulation variability. One skull shows a forward-jutting zygomatic arch and shovel-shaped incisors similar to those of present Asian populations. These skulls also resemble closely many American Indian skulls.

Europe   Just as the classic Neandertals were seen in terms of a single specimen, La Chapelle-aux-Saints, early modern humans are often seen in terms of Cro-Magnon. Discovered in 1868 in southwestern France, this skull of an old man has become the prototype of modern *H. sapiens*. Early scholars envisioned Cro-Magnon as a light-skinned, beardless, upright individual who invaded Europe and destroyed the bestial Neandertals. Actually, anatomically, Cro-Magnon is now known to represent only one individual of a highly variable population. In general, Cro-Magnon populations were characterized by broad, small faces with high foreheads and prominent chins. The cranial capacity was about 1,600 cubic centimeters, and their height has been estimated to be between 5 feet 4 inches and 6 feet.[45] Their skin color and amount of body hair can only be surmised.

Africa   By 10,000 years ago, the Sahara Desert was serving as a partial barrier to population movement and acted to separate the populations of North Africa, which resembled those of Europe, from the populations of sub-Saharan Africa.

The sub-Saharan finds fall into two major types. The older one can be termed the Boskop population, after the find made in 1914 in Boskop, South Africa. The dating of this specimen is very uncertain but is estimated to be between 10,000 and 30,000 years old. Other similar finds include Fish Hoek from South Africa and Gamble's Cave from Kenya; both date at about 15,000 years.

The Boskop individuals have very large cranial capacities, among the largest known for fossil hominids. The Fish Hoek brain case measures 1,600 cubic centimeters. This population is characterized by small brow ridges, a rather flattened vault, and a generally infantile appearance. The face is short, with a broad nose but without a depressed root, and very small teeth.

Many paleoanthropologists see in the Boskop material the ancestral population of the modern Bushman-Hottentot populations. However, unlike these short modern forms, the Boskop peoples were of average stature. Although the Bushman-Hottentot peoples today are found in restricted areas of South Africa, the distribution of the Boskop material indicates a much larger range throughout the grasslands of east Africa, as far north as Kenya.

A later population is represented by the Asselar skeleton, found in 1927 in what is today the middle of the Sahara Desert (Mali). This large skull, with a cranial capacity of 1,500 cubic centimeters, is long and narrow, with small brow ridges and a somewhat bulbous forehead. The nose is broad and the jaws are projecting. It is totally modern in appearance.

The New World   One of the major areas of debate in the earlier days of anthropology centered around the origin and antiquity of the American Indian. Most anthropologists today feel fairly certain that the New World was populated by Asian big-game hunters who followed their prey over a land bridge connecting Siberia to North America. The evidence of the Asian origin of American aboriginal populations goes beyond archaeological finds. American aborigines show similarities to Asian populations in body build, head shape, eye and body color, hair type, presence of the

---

[45] F. E. Poirier, *Fossil Man: An Evolutionary Journey* (St. Louis: Mosby, 1973), p. 199.

Diego antigen, and many other characteristics. Of course, different mutations, selective pressures, and drift have altered the gene pools of the original migrants to the New World. American Indian populations today show in their gene pools the results of interbreeding with many non-Asian populations.

Although very good archaeological evidence points to the presence of humans in the New World 10,000 to 20,000 years ago, many paleoanthropologists feel that humans have occupied the North American and South American continents far longer. While many sites have been studied which point to a great antiquity, dating of these sites has been far from satisfactory.

Human skeletal material from the New World is not extremely common, especially for the earliest periods. Perhaps one of the oldest finds in North America is the "Los Angeles Man," discovered in 1936. This skull fragment has been dated by carbon 14 to over 23,600 years old. The aspartic acid racemization method gives a date of 26,000 years old. Skeletal material from San Diego, California, has been dated by this latter method at 28,000, 44,000, and 48,000 years old.[46]

The Upper Paleolithic

During the Upper Paleolithic, human cultural development achieved a level of complexity which had never before existed, a level which exceeded that of most modern hunting and gathering peoples. The cultural traditions associated with the Upper Paleolithic are found throughout Europe, northern Asia, and the Middle East and northern Africa. It is on the northern plains of Europe and eastern Asia and in southwestern France that human cultural achievements appear most complex.

James R. Sackett writes:

In view of the sheer volume and elaboration of their cultural remains, there can be little doubt that Upper Paleolithic societies in the Dordogne [France] achieved one of the most successful hunting and gathering adaptations in culture history. . . . The factors accounting for this success presumably stemmed from an almost ideal combination of exploitative skills and environmental resources enjoyed by Upper Paleolithic men in this region.[47]

The idea that Europe and eastern Asia developed more elaborate and varied technological inventories than the rest of the world might be due to the fact that more research has been done in these areas. This section will deal with the technological developments of the Upper Paleolithic, the nature of people's relationship to their habitats, and finally, their aesthetic and religious achievements.

Upper Paleolithic technology The Upper Paleolithic is often defined in terms of the *blade*. Blades are not unique to this period, but the high frequency of their use is.

Blades are flakes with roughly parallel sides. They are manufactured from carefully prepared cores. The result is a blank from which a variety of specialized tools can be made. The edges are extremely sharp, and the blades can be made quickly in great numbers. The manufacture of

[46] J. L. Bada, R. A. Schroeder, and G. F. Carter, "New Evidence for the Antiquity of Man in North America Deduced from Aspartic Acid Racemization," *Science,* 184 (17 May 1974), 791–793.

[47] J. R. Sackett, "Method and Theory of Upper Paleolithic Archeology in Southwestern France," in S. R. Binford and L. R. Binford (eds.), *New Perspectives in Archeology* (Chicago: Aldine, 1968), p. 64.

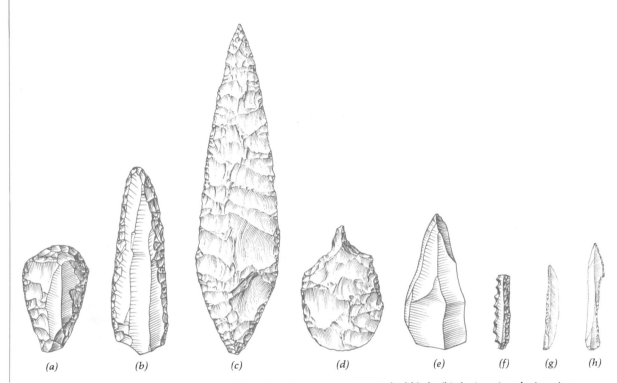

(a)   (b)   (c)   (d)   (e)   (f)   (g)   (h)

Figure 15-18   Upper Paleolithic tool types. (a) *Aurignacian: scraper on retouched blade,* (b) *Aurignacian: Aurignacian blade,* (c) *Solutrean: laurel-leaf point,* (d) *Solutrean: borer end scraper,* (e) *Perigordian: burin,* (f) *Perigordian: denticulated backed bladelet,* (g) *Magdalenian: backed bladelet,* (h) *Magdalenian: shouldered point.*

blades represents an efficient use of natural resources—in this case, flint. François Bordes points out that the Upper Paleolithic blade technique could produce 10 to 40 feet of cutting edge from a pound of flint, compared with only 40 inches using the early Mousterian technique.[48]

From the basic blade, a wide variety of highly specialized tools can be manufactured. Unlike the Lower Paleolithic use of the general-purpose hand ax, humans of the Upper Paleolithic used

tools designed for specific purposes. A number of these had the primary function of making other tools. Some of the tool types are illustrated in Figure 15-18.

Bone, along with antler, horn, and ivory, became a very common raw material. Bone has many advantages over stone. For example, it does not break as easily. The widespread use of bone resulted from the development of the burin; it had a thick point that did not break under pressure. Some of the later Upper Paleolithic cultures became very dependent on bone implements, such as spear points, and stone points practically disappeared.

[48] F. Bordes, *The Old Stone Age* (New York: McGraw-Hill, 1968).

One of the major reasons for the success of this period was the development of new projectile weapons. These were *compound tools*, that is, tools composed of several parts. Hafting appears in the archaeological record. The ax is no longer a hand ax but an ax with a handle.

Spears were made with bone points hafted to a shaft. To add to the force of penetration, the spear was often used with a spear thrower. Harpoons consisted of a barbed bone point which detached from the shaft after entering the animal yet remained tied to the shaft by some type of cord. The shaft dragging behind the animal would impede its flight. Later in the period, the bow and arrow appear. Several types of fishing gear, such as barbed fish hooks and fish spears, also are known.

Human relationship to the environment The development of the Upper Paleolithic must be seen in relation to the nature of the environment during this time. This was the latter part of the last glaciation, the Würm. Northern and western Europe was essentially a *tundra*, a land frozen solid during most of the year but thawing slightly during the summer. During the summer, plant life capable of supporting large herds of animal life proliferated. The tundra of Canada today teems with animal life, such as the moose and caribou. But this Pleistocene European tundra was a low-latitude tundra, receiving more solar radiation, and was able to support a fantastic mass of herd animals.

Upper Paleolithic peoples hunted the large herd animals, often specializing in one or two types, in contrast to the more individualistic hunting techniques of the Neandertals. This shift in orientation toward cooperative hunting of herd animals with improved projectile technology may have been responsible for the development of the Upper Paleolithic complex. Among the more important animals hunted were the reindeer,

horse, and bison. Fish, especially the salmon, were also important.

Unfortunately, growing mastery in the utilization of these natural resources may have been matched by the disruption of ecological balances. During the late Pleistocene, more than fifty genera of large mammals became extinct (Figure 15-19). The extinction of these large animals, the *megafauna* (all animals weighing more than 100 pounds) was not accompanied by the extinction of large numbers of smaller animals or plants. The analysis of fossils has shown no evidence of droughts in most areas, and although the Pleistocene was a time of climatic fluctuation, these changes do not usually correspond to the disappearance of the megafauna. Paul S. Martin has found one factor that does correspond to these extinctions—*H. sapiens*.[49] Most extinctions can be correlated with the movements of people into a specific area. Whether they actually caused or contributed to Pleistocene extinctions is debatable. Yet, it seems very possible that human technology and social efficiency had developed to a point at which the environment could have been endangered.

The Upper Paleolithic of Europe was essentially an adaptation to a very cold climate. People had to develop the technology to survive in such an environment. There is evidence in the archaeological record of tailored clothing. Bone needles have been found. In one case, a skeleton was found in Russia that was buried in a shirt covered with ivory beads. (The position of the beads permitted the reconstruction of the clothing.) The individual wore a pullover shirt with a round neck, a pair of trousers, boots, and some type of head covering.[50]

[49] P. S. Martin and H. E. Wright, Jr. (eds.), *Pleistocene Extinctions: The Search for a Cause* (New Haven: Yale Univ. Press, 1967).

[50] Chard, op. cit., p. 149.

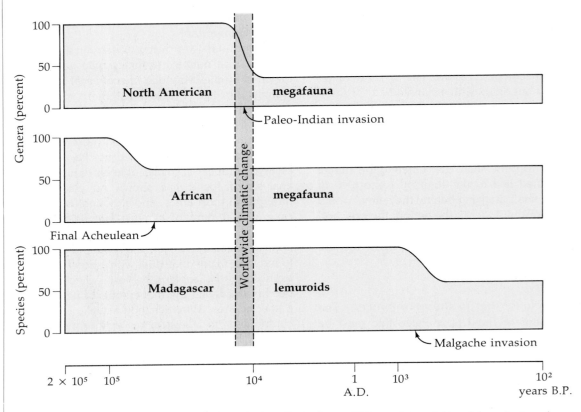

Figure 15-19 Pleistocene extinctions. *Large extinction of animals over 100 pounds in weight and the extinction of lemuroids, some 10,000 years ago, as the result of human activity.*

Humans in a cold environment also need housing. In southwestern France they used rock shelters. Many open settlements have also been found. Villages in this area were built in the river valleys, somewhat protected from the cold of the plateau.

Several sites in eastern Europe and Russia have shown the existence of dwellings. Chard describes them as "small round one-family habitations 12 to 18 feet in diameter, partly sunk into the ground and perhaps roofed over with skins supported on some sort of framework. Large bones or tusks might be used for various purposes in construction.[51]

Art of the Upper Paleolithic The Upper Paleolithic is characterized by a variety of artistic methods and styles. Paintings and engravings can be seen developing from early beginnings to the colorful and skillful renderings of the Magdalenian

[51] Ibid., pp. 149–150.

peoples. Realistic, stylized, and geometric modes were used.

Paleolithic art finds its expression in the modeling of clay, sculpturing in rock, bone, ivory, and antler, and painting and engraving on large surfaces, such as cave walls, as well as on small objects. Everyday utensils were decorated, but perhaps the most interesting works are the statues and cave paintings.

Some of the most famous statuary are the female statues, called *Venus figurines*. They are only a few inches high and are carved in the round from a variety of materials. They have extremely exaggerated breasts and buttocks and very stylized heads, hands, and feet (Figure 15-20). Perhaps they represent pregnant women. It has been assumed that the figures had ritual significance, probably involving the concept of fertility; however, this is not necessarily so. Peter Paul Reubens (1577–1640) painted fleshy women. Was his motivation fertility magic? The point is that it is perhaps not valid to make absolute statements about ancient peoples' motives. Upper Paleolithic artists also made models of animals, including the famous set of statues of a bison bull, cow, and calf found in France.

The cave art of the Upper Paleolithic is found in France, Spain, Italy, and the South Urals. The subject matter of most of this art is animals, although humans also are depicted. These were hunting peoples, and art expressed their relationship to the fauna that supported them (Figure 15-21). Most researchers believe that most representations of nature served magical purposes. Many cave paintings are in almost inaccessible areas of the caves, indicating that they were not done for totally aesthetic purposes. The cave art appears to have been used for both hunting and fertility magic. In the first instance, animals were often painted with mortal wounds. Perhaps this represents a type of imitative magic in which the "wounded" painting is supposed to have an effect on the animal it portrays. Animals were

Figure 15-20   Venus figurine. *The Venus of Willendorf, from Austria, 4⅓˚ inches high.*

often painted pregnant; and along with the statuary, this might have been an instance of imitative magic applied to fertility. This concept is supported by the suggestion that cave art reached its height when large herd animals were becoming increasingly scarce.

Since 1965, Alexander Marshack has been studying marks, dots, and lines of various configurations that accompanied Paleolithic art. He has concluded that these marks were not random scribblings but the beginnings of calendrics, arithmetic systems, and even writing. If this is true, the origin of these systems is earlier than it was considered to be just a few years ago.[52]

The Upper Paleolithic cultures The Upper Paleolithic is one of the best-documented periods of prehistory. One of the many reasons is that much material has been well preserved in rock shelters and has created a great interest in its study. Again, most research has been carried out in Europe; perhaps this gives a distorted picture of upper Paleolithic culture in other, less intensively studied parts of the world.

Some of the differences between the technologies of the various areas may be due to the different conditions for preservation and different amounts of research in each area. The variations can also be explained in terms of local adaptations. Various environments required different cultural inventories for successful adjustment and provided different potentials. The forest is characterized by different sources of foods, climatic conditions, and resources for shelter than those found in the tundra or desert. In addition, cultural

[52] A Marshack, "Upper Paleolithic Notation and Symbol," *Science*, 178 (24 November 1972), 817–828; A. Marshack, *The Roots of Civilization* (New York: McGraw-Hill, 1972).

Figure 15-21 Cave art. *Painted reindeer from the Dordogne, France.*

inventory depends on *diffusion*. That is, an idea for a particular artifact—or, for that matter, a social system—may originate in one area and then diffuse to surrounding areas. A group isolated by geographical barriers may be cut off from the innovations of others. Of course, there is always the possibility that an idea or artifact that diffuses to an area may not fit the ecological or cultural needs of a people and therefore will not be accepted. However, culture is cumulative, and every group has materials and behaviors that originated in areas distant from it.

The identification and correlation of the various Upper Paleolithic cultures is one of the great problems of research. Table 15-6 presents a generalized chronology and history of the cultures of the Upper Paleolithic of southwestern France, where much research has been carried out.

European-type assemblages are found in the Middle East, India, East Africa, the Mediterranean coast, the Crimea, and Siberia. On the other hand, some African traditions differed from those in Europe and maintained the hand ax as the main implement. The retention of the hand ax in some parts of Africa was not an indication of backwardness but an adaptation to forest conditions. The hand ax has a long history of development in these areas.

In East and Southeast Asia, simple chopper and chopping tools were used until the end of the Paleolithic. However, it has been suggested that this may be the result of the reliance on materials other than stone, such as bamboo, for tool manufacture.

Similarly, chopping tools and crude flake tools made up the majority of stone artifacts for the natives of Australia. The first inhabitants reached the continent about 35,000 years ago. They found an environment void of big game and

Table 15-6 The Upper Paleolithic of Southwestern France

Divisions of Würm Glaciation	Carbon 14 Dates	Cultural Tradition	
Würm IV	9,500	↑	
Würm III/IV	15,000	Magdalenian ↓	
	17,000	↑	
Würm III	19,000	Solutrean ↓ ↑	↑
		Perigordian	Aurignacian
	29,000		
Würm III/II	32,000	↓	↓
Würm II	37,000	Mousterian	

Adapted from François Bordes, *The Old Stone Age* (New York: McGraw-Hill, 1968), p. 222.

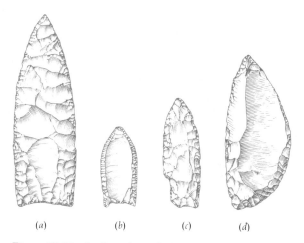

Figure 15-22 Artifacts from the New World. (a) *Clovis point,* (b) *Sandia point,* (c) *Folsom point,* (d) *knife or side scraper from Fell's Cave.*

The Evolution of the Genus Homo

lacking the types of raw materials needed for producing good blade tools. Although they did have resources of bone and wood and made a variety of tools out of these materials, their overall technology was restricted by lack of resources and their isolation from ideas that were developing elsewhere.

The exact date that the New World was first populated is debated. The Bering Strait was once a solid land bridge which at times was more than 1,000 miles wide from north to south. People from Siberia followed big game over the floor of the Bering Sea, which has been dry land several times during the last 100,000 years. However, open land routes were not available during all of this time, and the exact details of migrations have still to be worked out. Figure 15-22 shows some of the tools made by the inhabitants of the Americas, who were contemporaneous with the Upper Paleolithic hunters of the Old World.

Summary

Beginning about 35,000 years ago, all hominid fossils are placed into the subspecies *H. sapiens sapiens*. Fossil finds from this period on are found in all parts of the world, including Australia and North and South America.

In cultural terms, the period between 10,000 and 35,000 years ago in Europe, North Africa, northern Asia, and the Middle East is termed the Upper Paleolithic. The Upper Paleolithic is characterized by an intense exploitation of the large herd animals of the subarctic plains, with a refined technology based upon use of blades and bones as raw materials. Important in this technology is the development of hafting and new projectile implements, such as the spear thrower and, late in the period, the bow and arrow.

The richness of the Upper Paleolithic is seen in the elaboration of art, both in the decoration of utilitarian objects and in what appears to be religious and magical art. Magical art is seen in the many figurines from the period as well as the famous cave paintings of southwestern France.

SUGGESTED READINGS

In addition to the Suggested Readings for Chapter 14:

Chard, C. S. *Man in Prehistory.* New York: McGraw-Hill, 1969. A good general discussion of the Paleolithic.

Editors of Time-Life Books. *The Emergence of Man: The First Men.* New York: Time-Life, 1973. Part of The Emergence of Man series, this volume deals with *H. erectus.*

Shapiro, H. L. *Peking Man.* New York: Simon & Schuster, 1974. The story of the discovery, nature, and loss of the *H. erectus* fossils from Choukoutien.

Solecki, R. S. *Shanidar: The First Flower People.* New York: Knopf, 1971. The story of Solecki's excavation of Neandertal man in Iraq.

Chapter Sixteen

The Continuing Human Story

POST-PLEISTOCENE *HOMO SAPIENS*

The transition from *H. erectus* to *H. sapiens* of the Upper Paleolithic represents a substantial change in form and in technological capabilities. Yet the general mode of subsistence remained basically the same throughout this period. Gathering wild vegetables, hunting wild game, and collecting products of the seas, lakes, and rivers provided the nutritional needs of all Paleolithic populations. Of course, the relative dependence on gathering, hunting, and fishing differed from area to area and from time to time.

Also, during the Pleistocene the functioning group remained small, generally about twenty-five individuals (see Chapter 8), although certain lush local environments allowed for larger numbers. About 10,000 years ago, the nature of people's relationship to their environment and the social and cultural components of their being began to take on new perspectives. These new perspectives, which include larger population densities culminating in the formation of cities, the utilization of new sources of food and work energy, and the development of those social institutions that became elements of civilization, have been looked upon by some as the greatest developments of human evolution and by others as the beginning of the end for the human species.

The Mesolithic

The changes from a hunting and gathering existence to a farming economy did not occur overnight. The dependence on group living, along with the biological and technological developments of all of human evolution, created a potential for new systems of subsistence. This potential began to be expressed at an increased pace in the period between the retreat of the last glaciers and the advent of agricultural communities, a period known as the *Mesolithic*.[1]

[1] The term was originally used in reference to Europe, and difficulties often arise when the concept is used elsewhere.

During the Mesolithic, societies began to utilize the land around them more intensively. The last part of the Upper Paleolithic was characterized by enormous herds of large mammals in the grasslands of Eurasia. However, about 12,000 years ago, climatic changes began to occur which ultimately converted these grasslands into forests. With the advance of the forests came the disappearance of the herds. They were replaced by less abundant and more elusive animals, such as elk, red deer, and wild pigs.

"Man's best friend" In the areas where this forestation had occurred, hunters had to play hide and seek with well-hidden animals. It appears that to their aid came the dog. Juliet Clutton-Brock links the domestication of the dog with the increased pressure of hunting in the dense, dark forests. As discussed in the chapters on primates and the fossil record, the development of refined visual senses in primates was accompanied by a decrease in the sense of smell. The dog's nose seems to have been employed by people to sniff out nonvisible prey. The 9,500-year-old Mesolithic site of Star Carr in England gives the first European evidence for the domestication of the dog.[2]

Aquatic and vegetable resources Along with changes in hunting patterns came an intense exploitation of aquatic resources. Mesolithic sites are often found near seas, lakes, or rivers. A characteristic type of site is the *shell midden,* a large mound composed of shells, which indicates the

[2] J. Clutton-Brock, "The Origins of the Dog," in D. Brothwell and E. Higgs (eds.), *Science in Archeology* (London: Thames and Hudson, 1969), pp. 303–309.

Figure 16-1   Mesolithic artifacts. *Various artifacts from the Mesolithic of Palestine (Natufian), about 8000 ± 500* B.C.

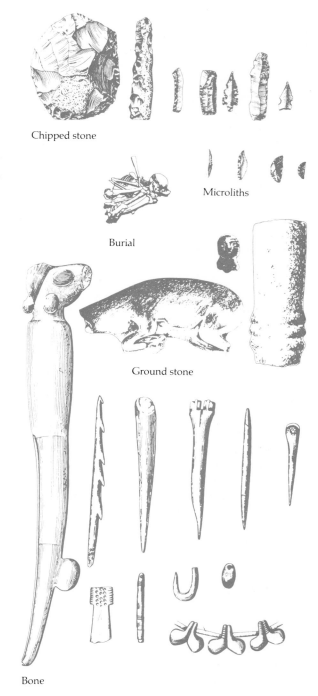

Chipped stone

Microliths

Burial

Ground stone

Bone

emphasis on shellfish as a food resource. Fishing was an important activity, and remains of boats and nets from this period have been recovered. Waterfowl also made up an important part of the diet in many areas.

In addition, people began to exploit the plant resources of their environment intensively. Much of this exploitation was made possible by the development of a technology for processing vegetable foods which cannot be eaten in their natural state. Included here are the milling stone and the mortar and pestle for breaking up seeds and nuts. In Mesolithic sites are found storage and container vessels, which allowed easy handling of small or pulverized foods (Figure 16-1). Out of this utilization of plant resources developed farming.

The origins of agriculture Domestication involves the control of the reproductive cycle of plants and animals. Use of agricultural techniques permits people to plant and harvest large quantities of food in specific areas. In time, people selected the best food-producing plants to breed. Domestication thus led to speciation initiated by humans, which over the centuries has created new types of plants. It is not our purpose here to explore the many theories of the origins of plant domestication, but it should be noted that agriculture probably was not a deliberate invention. It arose from an intensive utilization and dependence upon plant material, which developed out of Mesolithic economies.

Plant and animal domestication developed in the Middle East and in areas of Mexico and Peru. Domestication occurred in these two areas independently of each other and perhaps in Southeast Asia and West Africa as well.

The development of agriculture has been seen as the great revolution leading to modern civilization. It must be emphasized that agriculture was a revolution in potential only. Many hunting and gathering peoples rejected agriculture because it would have represented a decline in their

standard of living. Richard B. Lee notes that even in a semiarid region during a drought, the food supply of the Bushman is reliable and plentiful.[3] It is the farming and pastoral communities which suffer the most in such times.

The Neolithic

Ultimately, sometimes over a period of thousands of years and sometimes very quickly, food production came to dominate hunting and gathering in many parts of the world. With farming came the development of a new way of life — life in the village, the stage of human history known as the *Neolithic*.

The Neolithic was a time of great change in both technology and social organization. By producing food in one place rather than searching it out, societies could develop a more settled pattern of existence. Farming meant that more food could be acquired in less space, and population densities could increase. This, in turn, led to the interaction of greater numbers of people and hence to a greater degree of exchange of ideas and an increase in innovation, which is dependent on such exchanges.

The Neolithic was characterized by the elaboration of tool types dealing with food preparation, such as querns, milling stones, and mortars and pestles. Pottery, used only rarely by non-farming peoples, became refined and varied. The techniques of weaving and spinning cloth also were developed (Figure 16-2).

Most Neolithic villages were small, self-sufficient farming communities. However, during the Neolithic, many of the technological and social systems that would later be important in the first civilizations were being developed. This

[3] R. B. Lee, "What Hunters Do for a Living, or How to Make Out on Scarce Resources," in R. B. Lee and I. DeVore (eds.), *Man the Hunter* (Chicago: Aldine, 1968), pp. 30–48.

can be seen at the settlement of Çatal Hüyük in Turkey, dating from 8,500 to 7,700 years ago.[4]

Timber, obsidian, marble, stalactites, and shells were all imported. Skillfully made artifacts

[4] See L. Mellaart, "A Neolithic City in Turkey," *Scientific American*, 210 (April 1964), 94–104.

attest to the development of occupational specialization at Çatal Hüyük. Wooden bowls and boxes, jewelry, bone awls, daggers, spearheads, lance heads, arrowheads, ladles, spoons, spatulas, hooks and pins, and obsidian mirrors, as well as other beautifully made objects, make for a rich material inventory. The residents of Çatal Hüyük lived in plastered mud brick houses contiguous to

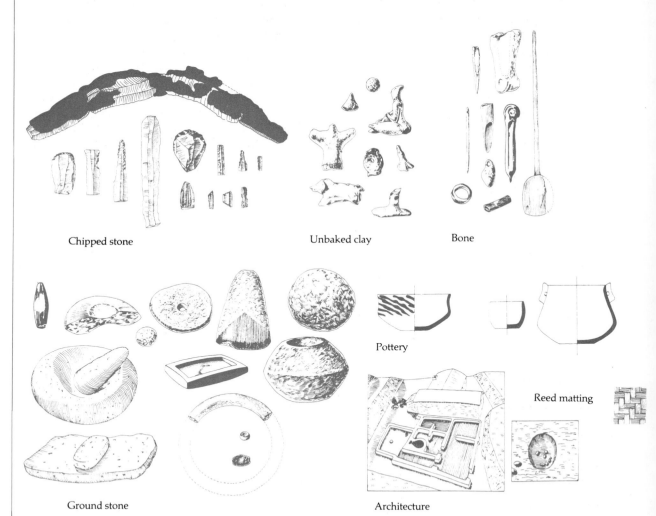

Chipped stone

Unbaked clay

Bone

Ground stone

Pottery

Reed matting

Architecture

Figure 16-2 Neolithic artifacts. *Various artifacts from the Neolithic site of Jarmo, Iraq (about 6750 ± 200 B.C.).*

each other and entered from the roof. The walls were painted with murals depicting animals, hunters, and dancers, and statues portrayed gods and goddesses as well as cattle. Much of this art has been interpreted as having religious significance.

The Development of Civilization

There are many thoughts on the origins of civilization. One of the major factors involved was the increase in population (Table 16-1). The development of techniques, primarily irrigation and flood control, which permitted agriculture in special areas such as the flood plain of the Tigris and Euphrates rivers, made possible the support of large populations. Once populations reach a certain number, the older pattern of social organiza-

tion breaks down and new ones develop. Specifically the older system, whereby each individual participated in food production and maintained a similar standard of living and whereby kinship served as the basic method of social organization, was replaced by the occupational division of labor, political and religious hierarchies, public works such as road and public building construction, class systems, codes of law, markets, new forms of warfare, and urban centers. Allied with these important sociological traits are material traits, such as monumental architecture and the development of science and, in many cases, metallurgy and writing systems.

The earliest civilization, Sumer, developed in the Middle East. This was the *Bronze Age* of the Old World, during which time people first developed the art of metallurgy. Civilizations also arose

Table 16-1   Human Population Growth*

Years Ago (from 1970)	Years Elapsed	World Population (thousands)	Comment
1,000,000		125	
300,000	700,000	1,000	
10,000	290,000	5,320	Domestication begins
6,000	4,000	86,500	
2,000	4,000	133,000	
220	1,790	728,000	Industrialization
70	150	1,610,000	Medical "revolution"
20	50	2,400,000	
10	10	3,000,000	
0 (the present)	10	3,632,000	
Year 2000†	30	5,400,000	

Note: (1) It took 700,000 years to reach the first million from a population of 125,000. (2) It took only 20 years (1950–1970) for an increase of more than 1 billion to take place. (3) Although the rate of population growth has slowed, it is estimated that between 1970 and 2000 about 1¾ billion people will be added to the world population.

* Data from Edward S. Deevey, Jr., "The Human Population," *Scientific American,* September 1960. Copyright © 1960 by Scientific American, Inc. All rights reserved.

† Projection for year 2000 based on a study by L. R. Brown of the Worldwatch Institute and reported by J. H. Douglas, "The Slowing Growth of World Population," *Science News,* 110 (13 November 1976), 316–317.

in other parts of the Old World, first in Egypt, China, and India, and later in Europe and Africa. At this time, civilization also developed independently in the New World, in the Mexican area, in Peru and its adjacent areas.

In the Old World the Bronze Age was followed by the *Iron Age,* which saw the rise and fall of great empires and the shift of power from the Middle East to Greece and Rome and then to western Europe. In the 1700s the *Industrial Age* began, leading directly to the modern civilizations of today.

Urbanization

Cities first arose about 5,000 years ago. However, they were small and represented nuclei for predominantly rural agricultural societies. *Urbanization* refers to the rise in the proportion of people living in cities in comparison to those who are rural. Although early urban centers were economically important, major urbanization did not occur in any part of the world until the end of the nineteenth century and is correlated with the rise of industrialism. It was the economic changes of industrialism which led to the migration of rural populations to the cities. An *urbanized society* is usually defined as one in which a majority of the people live in cities. Kingsley Davis states, "Before 1850 no society could be described as predominantly urbanized, and by 1900 only one, Great Britain, could be so regarded."[5]

Today, the story has changed greatly. As much as 70 percent of the United States is urban, about 65 percent of northwestern and central Europe, 47 percent of South America, and 45 percent of the USSR. If the present rate of urbanization remains the same, by 1990 more than 50 percent of the world's population will be living in cities of 100,000 or more.[6]

Most people who write about the consequences of urbanization do not realize how recent major urbanization is. One school of thought maintains that urbanization is a natural consequence of human evolution. John Buettner-Janusch poses the question, "Is there anything in the known archaeological sequence that enables us to determine whether adaptations for urban life developed in man's evolutionary history?" He answers his question by saying, "I believe the answer is affirmative."[7] There is no doubt that humans have a degree of preadaptation to city life and that in many ways the city has allowed for the expression of social systems not possible in rural or hunting and gathering societies. However, it would be a mistake to say that humans have developed or are developing a high selective fitness for city life.

Natural selection for most of human evolutionary history was operating on a hunting and gathering existence. In the last 10,000 years, selective pressures associated with farming have been having their effect. The relationship of sickle-cell anemia to farming and lactose tolerance to dairying have already been discussed in this light (Chapters 6 and 8). Urbanization is a phenomenon chiefly of the twentieth century. Some parts of the world have been urban for three to four generations, but urbanization for most of the world has been much more recent. There simply has not been sufficient time for a close fit to urban situations to occur. Also, the nature of urban environments has changed greatly even in this short time.

Mutations occur, natural selection works, and

---

[5] K. Davis, "The Urbanization of the Human Population," *Scientific American,* 213 (September 1965), 41.

[6] Ibid., pp. 41, 45.

[7] J. Buettner-Janusch, *Physical Anthropology: A Perspective* (New York: Wiley, 1973), p. 520.

drift and nonrandom mating operate in urban situations. Therefore, evolution is occurring in cities; this evolution may be different from that which is occurring in agricultural areas. These forces produce two basic results: survival (adaptation) or extinction. Extinction has been the most frequent result of evolution. It is premature to say how the conditions of urbanization will affect humankind. However, in the next few pages, we will present some of the data and ideas about the effects of both urbanization and industrialization on our evolution. Since all industrial societies today are highly urbanized, the term *industrial society* will be used to denote societies engaging in manufacturing, commerce, and services whose populations are largely urban.

Industrial societies and mutation With industrialism has come the use and development of physical and chemical materials that are known or suspected to cause mutation. Among these are many of the chemicals added to foods and used in medicines or for insect control. These elements, along with induced radiation, were discussed in Chapter 4. The long-term effect of the increase in mutagenic substances on human evolution is unknown. An increase in the rate of mutations might increase the genetic load of industrial societies. This, along with the fact that persons with genetic diseases can today survive to reproduce, could lower the general viability of a population.

Any increase in deleterious mutations within a population will cause human suffering. However, the benefits of the substances causing mutation may outweigh the suffering; some of them, such as the proper medical use of x-rays, have lengthened lives. Many things that can be harmful in one sense are beneficial in others. As Curt Stern says, "When, in prehistoric times, fire was made to serve human purposes it introduced a new danger which, in spite of extensive safeguards, still kills and maims many people every year."[8] Although mutagenic substances are not directly analogous to fire, further research is needed to determine whether mutagens of the industrial environment will balance out to be advantageous or destructive in our future.

Industrial societies and sampling error Sampling error is a phenomenon of small population size. As discussed in earlier chapters, genetic drift would easily occur in societies consisting of small bands. It would be hard to show that genetic drift is occurring in large urban centers. However, drift still would occur within small religious or ethnic isolates within the city. The founder effect is also limited in industrial societies. For example, when small groups left the cities to establish communes in the 1960s, they did not remain closed; new people entered and some of the original "settlers" left.

Industrial societies and nonrandom mating Industrial societies are characterized by both physical and social mobility. In the past 150 years, the invention of trains, individual motor vehicles, and aircraft has increased the ease with which people can travel intermediate and long distances. Such movement is important in industrial societies, in which jobs often become available in distant locations. In the last decades, for example, large numbers of engineers were needed in areas where the aerospace and automotive industries were developing. There were large movements of engineers to those areas. "This mobility has had the effect of widening the group among which the choice of mates is made and destroying or limiting previous isolation."[9]

---

[8] C. Stern, *Principles of Human Genetics,* 3d ed. (San Francisco: Freeman, 1973), p. 632.

[9] L. L. Cavalli-Sforza and W. F. Bodmer, *The Genetics of Human Populations* (San Francisco: Freeman, 1971), p. 784.

L. L. Cavalli-Sforza and W. F. Bodmer have listed the following genetic consequences of such mobility. First, there has been a tendency for "hybrid" groups to develop from populations once widely separated. Second, there has been a general decrease in genetic isolates, with an accompanying decrease in inbreeding (there are exceptions to this). Third, there also may be an increase in the number of heterozygotes when genetic isolates break down. Fourth, mating which now can take place in a larger group may become more selective and hence increase the probability of assortative mating.[10]

Once people become settled in an area, mates are often chosen from within a very close radius. As mentioned in Chapter 8, more than half of urban marriages in the last twenty years have been between people who lived less than a mile apart when they were married. The important thing is that the population density of a large city can be very high. For 1960 the following estimates of population density per square mile were calculated: Tokyo, 20,000; New York City, 25,000; and Manhattan, 75,000.[11] So, even within a small distance many potential mates are available in a large city. Also, because of mobility, the people who live close to you at the present may have diverse origins. Even though urbanites may choose their mates from among people living closer to them than members of hunting and gathering societies, the chances of marrying someone of a different ethnic background are, of course, vastly greater.

Industrial societies and differential fertility
With each environmental or cultural shift come new selective pressures and new fitness values for the potential genotypes of a population. The

[10] Ibid., pp. 784–785.

[11] P. R. Ehrlich and A. H. Ehrlich. *Population, Resources and Environment* (San Francisco: Freeman, 1970), p. 34.

processes of industrialism and urbanization have created many selective situations not found in farming or hunting and gathering societies. We will discuss only two of these: the spread of disease and pollution.

For most of human history, people have lived in small groups on sparsely populated continents. With the rapid growth of populations has come the spread of certain types of disease. Disease organisms are parasites that must move from host to host in order to propagate. If a small hunting camp was infected by a viral disease, most of the members who contracted the disease would either die or get well before coming into contact with another group. But in a crowded situation, disease can travel very rapidly from one person to the next. This can be seen in the rapid spread of flu epidemics around the world in recent times.

The disease can act as a selective agent. People more resistant to its effects will survive at a higher rate than others who are less resistant.

Pollution of various types—air, water, thermal, and noise, for instance—may also be creating differential mortality in industrial societies. The hunter-gatherer who moved camp usually left his garbage behind. However, as people began to build cities, not only did the population increase but so did the amount and persistence of filth and the levels of noise. The first urban centers also had a number of types of pollution. By at least 5,000 years ago, air pollution had started ravaging urbanites' lungs. It is known that at this time crude oil was being burned. In 1167 the army of Frederick Barbarossa found that the air of Rome "had become densely laden with pestilence and death." British kings of the Middle Ages decreed that polluting the air by burning coal was punishable by death. The industrial age ushered in new toxins for the atmosphere; more recently, the automobile has created a brownish haze hanging over the populations of many cities throughout the world (Figure 16-3).

What are the biological effects of smog? Ac-

Figure 16-3   Smog.

Table 16-2   Major Air-Pollution Episodes

Date	Place	Excess Deaths*
Feb. 1880	London, England	1,000
Dec. 1930	Meuse Valley, Belgium	63
Oct. 1948	Donora, Pa., United States	20
Nov. 1950	Poca Rica, Mexico	22
Dec. 1952	London, England	4,000
Nov. 1953	New York, United States	250
Jan. 1956	London, England	1,000
Dec. 1957	London, England	700–800
Dec. 1962	London, England	700
Jan./Feb. 1963	New York, United States	200–400
Nov. 1966	New York, United States	168

From Wilfrid Bach, *Atmospheric Pollution.* Copyright 1972 by McGraw-Hill Book Company. Used with permission of McGraw-Hill Book Company.

* Number of deaths above normal.

cording to the Surgeon General of the United States, air pollution from the automobile contains several extremely dangerous *pathogens.*[12] For example, one study showed that families living in areas of high nitrogen dioxide had a respiratory illness rate 18.8 percent greater than families living in relatively unpolluted areas. Children showed harmful effects of air pollution by the second grade.[13] In addition, such substances in smog as carbon monoxide, ozone, aldehydes, sulfates, and lead and nitrogen oxides are known to cause degeneration of the optic nerve, hearing impairment, skin disease, eye irritation, asthma attacks, bronchitis and emphysema, and headaches.[14]

[12] H. E. Hilleboe and G. W. Larimore (eds.), *Preventive Medicine,* 2d ed. (Philadelphia: Saunders, 1965), p. 74.

[13] C. M. Shy et al., "Chattanooga School Children Study: Effects of Community Exposure to Nitrogen Dioxide," *Journal of the Air Pollution Control Association,* 20 (1970), 539–545.

[14] Hilleboe and Larimore, op. cit.

Many substances contained in smog are known to be cancer-producing agents. In regard to cancer, a study done in New York has shown that "the lung cancer death rate for men over forty-five in the smoggiest part of Staten Island, New York, is 55 per 100,000. In a less smoggy area just a few miles away, the rate is 40 per 100,000.[15] Through such comparative data, it can be inferred that smog is a major contributing cause of death. Occasionally, when the level of smog builds up to unusually high levels, its effect can be even more dramatically seen. Table 16-2 shows several instances of a rise in the death rate correlated with an air-pollution episode.

The high population density in cities also has created problems of water pollution. In addition, the methods used to feed these large populations have created soils saturated with insecticides which eventually find their way into lakes, rivers, and oceans. Nuclear power plants spill boiling water into the ocean, causing thermal pollution.

As has been stressed in previous chapters, the precise effects of pollutants on human evolution are unknown. We do know that smog kills or contributes to the death of an increasing number of people. It is likely that pollutants affect some people more severely than others. Selective pressures are often very subtle. A shift of even a fraction of a percent in the fitness value of a genotype may lead to a major shift in gene frequencies over the generations.

Another major problem of modern life is noise. Noise is measured in decibels (*deci* means "ten," and *bel* is named after Alexander Graham Bell). The scale is a logarithmic one, which compresses very large differences into workable numbers. Thus, a 120-decibel sound is a trillion times the intensity of a sound on the threshold of hearing (Table 16-3). The city is an extremely noisy

[15] Ehrlich and Ehrlich, op. cit., p. 122.

place; and with each new roadway and each additional airplane route, it becomes noisier.

The consequences of extremely loud sound can be quite dramatic. The most obvious effect is the loss of hearing. Levels of noise about 80 decibels present dangers to hearing, and much city noise can far exceed that. The result can be seen in the fact that the hearing of Manhattanites in their twenties is often no better than that of rural agriculturalists in their seventies.[16]

Besides causing hearing loss, loud noises can cause anxiety and stress. Noise can initiate changes in the hormonal content of the blood, which results in the increased rate of heartbeat, constriction of blood vessels, increase in blood pressure, and digestive spasms. These events no doubt produce a wide range of physiological damage. There is also evidence that excessive and persistent noise can produce frustration and irritability that disturb social interaction and hence cut down on the efficiency of a social group attempting to accomplish some task.[17] Like chemical pollutants, noise may act as a selective agent; however, this can only be speculation at this time.

Industrialism and social deprivation Urbanization means that an increasing number of people live in crowded situations. Anthropologists, sociologists, and psychologists have been studying crowding and its possible effects on the biological and social characteristics of people. Unfortunately, architects and city planners usually have little knowledge of this research and construct

[16] A. Turk et al., *Ecology, Pollution, Environment* (Philadelphia: Saunders, 1972), p. 198.

[17] J. Smolensky and F. B. Haar, *Principles of Community Health*, 3d ed. (Philadelphia: Saunders, 1972), pp. 358–359. One study showed that steelworkers working in the noisiest part of a plant had a greater frequency of social conflicts at home and at work than did those working in quieter areas.

Table 16-3 Noise Levels (numbers in decibels)

Danger to Hearing	Moderately Loud	Quiet	Very Quiet	Barely Audible
180 Rocket engine				
150 Jet plane at takeoff				
125 Rock and roll music				
120 Thunder				
100 Heavy automobile traffic				
80 Garbage disposal				
	70 Vacuum cleaner			
	60 Normal conversation			
	50 Light traffic noise			
	100 feet away			
		45 Home		
			30 Soft whisper	
			20 Leaves rustling	
				10 Normal breathing
				1 Threshold of hearing

buildings and plan cities with little consideration of the cultural and social dimensions of the people who will live in them.[18] There is some encouragement that this condition is gradually changing for the better.

Much of the direct evidence of the biological effect of crowding has been gained from the study of nonhuman animals. With humans, the cultural dimension, which is absent or developed to a much smaller degree in the animals studied, must not be forgotten, for it has mediated many of the effects of crowding. However, with this caution in mind, we will look at the results of one of the more famous experiments on crowding.

This experiment was conducted by John B. Calhoun using domesticated white rats.[19] He built several rooms, dividing each one by electrified fences into four pens which were connected by ramps. Pens 1 and 4 were not connected, so that what he actually had was four pens in a row which he folded to save space. Windows cut in the top permitted the animals to be observed.

In one experiment, Calhoun placed one or two pregnant females in each pen and permitted the offspring to reproduce without human interference. As time went on, the population increased until it reached a population density twice that which had been observed to produce maximum stress in a wild colony. At this point a *behavioral sink* — a psychological state characterized by gross distortions of behavior — developed. The two end pens, each inhabited by a dominant male and a number of females, remained undisturbed, but the two center pens, which were intensely crowded, showed the development of this sink.

Without discussing this sink in detail, we will list a few of the abnormalities. A stable dominance hierarchy failed to develop, and territories were not respected. Hyperactive males would chase females and mount nonreceptive females and males. Many males simply withdrew from social and sexual intercourse. The mothers failed to complete the building of nests, so that the young became scattered. Many were eaten or simply stepped on. Only one-fourth of the young born survived to be weaned. The females suffered a high mortality rate, and pregnant females had a high rate of miscarriage. Aggressive behavior was generally increased.

Similar results have been found with other animals. Coypu (a South American aquatic rodent) colonies died out under crowded conditions. Examination of their adrenal cortexes "suggested that crowding stress had triggered overproduction of adrenal hormones, indirectly causing group death."[20]

Crowding has also been observed to have adverse effects on populations of deer, rabbits, and ducks.[21] Each species reacts somewhat differently to crowding. With humans, the general cultural background of a people affects the distance required between individuals both in direct interpersonal relationships and between dwellings and public buildings. The study of human perception and use of space in communication and social relations is called *proxemics*. One researcher in this area, Edward T. Hall, generalized that:

People of different ethnic origins need different kinds of spaces, for there are those who like to touch and those who do not. There are those who want to be auditorially involved with everybody else (like the Italians), and those who depend

[18] E. T. Hall, "Human Needs and Inhuman Cities," *Ekistics,* 27 (1969), 181–184.

[19] J. B. Calhoun, "A Behavioral Sink," in E. L. Bliss (ed.), *Roots of Behavior* (New York: Harper, 1962, chap. 22), and "Population Density and Social Pathology," *Scientific American,* 206 (February 1962), 139–146.

[20] E. Stoll, "Crowding," *The Sciences,* 11 (October 1971), 7.

[21] Ibid., 7, 28.

upon architecture to screen them from the rest of the world (like the Germans).[22]

City planning very seldom takes into consideration the spatial needs of the various ethnic groups. This can lead to a feeling of frustration and, hence, to stress and the "overtime working" of the adrenals.[23]

Frustration associated with crowding can originate from sources other than spatial relationships. For instance, the riots of the 1960s appear to have been at least partially initiated by a frustration of expectations: ". . . ambitious blue-collar blacks were unable to attain the middle-class prosperity flaunted by the mass media."[24] In addition, some groups of people can tolerate a greater amount of mobility than others. For instance, "very poor, uneducated people have a much lower tolerance for being displaced than people of the middle class. Even a move across the street can be traumatic because it alters the pattern of social relationships."[25]

The point is that cities, in addition to being high-pollution areas, also seem to be failing to serve people's social and cultural needs. This is shown in the flow of people out of cities into suburban areas and in the crime rates of cities. In cities with more than 250,000 people, the total crime rate is five times greater than in rural areas, with violent crimes eleven times greater.[26] Whether these problems of the city can be solved will depend on active experimentation with new methods of city planning that take into consideration the biological and social needs of city dwellers. At this time, such experimentation is

proceeding at a much slower rate than the increase in urban problems.

Urbanization and the ecosystem Most men and women in hunting and gathering societies are involved in food-getting activities, as are children from a young age. The same is basically true in farming societies in relationship to food production. In the city, the story is quite different. Most adults know little about the steps that result in bringing food to the table. Perhaps the most dangerous thing about city living is that it isolates the majority of the people from the ecosystems that support the city. It is not enough for the farmers in an industrial society to know the requirements of food production and the biologists to know the structure and dynamics of food chains and energy pyramids (see Chapter 1). An uninformed citizenry could allow the annihilation of the biological communities and natural resources that permit its existence through destructive legislation and a lack of proper controls. This lack of knowledge has already led to mass destruction of environments through pollution and improper resource management. We must realize quickly that many resources are finite and that a healthy ecosystem is needed if extinction is not to be a real and imminent danger.

In conclusion, urban *H. sapiens* is still biologically and socially evolving. Yet, the selective pressures created by technology and social change are multiplying and intensifying faster than our social institutions are dealing with them. It appears that humans may not have the potential to adapt biologically to their own technological and urban environments.

WILL THERE BE A NEXT MILLION YEARS?
Since modern evolutionary theory originated, people have wondered what is in store for the species in the future. Some have said that we will lose all of our hair and develop hooves, or

[22] Hall, op. cit., 183.

[23] Ibid., 181.

[24] Stoll, op. cit., 30.

[25] Hall, op. cit., 183.

[26] Stoll, op. cit., 30.

414

that our legs will degenerate from lack of use. The type of thinking behind these hypotheses is not only illogical but could be dangerous in the search for the solutions to contemporary problems. It is similar to the Lamarckian theory of evolution of the nineteenth century. The assumption is that when something becomes unnecessary, it will disappear; whereas when something becomes necessary, it will materialize. For instance, it might be reasoned that body hair will totally disappear because clothes can take its place. This type of thinking becomes dangerous when it is applied to something like smog, for example, where it is maintained that smog is not dangerous to humanity because people will simply develop lungs that can cope with it.

Evolution does not proceed by way of necessity or the lack of it. A trait will appear only if there is genetic potential for it and that potential expresses itself. The chance that any particular new trait will appear, and appear at the right time and in the right place, is infinitely small and not to be depended upon. Likewise, a trait will disappear only if it is selected against or diminishes because of random genetic drift. If it is selectively neutral, there will be no reason for it to vanish. Hair will not become more scarce unless the *lack* of hair has selective advantage over the retention of it. Lungs will not adapt to smog unless mutations occur that would allow this to happen, and *there is no reason to believe that this will happen*. Taking into account the ingredients of smog at high concentrations, extinction is a greater possibility.

Science provides no crystal balls. The anthropologist or other researcher cannot say what the human form will be in the future. We cannot predict random change or the effects that unknown environmental conditions of the future will have on the genetic material. However, there are some absolutes — existence or nonexistence, for instance. Since we know some of the requirements of life and some of the conditions that can

cause extinction, it is possible — and wise — to examine the chances we have for survival.

Human continuance depends on the realization of policymakers that certain conditions must exist for survival. First, it must be recognized that certain resources are nonreplenishable — for example, fossil fuels such as coal and oil or natural gases such as helium. Once they run out, there will be no guarantee of a substitute. Second, it is important to understand that the earth is a container with the ground acting as the bottom and the atmosphere as the sides and lid. Pollution pumped into the ground, water, and air is often trapped there. We reside in that container and depend on the conditions that exist within it. Third, the earth has a finite amount of space. Humans cannot occupy all of that space. The things they depend on for food and environmental stability must also have room to exist.

There are solutions to these problems. The first is population control. As seen in Table 16-1, the human species could eventually crowd everything else off the earth at its present rate of growth. Of course, before that could happen, widespread disease, mass starvation, and other catastrophic events would come into play. An increase in starvation occurred in many areas of the world because of crop failures in 1972 and 1975. As many as 1 million people died in India as a result of the 1972 decline in grain production.[27]

It appears that many of the world's governments have at least begun to tackle the problem of population growth. "In just five years the proportion of people living in countries where abortion is legal has jumped from a little over one-third of the world to nearly two-thirds."[28] Other

[27] J. H. Douglas, "The Slowing Growth of World Population," *Science News*, 110 (13 November 1976), 317.

[28] Ibid.

mechanisms of population control are being encouraged or actively enforced by different governments. These include male sterilization after a specified number of children have been born and economic or other social punishments for people who have what is defined by the country in question as too many children.

Many other factors are now working to slow the rate of population increase. In some countries such as the United States people are tending to marry later and have fewer children, more women are choosing careers other than motherhood, and general economic factors are making it difficult for large families to meet their basic needs. The widespread use of contraceptives has also had a major effect. The United Nations predictions made in 1970 of a world population of about 6.5 billion by the year 2000 has been reestimated by one researcher and set at 5.4 billion.[29] Although this is encouraging news, the increasing death rate from starvation suggests "that time has already run out for millions of people."[30]

Along with population control, people must learn to use resources better, recycling those which are scarce. Also, people must use their technological knowledge to prevent, not create, environmental deterioration. On July 10, 1976, in Seveso, Italy, an environmental catastrophe occurred that may help to focus world attention on the lethal potential of modern technology. As much as 60 kilograms (132 pounds) of dioxin escaped from a chemical plant. Just "three ounces (of dioxin) in New York's water supply would be enough to wipe out the entire city."[31] Hundreds of animals in the area died, and hundreds of people were treated for skin rashes and internal ailments. The contaminated area was evacuated, and some scientists believe that it cannot be decontaminated; it may become a pollution-created desert.[32]

Publicity about the above incident, massive pollution of bodies of water, recent nuclear accidents, the alteration of the earth's ozone layer, and other potentially cataclysmic tamperings with the ecosystem have at least focused some concern on environmental programs. Yet, whether the concern is great enough and whether we have the technology to deal with the negative effects of our technology is questionable. The willingness to attack these problems has generally not been very vigorous. At this time, the outlook for the human species appears dismal.

THE APPLICATION OF ANTHROPOLOGICAL KNOWLEDGE

The knowledge gained through anthropological investigation is not purely academic. The study of genetics has aided in building theories of inheritance that have been important in recognizing, treating, and—through counseling—preventing genetic disease. In this light, research into genetics and general evolutionary theory has awakened people to the dangers of increasing the genetic load by arresting a disease without curing it.

Studies of human variation have put these variations into an empirical perspective instead of one based on social and biological myths. This has very definitely affected policy making as well as the ideas held by the educated public. In fact, the works of an early anthropologist, Franz Boas, were extensively cited in the historic 1954 U.S. Supreme Court decision that ended racial segre-

[29] Ibid., pp. 316–317.

[30] Ibid., p. 316.

[31] M. S. Davis, "Under the Poison Cloud," *The New York Times Magazine* (10 October 1976), 20.

[32] Ibid.

gation legally in the United States. Anthropological studies have shown that the tendency of some groups within our society to score lower on IQ tests is due to social deprivation and environmental deterioration as well as to cultural bias in the tests themselves, rather than to supposed innate differences. This has been realized by some educators and administrators, and we hope that the implementation of policies aimed at correcting these situations will increase the standard of living for everyone.

Anthropology is an ecological discipline. One of the main contributions of anthropology has been to investigate our relationships with our environment. From these studies, it has become clear that people, like all animals, must maintain the proper balance with nature. Our great potential for cultural behavior provides adaptive flexibility but is limited; and if this potential is used carelessly, it could create a sterile environment.

The study of our closest relatives, the primates, and of evolutionary history has provided a multidimensional picture of human nature. Through these anthropological studies, many current biological and social problems, such as those that arise in urban situations, are put into understandable perspectives for which solutions can be sought.

SUGGESTED READINGS

Clark, J. D. *Aspects of Prehistory*. Berkeley: Univ. of California Press, 1970.

Mellaart, J. *Earliest Civilizations of the Near East*. New York: McGraw-Hill, 1966.

Piggott, S. (ed.). *The Dawn of Civilization*. New York: McGraw-Hill, 1961.

Woolley, L. *Excavations at Ur*. New York: Crowell, 1965.

The above volumes discuss the early cities and early civilizations.

Bodley, J. H. *Anthropology and Contemporary Human Problems*. Menlo Park: Cummings, 1976. This book considers current problems such as natural resource depletion, war, hunger, population growth, and attempts to put them into an anthropological perspective.

Ehrlich, P. R., and A. H. Ehrlich. *Population, Resources, Environment*. San Francisco: Freeman, 1970. An excellent survey of the current crises of overpopulation, resource depletion, and pollution.

Hardin, G. *Population, Evolution, and Birth Control*, 2d ed. San Francisco: Freeman, 1969. An interesting presentation of articles on subjects of controversy and importance in our understanding of ourselves and the earth that we must not abuse.

Scientific American, 213 (September 1965). The entire volume consists of articles on the city. Problems dealt with include the origins and growth of cities, as well as the social and biological conditions found within them.

Scientific American, 224 (September 1971). The entire volume deals with energy, including discussions of the flow of energy in societies at different technological levels.

Acknowledgments

Figure 1-1   Courtesy of Roy J. Pence, Department of Entomology, University of California, Los Angeles.

Figure 1-2   Reprinted with the permission of Hill and Wang, a division of Farrar, Straus & Giroux, Inc., from *Kalahari* by Jens Bjerre. © translation copyright 1960 by Michael Joseph, Ltd.

Figure 1-4   From *Science of Biology* by Paul Weisz. Copyright 1963 by McGraw-Hill Book Company. Used with permission of McGraw-Hill Book Company.

Figure 1-5   From *Fundamentals of Ecology,* 3d ed., by Eugene P. Odum. Copyright 1971 by W. B. Saunders Company. Used with permission of W. B. Saunders Company and Eugene P. Odum.

Figure 2-1   Ansel Adams, Magnum.

Figure 2-2   Photograph by Dodie Stoneburner.

Figure 3-1   From Wilhelm Strohmayer, "Die Vererbung des Habsburger Familientypus," *Nova Acta Leopoldina,* 5 (1937). Used with permission of Prof. Dr. Joachim-Hermann Scharf, Director Ephemeridum, Deutschen Akademie der Naturforscher, Leopoldina.

Figure 3-5   Courtesy of The National Foundation, March of Dimes.

Figure 4-1   Carolina Biological Supply Company.

Figures 4-2, 4-3, 4-8a, 4-10   Bio-Science Laboratories, Van Nuys, California.

Figure 4-4   Courtesy of the Medical Research Council, Clinical and Population Cytogenetics Unit, Western General Hospital, Edinburgh.

Figures 4-7, 4-17   From *Principles of Human Genetics,* 3d ed., by Curt Stern. W. H. Freeman and Company. Copyright © 1973.

Figure 4-8b   Courtesy of The National Foundation, March of Dimes.

Figure 4-14   From V. McKussick, *Mendelian Inheritance in Man.* Copyright © 1966, 1968, 1971, 1975 by The Johns Hopkins University Press, Baltimore.

Figure 4-16   From M. C. G. Israëls, et al., "Haemophilia in the Female," *The Lancet,* 260 (30 June 1951). Used with permission of M. C. G. Israëls.

Figure 4-21   From Johannes A. G. Rhodin, *An Atlas of Ultrastructure,* 1963. Copyright 1963 by W. B. Saunders Company.

Figure 4-23   Courtesy of P. Farnsworth.

Figure 5-2a   From J. G. Carlson, "Analysis of X-Ray Induced Single Breaks in Neuroblast Chromosomes of the Grasshopper," *Proceedings of The National Academy of Science,* 27 (1941). Used with permission of The National Academy of Science.

Figure 5-2b   From C. E. Purdom, *Genetic Effects of Radiation.* Copyright 1963 by Academic Press, Inc. Used with permission of Academic Press, Inc., and C. E. Purdom.

Figure 5-3 From L. L. Cavalli-Sforza, "Genetic Drift in an Italian Population," *Scientific American* (August 1969). Copyright © 1969 by Scientific American, Inc. All rights reserved.

Figure 6-1 Based on data from A. H. Booth, "Observations on the Natural History of the Olive Colobus Monkey, *Procolobus verus* (van Beneden)," *Proceedings of the Zoological Society of London,* 129 (1957). Used with permission of The Zoological Society of London.

Figure 6-3 From the experiments of Dr. H. B. D. Kettlewell, University of Oxford. Used with permission of Dr. H. B. D. Kettlewell.

Figure 6-5 Data from C. A. Clarke, "Blood Groups and Disease," *Progress in Medical Genetics,* vol. 1, Grune and Stratton, 1961. By permission of Grune and Stratton and C. A. Clarke.

Figure 6-7 From John Buettner-Janusch, *Origins of Man.* Copyright 1966 by John Wiley & Sons, Inc. Used with permission of John Wiley & Sons, Inc.

Figure 6-11 From William Elkin, "Reproductive Behaviors," in William Elkin (ed.), *Social Behavior and Organization among Vertebrates.* Copyright © 1964 by The University of Chicago Press. Used with permission.

Figures 6-12, 6-13 From David Lack, *Darwin's Finches,* 1947. Used with permission of Cambridge University Press.

Figure 7-1a, c Culver Pictures, Inc.

Figure 7-1b The Bettmann Archive, Inc.

Figure 7-2a, b, d, e, f Courtesy of The American Museum of Natural History.

Figure 7-2c Smithsonian Institution. National Anthropological Archives.

Figure 7-3 Photographs by Rick Freed.

Figure 7-4 From Morton Klass and Hal Hellman, *The Kinds of Mankind.* Copyright © 1971 by Morton Klass and Hal Hellman. Reproduced by permission of J. B. Lippincott Company.

Figure 7-5 From A. E. Mourant, A. C. Kopeć, and K. Domaniewska-Sobczak, *The Distribution of the Human Blood Groups and Other Polymorphisms,* 2d ed. (London: Oxford University Press, 1976). Used with permission of Oxford University Press.

Figure 7-6 From E. Sunderland, "Hair-Colour Variation in the United Kingdom," *Annals of Human Genetics,* 21 (1955–1956). Used by permission of Cambridge University Press.

Figure 8-1 Reprinted from C. F. Küchemann, A. J. Boyce, and G. A. Harrison, "A Demographic and Genetic Study of a Group of Oxfordshire Villages," *Human Biology,* 39 (1967). By permission of The Wayne State University Press and the authors. Copyright 1967 by Wayne State University Press.

Figure 8-2 Photograph by Philip L. Stein.

Figure 8-3 Reprinted with permission of Macmillan Publishing Co., Inc., from C. Loring Brace and M. F. Ashley Montagu, *Man's Evolution.* Copyright © 1965 by M. F. Ashley Montagu and C. Loring Brace.

Figure 8-4a Courtesy of The American Museum of Natural History.

Figure 8-4b Courtesy of D. F. Roberts, The University of Newcastle-upon-Tyne, England.

Figure 8-5 Adapted from N. L. Petrakis, "Evidence for a Genetic Cline in Earwax Types in the Middle East and Southeast Asia," *American Journal of Physical Anthropology,* 35 (1971). Used with permission of the Wistar Press.

Figures 8-6, 8-7, 8-8 From A. E. Mourant, A. C. Kopeć, and K. Domaniewska-Sobczak, *The Distribution of the Human Blood Groups and Other Polymorphisms,* 2d ed. (London: Oxford University Press, 1976). Used with permission of Oxford University Press.

Figure 8-9 Reproduced from R. A. Dart, "The Physical Characteristics of the Bushman," *Bantu Studies,* 11 (1937), with the permission of The Witwatersrand University Press, Johannesburg.

Figure 8-10 Data taken from tables in H. V. Meredity, "Findings from Asia, Australia, Europe, and North America on Secular Change in Mean Height of Children, Youths, and Young Adults," *American Journal of Physical Anthropology,* 44 (1976), 315–326. Original data published in R. E. Roth and M. Harris, *The Physical Condition of Children Attending Public Schools in New South Wales* (Sydney: Department of Public Instruction, 1908), and D. L. Jones, W. Hemphill, and E. S. A. Meyers, *Height, Weight and Other Physical Characteristics of New South Wales Children: Part 1, Children Age Five Years and Over* (Sydney: New South Wales Department of Health, 1973).

Figure 8-11a Smithsonian Institution. National Anthropological Archives.

Figure 8-11b Photograph by Rick Freed.

Figure 8-12 Adapted from Norman Kretchmer, "Lactose and Lactase," *Scientific American* (October 1972). Copyright © by Scientific American, Inc. All rights reserved. Additional data from Robert D. McCracken, "Lactase Deficiency: An Example of Dietary Evolution," *Current Anthropology,* 12 (1971).

Figure 8-13 From *Intelligence: Statistical Concepts of Its Nature* by L. J. Bischof. Copyright 1954 by Doubleday & Company, Inc. Used with permission of Random House, Inc.

Figures 9-1, 9-5a, 9-7 From George Gaylord Simpson and William S. Beck, *Life: An Introduction to Biology,* 2d ed. Copyright © 1957, 1965, by Harcourt Brace Jovanovich, Inc., and reproduced with their permission.

Figure 9-3 From Richard M. Tullar, *Life: Conquest of Energy.* Copyright © 1972 by Holt, Rinehart and Winston, Inc. Reprinted by permission of Holt, Rinehart and Winston, Inc.

419

Figures 9-6, 9-8 From A. S. Romer, *The Vertebrate Story.* Copyright 1959 by A. S. Romer. Used with permission of The University of Chicago Press and A. S. Romer.

Figure 9-9 From K. Johansen, "Evolution of Temperature Regulations in Mammals," in J. P. Hannon and E. Viereck (eds.), *Comparative Physiology of Temperature Regulation,* Arctic Aeromedical Laboratory, Department of the Army, 1962.

Figure 9-10*b* From W. E. LeGros Clark, *The Antecedents of Man,* 1959. Copyright © 1959 by Edinburgh University Press. By permission of Quadrangle/The New York Times Book Co.

Figure 9-11 San Diego Zoo photo.

Figure 9-12 Photograph by Ron Garrison. San Diego Zoo photo.

Figures 10-1, 10-3 From W. E. LeGros Clark, *The Antecedents of Man,* 1959. Copyright © 1959 by Edinburgh University Press. By permission of Quadrangle/The New York Times Book Co.

Figure 10-5 Photograph by Dodie Stoneburner.

Figure 10-7 From E. C. Amoroso, "Placentation," in *Marshall's Physiology of Reproduction,* 3d ed., vol. 2, 1952. Used with permission of Longmans, Green & Co. and E. C. Amoroso.

Figures 10-8, 10-11, 10-18 From C. F. Hockett, *Man's Place in Nature.* Copyright 1973 by McGraw-Hill Book Company. Used with permission of McGraw-Hill Book Company and C. F. Hockett.

Figures 10-9*a*, 10-12*a*, 10-14, 10-15, 10-16*a*, 10-17*b*, 10-19*a*, 10-20*a, c, d* San Diego Zoo photos.

Figure 10-9*b* Photograph by F. D. Schmidt. San Diego Zoo photo.

Figures 10-10, 10-13, 10-16*b*, 10-19*b*, 10-20*b* Photographs by Ron Garrison. San Diego Zoo photos.

Figure 10-12*b* San Diego Zoo photo by R. Van Nostrand.

Figure 10-17*a* Photography by John M. Bishop.

Figures 11-1, 11-2 From Irven DeVore (ed.), *Primate Behavior: Field Studies of Monkeys and Apes.* Copyright © 1965 by Holt, Rinehart and Winston, Inc. Reprinted by permission of Holt, Rinehart and Winston, Inc., and Irven DeVore/Anthro-Photo.

Figures 11-3, 11-4 Irven DeVore/Anthro-Photo.

Figures 11-5, 11-6 Copyright © National Geographic Society. Courtesy of The National Geographic Society.

Figure 11-7 Courtesy of Geza Teleki.

Figure 11-8 Reprinted from Richard B. Lee and Irven DeVore (eds.), *Man the Hunter* (Chicago: Aldine Publishing Company, 1968). Copyright © 1968 by Aldine Publishing Company. Reprinted by permission of the editors and Aldine Publishing Company.

Figure 11-9 James Malcolm/Anthro-Photo.

Figure 11-10 Courtesy of Drs. R. Allen and Beatrice T. Gardner, Department of Psychology, University of Nevada, Reno.

Figure 11-11 Courtesy of Roger S. Fouts.

Figure 11-12 Courtesy of M. Kawai, Primate Research Institute, Kyoto University, Japan.

Figure 12-1*a* Photograph by Ron Garrison. San Diego Zoo photo.

Figures 12-1*b, c, d* San Diego Zoo photos.

Figures 12-4, 12-5, 12-6, 12-19 From Adolph H. Schultz, *The Life of Primates.* Copyright 1969 by Adolph H. Schultz. Used with permission of Universe Books, Weidenfeld, and A. H. Schultz.

Figure 12-7 From John Buettner-Janusch, *Origins of Man,* 1966. Used with permission of John Wiley & Sons, Inc.

Figure 12-8 Reprinted from Adolph H. Schultz, "The Skeleton of the Trunk and Limbs of Higher Primates," *Human Biology,* 2 (1930). Copyright 1930 by Warwick and York, Inc. Used with permission of The Wayne University Press.

Figure 12-9 From William King Gregory, *Evolution Emerging,* vol. 2. Courtesy of The American Museum of Natural History.

Figure 12-10 Photograph by Rick Freed.

Figures 12-11, 12-12, 12-14 Photographs by Dodie Stoneburner.

Figure 12-13 From W. E. LeGros Clark, *History of the Primates,* 5th ed. Copyright © 1949, 1965, by the Trustees of the British Museum (Natural History). Used with permission of The University of Chicago Press.

Figures 12-15, 12-16 From George Gaylord Simpson and William S. Beck, *Life: An Introduction to Biology,* 2d ed. Copyright © 1957, 1965, by Harcourt Brace Jovanovich, Inc., and reproduced with their permission.

Figure 12-17 Reprinted with permission of Macmillan Publishing Co., Inc., from W. Penfield and T. Rasmussen, *The Cerebral Cortex of Man.* Copyright 1950 by Macmillan Publishing Co., Inc.

Figure 12-18 From G. J. Romanes, *Darwin, and after Darwin* (Chicago: Open Court, 1892). After Hackel.

Figure 12-20 Based on data from Ashley Montagu, "Sociogenic Brain Damage," *American Anthropologist,* 74 (1950).

Figure 12-21 From Phyllis Dolhinow and Vincent M. Sarich (eds.), *Background for Man,* p. 68. Copyright © 1971 by Little, Brown and Company. Reprinted by permission.

Figure 13-1 Courtesy of The American Museum of Natural History.

Figure 13-3 From M. Boule and H. V. Vallois, *Fossil Men,* 1957. Used with permission of Holt, Rinehart and Winston, Inc.

Acknowledgments

420

Figure 13-4 Photograph by Rick Freed.
Figure 13-5 Reproduced by permission of the American Association of Physical Anthropologists from Glenn Ll. Isaac, "Early Hominids in Action: A Commentary on the Contribution of Archeology to Understanding the Fossil Record in East Africa," *Yearbook of Physical Anthropology*, 19 (1975).
Figure 13-6 From John Buettner-Janusch, *Origins of Man*, 1966. Used with permission of John Wiley & Sons, Inc.
Figure 13-9 François Bordes, "Mousterian Cultures in France," in J. R. Caldwell (ed.), *New Roads to Yesterday: Essays in Archaeology*, Basic Books, New York, 1966. Copyright 1966 by The American Association for the Advancement of Science.
Figure 13-10 From Ashley Montagu, *An Introduction to Physical Anthropology*, 1960. By permission of Charles C Thomas, Publisher, Springfield, Illinois.

Figures 14-1, 14-2, 14-10 From E. L. Simons, "The Early Relatives of Man," *Scientific American* (July 1964). Copyright © 1964 by Scientific American, Inc. All rights reserved.
Figure 14-3 Reprinted with permission of Macmillan Publishing Co., Inc., from E. L. Simons, *Primate Evolution*. Copyright © 1972 by Elwyn L. Simons.
Figures 14-4, 14-6 Courtesy of Elwyn L. Simons and the Peabody Museum of Natural History, Yale University.
Figures 14-5, 14-15, 14-16 Copyright © National Geographic Society.
Figure 14-7 Courtesy of the British Museum (Natural History).
Figure 14-8 From E. L. Simons and P. C. Ettel, "Gigantopithecus," *Scientific American* (January 1970). Copyright © 1970 by Scientific American, Inc. All rights reserved.
Figure 14-9 From P. Andrews, "*Ramapithecus wickeri* Mandible from Fort Ternan, Kenya," *Nature*, 231 (21 May 1971), 193. Courtesy of Peter Andrews.
Figure 14-11 By permission of Professor Phillip V. Tobias. Photo by Alan R. Hughes.

Figures 14-13, 14-14 Courtesy of the Transvaal Museum.
Figure 14-17 Photograph by David Brill. © National Geographic Society.
Figure 14-19 From W. E. LeGros Clark, *History of the Primates*, 5th ed. Copyright © 1949, 1965, by the Trustees of the British Museum (Natural History). Used with permission of The University of Chicago Press.
Figure 14-20 From *Osteodontokeratic Culture of Australopithecus prometheus*, Transvaal Museum Memoir No. 10, 1957. Used with permission of the Transvaal Museum, Republic of South Africa.
Figure 15-1 Courtesy of R. E. F. Leakey, National Museums of Kenya.
Figures 15-2, 15-3, 15-4 From M. D. Leakey, *Olduvai Gorge*, vol. 3, *Excavations in Beds I and II, 1960–1963* (Cambridge: Cambridge University Press, 1971). By permission of Cambridge University Press.
Figures 15-7, 15-19, 15-20 Courtesy of The American Museum of Natural History.
Figures 15-9, 15-14, 15-17, 15-21 From François Bordes, *The Old Stone Age*. Copyright 1968 by François Bordes. Used with permission of McGraw-Hill Book Company and François Bordes.
Figure 15-10 Life Nature Library, *Early Man*, photograph by Dr. F. Clark Howell. © 1965, 1969, 1973 Time, Inc.
Figure 15-12 Photograph by Rick Freed.
Figure 15-15 From Grahame Clark, *The Stone Age Hunters*, 1967. Used with permission of Thames and Hudson, Ltd.
Figure 15-18 From Paul S. Martin, "African and Pleistocene Overkill," *Nature*, 212 (22 October 1966). Used with permission of Macmillan (Journals) Ltd. and Dr. Paul S. Martin.

Figures 16-1, 16-2 From Robert Braidwood, *Prehistoric Men*. Copyright © 1967 by Scott, Foresman and Company. Reprinted by permission of the publisher.
Figure 16-3 Elliott Erwitt, Magnum.

A Glossary has been incorporated into this index. Glossary terms in **boldface** are followed by their definitions. A *See also* entry indicates that a definition or a more detailed breakdown of the topic can be found under the term referred to. Names of species and genera are followed by the family to which they belong, and extinct taxa are indicated by a †.

Index

Arthropods. The members of the phylum Arthropoda; includes centipedes, spiders, butterflies, grasshoppers, lobsters, and horseshoe crabs, 197, 200

Artifact (*see* Archaeology)

Artificial gene, 110

Artificial insemination, 108

Asselar skeleton, 391–392

(See also *Homo sapiens*)

Assemblage (*see* Archaeology)

Assortative mating, 103, 105–106, 108, 157–158, 408

(See also Mating)

Atelinae. Subfamily of the Cebidae which includes the spider and woolly monkeys, 226

Atomic weight. A number given to each element which expresses how many times heavier or lighter it is compared to the weight of carbon 12.

Atoms. The building blocks of matter, 77

Australian aborigine, 144, 157

Australopiths. Members of the genus *Australopithecus* (Hominidae)† of the Pliocene and Pleistocene, 342–343, 345–362, 371

Australopithecus africanus†, 346–347

bipedalism, 352–354

brain, 355–356

cranial capacity, 352–353, 356, 359–360

culture, 354–355

dentition, 352–353, 359–360

gracile. Australopiths which are small and light in build relative to the robust forms, 347, 349–351, 353, 358

Hadar, 347, 349

(See also Hadar)

"*Homo habilis,*" 349, 358

(See also "*Homo habilis*")

Kromdraai. Site in the Sterkfontein Valley, South Africa, yielding the remains of robust australopiths, 347

Lake Turkana, 347, 350, 352, 359

(See also Lake Turkana)

locomotion, 352–354

Lothagam. Site in Kenya on the eastern shore of Lake Turkana yielding the earliest known australopith (5½ million B.P.), 345

"**Lucy.**" Nickname for AL 288, a gracile australopith skeleton from Hadar, Ethiopia, 349

Makapansgat. Site in South Africa yielding gracile australopiths, tentatively dated at 3.7 million B.P., 347–348

Olduvai Gorge, 347–349, 358

(See also Olduvai Gorge)

Omo, 347, 349

(See also Omo)

robust. Australopiths which are relatively larger and heavier than the gracile forms with relatively small incisors and canines but large premolars and molars and development of a sagittal crest, 347, 351, 353

stature, 353

Sterkfontein. Site in Sterkfontein Valley, South Africa, from which gracile australopiths have been recovered; tentatively dated at 3.3 million B.P., 347–349

Swartkrans. Site in Sterkfontein Valley, South Africa, yielding remains of robust australopiths; tentatively dated at 2.6 million B.P., 347–349, 355

Taung baby. The original *Australopithecus* found in 1925 at the Taung site in South Africa, tentatively dated at 900,000 B.P., 346–347

"***Zinjanthropus boisei.***" Robust australopith from Olduvai Gorge dated at 1.75 million B.P., 349

Autosome, 60

(See also Chromosome)

Avahi (Indriidae), 218, 221

Aye-Aye (Daubentoniidae), 218, 221, 286

Baboon (Cercopithecidae). Semiterrestrial African monkey, 218, 228–230, 238–248, 249, 258, 270, 278, 283, 287, 297, 300, 317, 336

chacma baboon, 225

Hamadryas baboon, 229, 249, 251, 292

savanna baboon: behavior, 238–245

diet, 239–240

dominance hierarchy, 241–243

[See also Dominance (behavioral)], 241–243

ecology, 239–240

sexual behavior, 242–244

social structure of troop, 241–245

Backcross. The process of crossing a hybrid with its homozygous recessive parent, 44

speech, and other higher mental activities, 9, 292–293

and association, 292–293

comparative anatomy, 217, 280, 289–294

cranial capacity, 289, 352–353, 356, 359–360, 367–368, 371, 378

(*See also* Cranial capacity)

encephalization quotient. A number reflecting the increase in brain size over and beyond that explainable by an increase in body size, 291–292

endocranial cast, 289, 356

(*See also* Endocranial cast)

mammalian, 290–291

neocortex. Gray covering on the cerebrum of some vertebrates, 290, 291

primate, 217, 280, 289–294

Branch running and walking, 270, 278

(*See also* Locomotion)

Branisella (Ceboidea?)†, 333

Broom, Robert, 347

Brose, David S., 384

Brother-sister mating, 103, 252

Brothwell, Don R., 390

Brow ridge (supraorbital torus). Ridge of bone above the eye sockets, 288–289

Buettner-Janusch, John, 300, 406

Buffon, Comte de, 26

Bush baby (Lorisidae), 222

Bushman, 5–6, 145, 175, 392

Calhoun, John B., 412

Callitrichidae. A family of New World monkeys consisting of the marmosets and tamarins, 218, 223–224

Campbell, Bernard, 342

Cannibalism, 377

Capuchin monkey (Cebidae), 218, 225, 270, 278

Carbohydrates. Organic compounds composed of carbon, oxygen, and hydrogen which include the sugars and starches.

Carbon 14 dating, 320–321

(*See also* Dating)

Carnivore. A meat-eating animal.

Carpenter, C. R., 238

Carrier. A person who possesses a recessive allele in the heterozygous condition.

testing for, 56

Cartmill, Matt, 215–216

Çatal Hüyük. A Neolithic site in Turkey, 404–405

Cataracts, 49, 52, 73

(*See also* Genetic abnormalities)

Catarrhine nose, 223–224

(*See also* Nose)

Cavalli-Sforza, L. L., 408

Cebidae. A family of New World monkeys which includes the squirrel, spider, howler, and capuchin monkeys, 218, 223–226

Cebinae. Subfamily of the Cebidae which includes the squirrel and capuchin monkeys, 225

Ceboidea. The superfamily of New World monkeys consisting of the Callitrichidae and Cebidae, 218, 224–226

Cell. The smallest unit which is considered to be alive. All living organisms are either one cell or composed of several cells, 58–59, 81

cytoplasm. Material within the cell between the plasma membrane and the nuclear membrane.

nuclear membrane. A structure that binds the nucleus.

nucleus. A structure found in the cell which contains the chromosomes.

plasma membrane. A structure that binds the cell but allows for the entry and exit of certain substances.

Cell division, 62–66, 71–72

centriole. A pair of small bodies found near the nucleus from which the spindle is formed.

meiosis. Form of cell division occurring in specialized tissue in the testes or ovary that leads to gamete production, 62–66, 71–72

mitosis. Form of cell division whereby one-celled organisms divide and whereby body cells divide in growth and replacement, 62–63

spindle. A structure consisting of fibers radiating out from the centriole which functions in cell division.

Cenozoic. The most recent era of geologic time, called the Age of Mammals because it represents the time of the adaptive radiation of mammals into the numerous ecological niches they occupy today, 325–327

Centriole (*see* Cell division)

Centromere (*see* Chromosome)

normal size but the limbs are quite short; in-inherited as a dominant, 51–53

colorblindness (red-green). The inability to distinguish between some shades of red and green; inherited as a X-linked recessive, 76, 171–172

control of, 56, 86, 125

detection and treatment of, 56, 86

diabetes. Failure of the body to produce insulin which controls sugar metabolism; has a complex genetic basis and is influenced by environmental factors, 50, 52, 123

Down's syndrome (Mongolism). Condition characterized by a peculiarity of eyefolds, malformation of heart and other organs, stubby hands and feet, short stature, and mental retardation; result of extra chromosome 21, 66–68

Ellis-van Creveld syndrome. A rare (except among the Amish) recessive abnormality characterized by dwarfism, extra fingers, malformations of the heart, 105

G6PD (Glucose-6-phosphate dehydrogenase) deficiency. Lack of an enzyme of the red blood cell inherited as a X-linked recessive; afflicted individuals develop severe anemia when in contact with the fava bean or certain antimalarial drugs, 76, 86, 95–96, 125, 171

galactosemia. A recessive abnormality involving the failure to produce the enzyme that converts galactose to glucose and other compounds, 52, 86

gout. Abnormal uric acid metabolism; inherited as a dominant with variable expression, 50, 52

hemophilia. A recessive X-linked trait characterized by excessive bleeding due to faulty clotting mechanism, 56, 75-76

incidence, 52

Kleinfelter's syndrome. A sex chromosome count of XXY; phenotypically male, tall stature, sterile, 68

lactase deficiency. Inability to digest milk sugar (lastose) because of an enzyme deficiency (lactase), 154–155, 182–184, 187

PKU (phenylketonuria). An absence of the enzyme responsible for the conversion of the amino acid phenylalanine to tyrosine, inherited as a recessive; phenylalanine accumulates in the blood and then breaks down into byproducts

which cause several mental retardation in addition to other symptoms, 52–53, 56, 85–86, 94–95, 111, 171, 176

retinoblastoma. A cancer of the retina of the eye in children, inherited as a dominant, 52, 121

sickle cell anemia. In individuals homozygous for hemoglobin S red blood cells will develop into a sickle shape which, in turn, will clog capillaries resulting in anemia, heart failure, etc., 52, 83–85, 112–113, 123–125, 154–155, 171, 176
(See also Sickle cell anemia)

sickle cell trait. The condition of being heterozygous for hemoglobins A and S, yet individual usually shows no abnormal symptoms, 84, 123–124, 154

table of genetic abnormalities and their inheritance, 52

Tay-Sachs disease. Enzyme deficiency of lipid (fat) metabolism inherited as a recessive; causes death in early childhood, 51–52, 56, 103–104, 171

thalassemia. Absence or reduction of alpha or beta chain synthesis in hemoglobin; in homozygous condition (thalassemia major) high frequency of hemoglobin F and fatal anemia; in heterozygous condition (thalassemia minor) highly variable but usually occurs with mild symptoms, 52, 125, 127, 171

Turner's syndrome. 45 chromosomes with a sex chromosome count of X-; phenotypically female, but sterile, 68–69

XYY syndrome. Chromosomal abnormality characterized by 47 chromosomes and a sex chromosome count of XYY; often associated with aggressive or criminal behavior, 68, 70

Genetic code, 79–80, 82, 85

Genetic counseling, 54–55

Genetic drift, 101–102, 105, 157, 407
(See also Population genetics)

Genetic equilibrium, 92–96
model of, 92–96
(See also Population genetics)

Genetic load, 95
(See also Population genetics)

Genetic traits:
ear wax, 165–166
Hapsburg lip, 39–40, 52